The Canterbury and York Society.

GENERAL EDITOR: ROSE GRAHAM, M.A., F.S.A.

T0326992

DIOCESE OF LINCOLN.

Visitations of Religious Houses

IN THE

DIOCESE OF LINCOLN.

VOLUME III.

Records of Visitations held by William Alnwick

BISHOP OF LINCOLN.

A.D. MCCCCXXXVI—MCCCCXLIX.

PART II.

EDITED BY

A. HAMILTON THOMPSON, M.A., D.Litt., F.S.A.

PROFESSOR OF MEDIEVAL HISTORY IN THE UNIVERSITY OF LEEDS

Oxford :

ISSUED FOR THE CANTERBURY AND YORK SOCIETY,

AT THE UNIVERSITY PRESS.

———

MDCCCCXXVII.

NOTE

Part LXXIX is a gift to the Society, in exchange, from the Lincoln Record Society.

ROSE GRAHAM.

6 March 1929.

Printed in Great Britain

PREFACE

The preparation of this volume, which concludes the records of Alnwick's visitations of monasteries and colleges, has been delayed by circumstances unforeseen by the editor when he entered upon his task, and has been carried on amid much pressure of work from other quarters. Some of the principal features of its contents have been summarized in the general introduction to the previous volume, in which their character and significance were defined at some length ; and to add anything to what was said there would be to embark upon a long and detailed discussion of numerous points of monastic life and discipline illustrated by the text, which would unduly swell the size of the book. The index of subjects, the compilation of which, in face of the great variety of detail included in these records and the difficulty of grouping it under general headings, has involved much labour and thought, cannot be offered as a complete analysis of the work ; but it provides at any rate some indication of the amount of material which has been preserved in these records for the consideration of the historian.

The editor has already expressed his thanks to those whose advice has aided him in his work. During the progress of this volume, however, death has deprived him of the constant encouragement of two scholars whose friendship was among his most valued privileges. As the second volume of this series of documents was dedicated to the memory of two others who did not live to see its publication, so this is offered to the memory of Sir William Henry St. John Hope, *facile princeps* of writers upon monastic architecture, and of William Brown, to whose self-effacing diligence and remarkable acquaintance with the history and topography of the North of England no tribute that can be offered is too high. Of both it may be truly said that their industry in collecting material for their publications was equalled only by their generosity in putting their knowledge at the disposal of all who sought their help with a genuine desire to learn ; and their example has left a permanent influence upon the mental habits and methods of work of all who were fortunate enough to feel its contact.

A. H. T.

Leeds,
    8 October, 1928.

CONTENTS

CONTENTS

XLIII.

[Fo. 84]

Visitacio prioratus de MARKEBY, ordinis Sancti Augustini, Lincolniensis diocesis, facta in domo capitulari ibidem xix⁰ die mensis augusti, anno Domini mccccxxxviij⁰, per reuerendum in Christo patrem et dominum, dominum Willelmum, Dei gracia Lincolniensem episcopum, anno suarum consecracionis xiij⁰ et translacionis secundo.

In primis, sedente dicto reuerendo patre in dicta domo capitulari die et anno supradictis iudicialiter pro tribunali in negocio visitacionis huiusmodi, comparuerunt coram eo prior et conuentus dicti prioratus, xij in numero, parati vt apparuit ad subeundum visitacionem huiusmodi. Et deinde prior ministrauit domino certificatorium citacionis sui et singulorum confratrum suorum ad mandatum domini facte in hec verba 'Reuerendo in Christo,' etc.; et deinde preconizatis citatis et comparentibus, propositum fuit verbum Dei per discretum virum magistrum Thomam Duffelde, in sacra theologia bacallarium, sequentem hoc thema, 'Omnia secundum ordinem fiant in vobis.'[1] Quo lingua latina laudabiliter finito, dominus peciit a priore exhiberi sibi confirmacionem sue eleccionis; qui dicit quod nullam habet nec habuit xl annis, et reddit causam eo quod combuste[2] erant in cella sua infra dormitorium, vbi et quando omnia sua indumenta et lectisternia et cetera inibi tunc existencia tunc[3] totaliter combusta erant. Tamen cum non habeat super hiis validum testimonium, dominus partim *eum* increpando dixit quod mediis vicibus potuit fecisse scrutari registra sua pro extrahendo testimonium, etc.; et cum ipse hoc ex necgligencia omiserit, ipse tamen hoc faciet fieri pro sui informacione super iure tituli sui et eius sufficiencia. Et cum exhibicio tituli confirmacionis sue foret fundamentum huius actus, vt per hoc probaretur eius ius in dignitate prioris, nec absque eo posset eius possessionem in[4] approbare, voluit tamen in aliis procedere iuxta formam mandati, et peciit a dicto priore exhiberi sibi fundacionem domus, statum domus et ordinaciones cantariarum, si que sint in prioratu fundate. Et exinde exhibuit prior statum domus

---

[1] 1 Cor. xiv, 40: 'Omnia autem honeste et secundum ordinem fiant.' The text is given as above in the Ulverscroft visitation (No. lxxvi), and with a slight variation in that of Thornholm (No. lxxiii).

[2] Sc. *littere*.

[3] *Sic*: repeated.

[4] *Sic*: *eadem* omitted.

[1] There appears to be no record of this : the date, however, was evidently 1398 or a little earlier. In spite of a note which qualifies the misstatement inadequately, the list of priors in V.C.H. *Lincs.* ii, 175, gives the date of election as 1433.

XLIII.

THE VISITATION OF THE PRIORY OF MARKBY, OF THE ORDER OF ST. AUSTIN, OF THE DIOCESE OF LINCOLN, PERFORMED IN THE CHAPTER-HOUSE THEREIN ON THE NINETEENTH DAY OF THE MONTH OF AUGUST, IN THE YEAR OF OUR LORD 1438, BY THE REVEREND FATHER IN CHRIST AND LORD, THE LORD WILLIAM, BY THE GRACE OF GOD BISHOP OF LINCOLN, IN THE THIRTEENTH YEAR OF HIS CONSECRATION AND THE SECOND OF HIS TRANSLATION.

In the first place, as the said reverend father was sitting in the said chapter-house, on and in the day and year abovesaid, in his capacity of judge as a tribunal in the business of such visitation, there appeared before him the prior and convent of the said priory, twelve in number, in readiness, as was apparent, to undergo such visitation. And then the prior furnished my lord with the certificate of the summons of him and of his several brethren which had been made at my lord's command, in these words, ' To the reverend [father] in Christ,' etc. ; and thereafter, when they that were summoned had been called by name and made their appearance, the word of God was set forth by the discreet master Thomas Duffelde, bachelor in divinity, after this text, ' Let all things be done among you in order.' Now when this had come to a praiseworthy end in the Latin tongue, my lord asked of the prior that the confirmation of his election should be shewn to him;[1] and he says that he has none nor has had it for forty years, and gives as the cause thereof that [the letters] were burned in his cell within the dorter[2], where and what time all his raiment and bedding and all else that was then therein were utterly burned up. Howbeit, since he has no valid evidence touching this matter, my lord said, partly rebuking him, that in the meantime he might have caused their registers[3] to be searched, that the evidence, etc., might be taken therefrom ; and, seeing that he has neglected this of his carelessness, yet he himself will cause this to be done for his own instruction concerning the right of his title and the sufficiency thereof. And albeit the displaying of the title-deed of his confirmation should be the foundation of this process, so that his right in the dignity of prior should be proved thereby, and without it he [himself] could not give approval to his possessory right in [the same], he was willing nevertheless to proceed in other matters according to the form of his mandate, and asked of the said prior that there should be shewn him the foundation of the house, the state of the house and the ordinations of the chantries, if there be any that are founded in the priory. And thereupon the

---

[2] The reference is apparently to a private room or *camera* constructed within the dormitory, rather than to a mere cubicle : see *Visitations* I, 40, note 1, and cf. the *loca quatuor monialium* appropriated to the prioress in the dormitory at Ankerwyke, *ibid.* II, 3.

[3] *I.e.* the registers of the monastery.

a festo Philippi et Jacobi, anno Domini mccccxxxiij⁰ vsque ad festum[1] anno Domini mccccxxxviij⁰, vt asserit et prout continebatur in quodam libro papireo. Exhibuit eciam quoddam registrum, continens eciam vt asserit fundacionem domus. Cantarias nullas habent in speciali in domo. Iniuncciones eciam dicunt se nullas habuisse citra tempus Oliueri episcopi dudum Lincolniensis. Et deinde dominus processit ad examinacionem prioris, qui examinatus dicit[2] ea que sequuatur.

Frater Johannes Fentone, prior, dicit quod silencium non seruatur in claustro vel ecclesia, sed valde male in refectorio vel[3] dormitorio.

Frater Thomas Dryby est suspectus cum quadam muliere manente in villa de Markeby.

Interrogatus prior dicit quod domus indebitatur in c marcis vel ibi circiter. Interrogatus qualiter exonerabitur de tanto debito, dicit quod oportebit eos retrahere se a superfluis et vt parcius viuant; et dicit quod non habetur instaurum de granis, frumento, braseo, antequam inhorreauerint fructus autumpnales iam instantes.

Item dicit quod iuniores canonici nec eciam seniores vacant contemplacioni in claustro horis debitis secundum regulam, sed sunt multum insolentes et circumvagantes, et presertim Johannes Alforde in hiis est multum culpabilis.

Frater Ricardus Leeke, supprior, dicit quod religio non obseruatur vt solito, et tamen in hoc multum delinquit Johannes Alforde: nullum habens officium *vult*[4] exire chorum, ecclesiam, claustrum et refectorium cum sibi libuerit nulla petita[5] licencia nec[6] aliquociens absentat se a refectorio temporibus refeccionum absque causa vel licencia; et siquis presidens ipsum pro huiusmodi[7] reprehendit, prorumpit in verba opprobriosa et inobediencie.

Item silencium non seruatur in aliquo loco[8] consueto secundum regulam, et in hoc delinquunt quasi omnes; et dicit quod domus indebitatur in lx li. vel circiter, et non habent ad exoneracionem nisi pauca debita, tamen desperata.

Item dicit quod frater Thomas Dryby notatur super incontinencia cum quadam muliere manente in villa de Markeby in quodam tenemento vocato Hanney thynge.

---

[1] Sic: *idem* omitted before *festum*.
[2] Written like *dicet*.
[3] *re* cancelled.
[4] Interlined above *vel* cancelled.
[5] *petita* repeated and cancelled.
[6] Sic: *obtenta et* probably omitted.
[7] Sic.
[8] *honesto* cancelled.

[1] 1 May, 1433.
[2] No chartulary of Markby is known to exist.
[3] Licences for the foundation and endowment of chantries in the priory church occur 24 May, 1327 (*Cal. Pat.* 1327-1330, p. 106), 7 March, 1336-7 (*ibid.* 1334-1338, p. 387), and 16 Feb., 1337-8 (*ibid.* 1338-1340, p. 13). See also an endowment for lights at the Lady mass (*ibid.* 1334-1338, p. 101). These chantries apparently had been discontinued: the office of warden of the Lady chapel, however, held by the precentor, indicates the existence of a special fund in that connexion, whether for masses or for the fabric.
[4] No copy of these is preserved in Sutton's register.

prior shewed him the state of the house from the feast of St. Philip and St. James in the year of our Lord 1433[1] until the [same] feast in the year of our Lord 1438, as he avouches and as it was contained in a paper book. He exhibited also a register which also contains, as he avers, the foundation of the house.[2] They have no chantries in the house that are specially [founded].[3] They also say that they have had no injunctions since the time of Oliver, sometime bishop of Lincoln.[4] And thereafter my lord proceeded to the examination of the prior, who says these things which follow.

Brother John Fentone, the prior,[5] says that silence is not kept in the cloister or the church, and very ill indeed in the frater or the dorter.

Brother Thomas Dryby is suspect with a woman that dwells in the town of Markby.

The prior says upon interrogation that the house is in debt a hundred marks or thereabouts. When interrogated after what manner it shall be discharged of so great a debt, he says that they must needs refrain themselves from superfluous living and live more sparingly; and he says that there is no store in hand of wheat, corn [and] malt, until they shall have garnered the autumn fruits that are now at hand.

Also he says that the younger canons, and the elder as well, give no time to contemplation in the cloister at the due seasons according to the rule, but are very disorderly and are gad-abouts, and John Alforde especially is very blameworthy in this respect.

Brother Richard Leeke, the sub-prior, says that religious discipline is not observed as is wont, and nevertheless[6] John Alforde is a sore offender herein: although he holds no office, he will go out of quire, church, cloister and frater whensoever it pleases him, without asking or [obtaining] any leave, [and] sometimes he withholds his presence from the frater at meal-times without cause or licence; and, if any of the presidents reproves him for such [doings], he breaks forth into reviling and disobedient words.

Also silence is not kept in any accustomed place according to the rule, and herein almost all do offend; and he says that the house is in debt sixty pounds or thereabout, and they have nothing for their discharge but a few sums that are owing, whereof they nevertheless despair.

Also he says that brother Thomas Dryby is defamed of incontinency with a woman who dwells in the town of Markby in a tenement that is called Hanney thynge[7].

---

[5] The names of the eleven canons indicate that five, viz. Alforde, Dryby, Malteby, Markeby and Welle, came from places near or only a few miles from the monastery, Leeke and Saltfletby also bear names derived from places somewhat further away, but at no great distance. Gouxhille (Goxhill) is in the north of the county, near Thornton abbey. Yorke and the novice Bunnebury bore names from outside the county: Bunbury is in Cheshire. The names Fentone and Thorntone are too general to be identified with certainty; but it is likely that their bearers were both Lincolnshire men. It will be noted that in the injunctions the prior's name is given as Fenthorpe, which is obviously local and is probably the correct form. The writer in V.C.H. *Lincs.* II, 175, who has read the name Dryby as ' Dugby,' has evidently not observed this point.

[6] *I.e.* in spite of general laxness, the case of Alforde was so conspicuous that it called for special censure.

[7] Hannay or Hannah is the next village to Markby on the north-east. Its name seems to appear in that of the tenement mentioned.

[Fo. 84*d*.] Frater Johannes Yorke, cellerarius, dicit quod religio in nullo obseruatur, et hoc propter impotenciam prioris et inaduertenciam[1] supprioris; et in horum defectu non habetur residencia in claustro, sed omnes vagantur in villam et alia exteriora secundum eorum desiderium temporibus tam diuini seruicii quam contemplacionis in claustro, non expectando in choro finem horarum sed insolenter egredientes.

Item frater Thomas Dryby notatur super incestu cum Margareta Portere de Markeby, ad cuius domum nimium habet et suspectum et quasi quotidianum accessum.

Item dicit quod Willelmus, cocus prioratus, non est vtilis pro domo, nam supponitur vt,[2] cum habeat corrodium suum omni septimana ad domum suam in villa pro se et familia sua, quod preter hoc vastat cibaria domus; et est pessimus detractor canonicorum et multum rebellis in verbis suis.

Item dicit quod iuuenes seculares iacent in dormitorio inter canonicos, et quidam cum canonicis in eisdem lectis, et presertim cum Johanne Alforde, qui frequencius aliis tales habet secum in lectis.

Item dicit quod omnes artentur ad obseruandum librum qui dicitur liber ordinis, quia in nullo obseruatur.

Item dicit quod seculares et presertim mulieres habent nimium accessum et suspectum ad loca interiora eciam claustralia prioratus in magnum scandalum domus.

Item petit vt omnino substituatur alius in officium supprioris, quia sub isto qui nunc est perit religio.

Frater Willelmus Saltfletby concordat cum York quo ad religionem, addendo quod quasi tota et omnibus[3] perit religio et obseruancie regulares pro nichilo habentur, quia per necgligenciam prioris et suppriorem obliuionem[4] et deducuntur in dissuetudinem; et dicit quod prior est nimis remissus in correccionibus faciendis, et propterea correcti proniores reddentur ad vetita.

Item dicit quod propter necligenciam officiariorum temporalia quasi tendunt ad non esse.

Item dicit quod Thomas Dryby notatur cum Margareta Portere de eadem.[5]

Item dicit quod canonici tanto intendunt potacionibus serotinis ante et post completorium, quod ex hoc grauati non veniunt ad matutinas, et si venerint propter sompnolenciam non proficiunt.

Item dicit quod quidam Johannes Kyrkeby habet secum duos pueros secum[6] sustentatos ex cibariis domus, et dicit vlterius quod domus multum aggrauatur per multitudinem talium puerorum.

Frater Thomas Dryby dicit quod silencium non seruatur vtrobique vt deberet secundum regulam.

---

[1] *s*, the first letter of *supprioris*, written and left uncancelled at the end of the line.

[2] *Sic*: *vt* is otiose.

[3] *Sic*: for *in omnibus*.

[4] *Sic*: either for *supprioris obliuionem* or *veniunt in obliuionem*.

[5] *Sic*: sc. *villa*.

[6] *Sic*: repeated.

[1] Cf. *Visitations* II, 11, note 6.

[2] *I.e.* the *Ordinale* of the monastery. On the general subject of Augustinian *ordinalia* see F. C. Eeles, *The Holyrood Ordinale*, Edinburgh, 1916.

Brother John Yorke, the cellarer, says that religious discipline is observed in naught, and this because of the incapacity of the prior and the subprior's carelessness: and in their default there is no abiding in cloister, but they all do roam into the town and elsewhere outside the precinct as the fancy takes them in time of divine service as well as of contemplation in cloister, and wait not in quire until the hours are ended, but go out in disorderly fashion.

Also brother Thomas Dryby is defamed of incest[1] with Margaret Portere of Markby, to whose house he has overmuch and suspect recourse almost daily.

Also he says that William, the cook of the priory, is of no profit to the house, for it is supposed, although he has his corrody every week for himself and his household at his house in the town, that apart from this he wastes the food of the house; and he backbites the canons very foully and is very rebellious in his words.

Also he says that secular youths do lie in the dorter among the canons, and some with the canons in the same beds, and especially with John Alforde, who more often than the others has such in bed with him.

Also he says that they all should be bound to observe the book that is called the book of the order,[2] for it is observed in naught.

Also he says that secular folk, and women especially, have overmuch and suspect recourse to the inner precincts, and even to the cloister buildings, of the priory, to the sore scandal of the house.

Also he prays that another person be substituted altogether in the office of subprior, for under him who now is [subprior] religious discipline cometh to naught.

Brother William Saltfletby agrees with York as touching religious discipline, adding that religion is almost utterly and in all things dead, and the regular observances are set at naught, because by the prior's neglect and by reason of the subprior they are brought [into] forgetfulness and disuse; and he says that the prior is very slack in making corrections, and therefore they that are corrected shall be made more inclined to things forbidden.

Also he says that because of the officers' neglect their temporal goods are coming almost to nothing.

Also he says that Thomas Dryby is defamed with Margaret Portere of the same [town.]

Also he says that the canons spend so much time in drinking in the evening before and after compline, that, being heavy herefrom, they do not come to matins, and, if they come, they are so sleepy that they profit not.

Also he says that one John Kyrkeby has with him two boys that are maintained out of the victuals of the house, and he says further that the house is sorely burthened by the multitude of such boys.[3]

Brother Thomas Dryby says that silence is kept nowhere[4] as it should be according to the rule.

---

[3] The boys mentioned at this visitation were apparently not ' children of the almonry,' the decrease in whose numbers is noted at Leicester (No. XL) and Thornton (No. LXXIV), but sons or relations of corrodars and servants of the house.

[4] Literally ' on neither side '; but *utrobique* is used at this date as an intensive form of *ubique*.

Item dicit quod filius fratris Johannis Kyrkeby multociens iacet de nocte in dormitorio cum Johanne Alforde in lecto suo.

[Fo. 85.] (Supprior.) Frater Ricardus Gouxhille, cantor et custos altaris beate Marie, dicit quod supprior,[1] qui occupat officium bursarii, non intendit religioni, quia occupatus dicto officio non potest sic intendere, et ideo multum absens ab ecclesia et claustro, et propterea perit quasi religio.

(Supprior.) Frater Robertus Welle, subcellerarius, dicit quod religio perit, eo quod supprior, vnus bursariorum, non intendit religioni; quia occasione dicti officii est multum absens a claustro et aliis locis religionis.

(Omnes.) Item dicit, canonici exeunt chorum et loca claustralia absque causa seu licencia.

(Dryby.) Item dicit quod frater Thomas Dryby notatur cum Margareta Portere.

(Alford.) Item dicit quod frater Johannes Alforde consueuit habere secum de nocte cubantem[2] in lecto iuuenes in dormitorio.

(Prior.) Item dicit quod non constat sibi de statu domus nec de commodis nec de expensis.

Frater Johannes Alforde dicit quod silencium non seruatur vtrobique secundum regulam, et quod religio non obseruatur, et hoc propter non intendenciam supprioris, eo quod occupatur in officio bursarii.

Item dicit quod supprior recepit pecunias pro vij^{xx} quarteriis fabarum et lanis venditis, et cum non habeatur frumentum in domo, et habebant pecunias in promptu et poterant habuisse quarterium frumenti pro vj$s$. viij$d$., noluerunt tunc aliquo; sed cum iam sit ad xs. iam emunt ad magnum domus detrimentum.

Item dicit quod Bunnebury non est doctus aut informatus in obsequio diuino et regularibus diciplinis,[3] et hoc in defectu Gouxhille, magistri sui, qui non intendit eius informacioni.

Item dicit quod Thomas Dryby notatur cum Margareta Portere de Markeby, de qua suscitauit duas proles; nam propter infamiam laborantem super similibus quidam, vt dominus Thomas Cumberworthe, subtrahunt elemosinas suas.

Item dicit quod quidam secularis est custos granarii, propter quod credit quod domus dampnificatur.

Frater Willelmus Thorntone dicit quod quidam canonici exeunt chorum ante finem horarum sine causa aut licencia; et dicit quod silencium non seruatur vtrobique[4] secundum regulam, et hoc in defectu supprioris, qui propter occupacionem officii bursarii multum est absens a locis claustralibus et sic perit religio.

---

[1] *quod* cancelled.
[2] *Sic*: for *cubantes*.
[3] *Sic*: for *disciplinis*.
[4] *vt* cancelled.

[1] See p. 220, note 3. Gouxhille was also novice-master, as appears below.
[2] Robert Welles or Well, canon of Markby, had papal dispensations in 1442 to choose his own confessor (27 Sept.) and to retain for life a benefice with cure of souls (17 Nov.). See *Cal. Papal Letters* IX, 309, 265.
[3] See note on Religio, *Visitations* I, 247.
[4] *I.e.* the novice.

Also he says that John Kyrkeby's brother's son lies oftentimes of a night in the dorter with John Alforde in his bed.

(The subprior.) Brother Richard Gouxhille, the precentor and warden of the altar of blessed Mary,[1] says that the subprior, who holds the office of bursar, pays no attention to religious discipline, for, being busied in the said office, and being therefore often absent from the church and cloister, he cannot pay such attention, and because thereof religious discipline is well-nigh dead.

(The subprior.) Brother Robert Welle,[2] the subcellarer, says that religion[3] is dead, in that the subprior, who is one of the bursars, pays no attention to religion; seeing that by reason of the said office he is often absent from the cloister and from the other places of religious observance.

(All.) Also he says [that] the canons go out of quire and the cloister precincts without cause or leave.

(Dryby.) Also he says that brother Thomas Dryby is defamed with Margaret Portere.

(Alford.) Also he says that brother John Alforde is wont to have youths lying with him of a night in his bed in the dorter.

(The prior.) Also he says that he is not certain of the state of the house or of its revenues or its expenses.

Brother John Alforde says that silence is kept nowhere according to the rule, and that religious discipline is not observed, and this because of the subprior's heedlessness, in that he is busied in the office of bursar.

Also he says that the subprior did receive money for seven score quarters of beans and for wool that was sold, and albeit they have no corn in the house, and they had ready money and might have had a quarter of corn for 6s. 8d., they would have it then in no wise; but now, though it is at ten shillings, they buy it to the great damage of the house.

Also he says that Bunnebury[4] is not taught or instructed in divine service and regular discipline, and this in the default of Gouxhille, his master, who pays no heed to his instruction.

Also he says that Thomas Dryby is defamed with Margaret Portere of Markby, of whom he has begotten two children; for, because of the ill report that is current touching the like, certain folk, such as sir Thomas Cumberworthe,[5] do withhold their alms.

Also he says that a secular person is keeper of the granary, by reason whereof he believes that the house suffers damage.

Brother William Thorntone says that certain canons do go out of quire before the end of the hours without cause or leave; and he says that silence is nowhere kept according to the rule, and this in the subprior's default, who, because he is busied in the office of bursar, is often absent from the cloister precincts, and thus religious discipline comes to naught.

---

[5] The will of sir Thomas Cumberworth of Somerby by Brigg, dated 15 Feb., 1450-1, is printed in full from Reg. xix in *Lincoln Dioc. Documents*, ed. Clark (E.E.T.S., orig. ser. CXLIX, 1914), pp. 45-57: abstract in *Early Lincoln Wills*, pp. 174, 175. The prior of Markby appears among the heads of religious houses to whom he bequeathed ' ilkon of tham a pare bedys of corall as far as that I haue m[a]y laste, & after yiff tham gette bedes.'

Item dicit quod Thomas Dryby notatur publice cum Margareta Portere de Markeby, ad quam habet multum accessum suspecte, quia dicitur quod suscitauit de ea duas proles.

Item dicit quod Johannes Alforde habet iuuenes secum in lecto suo in dormitorio de nocte cubantes, nunc vnum nunc duos, etc., et aliquociens temporibus completorii sedet in coquina aut vagatur circa friuola ad extra.

Item dicit quod compoti non redduntur singulis annis: ideo non constat de statu domus. Et dicit quod *non* seruitur canonicis de pecuniis pro habitu suo, et hoc in defectu supprioris.

Item dicit quod Gouxhille ex consuetudine et Alforde frequenter exercent tabernas publicas in villa de Markeby, et ibidem intendunt potacionibus cum secularibus publice diebus feriatis et non feriatis.

Item cum ipse Gouxhille sit cantor, non tamen sequitur chorum, sed est multum absens absque causa seu licencia, propter quod chorus non regitur in cantu in eius defectu.

Item dicit quod Malteby quasi omni die ante et post meridiem absque licencia accedit ad domum matris sue in villa ibidem, sic quasi apostatando.

Item dicit quod Welle et Alford multociens post completorium exeunt prioratum et intendunt publicis tabernis in villa absque vlla licencia et ex casum[1] necessitatis, et dictus Welle publice sagittat ad metas in villa inter seculares.

[Fo. 85*d*.] Frater Johannes Malteby dicit quod religio quasi in nullo obseruatur, et hoc propter impotenciam prioris et inaduertenciam supprioris, qui propter infirmitates et officium bursarii non intendit nec potest intendere religioni.

Item dicit quod status domus non ostenditur in communi: ideo nescitur. Fatetur se non ostendisse statum in communi.

Item dicit quod canonici nimium frequentant villam absque causa vel licencia.

Item dicit quod Thomas Dryby notatur cum Margareta Portere.

Item dicit quod silencium in nullo quasi seruatur.

Item dicit quod canonici soli accedunt ad villam, et[2] si duo exeant simul, vnus solus ad vnam villam vel locum, et alius solus ad alium locum accedunt, et hoc multum suspecte.

Frater Willelmus Markeby dicit quod[3] silencium nullicubi obseruatur, et dicit quod canonici seniores et iuniores ex consuetudine absque licencia[4] exeunt prioratum ad villam quasi apostatando.

Item reputat suppriorem inhabilem ad illud officium, quia adeo intendit officio bursarii quod non vacat religioni, propter quod perit; et nimis afficit lucratiua, vt ex illis possit aliquid commodi percipere.

Item dicit quod supprior consumit elemosinam ex mensa sua, nam omnia[5] remanencia ex ea mittit quo vult ad villam.

---

[1] *Sic*: for *extra casum*.
[2] *sim* cancelled.
[3] *se* cancelled.
[4] *exea* cancelled.
[5] *remia* cancelled.

[1] The reasons given in the text are awkwardly combined as though they referred to the subprior only.

Also he says that Thomas Dryby is publicly defamed with Margaret Portere of Markby, to whom he has often recourse in manner suspect, for it is said that he has begotten two children of her.

Also he says that John Alforde has youths that lie with him in his bed in the dorter of a night, now one, now two, etc., and sometimes in time of compline he sits in the kitchen or roams outside the priory after trifles.

Also he says that accounts are not rendered every year. Therefore there is no certainty of the state of the house. And he says that the canons are not furnished with money for their habit, and this in the subprior's default.

Also he says that Gouxhille of custom, and Alforde oftentimes, do haunt the public taverns in the town of Markby, and there sit at drinkings in public with secular folk on holidays and ordinary days.

Also, whereas the same Gouxhille is precentor, he nevertheless does not follow quire, but is often absent without cause or leave; wherefore in his default the quire is not ruled in song.

Also he says that Malteby almost every day, before and after noon, goes without leave to his mother's house in the town there, and is thus well-nigh guilty of apostasy.

Also he says that Welle and Alford do oftentimes go out of the priory after compline and resort to the public taverns in the town without any leave and in cases not of necessity; and the said Welle publicly shoots at the butts in the town among secular folk.

Brother John Malteby says that religion is almost in no wise observed, and this because of the incapacity of the prior and the carelessness of the subprior, [of] who[m the one] by reason of his infirmities and [the other by reason of] his office of bursar pays no heed and cannot attend to religion.[1]

Also he says that the state of the house is not shown in common: therefore it is unknown. He confesses that he has not shown the state in common.[2]

Also he says that the canons haunt the town exceedingly without cause or leave.

Also he says that Thomas Dryby is defamed with Margaret Portere.

Also he says that silence is kept almost in no respect.

Also he says that the canons go by themselves to the town, and, if two go out together, one goes by himself to one town or place, and the other by himself elsewhere, and this in a manner much suspect.

Brother William Markeby says that silence is observed nowhere; and he says that the canons, senior and junior, go of custom out of the priory to the town without leave, and are thus almost apostate.

Also he considers the subprior unfit for that office, because he is so busy in the office of bursar that he has no time for religion, whereby it cometh to naught; and he is too fond of offices of gain, that he may be able to get some profit out of them.

Also he says that the subprior wastes the alms from their table, for he sends all the leavings therefrom to the town whither he will.

---

[2] The confession is that of the prior, or of the subprior, who, from Markeby's deposition below, appears to have had the administration of the house in his hands.

Item dicit quod supprior xxx annis habuit totale regimen omnium prouentuum domus, et nullum reddit compotum, sic quod non constat de statu domus; nam ipse sedet in camera sua, vbi omnia recipit solus et omnia solus soluit, et in libris compotorum suorum petit allocaciones solucionum quas non fecit, et adeo cautus est in compotis quod nullus alius quantumcunque discretus ipsum percipiet in subtilitatibus suis.

Item dicit quod Johannes Alforde adeo est[1] inuidus quod si quis penes se deliquerit, gerit hoc in animo per tempus et tempora semper explorans quando posset se vendicare.

Frater Johannes Bunnebury dicit se nouicium et ide[2] nescire se quicquam[3] deponere.

Post nonas eiusdem diei Thomas Dryby comparuit; et obiecto sibi articulo cum Margareta Portere, negat crimen; vnde habet terminum et locum, videlicet incontinenti et in eadem domo, ad purgandum se cum v de confratribus suis et cetera facienda que iuris sunt. Tandem, quia dixit se nullam facere purgacionem de crimine, et fatetur se habuisse communem accessum ad domum dicte mulieris, ideo dominus habuit pro conuicto, et prestito iuramento de peragendo penitenciam, etc., et prestito eciam iuramento quod decetero non accedet ad domum dicte mulieris nec eam ad familiaritatem aliquam admittet, et[4] habet in penitenciam quod omni vj et iiij feria de hinc vsque proximum festum Sancti Martini in yeme ieiunet in pane, ceruisia et vno genere leguminum, et quod citra proximum festum Michaelis dicat in claustro ad duodecim vices sex psalteria Dauitica equaliter.

Johannes Alford monitus est sub pena excommunicacionis quod decetero non admittat aliquos ad cubandum secum in dormitorio nec extra nisi tantum inmineat et vrgens[5] necessitas ineuitabilis.

Dicto eciam xix° die mensis Augusti in domo capitulari prioratus predicti, prefatus frater Johannes Fentone, prior, dictum officium, statum et dignitatem sua pure et simpliciter in manus dicti reuerendi patris resignauit; et eisdem die et loco idem reuerendus pater resignacionem huiusmodi admisit, et deinde submissis in alto et in basso dictis resignante et suppriore coniunctim ordinacioni dicti reuerendi patris vt pro vite alimentis eidem resignanti ministrandis, et submissis huiusmodi per ipsum reuerendum patrem in se admissis, idem reuerendus pater ordinauit quod ipse resignans habeat vnam honestam cameram cum camino et latrina, et cum comederit in camera sua, percipiet de pane et ceruisia ac coquina quantum duo canonici domus percipiunt et quatuor marcas per annum ad vestitum; et cum comederit cum priore vel in conuentu, seruietur sibi honesto modo, et garcio eius cum garcionibus prioris aliter[6] de remanentibus ferculi sui, cui soluet stipendia sua. Habebit eciam focalia competencia de domo. Quibus quidem ordinacionibus tam resignans quam supprior et conuentus annuerunt et consencierunt; et deinde dominus continuauit visitacionem suam vsque in tunc crastinum,

---

[1] *est* repeated and cancelled.
[2] *Sic*: for *ideo*.
[3] *des* cancelled.
[4] *Sic*: *et* is otiose.
[5] *Sic*: for *urgeat* or *sit urgens*.
[6] *Sic*: for *aletur*.

[1] *I.e.* that he could not find compurgators.

Also he says that for thirty years the subprior has had the entire governance of all the revenues of the house, and renders no account, so that there is no certainty of the state of the house: for he himself sits in his lodging, where by himself he receives all things and by himself pays all, and in his books of accounts he claims allowances for payments which he has not made, and he is so cunning in his accounts that no other man, howsoever discreet, shall catch him in his wiles.

Also he says that John Alforde is so malicious that, if any one have transgressed against him, he bears this in his heart, ever watching for some time or another when he may be able to take his revenge.

Brother John Bunnebury says that he is a novice, and therefore cannot make any deposition.

After nones of the same day, Thomas Dryby appeared, and, the article [of incest] with Margaret Portere having been put to him, he denies his guilt; wherefore he has a term and place, to wit forthwith and in the same house, to clear himself with five of his brethren, and to do what else is in course of law. At length, because he said that he made no purgation of his guilt,[1] and confesses that he had had common resort to the said woman's house, therefore my lord held him to be convicted, and, when he had proffered an oath to perform penance, etc., and had also proffered an oath that he will not go to the said woman's house henceforward, or admit her to any familiar intercourse, he has for his penance that every Friday and Wednesday from now until the next feast of St. Martin in winter he shall fast upon bread, beer and one kind of vegetables, and that before next Michaelmas he shall say twelve times in cloister six psalters of David in equal portions.

John Alford was warned under pain of excommunication that henceforward he shall admit no persons to sleep with him in the dorter or out of it, save only in the imminence of pressing and unavoidable necessity.

On the said nineteenth day of August also, in the chapter-house of the aforesaid priory, the aforesaid brother John Fenton, the prior, resigned the said his office, state and dignity purely and simply into the hands of the said reverend father; and on and in the same day and place the same reverend father admitted such his resignation, and then, the said resignant and the subprior having submitted themselves jointly high and low to the ordinance of the said reverend father, as regards the ministration of nourishment of life to the same resignant, and such submissions having been admitted in themselves by the same reverend father, the same reverend father made ordinance that the same resignant shall have an honest lodging with a fire-place and a privy, and, whenever he shall eat in his lodging, he shall receive of bread and beer and from the kitchen as much as two canons of the house receive, and four marks a year for his raiment; and, whenever he shall eat with the prior or among the convent, service shall be done him in honest wise, and his groom, to whom he shall pay his wages, shall be nourished from the leavings of his meal with the prior's grooms. He shall also have sufficient fuel from the house.[2] To the which ordinances the resignant, as well as the subprior and convent, agreed and consented; and then my lord adjourned his visitation until the morrow, there being

---

[1] For the full form of an ordinance made in a similar case, see *Visitations* I, 39 (No. XVI).

presentibus Depyng, Bug et me Colstone. Quibus termino et loco idem reuerendus pater in huiusmodi visitacionis sue negocio iudicialiter sedebat, et comparuerunt coram eo omnes canonici dicti prioratus, et recitatis omnibus actis habitis in huiusmodi negocio et recognitis, dominus libera*uit*[1] eis certas iniuncciones scriptas et sigillatas, mandans eis omnibus vt ea obseruent sub[2] penis inibi latis. Iniunxit eidem suppriori vt iniuncciones ipsas illo die ante prandium in loco capitulari coram omnibus canonicis publice vt intelligantur legat. Et deinde continuauit visitacionem suam huiusmodi vsque in diem Lune proximam post dominicam in albis proxime futuram, presentibus Johanne Depyng, Johanne Bug, Thoma Thorpe et me Colstone.

[Fo. 90*d*.] Willelmus, permissione diuina Lincolniensis episcopus, dilectis filiis suppriori et conuentui prioratus de Markeby, ordinis Sancti Augustini, nostre diocesis, ipso prioratu per cessionem fratris Johannis Fenthorpe[3], vltimi prioris eiusdem, in manus *nostras* factam et per nos admissam vacante, *ac cuicunque futuro*[4] *priori in dicto prioratu canonice substituendo*, salutem, graciam et benediccionem. Ascendente ad nos clamore de et super diuersis excessibus, defectibus, culpis et delictis inter vos et per vos tam in religione et obseruanciis regularibus quam[5] regimine temporalium et spiritualium dicti prioratus, vt asseritur, enormiter perpetratis, *necessitate compulsi* descendimus, prout nobis ex officio nostro incumbebat,[6] vt videamus si clamor ille opere compleatur. Verum *vos et* dictum vestrum prioratum actualiter visitantes ac de et super[7] premissis solicite inquirentes, comperimus luculenter ad oculum nedum per inquisicionem huiusmodi verum eciam et famam in tota vicinia super hoc laborantem *dictum monasterium per incuriam et necligenciam ac per dilapidacionem et consumpcionem rerum, bonorum et nemorum et occasione insolenciarum irrecuperabile quasi, quod dolendum est, patitur detrimentum*,[8] quod in dicto prioratu nulla religio nec obseruancie regulares, sed *nec* eciam vix effigies religionis[9] *nisi* tantum signum cui signatum minime *corespondet*: ibi vtique omnis dissolucio, nulla obediencia ibi, omnis voluntaria euagacio, tabernarum publicarum exercitacio, potaciones, commesaciones et omnis ingluuies, temporalium sine quibus presens vita duci non potest voluntaria quinymo indebita consumpcio,[10] *non dicimus carnis lubricitas, sed* finaliter omnia puritati religionis contraria ibi vigent. Volentes igitur tot et tantis religionis miseriis et calamitatibus bonos mores sic impudenter corrumpentibus remediis quibus possumus obuiare, vobis uniuersis et singulis firmiter iniungimus et mandamus, vosque monemus[11] sub[12] pena excommunicacionis,[13] quam in personas vestras singulares, si hiis nostris *infrascriptis*

---

[1] Altered from *libera* . . [cancelled].
[2] Altered from *super*.
[3] *Sic*: possibly for *Fentone*.
[4] One or two letters cancelled.
[5] *admin* cancelled.
[6] Altered from *incumbit*.
[7] *mi* cancelled.
[8] Added in margin with *laborantem* repeated at beginning, and *volentes* added at end. There appear to be a few words more, quite obliterated.
[9] *sed* cancelled.
[10] *et* cancelled.
[11] *primo, secundo, tercio peremptorie* cancelled.

present Depyng, Bug and I, Colstone. At the which term and place the same reverend father was sitting in his capacity of judge in the business of such his visitation, and there appeared before him all the canons of the said priory, and, when all the acts that had been done in such business had been recited and recognised, my lord delivered to them certain injunctions written and sealed, bidding them all to keep them under the penalties therein contained. He enjoined upon the same subprior that he should read the same injunctions that day before breakfast in the place of chapter, publicly in presence of all the canons, so that they be understood. And then he adjourned such his visitation until Monday next after Low Sunday next to come,[1] there being present John Depyng, John Bug, Thomas Thorpe and I, Colstone.

William, by divine permission bishop of Lincoln, to our beloved sons the subprior and convent of the priory of Markby, of the order of St. Austin, of our diocese, the same priory being vacant by the cession of brother John Fenthorpe,[2] the last prior thereof, which has been made into our hands and admitted by us, and to whomsoever shall be the prior to be canonically substituted in the said priory, health, grace and blessing. As there came up to us loud report of and touching divers transgressions, defaults, faults and misdeeds that were with enormity wrought, as it is averred, among you and by you, both as regards religion and the regular observances and in the governance of the matters temporal and spiritual of the said priory, under the compulsion of necessity we came down, as was incumbent upon us by reason of our office, to see if that report were fulfilled in deed. But, in our actual visitation of the said your priory, and by our anxious inquiry concerning and touching the premises, we found it clearly apparent to the eye, not only by such inquiry, but also by the report that is current in the whole neighbourhood touching this, [that] the said monastery, by carelessness and negligence, and by the dilapidation and wasting of property, goods and woods, and by occasion of disorderlinesses, is suffering, which is a grievous thing, almost irrecoverable damage; that in the said priory there is no religion or regular observances, but hardly even so much as the outward form of religion, save only the sign whereto that which is marked with it answers not. There, to wit, is all manner of laxness; there is no obedience there; all manner of wilful gadding about, haunting of public taverns, drinkings, messes, and every sort of surfeit; wilful, nay, undue wastefulness of the things temporal without which this present life cannot be passed; we do not say fleshly concupiscence, but in short all things that are contrary to the purity of religion flourish there. We therefore, wishing to meet so many and so great miseries and disasters to religion, which thus shamelessly corrupt honest manners, with what remedies we may, firmly enjoin and command you all and several, and admonish you under pain of excommunication, which we with due effect intend to pronounce against your several persons, if you or any one of you

---

[12] Cancelled by mistake.
[13] *maioris* cancelled.

[1] 13 April, 1439. The bishop appears to have been at Buckden on this date (*Visitations* II, p. xxxiii).
[2] Called Fentone at the beginning of the visitation.

mandatis et monicionibus non parueritis seu non paruerit vestrum aliquis, debito cum effectu *intendimus fulminare,*[1] vt regulam illius gloriosi doctoris beati Augustini, quam dicitis vos professos secundum literam, *quatenus fragilitas sinat humana,*[2] penitus obseruetis; silenciumque in locis et horis secundum dictam regulam[3] districte seruetis: quodque ab omni potacione post completorium abstineatis, et illo decantato, lectos in dormitorio petatis, exinde nisi ad matutinas tantum vsque ad horam surgendi in crastino sequenti consuetam secundum regulam nullatinus exituri,[4] infirmis, senibus et hiis qui officiis exterioribus presunt dumtaxat exceptis; quodque[5] septa claustralia in villam de Markeby aut aliam vicinam, *nisi in comitiua honesta, sed neque chorum post incepcionem alicuius hore maioris vel minoris ante finem eiusdem completum* absque licencia et ex causa legitima et approbata petita et obtenta exire presumatis.[6]

Vobisque iniungimus et mandamus vosque monemus primo secundo et tercio peremptorie sub pena, etc., vt supra licet cancelletur, *vt nullo modo*[7] *in dicta uilla de Markeby vel alia infra vnum* milliare in circuitu circa eandem villam de Markeby bibatis quouismodo vel comedatis; quodque[8] mulierem aliquam quantumcunque honestam in dictum prioratum inducatis[9] nec per quemquam inductam ad familiaritatem aliquam admittatis, personis illis dumtaxat exceptis de quibus iura nichil mali posse suspicari presumant, *vobis eciam sub pena excommunicacionis fulminande, et*[10] horis debitis secundum regulam contemplacioni *in*[11] *claustro* vacetis et intendatis, et alias vos honeste occupetis circa ea *que* fructum in religione producant salubrem: *quodque nullos masculos seculares ad cubandum vobiscum in*[12] *dormitorio decetero admittatis.*

Ceterum iniungimus vobis et mandamus, vosque monemus primo, secundo et tercio peremptorie sub pena excommunicacionis in vos si contrarium feceritis quod mandamus, quatinus totam et integram elemosinam ex mensis prioris et conuentus prouenientem inter pauperes magis indigentes integraliter distribuatis, nichil penitus de huiusmodi elemosina subtrahendo aut cum miseris mulierculis aut meretricibus vt solito consumendo.[13]

Preterea iniungimus[14] et mandamus vobis sub pena excommunicacionis antedicte, quam vt prefertur tulimus in scriptis et[15] sub pena *perpetue amocionis et* priuacionis cuiuslibet prioris in dicto prioratu in futurum substituendi a statu, dignitate et officio suis, ne *alicui*[16] persone quantumcunque honeste quascunque pensiones, liberatas, corrodia

---

[1] *vestris dolo, culpa et offensa nostra nostraque* (sic) *trina canonica monicione premissa in hac parte precedentibus et id merito exigentibus exnunc prout extunc et .extunc prout exnunc ferimus in hiis scriptis* cancelled.

[2] *regulam* cancelled.

[3] *eo* cancelled.

[4] *quodque null* cancelled.

[5] *nullus* cancelled.

[6] *nec vllo modo* cancelled.

[7] All in margin. For the cancelled passage referred to see note 1 above.

[8] *cum secularibus, presertim mulieribus, infra dictum prioratum* cancelled.

[9] Sic: *non* omitted.

[10] Interlined above *et quod* cancelled.

[11] *infra loca* (interlined) cancelled.

[12] *decetero* (interlined) cancelled.

[13] Added at foot of leaf.

[14] *vobis* cancelled.

[15] *super* cancelled.

[16] Interlined above *cuicunque* cancelled.

obey not these our commands and admonitions hereunder written, to observe utterly, so far as human frailty allows, the rule of that glorious doctor, blessed Austin, which you say that you have professed according to the letter; and to keep silence strictly in [the due] places and hours according to the said rule; and to abstain from all drinking after compline, and, when that has been sung, to go to your beds in the dorter, and in no wise to go out therefrom, save only to matins, until the wonted hour for rising on the morrow following, according to the rule, with exception only of those who are infirm or old and of those who are in charge of external offices; and to presume [in no wise] to go out of the cloister precincts into the town of Markeby or any other neighbouring town, unless in honest companionship, or to go out of quire after the beginning of any hour, greater or less, before it has come to an end, without asking and obtaining leave and for a reason lawful and approved.[1]

And we enjoin, command and admonish you the first, second and third time peremptorily, under pain, etc., as above, albeit it is cancelled,[2] that in no wise you drink or eat in any manner in the said town of Markeby or in any other within a mile round about the same town of Markeby: and that you bring [not] any woman, howsoever honest, into the said priory, nor, if any such be brought by anyone, admit her to any friendly converse, with exception only of those persons of whom the laws presume that no ill can be suspected, under pain, moreover, of excommunication to be pronounced against you; and that you have time for and be busy upon contemplation in the cloister at the due hours according to the rule, and elsewhere busy yourselves honestly about such things as may bring forth healthful fruit in religion; and that from henceforth you admit no males of secular condition to sleep with you in the dorter.[3]

Further we enjoin, command and admonish you the first, the second and the third time peremptorily, under pain of excommunication against you if you do what is contrary to our command, that you distribute in its entirety the whole and entire alms that comes from the tables of the prior and convent among the poor that are most needy, withdrawing nothing at all from such alms, or wasting it, as is your wont, with wretched queans or harlots.[4]

Moreover we enjoin and command you, under penalty of the excommunication aforesaid, which, as is afore mentioned, we have passed in writing, and under pain of the perpetual removal and deprivation of any prior, who hereafter shall be put in place in the said priory, of his estate, dignity and office, that you sell not or grant in any manner to

---

[1] This comprehensive injunction, composed with much care and revision, is founded upon the general evidence. Six out of eleven canons testified to the decay of religious observance; six also referred specially to the breach of silence. For drinking after compline see Saltfletby's fourth *detectum*. Six canons witnessed to the habit of wandering without leave: leaving quire in time of service was mentioned in Yorke's first and Welle's second *detecta*.

[2] See the cancelled passage in note 1 (Latin).

[3] For the special grounds of the injunction relating to Markby, see Thorntone's first, fifth, sixth, seventh and eighth, and Malteby's third and sixth *detecta*. For women in the convent, see the evidence of eight canons, and Yorke's sixth *detectum*. Neglect of contemplation is founded upon the prior's fourth and Yorke's first *detecta*. The last clause is founded on the evidence of five canons.

[4] See Markeby's third *detectum*.

aut annuetates siue census annuos imperpetuum seu ad certum tempus vel ad terminum vite absque *nostra seu* successorum nostrorum *episcoporum* Lincolniensium licencia petita et obtenta, ac maioris et sanioris partis conuentus consensu et assensu vendatis quouismodo aut concedatis.

Ordinamus insuper, volumus et iniungimus quod omne[1] pecunie ex redditibus et prouentibus aliis quibuscunque ad dictum prioratum qualitercunque spectantibus[2] vel aliunde prouenientes per vnam fidelem, discretam et sufficientem personam colligantur, et duobus bursariis per tallia vel indenturas liberentur et per eosdem bursariis[3] aliis officiariis per tallia vel indenturas exsoluantur in vtilitatem domus exponende; et quod omni anno inter festa[4] Annunciacionis dominice et apostolorum Philippi et Jacobi plenus compotus de totali administracione bonorum dicti prioratus in loco capitulari coram conuentu vel personis ad hoc per conuentum assignandis omnino reddatur.

Hac[5] igitur iniuncciones ac ordinaciones et mandata nostra vobis transmittimus per vos vestrosque successores[6] sub penis supradictis inuiolabiliter obseruanda, salua et reseruata nobis potestate premissa moderandi, eis addendi et alia de nouo iuxta exigenciam detectorum et compertorum in visitacione nostra faciendi et mandandi, cum nobis visum fuerit expedire, libera potestate.[7] Data sub sigillo nostro in prioratu de Markeby[8] xx die mensis Augusti, anno Domini mccccxxxviij⁰, nostrarumque consecracionis anno xiij⁰ et translacionis secundo.

[At the foot of the page are added these words, which fit in at some point of the injunctions unspecified.]

Et quod horis aliis canonicis et diuinis obsequiis *intersint et intendant ab hiis nullatinus recedendo*[9] *nec in naui monasterii aut alibi vagando* nec *cum quocunque confabulando nisi* de licencia prioris petita et obtenta *ex causa racionabili priori cognita et approbata.*

---

[1] *Sic*: for *omnes.*
[2] *pro* cancelled.
[3] *Sic*: for *bursarios.*
[4] *sc* cancelled.
[5] *Sic*: for *has* or *hec.*
[6] *transm* cancelled.
[7] *Sic.*
[8] *xix* cancelled.
[9] *quousque* cancelled.

any person, howsoever honest, any pensions, liveries, corrodies or annuities or yearly allowances whatsoever, for ever or for a certain time or for term of life, without licence of us or of our successors, bishops of Lincoln, asked and had, and the consent and assent of the more and sounder part of the convent.[1]

We ordain, moreover, will and enjoin that all the monies from the rents and other revenues whatsoever in any wise belonging to the said priory or from elsewhere forthcoming, be collected by a trusty, discreet and sufficient person, and be delivered to two bursars by tallies or indentures, and be paid by tallies and indentures to the other officers by the same bursars, to be laid out to the advantage of the house; and that every year, between the feasts of the Annunciation of our Lady and of the apostles Philip and James, a full account of the whole administration of the goods of the said priory be rendered altogether in the place of chapter, in presence of the convent or of the persons to be appointed by the convent to this end.[2]

These our injunctions aud ordinances and mandates therefore we convey to you, to be observed without breach by you and your successors under the pains abovesaid, saving and with reservation to ourselves of the power of modifying the premises, adding to them, and free power of making and commanding others anew, according as the matters disclosed and discovered in our visitation require, whenever it shall seem expedient to us. Given under our seal in the priory of Markeby, on the twentieth day of the month of August, in the year of our Lord 1438, and of our consecration the thirteenth and our translation the second year.

And that they be present and diligent at the other canonical hours and divine services, in no wise departing from them, or strolling in the nave of the monastery or elsewhere, or chattering with anybody whomsoever, save with leave of the prior asked and had for a reasonable cause known to and approved by the prior.[3]

---

[1] See Yorke's third *detectum*. The case of John Kyrkeby (Saltfletby's third and Dryby's second *detecta*) is another instance.

[2] The financial straits of the priory are indicated in the prior's third, the subprior's fourth, Welle's fifth, Thornton's fifth and Malteby's second *detecta*. For the need of appointing bursars see Alforde's second and Markeby's fourth *detecta*.

[3] This appears to belong to the first injunction.

XLIV.

[Fo. 6]

VISITACIO PRIORATUS DE MARKEYATE, ORDINIS SANCTI BENEDICTI, LINCOLNIENSIS DIOCESIS, FACTA IN DOMO CAPITULARI IBIDEM VIJ⁰ DIE MENSIS MAIJ, ANNO DOMINI MCCCCXLIJ⁰, PER REUERENDUM IN CHRISTO PATREM ET DOMINUM, DOMINUM WILLELMUM, DEI GRACIA LINCOLNIENSEM EPISCOPUM, SUARUM CONSECRACIONIS ANNO XVJ⁰ ET TRANSLACIONIS SEXTO.

In primis, sedente dicto reuerendo patre die et loco supradictis in negocio visitacionis sue huiusmodi inchoando, comparuerunt coram eo priorissa et conuentus dicti loci, septem in numero; et exposito[1] eis per dominum causa aduentus sui, videlicet pro visitacione sua ordinaria inibi excercenda, peciit certificatorium mandati sui ipsi priorisse hoc in casu directe[2]. Que dixit quod non habuit clericum pro huiusmodi certificatorio scribendo paratum; super quo submisit se gracie domini et exhibuit exinde domino ipsum mandatum originale et nomina citatarum loco certificatorii. Quibus per dominum ex gracia admissis, iurauit eadem priorissa corporaliter tacto libro fidelitatem et obedienciam dicto reuerendo patri et ministris suis in licitis, etc. Deinde exhibuit fundacionem domus, statum domus et confirmacionem eleccionis sue, et dicit quod domus potest expendere lxxxxij li.; et dicit quod ad satisfaciendum creditoribus domus prostrauit vnum paruum boscum.

Domina Dionisia Louelyche, priorissa, dicit quod moniales nonnunquam loquuntur cum secularibus, nulla alia moniali audiente aut vidente quid dicunt vel faciunt.

Item quod aliquando moniales visitantes parentes et amicos suos stant cum eis per septem vel octo dies preter dies ad iter in eundo et redeundo.

Domina Isabella Reconge, suppriorissa, dicit quod tantum perciupiunt de domo panem, ceruisiam et ij marcas ad vestitum et cetera necessaria ad victum, que minus sufficiunt ad singula necessaria.

Item dicit quod non habetur lumen de nocte in dormitorio ad magnum tedium monialibus in surgendo de nocte.

Domina Anna Wylby dicit quod contra consuetudinem domus et ordinis *suppriorissa* occupat duo officia, videlicet supprioratus et sacristie.

---

[1] *Sic*: for *exposita*.
[2] *Sic*: for *directi*.

[1] Printed in *Monasticon* III, 372. No chartulary appears to remain. For the foundation see *Visitations* I, 157.

[2] Her election is not recorded. She had been compelled to resign in 1433 owing to the grave charges brought against her (see *Visitations* I, 82-6), and her re-appearance as prioress in 1442 is curious.

XLIV.

THE VISITATION OF THE PRIORY OF MARKYATE, OF THE ORDER OF
ST. BENET, OF THE DIOCESE OF LINCOLN, PERFORMED IN THE
CHAPTER-HOUSE THEREIN ON THE SEVENTH DAY OF THE MONTH
OF MAY, IN THE YEAR OF OUR LORD 1442, BY THE REVEREND
FATHER IN CHRIST AND LORD, THE LORD WILLIAM, BY THE GRACE
OF GOD BISHOP OF LINCOLN, IN THE SIXTEENTH YEAR OF HIS
CONSECRATION AND THE SIXTH OF HIS TRANSLATION.

In the first place, as the said reverend father was sitting on and in
the day and place abovesaid at the beginning of the business of such
his visitation, there appeared before him the prioress and convent of
the said place, seven in number; and after the reason of his coming,
to wit, that he might hold his visitation therein as ordinary, had been
set forth to them by my lord, he asked for the certificate of his mandate
which had been addressed in this event to the same prioress. And she
said that she had not a clerk who was equipped for writing such certificate; on the which head she submitted herself to my lord's grace and
then shewed my lord the original mandate itself and the names of [the
nuns] who had been summoned, in lieu of a certificate. The which
having been accepted by my lord of his grace, the same prioress sware
on her body, having touched the book, fealty and obedience to the said
reverend father and his ministers in things lawful, etc. Then she shewed
the foundation of the house,[1] the state of the house and the confirmation
of her election,[2] and she says that the house is able to spend £92; and she
says that, to satisfy the creditors of the house, she has felled one little
wood.

Dame Denise Louelyche,[3] the prioress, says that the nuns do sometimes talk with secular folk, with no other nun to hear or see what they
say or do.

Also that sometimes the nuns, when they visit their parents and
friends, do stay with them for seven or eight days, not counting the days
for their journey on the way there and back.

Dame Isabel Reconge, the subprioress, says that they receive of
the house only bread, beer and two marks for their raiment and what
else is necessary to their living, which are less than enough for their
sundry needful wants.

Also she says that a light is not kept at night in the dorter, to the
great nuisance of the nuns when they rise of a night.

Dame Anne Wylby says that, contrary to the custom of the house
and order, the subprioress holds two offices, to wit, those of subprioress
and sacrist.

---

[3] The numbers of the convent appear to have sunk from ten in 1433 to seven
in 1442, and there are no new names: see *Visitations* I, 85. Three place-names
occur, Wylby, Wyrehale and Tyttesbury, none of which seem to belong to the neighbourhood. Isabel Reconge, Joan Marchaund and Joan Wirale or Verser had been
professed, with four other nuns, 2 Dec., 1414, being already *tacite professe* (Reg.
xv, fo. 115d.).

Item dicit quod non habetur ibidem confessor aliquis[1] ad audiendum confessiones monialium auctoritate domini deputatus nisi vnus frater[2] de conuentu de Dunstaple nullam habens auctoritatem in ea parte.

Domina Johanna Marchaunt dicit quod ex permissu priorisse moniales confabulantur cum *secularibus*[3] [nulla] alia audiente sed ad votum et libitum.

Item dicit quod iuuenes nouicie portantes habitum non professe deputantur certis officiis in monasterio.

Item dicit quod priorissa semper tenet et per vij annos tenuit vnam et eandem monialem in capellanam absque aliqua alterius surrogacione, et[4] quando transit ad extra habet semper secum istam iuuenem monialem, et videtur quod haberet secum prouecciores.

Item memorandum est quod dominus loquatur priorisse quod cohibeat seruientes seculares ne ita rigide habeant se erga moniales, et quod melius respiciat ad moniales prius lapsas vt arcius custodiantur solito ne iterum labantur.

[Fo. 6*d*.] Domina Johanna Wyrehale dicit de confessore vt cum venerit diucius immoretur pro confessionibus maturius audiendis, etc., et de lumine habendo in dormitorio de nocte.

Item dicit de parcitate victus et vestitus monialium vt supra.[5]

Domina Katerina Tyttesbury dicit de parcitate victus et vestitus vt supra.

Item dicit quod moniales non habent aliquam mulierem que lauet vestes suas et paret cibaria sua, propter quod aut oportet eas abesse a diuinis circa premissa *aut*[6] semper cogitare de hiis parandis.

Item dicit quod priorissa percipit omnes oblaciones prouenientes ad ecclesiam ibidem que pertinerent officio sacristie, et nescitur quid agitur de huiusmodi pecuniis, sed et nouicias deputat in officiis huiusmodi.

Item dicit quod nouicie steterunt in habitu non professe et in etate legitima, quedam per duos, quedam per tres annos.

Domina Margareta Louelyche, cappellana priorisse, dicit quod stetit in huiusmodi officio per viij⁰ annos vltimos.

Fiat iniunccio de non admittendo alienos parochianos ad diuina diebus dominicis seu festiuis.

Quibus examinatis et demum huiusmodi inquisicione preparatoria publicata, habitaque communicacione per dominum cum priorissa et officiariis suis in temporalibus de et super regimine domus vt pro resolucione eris alieni quo in magna summa domus diuersis creditoribus

---

[1] *auctoritate domini* cancelled.

[2] *de conuentu* cancelled.

[3] Interlined above *monialibus* cancelled.

[4] *semper* cancelled.

[5] The margin is much torn, but *p*[*riorissa*] appears against this and one or two other of the *detecta*. It may be noted here that each paragraph of the *detecta* is marked with a marginal cross, doubtless made during the composition of the injunctions.

[6] Interlined above *p* cancelled.

---

[1] Markyate is 4½ miles S.E. of Dunstable, on the road to St. Albans.

[2] See Lyndwood, *Provinciale*, ed. 1679, p. 211 (tit. *de stat. regul.* c. *Omnem*, v. *ab Episcopis*.) The words of the constitution are: ' Confiteantur etiam moniales sacerdotibus sibi ab episcopis deputatis.' This, as Lyndwood remarks, involves a prohibition to nuns to choose their own confessor, unless they are specially privileged

Also she says that they have not therein any confessor appointed by my lord's authority to hear the nuns' confessions, save a friar of the convent of Dunstable[1] who has no authority in that behalf.[2]

Dame Joan Marchaunt says that the nuns hold speech with secular folk with the prioress's permission, when [none] other is in hearing, but at their wish and will.

Also she says that the young novices who wear the habit without having made profession are appointed to certain offices in the monastery.

Also she says that the prioress always keeps and for seven years has kept one and the same nun as her chaplain without substituting another in her place, and when she goes abroad she always has this young nun with her, and it seems that she should have with her persons of more mature years.

Also it should be kept in mind that my lord do speak to the prioress, to the end that she restrain the secular serving-folk from bearing themselves so stiffly towards the nuns and that she take better heed to the nuns who have previously erred, so that they be kept more strictly from erring again than is the wont.

Dame Joan Wyrehale says of the confessor that, when he comes, he should stay longer in order to hear confessions more thoroughly, and of the light that should be kept at night in the dorter.

Also she says as above concerning the scantiness of the nuns' victual and raiment.

Dame Katherine Tyttesbury[3] says as above concerning the scantiness of victual and raiment.

Also she says that the nuns have no woman to wash their clothes and get ready their food, for which reason they have either to stay away from divine service to look after the [food] aforeset or be always thinking about getting it ready.

Also she says that the prioress takes all the oblations accruing to the church in that place, which should belong to the office of the sacristy, and it is not known what is done with such monies, but she puts even novices in charge of such offices.

Also she says that novices who have not made profession and are of lawful age have continued wearing the habit, some for two, some for three years.

Dame Margaret Louelyche, the prioress's chaplain, says that she has continued in such office for the last eight years.[4]

Let an injunction be made that parishioners from elsewhere be not admitted to divine service on Sundays or feast-days.

Now, after these had been examined and such preparatory inquiry had at length been made public, and after counsel had been held by my lord with the prioress and her temporal officers concerning and respecting the governance of the house as regards the payment of the debt, wherein

---

or the custom of their order is otherwise. He refers to Gratian, ca. 18, qu. 2, c. 11: ' Qui religiosis feminis preponendus est ab episcopo comprobetur ' (4 Carthage, c. 39).

[3] Katherine Tyttesbury had gone into apostasy in 1433 (*Visitations* I, 83).

[4] This shows that Denise Lovelyche or Lowelyche had been restored as prioress as early, at any rate, as May, 1434. Her previous resignation took place in June, 1433.

obligatur, dominus, reseruata sibi potestate faciendi et transmittendi
iniuncciones et mandata sua super compertis predictis, visitacionem
suam huiusmodi dissoluit. Et monuit priorissam et singulas moniales
domus primo, secundo et tercio peremptorie sub pena excommunicacionis
ne earum aliqua[1] aliquam de ceteris improperet occasione detectorum
predictorum, presentibus magistro Johanne Leke, Thoma Thorpe et
me Colstone.

[INJUNCTIONS].

Wyllyam, by the grace of God bysshop of Lincolne, to our wele
belufed doghters in God the prioresse and the couent of the priorye of
Seynt Trynytee in the wode besyde Markeyate, of the order of Seynt
Benette, of our diocyse, helthe, grace and our blessyng. Now late we
visityng yow and your saide priorye fonde by our [in]quisicyone preparatory certeyn notable defautes requiryng dewe reformacyone, for
correccyone and reformacyone whereof we sende yow thise our iniunccyons
ordinaunces and commaundementes by yowe and yche one of yow and
your successours to be kepped vndere peynes here benethe writene.

In the fyrste, for as we fynde by [our] saide inquisicione that every
nunne takes in the yere to thaire sustynaunce and habyte alle onely
brede and ale and two marke of monye, where fore thai entende so bysyly
about purveying and dyghtyng of thair vytayle that often tymes thai
are absent fro the qwere in tyme of dyuyne seruyce, and ofte beyng ther
present thair myndes are rathere on thair mete purveying then vpone
the seruyce of God to kepyng of religyon, and here fore thai holde many
housholdes, wherthurghe as we drede comes many harmes and causes of
dissolucyone. Where fore we commaunde, enioyne and ordeyne[2] by
your allere assent *that* fro hense forthe ye all ete *to gedre* in one house,
oythere in the fraytour, fermorye or the prioresse halle or chaumbre, so
that no seculares sytte among the nunnes in tyme of mete ne sopere, and
that in tyme of mete ye hafe somwhat *redde* a fore yowe of holy wrytte or
seyntes lyfe, to the whiche redyng alle ye entende all other vayn talkyng
lafte, and that ye, prioresse, and your successours mynystre to your
sustres in commune brede and ale and *alle* other vitaile *necessary to youre*
sustynaunce of the commune godes of the house owte of one selare and
one kytchyne, and that ye pay euery nunne to thaire vesture a noble
yerely at termes vsuelle.[3]

Also we enioyne yowe, prioresse, vndere peyne of contempte that
euery yere ye chaunge your chapeleyn, and whan yow muste go owte of
the place ye take wyth *yowe* in your [com]pany a nunne wele appreuede
in religyone, so that ye hafe the[4] mo wyttenesses of your gode [con]uer-
sacyone.[5]

---

[1] Altered from *aliquos*.
[2] There is a reference in the text to a marginal note, which has disappeared.
[3] Founded on the first *detectum* of the sub-prioress, the second of Joan Wyrehale
and the first and second of Katherine Tyttesbury. No specific evidence is reported
with regard to the separate households or any abuse of frater.
[4] *most* cancelled.

the house is bound in a large amount to divers creditors, my lord, having reserved to himself the power of making and despatching his injunctions and commandments touching the discoveries aforesaid, dissolved such his visitation.   And he warned the prioress and the several nuns of the house the first, second and third time peremptorily under pain of excommunication, that none of them should rebuke any of the others on account of the disclosures aforesaid, there being present master John Leke, Thomas Thorpe and I Colstone.

Also we enioyne yow, prioresse, vndere the same peynes of contempte and cursyng that [when] your susters shalle visyte thayre frendes ye licence thaym *not* to be absent owtt of the place passed . . .[1] dayes at the moste oure resonable tyme to go and come, so that thai hafe wythe thayme a nunne approved in *the* religyon and honeste company.[2]

Also we enioyne yowe prioresse vnder the same peynes [that] ye suffre none of your susters to hafe any conuersacyone wythe seculere persones but if a nunne approved [in] religione be present to here and see what thai say or doo, ne that ye suffre none of your sustres to [Fo. 7] receyve ne sende owte lettres, tokens ne gyftes but ye fyrst see what is in conteyned in the l[ettres] and what are the tokens and gyftes.[3]

And also that ye diligently see to thoe of your susters that of freyle[te] hafe fallen here afore, that thai hafe none occasyone ne libertee to falle here aftere.[4]

And also that ye refreyne your seculere seruauntes that honestely and not sturdyly ne rebukyngly thai hafe thaym in thair langage to the susters, and that ye hafe an honest woman lauendere of the coste of the howse to wasshe your sustres clothes.[5]

Also we charge[6] and enioyne yowe, prioresse, vndere the same peynes that as sone as ye may and wythe haste possyble ye do your sustres now nouyces that are of lawfulle age and that hafe staide in religyon ouere j[7] yere of prefe to be expressely professed by a bysshop wythe oure autoritee, and to suche tyme as thai be so professede ye putte to occupye any office wyth ynne or wyth owte your place.[8]

Also we enioyne yow, prioresse, vndere the same peynes that nyghtly ye hafe competent lyght in the dormytory to the ease of your susters in rysyng to mattyns.[9]

---

[5] Founded on Joan Marchaunt's third *detectum* and the admission made by Margaret Louelyche.

[1] The number has disappeared: probably *three*.
[2] Founded on the prioress's second *detectum*.
[3] Founded on the prioress's and Joan Marchaunt's first *detecta* respectively.
[4] Founded on Joan Marchaunt's fourth *detectum*.
[5] Founded on Joan Marchaunt's fourth and Katherine Tyttesbury's second *detecta*.
[6] *yowe* cancelled.
[7] Interlined: *a* cancelled.
[8] Founded on Joan Marchaunt's second and Katherine Tyttesbury's fourth *detecta*.   There is a marginal note opposite this injunction, apparently summing up the contents in Latin, but most of it is torn away and the only word that can be made out is *quis*.   The last clause is defective: read 'ye put them not.'
[9] Founded on the sub-prioress's second and Joan Wyrehale's first *detecta*.

Also we charge vow prioresse, etc., vt in decima iniunccione Anker-wyk.[1]

Also we enioyne yow, prioresse, etc., vt in tercia decima iniunccione ibidem.

Also we enioyne yowe, prioresse and couent, vndere peyne of sus-pensyon of sayng of dyuyne seruyce and also vnde[re] peyne of enter-dytyng of your churche, that fro hense forthe specyally on Sondayes

---

XLV.

[Fo. 115]

VISITACIO PRIORATUS DE NEWENHAM, ORDINIS SANCTI AUGUSTINI, LINCOLNIENSIS DIOCESIS, FACTA IN DOMO CAPITULARI IBIDEM XVIIJ° DIE MENSIS JANUARIJ, ANNO DOMINI MCCCCXLIJ°, PER REUERENDUM IN CHRISTO PATREM ET DOMINUM, DOMINUM WILLELMUM, DEI GRACIA LINCOLNIENSEM EPISCOPUM, SUARUM CONSECRACIONIS ANNO XVIJ° ET TRANSLACIONIS VIJ°.

In primis, sedente iudicialiter dicto reuerendo patre in huiusmodi visitacionis sue inchoando negocio, comparuerunt coram eo prior et canonici dicti prioratus, parati vt apparuit ab[2] subeundum visitacionem eiusdem reuerendi patris. Et deinde primo et ante omnia propositum fuit verbum Dei iuxta actus futuri congruenciam per honorabilem virum magistrum Thomam Twyere, in sacra pagina scolarem, sequentem hoc thema, ' Nupcie facte sunt',[3] etc. Quo laudabiliter *in* lingua latina finito, prior loci liberauit dicto reuerendo patri certificatorium mandati domini sibi pro huiusmodi visitacione directi, in hec verba, ' Reuerendo in Christo patri,' etc.; quo perlecto idem prior liberauit domino copiam fundacionis prioratus que remanet penes registrarium. Exhibuit eciam confirmacionem eleccionis sue factam per magistrum Thomam Hore, auctoritate magistri Petri Partriche tunc officialis Lincolniensis sede vacante: et post hec idem prior iurauit obedienciam et fidelitatem domino in forma consueta. Postea exhibet statum domus, et deinde dominus processit ad inquisicionem suam preparatoriam sub forma sequenti.

---

[1] See No. i above (*Visitations* II, 9). The tenth injunction in question is the customary one against grants of corrodies and felling timber, while the thirteenth requires the presentation of an account twice a year. See the prioress's statement as to felling timber and Katherine Tyttesbury's third *detectum*.

[2] *Sic*: for *ad*.

[3] St. John ii, 1.

[1] See the note for a special injunction to be made on this head.

[2] *d* cancelled. For the Legbourne injunctions see *Visitations* II (No. xxxix).

[3] A note follows this: ' Joh. Gladman audito manente in Wendlyngburghe.' The word *manente* is written oddly, but this appears to be the right reading.

[4] 18 January, 1442-3.

[5] See *Visitations* II, 60, note 2. Twyer was appointed penitenciary in the diocese by Alnwick, 9 Nov., 1437, and on 1 Dec. following received a second appointment from the bishop ' ad ministrandum gregi suo pabulum verbi Dei ubique per suam diocesim ' (Reg. XVIII, ff. 30*d*., 31*d*.).

ne other festiuale day[es] ye receyve ne admytte or suffre any parysshens of townes abowte yowe to here any dyvyne seruyce in your churche fore preiudyce and harme and peryle of sowle that may fall there by.[1]

Ferthermore we monysshe yowe, etc., in inunccionibus Legburne, etc.[2]

Yeven vnder our seale, etc.[3]

XLV.

THE VISITATION OF THE PRIORY OF NEWNHAM, OF THE ORDER OF ST. AUSTIN, OF THE DIOCESE OF LINCOLN, PERFORMED IN THE CHAPTER-HOUSE THEREIN ON THE EIGHTEENTH DAY OF THE MONTH OF JANUARY, IN THE YEAR OF OUR LORD 1442,[4] BY THE REVEREND FATHER IN CHRIST AND LORD, THE LORD WILLIAM, BY THE GRACE OF GOD BISHOP OF LINCOLN, IN THE SEVENTEENTH YEAR OF HIS CONSECRATION AND THE SEVENTH OF HIS TRANSLATION.

In the first place, as the said reverend father was sitting in his capacity of judge, at the beginning of the business of such his visitation, there appeared before him the prior and canons of the said priory, ready, as was apparent, to undergo the visitation of the same reverend father. And then, first and before all else, the word of God was set forth as was agreeable to the act that was about to take place by the honourable master Thomas Twyere,[5] student in holy writ, after this text, ' A marriage was made,' etc. And, when this was come to a praiseworthy end in the Latin tongue, the prior of the place delivered to the said reverend father the certificate of my lord's mandate, which had been addressed to him for such visitation, in these words, ' To the reverend father in Christ,' etc.; and, after this had been read through, the same prior delivered to my lord the copy of the foundation of the priory,[6] which remains in the hands of the registrar. He exhibited also the confirmation of his election executed by master Thomas Hore, by authority of master Peter Partriche, at that time official of Lincoln in the voidance of the see;[7] and after this the same prior sware obedience and fealty to my lord in form accustomed. Thereafter he makes exhibition of the state of the house, and then my lord proceeded to his preparatory inquiry in form following.

---

[6] Presumably the charter of Simon de Beauchamp, granted about 1166: see V.C.H. Beds. II, 378. There is a chartulary of Newnham in MS. Harl. 3656, for the contents of which see Monasticon VI (i), 373. The confirmatory charter of Thomas Mowbray, earl marshal, embodying that of William Beauchamp, the founder's son, is printed ibid. 374-377.

[7] For Peter Partriche see Visitations II, 175. The vacancy referred to is that between Gray's death in February, 1435-6, and Alnwick's translation from Norwich in September following. This gives us the date of the accession of John Bromham as prior, which is not recorded elsewhere.

Frater Johannes Bromham prior dicit quod prior et conuentus elegerunt communi assensu fratrem Johannem Goldyngtone in suppriorem et Willelmum Wolastone in tercium priorem, qui sic electi renuunt subire officia huiusmodi.

Item idem Willelmus Wolastone est inobediens precept*is*[1] prioris vt in sequendo chorum et aliis regulariis.[2] Comparet et fatetur se non subisse onus officii tercii prioris et allegat se sequi chorum continue nocte et die.

Item fratres Willelmus Thornham et[3] Johannes Kempstone non seruant claustrum et nihil sciunt nec laborant ad scienciam; ymo contra preceptum prioris vagantur ad exteriora nec contentantur cibis appositis, ymo exquirunt lauciora. Comparent ambo et fatentur se exire loca claustralia absque licencia, non tamen extra prioratum. Iurati sunt quod decetero non exeant loca claustralia nisi de licencia prioris vel alterius presidentis petita et obtenta.

Frater Johannes Kempstone adulteratur cum Margareta Buchere coniugata de parochia Sancti Petri Mertone in Bedfordia. Comparet et fatetur accessum ad mulierem sed negat crimen ab omni tempore, vnde indicta est sibi purgacio cum tribus fratribus, qui produxit tres fratres cum quibus se purgauit. Postea abiurauit eam et omnia loca suspecta sub pena custodiendi claustrum et silencium per tres menses.

Idem quotidie mane visitat coquinam, maiorem curam habens de ventre quam de obsequio diuino. Iniunctum est eidem quod decetero abstineat ab huiusmodi insolenciis.

Item Willelmus Wolastone non contentatur cum cibis appositis in mensa sed currit ad coquinam sumens sibi ibidem fercula que sibi magis placent. Dicit quod seruitur sibi aliquociens de insulsis. Iniunctum est priori quod faciat deseruiri sibi competenter de cibariis et iniunctum est eidem Willelmo quod decetero abstineat a talibus.

Item Willelmus Thornham incontinenter viuit cum Matilde Irysshe[4] de[5] Bedeforde. Comparuit et negat articulum ab omni tempore: indicta est sibi purgacio cum duobus fratribus crastino die summo mane: quo crastino comparuit dictus Thornham et cum ij fratribus se purgauit. Postea abiurauit loca suspecta et dictam Matildem.

Frater Johannes Rothewelle adulteratur cum Alicia vxore Johannis Mountagu de Goldyngtone. Comparuit et negat articulum, vnde habet crastinum diem ad purgandum se cum iiij manu; quo crastino comparuit et cum iij confratribus se purgauit: abiurauit eciam dictam mulierem et loca suspecta.

---

[1] *is* interlined above *oris* cancelled.
[2] *Sic*: for *regularibus obseruanciis*.
[3] A word cancelled.
[4] *of* cancelled.
[5] *Goldyngtone* cancelled.

[1] Fourteen canons are named, of whom Bromham, the two Bedefordes, Carletone, Goldyngtone, Kempstone, Rounhale (Renhold), Stachedene (Stagsden) and Stevyngtone bore local place-surnames. Of the remaining five, Olney came from the neighbouring part of Buckinghamshire; Wolastone bore the name of a village just across the border of Northamptonshire; while Rothwelle probably came from the same county. The origin of Dardes and Thornham is not clear: Thornham may

Brother John Bromham, the prior,[1] says that the prior and convent by common assent elected brother John Goldyngtone to be subprior, and William Wolastone to be third prior; the which persons thus elected refuse to bear such offices.

Also the same William Wolastone is disobedient to the prior's commands as regards attendance in quire and the other regular observances. He appears and confesses that he has not undertaken the burthen of the office of third prior, and asserts that he constantly attends quire night and day.

Also brothers William Thornham and John Kempstone do not keep cloister, and they know nothing and take no pains after knowledge; but they wander out of doors contrary to the prior's order, and are not content with the meats that are set before them, but seek out more sumptuous diet. They both appear and confess that they go outside the cloister precincts without leave, but not outside the priory. They are sworn that henceforth they will not go out of the cloister precincts, unless with the leave of the prior or of another president asked and had.

Brother John Kempstone commits adultery with Margaret Buchere, married woman, of the parish of St. Peter Mertone[2] in Bedford. He appears and confesses his recourse to the woman, but denies his guilt at any time; wherefore he was appointed to make purgation with three of his brethren, and brought forward three brethren with whom he cleared himself. Thereafter he abjured her and all suspect places, under pain of keeping cloister and silence for three months.

The same [brother] daily visits the kitchen early in the morning, having more care for his belly than for divine service. He was enjoined to abstain from such disorderly habits henceforward.

Also William Wolastone is not content with the meats that are set before him at table, but runs to the kitchen, taking there for himself the dishes that please him better. He says that sometimes he is served with unsavoury food. The prior was enjoined to cause competent service to be done him in food, and the same William was enjoined to abstain henceforward from such doings.

Also William Thornham lives incontinently with Maud Irysshe of Bedford. He appeared and denies the article at any time; he was ordered to make his purgation with two of his brethren on the morrow at earliest morning. On the which morrow the said Thornham appeared and made his purgation with two brethren. Thereafter he abjured suspect places and the said Maud.

Brother John Rothewelle commits adultery with Alice, the wife of John Mountagu of Goldington.[3] He appeared and denies the article; wherefore he has the morrow for his purgation with three others. On the which morrow he appeared and made his purgation with three of his brethren. He abjured also the said woman and suspect places.

---

possibly have been transferred to Newnham from the priory of Thornholm in Lincolnshire.

    [2] St. Peter Martin, the church at the north end of High Street in Bedford.

    [3] Goldington is 1¾ miles N.E. of Bedford, on the road to St. Neots. Newnham priory was in this parish.

Frater Johannes Kempstone *quasi* illiteratus est nec intelligit quid legit nec laborat ad scienciam habendam.

Multi canonici non contentantur fercula[1] que sibi apponuntur, ymo semper murmurant, et tamen mittunt fercula sua non ad coquinam nec ad elemosinam sed quo voluerint.

[Fo. 115*d*.]   Frater Willelmus Bedeforde᛫ supprior dicit quod prior est remissus[2] et nimis necgligens in corrigendo excessus et defectus fratrum delinquencium: ymo ad faciendum correcciones est nimis meticulosus.

Prior est nimis leuis in concedendo canonicis licenciam exeundi prioratum, propter quod timetur de grauibus periculis.

Prior habet omnia officia domus in manu sua et per hoc dissipantur implementa eorum et nichil innouatur in eisdem.

Frater Willelmus Wolastone dicit quod prior excusat se ab interioribus propter exteriora agenda et sic religio perit.

Non habentur mappalia honesta pro canonicis in refectorio in defectu prioris.

In singulis officiis vt in sacristia et refectorio *ac hospicio et infirmaria* nichil innouatur sed antiqua consumuntur ita quod omnia tendunt ad non esse.

Prior non reddit claros compotos administracionis sue annuatim coram capitulo vt tenetur, et ideo nescitur qualiter stat cum domo. Iniunctum est priori quod citra proximum [*blank*] post festum natalis Domini plenum et planum compotum de totali administracione bonorum spiritualium et temporalium prioratus.[3]

Prior non assignat aliquem canonicum ad dicendum horas canonicas canonicis infirmis.

Prior consuluit quosdam nigromanticos pro rebus ecclesie alienatis.

[Fo. 116].   (Prior.)   Non habetur aliquis instructor in grammatica qui informet canonicos, et ideo sunt quasi mere laici et propterea non intendunt libris.   Iniunctum est priori[4] prouideat de instructore citra proximum festum Sancti Michaelis.

(Prior.)   Subtrahuntur elemosine que solent ex consuetudine dari pro animabus canonicorum in diebus obituum suorum, videlicet vnus panis et vnum ferculum de coquina.

(Prior.)   Omnia maneria pertinencia monasterio sunt quasi totaliter ruinosa.

(Prior.)   Seculares communiter prandent in refectorio tempore refeccionis canonicorum contra instituta regularia.

Petitur quod deputetur eis vnus auditor secularis qui audiat et terminet[5] compotos domus.   Iniunctum est prior[6] quod citra proximum festum Michaelis prouideat de auditore qui secundum legem auditorii audiat et terminet compotos monasterii per biennium.

---

[1] *Sic*: for *ferculis.*
[2] *meticulosus* interlined and cancelled.
[3] *Sic*: incomplete sentence.
[4] *vt infra annum* cancelled.
[5] A letter cancelled.
[6] *Sic*: for *priori.*

[1] Cf. the case of the abbot of Leicester, *Visitations* ii, 209, etc.
[2] The *recto* of fo. 116 is occupied with a series of *comperta*, apparently digested from the depositions of the remaining canons, which are given somewhat briefly on fo. 116*d*.

Brother John Kempstone is almost unlettered and understands not what he reads, nor does he work to acquire knowledge.

Many of the canons are not content with the dishes that are set before them, but are ever murmuring, and yet they send their dishes, not to the kitchen or to the almonry, but whither they will.

Brother William Bedeforde, the subprior, says that the prior is remiss and excessively careless in the correction of the transgressions and defaults of offending brethren: nay, he is excessively timid in making corrections.

The prior is over easy in granting the canons leave to go out of the priory, by reason whereof there is fear of grievous dangers.

The prior has all the offices of the house in his hand, and for this reason the implements that belong to them are scattered abroad and nothing is renewed in the same.

Brother William Wolastone says that the prior excuses himself from internal duties because of business out of doors, and thus religion comes to naught.

They have no seemly table-cloths for the canons in the frater, in the prior's default.

In the several offices, as in the sacristy and frater and the guest-house and infirmary nothing is renewed, but the old stuff is worn out, perishing, so that all things are on the way to perishing.

The prior does not render clear accounts of his administration yearly in presence of the chapter, as he is bound, and therefore it is not known how it stands with the house. The prior was enjoined to [render] a full and plain account of the entire administration of the spiritual and temporal goods of the priory before [blank] next after the feast of the nativity of our Lord.

The prior does not appoint any canon to say the canonical hours to the canons in the infirmary.

The prior has taken counsel with certain sorcerers for the goods of the church that have been alienated.[1]

(The prior.)[2] There is no teacher in grammar to instruct the canons, and therefore they are almost nothing but laymen, and because of this they pay no attention to books. The prior was enjoined [to] make provision of a teacher before the next feast of St. Michael.

(The prior.) The alms are withdrawn which of custom are wont to be given for the souls of the canons on their obit days, to wit, a loaf and a dish from the kitchen.

(The prior.) All the manors that belong to the monastery are almost utterly in ruin.

(The prior.) Secular folk commonly breakfast in the frater at the time of the canons' meal, contrary to the regular institutes.[3]

Prayer is made that a secular auditor be appointed them, who shall hear and determine the accounts of the house. The prior was enjoined to make provision, before the next feast of St. Michael, of an auditor who shall hear and determine the accounts of the monastery for two years according to the law of audit.

---

[3] The seculars in question, as appears from Thornham's first *detectum*, given later, were chiefly the lay servants and workmen of the monastery.

Fiat iniunccio quod nullus alii improperetur pro detectis.

(Prior.) Non deseruitur canonicis infirmis de cibariis congruis sed de grossis sicuti et sanis, sicuti deponit frater Johannes Goldyngtone.

(Prior.) Non habetur elemosinarius in domo qui elemosinas domus colligat et distribuat: ideo consumuntur elemosine.

(Prior.) Religio non obseruatur eo quod non habentur presides in religione.

Tempore quo canonici intenderent horis canonicis in choro vt tercie, vj^te et aliis, ymo intendunt iantaculis in quibus tanto saciantur quod in refeccionibus meridianis non possunt commedere sed emittunt fercula sua ad alia loca vbi sedent in solaciis suis tenentes ibidem claustrum suum.

Dum quidam sunt in minucionibus alii fingentes se indispositos absentant se a matutinis et aliis horis, tamen fortes sunt ad comedendum.

Est ibidem multitudo maxima canum rapiencium cibaria de mensa canonicorum per quod elemosina domus consumitur, cum quibus canibus[1] quidam canonici intendunt venacionibus.

Hore collacio, um non obseruantur in claustro et refectorio eo quod seculares commedunt et cenant ibidem.

Petitur vt quedam domus quam Londone canonicus edificauit subtus muros ecclesie et non proficit propter indecenciam dirimatur.

Non seruitur canonicis volentibus celebrare de pane et vino competentibus nisi cum murmure et strepitu.

Quidam magister Ricardus Rounhale dedit vasa argentea domui pro quo oratur pro eius anima singulis diebus in missa de beata Virgine, et nescitur vbi vasa ipsa deueniunt. Iniunctum est priori quod citra purificacionem exbeat[2] vasa huiusmodi conuentui.

[Fo. 116d.] Frater Johannes Dardes precentor dicit quod religio perit eo quod non sunt ibidem supprior et tercius prior qui intendant religioni. Fratres Willelmus Bedeforde subrogatur in suppriorem et

---

[1] *ibus* interlined above *onibus* cancelled.
[2] *Sic*: *ex* at end of one line, *beat* at beginning of next.

[1] See the prior's first and second *detecta*.
[2] The *jentaculum* was the early breakfast allowed to canons who needed refreshment before the mid-day *prandium*. Its frugal character under proper conditions is defined by the injunction founded on this *compertum*.
[3] *I.e.* instead of sitting in cloister at the proper hours, the canons retired to private rooms and other unauthorised places, where they consumed the food for which they had no appetite in the frater.
[4] See *Visitations* I, 227. The usual place for the delivery of the collation or homily before compline was the chapter-house. At Oseney it appears to have followed immediately upon supper (see p. 263 below). At Newnham the implication is that supper was prolonged, and the collation either delayed or omitted.
[5] The house in question was probably a mere shed or tool-house.
[6] Presumably Richard Rounhale (Renhold), LL.D., who was one of the receivers of petitions for Gascony and the English possessions beyond seas in the parliaments of 1390, 1391, 1392-3, 1394-5 and 1397 (*Rot. Parl.* III, 277, 284, 300, 329, 337, 348.) He succeeded Walter Skirlaw, then recently appointed keeper of the privy seal, as a clerk in chancery of the first grade on 8 Oct., 1382 (*Cal. Pat.* 1381-1385, p. 168), and was frequently employed as a commissioner in cases involving questions of maritime and mercantile law and the law of chivalry: *e.g.* he was one of the committee nominated to terminate and deliver judgment in the famous suit of Scrope v. Grosvenor, 28 Nov., 1390 (*ibid.* 1388-1392, p. 337). About 1384 he went on an

Let an injunction be made that no-one shall reproach another for matters disclosed.

(The prior.) The canons in the infirmary are not served with befitting food, but with coarse meats, like those who are sound in health, even as brother John Goldyngtone makes deposition.

(The prior.) There is no almoner in the house to collect and distribute the alms of the house: therefore the alms are wasted.

(The prior.) Religion is not observed, because there are no presidents in religion.[1]

At the time when the canons should be keeping the canonical hours in quire, that is, terce, sext and the rest, they are, on the contrary, busy with little breakfasts,[2] at which they are so surfeited that at their mid-day meals they cannot eat, but send out their dishes to other places where they sit at their ease, keeping their cloister in the same.[3]

While some [of the canons] are in their seynies, others, feigning themselves to be indisposed, absent themselves from matins and the other hours: nevertheless, they are hearty eaters.

There is a very great multitude of hounds in that place, which snatch their meat from the canons' table, whereby the alms of the house are wasted; and with these hounds certain of the canons go a hunting.

The times for collations[4] are not kept in the cloister and frater, because secular folk eat and sup there.

Prayer is made that a house which Londone, a canon, built adjoining the walls of the church and which is of no use, be destroyed because of its unseemliness.[5]

The canons who wish to celebrate are not served with befitting bread and wine, save only with grumbling and complaint.

One master Richard Rounhale[6] gave silver vessels to the house, and on his behalf prayer is made daily for his soul at the mass of the blessed Virgin; and no one knows what has become of the same vessels. The prior was enjoined to produce such vessels to the convent before the Purification.

Brother John Dardes, the precentor, says that religion is at an end, because there are not a subprior and third prior there to look after religion. Brother William Bedeforde is appointed subprior, and brother William

---

embassy from Richard II to his brother-in-law Wenzel, king of the Romans, was captured by enemies of England on the way, and put to ransom (*ibid.* 1381-1385, pp. 526, 527). On 10 June, 1386, he had a grant of Driffield preb. in York (*ibid.* 1385-1389, p. 159: cf. *ibid.* p. 401, 14 Feb., 1387-8). John Malvern names him among the envoys sent to negotiate preliminaries of peace with France at Calais in Nov., 1388 (Higden, *Polychr.* [Rolls Ser.] IX, 209). He was presented to the church of Aldington, Kent, 12 Sept., 1396 (*ibid.* 1396-1399, p. 23), and to Beckingham preb. in Southwell, 26 Jan. 1396-7 (*ibid.* p. 58: see also p. 103, 7 March following). On 26 Sept., 1397, he had ratification of his estate as rector of Cliffe-at-Hoo, Kent, and was presented to the church by the Crown on 22 Oct. following (*ibid.* pp. 202, 268). His estate in Driffield preb. was ratified by Henry IV, 18 Oct., 1399 (*ibid.* 1399-1401, p. 101); but he died before 4 March, 1400-1, when his successors in Beckingham and Driffield prebs. were appointed (York Reg. Scrope, ff. 3*d.*, 4). For various grants of pensions to him, see *Cal. Pat.* 1381-1385, pp. 526, 527; 1388-1392, p. 57; 1396-1399, p. 151. On 11 April, 1390, he had a grant for life of a messuage and 60 acres of land in Renhold, worth 20*s.* yearly, on the surrender of letters patent to a similar effect by John Wakefeld, yeoman of the chamber (*ibid.* 1388-1392, p. 235).

Willelmus Wolastone in tercium priorem. Iniunctum est Wolastone quod sumat in se officium huiusmodi et singulis de conuentu quod obediant eidem in officio illo et priori in virtute obediencie quod supportet ipsum in officio illo.

Frater Johannes Rothewelle: non seruitur canonicis de peculio suo pro vestura sua.

Est quedam mulier manens in prioratu quam canonici vocant sororem suam; ad quam et eius ancillas et pedisecas canonici frequentes accessus et cum quibus habent solacia sua in scandalum domus, et per hoc retrahuntur a diuinis.

Frater Willelmus Thornham dicit quod omnes seruitores domus vt bigarii, carucarii et alii inhonesti omni die commedunt in refectorio, quamobrem obseruancie regulares non seruantur ibidem.

In vltima visitacione fuerunt xxj canonici et iam non sunt nisi xiij et ideo[1] iam presentes sustinent maiorem et quasi intolerabilem laborem in diuinis.

Frater Johannes Stachedene dicit quod nihil occurrit menti sue deponendum.

> Frater Willelmus Olney sacrista[2]
> Frater Johannes Kempstone.
> Frater Johannes Rounhale.
> Frater Willelmus Carletone dicit omnia bene.
> Frater Thomas Bedeforde dicit omnia bene.
> Frater Nicholaus Stevyngtone dicit omnia bene.

[Fo. 117.] Willelmus permissione diuina Lincolniensis episcopus dilectis in Christo filiis priori et conuentui prioratus de Newenham, ordinis Sancti Augustini, nostre diocesis, presentibus et futuris salutem graciam et benediccionem. Visitantes iam pridem iure nostro ordinario dictum vestrum prioratum tam in capite quam in membris ac super statu eiusdem prioratus singulariumque personarum eiusdem solicite inquirentes, per huiusmodi inquisicionem nostram inuenimus nonnulla defectus[3] excessus et delicta nobis fore detecta et delata necessaria reformacione et correccione notorie digna.

In primis quia comperimus nobis fore detectum quod vos prior in corrigendis excessibus et moribus reformandis subditorum vestrorum dicti prioratus canonicorum adeo necgligens remissus fuistis et estis ac meticulosus quod crimina et defectus huiusmodi delinquencium transeunt impunita in vestre et suarum animarum graue periculum et aliorum recte viuencium perniciosum exemplum; vobis igitur in virtute obediencie et sub pena grauis contemptus firmiter iniungimus et mandamus quatinus omnem huiusmodi pigriciam necgligenciam meticulositatem et formidinem penitus excucientes cor animosum et virile cum Phynees[4] assumatis et taliter delinquentes in regula et obseruanciis regularibus[5]

---

[1] *quod* cancelled.
[2] *dicit q* cancelled.
[3] *des* cancelled.
[4] The name Phinees is indeclinable in the Vulgate.
[5] *taliter* cancelled.

[1] *I.e.* she had received letters of fraternity from the prior and convent.

Wolastone third prior. It was enjoined upon Wolastone that he should take such office on himself, and upon the several members of the convent that they should obey him in that office, and upon the prior in virtue of obedience that he should maintain him in that office.

Brother John Rothewelle: the canons are not furnished with their allowance for their raiment.

There is a woman dwelling in the priory whom the canons call their sister,[1] to whom and to her maid-servants and tirewomen the canons have often recourse, and take their ease with them to the scandal of the house; and hereby they are hindered from divine service.

Brother William Thornham says that all the serving-men of the house, such as the waggoners [and] carters, and other unhonest folk eat in the frater every day; wherefore the regular observances are not kept there.

At the last visitation there were twenty-one canons, and now there are only thirteen;[2] and therefore those who are now present endure more and almost intolerable toil in divine service.

Brother John Stachedene says that nothing worthy of deposition occurs to his mind.

Brother William Olney, the sacrist.

Brother John Kempstone.

Brother John Rounhale.

Brother William Carletone says all things are well.

Brother Thomas Bedeforde says all things are well.

Brother Nicholas Stevyngtone says all things are well.

William, by divine permission bishop of Lincoln, to our beloved sons in Christ the prior and convent of the priory of Newnham, of the order of St. Austin, of our diocese, that are now and shall be, health, grace and blessing. When sometime we, by our right as ordinary, were visiting your said priory in its head and members alike, and were making anxious inquiry concerning the state of the same priory and of the several persons thereof, we found by such our inquiry that certain defaults, transgressions and offences were discovered and reported to us, which were notoriously worthy of necessary reform and correction.

In the first place, because we found that it was discovered to us that you, the prior, have been and are so careless, remiss and timid in correcting the transgressions and reforming the manners of your subjects, the canons of the said priory, that the crimes and defaults of such offenders pass without punishment, to the grievous peril of your and their souls, and with disastrous example to the others who live aright:[3] we therefore firmly enjoin and command you, in virtue of obedience and under pain of grievous contempt, that, shaking off utterly all such sluggishness, carelessness, timidity and fear, you take to you, with Phynees, a stout and manly heart,[4] and correct and reform those who offend in such wise as regards the rule and regular observances according

---

[2] Actually fourteen canons are mentioned.

[3] Founded upon William Bedeforde's and Wolastone's first *detecta*.

[4] See Num. xxv, 6-15. Alnwick appears to allude to the meaning of the name Phinehas, viz. ' a bold countenance.'

secundum regulam vestram Sancti videlicet Augustini corrigatis et reformetis vt non impunitas sed correccio ceteris maneat in exemplum. Suppriori eciam et tercio priori vestris in similibus assistatis vt tantorum presidencium sagacitate delinquentes arceantur, memores quod de singulis vestre cure commissis in districto Dei iudicio reddetis racionem.

Preterea cum omnia officia dicti prioratus que per canonicos dudum occupari consueuerunt in manibus vestris teneatis ac eorum commoda percipiatis, volumus iniungimus vobis et eciam ordinamus sub eisdem penis vt implementa et alia necessaria in ipsis officiis diuisim exhibeatis et ministretis, sicuti olim ipsa officia occupantes melius exhibuerunt, cum nunc in vestri defectu omnia in ipsis officiis antiquitus prouisa iam conficiuntur et nichil penitus innouatur.

Item cum vagacio corporum sepius vagacionem mentis inducit,[1] iniungimus vobis vniuersis et singulis sub pena custodie claustralis et silencii per vnum mensem pro quolibet defectu in hac parte ne quis vestrum ad villas Bedefordie vel Goldyngtone vel alia loca ad vnum milliare circumposita accedere presumatis nisi ex causa necessaria priori vel suppriori aut tercio priori primitus exposita ac super hoc licencia petita et obtenta, sed neque ad familias quascunque infra situm prioratus in quibus mulieres conuersantur nullatinus et neque in hiis familiis nec aliis supradictis commedatis aut bibatis, et cum sic exieritis habeatis vobiscum personas honestas ad nutum licenciantis que vestre conuersacionis testes existant.

Iniungimus eciam vobis priori, suppriori et tercio priori sub pena excommunicacionis infrascripte ne in concedendo licencias huiusmodi exeundi sitis leues aut faciles, sed cognita causa licenciam et tempus exeundi ac redeundi ad claustrum discrecione preuia moderemini.

Item cum ingluuies siue crapula presertim in religiosis sit dampnata *et*[2] prohibita, nonnulli tamen vestrum prout nobis detectum est plus de ventre quam de mente curam habentes omni die summo mane ad coquinam discurrunt exquirentes qualia cibaria illo die sibi apponentur, alii temporibus horarum tercie et sexte choro penitus dimisso quasi vacuo ad coquinam accedunt et non adipatis seu modico sorbiciunculo que *confortande nature vsque horam prandendi sufficerent*[3] contentati fercula grandia exquirunt et tunc *tanto* saciantur quod in refeccione meridiana non commedunt sed et fercula tunc eis apposita quo voluerint tunc emittunt elemosinam domus nequiter subtrahentes, iniungimus igitur vobis vniuersis et singulis sub pena ieiunii in pane et aqua singulis quartis et sextis feriis per vnum mensem proxime sequentem postquam vestrum quisquis contra hanc nostram iniunccionem in hoc deliquerit, quod temporibus horarum tercie et sexte nec ante nec post tales commesaciones

---

[1] *et facilitas venie incentiuum tribuit delinquendi* cancelled.

[2] *sit* cancelled.

[3] Interlined above *nature sufficerent* cancelled.

[1] Founded upon William Bedeforde's third *detectum*: see also Wolastone's third.

[2] Founded upon the prior's third, fourth, seventh and eighth, and Rothewelle's second *detecta*.

[3] Founded upon William Bedeforde's second *detectum*.

[4] *Adipata* implies food smeared with lard or dripping.

to your rule, to wit, that of St. Austin, so that not their freedom from punishment, but their correction, may be an abiding example to the rest. You shall also give aid in like matters to your subprior and third prior, so that by the prudence of such notable presidents offenders may be restrained, remembering that at the strict judgment of God you shall render account concerning each one that is entrusted to your care.

Further, seeing that you hold all the offices of the said priory, which were wont aforetime to be filled by canons, in your own hands and receive their profits,[1] we will, enjoin upon you, and also ordain under the same penalties that you produce and supply severally the utensils and other things needful in the same offices, even in the best way as heretofore those who filled the same offices produced them, inasmuch as now in your default all things that were provided of old in the same offices are by this time used up, and nothing at all is renewed.

Also, inasmuch as bodily wandering very often gives occasion to wandering of the mind, we enjoin upon you all and several under pain of keeping cloister and of silence for a month for every default herein, that no-one of you take upon himself to go to the towns of Bedford and Goldington or other places for a mile round about, save for a necessary reason explained beforehand to the prior or subprior or third prior, and with leave concerning this asked and had, nor even to any household whatsoever within the site of the priory in any wise, wherein women have resort;[2] nor shall you eat or drink in these households or in the others above said. And, when you thus go out, you shall have with you at the bidding of him who gives you leave honest persons who shall be witnesses of your behaviour.

We enjoin also upon you, the prior, the subprior and the third prior, under pain of the excommunication hereunder written, that in granting such licences for going out you be not lenient or easy,[3] but that, having learned the reason, you shall regulate with discretion beforehand the licence and the time of leaving and returning to cloister.

Also, inasmuch as gluttony or drunkenness, especially among religious persons, is condemned and forbidden, and yet some of you, as has been discovered to us, taking more care of the belly than of the mind, run away the first thing in the morning every day to the kitchen, seeking out what sort of food shall be set before them that day, while others at the times of terce and sext, utterly neglecting quire, [so that it is] almost empty, go to the kitchen, and, not content with dripping cakes[4] or a little mess of broth, which should be enough to support nature until breakfast-time, ask for large helpings, and are then so surfeited that they do not eat at the noontide meal, but even at that time send out the dishes that are then set before them whither they will, wickedly withdrawing the alms of the house:[5] we therefore enjoin upon you all and singular, under pain of fasting on bread and water every Wednesday and Friday for a month next following, after that any one of you have offended herein against this our injunction, that [no one of you] presume at the times of terce and sext, or before or after, to require[6]

---

[5] Founded upon the prior's third, fifth, sixth and ninth *detecta*.

[6] Or ' hold,' if *exercere* be the right reading.

aut potaciones exigere[1] presumat, sed si quis quid indigeat pro[2] susten-
tanda natura in refectorio adipatis vel modico sorbiciunculo contentetur,
quodque id quod in refeccione meridiana aut in cenis post refeccionem
remanserit non vt solito emittatis, sed per elemosinarium solicite colli-
gatur et fideliter seruetur ac in elomasina[3] domus integre distribuatur.

Item cum nobis detectum existat quod plures in dicto sunt[4] prioratu
canes venatici et alii inutiles per quos elemosina domus perplurimum
consumitur, *et qui*[5] eciam[6] escas de mensis rapiunt canonicorum et eciam
claustrum ecclesiam refectorium et alia loca que nitida forent et munda
multum inhoneste[7] maculant et deturpant; iniungimus *vobis* priori in
virtute obediencie et sub pena[8] contemptus vt multitudinem canum
huiusmodi a dicto prioratu expellatis, sed et si quibus indigeatis ad
feras cohercendas ipsos in vna domo clausos per aliquem garcionem qui
eis intendat conseruari faciatis ne ad extra vagentur.

Item cum sit absurdum et inconsonum vt regulares qui temporibus[9]
refecceoneum[10] in silencio leccionem haberent[11] *et* laici simul in eadem
domo reficiantur, iniungimus vobis priori sub pena excommunicacionis
infrascripte vt decetero nullos seculares quantumcunque honestos neque
eciam domus seruientes aut artifices in refectorio, quod locus est *in quo*
obseruancie regulares debent obseruari, commedere permittatis aut
cenare, ne quies canonicorum discumbencium turbetur nec collaciones
ante completorium impediantur, sed huiusmodi seruientes et artifices
in domo quadam ad hoc antiquitus disposita vel in aula vestra omnino
refici faciatis, et si queque graues et honeste superuenerint persone ipsas
in camera vel[12] aula vestra aut alio loco honesto recipiatis et conuiuetis.

Item cum consuetudo quedam multum laudabilis in dicto prioratu
antiquitus obseruabatur vt in die obitus cuiuslibet canonici defuncti
vnus panis conuentualis et vnum ferculum de coquina pro anima ipsius
canonici[13] pauperi cuidam et indigenti distribueretur, que consuetudo
vt nobis detectum est[14] *modernis non seruatur temporibus*[15]; iniungimus
igitur vobis priori sub penis supra et infrascriptis vt elemosinam huiusmodi
in ipsis rebus et non pecunia vel aliis diebus obituum huiusmodi per
elemosinarium distribui faciatis.

Item cum secundum vulgare legere et non intelligere est necgligere,
ac nonnulli vt nobis detectum est dicti prioratus canonici adeo illitterati
sunt et quasi ideote quod vix legunt, sed et quod legunt non intelligunt

---

[1] *Sic*: probably for *exercere*. The negative is insufficiently implied in the clause.
[2] *confortanda* cancelled.
[3] *Sic*: for *elemosina*.
[4] *plures* cancelled.
[5] *qui* interlined above *cum* cancelled.
[6] *eciam* repeated and cancelled.
[7] *et* cancelled, and first stroke of the *m* of *maculant* interlined.
[8] *grauis* cancelled.
[9] *s* cancelled.
[10] *Sic*.
[11] *ac* cancelled.
[12] *ali* cancelled.
[13] *distr* cancelled.
[14] *tendit in abusum* cancelled.
[15] Added in the margin, probably in the bishop's handwriting.

such eatings or drinkings, but, if any one need aught for the support of nature, he shall be content with dripping or a little mess of broth in the frater; and that at the noontide meal or at supper you send not out, as is your wont, that which is left after the meal, but that it be carefully gathered up and faithfully kept by the almoner, and be distributed in its entirety in the alms of the house.

Also, whereas it is discovered to us that in the said priory there are many hounds for hunting and other useless [dogs], by reason of which the alms of the house are very greatly wasted, and which also snatch food from the canons' tables and do likewise very unbecomingly defile and befoul the cloister, church, frater and other places which should be spotless and clean;[1] we enjoin upon you the prior, in virtue of obedience and under pain of contempt, that you banish the multitude of such hounds from the said priory. But, if you are in need of any to keep down wild beasts, you shall cause them to be kept shut up in one house by some groom, who shall attend to them, so that they stray not outside.

Also, whereas it is absurd and inconsistent that men under rule, who at meal times should have their reading in silence, and laymen should have refreshment together in the same house,[2] we enjoin upon you the prior, under pain of the excommunication hereunder written, that henceforward you suffer no secular persons, how good soever their fame, or even the serving men of the house or the craftsmen[3] to eat or sup in the frater, which is a place wherein the regular observances ought to be kept, that the quiet of the canons as they sit at meals may not be disturbed, nor the collations before compline be hindered; but you shall cause such serving men and craftsmen to take all their refreshment in a house that of old time was set apart for this purpose, or in your hall, and, if any grave or honest persons chance to come, you shall receive and entertain them in your chamber or hall, or some other honest place.

Also, inasmuch as a very praiseworthy custom was observed of old in the said priory, that on the obit-day of each canon deceased a convent loaf and a dish from the kitchen should be distributed to a poor and needy person on behalf of the same canon's soul, the which custom, as has been discovered to us, is not kept in the times that now are:[4] we therefore enjoin upon you the prior, under the penalties written above and beneath, that you cause such alms to be distributed by the almoner in the same form, and not in money or in other goods, on such obit-days.

Also, seeing that, according to popular opinion, reading without understanding is carelessness, and, as it has been discovered to us, certain canons of the said priory are so unlettered and almost witless that they

---

[1] See the twelfth *compertum*.

[2] Founded upon Thornham's first *detectum*: see also the fourth and thirteenth *comperta*.

[3] *Artifex* is commonly employed to signify an artist craftsman. It is possible that works of repair were at this date being carried on in the church and buildings of the priory. In this connexion it should be noted that, although the temporal property of the monastery was in need of attention, no complaint was made of the state of the fabric of the convent buildings; and, although its financial position was uncertain owing to the usual slackness in rendering accounts, the house does not seem to have been in debt.

[4] See the second *compertum*.

et sic inutiles studio et contemplacione redduntur et inepti; iniungimus
igitur vobis *priori* sub penis supra et infrascriptis vt citra proximum
festum[1] *Pasche* proxime futurum prouideatis de vno instructore idoneo
qui canonicos huiusmodi ad vestri assignacionem in grammatica instruat
informet esculenta[2] et salarium *de domo et* de discipulis percipiendo, et
si qui canonici per vos assignati (fo. 117 *d*.] horis ad doctrinam huiusmodi
assignatis se subtraxerint seu desides et necgligentes fuerint aut in
addiscendo se ex propria desidia inhabiles reddiderint et non profecerint
tam diu sint vltimi in choro et refectorio et vno genere carnium vel
piscium prout dieta requirit absque pluri contentur[3] quousque eorum
instructor de eorum profectu testificetur.

Item cum humanum existat compati infirmis, iniungimus vobis
priori in virtute obediencie vt fratres vestros infirmantes sepius visitetis
et eis de talibus prouideri faciatis cibis quibus cicius et melius poterunt
recreari, assignetisque vnum canonicum sanum qui cum eis et coram
eis horas dicat canonicas et missas si quo modo fieri poterit celebret in
presencia eorundem.

Item iniungimus vobis vniuersis et singulis sub pena custodie claustralis per vnam septimanam vt omni die habita collacione et completorio
decantato omnes vniformiter dormitorium petatis ad quietem exinde
nullatinus exituri vsque septimam horam diei sequentis nisi dumtaxat
ad matutinas, ad quas decantandas omnes indifferenter assurgant senibus
infirmis et in minucionibus existentibus tantum exceptis; sed vt nobis
detectum est sunt quidam qui dum alii sunt in minucionibus fingunt
se indispositos et sic lectos suos seruant vsque septimam horam diei
sequentis sed et in refeccionibus sic habent ac si nichil mali sentirent;
iniungimus igitur vobis priori, suppriori et tercio priori vt de talibus
sedule precauentes quos in hoc delinquere reppereritis in futurum acerrime
corrigatis vt eorum correccio sit ceteris *in timorem.*[4]

Item iniungimus vobis priori nunc et cuilibet vobis succedenti in
dignitate ipsa sub pena suspensionis ab omni administracione spiritualium
et temporalium ad dictum prioratum spectancium vt omni anno inter
festa *Pasche et Penthecostes*[5] plenum et plenarium compotum de totali
administracione vestra in bonis huiusmodi coram toto conuentu vel
personis illis per conuentum ad hoc assignandis reddatis, et ad huiusmodi
compotos vestros seriosius componendos volumus iniungimus et
ordinamus quod citra proximum festum *Pasche*[6] prouideatis de vno
seculari auditore in hoc[7] bene experto qui compotos administracionis
bonorum dicti prioratus ad minus per biennium audiat et terminet.

---

[1] *Sancti Michaelis* cancelled.
[2] *de domo* cancelled.
[3] *Sic*: for *contententur.*
[4] *metum* cancelled.
[5] *Sancti Michaelis archangeli et Sancti Martini in yeme* cancelled.
[6] *Michaelis* cancelled.
[7] *me* cancelled.

[1] Founded upon the prior's first *detectum*: see also the first *compertum.*
[2] The introduction of a secular grammar-master is clearly implied. The
payment indicated would be supplied from the *peculium* allowed to each canon for
the ordinary necessaries of life which he could get for himself: see *Visitations* I,

barely read, and what they read they do not understand, and so are rendered profitless and unfit for study and contemplation:[1] we therefore enjoin upon you the prior, under the penalties written above and beneath, that before the next feast of Easter next to come you make provision of a serviceable teacher[2] to instruct and inform such canons in grammar at your appointment, receiving his food and stipend from the house and from his pupils; and, if any canons appointed by you stay away at the times assigned for such teaching, or be lazy and neglectful, or of their own laziness show themselves incapable and make no profit in learning, they shall be last in quire and frater, and shall be content with one kind of flesh or fish, as their diet requires, without more, for so long a time until their teacher shall bear witness of their profit.

Also, seeing that it is a humane thing to have compassion on the sick, we enjoin upon you the prior, in virtue of obedience, that you visit more often your brethren when they are ailing, and cause provision to be made them of such meats as shall most speedily and best tend to their refreshment;[3] and you shall appoint a canon in sound health to say with them and before them the canonical hours and celebrate masses in their presence, if in any wise it may be done.

Also we enjoin upon you all and singular, under pain of keeping cloister for a week, that every day, after you have had collation and compline has been sung, you all go to the dorter after one manner to your rest, to go out therefrom in no wise until seven o'clock on the following day, save only to matins, to sing which all shall rise without distinction, the old, infirm, and they that are in their seynies alone excepted. But, as it has been discovered to us, there are some who, while the others are in their seynies, feign themselves to be indisposed, and so keep their beds until seven o'clock on the following day, and yet so behave themselves at meals as if they felt no sickness;[4] we therefore enjoin upon you the prior, the subprior and the third prior, that, taking diligent precaution concerning such persons, you correct with great severity those whom you shall find hereafter offending herein, that their correction may be for the fear of the rest.

Also we enjoin upon you who are now prior, and upon everyone that shall succeed you in the same dignity, under pain of suspension from all administration of the spiritual and temporal goods to the said priory belonging, that every year between the feasts of Easter and Pentecost you render a full and complete account of your entire administration before the whole convent or the persons to be appointed by the convent for this purpose: and, for the more orderly drawing up of such your accounts, we will, enjoin and ordain that before the next feast of Easter you make provision of a secular auditor well skilled in this matter, who for the space of two years at least shall audit and determine the accounts of the administration of the goods of the said priory.[5]

---

243. On the subject of *peculium*, see Lyndwood, p. 205 (tit. *De stat. regul.*, c. *Quia nonnunquam*, v. *Denarii tribuantur*), who explains the excuse for the permission of this infraction of the stringent rules against *proprietas*.

[3] See Wolastone's fifth *detectum* and the seventh *compertum*.

[4] See the eleventh *compertum*.

[5] Founded upon Wolastone's fourth *detectum*: see also the request embodied in the fifth *compertum*.

Item iniungimus vobis vniuersis et singulis sub pena ieiunii in pane et aqua[1] singulis quartis et sextis feriis per vnam quindenam proxime sequentem postquam vestrum aliquis in hoc deliquerit ne vestrum aliquis alteri fratri suo occasione detectorum in hac visitacione nostra improperari presumat; quod si aliquis in hoc deliquisse deprehendatur vos presidentes penam predictam in personis delinquencium exequamini cum effectu.

Item iniungimus vobis priori in virtute obediencie et sub pena contemptus[2] vt domunculam illam quam quidam Londone dudum canonicus vester construi fecit subter muros ecclesie vestre propter indenciam[3] et deformitatem omnino demoliri faciatis et prosterni.

Item cum nichil facere et inutiliter facere equiparentur nobis*que* detectum existat quod cocus vester communis cibaria licet satis salubria et idonea sibi ad parandum pro refeccione conuentus liberata et tradita adeo inhoneste necgligenter et insulse parat et disponit quod cum conuentui fuerint apposita tanto ea propter eorum insulsitudinem et indisposicionem abhorrent quod ex eis quicquam gustare vel sumere non audent neque possunt; iniungimus igitur vobis priori in virtute obediencie et sub pena grauis contemptus vt ipsum cocum vestrum *presentem et ei similem futurum* mores suos in hoc reformare cogatis aut ipsum *et quemcumque talem futurum* ab officio illo penitus expellatis et alium qui se melius habeat subrogetis in eodem.

Numerum vero canonicorum augmentandum quousque nobis clare de prouentibus domus constiterit nobis specialiter reseruamus.[4]

[5]Monemus insuper vos omnes et singulos presentes et futuros *primo secundo et tercio peremptorie* sub pena excommunicacionis maioris quam in personas vestras singulares si premissis non obedieritis debito cum effectu intendimus fulminare quatinus premissa omnia et singula iniuncciones ordinaciones et mandata nostra quatenus ad vnumquemque vestrum attinet inuiolabiliter obseruetis et perficiatis ac obediatis eisdem sicuti canonicam effugere volueritis vlcionem.

Data sub sigillo nostro ad causas in monasterio de Elnestowe xxj die mensis Januarii anno Domini mccccxlij nostrarumque consecracionis anno xvij° et translacionis vij.

---

[1] *per vnam* cancelled.
[2] *si* cancelled.
[3] *Sic*: for *indecenciam*.
[4] Altered from *reseruatis*.
[5] In margin, *Memorandum de numero canonicorum augmentando* cancelled, probably by the bishop's hand. The italicised clause, *Numerum,* etc., added at the bottom of the injunctions.

Also we enjoin upon you all and singular, under pain of fasting on bread and water every Wednesday and Friday for a fortnight next following, after that any one of you shall offend herein, that no one of you take on himself to reproach another of his brethren by reason of the matters disclosed in this our visitation;[1] but, if any one be discovered to have offended herein, you that are presidents shall execute the penalty aforesaid with effect upon the persons of the offenders.

Also we enjoin upon you the prior, in virtue of obedience and under pain of contempt, that you cause that little house which one Londone, sometime your canon, caused to be built close to the walls of your church to be utterly destroyed and laid low by reason of its unseemliness and ugliness.[2]

Also, whereas doing nothing and doing things to no profit amount to the same thing, and it is discovered to us that your common cook prepares and serves up the food, albeit healthful and serviceable enough, that is delivered and supplied to him to prepare for the meals of the convent, so unfittingly, carelessly and unsavourily, that, when it has been set before the convent, [the canons] so abhor it because of its unsavouriness and ill appointment that they dare not and cannot taste or take aught of it:[3] we therefore enjoin upon you the prior, in virtue of obedience and under pain of grievous contempt, that you compel the same your cook that is now and him who shall be in like case hereafter to reform his ways in this matter, or you shall utterly expel him and any such person in future from that office, and substitute another in the same who shall behave himself better.

The increase of the number of canons we specially reserve to ourselves, until we have clear assurance concerning the revenues of the house.[4]

We admonish you, moreover, all and singular that now are and shall be, the first, second and third time peremptorily, under pain of the greater excommunication, which we intend to pronounce against your several persons, if you obey not the premises with due effect, to keep without breach and to perform all and several the aforeset our injunctions, ordinances and commands, and to obey the same, so far as concerns each one of you, even as you wish to escape from canonical vengeance.

Given under our seal *ad causas* in the monastery of Elstow[5] on the twenty-first day of the month of January in the year of our Lord 1442, and the seventeenth year of our consecration and of our translation the seventh.

---

[1] See the sixth *compertum*.
[2] See the fourteenth *compertum*.
[3] See the prior's sixth *detectum* and the seventh *compertum*.
[4] See Thornham's second *detectum*.
[5] The bishop visited Elstow on that day: see *Visitations* II, 89.

XLVI.

[Fo. 82]

Visitacio prioratus de Nouo Loco iuxta Stamfordiam, ordinis Sancti Augustini, Lincolniensis diocesis, facta in domo capitulari ibidem xxjᵒ die mensis octobris, anno Domini mccccxl, per reuerendum in Christo patrem et dominum, dominum Willelmum, Dei gracia Lincolniensem episcopum, anno suarum consecracionis xv et translacionis.[1]

In primis, sedente dicto reuerendo patre iudicialiter in dicte visitacionis negocio die, anno et loco predictis, comparuerunt personaliter coram[2] prior et conuentus dicti loci, vno canonico excepto qui grauiter vt[3] asseritur infirmatur. Et deinde lecto certificatorio prior exhibuit titulum suum incumbencie sue, et deinde iurauit idem prior obedienciam et fidelitatem domino in forma solita et consueta, et deinde exhibuit fundacionem domus. Et deinde dominus assignauit eidem priori ipsum diem xxjᵘᵐ Octobris apud Stamfordiam ad exhibendum pelnum[4] statum domus vt in omnibus prouentibus, instauramentis, creditoribus et debitoribus. Et deinde examinatus dicit ea que sequuntur.

Frater Willelmus Lylleforde, prior, dicit quod domus potest expendere circa xl marcas, et dicit quod domus indebitatur in xx marcis; et dicit quod indebitabatur tempore installacionis sue in v libris, et quod domus fuit pene destructa per alienaciones factas per Suttone vltimum priorem.

Frater Ricardus Spaldyng dicit quod non surgunt mediis noctibus ad matutinas propter paucitatem.

Frater Johannes Poluertofte, canonicus ibidem, dudum de Fynneshede, de ab illinc ad hunc locum migrando per priorem loci illius vt asserit licenciatus et hic professus ac in sacerdotum[5] ordinatus, habet terminum ad exhibendum licenciam migrandi citra proximum festum natalis Domini.

Item dicit quod frater Johannes Depyng, canonicus huius loci, de permissu prioris est in prioratu de Vluescrofte ad tempus.

Iniunctum est omnibus vt omni nocte media surgant ad matutinas decantandas,[6] licet voce dimissa.

Salua potestate prouidendi super statu domus cum fuerit exhibitus, dominus dissoluit visitacionem.

---

[1] Year (*quarto*) omitted.
[2] *Sic*: *eo* omitted.
[3] *apparuit* cancelled.
[4] *Sic*: for *plenum*.
[5] *Sic*.
[6] *eciam* cancelled.

[1] William Sutton, the prior's predecessor, resigned 31 January, 1435-6 (*Visitations* I, 92-94). There is no record of the date of Lylleforde's election or institution, but it must have followed shortly afterwards.
[2] No charter of foundation is known to exist. The priory was founded as a hospital temp. Henry III (see *Visitations* I, 164).

XLVI.

The visitation of the priory of NEWSTEAD BY STAMFORD, of THE ORDER OF ST. AUSTIN, OF THE DIOCESE OF LINCOLN, PER-FORMED IN THE CHAPTER-HOUSE THEREIN ON THE TWENTY-FIRST DAY OF THE MONTH OF OCTOBER IN THE YEAR OF OUR LORD 1440, BY THE REVEREND FATHER IN CHRIST AND LORD, THE LORD WILLIAM, BY THE GRACE OF GOD BISHOP OF LINCOLN, IN THE FIFTEENTH YEAR OF HIS CONSECRATION AND [THE FOURTH] OF HIS TRANSLATION.

In the first place, as the said reverend father was sitting in his capacity of judge in the business of the said visitation, on and in the day, year and place aforesaid, there appeared in person before [him] the prior and convent of the said place, with the exception of one canon who, as it is asserted, is grievously ill.   And then, when the certificate had been read, the prior exhibited his title of his incumbency;[1] and then the said prior sware obedience and fealty to my lord in the wonted and accustomed form, and then exhibited the foundation of the house.[2] And then my lord appointed to the same prior the same twenty-first day of October at Stamford for the exhibition of the full state of the house as regards all its revenues, stocks, creditors and debtors.   And then, upon examination, he says these things that follow.

Brother William Lylleforde, the prior,[3] says that the house can spend about forty marks, and says that the house is twenty marks in debt; and he says that at the time of his installation it was five pounds in debt, and that the house was almost destroyed by the alienations made by Suttone, the last prior.

Brother Richard Spaldyng says that, by reason of their fewness, they do not rise at midnight for matins.

Brother John Polvertofte, canon in the same, sometime of Fine-shade,[4] who, as he asserts, was licensed by the prior of that place to migrate to this place therefrom, and made his profession here and was ordained to the priesthood, has a term on this side the next feast of our Lord's Nativity for the production of his licence to migrate.

Also he says that brother John Depyng, canon of this place, is for a time in the priory of Ulverscroft with the prior's permission.

All were enjoined to rise in the middle of every night to sing matins, albeit without chant.[5]

Reserving the power of making provision concerning the state of the house when it shall be produced, my lord dissolved the visitation.

---

[3] There appear to have been five canons, one of whom bore the Northampton-shire name of Lilford, while the others had the Lincolnshire names of Spalding and Deeping.   The origin of the name of Polvertofte, the migrant from Fineshade, is uncertain.   The name of the sick canon is not given.

[4] Fineshade priory in Northamptonshire, a few miles south of Stamford. No record of a visitation of this house by Alnwick remains: for Gray's injunctions to the prior and convent see *Visitations* I, 63, 64.

[5] *Voce dimissa* seems to be equivalent to *voce submissa*, which implies the recita-tion of the hours *absque nota*, i.e. without chant or music.

Nouus locus iu[xta] Stamfordiam.

Fiant *hic* iniuncciones in forma qua fiunt priori de Noktoneparke cum hac addicione, quod canonicum suum fratrem Johannem Depyng, in prioratu de Vluescrofte existentem, ad proprium claustrum omni[1] celeritate qua poterit reducat.

XLVII.

[Fo. 81].

Visitacio prioratus de NOCTONE PARKE, ordinis Sancti Augustini, Lincolniensis diocesis, facta in domo capitulari ibidem[2] xij die mensis octobris, anno Domini mccccxl⁰, per reuerendum in Christo patrem et dominum, dominum Willelmum, Dei gracia Lincolniensem episcopum, anno consecracionis sue xv⁰ et translacionis quinto.

In primis, sedente dicto reuerendo patre iudicialiter in dictis[3] negocio, die, anno et loco predictis, comparentibusque coram eo priore et canonicis dicti loci, visitacionem huiusmodi vt apparuit subituri, primo et ante omnia propositum fuit verbum Dei iuxta actus futuri congruenciam per circumspectum virum magistrum Thomam Duffelde, in sacra theologia bacallarium, sequentem hoc thema, ' Veniunt ad monumentum,' etc.[4] Quo laudabiliter finito, prior dicti loci exhibuit domino certificatorium citacionis sui et conuentus eiusdem loci in hec verba, ' Reuerendissimo in Christo,' etc. Deinde exhibuit prefeccionem ipsius in priorem per Ricardum nuper Lincolniensem episcopum, et dimisit copiam: exhibuit eciam commissionem officialis archidiaconi Lincolniensis directam rectori de Blaunkeney ad installandum, etc., sed non ipsam installacionem; et vt pro fundacione exhibuit confirmacionem regis super donacione fundi siti[5] prioratus et ecclesiarum de Dunstone, Noktone et Calkewelle et aliorum terrarum et tenementorum; et postea iurauit obedienciam et fidelitatem dicto reuerendo patri. Et deinde examinatus super requisitis dicit ea que sequuntur.

Frater Johannes Shelforde, prior, dicit quod est ibi inter eos vnus canonicus de Thorntone professus, qui post varia hinc et inde [consilia] generalibus capitulis ordinis habita tandem ordinatum erat quod remoueretur ad domum professionis sue, qui illum [non prom]iserunt

---

[1] Written *coi* by mistake.
[2] *xx* cancelled.
[3] *Sic*: for *dicto*.
[4] St. Mark xvi, 2.
[5] *Sic*: for *situs*.

[1] A direction for the composition of injunctions added to the minutes.
[2] See No. xlvii below.
[3] There is no record of this in bishop Flemyng's register.
[4] *I.e.* Robert Fyssher, who was rector from 19 May, 1425, to *c.* 1446. (Reg. xvi, ff. 27 *d.*, 191 *d.*; *ibid.* xviii, ff. 97 *d.*, 98).
[5] The charter of confirmation granted by Henry iii, 22 April, 1271, is printed in *Monasticon* vi, 342, 343. For the ordination of vicarages in the three churches mentioned see *Rot. Hug. Welles* iii, 92 (Cawkwell), 170 (Nocton), 176 (Dunston).
[6] Three of the canons, Lincolne, Bostone and Wadyngworth bore Lincolnshire surnames. Shelforde and Newerk presumably came from Nottinghamshire.

NEWSTEAD BY STAMFORD.[1]

Let the injunctions in this case be made in the form wherein they are made to the prior of Nocton park,[2] with this addition, that [the prior] shall bring back to his own cloister, with all the speed he may, his canon, brother John Depyng, who is in the priory of Ulverscroft.

XLVII.

THE VISITATION OF THE PRIORY OF NOCTON PARK, OF THE ORDER OF ST. AUSTIN, OF THE DIOCESE OF LINCOLN, PERFORMED IN THE CHAPTER-HOUSE IN THE SAME, ON THE TWELFTH DAY OF THE MONTH OF OCTOBER IN THE YEAR OF OUR LORD 1440, BY THE REVEREND FATHER IN CHRIST AND LORD, THE LORD WILLIAM, BY THE GRACE OF GOD BISHOP OF LINCOLN, IN THE FIFTEENTH YEAR OF HIS CONSECRATION AND THE FIFTH OF HIS TRANSLATION.

In the first place, as the said reverend father was sitting in his capacity of judge in the said business, on and in the day, year and place aforesaid, and there appeared before him the prior and canons of the said place, to undergo, as was apparent, such his visitation, first and before all else the word of God was set forth, as was agreeable to the act about to take place, by master Thomas Duffelde, bachelor in sacred theology, after this text, ' They come unto the sepulchre,' etc.   And, when this had come to an end in praiseworthy fashion, the prior of the said place exhibited to my lord the certificate of the summons of himself and the convent of the same place in these words, ' To the right reverend in Christ,' etc.   Then he exhibited his own appointment as prior by Richard, late bishop of Lincoln,[3] and gave up a copy: he also exhibited the commission of the official of the archdeacon of Lincoln for his installation, etc., addressed to the rector of Blankney,[4] but not [the certificate of] the same installation; and in lieu of the foundation he exhibited the king's confirmation concerning the gift of the estate for the site of the priory and of the churches of Dunston, Nocton and Cawkwell and other lands and tenements.[5]   And thereafter he sware obedience and fealty to the said reverend father, and then, being examined upon matters requisite, he says these things which follow.

Brother John Shelforde, the prior,[6] says that there is there among them a canon professed of Thornton, and after divers [discussions] held at the general chapters of the order, it was at length ordained that he should be removed to the house of his profession.[7]   And they [undertook]

---

[7] The documents printed in Mr. Salter's *Chapters of Augustinian Canons* contain no allusion to this case, nor had any mention of it come up at the visitation of Thornton held by Alnwick during the previous July (No. LXXIV).   The question of the temporary relegation of refractory canons of one house to another formed the subject of an order made by the general chapter at Leicester in 1431, the particular case then under discussion being that of a canon of Haughmond (Salter, *op. cit.*, p. 81).   This method of discipline was frequently exercised, of course, by bishops as visitors of monastic houses, and the registers of the archbishops of York contain several valuable instances of its use in connexion with the numerous houses of Austin canons in that diocese.   See, *e.g.*, the case of two canons of Newstead in Sherwood, relegated by archbishop Corbridge in 1303, one to Kirkham, the other to St. Oswald's at Nostell (*Trans. Thoroton Soc.* XXIII, 77).

recipere, nisi staret in infimo et sic iuxta merita sua ascenderet ad altiora : quod ipse omnino recusauit, et sic expectauit in isto prioratu vsque visitacionem domini.

Frater Johannes Newerk, canonicus sacerdos,[1] quod Johannes Butylere, balliuus domus, non est vtilis domui, quia consulit priori vendere instaurum domus vili precio, et tunc ex necessario emunt cariori precio.

Item dicit quod iste canonicus de Thorntone, qui presens in domo est, alia vice propter eius demerita alienatus erat a domo, et iam regressus non fecit obedienciam.

Item dicit quod grangia de Dunstane est multum ruinosa in defectu prioris, et similiter domus supra voltam capituli in tantum quod pluit super voltam.

Frater Robertus Lincolne, diaconus,[2] quod tenementa domus in Noktone, Dunstane et Metheringham paciuntur magnam ruinam ob defectum reparacionis.

Item dicit quod frater Robertus Hidelstone, canonicus de Thorntone perhendinans in Noktone, habetur suspectus cum Katerina Pymme de Bardeney, cum qua dudum alia vice fuit diffamatus.

Item dicit de invtilitate Johannis Butylere vt supra.

Frater Ricardus Bostone, diaconus, dicit quod Johannes Butylere, balliuus, est inutilis, quia quod[3] fama est quod consumit bona domus frequentando tabernas, et cum nichil habuerat in aduentu suo, iam est multum locuples et vocatur inter seculares cellerarius vel supprior domus.

Item dicit[4] de canonico de Thorntone vt supra.

Frater Johannes Wadyngworthe in minoribus, professus tamen.

Quibus examinatis et iterato vocatis ad capitulum priore et *canonicis*[5] de gremio professis, dominus publicauit detecta. Tandem vocato ad capitulum dicto Roberto Hidelstone et petito ab eo quid iuris petit in isto prioratu, dicit pro conclusione quod de licencia sui abbatis generali admissus fuit hic per priorem in canonicum loci et fecit obedienciam priori loci, et sic stetit vt canonicus loci per plures annos. Et interim delinquens punitus fuit secundum canones, et licet vocatus ad capitulum generale, per quod ordinatum erat vt staret cum abbate Sancte[6] Osythe, vbi et stetit in quadam cella sua vocata Blakeney per aliquod tempus

---

[1] *dicit* omitted.
[2] *dicit* omitted.
[3] *Sic.*
[4] *quod* cancelled.
[5] Interlined above *capitulo* cancelled.
[6] *ol* cancelled.

[1] This mention of an upper story to the chapter-house suggests that here the chapter-house projected to the east of the eastern range of cloister buildings. Such upper rooms were a common feature of Cistercian chapter-houses, and probably were used as annexes to the dorter: cf. the room which remains above the chapter-house vault at Ford. In small Augustinian houses, such as Nocton park, the chapter-house was usually contained within the lower stage of the eastern range, without eastward projection, as at Newstead in Sherwood and in the nunnery at Lacock. If this was the case at Nocton, the *domus* must have formed an inter-mediate room between the dorter and the church.

to receive him only on condition that he should take the lowest place, and so go up higher according to his deserts; which he utterly refused to do, and so he has stayed in this priory until my lord's visitation.

Brother John Newerk, canon in priest's orders, [says] that John Butylere, the bailiff of the house, is of no advantage to the house, because he advises the prior to sell the store of the house at a cheap rate, and then they necessarily buy at a dearer price.

Also he says that this canon of Thornton, who is present in the house, was at another time removed from the house by reason of his ill deserts, and, now that he has returned, he has not done obedience.

Also he says that the grange of Dunston is very ruinous in the prior's default, and likewise the building above the vault of the chapter-house,[1] in so much that the rain falls upon the vault.

Brother Robert Lincolne, deacon, [says] that the tenements of the house in Nocton, Dunston and Metheringham suffer great ruin for default of repair.

Also he says that brother Robert Hidelstone,[2] canon of Thornton, who lodges at Nocton, is held suspect with Katherine Pymme of Bardney, with whom he was defamed at another time.

Also he says as above concerning the profitlessness of John Butylere.

Brother Richard Bostone, deacon, says that John Butylere, the bailiff, is useless, because the report is that he spends the goods of the house in haunting taverns, and, whereas he had nothing when he came, he is now exceedingly rich, and among secular folk he is called the cellarer or subprior of the house.

Also he says as above concerning the canon of Thornton.

Brother John Wadyngworthe, in minor orders, but professed.

Now, when these had been examined, and the prior and canons professed of the household[3] had been called to the chapter-house a second time, my lord made public the disclosures. Then the said Robert Hidelstone was summoned to the chapter-house, and, when it was asked of him what right he claims in this priory, he says for a conclusion that he was admitted here as a canon of the place by the prior, with the general licence of his abbot, and did obedience to the prior of the place, and so abode for several years as a canon of the place. And meanwhile, committing an offence, he was punished according to canon law, and, albeit he was summoned to the general chapter, by which it was ordained that he should stay with the abbot of St. Osyth's, and there also he abode in a cell of his called Blakeney[4] for some time as a canon of the place, he

---

[2] The name is given later as Hildestone, *i.e.*, Hilston. Hilston is in the East Riding of Yorkshire, on the sea-coast between Spurn Head and Withernsea: Thornton abbey had property in the neighbourhood, and the church of Humbleton, an adjoining parish, was appropriated to the abbot and convent.

[3] *I.e.* without the Thornton canon, who was not *de gremio*.

[4] The existence of this cell is otherwise unknown, and there is no place of this name connected with St. Osyth's. Mr. R. C. Fowler thinks that Blythburgh priory in Suffolk may be meant; but, if so, the mistake in the name is difficult to account for. It is just possible that Colstone, in making up his record, forgot the name of the place, and, knowing that it was in East Anglia and near the sea, confused it with Blakeney in Norfolk.

vt canonicus loci, rediit ad locum non missus, et sic dicit se canonicum loci. Ad quod prior respondens dicit quod credit litteras licencie sui abbatis in hoc non fore validas et sufficientes, et licet ipse tanquam simplex et iuris ignarus aliter fecerat ipsum admittendo quam facere debuit aut potuit, illud tamen quod ex post factum fuit et ordinatum per generale capitulum, quod est auctoritate apostolica, stare omnino oportebit vsque aliter statutum sit per capitulum generale, et cum nichil actum sic sit in contrarium facti premissi, videtur sibi se non teneri admittere ipsum vt canonicum suum; vnde dominus assignauit eisdem diem crastinum ad proponendum, dicendum et exhibendum quicquid sibi competit hinc inde, et ex hoc continuauit visitacionem vsque in diem crastinum ad procedendum et procedi videndum iuxta comperta in ceteris, presentibus Skayman et me Colstone. In quo termino et loco capitulari coram dicto reuerendo patre iudicialiter sedente comparuit dictus prie[1] et eciam conuentus; et deinde publicatis detectis dominus iniunxit priori in virtute obediencia quod cum omne accomoda accelera-cione amoueat dictum Johannem Butylere a prioratu et omnibus officiis eiusdem exterioribus et interioribus; et deinde, quia[2] repperit dictum Robertum Hildestone nichil iuris habere in dicto prioratu vt canonicus illius censeatur, dominus per litteras suas patentes remisit eum ad domum professionis sue;[3] et postea reseruata sibi potestate faciendi et transmittendi ipsis priori et conuentui iniuncciones necessarias, dominus dissoluit visitacionem suam, presente me Colstone.

[Fo. 79.] Noctone P[arke][4]

Willelmus, permissione diuina, etc., dilectis in Christo filiis priori et conuentui prioratus de Nokton park, ordinis Sancti[5] Augustini, nostre diocesis, presentibus et futuris, salutem, etc. Visitantes iam pridem vos et dictum prioratum vestrum et super eius statu inquirentes, quedam reperimus reformacione digna; pro quorum reformacione has nostras iniuncciones siue mandata vobis transmittimus per vos inuiolabiliter obseruanda.

In primis iniungimus vobis vniuersis et singulis vt omni die, dicto completorio, statim absque pluri dormitorium adeatis quietem petendo, exinde nisi *tantum* ad matutinas, ad quas omnes saltem sani et potentes accedant, vsque pulsetur ad primam in crastino nullatinus exituri; et quod delinquentes in horum aliquo iuxta regulam acriter puniantur, vt metu pene ad obseruandum regulares obseruancias arceantur.

Item iniungimus vobis priori in virtute obediencie et sub pena grauis contemptus, vt grangias et tenementa vestra in Nokton, Dunstone

---

[1] *Sic*: for *prior*.
[2] *non* cancelled.
[3] *presente* cancelled.
[4] These injunctions follow those addressed to the prior and convent of Kyme on the lower part of the same leaf.
[5] *Benedicti* cancelled.

[1] *I.e.* Nocton Park. The use of *locus* as practically equivalent to *monasterium* is noticeable in this passage. The same use may be remarked in the names given to many monasteries, especially in the Cistercian order: English examples are Bellus Locus (Beaulieu, Hants.), Locus Benedictus (Stanlaw, Cheshire, afterwards Whalley, Lancs., and Buckland, Devon), Locus Sancti Edwardi (Netley, Hants.),

returned to the place[1] unsent, and so says that he is a canon of the place. To which the prior says in answer that he thinks that the letters of licence of his abbot in this matter were not valid and sufficient, and, albeit he himself, as a plain man without knowledge of law, had done in admitting him otherwise than he ought or had power to do, nevertheless that which was afterwards done and ordained by the general chapter, which is of apostolic authority,[2] ought altogether to stand until it has been otherwise decreed by the general chapter, and, seeing that nothing has been so done to the contrary of the fact aforeset, it seems to him that he is not bound to admit him as his canon. Wherefore my lord appointed them the morrow for propounding, saying and exhibiting whatever is competent for them on both sides, and for this cause he adjourned the visitation until the morrow, to proceed and see process done according to the matters discovered as regards the rest, there being present Skayman and I Colstone. At the which term and place there appeared before the said reverend father, sitting as a judge, the said prior and also the convent; and then, having made public the matters disclosed, my lord enjoined the prior, in virtue of obedience, to remove the said John Butylere with all convenient speed from the priory and from all its external and internal offices. And then, because he found that the said Robert Hildestone[3] had no right in the said priory, so as to be reckoned a canon thereof, my lord by his letters patent sent him back to the house of his profession. And thereafter, having reserved to himself the power of making and conveying to the same prior and convent the necessary injunctions, my lord dissolved his visitation, I, Colstone, being present.

NOCTON PARK

William, by divine permission, etc., to our beloved sons in Christ the prior and convent of the priory of Nocton park, of the order of St. Austin, of our diocese, that now are and shall be, health, etc. In our sometime visitation of you and your said priory, and in our inquiry touching the state thereof, we found certain things worthy of reformation; for the reformation whereof we convey to you these our injunctions and commands, to be observed by you without breach.

In the first place, we enjoin upon you all and singular that every day, when compline has been said, you straightway go to the dorter without more ado in search of rest, and nowise go out therefrom, save only to matins, to which all at any rate who are in sound health and able shall go, until the bell rings for prime on the morrow; and that those who offend in aught of these things be severely punished, so that by fear of the penalty they may be constrained to keep the regular observances.[4]

Also we enjoin upon you the prior, in virtue of obedience and under pain of grievous contempt, that you diligently survey your granges and

---

and Regalis Locus (Rewley, Oxon.) Bellus Locus appears again in the small Benedictine priory of Beaulieu or Beadlow, Beds., and Locus Sancti Edwardi in the Benedictine nunnery of Shaftesbury. Cf. the sense of ' hallowed place ' which is frequently connected with the word ' stow ' in place-names.

[2] By the Benedictine constitutions (1339), cap. vii.

[3] See p. 242 note 2.

[4] This corresponds to none of the *detecta*.

et Metheryngham ac edificia infra situm prioratus, presertim supra domum capitularem, diligenter superuideatis et defectus in ipsis existentes cum omni celeritate possibili reparari faciatis, ne[1] in defectu reparacionis necessarie ruine pateant; quodque instaurum prioratus nullatinus absque consensu conuentus vendatis sub spe prouisionis future forte cariori foro faciende; et quod nichil arduum faciatis nec eciam firmas dimittatis nisi de consensu et assensu expresso sanioris partis conuentus.

Item iniungimus vobis priori vt omnino cohibeatis seruientibus vestris secularibus ne ipsi canonicis vestris improperent aut *eos* verbis opprobriosis vel contumelie infestent vel reprehendant; quodque decetero quemquam canonicum eiusdem ordinis in alia domo professum, licet per prelatum suum dimissum, ad vestrum conuentum nobis aut successoribus nostris episcopis Lincolniensibus inconsultis admittere vel recepire[2] nullatinus presumatis.

Item, etc., *vt in viij*ᵃ *iniunccione Welhowe et deinceps vsque in finem.*

XLVIII.

[Fo. 64d.]

VISITACIO MONASTERII SANCTI JACOBI IUXTA NORTHAMPTONI-AM, ORDINIS SANCTI AUGUSTINI, LINCOLNIENSIS DIOCESIS, FACTA IN DOMO CAPITULARI IBIDEM VIJ⁰ DIE MENSIS JULII, ANNO DOMINI MCCCCXLIJ⁰, PER REUERENDUM IN CHRISTO PATREM ET DOMINUM, DOMINUM WILLELMUM, DEI GRACIA LINCOLNIENSEM EPISCOPUM, ANNO SUARUM CONSECRACIONIS XVJ⁰ ET TRANSLA-CIONIS SEXTO.

In primis, sedente dicto reuerendo patre iudicialiter pro tribunali in huiusmodi visitacionis sue negocio die et loco antedictis, comparuerunt coram eo abbas et conuentus dicti loci, parati vt apparuit ad visitacionem huiusmodi subeundam. Et deinde primo et ante omnia propositum fuit verbum Dei iuxta actus futuri congruenciam in lingua materna per honorabilem virum magistrum Johannem Beuerley, sacre pagine professorem, sequentem hoc thema, 'Habete pacem, et Deus pacis erit vobiscum,[3] etc. Quo multum laudabiliter finito, abbas exhibuit confirmacionem eleccionis sue, et extunc iurauit fidelitatem et obedienciam eidem reuerendo patri in forma consueta. Postea exhibuit fundacionem monasterii, et deinde statum domus: exhibuit eciam fundaciones duarum cantariarum in ipso monasterio per canonicos

---

[1] *ob* cancelled.
[2] *Sic*: for *recipere*.
[3] 2 Cor. xiii, 11: ' pacem habete, et Deus pacis et dilectionis erit vobiscum'. Cf. Phil. iv, 9: ' et Deus pacis erit vobiscum.'

[1] See Newerk's first and third, and Lincolne's first *detecta*.
[2] There is no *detectum* relating to this: there may, however, be a reference to the conduct of the bailiff, John Butylere.
[3] This refers to the canon of Thornton, concerning whom all made depositions.
[4] See No. LXXVII. Cf. the similar clause in the injunctions to Kyme (No. XXXVI), visited two days later. Wellow had been visited on 6 July previously.
[5] See *Visitations* II, 34, note 3 (Eng.).

tenements in Nocton, Dunston and Metheringham, and the buildings within the site of the priory, especially that above the chapter-house, and cause the defaults that are in the same to be amended with all possible speed, lest in default of necessary repair they may be exposed to ruin; and that you in nowise sell the store of the priory without consent of the convent, in hope of making future provision, perchance in a dearer market; and that you do no serious business or even let farms, unless with the consent and express assent of the sounder part of the convent.[1]

Also we enjoin upon you the prior that you altogether restrain your secular serving-men from reproaching your canons, or from annoying or finding fault with them with words of reviling and insult;[2] and that henceforth you take upon yourself in no wise to admit or receive any canon of the same order who has made profession in another house to your convent, albeit he be sent by his superior, without taking counsel of us or our successors, bishops of Lincoln.[3]

Also, etc., as in the eighth injunction to Wellow[4] and thenceforward until the end.

XLVIII.

The visitation of the monastery of St. James by Northampton, of the order of St. Austin, of the diocese of Lincoln, performed in the chapter-house therein on the seventh day of the month of July, in the year of our Lord 1442, by the reverend father in Christ and lord, the Lord William, by the grace of God bishop of Lincoln, in the sixteenth year of his consecration and the sixth of his translation.

In the first place, as the said reverend father was sitting in his capacity of judge as a tribunal in the business of such his visitation, on and in the day and place aforesaid, there appeared before him the abbot and convent of the said place, in readiness, as was apparent, to undergo such visitation. And then, first and before all else, the word of God was set forth, as was agreeable to the act about to take place, in the mother tongue by the honourable master John Beverley, professor of holy writ,[5] after this text, ' Live in peace, and the God of peace shall be with you,' etc. And, when this had come to an end in very praiseworthy fashion, the abbot exhibited the confirmation of his election,[6] and then he sware fealty and obedience to the same reverend father in the form accustomed. Thereafter he exhibited the foundation of the monastery,[7] and then the state of the house: he exhibited also

---

[6] John Watford became abbot in July, 1430: the date of the confirmation is not recorded. See *Visitations* I, 161. He was one of the presidents of the order at the general chapter held at St. James' abbey in 1434 (Salter, *Chapters of Aug. Canons*, p. 82), and at Oseney in 1443 he was responsible for drawing up a form of the procedure to be observed in general chapters (*ibid.* p. 91).

[7] See *V.C.H. Northants.* II, 127, note 12, for references to copies of this document.

celebrandarum, et tercie cuius scriptum in martilogio monasterii regis-
tratum;[1] quorum omnium copias penes registrarium dimisit. Et postea
ad inquisicionem suam preparatoriam processit in hunc modum.

Frater Johannes Watforde, abbas, inquisitus an reddat compotum
omni anno secundum regulam, dicit quod non, et reddit causam eo quod
magna commoda domus consistunt in yconomia vt in granis, que omni
anno vendi non possunt.

Frater Ricardus Euerdone, sacrista et supprior, dicit quod tanto
grauatur infirmitate colica, propter quod oportebit eciam egredi chorum,
claustrum, refectorium et lectum; et ideo causa recessus huiusmodi
multociens culpatur per presidentes. Petit igitur super hiis remedium.

Frater Edmundus Grene, senescallus, dicit omnia bene.

Frater Simon Olyvere dicit omnia bene.

Frater Thomas Westone, coquinarius, dicit omnia bene.

Frater Johannes Pety dicit quod domini Edmundus Grene, Thomas
Westone, Willelmus Youn, non veniunt ad vesperas, matutinas aut
alias horas cum possent, neque Westone ad magnas missas.

Item dicit quod pauperes exhibiti in monasterio pro anima Thome
Wydevyle non sunt contentati de stipendiis suis.

Item dicit quod pietancie que olim dabantur conuentui iam subtrahuntur.

Item dicit quod certe lagene que dabantur celebrantibus missas
ad certa altaria iam subtrahuntur.

Item dicit quod coquinarius emit carnes pro conuentu a quodam
carnifice de Northamptonia cognato suo, que non sunt sapide, ymo
aliquociens sunt fetide et minime salubres.

Item dicit quod non seruitur canonicis infirmantibus de cibariis
suis temporibus suis et de subtilioribus quibus melius possent recreari.

Frater Johannes Mounceux, camerarius, dicit omnia bene.

Frater Nicholaus Youn, subsacrista.

Frater Johannes Symonde, claustralis: abbas non est indifferens in
vocando fratres ad refeccionem in camera vel aula sua, quia aliquando
vocat vnum bis vel ter et alios nulla vice.

Item dicit de carnibus prouisis per coquinarium vt supra pro
conuentu.

---

[1] *Sic*: sc. *est*.

[1] One licence for the endowment of a chantry in the abbey is recorded, dated
22 Nov., 1362 (*Cal. Pat.* 1361-4, p. 270). This provided for the alienation in mortmain by John Michel of Flore and others of a messuage, land, meadow and rents
in Duston, for the maintenance of a canon to celebrate for the souls of Richard de
Keselyngbury and his ancestors.

[2] Twelve canons were examined, but there were three more, mentioned in
Botylere's *detecta*. Of the fifteen, six bore surnames derived from places within a
few miles of Northampton, viz. Watford, Everdon, Weston [Favell], Orlingbury,
Braunston and Pattishall. The remaining nine had patronymics or other family
surnames. It is not unlikely that Edmund Grene, who filled the office of steward,
usually held by a layman, was a member of one of the well-known Northamptonshire families of the name, either that which owned the manor of Greens Norton,
or the Greenes of Drayton.

[3] Thomas Wydville was sheriff of Northamptonshire in 8 Hen. iv, 3, 8 and 9
Hen. v, 1, 7 and 12 Hen. vi, and knight of the shire in the parliaments of 2 Hen. v
and 4 Hen. vi (Bridges *Hist. Northants.* i, 6, 10). He appears to have been a brother
of Richard Wydville of Grafton, the father of Edward iv's queen.

the foundations of two chantries to be celebrated in the same monastery by the canons, and of a third, the deed whereof [is] registered in the martyrology of the monastery;[1] and of all these he left copies with the registrar.   And thereafter [my lord] proceeded to his preparatory inquiry on this wise.

Brother John Watforde,[2] the abbot, on inquiry whether he renders an account every year according to the rule, says that he does not, and gives as his reason that the great profits of the house consist in those coming from husbandry, such as corn, which cannot be sold every year.

Brother Richard Everdone, the sacrist and subprior, says that he is grievously oppressed with infirmity of the bowels, by reason of which he will even be obliged to go out of quire, cloister, frater and his bed; and therefore, because he so retires, he is very often blamed by the presidents.   He prays therefore for a remedy touching this.

Brother Edmund Grene, the steward, says that all things are well.

Brother Simon Olyvere says that all things are well.

Brother Thomas Westone, the kitchener, says that all things are well.

Brother John Pety says that dan Edmund Grene, dan Thomas Westone, [and] dan William Youn do not come to vespers, matins or the other hours when they might, nor does Westone come to high mass.

Also he says that the poor folk maintained in the monastery for the soul of Thomas Wydevyle[3] are not made content with their allowances.

Also he says that the pittances which aforetime were given to the convent are now withdrawn.

Also he says that certain gallons [of wine] that were given to those who celebrate masses at certain altars are now withdrawn.

Also he says that the kitchener buys meat for the convent from a butcher of Northampton who is his kinsman; and this is not savoury, but is sometimes stinking and unhealthy.

Also he says that the canons, when they are ailing, are not served with their food at the proper time, even with the more dainty food wherewith they might best be refreshed.

Brother John Mounceux, the chamberlain, says that all things are well.

Brother Nicholas[4] Youn, the sub-sacrist.

Brother John Symonde, in the cloister,[5] [says that] the abbot is not impartial in inviting the brethren to meals in his chamber or hall, for sometimes he invites one twice or thrice, and others never.

Also he says as above concerning the meat provided by the kitchener for the convent.

---

[4] Apparently an error for William.   William Youn or Yone succeeded Watford as abbot.   The *congé d'élire* on Watford's death was issued 9 Oct., 1445, and the royal assent to Youn's election was granted 26 Oct. following.   Youn died by 26 Sept., 1471 (*Cal. Pat.* 1441-1446, pp. 374, 394; 1467-1477, p. 278).   He was present at the general chapter held at Oseney in 1443 as proctor of the prior of Ravenstone, and was one of the assistants who aided abbot Watford in drawing up the form of procedure then adopted (Salter, *Chapters*, pp. 90, 91).

[5] The special meaning of *claustralis* in this passage is not quite clear.   Possibly he was third prior.

Idem conquinarius in diebus ferialibus vagatur in naui ecclesie et non venit ad chorum, cum non sit aliter prepeditus.

Item dicit quod abbas, Edmundus Grene et Willelmus Youn sunt executores testamentorum Thome Wydevyle et cuiusdam Longvyle, et tanto occupantur circa administracionem bonorum huiusmodi defunctorum quod non veniunt ad chorum nisi in dominicis et aliis principalibus et duplicibus festis.

Item dicit quod ministratur canonicis celebrantibus vinum *corruptum et* acetosum contra canones.

[Fo. 65.] Frater Willelmus Tryg, prior, dicit quod frater Johannes Pety est multum contumeliosus et suscitat dissensiones inter confratres, et licet sit correctus, tamen non desistit sed quasi ex consuetudine[1] labitur ad contumelias.

Item dicit quod canonici ludunt ad taxillos et tabellas contra religionem.

Item dicit quod canonici sunt discordes psallentes in choro, aliquando festine, aliquando retrahendo.

Frater Thomas Orlyngbere dicit quod omnia bene.

Frater Thomas Botylere dicit quod abbas fauet quibusdam canonicis et quibusdam non, ex quo generantur murmura et dissensiones inter fratres.

Item dicit quod fratres Johannes Pety, Ricardus Symonde, Johannes Symonde, Ricardus Braundestone et Robertus Patteshulle non contentantur, ymo murmurant contra victualia in refectorio, et vellent vt alii sic murmurare,[2] et adinuicem sunt isti quinque confederati. Moniti sunt sub pena excommunicacionis quod decetero abstineant ab huiusmodi conspiracionibus et confederacionibus.

Item dicti quinque murmurant contra abbatem, eo quod ipsos non prefert officiis, cum aliquando alios ipsis meliores idem abbas preferat.

Post nonas vero in eodem loco dominus iudicialiter sedens publicauit detecta, et habitis super eis cum hiis super quibus deteguntur racionibus et responsionibus, ac iniunccionibus factis vt prescribitur, dominus monuit omnes et singulos tam abbatem quam alios sub pena excommunicacionis maioris vt nullus alii improperet occasione detectorum huiusmodi, et extunc, reseruata potestate faciendi iniuncciones aliter quam prius fecerat si necesse sit, visitacionem suam huiusmodi dissoluit.

---

[1] *lib* cancelled.
[2] *Sic*: for *murmurarent*.

The same kitchener on ordinary week-days roams about in the nave of the church and comes not to quire, albeit he is not otherwise hindered.

Also he says that the abbot, Edmund Grene and William Youn are the executors of the wills of Thomas Wydevyle and of one Longvyle,[1] and they are so busied about the administration of the wills of such the deceased that they come to quire only on Sundays and on the other principal and double feasts.

Also he says that the canons who celebrate are served with wine that has gone bad and sour, contrary to canon law.

Brother William Tryg, the prior, says that brother John Pety is very abusive and promotes quarrels among his brethren, and, although he has been corrected, yet he ceases not, but almost of habit falls into words of abuse.

Also he says that the canons play at dice and tables, contrary to religion.

Also he says that the canons make discord when they sing in quire, sometimes hurrying and sometimes dragging behind.

Brother Thomas Orlyngbere says that all things are well.

Brother Thomas Botylere says that the abbot favours certain canons, and some not, whereby grumbling and quarrels come to pass among the brethren.

Also he says that brothers John Pety, Richard Symonde, John Symonde, Richard Braundestone and Robert Patteshulle are not content, but murmur against their victuals in the frater, and would that the others should so murmur, and these five are confederate together. They were admonished under pain of excommunication to abstain henceforth from such conspiracies and leagues.

Also the said five murmur against the abbot, because he does not put them in charge of offices, inasmuch as the same abbot sometimes gives such charges to others who are better than themselves.

Now, after nones, my lord, sitting in judgment in the same place, made public the matters disclosed, and, having taken, with those touching whom they are disclosed, their reasons and answers concerning them, and having made injunctions as is written beforehand,[2] my lord admonished all and singular, both the abbot and the others, under pain of the greater excommunication, that no one shall reproach another because of such disclosures; and then, having reserved the power of making injunctions otherwise than he had made them before, if it be necessary, he dissolved such his visitation.

---

[1] Probably one of the Longvyles of Little Billing. The living representative of the family was George Longvyle, sheriff of Northamptonshire in 8 Hen. vi, and still alive in August, 1455 (Bridges, *op. cit.* i, 6, 408, 409).

[2] These injunctions were verbal: no written injunctions remain, but the lower part of fo. 65 and the whole of fo. 65d. were left blank, probably to receive them.

XLIX.

[Fo. 38]

Visitacio hospitalis SANCTI JOHANNIS VILLE NORTHAMP-
TONIE, facta in vestibulo vt pro loco capitulari ibidem
xj die mensis julii, anno Domini mccccxlij⁰, per reuerendum
in Christo patrem et dominum, dominum Willelmum, Dei
gracia Lincolniensem episcopum, anno suarum consecracionis
xvj et translacionis vj^{to}.

In primis, sedente dicto reuerendo iudicialiter in huiusmodi visitacionis sue negocio die et loco huiusmodi, comparuerunt coram eo magister
et fratres dicti hospitalis parati vt apparuit visitacionem huiusmodi
subire. Et deinde[1]

L.

[Fo. 121 *d*].

Visitacio ecclesie collegiate beate Marie de NORTHYEVELLE,
Lincolniensis diocesis, facta in choro eiusdem ecclesie
loco vtique capitulari xxix⁰ die mensis januarii, anno
Domini mccccxlij⁰, per reuerendum in Christo patrem et
dominum, dominum Willelmum, Dei gracia Lincolniensem
episcopum, suarum consecracionis anno xvij⁰ et translacionis vij⁰.

In primis, sedente dicto reuerendo patre iudicialiter in huiusmodi
visitacionis inchoando negocio die, anno et loco antedictis, comparuerunt
coram eo magister et socii capellani ac alii ministri collegii antedicti,
parati vt apparuit ad subeundum visitacionem eandem. Et deinde
primo et ante omnia propositum fuit verbum Dei per egregium virum
magistrum Johannem Sperhawke, sacre pagine professorem, sequentem
hoc thema, ' Videamus si flores fructus parturiunt,' etc.[2] Quo in latino
sermone multum culte finito, magister dicti collegii certificatorium mandati domini sibi pro hoc negocio deputati dicto reuerendo patri exhibuit
in hec verba, ' Reuerendo,' etc. Quo perlecto magister liberauit domino

---

[1] All this is cancelled, and the report of the visitation of Rothwell priory (No.
LXII) follows immediately.
[2] Cant. VII, 12: ' Videamus si floruit vinea, si flores fructus parturiunt, si
floruerunt mala punica.'

[1] Probably the opening form was written in preparation for a visitation which
was postponed.
[2] *I.e.* 29 Jan., 1442-3.
[3] This clerk was not one of Alnwick's ordinary household, and does not appear
to have been connected with the diocese. He may be reasonably identified with
master John Sparhawke, LL.B., advocate of the consistory court of Wells in 1440-1

XLIX.

THE VISITATION OF THE HOSPITAL OF ST. JOHN, IN THE TOWN OF NORTHAMPTON, PERFORMED IN THE VESTRY, IN LIEU OF A PLACE OF CHAPTER THEREIN, ON THE ELEVENTH DAY OF THE MONTH OF JULY, IN THE YEAR OF OUR LORD 1442, BY THE REVEREND FATHER IN CHRIST AND LORD, THE LORD WILLIAM, BY THE GRACE OF GOD BISHOP OF LINCOLN, IN THE SIXTEENTH YEAR OF HIS CONSECRATION AND THE SIXTH OF HIS TRANSLATION.

In the first place, as the said reverend [father] was sitting in his capacity of judge in the business of such his visitation, on and in such day and place, there appeared before him the master and brethren of the said hospital, in readiness, as was apparent, to undergo such visitation. And then[1]

L.

THE VISITATION OF THE COLLEGIATE CHURCH OF BLESSED MARY OF NORTHILL, OF THE DIOCESE OF LINCOLN, PERFORMED IN THE QUIRE OF THE SAME CHURCH, THAT IS, IN THE PLACE OF CHAPTER, ON THE TWENTY-NINTH DAY OF THE MONTH OF JANUARY IN THE YEAR OF OUR LORD 1442,[2] BY THE REVEREND FATHER IN CHRIST AND LORD, THE LORD WILLIAM, BY THE GRACE OF GOD BISHOP OF LINCOLN, IN THE SEVENTEENTH YEAR OF HIS CONSECRATION AND THE SEVENTH OF HIS TRANSLATION.

In the first place, as the said reverend [father] was sitting in judgment at the beginning of the business of such his visitation, on and in the day, year and place aforesaid, there appeared before him the master and chaplain-fellows and the other ministers of the aforesaid college, in readiness, as was apparent, to undergo the same visitation. And then, first and before all else, the word of God was set forth by the excellent master John Sperhawke, professor of holy writ,[3] after this text, ' Let us see if the blossoms bring forth their fruits,'[4] etc. And, when this had come to an end very prettily in the Latin tongue, the master of the said college exhibited to the said reverend father the certificate of my lord's mandate deputed to him for this business, in these words, ' To the reverend,' etc. And, when this had been read

---

(*B. & W. Reg. Stafford* [Som. Rec. Soc.] II, 262), also S.T.D., who had collation of Ashill preb. in Wells, 4 Dec. 1445, and held it at his death in 1474 (MS. Harl. 6966, pp. 45, 60). Weaver (*Som. Incumbents*, p. 256) enters him as rector of Claverton, near Bath, in 1400-1; but this is an error.

[4] The allusion is to the vine: in A.V. the passage runs: ' Let us see if the vine flourish, whether the tender grape appear, and the pomegranates bud forth.'

titulum incumbencie sue, sic que domini Willelmus Charletone, Johannes Tempford et Willelmus Parkere iurauerunt obedienciam et exhibuerunt litteras ordinum. Dominus Willelmus Patone iurauit obedienciam sed non exhibuit litteras ordinum. Deinde magister exhibuit dispensacionem ad plura, etc., et deinde idem reuerendus pater processit ad inquisicionem suam preparatoriam in huiusmodi visitacione sua sub hac forma.

Magister Ricardus Hethe, magister collegii.

LI.

[Fo. 71 d.]

NUNCOTONE

Cum reuerendus in Christo pater et dominus, dominus Willelmus, Dei gracia Lincolniensis episcopus, diem *Sabbati* proximum post festum translacionis Sancti Thome martiris, anno Domini mccccxl, pro visitacione sua ordinaria in prioratu monialium de Nuncotone, ordinis Cisterciensis, Lincolniensis diocesis, per eum exercenda priorisse loci illius assignauerat, et litteras suas in forma solita et consueta eidem priorisse drexerat,[1] et ad locum illum ad premisse visitacionis sue negocium exequendum dicto die Sabbati accesserat, in loco tamen capitulari dicti prioratus die et anno predictis pro inchoando visitacionis sue huiusmodi negocium iudicialiter sedens, conuocatis coram eo ad hunc actum priorissa et conuentu dicti loci, aliis ingruentibus impedimentis quo minus ad vlteriora posset procedere, huiusmodi visitacionem suam et terminum[2] illum vsque in diem tunc crastinum continuauit et prorogauit, presentibus Depyng, Beuerley et me Colstone. Quibus die et loco, x videlicet die Julii, in dicta domo capitulari coram dicto reuerendo patre ipsis die et loco in huiusmodi visitacionis sue negocio iudicialiter sedente pro tribunali, comparuerunt personaliter priorissa et conuentus. Et deinde primo et ante omnia propositum fuit verbum Dei per venerabilem virum magistrum Johannem Beuerley, sacre pagine professorem, sequentem hoc thema, ' Egressus est Ysaak ad meditandum in agro,' etc.[3] Quo finito, priorissa liberauit dicto reuerendo patri certificatorium mandati domini sibi in hoc negocio directi sub hac forma conceptum, ' Reuerendissimo,' etc.; quo perlecto priorissa iurauit obedienciam in forma consueta, et deinde exhibuit fundacionem domus.

---

[1] *Sic*: for *direxerat*.
[2] *locum* cancelled.
[3] Adapted from Gen. xxiv, 63 : ' et egressus fuerat ad meditandum in agro.'

[1] See *Visitations* I, 190, for an account of Richard Hethe, at this time preb. of Caistor in Lincoln, rector of Shillington, Beds., and master of Northill from 1423. He died within some nine months of this visitation.
[2] The college of Northill had property at Tempsford, Beds. See *V.C.H. Beds.* I, 403.
[3] There is no record of this dispensation in *Cal. Papal Letters*.
[4] No depositions are entered. The college was, like most of the foundations of the kind in the diocese, of comparatively recent foundation. The letters patent by which its erection was licensed (8 Dec., 1404) are printed in *Monasticon* VI (3), 1399, 1400.

through, the master delivered to my lord the title of his incumbency,[1] and so did sir William Charletone, sir John Tempford[2] and sir William Parkere swear obedience and exhibit their letters of orders.   Sir William Patone sware obedience, but did not produce his letters of orders.   Then the master exhibited his dispensation for plurality;[3] and then the same reverend father proceeded to his preparatory inquiry in such his visitation under this form.

Master Richard Hethe, master of the college.[4]

LI.

NUNCOTON

Whereas the reverend father in Christ and lord, the lord William, by the grace of God bishop of Lincoln, had appointed Saturday next after the translation of St. Thomas the martyr, in the year of our Lord 1440,[5] for the holding by him of his visitation as ordinary in the priory of the nuns of Nuncoton, of the order of Cîteaux, of the diocese of Lincoln, to the prioress of that place, and had addressed to the same prioress his letters in the wonted and accustomed form, and had come to that place on the said Saturday to fulfil the business of his aforeset visitation, nevertheless, sitting in the chapter-house of the said priory on and in the day and year aforesaid in his capacity of judge to begin the business of such his visitation, when the prioress and convent of the said place had been called together in his presence to this process, since other matters came in the way as hindrances to his proceeding further, he adjourned and prorogued such his visitation and the term thereof until the morrow, there being present Depyng, Beverley and I Colstone.   On and in the which day and place, to wit, the tenth day of July, in the said chapter-house before the said reverend father, as he was sitting on and in the same day and place in his capacity of judge as a tribunal in the business of such his visitation, there appeared in person the prioress and convent.   And then first and before all else the word of God was set forth by the worshipful master John Beverley, professor of holy writ, after this text, ' Isaac went out to meditate in the field,' etc.[6]   And when this was done, the prioress delivered to the said reverend father the certificate of my lord's mandate which had been addressed to her in this business, composed under this form, ' To the right reverend,' etc.; and when this had been read through, the prioress sware obedience in the form accustomed and then exhibited the foundation charter of the house.[7]   Thereafter she exhibited the confirmation of her election, but

---

[5] *I.e.* 9 July, 1440.

[6] The application of this text is illustrated by Pierre Berthoire, *Reductorium morale*, I, xviii : ' Isaac vero, id est Christus, qui iam ad meditandum in agro paradisi per ascensionem ascenderat, ipsam puellam sibi matrimonialiter copulauit,' etc. Rebekah, of course, represents the church and, in a more restricted sense, the nun, who by her profession becomes the bride of Christ.

[7] This and other early charters are printed in *Monasticon* v, 676-8, from a chartulary which in 1649 belonged to sir Dudley North, K.B.

Postea exhibuit confirmacionem eleccionis sue, sed non installacionem. Deinde exhibuit statum domus: postea examinata dicit ea que sequuntur:

Domina Elizabetha Skypwythe, priorissa, petit vt existentes in minucionibus commedant aut in refectorio cum sequentibus chorum aut in aula priorisse, sic quod tercia familia destruatur.

Item dicit quod seculares persone iacent in dormitorio prope moniales.

Item quod plures habent mulieres seruientes quam sunt necessarie.

Domina Elena Frost, suppriorissa, petit quod seculares non communicent cum monialibus neque eciam seruiant eis in refectorio aut dormitorio.

Item petit quod refectorium seruetur omni die, cum sit vnum refectorium superius in quo vescuntur piscibus et lacticiniis, et aliud inferius in quo ex gracia vescuntur carnibus, et quod nullatinus compellantur ad aulam priorisse, ne misceantur secularibus.

Item petit vt panis et ceruisia in qualitate meliorentur.

Item dicit quod tante moniales in numero preficiuntur officiis exterioribus quod non possunt sequi chorum, et ideo residue moniales grauius pondus portant in diuino obsequio.

Item dicit quod consuerunt in preterito recepere[1] de[2] admittendis in moniales xx li. vel plus vel minus, alias eas non recepture.

Item dicit quod moniales temporibus autumpnalibus exeunt ad opera autumpnalia, per quod chorus non sequitur; et dicit quod moniales tempore seminatus purgant segetes a malis herbis in orreis, vbi ingrediuntur seculares, inter quos et moniales verba inhonesta proferuntur, ex quo malum timetur[3] subsequitur.

Item dicit quod reliquie et fragmenta mense conuentus non colliguntur nec distribuuntur in elemosinam, sed timet quod pereunt propter necgligenciam vel alias consumuntur.

Item dicit quod est vna senex monialis iacet[4] in[5] infirmaria, et cum

---

[1] *Sic*: for *recipere*.

[2] *mon* cancelled.

[3] *Sic*: for *ut timetur*.

[4] *Sic*: for *que iacet* or *iacens*.

[5] *dom* cancelled.

[1] Her accession is not recorded: see *Visitations* i, 160.

[2] The name Skipwith, still frequently found in Lincolnshire, though commonly under the form Skipworth, is derived from Skipwith in Yorkshire, near Selby. Of the other names, Benyngtone (Benington near Boston or Long Bennington near Grantham), Estone, Thorpe, Saltmershe (Saltmarshe in Yorkshire, near Howden) and possibly Jaktone are derived from places.

[3] *I.e.* the separate ' household ' in the infirmary.

[4] This passage is of considerable importance, with a corroborative passage from the visitation of Stixwould (No. lxx), as it affords the only documentary evidence hitherto forthcoming for the division of the Cistercian frater into an upper and lower story. This arrangement may still be seen at Ford abbey in Dorset and clearly existed at Kirkstall and Furness, and the reason has been recognised by Sir W. H. St. John Hope (see, e.g., *Kirkstall Abbey* [Thoresby Soc., vol. xvi, 1907],

not her installation.[1]   Then she exhibited the state of the house: afterwards on examination she says these things which follow.

Dame Elizabeth Skypwythe,[2] the prioress, prays that they who are in their seynies may eat either in the frater with them that go regularly to quire or in the prioress's hall, so that the third household may be done away with.[3]

Also she says that secular persons do lie in the dorter near the nuns.

Also that they have more serving-women than are needful.

Dame Ellen Frost, the subprioress, prays that secular folk may not hold converse with the nuns or do service to them also in the frater or dorter.

Also she prays that frater may be kept every day, since there is one upper frater wherein they feed on fish and food made with milk, and another down-stairs wherein they feed of grace on flesh,[4] and that they be in no wise bound to use the prioress's hall, lest they mingle among secular folk.

Also she prays that their bread and beer may be bettered in kind.

Also she says that so many nuns in number are set in charge of the external offices that they cannot go to quire regularly, and so the rest of the nuns bear too heavy a burthen as regards divine service.

Also she says that in the past they were wont to receive twenty pounds or more or less from persons to be admitted as nuns, and would not take them in otherwise.

Also she says that in the autumn season the nuns go out to their autumn tasks, whereby quire is not kept regularly; and she says that in seed-time the nuns clear the crops from weeds in the barns, and there secular folk do come in and unbecoming words are uttered between them and the nuns, wherefrom, [as] is feared, there are evil consequences.

Also she says that the leavings and broken meats of the table of the convent are neither gathered together nor distributed in alms, but she fears that by reason of carelessness they are destroyed or otherwise wasted.

Also she says that there is an old nun [who] lies in the infirmary and with her another nun who has been in religion twenty-two years,

---

p. 48) as the need of providing a misericord or flesh-frater near the cloister in addition to the regular refectory.   In 1335 the constitutions of Benedict XII restricted the eating of meat or *pulmenta cum carnibus condita vel decocta* to the infirmary, and forbade such viands to be prepared outside the infirmary or the special kitchen attached to it (*Nomasticon Cisterciense*, 1892, pp. 484-6).   Subsequently it became the custom in the order to eat meat on Sundays, Tuesdays and Thursdays, except in seasons of fasting, as is definitely implied in the articles of reform agreed upon at Paris in 1493 (*ibid.*, p. 552), so that the requirements of the constitution of 1335 were met in the fifteenth century by providing a special refectory and kitchen for flesh-days.   Sometimes, as at Jervaulx (see Hope and Brakspear in *Yorks. Archaeol. Journal* xxi, 334-6), the misericord was built as an annexe to the frater, with the meat-kitchen between it and the infirmary, which it also served; but at Kirkstall the frater was divided into two stories, the lower of which was served from a meat-kitchen at the south-east corner, while the upper or frater proper was served from the old cloister kitchen.   At other abbeys, however, as at Fountains, existing buildings seem to have been adapted without alteration to the new arrangements.

ea alia monialis habens in religione xxij annos, et commedunt in cellario conuentus et similiter infirme, imbecilles et existentes in minucionibus et alie officiarie commedunt in eodem cellario, sic quod omni die ad minus sunt in refectorio sex moniales.

Item petit quod perhendinantes amoueantur a domo sic quod non misceantur monialibus, quia, si nulle essent, priorissa posset sequi refectorium; et quod ad perhendinantes est magna confluencia extraneorum ad magnum onus domus.

Item dicit quod sunt duo corrodiarii, vnus a xx annis et alius a xij annis, pro quorum quolibet recepte erant xx marce.

Item dicit vbi quelibet monialis percipere consueuit ad vestitum in anno viij s., isto anno non[1] receperunt singule solum xij d.

Item dicit quod tempore suo fuerunt in habitu xviij[2] vel xx, et modo sunt nisi xiiij; et dicit quod moniales visitantes amicos suos in partibus nimis diutinas moras faciunt antequam redeant ad monasterium, eciam per septimanam.

[Fo. 72]   Domina Isabella Benyngton dicit quod panis et[3] ceruisia sunt multum debiles: ideo petit vt meliorentur.

Item dicit de secularibus seruientibus in refectorio vt supra, et de secularibus iacentibus in dormitorio vt supra.

Domina Cecilia Malet dicit quod aliquociens pauce moniales veniunt ad matutinas et completorium, et iste defectus non bene punitur; ideo transgredientes non curant.

Item dicit de secularibus iacentibus in dormitorio et seruientibus in refectorio vt supra, et petit vt refectorium seruetur vt supra.

Item petit vt dominus Willelmus Castre sit confessor mulierum.[4]

Domina Margareta Terry dicit quod magna confluencia est hospitum propter perhendinantes: petit refectorium seruetur vt supra.

Domina Margeria Estone dicit quod priorissa bona foret[5] si sanum habert[6] consilium, et dicit de corrodiis venditis et natiuis alienatis tempore istius priorisse absque licencia priorisse.

Item petit vt sacrista habeat secum vnam seruientem familiarem pro supportando onere suo in officio suo, sustentendam[7] in cibariis ad expensam conuentus.

Domina Alicia Aunselle petit vt omnes viuant in communi, et quod nulla monialis aliquid habeat quasi proprium, vt pote caupones et similia;

---

[1] *Sic*: probably *nisi* was intended to follow and *solum* written instead.
[2] *c* cancelled above line.
[3] *p* cancelled.
[4] *Sic*: possibly for *monialium*.
[5] *sil* cancelled.
[6] *Sic*: for *haberet*.
[7] *Sic*: for *sustentandam*.

[1] This should strictly imply the *cellarium* or cellarer's building which normally formed the lower part of the western cloister range.   Part of this building in houses of Cistercian monks was the frater of the lay brothers.   But it was inconveniently situated for the infirmary and meat-kitchen, and here the word should probably be taken to mean the under-frater already referred to, which might be called the *cellarium* to distinguish it from the frater proper, which formed the loft or *solarium* over it.   This is implied by the mention which follows of the daily use of the frater.

and they do eat in the cellar of the convent[1] and likewise the infirm, the weak-minded and they that are in their seynies and the other officers do eat in the same cellar, so that every day there are at least six nuns in the frater.

Also she prays that the lodgers be removed from the house so that they mingle not among the nuns, for, if there were none, the prioress might be able to come constantly to frater; and because there is great recourse of strangers to the lodgers, to the sore burthen of the house.

Also she says that there are two men who have corrodies, one for the last twenty years and the other for the last twelve years, for each of whom twenty marks were received.

Also she says that whereas each nun was wont to receive eight shillings a year for her raiment, this year they have received only twelve pence apiece.

Also she says that in her time there were eighteen or twenty wearing the habit and now there are but fourteen; and she says that the nuns when they visit their friends in the country do make too long tarrying, even for a week, before they return to the monastery.

Dame Isabel Benyngtone says that the bread and beer are very poor: she prays therefore that they may be bettered.

Also she says as above concerning the secular serving-folk in the frater, and as above concerning the secular folk that lie in the dorter.

Dame Cecily Malet says that sometimes few nuns come to matins and compline, and this default is not well punished; therefore they that transgress take no heed.

Also she says as above concerning the secular folk that lie in the dorter and serve in the frater, and she prays as above that frater may be kept.

Also she prays that Sir William Castre[2] may be the women's confessor.

Dame Margaret Terry says that there is great recourse of guests on account of the lodgers: she prays frater may be kept as above.

Dame Margery Estone says that the prioress would do well if she had sound advice, and she says of corrodies that they have been sold, and of bondmen that they have been alienated in this prioress's time without the prioress's licence.

Also she prays that the sacrist may have with her one serving-woman in her household to bear her burthen in her office, who shall be maintained in victuals at the charges of the convent.

Dame Alice Aunselle prays that they may all live in common, and that no nun may have anything, such as capons[3] and the like, as her

---

[2] Castre=Caistor, which is not far from Nuncoton. The women referred to in this petition are probably the lodgers. It is not clear, however, whether the recommendation implies that they should have a separate confessor from the nuns, or that the ordinary chaplain of the convent should hear their confessions. Probably the second alternative is meant, as the casual visits of priests from outside would add to the inconvenience and expense already caused by the boarders.

[3] Why capons should be mentioned specially is not clear. The allusion seems to be to delicacies sent to particular nuns from outside: these were to be considered common property.

set si que sint talia seruentur in communi per communem seruientem, nec habeant domos aut gardina separata¹ tanquam sibi ascripta.

Item petit vt mulieres perhendinantes apte ad matrimonium omnino amoueantur a domo, a refectorio et dormitorio propter plura incommoda que ex earum mora proueniunt domui.

Item dicit quod quedam moniales non veniunt ad completorium, sed vagantur illo tempore in gardinis pro herbis colligendis et alibi circa vana.

Item dicit et petit quod moniales prefecte officiis exterioribus exonerentur ab officiis illis et intendant choro, et hoc propter raritatem monialium.

Item petit vt moniales cohibeantur ne leuent pueros ad fontem aut crismacionem frontis, et quod non multum tardent ad extra cum visitent amicos; et quod moniales seruent interiora claustri.

Domina Elizabetha Thorpe dicit omnia bene.

Domina Isabella Gray dicit quod omnia bene.

Domina Matilda Saltmershe dicit de consuetudine recipiendi moniales precio vt supra.

Domina Agnes Jaktone, xv annis in religione, soluit in ingressu suo xx li.

Domina Johanna Ascyue, octennis in religione, soluit in ingressu suo xx li.

Domina Margareta Est dicit omnia bene.

Domina Alicia Skotte, quatuor annis in religione, soluit in ingressu suo, sed nescit quantum, sed vt credit xx li.

Item dicit de secularibus in refectorio et dormitorio vt supra, et de leuacione infancium dicit vt supra per priorissam.

[INJUNCTIONS].

[Fo. 77 *d*.] NUNCOTONE²

Willyam, by the suffraunce of God bisshope of Lincolne, to our wele belufede doghters in Criste the prioresse and the couent of the priorye of Nuncotone, of the ordre of Cistewes, of our diocese, *sendethe helthe, grace and his blessyng*.³ Late we visityng yow and your saide priorye by our inquisicyone⁴ fonde certeyn defautis theryn for⁵ reformacyon *of wich* we sende yowe thise our iniunccyons and commaundementes as thai are set bynethe here writene.

(1.) *[Quo]d nulla secularis [mini]stret in refectorio.* In the fyrste we enioyne and charge yow, prioresse, in virtue of your obedience and

---

¹ *q* cancelled.

² These injunctions follow those for Wellow and precede those for Thornton abbeys.

³ Written above the injunctions instead of *salutacyon in God wyth our blessyng* cancelled.

⁴ *we* cancelled.

⁵ *whose* cancelled.

¹ *I.e.* the nuns should not be allowed to stand as sponsors. *Chrismacio frontis,* as distinct from *chrismacio verticis* in baptism, is the anointing with chrism at con-

own; but that, if any such there be, they be kept in common by a common servant, and that they may not have houses or separate gardens appropriated, as it were, to them.

Also she prays that the women lodgers who are marriageable be altogether removed from the house, from the frater and dorter, by reason of the many disadvantages which arise to the house out of their stay.

Also she says that certain nuns do not come to compline, but stray about at that time in the gardens to gather herbs, and elsewhere in idle pursuits.

Also she says and prays that the nuns who are set in charge of the external offices may be discharged of those offices and attend quire, and this on account of the scarceness of nuns.

Also she prays that the nuns be restrained from presenting children at the font or when the chrism is put upon their foreheads,[1] and that they may not tarry long abroad when they visit their friends; and that the nuns may abide within the inner parts of the cloister.

Dame Elizabeth Thorpe says all things are well.

Dame Isabel Gray says that all things are well.

Dame Maud Saltmershe says as above concerning the custom of receiving nuns at a price.

Dame Agnes Jaktone, fifteen years in religion, paid twenty pounds at her entry.

Dame Joan Ascyue,[2] eight years in religion, paid twenty pounds at her entry. .

Dame Margaret Est says all things are well.

Dame Alice Skotte, four years in religion, paid at her entry, but she knows not how much, but, as she believes, twenty pounds.

Also she says as above concerning the secular folk in the frater and dorter, and of the presentation of infants she says as above [that it has been done] by the prioress.

---

vndere peyne of greuous contempte that ye suffre no seculers ministre in the fraytere ne lyg in the dormitory, women ne childerne; ne that ye take ne suffre to be taken any seculere persones to soiourne among yowe wythe owten specyal leve asked and had of vs or our successours, bysshop[3] of Lincoln; ne that ye suffre none of your susters to be in felowshipe wythe seculers nouthere in mete nere other occupacyons wythe yn ne

---

firmation, which took place as soon as the baptised child could be brought to the bishop. Archbishop Reynolds' constitution *Sacerdotes* orders: ' Item ad confirmacionem nullus puer teneatur a patre vel matre, vitrico vel noverca. Et volumus quod hec prohibicio sepe per sacerdotes in ecclesiis publicetur, ut sciant parentes ac alii qui pueros tenent ad confirmandum quod spirituale vinculum in hoc sacramento contrahitur ut in baptismo.' On the third day after confirmation the child was brought to church and his forehead washed by the priest at the font ' propter reverenciam chrismatis,' and the swaddling clothes burned in which he had been confirmed. The presence of godparents at confirmation is still required by the rubric.

[2] *I.e.* Ayscough or Askew.

[3] *Sic.*

wyth owte.   And the soiournauntes that are nowe, ameve thaym wythe yn[1] an halfe yere next comyng vndere the same peyne.[2]

(2.)[3] Also, for as muche as ther be but fewe in couent in regarde of tymes here to fore, and of thoe that now are ther are so manye putte to owtwarde officees that the qwere may not conuenyently be servede, we charge yow, prioresse, vndere payne aforesaide, that ye ordeyne that ther be more multitude to sarufe the qwere bothe nyght day,[4] other owtwarde officees lefte.[5]

(3.) Also we charge yowe alle that the relefe that remaynes after refeccyone of the couent and your borde, pryoresse, be not wastede, but truly keppede and distributede to pore peple.[6]

(4.) Also we wylle and charge yowe that thoe nunnes that are in seyneys for that tyme ete wythe the couent in that one[7] fraytour or that othere, or elles in the prioresse halle at a borde by thaym selfe, where no seculere shalle hafe communycacyone wythe thaym, so that no housholde be holden in any place at any tyme but in the fraytour or the prioresse halle in forme aforesayde.[8]

(5.) Also we enioyne yowe, prioresse, vndere peyne of deposicyone and vndere payne of the grete cursyng, that ye receyve no mo in to nunnes but as may be competently [Fo. 78] susteynede of the revenues of your house, ne that for receyvyng of any nunne ye exacte non erthely gode other wyse then thai or thaire frendes of thaire charytee wythe owtene any paccyone or couenaunt or promysse made be fore wylle gyfe yowe.[9]

(6.) Also, where by custom laudable of the place euery nunne shulde have viij s. in the yere to thaire vesture, we wylle and charge that thai in lyke wyse be payede so that thai hafe no cause to please owtwarde for thair necessitee.[10]

(7.) Also we charge yow, prioresse, vndere paynes abofe and bynethe conteynede, that ye oftere then ye are wonte kepe the fraytour in tyme of refeccyons, seyng that your rule be keppede.[11]

(8.) Also we enioyne yowe, prioresse, vndere lyke paynes, that when your susters shalle visite thaire frendes ye assigne theym a certeyn day be the whiche thai may come home, so that ouere thre dayes wythe owten grete and resonable cause thai abyde not wythe thair frendes.[12]

---

[1] *anhaf* cancelled.
[2] Founded on the prioress's first, the subprioress's first, sixth and ninth, Isabel Benyngtone's second, Cecily Malet's second, Alice Aunselle's second and Alice Skotte's second *detecta*.
[3] *Incipe* written in the margin.
[4] *Sic*.
[5] Founded on the subprioress's fourth and twelfth and Alice Aunselle's fourth *detecta*.
[6] Founded on the subprioress's seventh *detectum*.
[7] *fermorye* cancelled.
[8] Founded on the prioress's first, the subprioress's second and eighth, Margaret Terry's, Alice Aunselle's first and second and Alice Skotte's second *detecta*.
[9] Founded on the subprioress's fifth *detectum* and those of Maud Saltmershe, Joan Ascyue, Agnes Jaktone and Alice Skotte.
[10] Founded on the subprioress's eleventh *detectum*.
[11] Founded on the subprioress's ninth *detectum*.
[12] Founded on the subprioress's twelfth and Alice Aunselle's fifth *detecta*.

(9.) Also we enioyne eueryche one of yowe, vndere paynes obofe and bynethe writene, that ye alle that are not lawfully lettede be presente at complyne, and, that done, go ryght forthe to the dormytorye, and not come owte to the morne aftere that pryme rynge, save alle onely to matynes, to the whiche we wylle that all the nunnes come that are myghty, and that[1] *thoo* that trespase here yn be correcte so aftere your rule that other take fere by thaire correccyone.[2]

(10.) Also we enioyne yow alle and yche oon of yowe, vndere the same paynes, that none of yowe heve no childerne at the fount ne confirmyng.[3]

(11.) Also we charge yow, prioresse, vndere the same peynes, and yche of yow of the couent that ye hafe no mo seculere women seruauntes wythe[4] yow then hit is seen to yow, prioresse, necessary to be had.[5]

(12.) Also we enioyne yowe, prioresse, vndere peyne of finale priuacyone fro yowere office and dygnyte of prioresse, that ye neuer fro hens forthe gyfe, graunte or[6] selle any corrodye, lyverye, pensyone or annuetee to any persone what euer he be to terme of lyve, for euere or to a certeyn tyme; ne that *ye* alyene or selle any bondman but ye fyrste aske and hafe leve of *vs*[7] or our successours bysshope of Lincolne, and wythe fulle assente of the more partye of the couent.[8]

(13.) And also that in alle thynges that ye do ye take to *yow* sad and soubre consayle at the aduyse of the more party of the couent, wythe owte whiche aduyse ye do nothyng as on your owen hede here ouere we monesshe yow and yche one of yowe ones, twyes and thryes peremptorily that ye obserue.[9]

---

[1] *thoe* cancelled.

[2] Founded on Cecily Malet's first and Alice Aunselle's third *detecta*.

[3] *wythe outen specyall leve asked and had by nunnes of the prioresse and by the prioresse of vs or our successours bysshope of Lincolne* cancelled. The injunction is founded on Alice Aunselle's fifth and Alice Skotte's second *detecta*.

[4] *then h* cancelled.

[5] Founded on the prioress's third, the subprioress's first, Isabel Benyngtone's second, Cecily Malet's second and Alice Skotte's second *detecta*.

[6] Interlined above *ne* cancelled.

[7] Interlined above *hus* cancelled.

[8] Founded on the subprioress's tenth and Margery Estone's *detecta*.

[9] Founded on Margery Estone's *detectum*.

LII.

[Fo. 130.]

[VISITACIO][1] MONASTERII DE [NOT]TE[LEY, ORDINIS SANCTI AUGUS-
TINI, LINCOLNIENSIS DIOCESIS, FACTA IN DOMO CAPITULARI]
EIUSDEM XV DIE MENSIS [AUGUSTI, ANNO D]O[MINI MCC]CCXLVIJ⁰
PER REUERENDUM IN CHRISTO [PATREM ET] DOMINUM, DOMINUM
WILLELMUM, DEI GRACIA LINCOLNIENSEM EPISCOPUM, SUARUM
CONSECRACIONIS ANNO XXIJ⁰ ET TRANSLACIONIS [XJᵐᵒ]

In primis, sedente dicto reuerendo patre iudicialiter pro tribunali
die et loco antedictis in huiusmodi visitacionis sue negocio, comparuerunt
coram eo abbas et singuli canonici dicti monasterii, paucis canonicis
ibidem adextra in negociis domus agentibus et propter distanciam et
temporis breuitatem non citatis exceptis. Et deinde traditum fuit
dicto reuerendo patri pro parte abbatis certificatorium mandati dicti
reuerendi patris ipsi abbati pro hac visitacione directi; et quia in priori
visitacione dicti monasterii facta . . . . . . per Depyng idem abbas
iurauit obedienciam et exhibuit confirmacionem eleccionis sue, ideo
dominus nichil de hiis hoc instanti exegit. [Et deinde per]lecto certificatorio et preconizatis citatis et comparentibus, exceptis preexceptis,
dominus ad examinacionem abbatis processit; [qui] examinatus deponit
[. . . vt . . . . . .] plenius continetur. Et deinde nominauit Brehulle
ad occupandum . . . . et Thame ad occupandum officium. . .

(Medemenham.) Frater Edwardus Londone, prior, dicit quod
dissencio inter abbatem et Medemenham orta est eo quod [dictus] Medemenham stans apud Shiryngham v annis quorum quolibet reddidisset
monasterio xviij li. et nichil quasi in officio reddidit. [Prior] tamen
dicit quod Medemenham reddidit compotum talem qualem, abbas
tamen dicit non verum.

(Ewelme et Tylehurst.) Item dicit quod Thomas Ewelme et
Johannes Tylehurst fauent dicto Medemenham in huiusmodi maleficio
suo, et dicit quod non est verisimile quod pax aut quies non² erit in domo

---

¹ This part of the MS. is much torn and the upper portion of the leaf is not
easily legible.
² *Sic.*

¹ The date of the month is indicated by the dates of the injunctions and the
other document included in the records of this visitation. These dates have been
overlooked in the itinerary of Alnwick given in *Visitations* II, pp. xli, xlii, where
it is suggested that the visitation was held in January, 1447-8. The bishop was
probably at Liddington on 1 August; if he was at Nutley on 15 August, it is clear
that dates from Nettleham on the 13th and 14th, and from Sleaford on the 17th,
can bear no reference to his personal movements; while the date from Rothwell
on the 22nd is puzzling, if he went from Nutley to Bishops Wooburn. The abbey
of Nutley (*de Parco Thame*) was on the right bank of the Thame, in the parish of
Long Crendon, and about three miles north of Thame.
² It appears that this was a special visitation, held at short notice. It falls
into no scheme of visitation of the archdeaconry. See below, p. 254, note 4.
³ There is no further record of this visitation.
⁴ The abbot's depositions were clearly contained in a separate schedule, which
has not been preserved.

LII.

[THE VISITATION] OF THE MONASTERY OF [NUTLEY, OF THE ORDER OF
ST. AUSTIN, OF THE DIOCESE OF LINCOLN, PERFORMED IN THE
CHAPTER-HOUSE] OF THE SAME, ON THE FIFTEENTH DAY OF THE
MONTH OF [AUGUST,[1] IN THE YEAR OF OUR LORD] 1447 BY THE
REVEREND FATHER IN CHRIST AND LORD, THE LORD WILLIAM,
BY THE GRACE OF GOD BISHOP OF LINCOLN, IN THE TWENTY-
SECOND YEAR OF HIS CONSECRATION AND [THE ELEVENTH] OF HIS
TRANSLATION.

In the first place, as the said reverend father was sitting in his
capacity of judge as a tribunal on and in the day and place aforesaid
in the business of such his visitation, there appeared before him the abbot
and the several canons of the said monastery, with the exception of a
few canons therein who were engaged externally in the business of the
house, and, because they were at a distance and the time was short,[2]
had not been summoned. And then there was delivered to the said
reverend father on the abbot's behalf the certificate of the mandate of
the said reverend father addressed for this visitation to the same abbot;
and because, at the former visitation of the said monastery held . . . by
Depyng,[3] the same abbot sware obedience and exhibited the confirmation of his election, my lord therefore at this present demanded none of
these. [And then, when] the certificate had been read [through] and
those who were summoned had been called over and appeared, with
the exception of those before excepted, my lord proceeded to the examination of the abbot. [And he], on examination, deposes [. . . as . . . .]
is more fully contained.[4] And then [my lord] nominated Brehulle to
occupy . . . . . . and Thame to occupy the office . . .

[Medemenham.] Brother Edward Londone, the prior,[5] says that a
quarrel arose between the abbot and Medemenham, because [the said]
Medemenham, abiding for five years at Sheringham,[6] should have rendered
eighteen pounds every year to the monastery, and rendered almost
nothing in the office. [The prior] says, however, that Medemenham
rendered some sort of an account; but the abbot says it is not true.

(Ewelme and Tylehurst.) Also he says that Thomas Ewelme and
John Tylehurst abet the said Medemenham in such his mischief; and
he says that it is not likely that there will be peace or quiet in the house

---

[5] Sixteen canons are mentioned, nine of whom gave evidence. The abbot
was Nicholas Redyng, *i.e.* Reading. Eleven have names from places close to or
at no great distance from Nutley, viz. Ashendon, Crendon, Brill (Brehulle), Easington,
Marlow, and Medmenham in Bucks.; Thame and Ewelme, in Oxfordshire; Reading,
Tilehurst, Wallingford and Bray, in Berkshire. Of the other four, the prior was
called London, Borewelle and Altone are names of doubtful origin, and, while
Brystowe presumably came from Bristol, it is just possible that the form may be a
corruption of Boarstall, Bucks.

[6] Sheringham in Norfolk. The church of Sheringham was appropriated to
Nutley abbey. It is not mentioned in the foundation charter, but appears in Henry
II's confirmation charter among the gifts of the founders (*Monasticon* VI (i), 278).

dummodo ille Medemenham fuerit ibidem: ideo expediens foret quod amoueatur[1] a domo.

(Abbas.) Item dicit quod abbas nunquam tempore suo reddidit compotum administracionis sue in scriptis de quo iste recolit.

(Prior.) Frater Johannes Tylehurst dicit quod religio perit in defectu prioris et presidencium ordinis et nomina[2] Breulle vel Johannem Thame preficiendum in priorem quia prior modernus non intendit choro claustro[3] aliquando per iiij [dies].

(W. Walyngford.) Item dicit quod frater Willelmus Walyngford circa medietatem anni proxime preteriti captus fuit suspecto modo cum quadam muliere de[4] Chiltone cui ecclesie seruiebat vt capellanus parochialis et absque correccione abbas amouit eum vsque Mayden Bradley vt ibidem deseruiat in scandalum religionis. Iste non est presens in monasterio.

(Abbas.) Item dicit quod abbas non ministrat nec facit ministrari necessaria existentibus in infirmaria iuxta exigenciam ordinis et prout humanitas requirit, nec habetur ibidem custos qui deseruiat infirmis; et dicit quod iste idem deponens in infirmaria existens non habet focalia nec solacia de nocte sed solus iacet in infirmaria.

(Tawke.) Item dicit quod causa dissensionis in domo est eo quod quidam Tawke verberauit quendam famulum domus eo quod commitabatur Medemenham eunti ad dominum episcopum.

(Medemenham.) Frater Nicholaus Borewelle dicit quod causa dissensionis in domo est propter compotos de Shiryngham.

(Prior.) Item dicit quod dicit quod[5] propter senium et infirmitates prior non intendit obseruanciis regularibus: ideo perit religio.

(Prior.) Item dicit quod silencium non seruatur debite iuxta regulam.

(Prior.) Frater Johannes Altone dicit quod prior est nimis laxus et remissus in corrigendo defectus in religione.

(Medemenham.) Item dicit quod dissensio oritur ex compotis Shiryngham per Medemenham.

(Medemenham.) Frater Johannes Crendone dicit de dissensione inter abbatem et Medemenham.

---

[1] *ad* cancelled.
[2] Apparently this is the word: *nominat* seems to be meant.
[3] *ve* cancelled.
[4] *dicit* cancelled.
[5] *Sic*: *dicit quod* repeated by mistake.

[1] The word is quite gone in the original MS. ' Days ' is the most reasonable conjecture.
[2] Chilton, N.W. of the abbey, was one of the five neighbouring churches, the parishes of which formed a compact block, appropriated to the abbot and convent of Nutley, viz. Ashendon, Chilton, Dorton, Long Crendon and Lower Winchendon. In none of these was there a vicarage ordained, and the canons appear to have exercised the prescriptive right of serving them in person. In this respect, the position of Nutley is parallel to that of Dorchester with regard to its appropriated churches: see *Visitations* II, 80, note 2.
[3] Maiden Bradley is on the border of Wiltshire and Somerset, about five miles S.W. of Warminster. The church of Bradley was granted to the canons of Nutley

as long as that Medemenham is there. Therefore it would be expedient that he should be removed from the house.

(The abbot.) Also he says that the abbot in his time, so far as he recollects, has never rendered an account of his administration in writing.

(The prior.) Brother John Tylehurst says that religion is perishing in default of the prior and the presidents of the order, and names Breulle or John Thame as meet for preferment as prior, because the prior that now is sometimes does not keep quire [and] cloister for four [days][1] together.

(W. Walyngford.) Also he says that brother William Walyngford, about half a year last past, was taken in manner suspect with a woman of Chilton, the which church he was serving as parish chaplain,[2] and the abbot, without correcting him, removed him to Maiden Bradley[3] to serve there, to the scandal of religion. This man is not present in the monastery.

(The abbot.) Also he says that the abbot does not minister or cause things needful to be ministered to those who are in the infirmary, as the order demands and as human kindness requires, nor have they a warden there to do service to the infirm; and he says that this same deponent, who is in the infirmary, has no fuel or comforts at night, but lies by himself in the infirmary.

(Tawke.) Also he says that the cause of quarrelling in the house is that one Tawke beat a serving-man of the house, because he was Medemenham's companion when he went to the lord bishop.[4]

(Medemenham.) Brother Nicholas Borewelle says that the reason of the quarrel in the house is because of the accounts of Sheringham.

(The prior.) Also he says that, by reason of old age and sickness, the prior pays no heed to the regular observances: therefore religion is perishing.

(The prior.) Also he says that silence is not duly observed according to the rule.

(The prior.) Brother John Altone says that the prior is exceedingly slack and negligent in the correction of defaults in religion.

(Medemenham.) Also he says that quarrelling arises out of the accounts of Sheringham, because of Medemenham.

(Medemenham.) Brother John Crendone speaks of the quarrel between the abbot and Medemenham.

---

by Jocelyn, bishop of Salisbury, at the instance of Walter Giffard, earl of Buckingham and founder of the abbey. When, somewhat later, the hospital for leprous women which gave Maiden Bradley its distinctive epithet was founded, Jocelyn granted a special charter by which the indemnity of the parish church was secured (*Monasticon* VI (i), 279). The church remained appropriated to Nutley (cf. *ibid.* 280): Ecton and Bacon both make the mistake of noting it as appropriated to the local priory or hospital. No vicarage appears to have been ordained, in spite of the long distance from Nutley; and the church passed, with the other impropriations already mentioned, to the dean and canons of Christ Church, Oxford, after the suppression of the monastery.

[4] It may be inferred from this statement, coupled with the prominence given to the dispute between Medemenham and the abbot, that Medemenham had gone to the bishop to seek a remedy, and that the visitation was the consequence of this appeal. The special character of the visitation is indicated by the fact that only a limited number of canons were examined: the bishop had already heard Medemenham's side of the case, and wished to hear the other on the spot before coming to a conclusion.

(Medemenham.) Frater Robertus Asshendone dicit de dicta dissensione vt proxime supra.

[Fo. 130 *d.*] [1] Item dicit quod tenementa domus et . . . .
. . . . . . [reddi]tus domus diminuti sunt . . . . . [in de]fectu abbatis
vt credit in . . . . . et nescitur de statu domus quia compoti non
declarantur.

Item dicit quod propter defectum reparacionis testitudines[2] ecclesie
paciuntur dampnum tempore pluuioso et dicit quod . . . . . . patencia
oculo [et quod indigent] reparacione alia [edificia][3] monasterii.

Frater Johannes Thame dicit quod magne confabulaciones fiunt
inter canonicos in[4] coquinaria[5] in defectu prioris qui non intendit religioni
et ex hoc oriuntur dissensiones.

Item dicit quod contra solitum morem monasterii seruitur iiij[or]
canonicis . . . . . [de] vno ferculo in infirmaria ex quo oriuntur dissensiones.

Item dicit quod necessarium foret habere vnum officiarium qui
leuaret et congregaret reuentus domus et superuideret reparaciones ex
necessario faciendas et de sua administracione redderet compotum.

([Elemo]sinarius.) Frater Thomas Ewelme dicit quod reliquie mensarum conuentus non distribuuntur in elemosina sed post refecciones
deferuntur ad coquinam, et solebat esse ibidem vna domus in qua
elemosina[6] destruebatur[7] et iam non est illis domus.

(Tawke.) Item dicit de inieccione manuum violenta in famulum
domus per Tawke vt supra.

([Pri]or.) Item dicit de impotencia et ineptitudine prioris vt supra
et nominat ad illud officium vel Brehulle vel Thame. Iste fauet
Medemenham.

([Magister] nouiciorum.) Frater Johannes Brehulle dicit quod
nouicii non reddunt seruicia ad que reddenda tenentur secundum ordinis
obseruanciam, sed propter necgligenciam prioris seu magistri nouiciorum
hoc omittunt facere quousque promoueantur ad sacerdocium et tunc
dedignantur[8] et recusant ita quod tempore quo debent psalmodizare in
choro nocturnos in cantu non conueniunt nec sciunt seruicium cordetenus
vt deberent.

---

[1] Margin much torn and notes, if any, gone.
[2] *Sic*: for *testudines*.
[3] An interlineation.
[4] *infirmaria* cancelled.
[5] Apparently the word. It seems, however, from the injunctions that *refeccione*
or *refectorio* is the word wanted.
[6] *distrib* cancelled.
[7] *Sic*: for *distribuebatur*.
[8] *rec* cancelled.

[1] The *testudines* are the inner roofs of the church beneath the covering of lead
or tiles. The word is too general to make it certain whether wooden roofs or stone
vaulting are implied. See R. de Lasteyrie, *L'arch. relig. en France à l'époque romane*,
1912, p. 497 *n*: 'le vrai sens du mot *testudo*, au moyen age, est *couverture*. Quand
on l'emploie pour désigner une voûte, on l'accompagne ordinairement de l'épithète
lapidea.' This is possibly too general, as instances actually occur in which *testudo*
is used by itself to imply a roof which we know to have been of stone. In these
visitation records, where a stone vault is referred to, *volta* is the word used: see p. 242

(Medemenham.) Brother Robert Asshendone says of the said quarrel, as in the last deposition above.

Also he says that the tenements of the house and . . . . [and the rents] of the house are diminished . . . . . . [in] the abbot's [default], as he believes in . . . . and nothing is known of the state of the house, because the accounts are not published.

Also he says that, by reason of default in repair, the roofs[1] of the church suffer damage in rainy weather; and he says that . . . . [are] patent to the eye, [and that the] other [buildings] of the monastery [stand in need of] repair.

Brother John Thame says that great talkings take place among the canons in the kitchen, in the prior's default, who pays no heed to religion; and herefrom spring quarrellings.

Also he says that, contrary to the wonted custom of the monastery, four canons . . . . in the infirmary are served with one dish, whereout spring quarrellings.

Also he says that it should be necessary to have an officer, who should levy and bring together the revenues of the house and survey the repairs that are needful to be done, and render an account of his administration.

(The almoner.) Brother Thomas Ewelme says that the leavings of the tables of the convent are not distributed in alms, but are taken away to the kitchen after meals; and there used to be there a house in which the alms were distributed,[2] and now they have not the house.

(Tawke.) Also he says as above concerning the violent laying of hands upon the serving-man of the house by Tawke.

(The prior.) Also he says as above concerning the impotence and unfitness of the prior, and nominates for that office either Brehulle or Thame. This [deponent] is a supporter of Medemenham.[3]

([The master] of the novices.` Brother John Brehulle says that the novices do not render the services which they are bound to render[4] according to the observance of the order, but, by reason of the negligence of the prior or of the master of the novices, they omit to do this until they are advanced to the priesthood; and then they disdain and refuse to do it, so that, at the time at which they ought to be reciting the nocturn psalms in quire they are not in unison in song, nor do they know the service by heart, as they ought.

---

above. The form *testitudo* employed here is occasionally found: see, *e.g.* the passage quoted by Mortet, *Recueil*, p. 142, and Alanus de Insulis, *Distinctiones* (Migne *P.L.* ccx, col. 97).

[2] The error in the Latin text is obvious, though made with apparent deliberation.

[3] Apparently this is the meaning. The prior had already mentioned Ewelme as a friend of Medemenham, and the registrar entered this memorandum, it would appear, as a *caveat* against attaching undue weight to Ewelme's evidence in assessing the *comperta*.

[4] The ' rendering of services ' refers, of course, to the services in church, which the novices were expected to know intelligently and by heart, and to be able to chant correctly.

Item quo ad ineptitudinem prioris concordat cum aliis vt supra.

([Magister] nouiciorum.) Item *Johannes Thame* magister nouiciorum non ministrat nouiciis vestimenta et calciamenta competenter in tantum quod multociens incedunt vestibus et calciamentis ruptis et laceratis.

Frater *Henricus*[1] Esyngtone de ineptitudine prioris vt supra, et dicit quod magister nouiciorum non intendit illo[2] officio: ideo quasi vagabundi discurrunt.

Item dicit quod cum sit sacrista non ministratur sibi competenter de oleo, cera, vino et pane et aliis necessariis requisitis in defectu abbatis qui omnes redditus illius officii occupat.

[Confa]bulaciones [in re]fectorio.) Item habentur confabulaciones inter canonicos in refectorio nec vtuntur signis consuetis.

Memorandum de iniunccionibus mittendis in scriptis super detectis.

[Fo. 131.] . . . . vn . . . .

(Medemenham.) Superinde quidam frater Johannes Medemenham canonicus sumpsit querelam versus dictum Willelmum Tawke affirmans quod i[dem Tawke] violenciam fecit dicto Willelmo Thresshere pro eo quod comitabatur dicto fratri Johanni venienti ad dominum episcopum.

Insuper Thomas Ewelme, Willelmus Bury et Willelmus Brystowe canonici assistentes dicto fratri Johanni Medemenham cum fustibus insultum fecerunt super dictum Willelmum Tawke et ipsum insequebantur vsque ad cameram abbatis, et subsequenter de mandato abbatis primo per priorem et secundo per suppriorem moniti quod a talibus insolenciis abstinerent et claustrum seruarent noluerunt adquiescere, sed[3] ad chorum et ecclesiam armis inuasiuis muniti venerunt more guerrino contra abbatis preceptum inobedienciam committendo.

(Medemenham.) Frater Johannes Medemenham absque licencia abbatis exiuit monasterium eciam in habitu laicali dimisso habitu regulari animo et intencione interficiendi fratrem Walterum Merlowe canonicum tum manentem apud Shipyngham[4], et in itinere suo captus fuit apud Dunstaple ad magnum scandalum et sumptus monasterii.

Item tempore quo stetit sacrista monasterii fieri sibi fecit vnam diploidem anglice a Jak of fense de vestimentis ecclesie ad magnum dampnum ecclesie.

---

[1] Interlined above *Thomas* cancelled.
[2] *Sic*: for *illi*.
[3] *armis* and other words cancelled.
[4] *Sic*: for *Shiryngham*.

[1] For the language of signs in monasteries, carried in early religious houses to a very elaborate extent, see *Consuetudines Cluniacenses* (Migne, P.L. cxlix).
[2] This passage, owing to the torn state of the MS. is irrecoverable. There seems to have been no descriptive note attached to the series of *detecta* on fo. 121; but they appear to have been digested from the evidence given privately by the abbot. The missing passage evidently concerned the quarrel between Tawke and the serving-man Thresshere.
[3] Merlowe had probably superseded Medemenham as vicar or parish chaplain of Sheringham. The route from Nutley to Sheringham would lie *via* Aylesbury, Dunstable, Cambridge, Newmarket, Thetford and Norwich.

Also, as concerns the unfitness of the prior, he agrees with the others as above.

([The master] of the novices.) Also John Thame, the master of the novices, does not make competent provision of raiment and shoes for the novices, insomuch that they oftentimes walk about with their garments and shoes torn and tattered.

Brother Henry Esyngtone [says] as above concerning the unfitness of the prior, and says that the master of the novices pays no heed to that office: therefore [the novices] run about like vagabonds.

Also he says that, although he is sacrist, meet provision is not made him of oil, wax, wine and bread and other things needful when asked for, in the abbot's default, who holds all the rents of that office.

[Talkings in frater.] Also there are talkings among the canons in the frater, and they use not the accustomed signs.[1]

Be it remembered to send injunctions in writing touching the matters disclosed.

. . . .[2]

(Medemenham.) Thereupon one brother John Medemenham, a canon, took up the quarrel against the said William Tawke, affirming that [the same Tawke] did violence to the said William Thresshere because he was in the company of the said brother John when he came to the lord bishop.

Moreover Thomas Ewelme, William Bury and William Brystowe, canons, coming to the help of the said brother John Medemenham with clubs, made an attack upon the said William Tawke and pursued him as far as the abbot's lodging; and afterwards, when by order of the abbot they had been warned, first by the prior and secondly by the subprior, to desist from such disorderly doings and keep cloister, they would not agree, but came to quire and church, armed with weapons of offence in warlike guise, committing disobedience contrary to the abbot's command.

(Medemenham.) Brother John Medemenham went out of the monastery without the abbot's leave and in a layman's dress also, having put aside his regular habit, with the mind and purpose to kill brother Walter Merlowe, canon, who was then abiding at Sheringham;[3] and on his way he was taken at Dunstable, to the great scandal and cost of the monastery.

Also at the time when he was sacrist of the monastery he caused a doublet, in English 'a Jak of fense,'[4] to be made for him out of the vestments of the church, to the great damage of the church.

---

[4] ' Iakke of defence ' is rendered in *Prompt. Parv.* (Camden Soc.) I, 256, by the Latin *baltheus*, used properly as a sword-belt, but applied also *ibid.* to ' cote armure ' (p. 95), ' dobbelet ' (pp. 124, 125), and ' paltok ' (p. 380). See the notes by Way on the various entries. For ' dobbelet ' alternatives are given, ' *bigera* . . . *baltheus, diplois* . . . *anabatrum*,' the first and third being taken from Uguccio ' versificatus ' and the *Catholicon* of John of Genoa respectively. *Catholicon Anglicum* (E.E.T.S.), p. 194, has ' Iakke. *bombicinium*', glossed in another MS. as ' diplois, —idem or Dublett'; while ' Dublet ' (p. 110) is rendered *diplois*. ' Doublet ' is the natural translation of *diplois*, which is merely a cloak wrapped double and has no special military meaning by itself: cf. Ps. CIX, 28: ' et operiantur sicut diploide confusione sua.'

Item quodam tempore quo magister Johannes Walpole procurator monasterii fuit in monasterio dictus Medemenham cum sibi associatis cum baculis et aliis armis inuasiuis insurrexerunt in eundem magistrum Johannem intendentes illum interficere.

Idem[1] idem Medemenham subdole alienauit certos agnos qui fuerunt magistri Johannis Arundelle et quos abbas eidem magistro Johanni antea donauerat.

Item idem Medemenham contra voluntatem abbatis per vias insidiabatur Thome Felde ad ipsum verberandum et interficiendum.

Item idem Medemenham sica vel gladio accinctus cum baculo in manu sua venit obuiam abbati in claustro volens vt apparuit ipsum abbatem insilire, et cum abbas mandaret sibi vt huiusmodi arma dimitteret dixit plane quod noluit sed arroganter tenebat baculum suum eleuatum contra ipsum abbatem nolens sibi in aliquo obedire.

(Ewelm.) Frater Thomas Ewelme dummodo curam gereret apud Doretone commisit adulterium cum quadam muliere de eadem coniugata.

Item idem Thomas iacens de nocte in adulterio cum dicta muliere et requisitus per obstetricem vt ipse sacramenta ecclesie cuidam mulieri de eadem tunc in pariendo laboranti ministraret nollet adquiescere requisicionibus sic quod mulier decessit absque sacramentis in ipsius defectu.

Item idem Thomas de nocte deprehensus fuit in adulterio cum sepedicta muliere per constabularium et alios viros de eadem, contra *quos* faciens rescussum fregit pollicem vnius constabularii ad dampnum monasterii iiij marcarum.

Item idem Thomas seculari habitu indutus et regulari habitu dimisso fuit in apostasia adherens dicte mulieri in adulterio tribus anni vnius quarteriis.

Item idem Thomas in nocte festi beate Marie Magdalene vltimo preteriti absque licencia exiuit monasterium cum arcu et sagittis venando et ad secundam horam post mediam noctem bibit in taberna et post solis ortum diei sequentis venit ad monasterium et celebrauit missam de beata Virgine nulla habita digestione.

---

[1] *Sic*: for *item*.

[1] Presumably John Walpool, preb. of Leicester St. Margaret in Lincoln, who died in 1445 (Le Neve II, 169). A certain John Walpool, who may be the same person, was presented by the Crown to the church of Shipdham, Norfolk, for which he exchanged the vicarage of Swaffham Market, 25 Oct., 1436 (*Cal. Pat.* 1436-1441, p. 24). He was apparently instituted to the vicarage of Swaffham in 1434, and quitted Shipdham in 1438 (Blomefield and Parkin, *Hist. Norfolk* VI, 225; X, 247). He also became rector of Fincham St. Michael, Norfolk, in 1436 (*ibid.* VII, 62).

[2] The juxtaposition of this entry to the last suggests that John Arundell had succeeded Walpole as proctor or legal attorney of the house, and that the gift mentioned was by way of reward for his services. Such proctors were frequently rewarded by presentations to valuable benefices in the gift of the house to which they gave legal advice; but Nutley had no rewards of this kind.

The name John Arundell is not uncommon among the clergy of the fifteenth century, as several members of the various Cornish families of Arundell took holy orders. Three of these rose to some distinction, viz. (1) John Arundell, warden or dean of St. George's, Windsor, c. 1418-1454; (2) John Arundell, M.A., M.D., chaplain and first physician to Henry VI, archdeacon of Richmond 1457, and bishop of Chichester 1459-1477; and (3) John Arundell, dean of Exeter c. 1483, bishop of Coventry and Lichfield 1496, and of Exeter 1501-1504. The brief article on (2)

Also at a certain time when master John Walpole, the proctor of the monastery,[1] was in the monastery, the said Medemenham, with his confederates, rose up against the same master John with sticks and other arms of offence, with purpose to kill him.

Also the same Medemenham craftily alienated certain lambs which belonged to master John Arundelle,[2] and which the abbot had formerly given to the same master John.

Also the same Medemenham against the abbot's will laid an ambush on the roads for Thomas Felde, in order to beat and kill him.

Also the same Medemenham, being girt with a dagger or sword and with a stick in his hand, came to meet the abbot in cloister, with the mind, as it appeared, of assaulting the same abbot; and, when the abbot bade him put such arms aside, he said flatly that he would not, but arrogantly held his stick aloft against the same abbot, being unwilling to obey him in aught.

(Ewelm.) Brother Thomas Ewelme, while he was exercising the cure at Dorton[3], committed adultery with a married woman of the same.

Also the same Thomas, while lying by night in adultery with the said woman, and when asked by the midwife to administer the sacraments of the church to a woman of the same [town], who was then travailing in child-bed, would not hearken to her requests, so that the woman died without the sacraments in his default.

Also the same Thomas was caught by night in adultery with the oft-mentioned woman by the constable and other men of the same [town]; and, endeavouring to make reprisals upon them,[4] he brake the thumb of a constable, with four marks damage to the monastery.

Also the same Thomas, clothed in secular garb and having laid aside his regular habit, was in apostasy, cleaving to the said woman in adultery, for three quarters of a year.

Also the same Thomas, on the night of the feast of St. Mary Magdalene last past,[5] went out of the monastery a-hunting with bow and arrows without leave, and at the second hour after midnight he drank in a tavern, and after sunrise on the following day he came to the monastery and celebrated mass of the blessed Virgin with [his drink] undigested.

---

in *D.N.B.* confuses him with (1); while Hennessy, *Nov. Repert.* note *d*16, confuses all three. Newcourt's note on (2) in *Repert.* I, 174, 175, shows a degree of caution in identifying them to which these later writers have paid too little attention. Possibly (1) or (2) is referred to here: the younger man at this time, in addition to canonries and prebends in Hereford, Lichfield, Windsor, and possibly in Exeter, appears to have been rector of Kibworth and of the free chapel of Kibworth Harcourt, Leices., and of Chelmsford, Essex, and had coll. of Scamblesby preb. in Lincoln, 7 Sept., 1443 (Reg. XVIII, fo. 110 *d*). Here, where the identity is so uncertain, there is no need to discuss the careers of these contemporaries, namesakes and probably kinsmen, at length; but it is not irrelevant to notice the confusion which exists, here as in other cases, between two or more bearers of the same name.

[3] Dorton was one of the five parishes already mentioned on p. 256, note 3. The problems which arose from the privilege of a convent to serve its appropriated churches are well illustrated by this visitation and those of Dorchester. It will be noticed that the summary of the case against Medemenham is followed by the charges against Ewelme, his chief supporter in the monastery.

[4] ' *Rescous (Rescussus)* . . . is a forcible Resistance and a Rescuing of any Thing, or of a Person arrested, and procuring an Escape against Law.' (Jacobs, *Law Dictionary*).

[5] 22 July, 1447.

[Fo. 131 *d.*] . . . .
et quod infra fratres se . . . . habeant
. . . .

. . . . aut discordias suscitent aut suscitatas f[oue]ant
sub pena perpetue expulsionis a dicto [monasterio] et eius beneficio.[1]

Tyleshurst[2] quo ad bullam capellanie domini pape renunciauit
ipsi bulle et eius beneficio prestito primitus per eum iuramento quod
non nouit illum qui sibi obtinuit bullam illam.

Willelmus permissione diuina Lincolniensis episcopus dilectis in
Christo filiis fratri Johanni Brehulle canonico *regulari* et confratri
monasterii de Notteley ordinis Sancti Augustini nostre diocesis ac Willelmo
Foulere de Buckyngham eiusdem nostre diocesis salutem graciam et
benediccionem. Visitantes iam pridem dictum monasterium de Notteley
tam in capite quam in membris iure nostro ordinario et super statu
singulorum solicite inquirentes, quia nedum per inquisicionem huiusmodi
verum eciam per corporis inspeccionem *ac familiarem communicacionem*
luculenter comperimus quod dilectus in Christo filius frater Nicholaus
Redyng dicti monasterii abbas adeo per impotenciam corporis ex nimia
senectute *ac* paralisi aliisque morbis sonticis prouenientem debilis et
impotens est effectus quod hiis obstantibus nec ad sui dicti monasterii
regimen sufficit aut suorum, ad indempnitatem igitur dicti monasterii
conseruandam paterno affectu prospicientes et eidem monasterio ac persone dicti fratris Nicholai abbatis consideratis eius veneranda canicie
ac diutinis laboribus quos in laudabiliter regendo ipsum monasterium
multis annis sustinuit providere iuxta submissionem ipsius abbatis et
tocius conuentus *dicti monasterii* in nos in hac parte factam volentes,
vos fratrem Johannem et Willelmum predictum eidem abbati durantibus
huiusmodi infirmitatibus et impotencia *de consensu expresso dicti abbatis
ac singulorum de dicto conuentu* assignamus et deputamus coadiutores ita
quod sub iuramentis vestris in hac *parte* prestitis pleno et fideli inuentario
indentato omnium et singulorum bonorum iocalium et instauramentorum
dicti monasterii tam ad extra quam ad intra[3] cuius vna pars penes dictos
abbatem *et* conuentum et alia penes vos remaneat *prius* confecto, tu[4]
frater Johannes omnes et singulos redditus *et prouentus*[5] dicti monasterii
exigas et recipias ac eidem abbati iuxta status sui congruenciam ac
personis singulis de conuentu et aliis eiusdem monasterii ministris et
seruitoribus sufficienter et competenter *vite necessaria* ministres et *de*
tuis huiusmodi receptis et solutis quolibet anni quarterio . . . . . *dicto*
. . . . *per se* . . . . *conuentum* . . . . . *tandum* . . . . *ipsius*
. . . .[6] plenum compotum reddas et exhibeas: *onera eciam alia*

---

[1] Most of the upper part of this paragraph has been torn away, and only a
few words remain, some of which are illegible.
[2] *Sic*: for *Tylehurst.*
[3] *prius facto* cancelled.
[4] *fratres* cancelled.
[5] *reuentus et commoda* cancelled.
[6] Only fragments of this marginal addition are left.

[1] It is impossible to restore the whole text. The verbs are in the plural, and
the admonition was probably directed to the abbot and Medemenham. If so, *eius
beneficio* must refer to the abbot's office.

. . . .
and that they behave themselves among the brethren . . . .
. . . . or stir up quarrels
or [foster] any that be stirred up, under pain of perpetual expulsion
from the said [monastery] and from his benefice.[1]

Tylehurst, with respect to the bull [conferring upon him] the office
of chaplain of the lord pope, renounced the same bull and his benefice,[2]
after an oath had been proffered by him that he did not know the man
who got him the bull.

William, by divine permission bishop of Lincoln, to his beloved
sons in Christ brother John Brehulle, canon regular and one of the brethren
of the monastery of Nutley, of the order of St. Austin, of our diocese,
and William Foulere of Buckingham,[3] of the same our diocese, health,
grace and blessing. In our sometime visitation of the said monastery
both in its head and members by our right as ordinary, and in our anxious
inquiry concerning the state of each of them, because, not only by such
inquiry, but also by bodily view and familiar conversation, we plainly
discovered that our beloved son in Christ brother Nicholas Redyng,
the abbot of the said monastery, by reason of bodily impotence arising
from extreme old age and palsy and other grave diseases, is become so
weak and powerless that, with these impediments, he is sufficient to
govern neither his said monastery nor his own affairs: we therefore,
looking forward with fatherly affection to the preservation of the indemnity of the said monastery, and wishing to provide for the same
monastery and for the person of the said brother Nicholas the abbot,
in consideration of the reverence of his hoary hairs and the long toils
which he has endured for many years in the praiseworthy governance
of the same monastery,[4] according to the submission of the same abbot
and of the whole convent made to us in this behalf, appoint and depute
you, brother John and William aforesaid, with the express consent of
the said abbot and of the several persons of the said convent, to be
coadjutors to the same abbot for the duration of such his infirmities and
impotence, so that, under your oaths proffered in this behalf, having
first made a full and faithful inventory by indenture of all and sundry
the goods, jewels and stores of the said monastery, alike external and
internal, one part whereof shall remain in the hands of the said abbot
and convent, and the other part in yours, you, brother John, shall demand
and receive all and sundry the rents and revenues of the said monastery,
and shall make sufficient and fitting supply of the necessaries of life to
the same abbot, as is agreeable to his estate, and to the several persons
of the convent and to the other ministers and serving-folk of the same
monastery, and of such your receipts and payments you shall render
and produce every quarter of a year a full account . . . .
. . . .[5] and shall also undergo and fulfil out of the same rents
the other burthens, even of needful repairs, that are incumbent upon

[2] The benefice thus renounced was the papal chaplaincy. No mention of the
bull occurs in the foregoing depositions.

[3] A layman is associated in the commission with a canon.

[4] There is no record of the date at which Redyng became abbot of Nutley.

[5] The marginal note is so torn that the fragments of words left make no connected sense. The account was probably submitted to the abbot and then presented
to the convent as a whole.

ipsi monasterio incumbencia eciam reparacionum necessariarum de ipsis redditibus subeas et peragas ; tuque Willelme Foulere predicte[1] huiusmodi recepta et soluciones superuideas ac compotos dicti fratris Johannis in forma predicta exigas audias et termines et de factis vestrum vtriusque in fine anni cuiuslibet nos reddatis cerciores.   Data sub sigillo nostro ad causas *in manerio nostro de Woburne episcopi*[2] xxvj die mensis Augusti anno Domini mccccxlvij nostrarumque consecracionis anno xxij et translacionis xj⁰.

Willelmus permissione diuina Lincolniensis episcopus dilectis in Christo filiis abbati singulisque canonicis et confratribus *conuentus* monasterii beate Marie de Notteley ordinis Sancti Augustini nostre diocesis presentibus et futuris salutem graciam et benediccionem.   Sanctorum patrum sanxiuit auctoritas vt ecclesiarum prelati ad corrigendum subditorum excessus et reformandos mores eorundem prudenter ac diligenter intendant ne sanguis eorum de manibus suis requiratur nec admittatur pastoris excusacio si ipso nesciente oues luporum morsibus dilanientur cum ab eo tacente et sic consenciente permittatur securitas delinquendi.   Horum siquidem ammonicione vt ad vos et vestrum monasterium visitandum descenderemus cura nostra pastoralis nos coegit; verum quia per inquisicionem preparatoriam per nos in huiusmodi visitacione factam comperimus nonnulla puritati religionis contraria et inimica indies ibi committi infrascripta mandata nostra et iniuncciones ac ordinaciones vobis destinamus sub penis infrascriptis inuiolabiliter obseruanda.

In primis cum secundum regulares obseruancias ordinis vestri ac consuetudinem monasterii nouicii et alii iuuenes canonici antequam ad ordines sacros aspirent seruicia sua integraliter redderent et quod antequam *sic* reddiderint officiis quibusuis in monasterio intra vel extra nullatinus preficerentur, nobisque detectum existit quod nonnulli tam nouicii quam alii canonici eciam in sacerdocio constituti seruicia sua reddere contempserunt et iam reddere dedignantur[3] propter quod in psalmodizando nocturnos tempore matutinarum discordant ab aliis vt ignorantes in magnum tedium aliorum psallencium, quidam vero qui non reddiderunt contra laudabilem monasterii consuetudinem officiis preponuntur; idcirco iniungimus vobis abbati et ceteris huiusmodi nouiciorum magistris vt eos omnes qui non sic reddiderunt compellatis ad reddendum seruicia sua iuxta regularia vestra instituta et quod non reddentes nullis officiis vllatinus preponatis; quod si contrarium feceritis penam inobediencie vos abbas et vos magistri nouiciorum penam grauis contemptus non euadetis, ipsisque qui non reddiderunt et per vos iussi non reddiderunt penam ieiunii in pane[4] ceruisia et *vno genere* leguminum *absque piscibus* omni sexta feria quousque sic reddiderint iniungimus mandantes vobis vt non reddentes ad penas huiusmodi nostra auctoritate coherceatis.

---

[1] *obser* (apparently) cancelled.
[2] Interlined above *monasterio predicto* cancelled.
[3] *et non* and another word cancelled.
[4] *seruic* cancelled.

the same monastery; and you, William Foulere aforesaid, shall survey such receipts and payments and demand, audit and determine the accounts of the said brother John in form aforesaid; and you shall certify us at the end of every year concerning what each of you has done. Given under our seal *ad causas* in our manor of Bishops Wooburn on the twenty-sixth day of the month of August in the year of our Lord 1447, and in the twenty-second year of our consecration and the eleventh of our translation.

William, by divine permission bishop of Lincoln, to our beloved sons in Christ the abbot and the several canons and brethren of the convent of the monastery of blessed Mary of Nutley, of the order of St. Austin, of our diocese, that now are and shall be, health, grace and blessing. The authority of the holy fathers has sanctioned that the prelates of churches should with prudence and diligence take heed to correct the transgressions of their subjects and reform the manners of the same, that their blood may not be required of their hands, nor the shepherd be allowed excuse, if without his knowledge the sheep be torn to pieces by the bites of wolves, inasmuch as security to offence is allowed by his silence and, accordingly, by his consent. By their admonition therefore our pastoral care has constrained us to come down to visit you and your monastery; but, because, by the preliminary inquiry made by us in such our visitation, we have discovered that certain things contrary and hostile to the purity of religion are daily there committed, we direct to you our commands and injunctions and ordinances hereunder written, to be observed without breach under the penalties written beneath.

In the first place, inasmuch as, according to the regular observances of your order and the custom of the monastery, the novices and the other young canons, before they aspire to holy orders, should render their services in their entirety, and because, before they have so rendered them, they should in no wise be put in charge of any offices whatever, external or internal, in the monastery; and as it is disclosed to us that some, both novices and other canons, even in the order of priesthood, have treated the rendering of their services with contempt and do now disdain to render them, wherefore, while singing the nocturn psalms in time of matins, they are discordant with the others, inasmuch as they are ignorant, to the great affliction of the others while they sing; while some who have not so rendered are put in charge of offices, contrary to the praiseworthy custom of the monastery:[1] therefore we enjoin upon you the abbot, and upon the other masters of such novices, that you compel all those who have not so rendered to render their services according to your regular institutes, and that you put not those who do not render them in charge of any offices in any wise. But, if you do the contrary, you, the abbot, shall not escape the penalty of disobedience, nor you, the masters of the novices, the penalty of grievous contempt; and upon the same who have not so rendered, nor have rendered when bidden by you, we enjoin the penalty of fasting upon bread, beer and one kind of vegetables without fish every Friday, until they have so rendered, ordering you to force those who render not to [perform] such penalties by our authority.

---

[1] See Brehulle's first *detectum*.

Item iniungimus *tibi*[1] magistro nouiciorum qui pro tempore fueris vt eisdem nouiciis de peculio suo ministres[2] competenter de habitu suo et aliis que necessaria sunt tam in lectis quam vestibus et calciamentis ne decetero vt[3] *solito* vestibus laceratis aut calciamentis diruptis incedant, quodque eos in *lectura et cantu ac*[4] regula informes[5] *quodque* claustro[6] temporibus debitis intendant et non vagentur discurrentes[7] vt solebant sub pena ieiunii *in pane* et aqua proxima sexta feria postquam in hiis vel eorum aliquo necgligens vel remissus repertus fueris.

Preterea iniungimus tibi priori dicti monasterii *pro tempore existenti* vt huiusmodi magistrum nouiciorum in premissis diligenter superuideas et quociens [Fo. 132] . . . .[8]

Item cum contra solitam consuetudinem monasterii in . . . . iam [*nu*]*mero* sunt quatuor . . . . inter eos non intendentes ad lectorem habent . . . . . in quibus . . . . . aliquociens detracciones dissenciones *murmura* et dis[cordie] . . . . . . [iniun]gimus igitur vobis abbati vt decetero vt solito fuit bini canonici *et non plures* in vno ferculo et tot in alio in refectorio . . . . in esculentis et poculentis competenter *ad refeccionem* non ad voluptatem seu ingluuiem seruiatur[9] *ita quod sic moderentur refecciones huiusmodi canonicis* [*a*]*pponende quod*[10] . . . . *solitos* . . . . . *cedant* . . . . *tus quando plures ad vnum ferculum consedebant,* [et] quod vnus lector habeatur qui tempore refeccionis coram discumbentibus leccionem . . . de sacra scriptura vel vitis patrum legat ad quam omnes discumbentes aures habeant intentas *et* ab omni confabulacione . . . . .[11] se abstineant et si quid eos loqui oporteat sit in latino et voce submissa et breui ne alios *inquietent* aut signis vtantur et quociens aliquis canonicus in premissorum aliquo[12] deliqueret[13] proxima sexta feria sequenti in pane et aqua ieiunet.

Iniungimus eciam tibi priori et presidentibus religioni qui pro tempore fueritis et refectorio temporibus refeccionum interfueritis[14] canonicos discumbentes attente superuideatis et quos in premissorum aliquo delinquere reperitis iuxta regularia instituta et delicti qualitatem absque omni personarum accepcione acriter et taliter *per penam predictam* puniatis vt punicio et non impunitas sit ceteris in exemplum.

---

[1] Interlined above *vobis* cancelled.
[2] *s* interlined above *tis* cancelled.
[3] *antea* cancelled.
[4] Interlined above *primitiuis scienciis et* cancelled.
[5] *s* interlined above *tis* cancelled.
[6] *que* cancelled.
[7] *huc et illuc* cancelled.
[8] A long passage, beginning *fueris requisitus* is cancelled, and a large fragment is torn off from the top of the leaf.
[9] *et quod tercia pars conuentus omni die* [seruet] *refectorium nisi alia legitima causa subsistat* cancelled, and *ita quod*, etc., substituted in the margin.
[10] . . . *tos supra* cancelled.
[11] Interlineation illegible.
[12] *premissorum* cancelled.
[13] *Sic*: for *deliquerit*.
[14] *quod* omitted.

[1] See Brehulle's third *detectum*, and cf. Esyngtone's first *detectum*.
[2] This injunction is a supplement to the two preceding.

Also we enjoin upon you, the master of the novices for the time being, that you do sufficient ministry to the same novices out of their allowance, as regards their habit and the other things that are needful, whether in bedding, raiment or footwear, that henceforward they may not go about, as they are wont, in tattered clothes and broken shoon;[1] and that you instruct them in reading and song and the rule, and that they shall keep to cloister at the due times and roam not about, gadding here and there as they were wont, under pain of fasting on bread and water the next Friday after you shall have been found neglectful or slack in aught of these things.

Further we enjoin upon you, the prior of the said monastery for the time being, that you keep diligent oversight upon such the master of the novices as regards the premises, and as often as . . . .[2]

Also, inasmuch as, contrary to the wonted custom of the monastery in . . . . now they are four in number . . . . among them, not heeding the reader, they have . . . . in which . . . . sometimes backbitings, divisions, murmurs and dis[cords arise . . . .],[3] we therefore enjoin upon you the abbot, that henceforth, as was your wont, two canons and not more [shall be served] with one dish, and as many with another in the frater . . . . . [and that] they be served with food to eat and drink in sufficiency for their refection, not for their pleasure or surfeiting, so that the meals to be set before such canons be so moderated that they [exceed not] the wonted . . . . . . when more sat down to one dish,[4] [and] that a reader be had, who in time of refection shall read before them that sit at table a lesson . . . . from holy writ or the lives of the fathers; and all that are so sitting shall keep their hearing intent upon this and abstain . . . . . from all talking together, and, if they must say anything, it shall be in Latin and in a low voice and shortly, that they may not disturb the others, or they shall use signs; and, as often as any canon transgresses in aught of the premises, he shall fast on bread and water the next Friday following.

We enjoin also upon you the prior, and upon the presidents of religion for the time being, who shall be present in the frater at meal-times, [that] you diligently watch over the canons as they sit at table, and punish severely those whom you find to offend in any of the premises, according to the regular institutes and the quality of the transgression, without any acceptation of persons, and on such wise by the aforesaid penalty that their punishment, and not their freedom from it, may be for an example to the rest.

---

[3] See Thame's second *detectum*. The *detecta* say nothing about reading during meals, and Thame's *detectum* refers to the infirmary only. The injunction covers the whole question of meals, whether in the frater or in the infirmary. It probably has reference also to Thame's first *detectum*, the text of which, however, is imperfect; but Esyngtone's third *detectum* bears on the same subject and upon the disuse of signs, which are recommended in this injunction as an alternative to necessary speech.

[4] The apparent meaning is that, if four persons had been served with the allowance of two, there should be no attempt to enlarge this allowance, when it should be restored to the proper number of recipients. In the cases both of the *detecta* and of this injunction, the state of the MS. makes recovery of the full sense impossible.

Item cum vt nobis detectum est reliquie mensarum vestrarum inter pauperes non distribuitur[1] sed indebite consumitur et domus illa in qua distribui consueuit ad alios vsus conuertitur vel funditus dirimitur; iniungimus vobis abbati vt domum illam antiquo vsui restitui faciatis et quod deputetis vnum[2] canonicum idoneum et discretum qui fragmenta et reliquias mensarum tam vestri abbatis quam conuentus diligenter colligat et inter pauperes magis indigentes fideliter distribuat seu faciat distribui.

Item simili modo iniungimus vobis abbati vt hiis qui in[3] infirmaria non ex similacione sed infirmitate et debilitate sunt ministrari faciatis competenter secundum regulam et prout humanitas exigit cibaria competencia quibus melius refici poterunt ac eciam focalia et custodem honestum qui eis de die deseruiat et de nocte.

Item iniungimus vobis abbati simili modo vt exhiberi et ministrari faciatis sacriste pro tempore existenti expensas necessarias et competentes pro vino cera et[4] oleo[5] *ac* aliis necessariis in ecclesia per illud officium prouidendis.

Item iniungimus vobis vniuersis et singulis presentibus et futuris primo secundo et tercio peremptorie sub pena excommunicacionis maioris *quam*[6] in vestrum quemlibet intendimus fulminare si premissis vel infra-scriptis nostris iniunccionibus et mandatis non parueritis et ea non obseruaueritis, quod dicto abbati patri et pastori vestro qui pro animabus vestris racionem est redditurus in omnibus *et* per[7] omnia humiliter obediatis et intendatis eidemque reuerenciam et honorem impendatis secundum regularia instituta, quodque *ab* omni detraccione similacione discordiarum inimiciarum et iurgiorum seminacione et fomento penitus abstinentes vos ipsos in omni caritate et dileccione[8] ac honore *simul* preueniatis sicuti Dei et canonicam[9] effugere volueritis vlcionem. Data sub sigillo nostro ad causas in manerio nostro de Wobourne episcopi xxvij⁰ die mensis Augusti anno Domini mccccxlvij⁰ nostrarumque consecracionis anno xxij⁰ et translacionis xj⁰.[10]

CERTIFICATORIUM SUPER PENITENCIA PERACTA PER
RELIGIOSUM VIRUM IN ALIO[11] DOMO.
[Reg. XVIII, fo. 73].

Reuerendo in Christo[12] et domino, domino Willelmo, Dei gracia Lincolniensi episcopo vester humilis et deuotus in Christo filius Thomas, abbas monasterii Oseneie, ordinis sancti sancti[13] Augustini, vestre Lincolniensis diocesis, obedienciam, reuerenciam et honorem cum omni

---

[1] *Sic*: *elemosina* was possibly in the mind of the writer.
[2] *s* cancelled.
[3] *infirmitate* cancelled.
[4] A letter cancelled.
[5] *ad* cancelled.
[6] Interlined above *excommunicacionis* cancelled.
[7] A letter, apparently *e*, cancelled.
[8] Altered, with one or more letters cancelled at the end.
[9] A letter cancelled.
[10] Ff. 132 *d.* to 135 *d.* are blank.
[11] *Sic*: for *alia*.
[12] *patri* omitted.
[13] *Sic*.

Also, inasmuch as it is disclosed to us that the leavings of your tables are not distributed among the poor, but unduly wasted, and the house wherein they were wont to be distributed is turned to other uses or utterly destroyed,[1] we enjoin upon you the abbot that you cause that house to be restored to its ancient use, and that you appoint a fit and discreet canon, who shall diligently gather up the fragments and leavings of the tables, both of you the abbot and of the convent, and faithfully distribute or cause them to be distributed among the poor that are most needy.

Also in like manner we enjoin upon you the abbot that to such as are in the infirmary, not of feigning, but because of sickness and weakness, you cause sufficient service to be done, according to the rule and as humanity demands, of fitting foods wherewith they may best be refreshed, and also of fuel and of an honest warden, who shall serve them by day and by night.[2]

Also we enjoin upon you the abbot in like manner that you cause to be paid and furnished to the sacrist for the time being, the expenses needful and sufficient for wine, wax and oil, and for the other things needful in the church which should be provided by that office.[3]

Also we enjoin upon you all and several that now are and shall be, the first, second and third time peremptorily, under pain of the greater excommunication, which we intend to pronounce against each one of you, if you obey not the premises or our injunctions and mandates herein written, and observe them not, that in all things and through all things you humbly obey and hearken to the said abbot, your father and shepherd, who shall render account for your souls, and pay him reverence and honour according to the regular institutes, and that, utterly abstaining from all backbiting, falsehood, sowing and fostering of quarrels, enmities and strifes, you all together be beforehand with one another in all charity and love and honour, even as you will avoid the vengeance of God and of canon law. Given under our seal *ad causas* in our manor of Bishops Wooburn, on the twenty-seventh day of August in the year of our Lord 1447, and in the twenty-second year of our consecration and of our translation the eleventh.

CERTIFICATE TOUCHING THE PERFORMANCE OF PENANCE BY A MAN OF RELIGION IN ANOTHER HOUSE.[4]

To the reverend [father] in Christ and lord, the lord William, by the grace of God bishop of Lincoln, your lowly and devout son in Christ Thomas, abbot of the monastery of Oseney,[5] of the order of St. Austin, of your diocese of Lincoln, obedience, reverence and honour with all

---

[1] See Ewelme's first *detectum*.
[2] See Tylehurst's third *detectum*.
[3] See Esyngtone's second *detectum*.
[4] This document, preserved in Alnwick's register as a specimen of its type, supplies the sequel to the inquiry into Medemenham's character at the visitation.
[5] Thomas Hokenorton, abbot of Oseney, 1430-53: see *Visitations* I, 64, note 4, and No. LIII below.

subieccione filiali. Litteras vestras reuerendas ad recipiendum et admittendum fratrem Johannem Medemenham, canonicum monasterii de Notley, ad certam penitenciam iuxta decretum venerabilis magistri Thome Ballescote, vestri in hac parte commissarii, eidem Johanni pro suis demeritis iniunctam et in monasterio nostro de Oseney peragendam, xiij die mensis Decembris cum ea qua decuit reuerencia recepi. Quarum quidem [fo. 73 d.] litterarum auctoritate et uigore prefatum fratrem Johannem Medemenham canonicum in monasterio nostro de Oseney eodem xiijº die recepi, et ad peragendum penitenciam suam in forma michi[1] descripta admisi, ac vlterius pro vt ordinis nostre[2] disciplina et anime sue saluti[3] exigit et requirit, attenta ipsius gestura, eundem fratrem Johannem iuxta scire meum in futurum regulariter pertractabo. Et sic mandatum vestrum reuerendum in parte executus sum et in futurum exequar iuxta posse. Que paternitati vestre notifico per presentes sigillo nostro signatas. Data in monasterio vestro[4] de Oseney vicesimo die Decembris, anno Domini mccccxl septimo.

LIII.

[Fo. 30 d.]

Visitacio monasterii de OSENEYA, ordinis Sancti Augustini, Lincolniensis diocesis, facta in domo capitulari ibidem iiij^{to} die mensis Junii, anno Domini mccccxlquinto, per reuerendum in Christo patrem et dominum, dominum Willelmum Alnewyke, Dei gracia Lincolniensem episcopum, suarum consecracionis anno XIXº et translacionis nono.

In primis, sedente dicto reuerendo patre iudicialiter pro tribunali in huiusmodi sue visitacionis negocio inchoando die et loco antedictis, comparuerunt coram eo abbas et conuentus dicti monasterii, parati vt apparuit huiusmodi visitacionem subire. Et deinde primo et ante omnia propositum fuit verbum Dei iuxta actus futuri congruenciam per honestum virum magistrum Thomam Twyere, in sacra theologia scolarem, sequentem hoc thema, ' Ecce sponsus venit et intrauerunt ad nupcias,[5] etc. Quo in latino sermone laudabiliter finito,[6] abbas dicti loci exhibuit dicto reuerendo patri certificatorium mandati sibi pro huiusmodi exercenda visitacione directi confectum in hec verba, ' Reuerendo in Christo,' etc.; quo in publica audiencia perlecto, idem abbas exhibuit domino

---

[1] Apparently altered from *inibi*.
[2] *Sic*: for *nostri*.
[3] *Sic*: for *salus*.
[4] *Sic*: possibly a deferential substitution for *nostro*.
[5] St. Matth. xxv, 6 and 10: ' Ecce sponsus venit . . . . venit sponsus; et quae paratae erant intraverunt cum eo ad nuptias.'
[6] Written *finalito*: *ali* cancelled.

[1] Thomas Balscote, canon of Wroxton priory (see No. lxxviii), bachelor and licentiate in canon law. He had a papal dispensation to hold a benefice with cure of souls, 23 Sept., 1441 (*Cal. Papal Letters* ix, 217). He took a prominent part in the general chapters of the order. At Oseney in 1443 he was unanimously chosen

filial subjection. On the thirteenth day of the month of December, I received, with the reverence that beseemed them, your reverend letters for the reception and admission of brother John Medemenham, canon of the monastery of Nutley, to a certain penance which, according to the decree of the worshipful master Thomas Ballescote,[1] your commissary in this behalf, was enjoined upon the same John for his ill deserts, and is to be performed in our monastery of Oseney. By the authority and force of the which letters I received the aforesaid brother John Medemenham, canon, in our monastery of Oseney on the same thirteenth day, and admitted him to perform his penance in the form described to me, and further, as the discipline of our order and the health of his soul demand and require, with consideration to his behaviour, I will in future treat the same brother John after my knowledge according to rule. And so I have executed your reverend commandment in part, and will execute it in future as I am able. Of the which things I give your fatherhood notice by these presents sealed with our seal. Given in your monastery of Oseney on the twentieth day of December, in the year of our Lord 1447.

LIII.

THE VISITATION OF THE MONASTERY OF OSENEY, OF THE ORDER OF ST. AUSTIN, OF THE DIOCESE OF LINCOLN, PERFORMED IN THE CHAPTER-HOUSE THEREIN ON THE FOURTH DAY OF THE MONTH OF JUNE, IN THE YEAR OF OUR LORD 1445, BY THE REVEREND FATHER IN CHRIST AND LORD, THE LORD WILLIAM ALNEWYKE, BY THE GRACE OF GOD BISHOP OF LINCOLN, IN THE NINETEENTH YEAR OF HIS CONSECRATION AND THE NINTH OF HIS TRANSLATION.

In the first place, as the said reverend father was sitting in his capacity of judge as a tribunal at the beginning of the business of such his visitation on and in the day and place aforesaid, there appeared before him the abbot and convent of the said monastery, in readiness, as was apparent, to undergo such visitation. And then first and before all else, the word of God was set forth in agreement with the act that was about to take place by the honest master Thomas Twyere, student in sacred theology, after this text, ' Lo, the bridegroom came, and they went in to the wedding,' etc. And, when this had come to an end praiseworthily in the Latin tongue, the abbot of the said place exhibited to the said reverend father the certificate of the mandate which had been addressed to him for the holding of such his visitation, drawn up in these words, ' To the reverend in Christ,' etc.; and, after this had been read through in the public hearing, the same

---

as the scribe of chapter, produced a memorandum upon procedure, and was one of the counsel who assisted the abbot of St. James', Northampton, in drawing up an order of procedure for future chapters (Salter, *Chapters of Aug. Canons*, pp. 85, 86-7, 91). At the same chapter he was appointed collector general of fines and sub-ventions in the province (*ibid.* p. 104). His initials occur in the form composed for the conduct of the chapter at Oseney in 1449, when he evidently acted again as scribe (*ibid.* p. 119).

confirmacionem eleccionis sue ac installacionem et induccionem, et deinde iurauit obedienciam et fidelitatem in forma consueta, et deinde exhibuit idem abbas domino fundacionem monasterii. Postea examinatus dicit ea que sequuntur.

Frater Thomas Hokenortone abbas dicit omnia bene et exhibet statum monasterii.

Frater Hugo Westone prior dicit omnia bene.

Frater Johannes Holbeche dicit omnia bene.

Frater Thomas Westone dicit omnia bene.

Frater Johannes Aas dicit omnia bene.

Frater Johannes Alryngtone dicit omnia bene.

Frater Johannes Garsyngtone dicit omnia bene.

Frater Johannes Londone canonicus manet in Hibernia deseruiens ibidem cure vnius ecclesie pertinentis monasterio.

Frater Bartholomeus Bysshopstone dicit omnia bene.

Frater Petrus Oxonforde dicit omnia bene.

Frater Johannes Tettebury dicit omnia bene.

Frater Edmundus Wycumbe senescallus dicit omnia bene.

Frater Thomas Stanforde dicit quod omnia bene.

Frater Walterus Godefray dicit quod omnia bene.

Frater Ricardus Adderbury dicit quod omnia bene.

Frater Johannes Wycumbe dicit quod minister deputatus pro infirmaria non bene se gerit in officio suo circa custodiam infirmorum.

Frater Thomas Wolgarcote dicit quod omnia bene.

Frater Willelmus Hertewelle dicit quod existentes in minucionibus compelluntur ad statim surgere a cena et accedere ad collacionem, quod est eis tediosum.

Frater Johannes Quenyntone dicit omnia bene.

Frater Johannes Lye dicit omnia bene.

Frater Petrus Janyns dicit quod non seruitur infirmis de subtilioribus cibariis nec est distinccio inter ipsos et sanos, nam equaliter eis seruitur.

Item dicit quod prior in correccionibus non est indifferens, nam quosdam segniter et quosdam acriter punit.

Frater Johannes Waltone dicit quod de consuetudine loci omni die cellerarius vel subcellerarius mane visitaret infirmos vt sciat quali dieta melius recreentur.

---

[1] See *Visitations* I, 64, note 4, for the date of abbot Hokenorton's election, between 24 Nov. and 4 Dec. (not, as given there, 12 Dec.), 1430. The record of his confirmation, which probably took place before bishop Flemyng's death (25 Jan., 1431), is not preserved, as Flemyng's register for the archdeaconry of Oxford is wanting between April, 1425, and his death. See p. 261 above, for a letter from Hokenorton to Alnwick. He was one of the presidents of the general chapter at Oseney in 1443 and at Northampton in 1446 (Salter, *Chapters of Aug. Canons*, pp. 84, 105, 115).

[2] Of the twenty-seven canons, twelve bore surnames derived from places in Oxfordshire, viz. Oxford (two), Adderbury, Alkerton (Alryngtone), Aston, Barton (probably Steeple Barton, the church of which was appropriated to Oseney), Garsington, Hook Norton (church appropriated to Oseney), Lye (North or South Leigh), Weston (two: Weston on the Green, church appropriated to Oseney), and Wolvercote. Hartwell, Wycombe (two), and possibly Bishopstone and Walton, are from Buckinghamshire; Quenington and Tetbury from Gloucestershire; Stanford may be from Berkshire; Holbeach is in Lincolnshire; Ogbourne (Okebourn) seems to

abbot exhibited to my lord the confirmation of his election, and his [certificates of] installation and induction,[1] and then he sware obedience and fealty in the form accustomed. And then the same abbot exhibited the foundation of the monastery to my lord. Thereafter, on examination, he says those things which follow.

Brother Thomas Hokenortone, the abbot,[2] says all things are well, and produces the state of the monastery.

Brother Hugh Westone, the prior, says all things are well.

Brother John Holbeche says all things are well.

Brother Thomas Westone says all things are well.

Brother John Aas says all things are well.

Brother John Alryngtone says all things are well.

Brother John Garsyngtone says all things are well.

Brother John Londone, canon, abides in Ireland, where he serves the cure of a church that belongs to the monastery.[3]

Brother Bartholomew Bysshopstone says all things are well.

Brother Peter Oxonforde says all things are well.

Brother John Tettebury says all things are well.

Brother Edmund Wycumbe, the steward, says all things are well.

Brother Thomas Stanforde says that all things are well.

Brother Walter Godefray says that all things are well.

Brother Richard Adderbury says that all things are well.

Brother John Wycumbe says that the servant appointed for the infirmary does not bear himself well in his office as regards his wardenship of the infirm.

Brother Thomas Wolgarcote[4] says that all things are well.

Brother William Hertewelle says that those who are in their seynies are compelled at a moment's notice to get up from supper and go to the collation,[5] which is troublesome to them.

Brother John Quenyntone says all things are well.

Brother John Lye says all things are well.

Brother Peter Janyns says that the infirm are not served with more delicate food, nor is there distinction between them and the sound in health; for they are served alike.

Also he says that the prior is not impartial in his corrections; for some persons he is slow to punish, and some he punishes severely.

Brother John Waltone[6] says that, by the custom of the place, the cellarer or subcellarer should visit the infirm every day in the morning to know with what sort of diet they may best be refreshed.

---

be from Wiltshire. Of the remaining five, London is obvious, the others indefinite.

[3] Oseney abbey possessed in Ireland the churches of Balibrenan and Kiltevenan (*V.C.H. Oxon.* II, 90), viz. Ballybrennan and Kildavin in the barony of Forth, co. Wexford.

[4] Thomas Walgarcot, canon of Oseney, had a papal dispensation to hold a benefice *curatum dumtaxat* for life, 9 August, 1441 (*Cal. Papal Letters* IX, 212).

[5] See p. 234 above, note 4. This complaint, as contrasted with the *detectum* at Newnham to which that note alludes, speaks well for the discipline at Oseney under Hokenorton.

[6] Walton succeeded Hokenorton as abbot in 1452: *congé d'élire* 5 Oct., temporalities restored 1 Nov. (*Cal. Pat.*, 1452-61, pp. 50, 63). He vacated the abbey on his promotion to the archbishopric of Dublin in 1472 (*congé d'élire* 27 Aug., *ibid.* 1466-77, p. 342), which he held until 1484 (Gams, *Ser. Episc.*, p. 218).

Item dicit quod ille qui deputatur custodie infirmarie adeo debilis est quod non sufficit exercicio officii sui.

Frater Robertus Okeburne dicit omnia bene.

Frater Johannes Astone dicit omnia bene.

Frater Robertus Oxonforde dicit quod omnia bene.

Frater Henricus Bartone dicit quod omnia bene.

Frater Thomas Slade moratur apud Bybury in diocesi Bathoniensi.

LIV.

[Fo. 98.]

VISITACIO MONASTERII DE OSOLUESTONE, ORDINIS SANCTI AUGUSTINI, LINCOLNIENSIS DIOCESIS, FACTA IN DOMO CAPITULARI IBIDEM XXIJ DIE MENSIS NOUEMBRIS, ANNO DOMINI MCCCCXL, PER REUERENDUM IN CHRISTO PATREM ET DOMINUM, DOMINUM WILLELMUM, DEI GRACIA LINCOLNIENSEM EPISCOPUM, ANNO SUARUM[1] CONSECRACIONIS XV ET TRANSLACIONIS QUINTO.

In primis, sedente dicto reuerendo patre in huiusmodi negocio visitacionis sue inchoando, die, anno et loco predictis, comparuerunt coram eo abbas et conuentus dicti loci, visitacionem suam huiusmodi vt apparuit subituri. Et deinde primo et ante omnia propositum fuit verbum Dei per egregium virum magistrum Thomam Duffelde, in sacra theologia bacallarium, sequentem hoc thema, ' Visita vineam istam,' [2] etc. Quo laudabiliter finito, abbas liberauit domino certificatorium execucionis mandati sibi pro hoc negocio primitus destinati in hec verba, ' Reuerendo in Christo patri,' etc.; quo publice in audiencia perlecto, abbas exhibuit confirmacionem eleccionis sue facte per priorem de Ouere, auctoritate domini Ricardi, Lincolniensis[3] episcopi, sed nichil exhibuit de installacione. Dicit tamen quod certi confratres sui fuerunt presentes, videlicet Thomas Rysshetone et Johannes Lychefelde, quos productos et iuratos dominus examinauit; qui examinati deponunt quod presentes fuerunt in monasterio illo in festo Sancte Petronille virginis, anno Domini mccccxxij, vbi et quando viderunt et audierunt quod dominus Ricardus Eluet, tunc archidiaconus Leycestrie, iure suo archidiaconali in propria sua persona ipsum dominum abbatem in dictum monasterium installauit et in corporalem possessionem eiusdem[4] induxit;

---

[1] *transla[cionis]* cancelled.
[2] Ps. LXXX, 14.
[3] *tunc* cancelled.
[4] *d'* cancelled.

[1] Robert Okeborne had been one of the alternative persons chosen, at the general chapter of the order held at Oseney in 1443, to preach the Latin sermon at the next chapter, the other being William Wyskare or Westkare, S.T.P., prior of the students at Oxford. Accordingly, at the Northampton chapter in 1446, Robert Okborne, ' scolaris de Oseney,' preached ' multum eleganter et fructuose ' from St. Matth. VI, 28, ' Considerate lilia agri, quomodo crescunt ' (Salter, *Chapters of Aug. Canons*, pp. 104, 112).

Also he says that he who is appointed to the wardenship of the infirmary is so feeble that he is not competent to exercise his office.

Brother Robert Okeburne[1] says all things are well.

Brother John Astone says all things are well.

Brother Robert Oxonforde says that all things are well.

Brother Henry Bartone says that all things are well.

Brother Thomas Slade is staying at Bibury in the diocese of Bath.[2]

LIV.

THE VISITATION OF THE MONASTERY OF OWSTON, OF THE ORDER OF
ST. AUSTIN, OF THE DIOCESE OF LINCOLN, PERFORMED IN THE
CHAPTER-HOUSE THEREIN ON THE TWENTY-SECOND DAY OF THE
MONTH OF NOVEMBER, IN THE YEAR OF OUR LORD 1440, BY THE
REVEREND FATHER IN CHRIST AND LORD, THE LORD WILLIAM,
BY THE GRACE OF GOD BISHOP OF LINCOLN, IN THE FIFTEENTH
YEAR OF HIS CONSECRATION AND THE FIFTH OF HIS TRANSLATION.

In the first place, as the said reverend father was sitting in the beginning of such the business of his visitation, on and in the day, year and place aforesaid, there appeared before him the abbot and convent of the said place, to undergo, as was apparent, such his visitation. And then first and before all else, the word of God was set forth by the excellent master Thomas Duffelde, bachelor in sacred theology, after this text, ' Visit this vine,' etc. And, when this had come praiseworthily to an end, the abbot delivered to my lord the certificate of his execution of the mandate at first addressed to him for this business, in these words, ' To the reverend father in Christ,' etc.; and, after this had been read through publicly in the audience, the abbot exhibited the confirmation of his election, made by the prior of Overy,[3] by authority of the lord Richard, bishop of Lincoln,[4] but exhibited nothing concerning his installation. But he says that certain of his brethren were present, to wit Thomas Rysshetone and John Lychefelde, whom, being brought forward and sworn, my lord examined. And, upon examination, they depose that they were present in that monastery on the feast of St. Pernell the virgin in the year of our Lord 1422,[5] where and when they saw and heard that sir Richard Elvet, then archdeacon of Leicester, by his right as archdeacon, did in his proper person install the same lord abbot into the said monastery and inducted him into bodily possession

---

[2] *Sic.* Bibury, Glouces., the church of which was appropriated to Oseney, was in the diocese of Worcester. Slade possibly served the church as vicar, but I have been unable to verify this from the registers at Worcester.

[3] *I.e.* St. Mary Overies in Southwark.

[4] See *Visitations* I, 92, note 3 (Eng.) Bishop Flemyng's commission for the confirmation of the election was issued at the Old Temple, 7 May, 1421 (Reg. XVI, fo. 90 *d.*). The prior of Southwark at this date was Henry Werkworth (1414-c. 1452): see the list of priors in *Monasticon* VI, 169. Kilpesham was abbot of Owston for forty-five years, dying shortly before 6 Aug., 1467 (*Cal. Pat.* 1467-77, p. 23). His successor was Robert Kirkeby, canon of Kirby Bellars, presumably the canon mentioned there in 1440 (*Visitations* II, 166).

[5] *I.e.* 31 May, 1422.

et super depositis per eos est publica vox et fama, etc. Et deinde iurauit abbas obedienciam et fidelitatem in forma consueta. Postea examinatus dicit ea que sequuntur.

Frater Willelmus Kylpesham dicit quod domus indebitatur in c marcis, et quod reuentus domus vltra resoluta solum extendunt se de claro ad xl libras.

Frater Thomas Seusterne, prior, dicit quod omnia bene.

Frater Thomas Russhetone dicit quod omnia bene.

Frater Johannes Ryalle dicit quod omnia sunt bene.

Frater Johannes Lychefelde dicit omnia sunt bene.

Frater Simon Bostone dicit omnia bene.

Frater Willelmus Osoluestone, pietanciarius, dicit omnia bene.

Frater Thomas Wyssendene, cantor et magister nouiciorum, dicit omnia bene.

Frater Johannes Tyltone, diaconus, elemosinarius, dicit omnia bene.

Frater Thomas Asfordeby, accolitus, dicit quod omnia bene.

Frater Willelmus Braunstone, nouicius, dicit quod omnia bene.

Frater Willelmus Leycestre, nouicius, dicit quod omnia bene.

Frater Ricardus Querndone, infatuatus.

Frater Willelmus Hungartone dicit omnia bene.

Frater Johannes Osoluestone, subdiaconus, dicit quod omnia bene.

LV.

[Fo. 30.]

VISITACIO PRIORATUS SANCTE FRIDESWIDE IN OXONIA, LIN-COLNIENSIS DIOCESIS, FACTA IN DOMO CAPITULARI IBIDEM TERCIO DIE MENSIS JUNII, ANNO DOMINI MCCCCXL QUINTO, PER REUEREN-DUM IN CHRISTO PATREM ET DOMINUM, DOMINUM WILLELMUM ALNEWYKE, DEI GRACIA LINCOLNIENSEM EPISCOPUM, SUARUM CONSECRACIONIS ANNO XIXᵒ ET TRANSLACIONIS IXᵒ.

In primis, sedente dicto reuerendo patre iudicialiter pro tribunali in huiusmodi visitacionis sue negocio inchoando die et loco supradictis, comparuerunt coram eo prior et canonici dicti prioratus, parati, vt apparuit, visitacionem huiusmodi subire. Et deinde primo et ante omnia propositum fuit verbum Dei iuxta actus futuri congruenciam in lingua latina per honorabilem virum magistrum Johannem Beuerley, sacre pagine professorem, sequentem hoc thema, 'Estote prudentes *et*

---

[1] For Richard Elvet and his brothers Gilbert and John, see a reference in *Assoc. Soc. R. & P.* XXXII, 523. He had coll. of the fourth prebend in the Newarke college, Leicester, 3 Dec., 1390, at the presentation of John of Gaunt, and was promoted to the deanery and first prebend, 1 Oct., 1396 (Reg. XI, ff. 217, 233). On the death of his brother, John Elvet, archdeacon of Leicester, who succeeded him in the fourth prebend, he obtained the archdeaconry of Leicester (see Le Neve, II, 61, who, however, has confused the date with that of his exchange in 1424). He continued to hold his deanery with the archdeaconry, which he exchanged with John Legbourne in 1424 for the church of Sedgefield, co. Durham. The letters patent presenting Legbourne to the archdeaconry bear date 23 Oct., 1424 (*Cal.*

of the same;[1] and, touching the things deposed by them there are public rumour and report, etc. And then the abbot sware obedience and fealty in form accustomed. Thereafter, upon examination he says these things which follow.

Brother William Kylpesham[2] says that the house is in debt a hundred marks, and that the revenues of the house, over and above its payments, extend only to forty pounds net.

Brother Thomas Seusterne, the prior, says that all things are well.

Brother Thomas Russhetone says that all things are well.

Brother John Ryalle says that all things are well.

Brother John Lychefelde says all things are well.

Brother Simon Bostone says all things are well.

Brother William Osulvestone, the pittancer, says all things are well.

Brother Thomas Wyssendene, the chanter and master of the novices, says all things are well.

Brother John Tyltone, deacon, the almoner, says all things are well.

Brother Thomas Asfordeby, acolyte, says that all things are well.

Brother Willian Braunstone, novice, says that all things are well.

Brother William Leycestre, novice, says that all things are well.

Brother Richard Querndone, out of his wits.

Brother William Hungartone says all things are well.

Brother John Osulvestone, subdeacon, says that all things are well.

LV.

The visitation of the priory of ST. FRIDESWIDE IN OXFORD, of the diocese of Lincoln, performed in the chapter-house therein on the third day of the month of June, in the year of our Lord 1445, by the reverend father in Christ and lord, the lord William Alnewyke, by the grace of God bishop of Lincoln, in the nineteenth year of his consecration and the ninth of his translation.

In the first place, as the said reverend father was sitting in his capacity of judge as a tribunal at the beginning of the business of such his visitation, on and in the day and place abovesaid, there appeared before him the prior and canons of the said priory, in readiness, as was apparent, to undergo such visitation. And then, first and before all else, the word of God was set forth, as was agreeable to the act about to take place, in the Latin tongue by the honourable master John Beverley, professor of holy writ, after this text, ' Be ye prudent and sober, and keep

---

Pat. 1422-9, p. 234) : the certificate of the exchange, effected by the bishop of Durham, was received by archbishop Chichele on 29 Oct. (Lambeth Reg. Chichele I, ff. 249 *d.*, 250). He died in 1431 : his successor in the deanery of the Newarke was inst. 18 Dec. (Reg. XVII, f. 37). For the chantry founded by him in the church of the Newarke college, see *Assoc. Soc. R. & P., u.s.,* p. 524.

² Of fifteen names, eight are from Leicester, viz. Leicester, Asfordby, Hungarton, Owston (Osolvestone,) Quorndon (Querndone), Sewstern and Tilton; three from Rutland, viz. Clipsham (Kylpesham), Ryhall and Whissendine, and possibly Braunston. Rushton is from Northamptonshire, Boston from Lincolnshire, and Lichfield from Staffordshire.

sobrii et vigilate in oracionibus,' etc.[1] Quo laudabiliter finito, dictus prioratus predicti prior certificatorium mandati domini sibi pro huiusmodi visitacione subeunda directi confectum eidem reuerendo patri exhibuit in hec verba, ' Reuerendo in Christo patri,' etc.; quo in publica audiencia perlecto, dictus prior confirmacionem eleccionis sue,[2] installacionem vero non exhibuit. Exhibuit eciam fundacionem prioratus per Ethelredum regem Anglie sub anno Domini miiij[to] post cedem Danorum, partim sub lingua teutonica et partim latina: exhibuit eciam confirmacionem regiam. Deinde prior examinatus dicit vt sequitur.

Frater Robertus Downham, prior, dicit quod domus potest expendere ccxl marcas in anno, et dicit quod ipse reddidit compotum administracionis sue de anno in annum vt deberet.

Frater Johannes Mountagwe senior, supprior, dicit omnia bene.

Frater Ricardus Godalmynge dicit omnia bene.

Frater Johannes *Haselle*[3] junior dicit omnia bene.

Frater Johannes Westbury dicit quod quidam Edwardus rex post conquestum, visitans feretrum Sancte Frideswide, quia euasit sine verecundia vel dampno dedit per cartam suam domui x marcas annuas percipiendas de scaccario in perpetuum in vsus fabrice et ornamentorum ecclesie conuertendas, quas prior recipit et in alios vsus conuertit.

Item prior contra consuetudinem domus oblaciones factas ad feretrum Sancte Frideswide, que olim conuertebantur per sacristam in vsus fabrice ecclesie, hiis diebus percipit et in alios vsus conuertit.

Frater Johannes Chichestre dicit quod soror prioris habens duas filias manet in prioratu iuxta coquinam; que omnes viuunt de bonis domus absque consensu conuentus, et sic vixerunt vno anno et amplius: nam, vt dicit, tres canonici bene possent sustentari expensis quas habent iste tres mulieres.

Item frater naturalis eiusdem prioris, manens in partibus prope Oxoniam, percipit de domo quociens et quando sibi placet, eciam sine consensu conuentus, frumenta, braseum et alia genera granorum et ducit ea a domo vsque mansum suum; et si quis canonicus aliquid dixerit vocat eum garcionem. Et dicit de compoto non reddito per priorem nec tempore quo stetit senescallus nec citra.

Frater Johannes Wodebryge dicit quod celle in dormitorio non bene reparantur.

Frater Robertus Oxonford dicit quod prior non iacet in dormitorio de nocte.

---

[1] 1 Pet. iv, 7: ' Estote itaque prudentes, et vigilate in orationibus.' The inserted words are a reminiscence of 1 Thess. v, 6: ' vigilemus, et sobrii simus.'

[2] *et* cancelled.

[3] Interlined above *Mountagwe* cancelled.

[1] Robert Downham was elected prior of St. Frideswide's on the death of Edmund Andever (see *Visitations* I, 101, note 1 Eng.). His election received royal assent 13 May, 1439, and temporalities were restored 8 July following (*Cal. Pat.* 1436-41, pp. 256, 292-3). There is no record of his confirmation in Alnwick's register. He died before 3 May, 1458 (*ibid.* 1452-61, p. 420).

[2] See *Monasticon* II, 144, where this document is printed from the register of Oseney (MS. Cotton, Vitellius F. xvi) and from a MS. which belonged to Gerard Langbaine.

[3] The twelve canons seem to have been drawn from a wide area, the only local names being Oxford and Wallingford, and possibly Haselle (Haseley). Westbury may have come from the place of that name near Buckingham. The prior seems to

watch in prayers,' etc. And, when this had come to an end in praiseworthy fashion, the said prior of the priory aforesaid exhibited the certificate of my lord's mandate addressed to him for the undergoing of such visitation to the same reverend father, drawn up in these words, ' To the reverend father in Christ,' etc. And, when this had been read through in the public hearing, the said prior exhibited the confirmation of his election, but not his installation,[1] He exhibited also the foundation charter of the priory by Ethelred, king of England, bearing date in the year of our Lord 1004 after the slaughter of the Danes, and written partly in the Teutonic, and partly in the Latin tongue: he exhibited also the royal charter of confirmation.[2] Then the prior, upon examination, says as follows.

Brother Robert Downham,[3] the prior, says that the house is able to spend 240 marks in the year; and he says that he has rendered the account of his administration from year to year as he ought.

Brother John Mountagwe the elder, the subprior, says all things are well.

Brother Richard Godalmynge says all things are well.

Brother John Haselle the younger says all things are well.

Brother John Westbury[4] says that a certain king Edward after the conquest, being on a visit to the shrine of St. Frideswide, because he had escaped without shame or loss, gave to the house by his charter ten marks to be paid yearly out of the exchequer for ever, which should be applied to the uses of the fabric and ornaments of the church,[5] which the prior receives and turns to other uses.

Also the prior, contrary to the custom of the house, receives in these days the offerings made at the shrine of St. Frideswide, which aforetime were applied by the sacrist to the uses of the fabric of the church, and turns them to other uses.

Brother John Chichestre says that the prior's sister, who has two daughters, dwells in the priory, hard by the kitchen; and these all do live of the goods of the house without the consent of the convent, and so have lived for a year and more: for, as he says, three canons might well be maintained at the cost which these three women keep.

Also the same prior's natural brother, who dwells in the country near Oxford, receives of the house, as often as and when it pleases him, even without the consent of the convent, corn, malt and other sorts of grain, and takes them from the house to his dwelling; and, if any canon say aught, he calls him varlet. And [the deponent] says concerning the account, that it was not rendered by the prior, either at the time when he was steward or since.

Brother John Wodebryge says that the cells in the dorter are not well repaired.[6]

Brother Robert Oxonford says that the prior does not lie in the dorter of a night.

---

have belonged to the neighbourhood of Oxford, from the internal evidence of the visitation.

[4] Westbury succeeded Downham as prior in 1458: royal assent 21 May, temporalities restored 23 Aug. (*Cal. Pat.* 1452-61, pp. 423, 431).

[5] I have found no other reference to this circumstance.

[6] The cells are the cubicles in the dorter: see *Visitations* I, 231. It is possible that by this date the dorter was divided by partition walls into a number of private rooms, as *cella* implies rather more than a mere partition by screens.

Item dicit quod domus male opprimitur per cognatos, sorores et fratres prioris.

Item dicit quod soror prioris et eius filie, que dudum manebant in partibus, iam manet[1] in prioratu serate infra vnum mansum ne hoc temere exeant.

Item dicit quod non seruitur canonicis infirmantibus in infirmaria de cibis subtilioribus et medicinis secundum exigenciam regule.

Frater Johannes Walope dicet quod domus deberet exhibere vnum[2] canonicum in studio, et non exhibetur talis.

Item dicit de dictis x marcis conuersis in alios[3] vsus quam ad quos donabantur.

Frater Johannes Mountagwe junior dicit quod redditus domus in villa Oxonie decrescunt, eo quod tenementa non reparantur in defectu prioris.

Frater Ricardus Walyngforde dicit omnia bene.

Frater Johannes Londone, canonicus domus, dicit quod omnia bene.

LVI.

[Fo. 29 *d.*]

Visitacio collegii BEATE MARIE ET OMNIUM SANCTORUM OXONIE, Lincolniensis diocesis, facta in capella eiusdem collegii vt pro loco capitulari primo die mensis junii, anno Domini mccccxl quinto per reuerendum in Christo patrem et dominum Willelmum, Dei gracia Lincolniensem episcopum, eiusdem collegii ordinarium et patronum, anno suarum consecracionis xix° et translacionis ix°.

In primis, sedente dicto reuerendo patre iudicialiter in huiusmodi sue visitacionis negocio pro tribunali, comparuerunt coram eo rector et socii dicti collegii, parati vt apparuit visitacionem huiusmodi subire. Primo et ante omnia propositum fuit verbum Dei in latino sermone iuxta actus futuri congruenciam per honestum virum magistrum Johannem Beke, sacre theologie bacallarium, eiusdem collegii rectorem, sequentem hoc thema, ' Visita nos, Domine, in salutari tuo,' etc.[4] Quo laudabiliter finito, idem rector exhibuit dicto reuerendo patri fundacionem collegii ac institucionem et induccionem suas in dicto collegio; sed primo exhibuit domino certificatorium mandati domini sibi pro

---

[1] *Sic*: for *manent*.
[2] *scol* cancelled.
[3] *d* cancelled.
[4] Ps. cv, 4.

[1] The Benedictine constitutions of 1339, cap. xi, required that out of every twenty canons in a monastery, one should be sent to a university. This rule applied to any house which had more than six and less than twenty members, provided that its resources were sufficient (see text ap. Salter, *Chapters of Aug. Canons.* pp. 230-2).

[2] *I.e.* Lincoln college.

[3] John Beke was the second rector of Lincoln and was vice-chancellor of the university 1450-2 (Le Neve iii, 556, 472). He was instituted 11 Nov , 1422, to the

Also he says that the house is sorely burthened by the kinsfolk, sisters and brethren of the prior.

Also he says that the prior's sister and her daughters, who sometime dwelt in the country, do now dwell in the priory within a lodging under lock and key, so that they may not go out therefrom as they list.

Also he says that the canons who are sick in the infirmary are not served with more delicate meats and medicines, as the rule requires.

Brother John Walope says that the house ought to maintain a canon at the university,[1] and no such canon is maintained.

Also he says, concerning the said ten marks that were turned to other uses, how [and] to what persons they were given.

Brother John Mountagwe the younger says that the rents of the house in the town of Oxford are decreasing, because the tenements are not repaired in the prior's default.

Brother Richard Walyngforde says all things are well.

Brother John Londone, canon of the house, says that all things are well.

LVI.

The visitation of the college of BLESSED MARY AND ALL SAINTS OF OXFORD,[2] of the diocese of Lincoln, performed in the chapel of the same college as in lieu of the place of chapter, on the first day of the month of June in the year of our Lord 1445, by the reverend father in Christ and lord William, by the grace of God bishop of Lincoln, the ordinary and patron of the same college, in the nineteenth year of his consecration and of his translation the ninth.

In the first place, as the said reverend father was sitting in his judicial capacity as a tribunal in the business of such his visitation, there appeared before him the rector and fellows of the said college, in readiness, as was apparent, to undergo such visitation.   First and before all things the word of God was set forth in the Latin speech, as was agreeable the process about to take place, by the honest master John Beke, bachelor of sacred theology, rector of the same college,[3] after this text, ' Visit us, O Lord, in Thy salvation,' etc.   And when this had come to an end in praiseworthy wise, the same rector exhibited to the said reverend father the foundation of the college,[4] and his letters of institution and induction in the said college; but first he exhibited to my lord the certificate of

---

vicarage of St. Michael's at the North gate, Oxford (Wood, *City of Oxford*, ed. Clark, III, 93), one of the churches united by the founder of the college.   He was elected rector of Lincoln 7 May, 1434, and resigned in 1460-1.   On 2 Oct., 1435, he exchanged the church of Welbourn, Lincs., for that of Rollright, Oxon. (Reg. XVII, fo. 65), with which he had a papal dispensation, 24 Nov., 1438, to hold another cure (*Cal. Papal Letters* IX, 35).   He vacated Rollright by death before 4 June, 1465 (Reg. XX, fo. 241).   For an account of his rule and the great advantages which it brought to the college see Clark, *Oxford College Histories: Lincoln*, pp. 7 sqq.

⁴ The licence for the foundation of the college was granted to Bishop Flemyng, 13 Oct., 1427: see *Cal. Pat.* 1422-9, p. 455.

huiusmodi visitacione subeunda directi, cuius tenor talis est, ' Reuerendo in Christo patri ac domino,' etc.; ipsoque in publica audiencia perlecto, idem rector iurauit canonicam obedienciam in forma consueta.   Postea examinatus dicit ea que sequuntur.

Magister Johannes Beke, rector, petit vt dominus iniungat eisdem rectori et sociis vt prosequantur pro reformacione et confirmacione statutorum collegii.

Magister Johannes Segefeld, primam habens tonsuram, iurauit obedienciam, et examinatus dicit omnia bene.

Magister Johannes Malberthorpe, presbyter socius, iurauit obedienciam et exhibuit: examinatus dicit omnia bene.

Magister Willelmus Layly, socius presbyter, iurauit obedienciam et exhibuit: examinatus dicit omnia bene.

Magister Johannes Trysthorpe, socius presbyter, iurauit obedienciam et exhibuit, et examinatus dicit omnia bene.

Magister Johannes Portreue, socius presbyter, iurauit obedienciam et exhibuit, et examinatus dicit omnia bene.

LVII.

[Fo. 29 *d*.]

VISITACIO COLLEGII BEATE MARIE DE LY ORYELLE OXONIE, LINCOLNIENSIS DIOCESIS, FACTA IN CAPELLA EIUSDEM COLLEGII VT PRO LOCO CAPITULARI SECUNDO DIE MENSIS JUNII, ANNO DOMINI MCCCCXL QUINTO, PER REUERENDUM IN CHRISTO PATREM ET DOMINUM WILLELMUM ALNEWYKE, DEI GRACIA LINCOLNIENSEM EPISCOPUM, SUARUM CONSECRACIONIS ANNO XIX⁰ ET CONSE-CRACIONIS[1] IX⁰.

In primis, sedente dicto reuerendo patre iudicialiter in huiusmodi visitacionis negocio pro tribunali, comparuerunt coram eo prepositus et socii eiusdem collegii, parati vt apparuit visitacionem huiusmodi subire.   Et deinde primo et ante omnia propositum fuit verbum Dei per magistrum Johannem Maunselle, in sacra theologia bacallarium, eiusdem collegii socium, sequentem hoc thema, ' Depositum custodi,'[2] etc.   Quo latino sermone laudabiliter finito, dictus prepositus iurauit obedienciam et exhibuit certificatorium mandati sibi pro visitacione huiusmodi directi in hec verba, ' Reuerendo in Christo,' etc.; preconiti[3] que singuli socii comparuerunt, et iurauit eorum[4] quilibet canonicam obedienciam et exhibuit literas ordinum suorum, et deinde examinati dicunt ea que sequuntur.

---

[1] *Sic*: for *translacionis.*
[2] 1 Tim. vi, 20.
[3] *Sic*: for *preconizati.*
[4] *aliquis* cancelled.

[1] The rector's surname indicates his Lincolnshire origin. Two of the fellows bore names from the same county, viz. Mablethorpe and Trusthorpe.

my lord's mandate addressed to him for the undergoing of such visitation, whereof the purport is on such wise, ' To the reverend father in Christ and lord,' etc.; and, when the same had been read through in the public hearing, the same rector sware canonical obedience in the form accustomed. Thereafter, upon examination, he says these things which follow.

Master John Beke,[1] the rector, prays that my lord will make injunction to the same rector and fellows, that they make suit for the reformation and confirmation of the statutes of the college.[2]

Master John Segefeld, having the first tonsure, sware obedience, and upon examination says all things are well.

Master John Malberthorpe, priest fellow, sware obedience and made exhibition:[3] upon examination he says all things are well.

Master William Layly, priest fellow, sware obedience and made exhibition: upon examination he says all things are well.

Master John Trysthorpe,[4] priest fellow, sware obedience and made exhibition, and upon examination says all things are well.

Master John Portreue, priest fellow, sware obedience and made exhibition, and upon examination says all things are well.

LVII.

The visitation of the college of BLESSED MARY OF LY ORYELLE OF OXFORD, of the diocese of Lincoln, performed in the chapel of the same college, as in lieu of the place of chapter, on the second day of the month of June in the year of our Lord 1445, by the reverend father in Christ and lord William Alnewyke, by the grace of God bishop of Lincoln, in the nineteenth year of his consecration and of his [translation] the ninth.

In the first place, as the said reverend father was sitting in his capacity of judge as a tribunal in the business of such his visitation, there appeared before him the provost and fellows of the same college, in readiness, as was apparent, to undergo such visitation. And then, first and before all else, the word of God was set forth by master John Maunselle, bachelor in sacred theology, fellow of the same college, after this text, ' Keep that which is committed to thee,' etc. And, when this had come to an end in praiseworthy wise in the Latin speech, the said provost sware obedience and presented the certificate of the mandate addressed to him for such visitation, in these words, ' To the reverend [father] in Christ,' etc.; and, being called by name, the several fellows appeared, and each of them sware canonical obedience and exhibited the letters of his orders, and then upon examination they say these things which follow.

---

[2] The statutes finally adopted were those given by bishop Rotherham, 11 Feb., 1479-80 (Clark, op. cit., p. 29).

[3] I.e. of his letters of orders.

[4] Proctor in 1443 (Le Neve III, 482). He was elected rector 28 Feb., 1460-1, and held the office till 1479 (Clark, op. cit., pp. 21 sqq).

Magister[1] Johannes Mawnshulle dicit quod statutum erat dudum quod socii collegii infra illud semper loquerentur mutuo latinum vel gallicum, quod quidem statutum male iam seruatur.

Magister Thomas Wyche dicit quod socii in sacerdocio constituti preter collegium celebrant annalia de permissu statutorum.

Magister Henricus Sampsone, decanus, dicit omnia bene: exhibuit domino statuta domus facta per Henricum Burgershe dudum Lincolniensem episcopum.

Magister Johannes Westone dicit omnia bene.

Magister Ricardus Wylshere dicit omnia bene.

Magister Willelmus Edwarde dicit omnia bene.

Magister Johannes Cambyrlayne dicit omnia bene.

Magister Johannes Swane dicit quod theologi non laborant in predicando, sed semper domi resident non proficientes in predicando.

Magister Walterus Lyhart, prepositus.

Magister Andreas Maukeswelle nichil dicit.

Magister Rogerus Stephyne.

Magister Ricardus Trynge.

Henricus Fraunceys.

LVIII.

[Fo. 1.]

VISITACIO MONASTERII DE BURGO SANCTI PETRI, ORDINIS SANCTI [BENEDICTI, LINCOLNIENSIS] DIOCESIS, FACTA ET INCHOATA IN [DOMO] CAPITULARI IBIDEM X° [ET XJ°] DIEBUS MENSIS [DECEM]-BRIS, ANNO [DOMINI] M°CCCCXXXVIJ°, PER REUERENDUM IN CHRISTO PATREM [ET] DOMINUM, DOMINUM WILLELMUM, [DE]I GRACIA LINCOLNIENSEM EPISCOPUM, ANNO SUE[2] CONSECRACIONIS XIJ° ET TRANSLACIONIS [SECUNDO][3]

In primis dictus reuerendus pater in huiusmodi sue visitacionis negocio in[choa]ndo sedebat iudicialiter pro tribunali in d[ie, anno et

---

[1] Interlined above *Frater* cancelled.
[2] *translacionis xj* cancelled.
[3] Word in brackets torn in original.

[1] The names of the fellows afford no indication of a special district of origin.
[2] The original statutes bear date 1 Jan., 1325-6: for a general summary of their contents see Rannie, *Oxford College Histories: Oriel*, pp. 6-10. Bishop Burghersh's statutes bear date 23 May following, and were confirmed on 11 June (*ibid.* p. 11).
[3] *I.e.* masses celebrated for a year or for some other limited period, involving a merely temporary engagement, 'sic quod non sint ad officia talia dicenda intitulati, nec perpetui, sed temporales et elapso tempore remotivi' (Lyndwood, ed. 1679, p. 228: tit. *de celebr. miss.*, c. *Sacerdotes*, ver. *anualia*).
[4] Henry Sampson, S.T.P., became provost of Oriel in 1449 (Le Neve III, 549): he was principal of the subordinate foundation of St. Mary's hall in 1438 (*ibid.* 584). As an old friend of John Carpenter, bishop of Worcester (see *Visitations* I, 193), he was appointed by him to the deanery of the collegiate church of Westbury-on-Trym, Glouces., 20 Jan., 1458-9 (Worcester Reg. Carpenter I, fo. 149 *d.*). He resigned this on 3 June, 1469, exchanging the office with William Cannyng for the prebend of Goodringhill in the same church (*ibid.* ff. 240 *d.*, 241). He vacated this prebend by death before 10 March, 1482-3 (Worcester Reg. Alcock, fo. 113 *d*).

Master John Mawnshulle[1] says that it was some time ordained by statute that the fellows of the college, being therein, should always talk with one another in Latin or French,[2] the which statute is now ill kept.

Master Thomas Wyche says that the fellows in priest's orders do by permission of the statutes celebrate annuals[3] outside the college.

Master Henry Sampsone, the dean,[4] says all things are well: he exhibited to my lord the statutes of the house made by Henry Burgershe, sometime bishop of Lincoln.

Master John Westone says all things are well.

Master Richard Wylshere[5] says all things are well.

Master William Edwarde says all things are well.

Master John Cambyrlane says all things are well.

Master John Swane says that the theologians take no pains in preaching, but stay ever at home, making no profit in preaching.

Master Walter Lyhart, the provost.[6]

Master Andrew Maukeswelle says nothing.

Master Roger Stephyne.

Master Richard Trynge.

Henry Fraunceys.

LVIII.

THE VISITATION OF THE MONASTERY OF PETERBOROUGH, OF THE ORDER OF ST. [BENET], OF THE DIOCESE [OF LINCOLN], PERFORMED AND BEGUN IN THE CHAPTER-[HOUSE] THERE ON THE TENTH [AND ELEVENTH] DAYS OF THE MONTH OF [DECEM]BER, IN THE YEAR OF [OUR LORD] 1437, BY THE REVEREND FATHER IN CHRIST [AND] LORD, THE LORD WILLIAM, BY THE GRACE OF [GOD] BISHOP OF LINCOLN, IN THE TWELFTH YEAR OF HIS CONSECRATION AND [THE SECOND] OF HIS TRANSLATION.

In the first place the said reverend father, in the beginning of the business of such his visitation, sate in his capacity of judge as a tribunal

---

He also held the church of Tredington, Worces. There is no record of his institution, but there can be no doubt that he received collation from Carpenter after the death of John Macworth in 1450 (see *Visitations* I, 69, note 1, and 174). Nash, *Hist. Worces.* II, gives the inscription from the brass of Henry Simpson (*sic*) at Tredington, which supplies the date of his death, 17 Nov., 1482.

[5] Principal of St. Mary's hall, 1445 (Le Neve III, 584).

[6] Walter Lyhart (le Hart), B.A., was admitted to a fellowship of Oriel by Carpenter, 6 July, 1425, after a dispensation granted on behalf of him and three other fellows by archbishop Chichele from fulfilling their statutory year of probation (Lambeth Reg. Chichele I, fo. 260 d.). He was instituted to the church of Lamarsh, Essex, 7 Oct., 1427 (Newcourt II, 361), which he exchanged for that of West Tilbury, 4 Nov., 1428 (*ibid.* II, 598: pres. by Crown 24 Oct., *Cal. Pat.* 1422-9, p. 521). He resigned this benefice 1 March, 1434-5 (Newcourt, u.s.), having exchanged it for the church of Nettleton, Wilts. (*Cal. Pat.* 1429-36, p. 448). About this time he succeeded John Carpenter, afterwards bishop of Worcester, as provost of Oriel; he is mentioned under that title in a dispensation, dated 23 Aug., 1435, licensing him to hold an incompatible benefice with Nettleton (*Cal. Papal Letters* VIII, 539); but Rannie (op. cit., p. 58) says that he was elected 1 June, 1436. He was presented by the Crown to Bradwell-juxta-Mare, Essex, 24 Feb. 1440 (*Cal. Pat.* 1436-41, p. 513), and was instituted on 3 March (Newcourt II, 74). On 9 March, 1443-4,

loco predictis]; et d[einde c]omparuerunt [cor]am eo sic iudicialiter sedente frater Johannes Depyng, abbas dicti monasterii, ac ceteri monachi eiusdem omnes et singuli, xliiij in numero, duobus Oxonie studentibus et vno lepra percusso infirmante dumtaxat exceptis. Quibus sic presentibus primo et ante omnia propositum fuit verbum Dei per fratrem Thomam Depyng, monachum eiusdem monasterii, sacre pagine professorem, sequentem hoc thema, ' Vt filii lucis ambul[ate.'¹ Q]uo laudabiliter finito, dictus d[ominus] abbas liberauit prefato reuerendo patri certificatorium mandati domini sibi pro hac [visita]cione directi sigillo suo sigillatum, cuius tenor talis est, ' Reuerendo in Christo patri,' etc. Quo quidem certificatorio per me scribam infrascriptum de mandato dicti reuerendi patris in publica audiencia perlecto, preconizatis*que* singulis huiusmodi monachis citatis et comparentibus, exceptis preexceptis, dictus dominus abbas primo et ante omnia exhibuit dicto reuerendo patri titulum confirmacionis eleccionis sue sub data mensis J[anuarii] anno Domini mccccviij, et eciam installacionis sue, etc.; et deinde iurauit idem dominus abbas canonicam obedienciam dicto reuerendo patri in forma consueta. Postea exhibuit fundacionem monasterii; et deinde idem reuerendus pater processit ad inquisicionem suam preparatoriam in huiusmodi visitacione sua, examinando primo dictum dominum abbatem ac fratrem Ricardum Harltone priorem, postea fratrem Willelmum Extone senescallum. Et deinde commisit potestatem et vices suas magistris Johanni Depyng et Johanni Leke coniunctim et diuisim ad examinandum ceteras personas conuentus; qui assumptis

---

he had a grant of the wardenship of St. Anthony's hospital in Threadneedle Street, in succession to Carpenter, who had resigned it on his promotion to the see of Worcester (*Cal. Pat.* 1441-6, p. 266). He resigned Bradwell by 10 Nov. 1444 (Newcourt, u.s.), having been instituted, at the presentation of the abbot and convent of Glastonbury, to High Ham, Somerset, on 3 Nov. (Weaver, *Somerset Incumbents*, p. 101, where he is wrongly called Hihert). As rector of High Ham, he had a papal indult to retain his hospital and provostship, 18 May, 1445 (*Cal. Papal Letters* IX, 497). At the end of 1445 he was appointed to the bishopric of Norwich, vacant by the death of Thomas Brouns (see *Visitations* I, 16, note 1, and 201-2). The *congé d'élire* was issued 15 Dec., 1445; he was given custody of the temporalities 10 Jan. following, which were restored to him on 26 Feb. (*Cal. Pat.* 1441-6, pp. 407, 428, 405,) after his provision on 24 Jan. (*Cal. Papal Letters* IX, 513). He was consecrated by archbishop Stafford on 20 or 27 March, 1446, and held the see for sixteen years, dying on 17 May, 1472. It was during his episcopate that the beautiful vault of the nave of Norwich cathedral was completed, the continuation of the work which Alnwick's refacing of the west doorway and provision for the construction of the new west window (see *Visitations* II, xxiii, xxvii) had begun. His successor at Oriel was John Hals, a probationer fellow, who was consecrated bishop of Lichfield in 1459, but resigned the provostship in 1449.

¹ Eph. v, 8.

¹ See *Visitations* I, 101, note 2 Eng.
² These, with the three exceptions mentioned, are all accounted for at this visitation. The total numbers at the visitations of 1442 and 1446 are less easy to compute. In 1442 thirty-four monks gave evidence, and another is mentioned; while we may reasonably infer that three others, who were present in 1437 and 1446 and include the prior, may be added to the total, which thus reaches thirty-eight, and another, of whom we learn from another source, brings it to thirty-nine. In 1446 only twenty-two monks were apparently examined, but seven more were mentioned in the depositions. If twenty-nine was the full number, the convent must have lost nine monks in a little over four years; but there must have been at least thirty-two, as the list of thirty-seven monks present at abbot Ramsey's election

[on and] in [the day, year and place aforesaid]; and then there appeared [before] him as he so sate in judgment brother John Depyng, the abbot of the said monastery,[1] and the rest of the monks thereof all and sundry, forty-four in number,[2] save only two that were students at Oxford and one that, being stricken with leprosy, was sick.   And, these being thus present, first and before all else the word of God was set forth by brother Thomas Depyng, monk of the same monastery, professor of holy writ, after this text, ' Walk as children of light.'   The which being come to a praiseworthy end, the said [lord abbot] delivered to the aforesaid reverend father the certificate of my lord's mandate which had been addressed to him for this visitation, sealed with his seal, the purport whereof is on such wise, ' To the reverend father in Christ,' etc.   Now, after this certificate had been read through in the public hearing, at the command of the said reverend father, by me the scribe hereunder written, and such several monks who had been summoned had been called by name and made their appearance, save those before excepted, the said lord abbot first and before all else exhibited to the said reverend father his title of the confirmation of his election under the date of the month of J[anuary], in the year of our Lord 1408,[3] and also that of his installation, etc.; and then the same lord abbot sware canonical obedience to the said reverend father in form accustomed.   After these things he exhibited the foundation of the monastery;[4] and then the same reverend father proceeded to his preparatory inquiry in such his visitation, examining first the said lord abbot and brother Richard Harltone the prior, [and] afterwards brother William Extone the steward.   And then he committed his power and place to masters John Depyng and John Leke jointly and severally to examine the rest of the persons of the

---

in 1471 (*Monasticon* II, 363, note 6) contains three names, mentioned in 1437 or 1442, but not in 1446.

On this calculation, of the forty-one monks present in 1437, thirty-two were in the monastery in 1442, and twenty-two in 1446; and, of the total of thirty-eight in 1442, we can account for twenty-six out of twenty-nine in 1446.   Nine names are peculiar to the list of 1437, two to that of 1442, three to that of 1446.

An analysis of the fifty names thus obtained shows that the convent drew largely for its members upon local sources.   The name Burgh occurs three and possibly four times, the name Deeping five times, the name Stamford twice.   From Northamptonshire, and in each case from places on the estates of the monastery, come Aldwinkle, Ashton (near Oundle), Barnack, Maxey, Pyghtesley (Pytchley), Warmington and Walmesford (Wansford).   South Lincolnshire is represented by Brune (Bourne), Freshney, Gedney, Gosberkyrk (Gosberton), Leasingham, Morton (near Bourne), Spalding and Tallington; Rutland by Exton, Liddington and Wyssendene (Whissendine); Huntingdonshire by Winwick and Jakesle (Yaxley); Bedfordshire by Turvey; Cambridgeshire by Harlton; Norfolk by Lynn and possibly Burnham. ' Stanerne' (1437) should be Stanion in Northants; but the form 'Statherne ' (1446) points to Stathern in Leicestershire, from which also comes Melton. Markham, Newark and Nottingham belong to a district further north; while Bisley, Lindfield, Oxford and York indicate a more distant origin than the others.   Out of forty-one separate surnames, only four, Barton, Beaufo, Brewster, and More, are without definite local characteristics.

Five names given in this series of visitations are mentioned in Gray's injunctions of 1432 (*Visitations* I, 101, note 2 Eng.).   Of these only Richard Harlton remained in 1446, when he still held the office of prior.

[3] The date is a year wrong: it should be 25 Jan., 1409-10 (Reg. XIV, ff. 240 *d.*, 241).

[4] Modern texts of the charter of Wulfhere (664) are printed in *Monasticon* II, 377-8, Kemble, *Cod. Dipl.* No. 984, Birch, *Cartul. Sax.*, No. 22 (I, 33-41).

sibi diuisis[1] scribis secesserunt ad loca separata in inferiori parte dicte domus capitularis, et ibidem ad similem inquisicionem processerunt, ceteras personas monasterii examinando. Et subsequenter idem reuerendus[2] post refeccionem *meridianam*[3] ad capitulum rediens examinauit fratres Willelmum Stamford, Johannem Jakesley suppriorem, Johannem Burghe gardianum de Oxney, Ricardum Stamford camerarium, Johannem Burtone sacristam, Thomam Depyng seniorem elemosinarium, Thomam Depyng juniorem receptorem ex parte abbatis et fratrem Walterum Fressheney cellerarium ex parte conuentus. Quibus per ipsum reuerendum patrem et ceteris omnibus, Johanne Turvey excepto et exceptis preexceptis, per dictos dominos commissarios examinatis et eorum deposicionibus vt infra sequitur in scriptis redactis, idem reuerendus pater, vocatis ad se dictis abbate, priore et cellerario conuentus, continuauit huiusmodi visitacionem suam in statu quo tunc erat vsque in diem tunc crastinum, xj videlicet diem dicti mensis Decembris, in loco predicto, presentibus magistro Johanne Leke et me Colstone notario et scriba. In quibus termino et loco coram dicto reuerendo patre in huiusmodi visitacionis sue negocio iterato iudicialiter sedente pro tribunali comparuerunt personaliter dictus abbas ac omnes et singuli monachi dicti monasterii, exceptis tribus preexceptis. Et deinde idem reuerendus pater publicauit dicta et deposiciones ac comperta in huiusmodi visitacione sua; et deinde obiecit abbati omnia que de ipso detecta sunt, que omnia, vt ipsemet alias fatebatur se minus idoneum ad regendum[4] ipsum monasterium, sapebant improuidam gubernacionem dicti monasterii in temporalibus et spiritualibus pro parte saltem a[bba]tis. Vnde idem reuerendus pater mandauit ipsi abbati vt, vocatis ad se priore et diuicioribus fratribus suis in quibus confidebat, ex[qui]rerent inter se communicato consilio viam idoneam pro regimine maturiori dicti monasterii vt pro parte sua et exquisitam sibi referret. Vnde, secedente dicto reuerendo patre paulisper et postmodum redeunte, idem abbas dixit quod visum [est] sibi de consilio fratrum suorum expediens quod prior, vocando ad eum de fratribus quos vult, habeat total[e] regimen in spiritualibus et temporalibus dicti monasterii. Vnde idem reuerendus pater de consensu eiusdem abbatis suspen[sit] eundem abbatem ab omni administracione spiritualium et temporalium dicti monasterii, sacramento penitencie sibi confiteri volent[ibus]et reuerencia obedienciali tantum exceptis et sibi reseruatis modo debito. Et deinde de consensu eiusdem abbatis et tocius conuentus idem reuerendus pater deputauit fratrem Ricardum Harltone, priorem eiusdem monasterii, in coadiutorem ei[dem] abbati et commisit ipsi fratri Ricardo totalem administracionem spiritualium et temporalium dicto monasterio pertinencium, saluis

---

[1] This word is indistinct in the original, as the minims have been run together.
[2] *Sic: pater* omitted.
[3] Interlined above *quotidianam* cancelled.
[4] Written *regiend.*'

[1] This method of expediting an inquiry, when the monastery was large, and the chapter-house afforded room for two simultaneous private examinations, deserves notice.
[2] Oxney was the cell or ' seny place,' a short distance north-east of Peterborough, used by monks in need of change of air. See *Visitations* I, 37, note 5, and cf. II, 14, note I.

convent; and they, having taken to them separate scribes, went aside to places set apart at the lower end of the said chapter-house and there proceeded to a like inquiry, examining the other persons of the monastery.[1]   And thereafter the same reverend father, returning to the chapter-house after the noon-day meal, examined brothers William Stamford, John Jakesley the sub-prior, John Burghe the warden of Oxney,[2] Richard Stamford the chamberlain, John Burtone the sacrist, Thomas Depyng the elder the almoner, Thomas Depyng the younger the receiver on behalf of the abbot, and brother Walter Fressheney the cellarer on behalf of the convent.   And when these had been examined by the same reverend father and all the rest, save John Turvey and save those before excepted, by the said sirs commissaries, and their depositions had been taken down in writing as follows hereafter, the same reverend father, having called to him the said abbot, prior and cellarer of the convent, adjourned such his visitation in the state wherein it then was until the morrow of that day, the eleventh day to wit of the said month of December, in the aforesaid place, there being present master John Leke and I Colstone the notary and scribe.   At and in the which term and place, before the said reverend father, as he was sitting a second time in his capacity of judge as a tribunal in the business of such his visitation, there appeared in person the said abbot and all and singular the monks of the said monastery, save the three before excepted.   And then the same reverend father made public what had been said and deposed and the matters discovered in such his visitation; and then he laid to the abbot's charge all the matters that were disclosed concerning him, all the which, as he himself confessed at another time that he was but little fit to rule the same monastery, savoured of the unthrifty governance of the said monastery in things temporal and spiritual, at any rate on the abbot's part.   Wherefore the same reverend father bade the same abbot call to him the prior and his better endowed[3] brethren in whom he trusted, that so, taking counsel together, they might seek out a fit way for the more discreet rule of the said monastery as regards his own part,[4] and that [the abbot] should tell it to him when it had been sought out. Wherefore, the said reverend father going away for a little while and returning afterwards, the same abbot said that with the advice of his brethren it seemed expedient to him that the prior, calling to him of the brethren whom he will, should have the entire governance of the said monastery in matters temporal and spiritual.   Wherefore the same reverend father with the consent of the same abbot suspended the same abbot from all the administration of the spiritual and temporal affairs of the said monastery, saving only and reserving to him in manner due [the ministry of] the sacrament of penance to them that will make confession to him, and the reverence of obedience.   And then with the consent of the same abbot and the whole convent the same reverend father deputed brother Richard Harltone, the prior of the same monastery, to be coadjutor to the same abbot, and committed to the same brother Richard the whole administration of the matters spiritual and temporal

---

[3] The word in the original appears to be *diuicioribus*, although the initial letter is more like *e* than *d*.   The use of such a word in the context is very peculiar, as the endowments referred to must be mental.

[4] *I.e.* the abbot's household, to the maintenance of which, as appears later, nearly half of the revenues were devoted.

[reuer]encia obedienciali debita abbati et ministracione sacramenti penitencie sibi confiteri volentibus. Et deinde iuratus [est] abbas de hiis parendo et coadiutor de fideliter administrando et computando quibus ipse reuerendus pater manda[ret]; et eciam iuratus est frater Thomas Depyng receptor abbatis de fideliter faciendo que pertinent ad officium suum [secundum] aduisamentum et deliberacionem dicti coadiutoris. Et subsequenter quia nedum per inquisicionem sed per communem famam ve[nit] ad aures dicti reuerendi patris de magna et insolenti vagacione et commesacione monachorum in villa Burgi et communicacione [sus]pecta cum mulieribus, idem reuerendus pater monuit omnes et singulos monachos predictos vt prefertur presentes primo, secundo et tercio ac peremptorie sub pena excommunicacionis maioris, *quam in personas contraueniencium intendit fulminare vt dixit*, ne eorum quilibet quauis occasione bibat aut commedat quouis quesito colore in villa Burgi de hinc vsque vltimum diem Marcii proxime futurum, nec *quod cum aliquibus mulieribus in ipsa villa salte[nt, nec]* quod aliquas [mu]lieres intra monasterium introducant seu ab aliis introductas ad familiaritatem admittant aliqualem su[spectam], personis illis de quibus iura nichil mali suspicantur dumtaxat exceptis; et eandem monicionem fecit idem reuerendus pater magistro operum. Monuit eciam gardianum de Oxney vt in fine singulorum mensium reddat compotum administracionis sue ibidem *per illum mensem*; cui monicioni annuit idem gardianus. Hortabatur eciam sacristam et camerarium, de quibus plures quere[le] facte sunt, vt, si[1] bene vel non bene in omnibus in suis huiusmodi officiis se[2] gesserint, melius in futurum se haberent. Et hiis ita gestis, idem reuerendus pater continuauit visitacionem suam huiusmodi in statu quo tunc erat vsque dictum vlt[imum] diem Marcii in eadem domo capitulari, et tribuit presidentibus religionis[3] facultatem et licenciam corrigendi pu[ni]endi et reformandi omnia et singula delicta, defectus, excessus et crimina interim contingencia, presentibus magistris Johanne D[epyng], licenciato in legibus, Johanne Leke, in decretis bacallario et me Thoma Colstone notario et scriba.

[Fo. 1 *d*.] [Frater][4] Johannes Depyng, abbas, dicit quod propter i[mpotenciam et seni]um suum et graues infirmitates quas indies patitur et indies [magis] crescunt super eum sentit se inhabilem et impotentem ad onus dignitatis [sue] abbacialis debite supportandum, eo quod nec potest nec scit exequi illud officium. Petit igitur s[e] exonerari ab huiusmodi onere. [Interrogatus] de statu domus, nescit respondere ad hoc, vt dicit, quia vt dicit omnes officiarii monasterii annuatim reddunt compotos administracionum suarum coram conuentu vel saltem priore et senioribus.

---

[1] Written *sibi*: *bi* cancelled.
[2] *non* cancelled.
[3] *corri* cancelled.
[4] This leaf is in very bad condition, and many words are torn and illegible. The first paragraph has been much altered in the original, and its syntax is very defective.

[1] For the snare of dancing cf. the case of the two nuns of Catesby who danced with friars at Northampton, and that of the monk at Humberstone who climbed a gate to watch the dancers in the churchyard (*Visitations* II, 50, 140).
[2] See the note on this office, *Visitations* I, 237, and cf. II, 55, note 3. The identity of the master of the works at Peterborough is not disclosed in the sequel.

belonging to the said monastery, saving the reverence of obedience due to the abbot and the ministry of the sacrament of penance to them that will make confession to him. And then the abbot [was] sworn to obey these things, and the coadjutor to make faithful administration and render an account to them to whom the same reverend father [should] give command; and brother Thomas Depyng, the abbot's receiver, was also sworn to perform faithfully those things which appertain to his office according to the counsel and determination of the said coadjutor. And thereafter, because, not only by inquiry but by common report, there came [news] to the said reverend father's ears of the great and unruly roaming about of the monks and their eating in the town of Peterborough and their [sus]pect conversation with women, the same reverend father warned all and singular the monks aforesaid that were present as is aforeset, a first, second and third time and peremptorily, under pain of the greater excommunication, which he intends, as he said, to declare against the persons of them that go counter thereto, that none of them for any cause whatever shall drink or eat under colour of any pretext soever in the town of Peterborough from this time until the last day of March next to come, and that they dance[1] not with any women in the same town or bring in any women within the monastery or receive them that are brought in by others to any familiar converse suspect, save only those persons concerning whom the laws have no evil suspicion; and the same warning did the same reverend father give to the master of the works.[2] He warned also the warden of Oxney to render at the end of each month an account of his administration in the same place through that month; to the which admonition the same warden gave assent. He exhorted also the sacrist and the chamberlain, concerning whom many complaints were made, that, whether they have borne themselves well or not well in all things in such their offices, they should behave themselves better for the future. And, when these things had thus been done, the same reverend father adjourned such his visitation in the state wherein it then was until the said last day of March in the same chapter-house, and gave power and licence to the presidents of religion[3] to correct, punish and reform all and sundry the offences, defaults, transgressions and crimes that happen in the meantime, there being present masters John Depyng, licentiate in laws, John Leke, bachelor in decrees, and I Thomas Colstone the notary and scribe.

Brother John Depyng, the abbot, says that by reason of his [want of strength and old age] and the sore infirmities which he daily suffers and that daily grow upon him [more] he feels himself unable and powerless to endure the burthen of [his] dignity of abbot as he ought, in that he cannot and knows not how to fulfil that office. He prays therefore that he may be discharged of such burthen. [Interrogated] concerning the state of the house, he knows not how to answer hereunto, as he says, because, as he says, all the officers of the monastery do render yearly the accounts of their administrations before the convent or at any rate [before] the prior and the elder [monks].

---

[3] *I.e.* the prior, subprior, third and fourth priors.

Frater Ricardus Harletone, prior, exhortatus in periculum anime sue, dicit quod sunt in numero xliiij et ex hiis omnibus non sunt in choro *tempore diuini seruicii*[1] vltra x vel xij; et hoc quia abbas habens secum iiij monachos officiarios, et sunt[2] *senescallus, r[ecep]tor, cellerarius, capellanus,* non *sequuntur*[3] chorum, et ij scolares excusati *sunt,* et v officiarii ex parte conuentus, *sacrista, [cel]lerarius, [ele]mosinarius,* th[esaurarius], *magister oper[um]*, qui non veniunt ad chorum nisi certis[4] festis, et vj stant continue apud Oxney, et omni septimana *adminus* ij diebus vij *sunt* in minucionibus, et aliquociens ij vel tres licenciati per abbatem morantur in maneriis et grangiis *vel alibi cum amicis suis extra monasterium*; et sic aliquociens contingit vt dum sint iiij, v vel sex ministri circa altare, non remanent vltra duos in vna et duos in altera parte chori, *sic quod seculares videntes hec obloquuntur de ista raritate presencium in choro*; et preter hoc sunt[5] valitudinarii qui propter infirmitates *et etates* excusantur a choro. Petitur quod de hiis fiat remedium et quod tales licencie de facili non concedantur, cum ex ipsis oriantur dissoluciones [et grauia] scandala.

Item dicit quod tante fiunt quasi quotidie[6] vigilie et serotine potaciones quod ex hoc huiusmodi exercentes redduntur indispositi ad celebrandum sequentibus diebus, et sic non celebrantur misse iuxta numerum . . . . [monac]horum. Petitur igitur vt ordinetur ne decetero fiant tales vigilie aut potaciones in monasterio, nec apud Oxney[7] vltra horam viij sub pena graui.

Item dicit quod ex parte abbatis expense facte excedunt receptam per c li. *in anno,* et hoc quia redditus sui non exiguntur, et omni anno magis ac magis incurrit maiora onera eris alieni. Petitur igitur vt abbas sit con[tentus pro] vestitu suo et aliis necessariis summa quam percipit de diuersis officiariis conuentus et redditu pertinente ad cameram suam cum denariis quos percipit [de balliuis] libertatis et non oneret receptorem suum cum talibus expensis ex causa excessus expensarum vltra receptam vt supra.

Item dicit vbi minuti solebant comedere per se in vno loco, et alii excusati a refectorio propter eorum recreacionem[8] in aliis separatis locis per se, facta fuit magna consumpcio bonorum, iam eius laborbus[9] omnes hii iam comedunt insimul in vno loco. Petit igitur vt dominus *in* hoc commendet eos et idem ratificet, etc.

Item dicit quod pars abbatis potest expendere dcc li. et pars conuentus dccc li.

---

[1] This seems to be the reading: *tempore* is certain, but the other words are difficult to make out.

[2] *idem* cancelled, and the titles of the officers written in margin.

[3] Interlined: *frequentant* cancelled.

[4] *principalibus* cancelled.

[5] *sex vel octo* cancelled.

[6] *tante* cancelled.

[7] *sed* cancelled.

[8] A word, apparently *vbi,* cancelled.

[9] *Sic*: for *laboribus.*

[1] See the note on *stagiarius, Visitations* i, 249, and cf. ii, 56, note 2. It may be remarked that, with these constant and customary absences, there was probably some arrangement for attendance in quire by rotation; but, if there was such an arrangement, it was evidently not very systematic.

Brother Richard Harletone, the prior, being exhorted on peril of his soul, says that they are forty-four in number, and out of all these there are not more than ten or twelve in quire in time of divine service; and this because the abbot has four monks with him as his officers, and they are his steward, receiver, cellarer [and] chaplain, [and] do not attend quire, and there are two excused at the university, and five officers on the side of the convent, the sacrist, [cel]larer, [al]moner, t[reasurer], master of the works, who come to quire only on certain feasts, and there are six abiding continually at Oxney, and at least two days in every week there are seven in their seynies, and sometimes two or three, with the abbot's licence, stay in the manors and granges or with their friends elsewhere without the monastery; and so it sometimes happens that, while there may be four, five or six ministers at the altar, there are left no more than two on one and two on the other side of the quire, so that the secular folk who see these things speak harm of this scantiness of persons present in quire; and beside this there are the feeble-bodied who, by reason of their infirmities and age, are excused from quire.[1] Prayer is made that remedy be taken for these things and that such licences be not readily granted, seeing that from the same there arise disorders [and grievous] scandals.

Also he says that almost every day there take place so much late watching and drinking in the evening that for this cause they that use such doings are left indisposed to celebrate on the following days, and so masses are not celebrated according to the [full] number of [the monks]. Prayer is therefore made for an ordinance that from henceforth such watchings or drinkings be not held in the monastery, or at Oxney after eight o'clock, under a heavy penalty.[2]

Also he says that on the abbot's side the money spent exceeds that received by a hundred pounds in the year, and this because his rents are not levied, and every year more and more he incurs greater burthens of debt. Prayer therefore is made that [for] his raiment and other needful matters the abbot shall be con[tent] with the sum which he receives from the divers officers of the convent and with the rent that belongs to his privy purse,[3] together with the money which he receives [from the bailiffs] of the liberty, and shall not burthen his receiver with such expenses by reason of the excess of the expenses over the receipt, as above.

Also he says [that] whereas those who are in their seynies were wont to eat by themselves in one place, and the others who are excused from frater for their refreshment, in other places apart by themselves, there came to pass great waste of goods; [but] now by his labours all these do now eat together in one place. He prays therefore that my lord will commend them herein and ratify the same, etc.

Also he says that the abbot's side can spend seven hundred pounds and the convent's side eight hundred pounds.

---

[2] The limited permission with regard to Oxney is due to the fact that at such cells, where monks went for their health, some relaxation of strictness was customary.

[3] See note on the various meanings of *camera*, *Visitations* I, 222. The origin of *garderoba* and *camera* as names for departments of finance is explained at length by T. F. Tout, *Chapters in Mediaeval Admin. Hist.*, 1920, I, 67-71.

Item dicit quod ipsemet de aduisamento seniorum ordinatum est[1] quod quilibet remittet de suo peculio annuatim ad tres annos, *quod extendit ad l li.*, ad releuamen minorum officiorum *ex parte conuentus*, que propter exilitatem rerum eis pertinencium non sufficiebant ad onera eis incumbencia. Petit vt dominus eos [in hoc] commendet et factum hoc approbet.

Item dicit quod maneria et tenementa pertinencia parti abbatis tendunt ad magnam ruinam et quasi [irrep]arabilem nisi cicius respiciatur ad eorum reparacionem, nec habentur instauramenta in ipsis maneriis. Petitur vt senescallus vel custos maneriorum melius intendant eorum reparacioni.

Item dicit quod abbas tempore suo vendidit diuersa corrodia, vnum videlicet cuidam Vnderwode pannario [d]e quo habuit c li., *et lx li. pro bosco vendito apud Estewode et alibi et c marcas de fratre Thome Perpount et vendidit* alium *corrodium* Thome Mortymer, recipiendo ab eo ccc li., quod[2] corrodium *valet annuatim* xx li. annuas, et nescitur qualiter pecunie recepte expenduntur. Petitur igitur quod abbas de hiis reddat racionem.

[Item] exigatur quod inutiles expense facte ex parte abbatis omnimodo subducantur, et quod nullus seculares[3] [habeat] aliquos equos pastos expensis domus, sicut frater abbatis nunc habet duos, nisi corrodiarius regis [vel] Castell vel alius qui forte occupabit officium suum.

Item dicit quod abbas fecit inutiliter construi vnum molendinum ad ventum pro granis et oleo de rapis conficiendo. Petitur vt abbas abstineat a huiusmodi et aliis inanibus expensis, cum nullo modo cedere monasterio [s]per[etur] commodum; nam seminari fecit plures

---

[1] *Sic*: the construction changes.
[2] *quidem ter* cancelled.
[3] *Sic*: for *secularis*.

[1] This appears to be calculated on a basis of a complement of fifty monks at 6s. 8d. a head per annum. It will be seen that in 1446 the recognised custom was to allow the monks £60 a year in equal shares for their private allowances. If, however, as stated by one of the deponents in 1446, each monk in priest's orders should have received £2 13s. 4d. and each deacon £2, the amount would be considerably above £60. For *peculium* see p. 238, note 2.

[2] The abbot's steward was a monk, William Exton. None of the monks at this visitation is mentioned as warden of the manors, and the office was probably filled by a layman. At Westminster one of the obedientiaries was warden of the manors which formed the endowment of Eleanor of Castile's obit, and probably also of the manors belonging to later royal foundations of a similar kind (Pearce, *The Monks of Westminster*, 1916, pp. 15-21).

[3] The grant of the corrody to John Underwode of Deeping is entered without a date in the register of abbots Genge and Depyng (B.M. Add. MS. 25288), fo. 142. He had a weekly allowance of eight convent loaves and eight gallons of the best ale from the abbot's pantry and cellar, to be fetched twice a week, and twopence daily for his kitchen to be paid at the end of each week by the receiver. He had further one furred robe (*i.e.* suit), such as the abbot's yeomen wore, when the abbot gave full livery, a robe without fur when he gave summer livery, and a cloth robe of the .colour of the suit for Isabel his wife; two stone of cheese, two dozen Paris candles, two skeps of oatmeal, two skeps of salt; four cart-loads of fuel of ' baluwoode ' (*i.e.* logs; for ' ballow '= a cudgel, cf. Shakespeare, *King Lear* II, vi, 247), at Midsummer, to be carried at the abbot's expense; and a tenement with a stall in the market stead, formerly held by Richard Bracier without lands and tenements. He was excused summons to the market court at Peterborough and the hundred court at Castor. By the usual arrangement half the corrody was to be

Also he says that it was ordained [by] himself with the advice of the elder [monks] that everyone shall yearly make a remittance from his private allowance for three years, to the amount of fifty pounds [in all],[1] towards the relief of the lesser offices on the side of the convent, which because of the scantiness of the goods pertaining to them have not been sufficient for the burdens incumbent upon them. He prays that my lord will commend them [herein] and approve of this that they have done.

Also he says that the manors and tenements which belong to the abbot's side are going to great and almost [irrep]arable ruin unless heed be taken speedily to their repair, nor are there stocks of goods kept in the same manors. Prayer is made that the steward or the warden of the manors[2] may take better order for their repair.

Also he says that the abbot in his time has sold divers corrodies, one to wit to one Underwode, a clothier, [from] whom he had a hundred pounds,[3] and [he has had] sixty pounds for wood sold at Eastwood[4] and elsewhere and a hundred marks from the brother of Thomas Perpount,[5] and he sold another corrody to Thomas Mortymer, receiving from him three hundred pounds, the which corrody is worth yearly twenty pounds a year;[6] and it is not known after what manner the monies received are spent. Prayer is therefore made that the abbot will render a reckoning concerning these things.

Also let it be required that the profitless expenses that are caused on the abbot's side be altogether brought to an end, and that no secular person [shall have] any horses that are fed at the costs of the house, even as the abbot's brother now has two, unless he be one that has a king's corrody[7] [or] Castell[8] or another who by chance shall hold his office.

Also he says that the abbot caused a windmill for corn and for making oil out of rape-seed to be built to no profit. Prayer is made that the abbot may refrain from such and other senseless expenses, seeing that in no wise [is] profit [expected] to come to the monastery; for he

---

continued to his wife at his death. The register contains several examples of such grants, with interesting varieties of detail. In view of the two weekly visits arranged for the conveyance of victuals from the monastery, it may be noted that these were probably on Saturday and Wednesday, which, according to a grant made on 5 May, 1414, to Robert Bulwer (*ibid.* fo. 60), were the two days ' portacioni noue ceruisie consuetis.'

[4] Three miles N.NE. of Peterborough, between Dogsthorpe and Eye.

[5] I assume that *Thome* is the right extension of *Thom'*, although on fo. 4 it is written in full as *Thoma*. There are obvious reasons against supposing that ' brother Thomas Perpount,' presumably a man in religion, paid this large sum for a corrody.

[6] *I.e.* the corrody was granted for life at fifteen years' purchase. The grants contain no statement of the sums paid for them.

[7] *I.e.* a person to whom a corrody was granted at the special request of the king, who had this right in monasteries of which he was patron.

[8] Apparently one of the lay officials attached to the monastery. After the resignation of abbot Depyng he went with brother William Exton and others to Warwick to obtain the king's *congé d'élire* and subsequently was sent to the clerk of the privy seal and the chancellor for writs connected with the same business (Peterborough Reg. Assheton, fo. 4).

terras cum rapis que multum fertiles erant, id . . . . . . et hoc vtilius fuisset monasterio.[1]

Item petitur quod ille xl li. quas abbas accomodauit fratri suo Ricardo Gyldhale restituantur receptori abbatis pro releuamine officii sui.

[Fo. 2.] Frater Willelmus Extone, senescallus ex parte abbatis, hortatus dicit cum priore secundum sceduliam[2] ministrat[am].

(Contra abbatem.) Item dicit quod dominus Ricardus Flemmyng, nuper Lincolniensis episcopus, commisit nunc priori[3] omnem administracionem partis abbatis, et tunc prosperabatur illa pars; et postquam dimisit illud regrimen,[4] retrocessit in tantum quod illa pars iam indebitatur in ccc marcis.

(. . . priorem . . . scedula.) Item dicit quod de pecuniis receptis per abbatem pro corrodiis venditis Vnderwode et Mortymere et alivnde ad magnas summas consumuntur per abbatem, et nescitur quo modo: creditur per fratrem suum.

([Contra] fratrem abbatis.) Item dicit quod monasterium multum oneratur per Ricardum fratrem abbatis; et refert se vlterius ad dictam scedulam ministratam per priorem.

(Contra abbatem.) Item dicit quod abbas est nimis facilis[5] in concedendo licencias iuuenibus monachis visitandi partes exteras, ad magnos sumptus et scandalum monasterii.[6]

(Contra sacristam.) [7]Frater Willelmus Stamford dicit quod frater Johannes Bartone, sacrista, inutilis est in officio illo, nam maneria et tenementa pertinencia officio suo minantur ruinam et ad terram quasi collabuntur: ideo officium non prosperatur sub regimine suo.

Item dicit quod non venit ad chorum ad diuina celebranda, vix ad vesperas; et cum sit stagiarius, non conuenit sibi occupare officium illud.

Idem spaciatur et vagatur in campis cum solo puero diebus dominicis et aliis festiuis tempore diuinorum, ex quo scandalum generatur monasterio.

[8](Contra abbatem.) Item petit quod decetero non vendantur vel concedantur aliqua corrodia vel liberaciones sine licencia episcopi, sicut iam nuper concessum erat vnum Thome Mortymere, pro quo recepte erant cccc li.; et conuentus nescit qualiter expenduntur.

Item dicit quod abbas[9] multum regitur per senescallum et alios officiarios ex parte sua, quod non multum cedit monasterio in commodum.

---

[1] Much of this passage is illegible. It is followed by . . . . *ministrat scedulam* cancelled, apparently referring to the prior's written schedule of *detecta*, which will be found later on.

[2] *Sic*: for *scedulam*.

[3] Altered from *priorem*.

[4] *Sic*: for *regimen*.

[5] *liberal* cancelled.

[6] *Frater Thomas Depyng receptor ex parte abbatis* (separate line) cancelled.

[7] This and the next two entries are bracketed together, as referring to the sacrist.

[8] This and the next entry are bracketed under the same marginal reference.

[9] *per* cancelled.

[1] See *Visitations* I, 119, 120, for the summons, made in or about 1430, to Richard Gildhalle of Peterborough in respect of his claim to the mastership of the hospitals of St. Thomas the martyr and St. Giles at Stamford. This was no doubt the same

has caused several plots of land that were very fertile to be sown with rape-seed, ... , and this would have been of more advantage to the monastery.

Also prayer is made that the forty pounds which the abbot lent to his brother Richard Gyldhale[1] may be restored to the abbot's receiver for the relief of his office.

Brother William Extone, steward on behalf of the abbot, being exhorted, says as does the prior according to the schedule furnished by him.

Also he says that the lord Richard Flemmyng, of late bishop of Lincoln, committed all the administration of the abbot's side to him who is now prior,[2] and then that side fared well; and after that he gave up that governance, it went so far backward that now that side is three hundred marks in debt.

([See] the prior [as in his] schedule.) Also he says that of the monies which were received by the abbot for the corrodies sold to Underwode and Mortymere and from other sources for large sums, they are consumed by the abbot and it is not known how: it is believed to be by means of his brother.

([Against] the abbot's brother.) Also he says that the monastery is sorely burthened by Richard, the abbot's brother; and he refers himself further to the said schedule which was furnished by the prior.

(Against the abbot.) Also he says that the abbot is too easy in the matter of granting leave to the young monks for visiting places outside the house, to the great cost and scandal of the monastery.

(Against the sacrist.) Brother William Stamford says that brother John Bartone, the sacrist, is of no profit in that office, for the manors and tenements that belong to his office are threatening ruin and are almost falling to the ground: therefore the office fares not well under his governance.

Also he says that he does not come to quire for the celebration of divine service [and] hardly to vespers; and, since he is a stagiary, it is not seemly that he should hold that office.[3]

He also walks and roams in the fields with a boy alone on Sundays and other feast-days in time of divine service, whereby scandal is bred to the monastery.

(Against the abbot.) Also he prays that from henceforth no corrodies or liveries may be sold or granted without the bishop's leave, even as now of late there was one granted to Thomas Mortymere, for the which four hundred pounds[4] were taken; and the convent knows not after what manner they are spent.

Also he says that the abbot is greatly governed by the steward and the other officers of his side, which goes not greatly to the advantage of the monastery.

---

man. Among the chambers in the monastery granted to John Delabere in 1454 (p. 288, note 3) was one which bore the name of ' Gyldalles chamber.'

  [2] There is no other record of this. Flemyng was at Peterborough on 27 Sept., 1420 (*Visitations* I, xx), and probably visited it during his primary visitation of the archdeaconry of Northampton, between 22 and 27 Oct., 1421 (*ibid.* xxi).

  [3] See p. 273, note 1. Cf. the evidence of the almoner of Croyland, *Visitations* II, 56.

  [4] The sum has been stated previously as £300.

(Contra Hunte et Drake.) Item dicit se audisse receptorem ex parte abbatis dicere quod citra festum Magdalene vltimum expendite sunt in familia abbatis sex pipe vini, et dicit hoc esse in defectu Johannis Hunt et Johannis Drake, qui consumunt huiusmodi vina per vtres, et aliunde, et quod nunquam prosperabitur pars abbatis quam diu illi duo steterint prout iam stant.

Frater Johannes Jakesley, supprior: omnia bene.

(Contra vigilias et potaciones.) Frater Johannes Burgh, custos de Oxeney, adiuratus per dominum, etc., dicit de vigiliis et potacionibus vt supra cum priore.

Item petit vt abbas ministret monachis apud Oxney quolibet quarterio anni iij modios salis.

(Contra camerarium.) Item dicit quod camerarius non est vtilis in officio suo, ministrando femeralia et alia similia monachis.

Frater Ricardus Stamford, *camerarius*, dicit quod, quid per senium abbatis et infirmitates eius et prioris et simplicitatem supprioris, quasi perit religio; et dicit quod temporalia non diriguntur vt ad vtilitatem monasterii: ideo petit vt dominus [requirat] compotos singularium officiorum.[1]

(Contra sacristam.) Item dicit quod sacrista non est vtilis in officio suo vt supra: concordat cum Willelmo Stamford.

(Contra suppriorem.) Item dicit quod *supprior*,[2] dudum *cellerarius*[3] ex parte conuentus, dimisit officium illud multum indebitatum.

(Contra abbatem.) Item dicit de facilitate abbatis in concedendo licenciam monachis exeundi, etc. vt supra.

(Contra abbatem.) Item dicit quod plures redditus assise ad valorem xl li., etc., vltra, *remanent non leuati*[4] *et* non est[5] qui petat; et si quis petat discit v[anum].[6]

(Contra abbatem.) Frater Johannes Bartone, sacrista, adiuratus dicit de diuino obsequio non debite obseruato, et quod temporalia non dirig[untur] ad vtilitatem monasterii; et petit quod non artetur ad matutinas de nocte[7] quousque conualescat de infirm[itatibus] quas patitur in capite et oculis.

(Contra abbatem.) Frater Thomas Depyng, doctor in theologia, *elemosinarius*, adiuratus, etc., dicit quod propter facilem licenciam concessam monachis de exeundo, et eo quod abbas vocat aliquociens ad mensam suam tales qui interessent altis missis, perpauci . . . .[8] choro.

(Contra magistrum operum et omnes.) Item dicit quod scandalum generatur per frequentes communicaciones monachorum cum mulieribus,

---

[1] *Contra non computantes* is written in the margin against the last part of this deposition.
[2] Interlined above *prior* cancelled.
[3] Interlined above *thes[aurarius]* cancelled.
[4] Altered from *leuata*.
[5] *quod* cancelled.
[6] The last word has been torn away: *discit* is written very indistinctly, like *discid*.
[7] *propter* cancelled.
[8] The missing words have utterly disappeared.

[1] *I.e.* since 22 July.
[2] Sc. *de veritate dicenda*.

(Against Hunt and Drake.) Also he says that he heard the receiver on behalf of the abbot say that since the feast of [St. Mary] Magdalene last[1] there were six pipes of wine consumed in the abbot's household, and he says that this is in the default of John Hunte and John Drake, who make away with such wine by skins-full, and for other reasons, and that the abbot's side will never do well so long as they two shall abide even as they are now.

Brother John Jakesley, the subprior: all things are well.

(Against watchings and drinkings.) Brother John Burgh, the warden of Oxney, being adjured by my lord, etc.,[2] says as above, in agreement with the prior, concerning watchings and drinkings.

Also he prays that the abbot may furnish the monks at Oxney with three measures of salt every quarter of a year.

(Against the chamberlain.) Also he says that the chamberlain is of no profit in his office, as regards furnishing drawers[3] and other like things to the monks.

Brother Richard Stamford, the chamberlain, says that, what for the abbot's old age and his infirmities and those of the prior and the subprior's simpleness, religious discipline is well-nigh dead; and he says that their temporal affairs are not guided to further the profit of the monastery: therefore he prays that my lord [demand] the accounts of the several offices.

(Against the sacrist.) Also he says as above that the sacrist is of no profit in his office: he agrees with William Stamford.

(Against the subprior.) Also he says that the subprior, who was sometime the cellarer on behalf of the convent, left that office much in debt.

(Against the abbot.) Also he says as above concerning the abbot's easiness in granting leave to the monks to go out, etc.

(Against the abbot.) Also he says that many rents of assize to the value of more than forty pounds, etc., remain unlevied, and there is no one to demand them; and, if any one should ask them, he learns [that it is useless].

(Against the abbot.) Brother John Bartone, the sacrist, says upon adjuration concerning divine worship, that it is not duly kept, and that their temporal affairs are not guided to the advantage of the monastery; and he prays that he be not compelled to [go to] matins of a night, until he shall recover of the ailments which he suffers in his head and eyes.

(Against the abbot.) Brother Thomas Depyng, doctor in theology, the almoner, being adjured, etc., says that by reason of the easy leave that is granted to the monks for going out, and because the abbot sometimes invites to his table such as should be present at the high masses,[4] very few [are sometimes present in] quire.

(Against the master of the works and all.) Also he says that scandal is bred by the often conversation of the monks with women, especially

---

[3] *Consuetudinarium S. Aug. Cantuar.* (Henry Bradshaw Soc.) i, 197, prescribes that the monks should have vests and drawers supplied as often as they had need of them. The Rule of St. Benedict, cap. lv, contemplates the use of drawers only on a journey: ' femoralia hi qui in via diriguntur de vestiario accipiant. Qui revertentes lota ibi restituant.'

[4] The principle of rotation of attendance in quire seems to be implied here.

presertim vxore . . . . . ,[1] et per accessum similium mulierum ad[2] officium monachi magistri operum.

(Contra Gyldhale.) Item dicit quod frater abbatis fuit in causa quod prior dimisit regimen partis abbatis, et quod post dimissionem suam [non] prosperabatur pars illa; nam idem frater habet ij equos ad expensas domus in [3] et feno et auenis, et quatuor in fer[rura].

(Contra omnes.) Item fiat orimacio[4] quod monachi non commedant aut bibant in villa Burgi eciam tempore completo[rii].

[Fo. 2*d*.] Frater Thomas Depyng junior, receptor ex parte abbatis, dicit quod recepta sua de vltimo anno extendit se ad dcc li.

Item dicit quod si foret vnus abbas qui posset intendere regimini monasterii, melius foret pro commodo domus quam nunc est.

Item dicit quod familia abbatis est nimis excessiua et onerosa.

Item dicit quod commoda domus subtrahuntur, vt in reddituum releuiis, et non est qui exigit; et quidam balliui non computarunt hiis tribus annis, nec est qui eos compellat.

Item dicit quod ignorat quid factum fuit de illis ccc libris receptis pro corrodio vendito Thome Mortimere; et omni anno valet xx li.

(Contra omnes.) Frater Walterus Fressheney, cellerarius ex parte conuentus, adiuratus, etc., petit quod fiat ordinacio quod monachi non bibant nec comedant in villa de Burgo.

(Contra abbatem.) Item dicit quod multociens misse perpauce se[5] celebrantur in monasterio.

Item dicit quod credit quod abbas habet[6] modicum instaurum in maneriis suis et tamen[7] nisi in vno, et tamen illa pars, videlicet abbatis, est valde tenuis.

Quibus examinatis et presentibus abbate, priore et cellerario ac Johanne Leek et me Colstone, dominus continuauit visitacionem suam vsque in diem tunc crastinum, videlicet xj diem dicti mensis Decembris inter horas vij et octavam in mane.

[Fo. 3.] Ricardus Oxforde, monachus professus celle de Oxney, petit vt[8] dominus mutet matutinas ad [gallo]cinium[9] celebratas circiter horam quartam *in mane* fore celebrandas.

(Contra priorem.) Item dicit quod solent habere commune depositum ad ponendum thesaurum superueniens de certis officiis, quod quidem solebat esse sub tribus clauibus: modo existit tantum in custodia prioris,

---

[1] The name has disappeared.
[2] *hoc* cancelled.
[3] *ferrura* cancelled: *iiij* interlined and cancelled.
[4] *Sic*: for *ordinacio*.
[5] *Sic*: left uncancelled.
[6] *non* cancelled.
[7] *Sic*: the words *et tamen* should have been cancelled.
[8] Interlined above *quod* cancelled.
[9] This appears to be the word: the first part has disappeared.

[1] Brother Walter ' Frysney ' was one of the proctors sent by the convent to the general chapter of the province at Northampton in July, 1444 (Reg. Assheton, ff. 12 *d*., 13). He must therefore have been a member of the convent at the time of the visitation in 1442, when his name is not mentoned.
[2] This refers to Oxney only. Cf. the petition of the secular canons of Ottery St. Mary to Martin v in 1422-3, representing the difficulty of observing the statutory hours for matins, which from Holy Cross day to Maundy Thursday were sung at midnight, and from Easter Monday to Holy Cross day about sunrise. The canons,

with the wife of . . . . . , and by the recourse of like women to the office of the monk who is the master of the works.

(Against Gyldhale.) Also he says that the abbot's brother had to do with the reason that the prior gave up the governance of the abbot's side, and that that side, after he gave it up, fared not well; for the same brother keeps two horses at the cost of the house both in hay and oats, and four in shoeing.

(Against all.) Also let an ordinance be made that the monks shall not eat or drink in the town of Peterborough, especially at the time of compline.

Brother Thomas Depyng the younger, the receiver on behalf of the abbot, says that his receipt for the last year amounts to seven hundred pounds.

Also he says that if there were an abbot who could pay heed to the government of the monastery, it would be better for the profit of the house than it is now.

Also he says that the abbot's household is too great in numbers and burthensome.

Also he says that the profits of the house are taken away, as in respect of the levying of rents, and there is no-one who demands them; and certain bailiffs have not given an account these three years, nor is there any one to constrain them.

Also he says that he does not know what has been done with the three hundred pounds received for the corrody sold to Thomas Mortimere; and it is worth twenty pounds every year.

(Against all.) Brother Walter Fressheney,[1] the cellarer on behalf of the convent, being adjured, etc., prays that an ordinance be made that the monks drink not nor eat in the town of Peterborough.

(Against the abbot.) Also he says that oftentimes very few masses are celebrated in the monastery.

Also he says that he believes that the abbot has a small store in his manors, save in one only, and nevertheless that side, to wit the abbot's, is very slenderly endowed.

Now, when these had been examined, the abbot, prior and cellarer and John Leek and I Colstone being present, my lord adjourned his visitation until the morrow of that day, to wit, until the eleventh day of the said month of December between the hours of seven and eight in the morning.

Richard Oxforde, monk professed of the cell of Oxney, prays that my lord change matins, which are celebrated at [cock-]crow, that they may be celebrated about four o'clock in the morning.[2]

(Against the prior.) Also he says that they are wont to have a common place of deposit for putting by the treasure which comes as a surplus from certain offices, the which was accustomed to be under three keys: now it is in the keeping of the prior only, who sometimes

---

owing to the smallness of their salaries, refused to attend midnight matins, and asked that they should be allowed to change them to a more convenient hour   They obtained a dispensation empowering them to have matins at 4 a.m. during the winter half of the year (*Cal. Papal Letters* vii, 277; 24 March, 1422-3).   Their plea that the later hour would be more convenient for parishioners would not be applicable to Peterborough.

qui *quandoque* expendit thesaurum huiusmodi [ad] libitum suum conuentu inconsulto.

(Contra abbatem.) Dominus Willelmus Markham, monachus professus celle Oxney predicte,[1] dicit quod officiarii ex parte abbatis onerantur[2] ultra recepta sua in compotis suis, et sic multociens arreragia remanent incollecta ; et, vt sibi videtur, expediens esset vt aliquis secularis ad arreragia huiusmodi leuanda deputetur pro stipendio competenti ; nam dicit quod post exoneracionem officiariorum[3] onus leuandi huiusmodi arreragia committitur suis successoribus, qui successores cum pluribus equis arreragiis leuandis equitantur *in detrimentum monasterii*, vbi vnus secularis pro competenti stipendio potuit huiusmodi arreragia[4] omnium officiorum[5] leuare.

Petit releuari in vigiliis in minucionibus suis.

(Contra abbatem.) Item dicit quod congrue sibi misericordie ministratur[6] in ferculis in refectorio.

(Contra abbatem.) Quantum ad depositum ponit vt prius, et addit quod prior thesaurum huiusmodi depositum[7] conuertit ad ea que n[on] proficiunt monasterio et que facienda sunt magis necessaria penitus omittit, conuentu in factis suis inconsulto.

(Contra abbatem.) Frater Willelmus Beupho, monachus professus in ordine sacerdotali constitutus, *tercius supprior*, dicit quod abbas nimis petentibus *concedit* licenciam exeundi chorum, cuius rei pretextu diuinus cultus in choro diminuitur in tantum quod [rema]nent ex vtraque parte chori tres vel quatuor in magnum scandalum monasterii.

(Contra abbatem.) Item petit quod dominus auferatur[8] ab abbate potestatem regiminis tam temporalium quam spiritualium, nam sue vires minime sufficiunt ad regendum monasterium ; et quod alii deputentur *qui* plenam potestatem *abbacialem* regendi habeant.

(Contra abbatem.) Frater Johannes Burnham, monachus professus in ordine sacerdotali constitutus, *cellerarius ex parte abbatis*, petit vt prior habeat [regimen] tam *spiritualium* quam temporalium, abbate nimia senectute confracto, reseruata abbati dignitate abbatis.

Frater Thomas Newerke, monachus, nichil deponit, nam iuuenis est.

(Contra abbatem.) Frater Johannes Brewster, monachus, petit vt fiat deputacio tam temporalium quam spiritualium priori.

(Contra abbatem.) Frater Petrus Lynne, monachus, etc., dicit quod diuinus cultus congrue non obseruatur propter paucitatem [monac]ho[rum] in choro, et quod[9]

(Contra suppriorem.) Item dicit quod[10] monasterium indebitatur per suppriorem de tempore quando officium cellerarii [occupauit in]

---

[1] *petit* cancelled.
[2] *in* cancelled.
[3] Altered from *officiorum*.
[4] *leuare* cancelled.
[5] Altered from *officiarum*.
[6] *Sic*: for [*non*] *ministrantur*.
[7] *ad* cancelled.
[8] *Sic*: for *auferat*.
[9] The deposition is not finished.
[10] *Supprior* cancelled.

spends such treasure as he pleases, without the advice of the convent.

(Against the abbot.) Dan William Markham, monk professed of the cell of Oxney aforesaid, says that the officers on the abbot's side are charged in their accounts for more than their receipts, and so oftentimes their arrears remain uncollected; and, as it seems to him, it would be expedient that some secular person should be appointed to levy such arrears for a sufficient salary; for he says that after the discharge of the officers the task of raising such arrears is entrusted to their successors, the which successors ride about to raise the arrears with several horses to the harm of the monastery, whereas one secular person could levy such the arrears of all the offices for a sufficient salary.

He prays that they may be eased as regards vigils during their seynies.[1]

(Against the abbot.) Also he says that fitting mercies[2] are [not] furnished them in the matter of courses in the frater.[3]

(Against the abbot.) As concerns their deposit he deposes as before, and adds that the prior applies such treasure that is laid up to ends which are of no profit to the monastery and leaves out altogether the things that are more needful to be done, without asking advice of the convent in what he does.

(Against the abbot.) Brother William Beupho, monk professed, in priest's orders, the third subprior,[4] says that the abbot gives overmuch leave for going out of quire to them that ask him, by occasion of the which thing divine worship in quire is scanted in so much that there [remain] on either side of the quire [only] three or four [monks], to the great scandal of the monastery.

(Against the abbot.) Also he prays that my lord will take from the abbot his power of governance over both temporal and spiritual matters, for his strength does not avail to rule the monastery; and that others be put in charge who shall have the full power of the abbot to govern.

(Against the abbot.) Brother John Burnham, monk professed, in priest's orders, the cellarer on behalf of the abbot, prays that the prior may have the governance both of spiritual and temporal affairs, since the abbot is sore stricken in years, with reservation to the abbot of the dignity of abbot.

Brother Thomas Newerke, monk, makes no deposition, for he is a youth.

(Against the abbot.) Brother John Brewster, monk, prays that the charge both of temporal and spiritual affairs may be given to the prior.

(Against the abbot.) Brother Peter Lynne, monk, etc., says that divine worship is not fittingly observed because of the fewness of the monks in quire, and that . . . . .

(Against the subprior.) Also he says that the monastery is about sixty pounds in debt by reason of the subprior, from the time when he

---

[1] A repetition of Oxforde's request for relaxation of the hour of matins.

[2] See note on *misericordia*, *Visitations* I, 238. Here the *misericordia* is a pittance or extra allowance of food, furnished on certain days in the frater.

[3] Although there is no negative in the original, the context evidently requires one.

[4] *Sic*: third prior is meant.

circiter lx li. racione officii *illius,* nec est pacificus cum fratribus suis.

(Contra presidentem.) Frater Ricardus Stanerne, monachus, dicit quod diuinum officium ob paucitatem monachorum non obse[ruatur], et quod vix in alta missa sunt v vel vj monachi.

(Contra tercium suppriorem.) Item dicit quod expediens esset si frater Willelmus Beupho, tercius supprior, amoueatur ab officio suo omnino[1] et non[2]

[Fo. 3 *d.*] Frater Radulphus Brune dicit omnia bene.

(Contra suppriorem.) Frater Willelmus Gedney, monachus, dicit quod frater Ricardus[3] Jakesley, nuper cellerarius conuentus, nunc supprior, onerauit officium cellerarii *in voluptuosis expensis* circiter xx li. et vltra, et nesciunt inde computare.

([Contra] abbatem.) Item dicit quod duo, videlicet Johannes Drake et Johannes consanguineus abbatis, conuertunt abbatem iuxta votum suum, itaque nullus monachus audet eos offendere propter obloquium sinistrum quod ab eis perpetratur penes bonos.

Item dicti duo deuastunt[4] bona dicti abbatis *penes*[5] seculares.

([Contra] omnes.) Frater Willelmus Gretforthe, monachus in ordine diaconatus, dicit quod diuinum officium non obseruatur propter paucitatem monachorum.

Item dicit quod frater Johannes Bartone, sacrista, gaudebat officio illo per xx annos et vltra, et in eius defectu tenementa eidem officio incumbencia non modicam paciuntur ruinam.

([Stath]erne.) Item dicit quod frater Ricardus Statherne patitur morbum caducum et multociens in nocte surgit in dormitorio, requiem monachorum quam maxime perturbando.

([Contra tercium su]ppriorem.) Item dicit quod frater Willelmus, tercius supprior, vtitur obloquio, famam monachorum denigrando.

Frater Henricus[6] Burugh dicit omnia bene.

(Oxney.) Frater Willelmus Walmesforthe petit quod dominus prouideat de relaxacione vigilie ad matutinas *pro* minutis remissis celle Oxney, vt sic dignetur prouidere vt huiusmodi minuti sic apud Oxney missi valeant conuolare ad requiem ad horam octauam et resurgere ad horam quartam, vt munitatis[7] gracia in re.[8]

Item dicit quod tenementa ex parte abbatis in defectu officiorum[9] ruinam irrecuperabilem paciuntur.

Item dicit quod officiarii huiusmodi[10] opinantur quod loca edificata ad pasturam et ruinam conuersa magis in commodum conuertuntur quam si repararentur aut reedificarentur.

---

[1] This is apparently the word, but there is very little left of it.
[2] The deposition is not concluded.
[3] *Sic*: for *Johannes.*
[4] *Sic*: for *deuastant.*
[5] Interlined above *circa* cancelled.
[6] *Burgh* cancelled.
[7] *Sic*: *immunitatis* appears to be meant.
[8] Possibly *re* is an abbreviation for *recedendo,* i.e. ' in their absence from the monastery.' Cf. the rolls of *Re* and *Ve,* i.e. *Recedendi* and *Veniendi,* at Lincoln, on which the attendance of residentiaries in quire was noted.
[9] *Sic*: for *officiariorum.*
[10] *iuniorum* cancelled.

held the office of cellarer, on account of that office, and he is not peaceable with his brethren.

(Against the president.)[1] Brother Richard Stanerne,[2] monk, says that the divine office is not observed by reason of the fewness of the monks, and that at high mass there are hardly five or six monks.

(Against the third subprior.) Also he says that it would be expedient that brother William Beupho, the third subprior, be utterly removed from his office, and not . . . .

Brother Ralph Brune says all things are well.

(Against the subprior.) Brother William Gedney, monk, says that brother Richard[3] Jakesley, of late the cellarer of the convent, now the subprior, burthened the cellarer's office with about twenty pounds and more in wanton expenses, and they know not how to make account thereof.

([Against] the abbot.) Also he says that two men, to wit John Drake and John the abbot's kinsman,[4] do turn the abbot about at their liking, and so no monk dares to offend them on account of the malicious abuse which is wrought by them among honest folk.

Also the said two do waste the said abbot's goods among secular folk.

([Against] all.) Brother William Gretforthe, monk in deacon's orders, says that the divine office is not observed on account of the fewness of the monks.

Also he says that brother John Bartone, the sacrist, has enjoyed that office for twenty years and more, and in his default the tenements which are the charge of the same office suffer no small decay.

(Statherne.) Also he says that brother Richard Statherne suffers from the falling sickness and rises up in the dorter oftentimes in the night, troubling the monks' rest exceedingly.

(Against [the third] subprior.) Also he says that brother William, the third subprior, uses evil speech, blackening the fame of the monks.

Brother Henry Burugh says all things are well.

(Oxney.) Brother William Walmesforthe prays that my lord will make provision for the remission of waking for matins on behalf of them that are sent in their seynies to the cell of Oxney, that he will so deign to make provision that such in their seynies that are so sent to Oxney may be able to resort together to their rest at eight o'clock and rise again at four o'clock, to wit, by his gracious grant of immunity in the matter.

Also he says that the tenements on the abbot's side suffer irreparable ruin in the default of the office[r]s.

Also he says that such officers suppose that sites which were built upon are turned to greater advantage, when they are converted into pasture-land and ruin, than were they to be repaired or built upon anew.

---

[1] The officer responsible for discipline in cloister, presumably one of the four priors.

[2] *Rectius* Statherne: see p. 270, note 2.

[3] *Rectius* John.

[4] Possibly John Hunte, mentioned above.

Frater Johannes More, monachus, dicit quod quidam seniores monachi a diuinis seruiciis se absentant in simile exemplum[1] monachorum[2] nouiciorum.

Frater Ricardus Herltone iunior, monachus, etc., subsacrista, dicit quod vestimenta sua *reuestiario pertinencia* accomodantur magnatibus, *videlicet domino de la Zouche*, et aliis viris in magnum scandalum monasterii.

[Fo. 4 *d*.] [3]Primo quod numerus fratrum in[4] officio diuino in choro est frequenter nimis diminutus, quia, cum sint xliiij monachi in congregacione, vix erunt aliquando x vel xij in choro.[5]

Item cum diuturne siue excessiue vigilie et potaciones in noctubus multum indisponant confratres ad opus diuinum et precipue ad celebracionem missarum, petitur quod tam in monasterio quam apud Oxeneye non vigiletur vltra octauam horam sub pena.

(Extra monasterium.) Item quod abbas est nimis facilis ad concedendum fratribus licencias equitandi in patriam *et trahendi moram*, quia ex talibus licenciis oriuntur quandoque dissoluciones et scandala: ideo petitur reformacio.

(Confirmetur per dominum.) Item *petitur* quod vna sit mensa, *prout iam ordinatum est ex consensu fratrum*, confratrum comedencium extra refectorium tam diebus carnium quam piscium, etc.

Item petitur quod contribucio 1 li. concessa per conuentum ad releuandum diuersa officia ex parte conuentus cedat ad dictum vsum auctoritate et approbacione domini episcopi, etc.

Item petitur quod dominus abbas sit contentus pro vestitu suo et aliis sibi necessariis summa quam percipit de diuersis officiariis conuentus et de redditu pertinente ad cameram suam, cum denariis quos percipit de balliuis libertatis,[6] et non oneret receptorem suum cum talibus expensis, quia expense receptoris excedunt annuatim *receptum*[7] eiusdem ad summam c li.

Item petitur quod nullus secularis ex parte abbatis teneat aliquem vel aliquos equos ad custus ipsius abbatis, nisi tantum corrodiarius domini regis et Willelmus Castel vel alius ocupans officium eiusdem.

---

[1] *iuniorum* cancelled again.
[2] *in* cancelled in interlined passage.
[3] Fo. 4 is a narrow sheet of paper inserted so that the recto and verso have changed places.
[4] *ad seruiend* cancelled.
[5] Each paragraph of the schedule, except the last two, where the marks can no longer be made out, has a mark against it in the margin. The first five and the eighth to tenth paragraphs are marked with crosses: the sixth has a small circle with a horizontal stroke on one side, the seventh a small circle with a vertical downward stroke; the eleventh a small circle only.
[6] *quia* expunged and cancelled.
[7] Interlined above *expen* expunged and cancelled.

[1] This series of depositions is followed by a summary list of the principal *detecta* and the petitions accompanying them. It is in a somewhat larger handwriting than the rest, and, as the petition relating to Maxey church is in the first person, it may have been drawn up by the prior, and is probably the schedule referred to in the minutes and by the precentor in his deposition before Depyng. At this point the minutes of the examination personally conducted by the bishop close, and the remainder of the document is occupied with those of the inquiry separately conducted by Depyng.

Brother John More, monk, says that certain elder monks withhold their presence from divine service, to the like example of the monks who are novices.

Brother Richard Herltone the younger, monk, etc., the subsacrist, says that their vestments which belong to the revestry are lent to great folk, to wit, to the lord la Zouche, and to other men to the great scandal of the monastery.[1]

In the first place, that the number of the brethren at the divine office in quire is oftentimes sorely scanted, for, albeit there are forty-four monks in their congregation, there shall sometimes be hardly ten or twelve in quire.[2]

Also seeing that long or overmuch watching and drinking at night time do much unfit the brethren for God's work[3] and especially for the celebration of masses, prayer is made that, both in the monastery and at Oxney, watch may not be kept beyond eight o'clock, under penalty.[4]

(Without the monastery.) Also that the abbot is too easy in granting the brethren leave to ride into the country round and prolong their stay, for out of such licences there sometimes arise disorders and scandals: therefore prayer is made for reform.[5]

(Let it be confirmed by my lord.) Also prayer is made that, even as it is now ordained with the consent of the brethren, there may be one board for the brethren who take their food outside the frater, on days both of flesh and fish, etc.[6]

Also prayer is made that the contribution of fifty pounds that was granted by the convent for the relief of divers offices on the side of the convent may go to the said use with the authority and approval of the lord bishop, etc.[7]

Also prayer is made that, for his raiment and other things needful for him, the lord abbot may be content with the sum which he receives from divers officers of the convent and with the rent that belongs to his privy purse, together with the monies which he receives from the bailiffs of the liberty, and that he may not charge his receiver with such expenses, inasmuch as the receiver's expenses do yearly surpass his receipts to the amount of a hundred pounds.[8]

Also prayer is made that no secular person of the abbot's side may keep any horse or horses at the costs of the same abbot, save only he that has a corrody from our lord the king and William Castel or any other who holds his office.[9]

----

[2] See the prior's first deposition, Thomas Depyng's first, Beupho's first, Stanerne's second, Lynne's first, Gretforthe's first, Lesyngham's first, Yorke's second, Bernak's first.

[3] The *opus Dei*, St. Benedict's synonym for the divine office: see, e.g., cap. xiii of the Rule.

[4] See the prior's second, John Burgh's first, Fressheney's second, Markham's second and Walmesforthe's first depositions.

[5] See Extone's fifth, Richard Stamford's fourth, Thomas Depyng's first, Beupho's first, Lesyngham's second, and Warmyngtone's depositions.

[6] See the prior's fourth deposition.

[7] See the prior's sixth deposition.

[8] See the prior's third (cf. his fifth), Thomas Depyng the younger's third, and Fressheney's third depositions.

[9] See the prior's ninth and Thomas Depyng's third depositions.

Item petitur quod xl li. quas abbas accommodauit fratri suo Ricardo Gyldale restituantur et liberentur receptori abbatis ad releuamen officii sui.

Item petitur quod non fiant expense superflue circa molendinum pro oleo faciendo et alia huiusmodi non necessaria.

Item petitur quod senescallus *vel custos maneriorum* abbatis sit[1] sollicitus circa reparacionem maneriorum et tenauntrie ex parte abbatis, quia paciuntur ruinam magnam.

[Fo. 4.] Item petitur quod abbas reddat racionem de[2] c li. quas recepit de Johanne Vnderwode et de lx li. receptis de bosco vendito apud Estwode et alibi, et de c marcis receptis de fratre Thoma[3] Perponte et de ccc li. quas recepit *pro*[4] corrodio vendito Thome Mortymere armigero.

Item cum sit contencio inter elemosinarium Burgi et vicarium de Makeseye pro reparacione cancelli ibidem, humiliter supplicamus dominacioni vestre quatinus visis et auditis euidenciis vtriusque partis contencionem huiusmodi sedare et quod iuris est fieri iudicetis.

Item cum prior claustralis propter invalitudinem corporalem minus sufficiat ad officium suum debite exercendum, petitur quod in fine instantis anni ab officio prioratus excusetur et alter magis ydoneus ordinetur.

[Fo. 5.] Examinacio facta per Depyng.

(Contra presidentem.) Frater Johannes Lesyngham, quartus prior, examinatus dicit quod *multociens* pauci sunt in choro in diuinorum tempore ministrantes.

([Contra a]bbatem.) Item dicit quod quidam monachi per abbatem licenciati aliquando cum eorum parentibus et amicis potaciones et comessaciones in villa frequentant.

([Contra a]bbatem.) Item dicit quod edificacio noui molendini fuit, est et erit sumptuosa et onerosa.

([Contra] abbatem.) Frater Johannes Spaldyng, succentor, examinatus dicit de comessacionibus et potacionibus exteris prout supra deponitur.

(Contra gardianum de Oxney.) Frater Willelmus Moretone examinatus dicit quod ex antiqua monasterii consuetudine gardianus de Oxeney s[olebat] *pro*[5] communis monachorum ibidem existencium *singulis*

---

[1] *magis* expunged and cancelled.
[2] *de* expunged and cancelled.
[3] *Sic*: for *Thome*.
[4] Interlined above *de* expunged and cancelled.
[5] Interlined above *septimanatim pro* cancelled.

[1] See the prior's eleventh, and cf. Extone's and Thomas Depyng's third depositions.
[2] See the prior's tenth and Lesyngham's third depositions.
[3] *I.e.* the tenements in general.
[4] See the prior's seventh and Byseley's deposition.
[5] See the prior's eighth, Extone's third, William Stamford's fourth, and Thomas Depyng the younger's fifth depositions.
[6] Between Peterborough and Market Deeping. The statement of the ordination of the vicarage in *Rot. Hug. Welles* I, 90, II, 192, gives merely the general direction that the vicar shall bear all the ordinary, due and accustomed burthens. Lyndwood, ed. 1679, p. 66 (tit. *de off. vicar*, c. *Quoniam*, ver. *onera ecclesiastica*) discusses at length the question whether the repair of the chancel is an ordinary or extraordinary burthen, inclining to the opinion that it may be classed as ordinary, ' nam

Also prayer is made that the forty pounds which the abbot lent to his brother Richard Gyldale may be restored and paid to the abbot's receiver for the relief of his office.[1]

Also prayer is made that no superfluous costs may be spent on the mill for making oil and other such needless matters.[2]

Also prayer is made that the abbot's steward or the warden of his manors may be instant about the repair of the manors and tenantry[3] on the abbot's side, inasmuch as they suffer sore decay.[4]

Also prayer is made that the abbot may render a reckoning concerning the hundred pounds which he received of John Underwode and concerning the sixty pounds received from the sale of wood at Eastwood and elsewhere, and concerning the hundred marks received of [the] brother [of] Thomas Perponte and concerning the three hundred pounds which he received for the corrody which was sold to Thomas Mortymere, esquire.[5]

Also, seeing that there is a dispute between the almoner of Peterborough and the vicar of Maxey[6] as concerns the repair of the chancel in that place, we humbly beseech your lordship that, when you have seen and heard the evidence on both sides, you will [deign] to settle such dispute and adjudge what is lawful to be done.

Also, seeing that the prior of cloister,[7] by reason of his bodily ill-health, is but little sufficient for the due exercise of his office, prayer is made that, at the end of the year that now is, he may be excused from the office of his priorship and another fitter person may be appointed.

The examination made by Depyng.

(Against the president.) Brother John Lesyngham, the fourth prior, says upon examination that oftentimes there are few persons ministering in quire in time of divine service.

([Against] the abbot.) Also he says that certain monks with leave of the abbot do sometimes attend drinkings and eatings in the town with their kinsfolk and friends.

([Against] the abbot.) Also he says that the building of the new mill has been, is and will be costly and burthensome.

([Against] the abbot.) Brother John Spaldyng, the subchanter, upon examination, says even as deposition is made above concerning eatings and drinkings without the monastery.

(Against the warden of Oxney.) Brother William Moretone says upon examination that, according to the ancient custom of the monastery, the warden of Oxney [was wont] to render an account and reckoning every week for the commons of the monks who are in that place; the

----

onera ordinaria sunt illa quae habent regularem praestationem.' Thus, while it was customary for the rectors of churches to keep their chancels in repair, with an occasional stipulation that the vicar should contribute a fixed share, the question of responsibility might be raised where there was no definite composition in existence. The present dispute is not mentioned in the depositions.

[7] The subprior seems to be meant, but the complaints against him (see Richard Stamford's first and Lynne's and Meletone's second depositions) do not amount to a statement of his ill-health, although his *simplicitas* doubtless was a manifest sign of his incapacity. The prior at Peterborough had his separate lodging on the site of the present deanery, and was probably seldom in cloister.

septimanis compotum reddere et racionem; quod tamen[1] [in] modernis diebus per gardianum huiusmodi factum non est.

(Contra abbatem.) Frater Thomas Gosberkirke examinatus[2] petit et instanter affectat quod prior totam habeat in spiritu[alibus] disposicionem et regimen, saluis semper abbatis reuerencia et honestate.

Frater Ricardus Depyng examinatus dicit omnia bene esse.[3]

(Contra precentorem.) Frater Johannes Yorke examinatus dicit quod gradalia chori sunt multum in *notacione*[4] discrepa[ncia] ex defectu precentoris, qui quidem corrigere deberet librorum cantalium defectus.

(Contra presidentem.) Item[5] quantum ad paucitatem monachorum in choro famulancium, deponit vt supra.

(Contra abbatem.) Frater Walterus Warmyngtone examinatus dicit quod abbas in licenciarum[6] concessione ad[7] egressus *monachorum* est nimium liberalis: propterea dicit quod salubre foret quod huiusmodi licenciandi pot[estas] priori attribueretur.

(Contra abbatem.) Frater Johannes Bernak, examinatus, de paucitate monachorum in choro deponit vt [supra].

Frater Johannes Wynwyke, refectorarius, dicit omnia bene esse.

(Contra abbatem.) Frater Ricardus Byseley examinatus dicit omnia bene, preterquam de maneriorum reparacione.

(Contra Mortymere.) Frater Thomas Maxey, thesaurarius pro conuentu, examinatus dicit quod vxor et familie[8] [Thome] Mortymere mane et sero ac frequenter ingrediuntur et egrediuntur per monasterii clau[strum].[9]

(Contra Drake.) Item quidam Johannes[10] Drake, camerarius abbatis, magnam facit *et freq*[uentem] vi . . .[11] dicti abbatis.

(Fo. 5d.) [Frater W]illelmus Meletone, subelemosinarius, examinatus dicit quod vt audiuit monasterium est vehementer indebitatum, set in quanto ignorat.

Item dicit quod supprior correcciones fratrum suorum facit nimis rigorose et multum indiscrete, sopita eciam[12] fratrum suorum scelera sepius *quasi*[13] ex odii rancore eis obiciendo et imoderanter iterando.

Frater Augustinus Depyng examinatus deponit omnia bene.

Frater Johannes Lyndefelde, precentor, examinatus deponit secundum quod in quadam scedula per priorem domino exhibita continetur.[14]

Require inincciones factas tempore huius visitacionis in v folio secundi quaterni memorandorum de tempore domini nunc.

---

[1] *mod* cancelled.
[2] *dicit* cancelled.
[3] *Frater Willelmus Beaufo examinatus dicit* (separate line) cancelled.
[4] Interlined above *nota* cancelled.
[5] *q* cancelled.
[6] *monachis* interlined and cancelled.
[7] *extra ex*[*eundi*] cancelled: another word interlined and cancelled, the last letters being apparently altered to *ad*.
[8] *Sic*: for *familia*.
[9] *in nocu* cancelled.
[10] *Da* cancelled.
[11] The rest of the word is torn away.
[12] *et quasi* cancelled.
[13] *quasi* again interlined and cancelled.
[14] There is a marginal note against this paragraph, torn and no longer legible. All that can be made out is . . . *in* . . . *traneis* . . . . *habet* . . . *endam.*

which nevertheless has not been done by such warden in the days that now are.

(Against the abbot.) Brother Thomas Gosberkirke, upon examination, prays and earnestly craves that the prior may have the entire ordering and governance in matters spiritual, saving always the abbot's reverence and honourable estate.

Brother Richard Depyng, upon examination, says that all things are well.

(Against the precentor.) Brother John Yorke says upon examination that the grayles[1] which belong to the quire have many differences in their notation, by default of the precentor, who verily ought to correct the faults of the song-books.

(Against the president.) Also, as concerns the fewness of the monks who do service in quire, he deposes as above.

(Against the abbot.) Brother Walter Warmyngtone says upon examination that the abbot is over bounteous in granting leaves for the monks to go out: he says therefore that it would be healthful that such power of giving leave should be committed to the prior.

(Against the abbot.) Brother John Bernak, upon examination, deposes as above concerning the fewness of the monks in quire.

Brother John Wynwyke, the fraterer, says that all things are well.

Brother Richard Byseley, upon examination, says all things are well, except as regards the repair of the manors.

(Against Mortymere.) Brother Thomas Maxey, the treasurer on behalf of the convent, says upon examination that the wife and household of [Thomas] Mortymere do go in and out, early and late and often, through the cloister of the monastery.

(Against Drake.) Also one John Drake, the abbot's chamberlain, makes great and often . . . . . of the said abbot.

[Brother] William Meletone, the subalmoner, says upon examination that, as he has heard, the monastery is deeply in debt, but to what amount he knows not.

Also he says that the subprior makes correction of his brethren over harshly and very indiscreetly, oftentimes, as it were out of the malice of hatred, laying to their charge and rehearsing beyond measure the ill-doings of his brethren, even when they are things of the past.[2]

Brother Austin Depyng, upon examination, deposes all things to be well.

Brother John Lyndefelde, the precentor, deposes upon examination according to that which is contained in a schedule exhibited to my lord by the prior.

Look for the injunctions made at the time of this visitation on the fifth leaf of the second quire of the *memoranda* of the time of my lord that now is.[3]

---

[1] The *graduale* was the book containing the scriptural passages, *i.e.* introit, gradual, Alleluia, tract, offertory and communion, which were sung at mass. See Wordsworth and Littlehales, *Old Service Books of the English Church*, 1904, pp. 203-6.

[2] This indicates that the subprior's *simplicitas*, coupled with the general complaint of his ill-health in the schedule (see p. 281, note 7), took the form of an enfeebled mind dwelling upon old grudges.

[3] This reference applies to a quire of *memoranda* which no longer exists. The *memoranda* bound up in Reg. xviii do not include the injunctions here mentioned.

LIX.

[Fo. 91.]

VISITACIO MONASTERII BEATI PETRI DE BURGO, ORDINIS SANCTI
BENEDICTI, LINCOLNIENSIS DIOCESIS, FACTA IN DOMO CAPITULARI
IBIDEM ET INCHOATA XXIIJ° DIE MENSIS JUNII, ANNO DOMINI
MCCCCXLIJ°, PER REUERENDUM IN CHRISTO PATREM ET DOMINUM,
DOMINUM WILLELMUM[1] ALNEWYKE, DEI GRACIA LINCOLNIENSEM
EPISCOPUM, SUARUM CONSECRACIONIS XVJ ET TRANSLACIONIS
VJ^{to} ANNO.

In primis, sedente dicto reuerendo patre iudicialiter die, anno et
loco predictis in huiusmodi visitacionis sue[2] negocio inchoando et ex-
pediendo, comparuerunt coram eo abbas et conuentus dicti loci, ad
subeundum visitacionem huiusmodi vt apparuit parati. Et deinde
primo et ante omnia propositum fuit iuxta actus futuri congruenciam
verbum Dei per fratrem Willelmum Burghe, monachum eiusdem monasterii, sequentem hoc thema, ' Vide *ne*[3] lumen quod in te est[4] tenebre
sint.'[5] Quo laudabiliter in latino finito.[6]

Frater Ricardus Astone, abbas, examinatus.[7]

Frater Walterus Wermyngtone, stans apud Oxney, dicit quod abbas
de parco Lude tenetur monasterio de Burgo in annuo redditu ij marcarum annuatim et detinuit per triennium; qui redditus deberet applicari
infirmorum sustentacioni monachorum, et racione detencionis huiusmodi
peius eis seruitur.

Frater Johannes Lynfelde, eciam stans apud Oxney, examinatus
dicit omnia bene, et quod iniuncciones facte per dominum debite
obseruantur.

Frater Johannes Yorke, stans apud Oxney.

---

[1] *Gra* and the first stroke of *y* cancelled.
[2] Altered from *suo*.
[3] Interlined above *vt* cancelled.
[4] *non sint* cancelled.
[5] St. Luke xi, 35.
[6] The paragraph ends abruptly here, with a broad space left for more below.
[7] *Sic.* The abbot's depositions are not copied in.

[1] This monk was not in the monastery in 1437, and appears not to have been
examined on the present occasion.
[2] The temporary rule of prior Harlton as coadjutor to the abbot lasted for less
than nine months. Abbot Depyng resigned in the summer of 1438: the *congé
d'élire* was issued 27 Aug., and assent to the election of Richard Assheton was given
on 24 Sept. The temporalities were restored on 14 Oct. (*Cal. Pat.* 1436-41, pp.
185, 203, 220). An interesting account of the heavy expenses incurred by the
abbot and convent in the transaction of the business necessary for the royal and
episcopal confirmation of the new abbot and his installation is given in the register
of abbots Assheton and Ramsey, now in the library of the dean and chapter of
Peterborough (fo. 4), and has been printed in English by the present editor in *Assoc.
Soc. R. & P.* XXXIV, 275-7. There is no notice of the episcopal confirmation in
Reg. XVIII; but the order of the account in Reg. Assheton shows that it took place
between 24 Sept. and 14 Oct. at Buckden, where Alnwick stayed from about 20
Sept. to 18 Oct. (*Visitations* II, xxxiii). On this occasion the abbot elect stayed for
four nights at Huntingdon; the prior, with brother Thomas Makesey and a notary,

LIX.

The visitation of the monastery of BLESSED PETER OF BURGH, of the order of St. Benet, of the diocese of Lincoln, performed in the chapter-house therein and begun upon the twenty-fourth day of the month of June, in the year of our Lord 1442, by the reverend father in Christ and lord, the lord William Alnewyke, by the grace of God bishop of Lincoln, in the sixteenth year of his consecration and the sixth of his translation.

In the first place, as the said reverend father was sitting in his capacity of judge, on and in the day, year and place aforesaid, in the beginning and dispatch of the business of such his visitation, there appeared before him the abbot and convent of the said place in readiness, as was apparent, to undergo such visitation. And then first and before all else the word of God was set forth as was agreeable to the process about to take place by brother William Burghe[1], monk of the same monastery, after this text, ' See that the light which is in thee be not darkness.' And when this had come to a praiseworthy end in Latin. . . . .

Brother Richard Astone, the abbot,[2] examined.

Brother Walter Wermyngtone, abiding at Oxney, says that the abbot of Louth park is bound to the monastery of Burgh in a yearly rent of two marks a year and has kept it back by the space of three years; the which rent ought to be applied to the maintenance of the monks who are ailing, and by reason of such withholding they have worse service.

Brother John Lynfelde,[3] also abiding at Oxney, upon examination says all things are well, and that the injunctions made by my lord are duly kept.

Brother John Yorke, abiding at Oxney.

---

rode to Buckden to present the decree of election to the bishop, and the prior and John Burgh stayed there overnight, while it was discussed and examined.

Assheton was not in the monastery in 1437, but may have been one of the monks then at Oxford, and William Burghe the other. It seems unlikely that, where there was so wide a choice, he would have been introduced from another house.

Abbot Depyng continued to reside in the monastery after his resignation. In Reg. Assheton, fo. 6, the ordination made for his maintenance is given in a letter, without date, from the abbot and convent to the bishop, who had required them to take order to this effect. His household was to consist of a monk as chaplain, and two serving-men, a yeoman and a groom. He was allowed three white loaves on fast-days, four on others; while his serving-men had four brown loaves every day. The weekly allowance of beer was twenty gallons, with four shillings' worth of meat and fish. In yearly allowances he had: fuel, ten cart-loads; candles and cressets, 13s. 4d.; table-cloths, towels and napkins, 6s. 8d.; two dozen vessels *de plectro* (more probably *electro*). The servants had 30s. and two robes a year. Certain clothes were assigned to the ex-abbot from the chamberlain's office, and he had an additional allowance of 100s. a year in money for other necessary raiment, ' necnon et ad sue grandeue senectutis solacium.'

[3] Precentor in 1437. Apart from the titles of the abbot, prior and fourth prior, and the specification of the monks at Oxney, no offices are mentioned.

Frater Willelmus Walmesforde, stans apud Oxney, petit modificacionem iniunccionis de non bibendo in villa.

Frater Ricardus Harletone, prior, dicit quod omnia bene.

Frater Robertus Wyssendene, stans apud Oxney.

Frater Thomas Gosberkyrke dicit omnia bene.

Frater Thomas Depyng dicit omnia bene.

Frater Ricardus Harletone dicit omnia bene.

Frater Augustinus Depynge dicit omnia bene.

(Thorntone.) Frater Willelmus Aldewyncle dicit omnia bene.

Frater Thomas Maksey petit vt abbas cogat seruientes suos tenentes officio dicti Thome soluere annuos redditus suos pro tenementis que tenent de dicto officio: alioquin oportebit eum illos distringere, quod nolle.[1]

Frater Willelmus Meltone dicit omnia bene.

Frater Willelmus Mortone dicit omnia bene.

Frater Willelmus Beaufo dicit omnia bene.

Frater Johannes Burnham dicit omnia bene.

Frater Johannes Breustere dicit omnia bene.

Frater Johannes Barnake dicit omnia bene.

Frater Willelmus Markham dicit omnia bene.

Frater Willelmus Stamford dicit omnia bene.

Frater Willelmus Gretfforde dicit omnia bene.

Frater Johannes Spaldyng deponit omnia bene.

Frater Johannes Wynwyk deponit omnia bene.

Frater Johannes More, quartus prior. Dicitur a pluribus quod iste non est discretus in audiendo confessiones fratrum et iniungendo eis penas.

Frater Thomas Newerk dicit omnia bene.

Frater Johannes Burghe dicit omnia bene.

(Fo. 91 *d*.] (Depyng.) Frater Ricardus Oxenforde dicit omnia bene.

---

[1] *Sic*: for *nollet*.

[1] New names. Richard Harlton the younger resigned his office of abbot's receiver and steward at Michaelmas 1460. The inventory which he delivered to his successor, William Leicester, is given in Reg. Assheton, ff. 52-54, and includes the contents of the abbot's hall with its adjacent rooms and outbuildings, viz. ' le Oryell,' the chamber at the south end of the oriel, the hall of the oriel, the pantry in the oriel, the checker by ' heven yate ' (Heaven's gate), the kitchen, larder, and storehouse for dried fish and cheese. Apart from much silver plate in the hall, the main item of interest is the furniture and contents of the great chamber south of the oriel. This contained four new feather beds bought by Harlton; four bolsters; four couchers; six new pillows; seven ' *superpelliciae* called coverlettes,' viz. four white, embroidered with the letter M, and three green, embroidered with leopards' heads and flowers; six bed-coverings of red say; a pair of blankets of white fustian, containing 30 yards; six pairs of white cloth blankets; nine pairs of sheets, viz. a pair of new hempen cloth and eight of new linen, with one from the old store; two blue silk curtains from the old store; one new ' male de corpo ' (*sic*), apparently a leather trunk; a pair of ' boges ' (bows) in the sacrist's keeping; four ' *arcus* called bowes ' with six sheaves of arrows for the same; a brass bushel, a brass gallon-pot, a brass pint-pot, and a seal for sealing bushels, in the keeping of Richard Horton; a tailor's yard-measure of brass, broken; and a pair of weights for weighing bread. The names of famous registers or chartularies then follow, viz. ' le Swaffan ' (*sic*), then remaining in the exchequer; ' le blak Registre '; and two other registers called ' Acherches,' in the sacrist's keeping. Beside these there were two *breuiaria* (probably registers of writs rather then breviaries in the usual sense), belonging to the receiver's office and formerly to brother B. Aslakby; one

Brother William Walmesforde, abiding at Oxney, prays for a modification of the injunction against drinking in the town.

Brother Richard Harletone, the prior, says that all things are well.

Brother Robert Wyssendene,[1] abiding at Oxney.

Brother Thomas Gosberkyrke says all things are well.

Brother Thomas Depyng[1] says all things are well.

Brother Richard Harletone[1] says all things are well.

Brother Austin Depynge says all things are well.

(Thorntone.)[2] Brother William Aldewyncle[3] says all things are well.

Brother Thomas Maksey[4] prays that the abbot shall compel his tenants by serjeanty to pay to the office of the said Thomas their yearly rents for the tenements which they hold of the said office: otherwise it needs must be that he shall distrain them, which he fain would not.

Brother William Meltone[5] says all things are well.

Brother William Mortone says all things are well.

Brother William Beaufo[6] says all things are well.

Brother John Burnham[7] says all things are well.

Brother John Breustere says all things are well.

Brother John Barnake says all things are well.

Brother William Markham[8] says all things are well.

Brother William Stamford says all things are well.

Brother William Gretfforde[9] says all things are well.

Brother John Spaldyng[10] makes deposition that all things are well.

Brother John Wynwyk[11] makes deposition that all things are well.

Brother John More, the fourth prior.[12] It is said by divers persons that this deponent is not wary in hearing the brethren's confessions and enjoining penalties upon them.

Brother Thomas Newerk[13] says all things are well.

Brother John Burghe[14] says all things are well.

(Depyng.)[15] Brother Richard Oxenforde[16] says all things are well.

---

great locked coffer full of royal charters and other muniments; a table with two trestles; and a box or ' cofyn ' half full of glass of divers colours and beryl.

[2] This marginal note indicates that the examination of Aldewyncle and the next fifteen monks was deputed to Robert Thornton, archdeacon of Bedford (see *Visitations* I, 60, note 2), to whom and to John Depyng (*ibid.* I, 190) the bishop seems to have delegated part of the inquiry, after the method pursued in 1437.

[3] New name. He was presented for holy orders 19 Feb., 1444-5 (Reg. Assheton, fo. 14 *d*.).

[4] Treasurer of the convent in 1437, an office which he apparently still held.

[5] Subalmoner in 1437.

[6] Third prior in 1437.

[7] Abbot's cellarer in 1437.

[8] At Oxney in 1437.

[9] Presented as deacon in 1439-40 for ordination to the priesthood (Reg. Assheton, fo. 7 *d*.).

[10] Subchanter in 1437.

[11] Fraterer in 1437.

[12] Robert Lesyngham, not mentioned in 1442, was fourth prior in 1437.

[13] Presented as deacon in 1439-40 for priest's orders (Reg. Assheton, fo. 7 *d*.).

[14] Warden of Oxney in 1437.

[15] Here begin the depositions of the monks examined by Depyng.

[16] At Oxney in 1437. Acolyte on 15 Dec., 1445, when he was presented for subdeacon's orders, and presented for the diaconate 9 March, 1445-6 (Reg. Assheton, ff. 16 *d*, 17). His delay in proceeding from minor to holy orders is noticeable. He is not mentioned in the 1446 visitation, but was subalmoner in 1471 (*Monasticon* II, 363, note b).

Frater Petrus Lynne petit vt dominus modificet iniunccionem suam de non exeundo ad villam et bibendo ibidem.

Frater Ricardus Byseley dicit omnia bene.

Frater Ricardus Depyng dicit omnia bene.

Frater Robertus Notyngham dicit omnia bene.

Frater Robertus Lidyngtone dicit omnia bene.

Frater Johannes Lesyngham dicit omnia bene.

Quibus sic examinatis, magister Robertus Thornetone, commissarius domini, de consensu magistri Johannis Depyng, college sui, auctoritate domini eis commissa continuauit visitacionem huiusmodi in statu quo tunc erat vsque in diem tunc crastinum, xxiiij videlicet diem dicti mensis Junii et eodem loco, presentibus Thorpe, Bug et me Colstone.

LX.

[Fo. 123.]

VISITACIO MONASTERII DE BURGO SANCTI PETRI, ORDINIS SANCTI BENEDICTI, LINCOLNIENSIS DIOCESIS, IAM TERCIO VISITATI, FACTA IN DOMO CAPITULARI IBIDEM X⁰ DIE MENSIS SEPTEMBRIS, ANNO DOMINI MCCCCXLVJ⁰, PER REUERENDUM IN CHRISTO PATREM ET DOMINUM, DOMINUM WILLELMUM ALNEWYK, DEI GRACIA LINCOLNIENSEM EPISCOPUM, ANNO SUARUM CONSECRACIONIS XXJ⁰ ET TRANSLACIONIS Xᵐᵒ.

In primis, sedente dicto reuerendo *patre* iudicialiter in huiusmodi visitacionis sue negocio exercende pro tribunali die et loco antedictis, comparuerunt coram eo sic iudicialiter sedente abbas et conuentus dicti monasterii pariti¹ vt apparuit huiusmodi visitacionem subire. Et deinde primo et ante omnia propositum fuit verbum Dei iuxta actus futuri congruenciam per honestum virum magistrum Thomam Twyere, in sacra theologia scolarem, sequentem hoc thema, " Videamus si floruerit vinea."² Quo in latino sermone laudabiliter finito, abbas liberauit domino litteras certificatorias confectas super mandato domini ipsi abbati pro huiusmodi acto³ directo. Quo recepto et de mandato domini publice perlecto in hec verba, " Reuerendo in Christo patri," etc., idem abbas liberauit domino statum domus et ini800cciones per ipsum dominum in priore visitacione sua factas. Et deinde processit ad examinacionem et inquisicionem suas in hoc negocio.

(Sorores.) Frater Ricardus Asshtone, abbas, inquisitus dicit quod de domo sororum est vnus introitus in villam, est et alius in monasterium, per quos introitus habetur concursus de villa in monasterium et de

---

¹ *Sic*: for *parati*.

² Cant. vii, 12: Vulgate has *floruit*.

³ *Sic*: for *actu*.

¹ New name. Not mentioned in 1446, but subprior at the election of abbot Ramsey in 1471 (*Monasticon* II, 363, note b).

² New name.

³ Robert Lesyngham was fourth prior in 1437.

Brother Peter Lynne prays that my lord will modify his injunction against going out to the town and drinking therein.

Brother Richard Byseley says all things are well.

Brother Richard Depyng says all things are well.

Brother Robert Notyngham[1] says all things are well.

Brother Robert Lidyngtone[2] says all things are well.

Brother John Lesyngham[3] says all things are well.

Now, when these had been thus examined, master Robert Thornetone, my lord's commissary, with the consent of master John Depyng his colleague, by my lord's authority committed to them adjourned such visitation in the state wherein it then was until the day which was then the morrow, the twenty-fourth day to wit of the said month of June and in the same place, there being present Thorpe, Bug and I Colstone.

LX.

THE VISITATION OF THE MONASTERY OF PETERBOROUGH, OF THE ORDER OF ST. BENET, OF THE DIOCESE OF LINCOLN, VISITED NOW FOR THE THIRD TIME, PERFORMED IN THE CHAPTER-HOUSE THERE ON THE TENTH DAY OF THE MONTH OF SEPTEMBER, IN THE YEAR OF OUR LORD 1446, BY THE REVEREND FATHER IN CHRIST AND LORD, THE LORD WILLIAM ALNEWYK, BY THE GRACE OF GOD BISHOP OF LINCOLN, IN THE TWENTY-FIRST YEAR OF HIS CONSECRATION AND THE TENTH OF HIS TRANSLATION.

In the first place, as the said reverend father was sitting in his capacity of judge as a tribunal on and in the day and place aforesaid, in the business of holding such his visitation, there appeared before him as he so sate in his capacity of judge the abbot and convent of the said monastery, in readiness, as was apparent, to undergo such visitation. And then, first and before all else, the word of God was set forth as was agreeable to the process about to take place by the honest master Thomas Twyere, student in divinity, after this text. ' Let us see if the vine have flourished.' And when this had come to a praiseworthy end in the Latin speech, the abbot delivered to my lord his letters of certificate composed concerning my lord's mandate which had been addressed to the same abbot on behalf of such process.[4] The which having been received and read through in public by my lord's command in these words, ' To the reverend father in Christ,' etc., the same abbot delivered to my lord the state of the house and the injunctions made by the same my lord in his former visitation.[5] And then [my lord] proceeded to his examination and inquiry in this business.

(The sisters.)[6] Brother Richard Asshtone, the abbot, says upon inquiry that from the sisters' house there is one entry into the town, and there is another into the monastery, through the which entries there is a concourse of people from the town into the monastery and from the

---

[4] The mandate and certificate have been printed in full from abbot Assheton's register, *Visitations* II, lxiv-lxvi.

[5] See p. 282, note 3.

[6] For the ' sisters' house,' the dwelling of the bedeswomen in the almonry, see the note on the similar institution at Croyland, *Visitations* II, 55, note 5.

monasterio in villam, ex quo generatur monasterio magnum scandalum; que domus[1] nunc vocatur thesauraria, vbi de nouo construitur noua aula et nouum gardinum quod iam clausum est sepe, et propterea dicunt quod est infra septa monasterii et propterea ibidem comedunt et bibunt[2] monachi[3] ingredientes per illam sepem iam effractam; et ante clausuram huiusmodi factam reputabatur locus ille extra septa monasterii.

(Sorores.) Item dicit quod principales officiarii monasterii habebant in cultura sua certa maneria officiis[4] suis pertinencia et sub se alios balliuos et alios seruientes, et ea de causa ad tunc non potuerunt intendere religioni et diuino obsequio in monasterio ipsi officiarii, sed iam cessante causa occupacionum huiusmodi, omnia maneria illa tradantur[5] ad firmam et illi officiarii non sunt tanto occupati. Petit vt ipsi officiarii magis solito intendant choro.

(Abbas.) Frater Willelmus Extone, elemosinarius, dicit quod abbas facit prosterni nemora in diuersis locis quorum noticiam Henricus Hopkyn, custos et bedellus nemorum illorum, habet, et nescitur vbi deuenit pecunia.

(Abbas.) Item dicit quod abbas notatur cum vxore Willelmi Parkere, que ornatur vltra statum viri sui, et cum Margareta[6] Willelmi Clerk commorantis ad portam monasterii, et de hiis est communis fama, et cum vxore Willelmi Est de Oundelle.

(Abbas.) Item dicit quod abbas non reddidit compotum de administracione sua singulis annis secundum quod antiquitus est consuetum[7] in monasterio.

(Abbas.) Item quod certi officiarii habent mulieres lotrices que accedunt ad domus officiorum suorum, et sic alie mulieres habent communem accessum ad officia huiusmodi.

Item quod in officio sacristie mulieres lauant pannos.

(Abbas.) Frater Johannes Barnak dicit de compoto non reddito per abbatem et de nemoribus monasterii prostratis per abbatem absque consensu[8] conuentus et inconsulti,[9] pro quibus recipit magnas summas, et nescit in quo domus melioratur.

(Abbas.) Item dicit quod abbas notatur cum vxore Willelmi Clerk, merceri de Burghe, et cum vxore Willelmi Parkere de Yvebury

---

[1] *es* cancelled.
[2] *ibidem* cancelled.
[3] *dictam* cancelled.
[4] Altered from *officia*.
[5] *Sic*: *cum* is probably omitted.
[6] Sc. *vxore*.
[7] *est* cancelled.
[8] *abb* cancelled.
[9] *Sic*: for *absque consilio*.

[1] *I.e.* a new infirmary hall.
[2] This marginal note is evidently a mistake, as the deposition does not refer to the ' sister-house.'
[3] Extone did not appear at the visitation of 1442: he had been the abbot's steward in 1437.   On 30 June, 1441, he was sent as proctor for the abbot and convent to the general chapter of the province held at St. Andrew's priory, Northampton, on 2 July (Reg. Assheton, fo. 8 *d*.).   It will be seen that after this visitation he succeeded Harlton as prior.

monastery into the town, and hereout is great scandal bred to the monastery; and this house is now called the treasury, where there is newly made the new hall[1] and the new garden which is now enclosed by a hedge, and therefore they say that it is within the bounds of the monastery, and therefore do the monks, entering through that hedge, which has now been broken, eat and drink in that same; and before such enclosure was made, that place was reckoned to be without the bounds of the monastery.

(The sisters.)[2] Also he says that the principal officers of the monastery used to have in their tillage certain manors belonging to their offices, and under themselves others, bailiffs, and others, serving-folk, and for this cause the same officers could not at that time take heed to religion and divine worship in the monastery; but now that there is no longer cause why they should be thus busy, [since] all those manors are let out to farm, those officers are not so greatly busied. He prays that the same officers may attend quire more often than is their wont.

(The abbot.) Brother William Extone, the almoner,[3] says that the abbot causes copses to be felled in divers places whereof Henry Hopkyn, the warden and beadle of those woods,[4] has knowledge, and it is not known where the money has gone.

(The abbot.) Also he says that the abbot is defamed with William Parkere's wife, who is decked out beyond her husband's estate, and with Margaret, the wife of William Clerk who dwells at the monastery gate, and concerning these there is common report, and with William Est's wife of Oundle.

(The abbot.) Also he says that the abbot has not rendered an account of his administration every year according to the custom which was used of old time in the monastery.

(The abbot.) Also that certain officers have washerwomen who go to the houses of their offices,[5] and so do other women have common resort to such offices.

Also that women wash clothes in the office of the sacristy.

(The abbot.) Brother John Barnak says concerning the account, that it is not rendered by the abbot, and concerning the copses of the monastery, that they have been felled by the abbot without the consent and without the advice of the convent; and for these he receives large sums, and [this deponent] knows not wherein the house is bettered.

(The abbot.) Also he says that the abbot is defamed with the wife of William Clerk, mercer, of Peterborough, and with William Parkere's

---

[4] A grant of a corrody for life to Henry Hopkyn of Peterborough, made 28 July, 1447, gave him a weekly allowance of twelve convent loaves, twelve loaves called 'spitelbreed,' twelve gallons of the best convent ale, and twelve gallons of middling ale called 'howsoldale' from the abbot's pantry and cellar. He had yearly six cartloads of fuel called 'baloughwode' and four of underwood called 'kydes,' to be felled and carried at the costs of the abbot and convent; a quarter of oats for making flour; four bushels of salt; and 37 pounds of Paris candles; and one furred robe which was a mixture of the livery of the abbot's gentlemen and yeomen. If his wife Alice survived him, she was to have half the corrody, the robe excepted (Reg. Assheton, fo. 21 d.). For the meaning of 'baloughwode' see p. 274, note 3: 'baloughwode' = logs, and 'kydes' = faggots.

[5] *I.e.* the checkers belonging to the several offices.

et cum vxore Willelmi Est de Oundelle, et super hiis publica fama.

(Prior.) Item dicit quod religio perit propter absenciam continuam prioris, qui ad extra manet et non intendit claustralibus nec religularibus[1] obseruanciis et ideo inutilis: ideo necessarium vt alius subrogetur.

(Presidentes). Item alii priores sub se nichil faciunt in officiis suis, in tantum quod iuuenis[2] lasciuant nec obediunt suis prepositis nec gerunt reuerenciam senioribus, et hoc propter leues penes.[3]

[Fo. 123 *d.*] (Abbas.) Item tenementa monasterii tendunt ad ruinam in defectu abbatis.

(Abbas.) Item dicit quod non seruitur monachis de pecuniis quas abbas eis solueret, nec[4] eciam seruientibus monasterii.

(Abbas.) Frater Ricardus Harleton, prior, dicit quod abbas notatur cum vxore Parkere de Ivebury, quam iste prior consuluit sibire[5] amouere, et tamen non fecit; cuius marito abbas concessit officium parci ad terminum vite, et cum vxore Willelmi Clerk, merceri de Burghe, et cum vxore Willelmi Est de Oundelle.

(Abbas.) Item dicit quod abbas prosternit grossa nemera[6] monasterii; et dicit plane quod penitus ignorat statum monasterii, eo quod abbas non reddit compotum secundum consuetudinem monasterii, et propter hoc potissime quod plures sunt receptores nec sciunt conficere compotos suos, et hoc pluribus annis.

(Abbas.) Item abbas solueret conuentui singulis annis ad Pascha et festum Sancti Michaelis equaliter lx li. ad vestitum, et aretro est et de vltimo Pascha.

(Abbas.) Item dicit quod si *de* dilapidacione sit suspectus erat tempore incepcionis sue, et eo quod duobus vel tribus annis tenuit tres vel quatuo[7] seruientes omnino inutiles, eciam plures, vltra solitum numerum.

(Prior.) Item propter senium et impotenciam petit se exonerari ab officio prioris.

(Abbas.) Frater Willelmus Markham dicit quod abbas notatur cum vxore Willelmi Parkere de Ibury, vxore Willelmi Clerk de Burghe et[8] vxore Willelmi Est de Oundelle. Petit vt mulieres ipse amoueantur a locis more sue propter scandalum summouendum.

(Abbas.) Item abbas est aretro de xxx li. de vltimo Pascha, et quod expendit plura bona monasterii in sustentacione mulierum huiusmodi.

(Abbas.) Item abbas dat grossas arbores in magno numero amicis suis de nemore apud Oundelle et in aliis pluribus locis, et tamen officiarii monasterii non possunt habere vix vnam arborem pro reparacione tene-

---

[1] *Sic:* for *regularibus.*
[2] *Sic:* for *iuuenes.*
[3] *Sic:* for *penas.*
[4] *est* cancelled.
[5] *Sic:* for *sibi.*
[6] *Sic:* (*nem'a*).
[7] *Sic:* for *quatuor.*
[8] *Wi* cancelled.

[1] William Parker was evidently the park-keeper in the manor of Eyebury, north of Peterborough.

wife of Eyebury[1] and William Est's wife of Oundle, and touching these things [there is] public rumour.

(The prior.)   Also he says that religion is near an end by reason of the constant absence of the prior, who stays outside and heeds not the observances of cloister or of the rule, and is therefore profitless: needs therefore that another be put in his place.

(The presidents.)   Also the other priors under him do naught in their offices, insomuch that the young [monks] do wanton and obey not them that are set over them, and pay no reverence to their elders, and this by reason that the penalties are light.

(The abbot.)   Also the tenements of the monastery are going to ruin in the abbot's default.

(The abbot.)   Also he says that the monks are not served with the monies which the abbot should pay them, nor also are the serving-folk of the monastery.

(The abbot.)   Brother Richard Harleton, the prior, says that the abbot is defamed with Parker's wife of Eyebury, whom this prior advised him to send away, and yet he did it not, and to her husband the abbot granted the office of his park for the term of his life; and with the wife of William Clerk, mercer of Peterborough, and with William Est's wife of Oundle.

(The abbot.)   Also he says that the abbot fells the thick copses of the monastery; and he says outright that he is altogether ignorant of the state of the monastery, because the abbot renders no account according to the custom of the monastery, and for this cause especially, that there are several receivers, and they do not know how to cast up their accounts; and so has it been for many years.

(The abbot.)   Also the abbot should pay every year at Easter and the feast of St. Michael in equal shares sixty pounds to the convent for their raiment, and he is in arrears even from Easter last.

(The abbot.)   Also he says that, if [the abbot] be suspected of dilapidation, he was [suspected] during the time when he began [his rule] and that because for two or three years he kept three or four servants who were utterly profitless [and] even more above the accustomed number.

(The prior.)   Also because of his old age and powerlessness he prays that he may be discharged of the office of prior.

(The abbot.)   Brother William Markham[2] says that the abbot is defamed with William Parkere's wife of Eyebury, William Clerk's wife of Peterborough and William Est's wife of Oundle.   He prays that the same women may be removed from the places where they dwell, that scandal may so be taken away.

(The abbot.)   Also the abbot is thirty pounds in arrear from last Easter, and [he says] that he spends many of the goods of the monastery upon the maintenance of such women.

(The abbot.)   Also the abbot gives thick trees from the wood at Oundle and in several other places in large number to his friends, and yet the officers of the monastery can have scarce one tree for the repair

---

[2] At Oxney in 1437.   He is mentioned as treasurer of the monastery in the proceedings consequent upon the present visitation.

mentorum in villa pertinencium officiis suis; et hec facit absque vlla communicacione cum conuentu.

(Abbas.) Item tenementa in villa sunt diruta de quibus abbas consueuit recipere annuatim lij marcas, et iam propter non reparacionem nichil vel modicum recipit.

(Abbas.) Item quod xvj bouate apud Fiskertone sunt in manibus abbatis et conuentus prop[1] non reparacionem domorum tenencium.

(Abbas.) Item dicit quod in agendis et tractandis negociis domus, innitur[2] suo proprio sensui absque communicacione conuentus, et multum in hoc regitur per seculares.

(Abbas.) Item propter infamiam quam abbas incurrit non est ausus defendere iura monasterii nec contradicere ea infringentibus.

(Abbas.) Item dicit abbas[3] posuit in morgagium siue apothecam pro debitis monasterii manerium de Keteryng magistro Johanni de la Bere pro pecuniis eidem abbati per Delabere mutuatis, et manerium de

---

[1] *Sic*: for *propter*.
[2] *Sic*: for *innititur*.
[3] *Sic*: *quod* omitted.

[1] Five miles east of Lincoln. See *Lincolnshire Domesday* (L.R.S.) I, 54.

[2] *I.e.* the tenants had left their ruinous houses, and the land was consequently left uncultivated.

[3] John Delabere, bachelor of decrees, appears for the first time in 1421, when, on 10 August, he exchanged the chantry or free chapel of St. Radegund in St. Paul's for the prebend of Putson major in Hereford cathedral (*Hereford Reg. Spofford* [Cantilupe Soc.], p. 368). He subsequently obtained the rectory of the church or free chapel of Tormarton, Glouces., which he held in 1424 with the church of St. Martin's, Oxford (date of institution to the latter not recorded) in the hope of obtaining a dispensation. From the somewhat intricate terms of a later dispensation (*Cal. Papal Letters* VIII, 273-4) it appears that he was at first dispensed to hold the two churches for three years, but later, 30 Dec., 1425, to hold two incompatible benefices for life (*ibid.* VII, 470); while, on 8 March 1426-7, he received a further indult to hold Tormarton for life with other benefices (*ibid.* VII, 532). He resigned his prebend in Hereford before 16 Dec., 1427 (*Hereford Reg. Spofford*, u.s. p. 354). He became king's almoner not long after this period: he apparently resigned this post in 1433 or 1434, but held it again in 1440 and later. On 20 Dec., 1432, he obtained Hurstbourn preb. in Salisbury (Jones, *Fasti Eccl. Sar.*, p. 395), and on 1 Feb., 1433-4 was presented to the deanery of Tamworth, which he exchanged later in the year for a canonry of Exeter (*Cal. Pat.* 1429-36, pp. 332, 337). He received collation of this on 11 Dec., 1434 (*Exeter Reg. Lacy*, ed. Randolph, I, 182). He had resigned St. Martin's, Oxford, by 24 Nov., 1433 (Wood, *City of Oxford*, ed. Clark, III, 88). On 3 April, 1440, he was presented by the Crown to the church of Aveton Giffard, Devon (*Cal. Pat.* 1436-41, p. 383). This, however, had no effect (see *Exeter Reg. Lacy*, u.s. I, 257), and it was possibly in compensation for this that he was preferred by bishop Lacy, 18 June, 1440, to a canonry and preb. in the church of Bosham (*ibid.* I, 260). On 5 Jan., 1440-1, he had collation of Wedmore secunda preb. in Wells (*Wells Reg. Stafford* [Somerset Rec. Soc.] II, 261), and on 28 Oct. following was presented to a stall in St. Stephen's, Westminster (*Cal. Pat.* 1441-6, p. 3). He appears to have resigned Tormarton about this period: the dispensation already referred to states that, after doing so, he held divers benefices without cure not exceeding three, but in 1440 he was holding three, and at the end of 1441 five. See also papal letters of 12 June, 1441-2, and 23 May, 1443, giving him further facilities for benefices and validating former dispensations (*Cal. Papal Letters* VIII, 327, 312-14). His preferments were considerably increased in 1443, when he obtained a cure of souls by his institution on 2 June to St. Mary Abchurch, London (Hennessy, *Nov. Rep.*, p. 296). He resigned this by 11 July, and on 20 Aug. was presented by the abbot and convent of Peterborough to the church of Oundle (Reg. Assheton, fo. 10), to which he was instituted on 23 Aug. (Bridges, *Hist. Northants.* II, 408). On 15 Oct. he was appointed warden of St.

of the tenements in the town that belong to their offices; and these things he does without any common counsel with the convent.

(The abbot.) Also the tenements in the town, wherefrom the abbot was wont to receive fifty-two marks yearly, are in ruin, and now, because they are not repaired, he receives nothing or but little.

(The abbot.) Also that sixteen bovates at Fiskerton[1] are in the hands of the abbot and convent, because the tenants' houses are not repaired.[2]

(The abbot.) Also he says that, in performing and handling the business matters of the house, [the abbot] depends upon his own wit without taking counsel with the convent, and herein is he greatly ruled by secular folk.

(The abbot.) Also, by reason of the defamation which the abbot has incurred, he has not dared to defend the rights of the monastery or gainsay them that infringe them.

(The abbot.) Also he says [that] the abbot, for the debts of the monastery, put the manor of Kettering into mortgage or forfeit to master John de la Bere,[3] in return for monies lent by Delabere to the same abbot,

Katherine's hospital by the Tower (*Cal. Pat.* 1441-6, p. 206); on 31 Oct. he had collation of Cutton preb. in Exeter castle, in which he succeeded Thomas Bekynton, recently appointed bishop of Bath and Wells (*Exeter Reg. Lacy*, u.s. I, 281), and on 3 Feb., 1443-4, obtained Barnby preb. in York (York Reg. Kempe, fo. 50 *d.*). After the death of John Forest, dean of Wells, on 25 March, 1446 (see *Visitations* I, 186-7), a determined attempt was made by his friends at court to thrust him into the deanery against the will of the sub-dean and chapter. He had licence to sue for provision on 16 July, 1446 (*Cal. Pat.* 1441-6, p. 442); but the chapter had already received the king's consent, by an act made in the Star chamber on 11 July, to proceed to a free election (*Cal. MSS. D. & C. Wells* [Hist. MSS. Comm.] II, 675-7). On 22 Aug. they elected Nicholas Carent, and the election was confirmed on 28 Aug. by bishop Bekynton (Harl. MS. 6966, p. 61). Meanwhile, Delabere's provision had been granted, and one of the executors, the prior of Southwark (see p. 264, note 4), excommunicated the canons. The messenger who attempted to fix the sentence upon the cathedral doors was threatened with death and imprisoned. On 13 Nov. a peremptory mandate from the pope ordered the chapter to receive Delabere and quashed the proceedings which were pending in the court of Canterbury (*Cal. Papal Letters* VIII, 311-12); but in spite of this the chapter held its own. It seems also that Delabere had a simultaneous provision to Forest's archdeaconry of Surrey; for he was dispensed, 3 Oct., 1446, to hold it for life with the deanery of Wells and Oundle (*ibid.* VIII, 273-4). The dispute was compromised by the provision of Delabere to the see of St. Davids, which fell vacant on 22 May, 1447, by the death of John Langton after an episcopate of a fortnight. This bears date 15 Sept. (*ibid.* IX, 294): the temporalities were restored 14 Nov., 1447 (*Cal. Pat.* 1446-52, p. 114), and Delabere was consecrated by archbishop Stafford on 19 Nov. (Stubbs, *Reg. Sac.*, p. 90). He now resigned Oundle and his nine compatible benefices. His connexion with Peterborough, however, did not cease. He had lent money freely to the abbot and convent. On 30 March, 1454, he released them from all obligations, receiving in return on 16 April the grant of a yearly rent of £32 for life out of the manor of Kettering (Reg. Assheton, ff. 46, 47), and of a lodging for life in the monastery and in the prior's manor house at Eyebury (*ibid.* ff. 44 *d.*-45 *d.*). This second grant, which is in English and contains much interesting detail, is printed in full in *Assoc. Soc. R. & P.* XXXIV, 278-9: it includes the grant of an obit, and was made ostensibly on account, among other benefits, of his gift of his episcopal vestments to the monastery. On 24 Dec., 1457, he gave a receipt to the abbot and convent for £132 of the rent from Kettering, and for £44 which he had lent them (Reg. Assheton, fo. 45 *d.*). He resigned his see in 1460, and probably retired to Peterborough. He was one of Gascoigne's *bêtes noires*: the transaction by which he became a bishop receives vigorous comment in *Loci e libro veritatum*, ed. Rogers, pp. 25-6, and he is accused (*ibid.* 35-6) of converting the misdemeanours of his

Oundelle eidem Delabere, vt credit, eciam pro pecuniis simili modo, sub sigillo suo proprio absque consensu conuentus.

(Abbas.) Item conuentu inconsulto dimisit manerium de Thorpe Willelmo Est ad terminum lix annorum sub sigillo suo proprio pro ix marcis annuatim soluendis, et ipse Willelmus dimisit idem manerium alii viro pro x marcis annuis.

[Fo. 124.] (Abbas.) Item manerium de Suthorpe pertinens conuentui dimissum erat cuidam Mortymere cum reparacione, et iam ipso Mortymere defuncto nulla reparacione facta, abbas detinet ab executoribus dicti Mortymere xl li. *nomine reparacionis huiusmodi*, quas idem abbas debuit dicto Mortymere. Petit igitur vt dicte xl li. restituantur conuentui ad reparacionem predictam faciendam.

(Abbas.) Item abbas subtrahit prebendas debitas pauperibus in villa de Burghe, occasione cuius subtraccionis credit plura mala monasterio euenire.

(Abbas.) Frater Ricardus Stamforde dicit quod diuinum officium non fit in ecclesia prout consuetum est, et hoc quod iuuenes monachi in hiis delinquentes recurrunt ad abbatem, qui eis facile[1] indulget, et sic facilitas venie[2] facit eos audaciores ad delinquendum, et eo *magis*[3] paruipendunt suos seniores religioni presidentes.

(Abbas.) Item dicit quod abbas vendit wardas et maritagia que sunt multi valoris pro vili precio, et in hiis solum vtititur[4] consilio cuiusdam Es꞉ et non conuentus, et tamen pecunias conuertit in vsus proprios.

(Abbas.) Item dicit quod abbas tempore suo donauit plures grossas arbores amicis et beneuolis suis absque consensu conuentus.

(Abbas.). Item concordat de eo quod abbas est diffamatus[5] cum prefatis tribus mulieribus vt predicitur.

(Abbas.) Item abbas solueret annuatim coquine conuentus lij marcas de redditibus villa de Burgo soluendas septimanatim per manus balliui ville, et dicit quod iam *non* potest soluere propter decasum tenementorum.

(Abbas.) Item[6] videtur quod officium cellerarii conuentus posset releuari per prouentus prouenientes de nundinis siue feriis ibidem, que tenentur in solo pertinente officio dicti cellerarii.

(Abbas.) Frater Johannes Burghe senior dicit quod religio non seruatur in domo, quia iuuenes post completorium descendunt de dormitorio et ita intendunt potacionibus, aliquociens cum abbate, adeo libere ac si hoc eis liceret, et ad interessendum matutinis vel cele-

---

diocesan clergy into a licensed source of profit to his revenues. His dealings with Peterborough were certainly not without advantage to himself, and his presentation to Oundle, a profitable living, is hardly free from the suspicion of simony at a date when he was a creditor of the convent.

[1] *indig* cancelled.
[2] Altered from *venia*.
[3] Interlined above *pocius* cancelled.
[4] *Sic*: for *vtitur*.
[5] *est* cancelled.
[6] *abbas sub* cancelled.

[1] This and the other leases mentioned are not recorded in Reg. Assheton. It may be noted that on fo. 17 there is a grant of the next presentation to Oundle

and also, as he believes, for monies in like manner, the manor of Oundle to the same Delabere, under his own seal without the consent of the convent.[1]

(The abbot.) Also the abbot, without the advice of the convent, leased the manor of Thorpe[2] to William Est for the term of fifty-nine years under his own seal, in return for the yearly payment of nine marks, and the same William leased the same manor to another man for ten marks a year.

(The abbot.) Also the manor of Southorpe,[3] which belongs to the convent, was leased to one Mortymere with the repairs thereof, and, now that the same Mortymere is dead and no repairs have been done, the abbot is keeping back under the name of such repairs from the said Mortymere's executors forty pounds, which the same abbot owed to the said Mortymere. He prays therefore that the said forty pounds be restored to the convent, that they may do the repairs aforesaid.

(The abbot.) Also the abbot withdraws the allowances which are due to the poor folk in the town of Peterborough, by reason of the which withdrawal he believes that many evils will betide the monastery.

(The abbot.) Brother Richard Stamforde[4] says that the divine office is not performed in church as has been their wont, and this because the young monks who offend in these respects have recourse to the abbot, who readily gives them indulgence, and so the ease wherewith they are excused makes them more bold to offend, and therefore do they reck less of their elders that are the presidents of religion.

(The abbot.) Also he says that the abbot sells wardships and marriages which are of much value at a cheap rate, and herein does he use the advice of one Est only and not of the convent, and yet he turns the monies to his own uses.

(The abbot.) Also he says that the abbot in his time has given many thick trees to his friends and well-wishers without the consent of the convent.

(The abbot.) Also he agrees concerning this, that the abbot is defamed with the aforesaid three women, as is said before.

(The abbot.) Also the abbot should pay yearly to the convent kitchen fifty-two marks out of the rents of the town of Peterborough, to be paid weekly by the hands of the bailiff of the town, and he says that now he cannot pay, because the tenements are in decay.

(The abbot.) Also it seems that the office of the cellarer of the convent could be lightened by the profits that come out of the marts or fairs in the same place, which are held on ground that belongs to the office of the said cellarer.

(The abbot.) Brother John Burghe the elder[5] says that religious discipline is not kept in the house, for after compline the young [monks] come down from the dorter and so do set to drinking, sometimes with the abbot, as freely as if this were allowed them, and are rendered altogether unfit for being present at matins or celebrating on the day following,

---

to Thomas Catworth, alderman of London, and John Everdon and John Parke, clerks of the green cloth, dated 7 Nov., 1445.
[2] Immediately west of Peterborough.
[3] Eight miles N.W. of Peterborough, in the parish of Barnack.
[4] Chamberlain in 1437, not mentioned in 1442.
[5] Warden of Oxney in 1437.

brandum die sequenti sunt omnino indispositi, ita quod nisi senes et officiarii velint celebrare missam matutinalem et de beata virginis[1] non reperitur aliquis de iuuenibus qui velit hoc facere.

(Iuuenes.) Item iuuenes monachi in capitulo quando deberent corrigi pro excessibus murmurant contra presidentes, eis comminando.

(Abbas.) Item dicit quod monasterium quo ad temporalia stat in pessimo statu,[2] nam abbas ex vendacione[3] arborum grossarum magnas et graues summas recepit, quia istis c annis *proxime* precedentibus *tempore alicuius abbatis* non fuit facta tanta vendicio nemorum quantam ipse fecit octo annis quibus iste stetit abbas; et tamen non releuatur monasterium a debitis quibus tenebatur et tenetur, ita quod magna presumitur dilapidacio.

(Abbas.) Item abbas necgligens est in petendo et defendendo iura et libertates monasterii, ita quod ea occasione perduntur hundrede et diuerse curie quas dudum habuerunt in diuersis locis.

(Abbas.) Item quo ad mulieres concordat cum aliis vt supra deponentibus. Obiectis abbati articulis cum tribus hiis mulieribus, negat crimen cum omnibus hiis mulieribus ab omni tempore: monitus est quod amoueat vxorem Parkere ab illo loco citra festum Omnium Sanctorum in virtute obediencie et sub pena excommunicacionis, et eciam quod vxor Clerk amoueatur a loco vbi manet, et quod non communicet cum illis suspecte sub pena excommunicacionis.

(Abbas.) Item dicit quod diffamatus est abbas quod noctanter exiuit monasterium, exutus vestibus regularibus, indutus secularibus, et cum secularibus personis ad domum Willelmi Clerk manentis iuxta portas monasterii. Negat articulum.

(Aldewyncle, Ricardus Depyng.) Item quod frater Willelmus Aldewyncle habens vnum jak et frater Ricardus Depyng eciam habens vnum jak habent arma inuasiua in dormitorio, presertim arcus et sagittas, cum quibus illi et alii iuuenes soli vadunt de villa ad villam sic[4] laici.

(Abbas.) Item mulieres leues et suspecte nimium habent accessum ad monasterium et potissime in hostalariam,[5] quem licet abbas bene nouerit, non tamen corrigit.

(Precentor.) Item dicit vbi[6] precentor ex onere officii chorum sequeretur, iam tamen deputatus[7] subcellerarius ex parte conuentus, propter cuius occupacionem non intendit choro iuxta officium precentoris.

(Abbas.) Item dicit quod nisi monasterium ponatur sub meliori regimine penitus destruetur.

[Fo. 124 *d*.] (Abbas.) Frater Thomas Makesey dicit quod abbas dedit vxori Willelmi Parkere de Ibury vnum mantellum furruratum

---

[1] *Sic*: for *virgine*.
[2] *ob defectum abbatis* cancelled.
[3] *Sic*: for *vendicione*.
[4] *Sic*: for *sicut*.
[5] *Sic*: for *hostilariam*.
[6] *Sic*: *quod* omitted.
[7] *Sic*: for *deputatur* or *deputatus est*.

[1] The Lady chapel was on the east side of the north transept, adjoining the north aisle of the presbytery, against the outer wall of which remains of it still exist.
[2] *I.e.* the hundred courts with their perquisites.

so that, unless the old [monks] and officers will celebrate the morrow mass and [the mass] of the blessed Virgin,[1] there is found none of the young [monks] who will do this.

(The young [monks].)   Also the young monks in chapter, when they should be corrected for their transgressions, murmur against the presidents, threatening them.

(The abbot.)   Also he says that the monastery stands in very ill plight as regards things temporal, for the abbot has received great and heavy sums from the sale of thick trees, in that there has not been made in the last hundred years that are gone before, in the time of any abbot, so great a sale of copses as he has made in the eight years wherein he has been abbot ; and yet the monastery is not relieved from the debts wherewith it was and is bound, so that there is presumed to be sore dilapidation.

(The abbot.)   Also the abbot is neglectful in claiming and defending the rights and liberties of the monastery, so that because thereof the hundreds[2] and sundry courts that they had aforetime in divers places are lost.

(The abbot.)   Also, as regards the women, he agrees with the other deponents as above.   When the articles [of his defamation] with these three women had been put to the abbot, he denies his guilt with all these women at any time: he was warned to remove Parkere's wife from that place on this side the feast of All Saints in virtue of obedience and under pain of excommunication, and also that Clerk's wife be removed from the place where she dwells, and that he shall not have suspect converse with them under pain of excommunication.

(The abbot.)   Also he says that the abbot is defamed because he went out of the monastery by night, having put off his regular habit, dressed in secular raiment and with secular folk, to the house of William Clerk, who dwells by the gates of the monastery.   He denies the article.

(Aldewyncle, Richard Depyng.)   Also that brother William Aldewyncle, who has a jack,[3] and brother Richard Depyng, who also has a jack, do keep arms of offence in the dorter, especially bows and arrows, wherewith they and the other young [monks] go by themselves from town to town, like laymen.

(The abbot.)   Also light women and suspect have overmuch access to the monastery and especially into the hostry ;[4] and this, albeit he well knows it, the abbot nevertheless does not correct.

(The precentor.)   Also he says [that], whereas the precentor, out of the charge belonging to his office, should attend quire regularly, now, however, he has been appointed subcellarer on behalf of the convent, and, because he holds this [office], he does not attend quire as befits the office of precentor.

(The abbot.)   Also he says that, except the monastery be put under better governance, it will be utterly destroyed.

(The abbot.)   Brother Thomas Makesey[5] says that the abbot gave a mantle furred with vair,[6] which belonged to the abbot who is

---

[3] *I.e.* a jack of defence: see p. 256, note 4.   For armour in the monastery, cf. the inventory of 1460, p. 284, note 1.   The same inventory mentions a hauberk which was in the oriel pantry, to be cleaned and scoured.

[4] The buildings, including stables, south of the infirmary and S.E. of the cloister.

[5] Convent treasurer in 1437.

[6] Cf. *Visitations* II, 3, note 4.

cum vario quod fuit abbatis mortui, et vxori Willelmi Est vnam murram ornatam cum argento deaurato.

(Abbas.) Item concessit Willelmo Est tenenti curias monasterii vij marcas et dimidiam vltra iiij marcas quas prius percepit nomine feodi, et hoc ad totam vitam suam.

(Abbas.) Item concessit vicario de Burghe vnam cameram infra monasterium in qua iacet de nocte, dimisso manso vicarie sue, absque consensu conuentus, ex quo verisimiliter orietur dissensio inter futurum vicarium et conuentum.

(Derby. Abbas.) Frater Willelmus Stamforde dicit quod abbas non reddidit compotum administracionis sue per biennium.

(Abbas.) Item dicit quod abbas vendidit et prostrauit quasdam siluas non ceduas, se[1] que sunt ignorat.

(Abbas.) Item dicit quod abbas non soluit confratribus suis salaria sua, sed est aretro cuilibet confratri suo in huiusmodi solucionibus.

(Meltone, Markham, Gosberkyrk.) Item dicit quod fratres Willelmus Meltone, Thomas Gosberkyrk et Willelmus Markham vacant indies potacionibus serotinis, sedendo in thesauraria et cameraria, ita quod non disponuntur[2] ad diuina officia, in tanto quod aliquociens vix semel in septimana veniunt ad matutinas vel missas celebrant.

(Gosberkyrk.) Item quod sepius frater Thomas Gosberkyrk maledixit domino pro iniunccione facta de non bibendo in villa de Burghe.

(Burnham.) Item dicit quod frater Johannes Burnham vtitur camiseis et aliis vestimentis lineis ad carnem contra regulam.

(Burnham.) Item dicit quod idem frater Johannes, dum stetit magister operum, induxit in domum suam modo suspecto mulieres suspectas, per quod monasterium pessime diffamabatur.

(Lynfelde.) Item dicit quod frater Johannes Lynfelde precentor occupat officium subcellerarii ex parte conuentus, per quod multum impeditur a choro tempore diuinorum temporibus quibus vt precentor tenetur choro intendere.

(Turvey.) Item frater Johannes Turvey sub vsuris mutuauit cuidam Thome Mason de Burghe xx li., recipiendo pro huiusmodi mutuo a dicto Thoma xx s. quolibet quarterio anni vltra sortem.

(Turvey.) Item dicit quod idem frater Johannes, dum stetit custos infirmarie, absque consensu conuentus impignorauit diuersa iocalia pertinencia dicto officio, videlicet vnam pixidem argenteam pro corpore Christi et alia plura, nec ea redemit et pecuniam inde receptam in suos vsus conuertit.

---

[1] The date of abbot Depyng's death is not known. See p. 283, note 2.

[2] Presumably John Hare, instituted to the vicarage 6 July, 1439 (Bridges, *Hist. Northants.* II, 544).

[3] The examination passes at this point to the bishop's clerk, John Derby, at this time canon of Lincoln and prebendary of Bedford major.

[4] See *Visitations* II, p. 180, note 4.

[5] Neither of these gave evidence. Meltone was subalmoner in 1437. Gosberkyrk had recently been cellarer and was now at Oxney (see More's first and second *detecta*).

[6] Abbot's cellarer in 1437. He did not appear at this visitation.

dead,[1] to William Parkere's wife of Eyebury, and to William Est's wife a mazer adorned with silver gilt.

(The abbot.)   Also he granted to William Est, who holds the courts of the monastery, seven and a half marks over and above the four marks which he erstwhile received by the name of his fee, and this for his whole life.

(The abbot.)   Also he granted to the vicar of Peterborough[2] without the consent of the convent a chamber within the monastery, wherein, leaving his vicarage-house, he lies of a night; wherefrom in likelihood shall arise bickering between the vicar that shall be and the convent.

(Derby.[3]   The abbot.)   Brother William Stamforde says that the abbot has not rendered an account of his administration by the space of two years.

(The abbot.)   Also he says that the abbot sold and felled certain woods that were not fit for cutting,[4] but which they are he knows not.

(The abbot.)   Also he says that the abbot does not pay his brethren their stipends, but is in arrears to every one of his brethren as regards such payments.

(Meltone, Markham, Gosberkyrk.)   Also he says that brothers William Meltone, Thomas Gosberkyrk[5] and William Markham spend their time daily in drinking at eventide, sitting in the treasury and the chamberlain's checker, so that they are indisposed for the divine offices, insomuch that they come to matins or celebrate masses hardly once in the week.

(Gosberkyrk.)   Also that brother Thomas Gosberkyrk has very often reviled my lord for the injunction which he made against drinking in the town of Peterborough.

(Burnham.)   Also he says that brother John Burnham[6] wears shirts and other raiment of linen next his skin, contrary to the rule.

(Burnham.)   Also he says that the same brother John, while he was master of the works, brought suspect women into the house in manner suspect, whereby the monastery has been most grievously defamed.

(Lynfelde.)   Also he says that brother John Lynfelde the precentor[7] holds the office of subcellarer on behalf of the convent, whereby he is much hindered from quire in time of divine service at the times when, as precentor, he is bound to attend quire.

(Turvey.)   Also brother John Turvey[8] lent twenty pounds usuriously to one Thomas Mason of Peterborough, receiving in return for such loan from the said Thomas twenty shillings beyond his share every quarter of a year.[9]

(Turvey.)   Also he says that the same brother John, while he was warden of the infirmary, put divers jewels which belong to the said office in pawn, without the consent of the convent, to wit, a silver pyx for the body of Christ, and many others, and he has not bought them back and has turned the money which he received therefrom to his own uses.

---

[7] Lynfelde was precentor in 1437, and at Oxney in 1442.   He gave no evidence on this occasion.

[8] This monk, present in 1437, appeared neither in 1442 nor now.

[9] *I.e.* the loan was at 20 per cent interest.

(Abbas.) Frater Willelmus Morton dicit quod cellerarius conuentus haberet prouentus nundinarum et feriarum iam de nouo institutarum, et hoc impedit abbas.

(Abbas.) Item abbas absque consensu conuentus vendidit siluas non ceduas vocatas Estwode et Westwode et alias plures.

(Abbas.) Item dicit quod abbas non reddidit compotum pluribus annis nec soluit confratribus suis eorum stipendia, in tantum quod aliquibus debet vj marcas, aliquibus plus vel minus, nec reparat tenementa monasterii: ymo sunt quasi in toto ruinosa.

(More.) Item dicit quod frater Johannes More, confessor abbatis, suscitat discordias et debatas inter abbatem et conuentum.

(Abbas.) Item dicit seculares[1] seruientes abbatis, presertim cubicularii siue camerarii, ex necessario amouerentur, quia ex eis, cum iuuenes sunt et lasciui, magnum scandalum monasterio generatur.

(Abbas.) Item dicit de incontinencia abbatis, prout deponit frater Johannes Burghe.

(Abbas.) Frater Ricardus Statherne dicit quod abbas non venit ad chorum sicut alii predecessores consueuerunt ad magnas missas et processiones, nec superintendit vt silencium in claustro et aliis locis consuetis obseruetur secundum regulam.

(Prior.) Item dicit quod prior non intendit choro, claustro aut refectorio, sed semper residet apud Oxney, propter quod diuinum officium necgligitur, regulares obseruantur[2] non obseruantur, sed neque silencium.

(Harletone cellerarius.) Item dicit quod frater Ricardus Harletone, cellerarius ex parte conuentus, non ministrat isti deponenti infirmanti cibaria secundum regulam.

[Fo. 125.] (Gosberkyrk.) Frater Johannes More dicit quod frater Thomas Gosberkyrke, dudum refectorarius, nondum reddidit compotum suum de illo officio de anno proxime elapso.

(Gosberkyrk.) Item idem frater Thomas nunc est in minucionibus apud Oxeney. Accedit frequenter post prandium et cenam ad villam de Burghe et ibidem expectat in solaciis suis cum secularibus, eciam mulieribus, vsque x vel xj horam in nocte, antequam redeat ad Oxeney.

(Gosberkyrk.) Item frater Thomas vix semel in septimana celebrat nec cursum suum in celebrando missas septimane sue obseruat.

(Gosberkyrk, Markham.) Item frater Thomas et frater Willelmus Markham vtuntur potacionibus serotinis in thesauraria, vbi cum eis conueniunt mulieres suspecte in scandalum domus; et de eorum a choro absentacione tempore diuinorum deponit prout deposuit frater Willelmus Aldewyncle.

(Mortone,) Item frater Willelmus Mortone vtitur deambulacionibus serotinis inter monasterium et Oxney, bibendo in villulis intermediis in monasterii scandalum.

---

[1] *Sic*: *quod* omitted.
[2] *Sic*: for *observancie*.

[1] It is not clear what recently instituted markets and fairs are alluded to.
[2] For Eastwood see p. 274, note 4. Westwood lay west of the town, and to the north of Thorpe.
[3] Called Stanerne (but also Statherne) in 1437. He did not appear in 1442.

(The abbot.) Brother William Morton says that the cellarer of the convent should have the profits of the marts and fairs that have now of late been ordained,[1] and this the abbot hinders.

(The abbot.) Also the abbot has sold woods not meet for felling, which are called Eastwood and Westwood,[2] and many besides.

(The abbot.) Also he says that the abbot has not rendered an account for several years and does not pay his brethren their stipends, insomuch that to some he owes six marks, to some more or less, nor does he repair the tenements of the monastery: nay, they are almost altogether in ruins.

(More.) Also he says that brother John More, the abbot's confessor, stirs up strifes and debates between the abbot and convent.

(The abbot.) Also he says [that] the abbot's secular serving-folk, especially the men of his bed-chamber or chamberlains, must needs be removed, because by reason of them, since they are youths and wanton, sore scandal is bred to the monastery.

(The abbot.) Also he says, even as brother John Burghe makes deposition, concerning the abbot's incontinence.

(The abbot.) Brother Richard Statherne[3] says that the abbot comes not to quire for high masses and processions, as the others his predecessors were wont, nor does he keep watch that silence be observed according to the rule in cloister and elsewhere.

(The prior.) Also he says that the prior does not attend quire, cloister or frater, but stays always at Oxney, on which account the divine office is neglected [and] the regular observances, and silence also, are not kept.

(Harletone the cellarer.) Also he says that brother Richard Harletone,[4] the cellarer on behalf of the convent, does not serve this deponent, when he is ailing, with victuals according to the rule.

(Gosberkyrk.) Brother John More[5] says that brother Thomas Gosberkyrke, sometime the fraterer, has not yet rendered his account concerning that office for the year last gone by.

(Gosberkyrk.) Also the same brother Thomas is now in his seynies at Oxney. He goes oftentimes after breakfast and supper to the town of Peterborough and stays therein amusing himself with secular persons, even women, until ten or eleven o'clock at night, before he goes back to Oxney.

(Gosberkyrk.) Also brother Thomas celebrates hardly once in the week, nor does he keep his course in celebrating the masses of his week.

(Gosberkyrk, Markham.) Also brother Thomas and brother William Markham do use to drink at eventide in the treasury, where suspect women come in their company to the scandal of the house; and concerning their absence from quire in time of divine service he makes deposition even as brother William Aldewyncle has deposed.

(Mortone.) Also brother William Markham uses to walk up and down of an evening between the monastery and Oxney, drinking in the thorpes that lie between, to the scandal of the monastery.

---

[4] *I.e.* the younger Harletone. He did not give evidence.
[5] Fourth prior in 1442: he was now abbot's confessor (see Morton's fourth deposition).

(Abbas.) Frater Johannes Pyghtesley dicit quod abbas non reddidit compotum de administracione sua secundum regulam per biennium elapsum.

(Gosberkyrk.) Item dicit quod frater Thomas Gosberkyrk non venit vllo die ad matutinas, missas vel horas, eciam si abbas presens sit, quia non curat de aliquo.

(Turvey.) Item dicit quod frater Johannes Turvey est vsurarius vt supra, et quod impignorauit pixidem et alia vt supra.

(Abbas.) Frater Johannes Burghe junior dicit quod abbas detinet iniuste a confratribus suis stipendia sua.

(Abbas.) Item dicit quod abbas dedit vnam murram ornatam argento aureato de bonis communibus domus vxori Willelmi Est absque consensu conuentus, cum qua notatur super adulterio, vt fama publica laborat.

(Abbas.) Item dicit quod abbas notatur super graui crimine adulterii cum Margareta vxore Willelmi Clerk commorantis ad portam exteriorem monasterii et cum Alicia vxore Willelmi Parker de Ivebury.

(Abbas.) Item abbas inconsulto conuentu sub sigillo dedit custodiam parci de Ivebury dicto Willelmo Parkere ad terminum vite sue.

(Abbas.) Item abbas non reddidit conuentui compotum administracionis sue secundum regulam per quatuor annos.

(Abbas.) Item abbas absque consensu conuentus vendidit siluas non ceduas apud Fyskertone in dilapidacionem bonorum monasterii.

(Abbas.) Item abbas obligauit vnam villam pertinentem monasterio absque consensu conuentus domino de Cromwelle sub ypotheca pro certa summa pecunie, et quod tenementa monasterii in defectu abbatis sunt in maxima ruina; sicque ex multis causis est dilapidator bonorum communium monasterii.

(Abbas.) Item abbas dedit vxori dicti Willelmi Parkere[1] vnam clamidem cum vario furruratam quam frater Johannes Depyng, vltimus abbas ibidem, pro[2] expressum reliquit successoribus suis abbatis[3] nulli alii conferendam.

(Makesey.) Frater Robertus Lidyngtone dicit quod frater Thomas Maksey irreligiose deambulat inter studentes in claustro, confabulando cum eis et impediendo eorum studium, et cum nihil habeat cum nouiciis, de ipsis se semper intromittit.

(Abbas.) Item abbas non reddit compotum de administracione sua secundum regulam, et vendit siluas monasterii absque consensu conuentus, nec soluit salaria confratribus suis.

(Gosberkyrk.) Item frater Thomas Gosberkyrk non venit ad matutinas cum est presens in monasterio.

---

[1] *per expre* cancelled.
[2] *Sic*: for *per*.
[3] *Sic*: for *abbatibus*.

[1] A new name. He was one of the acolytes presented for subdeacon's orders, 15 Dec., 1445, and for deacon's orders, 9 March, 1445-6 (Reg. Assheton, ff. 16 *d*, 17). He was presented for priest's orders 1 June, 1447 (*ibid.* fo. 21). At the election of abbot Ramsey, 27 March, 1471, he was warden of Oxney (*Monasticon* I, 363, note b).

(The abbot.)   Brother John Pyghtesley[1] says that the abbot has not rendered an account of his administration according to the rule by the space of two years past.

(Gosberkyrk.)   Also he says that brother Thomas Gosberkyrk comes not to matins, masses or the hours on any day, even if the abbot be present; for he takes no care of anything.

(Turvey.)   Also he says as above that brother John Turvey is an usurer, and that he has put the pyx and other things in pawn, as above.

(The abbot.)   Brother John Burghe the younger[2] says that the abbot wrongfully withholds their pay from his brethren.

(The abbot.)   Also he says that the abbot gave a mazer adorned with silver gilt out of the common goods of the house to William Est's wife without the consent of the convent, and he is defamed of adultery with her, as is the constant public rumour.

(The abbot.)   Also he says that the abbot is defamed of the grievous crime of adultery with Margaret the wife of William Clerk, who dwells at the outer gate of the monastery, and with Alice, William Parker's wife of Eyebury.

(The abbot.)   Also the abbot, without the advice of the convent, gave the wardenship of the park of Eyebury to the said William Parkere under seal for the term of his life.

(The abbot.)   Also the abbot has not rendered an account of his administration to the convent according to the rule for four years.

(The abbot.)   Also the abbot, without the consent of the convent, has sold woods at Fiskerton not meet for felling, to the dilapidation of the goods of the monastery.

(The abbot.)   Also the abbot, without the consent of the convent, has bound a town which belongs to the monastery to lord Cromwell[3] under mortgage for a certain sum of money, and [he says] that the tenements belonging to the monastery are in the worst state of ruin in the abbot's default; and so for many reasons [the abbot] is a dilapidator of the common goods of the monastery.

(The abbot.)   Also the abbot gave to the said William Parkere's wife a mantle furred with vair, which brother John Depyng, the last abbot in the same place, expressly left to the abbots his successors, to be bestowed upon no-one else.

(Makesey.)   Brother Robert Lidyngtone[4] says that brother Thomas Maksey, contrary to religious discipline, walks up and down among [the monks] at study in cloister, chattering with them and hindering their study, and albeit he has naught to do with the novices, he is ever intermeddling with them.

(The abbot.)   Also the abbot renders no account of his administration according to the rule, and he sells the woods of the monastery without the consent of the convent, nor does he pay his brethren their stipends.

(Gosberkyrk.)   Also brother Thomas Gosberkyrk comes not to matins when he is present in the monastery.

---

[2] A new name. Presented for subdeacon's and deacon's orders with Pyghtesley and others (see previous note).
[3] Ralph, lord Cromwell, treasurer 1433-43. See *Visitations* II, 24, note 2.
[4] Present at the election of abbot Ramsey in 1471 (*Monasticon* u.s.)

(Gosberkyrk.) Frater Willelmus Aldewyncle dicit quod frater Thomas Gosberkyrk iactauit se quod, si quis quicquam de eo deponeret, sciet adstatim de deponente.

(Abbas.) Item abbas detinet a confratribus suis stipendia sua.

(Abbas.) Item dicit quod vbi Henricus Ouertone, dudum abbas, ordinauit circa tenementa, ex quorum prouentibus tempore exequiarum suarum in monasterio annuatim celebrandarum quilibet monachus perciperet per manum abbatis pro tempore existentis vnam libram cere et xl d., abbas nunc subtraxit omnia predicta toto tempore suo, cuius pretextu exequie huiusmodi non celebrantur.

(Abbas.) Item abbas notatur super crimine adulterii cum Margareta et Alicia supradictis.

(Turvey.) Item dicit de vsuria commissa per fratrem Johannem Turvey vt supra, et quod impignorauit duas phiolas et vnam craterem de bonis communibus domus absque consensu conuentus, sed nescit cui vel quibus.

(Markham.) Item frater Willelmus Markham exercet potaciones serotinas post completorium in thesauraria, vbi conueniunt in noctis crepusculo mulieres suspecte de villa, et presertim Johanna vxor Willelmi Steynour de Burgo, cum dicto Markham.

[Fo. 125 *d.*] Item dicit quod frater Thomas Gosberkyrke habet communem accessum ad thesaurariam diebus et noctibus ac aliis temporibus indebitis, exercendo ibidem potaciones serotinas; et non venit ad chorum et diuina obsequia, et habet frequentem accessum ad domum Willelmi Castelle in villa de Burghe, ibidem indulgendo potacionibus contra iniuncciones domini.

Idem frater Thomas est incorrigibilis, quia non vult gubernari in aliquo per abbatem aut priorem, et idem maledixit domino propter suas iniuncciones, et hoc apud Oxney.

Item dicit quod tenementa monasterii in toto sunt ruinosa in defectu abbatis.

Item dicit de fratre Johanne Lynfelde vt supra, qui est precentor et subcellerarius pro conuentu.

Frater Willelmus Burghe dicit quod abbas notatur super incontinencia vt supra, propter quod dicit monasterium fore grauiter apud omnes diffamatum.

Item dicit quod abbas vendidit siluas monasterii plurimum indiscrete absque consensu conuentus.

Item dicit quod frater Thomas Maksey, quando abbas monuit eum in virtute obediencie quod permittere[1] eum intrare per portam sacristarie, resistebat abbati in facie sua cum cultello extracto in manu sua in pessimum exemplum.

Item dicit quod frater Thomas Gosberkyrke, postquam abbas receperat litteras domini pro ista visitacione, fecit conspiraciones inter

---

¹ *Sic*: for *permitteret.*

¹ See p. 284, note 3.
² Abbot 1361-91.
³ *I.e.* the obits to be celebrated for the donors of this property.
⁴ See p. 274, note 8.

(Gosberkyrk.)   Brother William Aldewyncle[1] says that brother
Thomas Gosberkyrk boasted of himself that, if anybody should depose
aught concerning him, he shall know at once of the deponent.

(The abbot.)   Also the abbot keeps back their pay from his brethren.

(The abbot.)   Also he says that whereas Henry Overtone,[2] sometime
the abbot, did make an ordinance about the tenements, from the profits
whereof, at the time of the yearly celebration of their obits[3] in the monastery, every monk should receive a pound of wax and forty pence at the
hand of the abbot for the time being, the present abbot has withdrawn
all the [payments] aforesaid during his whole time, by occasion whereof
such obits are not celebrated.

(The abbot.)   Also the abbot is defamed of the crime of adultery
with Margaret and Alice abovesaid.

(Turvey.)   Also he says as above concerning the usury committed
by brother John Turvey, and that he has put two phials and a bowl of
the common goods of the house in pawn without the consent of the
convent, but he knows not to what person or persons.

(Markham.)   Also brother William Markham holds drinkings of
an evening in the treasury after compline, where there come together
at dusk of night suspect women from the town, and especially Joan,
William Steynour's wife of Peterborough, in company with the said
Markham.

Also he says that brother Thomas Gosberkyrke has common access
to the treasury by day and by night and at other undue seasons, holding
drinkings therein at eventide; and he comes not to quire and divine
worship and has often recourse to William Castelle's [4] house in the town
of Peterborough, indulging in drinkings in the same contrary to my
lord's injunctions.

The same brother Thomas is past correction, for he will not be ruled
in aught by the abbot or the prior, and he likewise has reviled my lord
because of his injunctions, and this at Oxney.

Also he says that the tenements belonging to the monastery are
utterly in ruins in the abbot's default.

Also he says as above concerning brother John Lynfelde, who is
precentor and sub-cellarer for the convent.

Brother William Burghe[5] says as above that the abbot is defamed
of incontinence, for the which reason he says that the monastery is
grievously defamed on all hands.

Also he says that the abbot has sold the woods of the monastery
with very little discretion, without the consent of the convent.

Also he says that brother Thomas Maksey, when the abbot admonished him in virtue of obedience to suffer him to enter by the door
of the sacristy,[6] withstood the abbot to his face with a dagger drawn in
his hand, to the most evil example [of others].

Also he says that brother Thomas Gosberkyrke, after that the
abbot had received my lord's letters for this visitation, made conspiracies

---

[5] The preacher at the visitation of 1442. From the proceedings recorded at
the end of the visitation, he was steward of the monastery at this date. He was
still in the monastery in 1471 (*Monasticon*, u.s.).

[6] The doorway on the west side of the building between the cloister and south
transept.

fratres, dicens eis ' Cum quo vis tu esse, vtrum ex parte mea vel abbatis ? Si ex parte abbatis, tu primo accusaberis.'

Item frater Thomas maledixit domino vt supra, et pessime se habet in regimine suo.

Frater Ricardus Bysley dicit quod abbas succidit quandam siluam pertinentem monasterio vocatam Longwode iuxta Lincolniam, sed ignorat quantum.[1]

Item dicit quod diffamatur super incontinencia cum pluribus mulieribus, prout laborat publica fama, et detinet a confratribus magnam partem communarum suarum.

Frater Walterus Wermyngtone dicit quod iuuenes monachi in noctibus post completorium ascendunt ad abbatem in camera sua et ibidem intendunt confabulacionibus, potacionibus, commesacionibus cum abbate vsque x vel xj horam in nocte, et ex hoc redduntur inepti ad surgendum ad matutinas.

Item abbas notatur super incontinencia cum Alicia vxore Willelmi Parcare de Ibury.

Item dicit quod abbas dilapidat nemora non cedua monasterii apud Fyrkertone[2] iuxta Lincolniam, iuxta Oundelle et Burghe, quorum nomina nescit describere.

Item dicit quod abbas solueret cuilibet monacho annuatim duas marcas, et de hac solucione est aretro per plures annos.

Frater Willelmus Talyngtone dicit quod abbas notatur super adulterio cum Margareta Clerk, manente ad portam exteriorem monasterii, et cum Alicia vxore Willelmi Parcare de Ibury, prout fama publica laborat.

Item dicit quod monachi sacerdotes recipiunt per annum nomine stipendiorum suorum quatuor marcas et diaconi xl s., qui pro magna parte iam subtrahuntur.

Item dicit quod seruientes in monasterio per tres annos non habuerunt nisi vnam liberatam, vbi singulis annis eam haberent.

Item dicit quod parci franguntur et dame ac hinnuli[3] capiuntur, et plura alia iura et libertates monasterii[4] violantur in defectu abbatis non defendentis iura huiusmodi.

Item dicit quod monachi officiarii non reddunt annuatim compotos de suis officiis, in tantum quod quidam sunt aretro de vij annis.

Frater Willelmus Gretforde dicit quod frater Thomas Gosberkyrk, licencia petita[5] nec obtenta, sepius ad villam de Burghe[6] sedens in ortis laicorum, et presertim Willelmi Steynour, bibens et commedens cum mulieribus, aliquando per duas vel tres horas, aliquociens vsque horam x vel xj in nocte, et non venit ad chorum tempore diuinorum fere per

---

[1] *Sic.*
[2] *Sic*: for *Fyskertone.*
[3] *capiant* cancelled.
[4] *vil* cancelled.
[5] *Sic*: probably *non petita* was meant.
[6] *Sic*: *accedit* omitted.

[1] At Oxney in 1442.
[2] See *Visitations* I, 222.
[3] New name. Presented for subdeacon's and deacon's orders with Pyghtesley, John Burgh, etc. (see p 293, note 1).

among the brethren, saying to them, ' With whom will you be, on my side or the abbot's ?   If on the abbot's side, you will be accused first.'

Also brother Thomas has reviled my lord as above, and very ill does he behave himself in his ruling.

Brother Richard Bysley says that the abbot has cut down a wood belonging to the monastery hard by Lincoln, called Longwood, but he knows not to what extent.

Also he says that the abbot is defamed of incontinence with several women, as public rumour persists, and he withholds from his brethren a large part of their commons.

Brother Walter Wermyngtone[1] says that the young monks go up at nights after compline to the abbot in his chamber,[2] and there do they stay chattering, drinking [and] eating with the abbot until ten or eleven o'clock at night, and hereby are they rendered unfit to rise for matins.

Also the abbot is defamed of incontinence with Alice, William Parcare's wife of Eyebury.

Also he says that the abbot dilapidates the copses of the monastery that are not meet for cutting at Fiskerton by Lincoln, by Oundle and [by] Peterborough, the names whereof he knows not how to write down.

Also he says that the abbot should pay two marks yearly to every monk, and he is several years in arrear as regards this payment.

Brother William Talyngtone[3] says that the abbot is defamed of adultery with Margaret Clerk, who dwells at the outer gate of the monastery, and with Alice, William Parcare's wife of Eyebury, as public rumour persists.

Also he says that the monks who are priests receive four marks a year under the name of their pay, and they who are deacons forty shillings, the which is now in great part withdrawn.[4]

Also he says that the serving-folk in the monastery have had but one livery for three years, whereas they should have it every year.

Also he says that the parks are broken and the hinds and foals are taken, and many other rights and liberties of the monastery are violated in the abbot's default, since he does not defend such rights.

Also he says that the monks who are officers do not render accounts of their offices every year, insomuch that some are seven years behind-hand.

Brother William Gretforde[5] says that brother Thomas Gosberkyrk, [without] asking or obtaining leave, [goes] very often to the town of Peterborough, where he sits in laymen's, and especially in William Steynour's orchard, drinking and eating with women, sometimes for two or three hours, sometimes until ten or eleven o'clock at night, and almost for two years he has come to quire in time of divine service only

---

[4] The total sum, as previously stated, was reckoned at £60. As the exact number of monks at this date was certainly somewhat larger than the twenty-nine of whom we hear (see p. 270, note 2), and we do not know the relative proportion of priests and deacons, it is difficult to make an approximately accurate statement on this point. We know of three who at this time were deacons. As the remaining twenty-five, not counting the abbot, were senior to them and probably all priests, the allowances required would come to a total of £72 13s. 4d. at least, if properly paid.

[5] See p. 284, note 9.

biennium nisi cum voluerit, et semper clamat de religione obseruanda. et ipsemet eam in nullo obseruat, nec iacet in dormitorio cum fratribus suis.

Item dicit quod honor foret monasterio et abbati quod Margareta Clerk et Alicia Parkere longius amouerentur a monasterio propter infamiam regnantem super criminibus commissis inter eosdem abbatem et mulieres.

[Fo. 126.] (Turvey.) Item dicit quod frater Johannes Turvey impignorauit diuersa bona et iocalia domus Roberto Barnak absque abbatis et conuentus consensu, que nondum redemit.

(Abbas.) Item quod in defectu abbatis non est satisfactum monachis de communis suis.

(Gosberkyrk.) Item quod in defectu fratris Thome Gosberkyrke, qui quasi communis susurro est, non est caritas neque pax in monasterio.

(Abbas.) Frater Willelmus Walmesforde dicit quod abbas est necgligens in reparando tenementa et domus reddituales monasterii que omnia paciuntur notabilem ruinam et ad terram quasi dilabuntur, nam ex huiusmodi redditibus resulteret[1] magna pars exhibicionis monachorum.

(Abbas.) Item abbas absque consensu conuentus vendidit et alienauit nemora non cedua prot. . . . d' videlicet de Fiskertone et de Estwode et Westwode, et pecunias exinde receptas consumpsit et dilapidauit ac nemus de Thurleby succidit et dedit amicis suis illis, et quia non clausit illud nemus, stipites renascentes per animalia ingrediencia consumuntur in finalem destruccionem nemoris huiusmodi.

(Abbas.) Item abbas non venit ad processiones diebus dominicis et festiuis et in quadragesima secundum antiquam consuetudinem monasterii.

(Abbas.) Item dicit quod abbas toto tempore suo defaltauit stipendia monachorum absque eorum consensu.

(Abbas.) Item dicit quod abbas habet iuuenes lasciuos sibi seruientes, cum quibus est nimis familiaris et secundum eorum consilium regitur; per quod et bona fama monasterii et abbatis multum leduntur.

(Abbas.) Item dicit quod abbas per tres annos subtraxit stipendia et liberatam seruiencium monasterii ad eorum magnam lesuram et monasterii scandalum.

(Abbas.) Item dicit quod si due mulieres cum quibus abbas diffamatur forent procul a monasterio amote, cederet monasterio et abbati in magnum honorem.

(Abbas.) Item dicit quod abbas sub sigillo suo,' conuentu inscio, concessit officium parcarie de Ibury Willelmo Parkere ad terminum vite sue, et Willelmo Est manerium de Thorpe et viij bigatas lignorum ad lx annos, pro minore pensione quam ipsum manerium per se reddere solebat.

(Abbas.) Item dicit quod in vltima quadragesima abbas equitauit vsque Stamfordiam et ibidem publice in omnium conspectu inter laicos

---

[1] *Sic*: for *resultaret*.

[1] At Oxney in 1442. At abbot Ramsey's election in 1471 he was an old man in the infirmary, together with John Yorke, then a very old man. Yorke, who was at Oxney in 1442, is not mentioned at this visitation.

whenever he wishes, and he is always clamouring about the observance of religion, and he himself observes it in naught, nor does he lie in the dorter with his brethren.

Also he says that great credit would come to the monastery and the abbot, were Margaret Clerk and Alice Parkere sent farther away from the monastery, because of the defamation which prevails touching the crimes committed between the same abbot and the women.

(Turvey.) Also he says that brother John Turvey has pawned divers goods and jewels of the house to Robert Barnak without the consent of the abbot and convent, the which he has not yet bought back.

(The abbot.) Also that in the abbot's default satisfaction is not made of their commons to the monks.

(Gosberkyrk.) Also that in default of brother Thomas Gosberkyrke, who is as it were a common whisperer, there is not love or peace in the monastery.

(The abbot.) Brother William Walmesforde[1] says that the abbot is neglectful as regards the repair of the tenements and houses that bring rent to the monastery, which all suffer noteworthy dilapidation and are almost falling to the ground, for out of such rents a large part of the monks' payments should arise.

(The abbot.) Also the abbot, without the consent of the convent, has sold and alienated copses not meet for felling . . . . . . , those to wit of Fiskerton and of Eastwood and Westwood, and the monies received therefrom he has spent and squandered, and he has cut down the wood of Thurlby[2] and given it to these friends of his, and, because he did not enclose the wood, the stumps as they shoot again are spoiled by the beasts that enter in, to the final destruction of such wood.

(The abbot.) Also the abbot comes not to processions on Sundays and feast-days and in Lent according to the ancient custom of the monastery.

(The abbot.) Also he says that the abbot, during his whole time, has failed to pay the monks' stipends, without their consent.

(The abbot.) Also he says that the abbot has wanton youths that serve him, with whom he is over kindly and is ruled after their counsel; whereby the good report both of the monastery and of the abbot is sorely injured.

(The abbot.) Also he says that for three years the abbot has withdrawn the pay and livery of the serving-folk of the monastery, to their great hurt and the scandal of the monastery.

(The abbot.) Also he says that, if the two women with whom the abbot is defamed were sent far away from the monastery, it would turn out to the great fame of the monastery and the abbot.

(The abbot.) Also he says that the abbot, without the knowledge of the convent, granted the office of the parkership of Eyebury to William Parkere for the term of his life, and the manor of Thorpe and eight waggon-loads of logs to William Est for sixty years, for a smaller payment than the same manor used to render by itself.

(The abbot.) Also he says that last Lent the abbot rode to Stamford and there did publicly in the sight of all shoot at the mark, like a layman,

---

[2] Between Bourne and Market Deeping.

vt laicus sagittauit; et aliquociens equitat ad le Bellesyese et ibidem conuocat et lautissime conuiuat generosos, armigeros et laicos in graue dampnum monasterii.

(Abbas.) Item dicit quod abbas multum ducitur consilio iuuenum monachorum, qui si quid audierint in conuentu statim referunt abbati, et sic suscitant et nutriunt discordias inter abbatem et conuentum.

(Abbas.) Item dicit quod abbas solus vagatur circumquaque, eciam ad officinas monasterii, et inter monasterium et[1] Ibury cum vno solo monacho.

(Abbas.) Item dicit quod curie temporales tam in villa de Burgo quam extra non tenentur vt deberent : propterea priuilegia monasterii pereunt, et si quid in eis cum tenentur iudicatur, non exequitur in magnum preiudicium monasterii in defectu abbatis.

(Abbas.) Item vbi monasterium habere consueuit piscatores ad pisces capiendos ad commodum monasterii in paludibus et mariscis monasterii, iam nulli tales habentes,[2] sed et alii extranei absque licencia piscantur in eisdem, et tamen abbas nichil agit contra eos.

(More.) Item frater Johannes More quotidie quasi, quando abbas est in monasterio post completorium, venit de dormitorio et vadit ad abbatem ad cameram suam cum aliis iuuenibus monachis et ibidem intendit commesacionibus et potacionibus vsque decimam vel xj horam in nocte, et si quid audierit in conuentu refert abbati, et sic suscitat et fouet dissensiones inter abbatem et conuentum. Petitur igitur vt ad tempus aliquod ponatur in alio monasterio, quia quamdiu est in isto non erit in eo pax neque caritas.

Quibus omnibus sic examinatis ac ipsis abbate et conuentu simul conuocatis coram dicto reuerendo patre in huiusmodi negocio dicto loco capitulari et decimo die Septembris et anno predictis iudicialiter sedente et comparentibus, dictus reuerendus pater communicauit cum eis simul primo, et postea, abbate a capitulo amoto, cum conuentu, super compertis et detectis super et de persona abbatis. Tandem reuocato ad capitulum abbate, dominus iniunxit eidem abbati vt se in persona et regimine suis emendaret absque alio processu tunc contra eum iuxta detecta faciendo, volens vt asseruit eum sub paciencia tolerare vsque certum terminum futurum ad quem proposuit negocium istud sub spe melioracionis gesture abbatis continuare. Et demum obiecit dicto abbati crimina adulterii cum dicta Alicia Parkere, Margareta Clerke et Alicia Est, et eciam exitum monasterii in habitu seculari dimisso habitu regulari. Que omnia idem abbas expresse negauit ; tamen propter infamiam in hac parte laborantem monuit ipsum abbatem quod amoueat vxorem Parkere ab illo loco Ibury citra proximum proximum[3] festum Omnium Sanctorum, et dictam Margaretam a loco quo inhabitat cum

---

[1] *E* cancelled.
[2] *Sic*: for *habentur*.
[3] *Sic*.

[1] Belsize (i.e. *bel assis*), now a farm some four miles N.W. of Peterborough, near Marholm.
[2] Continued negligence of this kind no doubt contributed at a later period in the century to the straits into which the monastery was brought for obtaining fish, described in the petition for the appropriation of North Collingham church, Notts., in 1499 (York Reg. Rotherham I, fo. 286 *d*.). The passage is quoted and translated

among lay-folk; and sometimes he rides to Bellesyese[1] and there calls together and regales most sumptuously gentlemen, esquires and lay-folk, to the grievous damage of the monastery.

(The abbot.)   Also he says that the abbot is greatly led by the advice of the young monks, who straightway tell the abbot whatsoever they hear in the convent, and so stir up and cherish quarrels between the abbot and convent.

(The abbot.)   Also he says that the abbot wanders all about by himself, even to the offices of the monastery, and [goes] between the monastery and Eyebury with one monk only.

(The abbot.)   Also he says that their courts temporal, both in the town of Peterborough and outside, are not held as they should be: therefore do the privileges of the monastery come to naught, and whatsoever judgment is given in them when they are held is not executed, to the great prejudice of the monastery, in the abbot's default.

(The abbot.)   Also, whereas the monastery was wont to have fishermen to catch fish for the profit of the monastery in the fens and marshes of the monastery, now there are kept none such, but even other folk, strangers, do fish in the same without leave, and yet the abbot does naught against them.[2]

(More.)   Also brother John More almost every day, when the abbot is in the monastery after compline, comes from the dorter and goes to the abbot in his chamber with the other young monks and stays eating and drinking therein until ten or eleven o'clock at night, and he tells the abbot whatsoever he hears in the convent, and so kindles and feeds quarrels between the abbot and convent.   Prayer is therefore made that he be put for some time in another monastery, for, so long as he is in this, there shall be therein neither peace nor love.

Now, when all these had been thus examined and the same abbot and convent had been called together and made their appearance before the said reverend father, as he sate in his capacity of judge in such business in the said place of chapter and on the tenth day of September and in the year aforesaid, the said reverend father held counsel with them, at first all together, and thereafter, having sent the abbot out of the chapter-house, with the convent, touching the matters discovered and disclosed touching and concerning the abbot's person.   At last, having recalled the abbot to the chapter-house, my lord enjoined upon the same abbot that he should make amends in his person and governance, without at that time holding any other process against him in accordance with the disclosures, [but] wishing, as he averred, to bear with him patiently until a certain term to come, to the which he proposed to adjourn this business in hope of the betterment of the abbot's behaviour.   And at length he charged the said abbot with the crimes of adultery with the said Alice Parkere, Margaret Clerke and Alice Est, and also with his going out of the monastery in secular attire, having laid aside his regular habit.   All the which things the same abbot expressly denied; howbeit, because of the ill fame which persists in this behalf, [my lord] admonished the same abbot to remove Parkere's wife from that place of Eyebury on this side the next feast of All Saints, and the said Margaret with all speed from the

---

in *Assoc. Soc. R. & P.* xxxiv, 272-3.   The ostensible reason given is a series of long droughts which had checked the supply of fish.

festinacione, et quod non communicet cum illis nec Alicia Est suspecto modo, et quod abstineat ab illa Alicia Est sub pena excommunicacionis. Et deinde monuit abbatem et singulos monachos dicti conuentus quod nullus alii improperetur publice vel occulte occasione delatorum[1] et detectorum in huiusmodi negocio sub pena excommunicacionis quam in singulares personas contraueniencium intendit fulminare; et deinde continuauit huiusmodi negocium in statu quo tunc erat vsque in diem Mercurii proximum post festum purificacionis beate Marie proxime futurum, et ad quemlibet diem citra de quo pro tempore prouidebit, in eadem domo capitulari coram eo aut commissario suo ad vlterius procedendum, etc., presentibus magistro Roberto Thorntone, Johanne Derby, Johanne Malyns et Thoma Colstone. In crastino vero, xj vide-licet die mensis Septembris, in dicta domo capitulari idem reuerendus pater ex gracia sua et ad supplicacionem dicti abbatis admisit ipsum abbatem ad purgacionem suam faciendam super crimine adulterii cum prefata Alicia Est; qui se coram toto conuentu purgauit se[2] de dicto crimine ab omni tempore cum priore et aliis vij commonachis confratribus suis. Et deinde idem reuerendus pater monuit ipsum abbatem sub pena excommunicacionis quod non admittat aliquos detractores nec eos audiat detrahentes fratribus suis, sed eos omnino repellat et in nullo eis credenciam adhibeat, presentibus vt supra.

(Require actum contra mulieres habitum in scedula in hoc libro post.)

[Fo. 126 *d.*] Preterea vero x° die mensis Septembris in dicta domo capitulari coram prefato reuerendo patre venit prefatus frater Ricardus Harletone, prior, et exposuit dicto reuerendo patri quod adeo senectute et variis infirmitatibus depressus et attenuatus est, quod religioni et obseruanciis regularibus claustralibusque excubiis ac aliis que vtilitatem conuentus concernunt absque graui corporis dispendio intendere non potest, propter quod bene sibi constitit quod religio sub eius regimine non fructificat, sed et communitas conuentus grandia patitur dampna et iacturas. Propter que peciit a dicto reuerendo patre vt ipsum ab ipso officio prioris et eius solicitudine absoluere et alium in ipsum officium substituere dignaretur. Dictus vero reuerendus pater grandeuam[3] etatem ipsius prioris et prolixos labores suos quos in dicto monasterio ad eius commodum et honorem multis diebus sustinuit considerans, et propterea nolens eum tam subito exonerare, commisit et mandauit abbati vt ad proximum festum Sancti Michaelis ipsum priorem de dicto officio ipsius reuerendi patris auctoritate exoneret et alium suo loco surroget secundum monasterii consuetudinem approbatam, etc., pre-sentibus vt supra . xvij die mensis Septembris anno supradicto apud Bugdene dominus commisit vices suas magistro Roberto Thorntone, officiali Lincolniensi, ad recipiendum purgacionem dicti abbatis cum tribus abbatibus, tribus confratribus suis dicti monasterii monachis senioribus, et quinque capellanis honestis noticiam conuersacionis sue habentibus, super crimine adulterii cum Margareta et Alicia Parkere

---

[1] Altered from *delectorum.*
[2] *Sic: se* repeated.
[3] *r* or *p* cancelled.

[1] 8 February, 1446-7.
[2] This clerk is not mentioned in any of the other visitations.

place wherein she dwells, and not to hold converse with them or with Alice Est in manner suspect, and to keep from this Alice Est under pain of excommunication. And then he admonished the abbot and the several monks of the said convent that no-one should reproach another openly or in secret because of the matters reported and disclosed in such business, under pain of excommunication, which he intends to pronounce against the several persons of them that go counter hereto; and then he adjourned such business in the state wherein it then was until the Wednesday next after the feast of the purification of blessed Mary next to come,[1] and to any day this side thereof concerning which he shall make provision for the time, in the same chapter-house before him or his commissary, to take further process, etc., there being present master Robert Thorntone, John Derby, John Malyns[2] and Thomas Colstone. But on the morrow, the eleventh day to wit of the month of September, in the said chapter-house, the same reverend father of his grace and at the said abbot's supplication admitted the same abbot to make his purgation touching the crime of adultery with the aforesaid Alice Est; and he made purgation of the said crime for all time before the whole convent with the prior and seven other fellow-monks his brethren. And then the same reverend father admonished the same abbot under pain of excommunication to give place to no back-biters nor to give ear to them when they speak ill of their brethren, but to drive them utterly away and put no belief in them in any matter, there being present, as above.

(Look for the process held against the women in the sheet that follows after in this book.)[3]

Moreover, on the tenth day of the month of September in the said chapter-house, there came before the aforesaid reverend father the aforesaid brother Richard Harletone, the prior, and set forth to the said reverend father that he is so weighed down and weakened by old age and divers infirmities that he cannot take heed to religion and the regular observances and the watchings in cloister and other things that concern the profit of the convent without grievous bodily exhaustion, by reason whereof he has well assured himself that under his rule religious discipline bears no fruit, but rather the commonwealth of the convent suffers serious damage and loss. Wherefore he besought the said reverend father to deign to acquit him of the same office of prior and the anxiety thereof and to set another in his place in the same office. Now, the said reverend father, considering the great age of the same prior and his lengthy toils which he has undergone for many days in the said monastery to its profit and honour, and being therefore unwilling to discharge him so suddenly, gave commission and commandment to the abbot to discharge the same prior of the said office by the same reverend father's authority at the next feast of St. Michael and to substitute another in his room according to the approved custom of the monastery, etc., there being present, as above. On the seventeenth day of the month of September in the year abovesaid, at Buckden, my lord committed his part to master Robert Thorntone, the official of Lincoln, to receive the said abbot's purgation with three abbots, three of his brethren, being elder monks of the said monastery, and five honest chaplains who have knowledge of his conversation, of the guilt of adultery with Margaret [Clerk] and Alice Parkere and of the

---

[3] *I.e.* fo. 96 sched., given at the end of this visitation.

et super crimine apostasie vt in detectis, etc., die dominica proxima post festum Sancti Mathei proximum in ecclesia Sancti Johannis de Burghe, vocatis vocandis, etc., vt in genere, et ad certificandum citra festum Sancti Dionisii proxime futurum vna cum nominibus compurgatorum, etc.

Memorandum de fratre Johanne More qui est confessor abbatis.

Memorandum de loquendo abbati de resolucionibus fiendis cellerario.

Memorandum de loquendo abbati pro fratre Johanne Burghe, cecitate percusso, vt tractetur secundum consuetudinem vt stagriarius.[1]

Memorandum de tercio et quarto priore vt exonerentur de exaudicione confessionum.

Monachi habent separatim arma inuasiua et defensiua in cellis suis.

Item in locis minucionum tempore refeccionum fiunt oblocaciones,[2] detracciones contra absentes, que sunt cause diuisionis in conuentu.

De officiariis qui potuerunt ex antiquo interesse officio diuino, de cetero non eximantur ab hoc.

De noua domo constructa in elemosinaria versus villam, per quam mulieres ingrediuntur officium ele[mosinarii.][3]

In quo termino, octavo videlicet die mensis Februarii, anno Domini mccccxlvj, in domo capitulari dicti monasterii de Burgo Sancti Petri, coram prefato reuerendo patre in huiusmodi sue visitacionis negocio iudicialiter sedente et secundum retroacta in eodem negocio per eum et coram eo habita procedente, comparuerunt personaliter dicti abbas et singuli monachi de conuentu dicti monasterii. Et deinde recitato per ipsum reuerendum patrem processu per ipsum in hac parte habito, tota illa die octava Februarii tractauit inter dictos abbatem et conuentum et cum eis super regimine illius monasterii in temporalibus, in quibus illud monasterium idem reuerendus pater inuenit grauiter collapsum. Tandem quasi in noctis tenebris eiusdem diei viij Februarii, dictus abbas coram dicto reuerendo patre in dicta domo capitulari iudicialiter sedente, eciam presente ibidem toto conuentu, dixit quod voluit et plane[4] consenciit quod quatuor monachi dicti monasterii tunc nominati, videlicet frater Willelmus Extone prior, Ricardus Harletone nuper prior ac fratres Willelmus Burghe senescallus et Willelmus Markham thesaurarius dicti monasterii habeant administracionem omnium bonorum temporalium dicti monasterii de hinc vsque biennium proximum in sua superuisione, et quod in administracione huiusmodi illos nullatinus impediret iuramentum prestare vellet; quibus sic habitis, idem reuerendus pater negocium visitacionis sue huiusmodi in statu quo tunc erat vsque in diem tunc

---

[1] *Sic*: for *stagiarius*.

[2] *Sic*: for *oblocuciones*. There seems to have been a careless attempt to alter the *a* into *u*.

[3] The last part of this word is wanting, and the sentence does not appear to be finished.

[4] Probably *plene* was intended.

[1] *I.e.* of leaving the monastery and going about in public in lay costume.

[2] 25 Sept., 1446.

[3] 9 Oct., 1446.

[4] *I.e.* 1446-7.

guilt of apostasy,[1] as in the disclosures, etc., on Sunday next after the next feast of St. Matthew[2] in the church of St. John of Peterborough, after summoning those who should be summoned, etc., as in general, and to make certificate thereof on this side the feast of St. Denis next to come,[3] together with the names of the compurgators, etc.

Note should be made of brother John More, who is the abbot's confessor.

Note should be taken to speak to the abbot concerning the payments to be made to the cellarer.

Note should be taken to speak to the abbot on behalf of brother John Burghe, who is stricken with blindness, that he may be treated according to custom as a stagiary.

Note should be made of the third and fourth prior, that they may be discharged from hearing confessions.

The monks keep weapons of attack and defence in places apart in their cells.

Also in the places of their seynies there take place at meal-times despiteful words [and] backbitings against the absent, which are sources of strife in the convent.

As to the officers who could of old time be present at the divine office, let them not be exempted herefrom from henceforward.

Concerning the new house that is built in the almonry towards the town, wherethrough women come into the almoner's office.

At the which term, the eighth day to wit of the month of February, in the year of our Lord 1446,[4] in the chapter-house of the said monastery of Peterborough, before the aforesaid reverend father as he sate in his capacity of judge in the business of such his visitation and was proceeding according to the process previously done and held by him and before him in the same business, there appeared in person the said abbot and the several monks of the convent of the said monastery. And then, after the rehearsal by the same reverend father of the process held by him in this behalf, all that eighth day of February he held treaty among the said abbot and convent and with them touching the governance of that monastery in things temporal, wherein the same reverend father found that monastery grievously fallen to ruin. At last, almost in the darkness of the night of the same eighth day of February, the said abbot, in the presence of the said reverend father as he sate in his capacity of judge in the said chapter-house, the whole convent also being present in the same, said that it was his will and clear consent that four monks of the said monastery who were then named, to wit, brother William Extone the prior, Richard Harletone, late the prior, and brothers William Burghe the steward and William Markham the treasurer of the said monastery, should have the administration of all the temporal goods of the said monastery from henceforth until two years' time from now in their supervision, and that he was willing to proffer his oath to hinder them in no wise as regards such administration; and, when these things had thus taken place, the same reverend father adjourned the business of such his visitation in the state wherein it then was until the day which

crastinum et in eodem loco continuauit. In quibus termino et loco,
ix videlicet die mensis Februarii et domo capitulari predicta, coram
eodem reuerendo patre in huiusmodi visitacionis sue negocio vt premittitur iudicialiter sedente et procedente, comparuerunt personaliter dicti
abbas et singuli monachi conuentus predicti; et deinde recitato per
dictum reuerendum patrem promisso dicti abbatis de administracione
bonorum temporalium dicti monasterii et modo eiusdem vt premittitur
per ipsum abbatem facto, et super hoc certa scriptura confecta ipsi
abbati ostensa et per eundem reuerendum patrem in publico perlecta,
petitoque per eundem reuerendum patrem ab eodem abbate an huic
scripture annuere et eam obseruare vellet, idem abbas dicto reuerendo
patri humiliter supplicauit vt suis honori et honestati ex gracia sua
parcere dignaretur; nam si omnis administracio temporalium sibi adi-
meretur, esset sibi in perpetuum nominis sui scandalum. Peciit igitur
a dicto reuerendo patre vt ipsemet habeat administracionem huiusmodi,
adiunctis sibi dictis quatuor monachis in consiliarios et assessores. Vnde
idem reuerendus patre peciit a dicto abbate si se ordinacioni ipsius
reuerendi patris in hac parte submittere vellet; qui se ordinacioni et
voluntati dicti reuerendi patris in hac parte in alto et in basso *submisit,*
iurans fide sua media, dextera sua in manum dexteram dicti reuerendi
patris data, quod voluntati et ordinacioni dicti reuerendi patris in premissis *in alto et in basso* stabit et parebit in omnibus et per omnia prout
idem reuerendus pater voluerit et ordinauerit. Et deinde singulares
persone dicti conuentus per dictum reuerendum patrem singillatim inqui-
site se ordinacioni et voluntati dicti reuerendi patris in premissis in alto
et in basso submiserunt. Et deinde admissis per dictum reuerendum
patrem huiusmodi submissionibus, idem reuerendus pater voluit, ordinauit
et decreuit quod dictus abbas de hinc vsque biennium proxime futurum
habeat administracionem bonorum temporalium dicti monasterii, adiunctis sibi dictis quatuor monachis; et si eorum aliquis per mortem, infirmitatem vel alias legitime impeditus fuerit quo minus hiis possit intendere,
loco primi sic impediti alius de conuentu per abbatem assumatur, et loco
secundi sic impediti alius per conuentum assumatur, et sic semper locis
impeditorum alii per abbatem et conuentum diuisim assumantur, sine
quorum quatuor consilio, aduisamento et consensu adhibitis abbas
nichil grande vel arduum agat, neque nemora non cedua vendat vel
donet nec aliquid aliud agat quod in dilapidacionem sonare poterit;
quodque durante dicto biennio in cella de Oxney cum vno honesto
monacho[1] capellano suo, duobus generosis, tribus valettis et duobus
garcionibus honestis bone fame et nominis, non lubricis aut male fame
vel nominis, immoretur, et quociens necessarium foret pro superuidenda
huiusmodi administracione ac regimine monasterii in regularibus obseruanciis et diuino obsequio habeat accessum *ad monasterium,* non diu ibi

---

[1] Part of word, apparently *mitt,* followed by *d,* cancelled.

was then the morrow and in the same place.   At and in the which term and place, on the ninth day to wit of the month of February and in the chapter-house aforesaid, there appeared in person before the same reverend father, as he sate in his capacity of judge, and was proceeding, as is aforeset, in the business of such his visitation, the said abbot and the several monks of the convent aforesaid; and then, after the said abbot's promise concerning the administration of the temporal goods of the said monastery and the manner thereof, which had been made, as is aforeset, by the same abbot, had been rehearsed by the said reverend father, and a certain writing drawn up touching this matter had been shown to the same abbot and read through in public by the same reverend father, and after the same abbot had been asked by the same reverend father whether he would consent to this writing and keep it, the same abbot humbly besought the said reverend father that he would deign of his grace to spare his honour and good repute; for, if all the adminis-tration of temporal goods were taken away from him, it would be to the everlasting scandal of his name.   He prayed the said reverend father therefore that he may have such administration himself, taking into union with him the said four monks, to be his advisers and assessors. Wherefore the same reverend father asked of the said abbot whether he would submit himself to the same reverend father's ordinance in this behalf; and he submitted himself to the ordinance and will of the said reverend father in this behalf in high and in low, swearing upon his word of honour, having given his right hand into the said reverend father's right hand, that he will abide by and obey the will and ordinance of the said reverend father as regards the premises in high and in low, in all and through all things, even as the same reverend father shall will and ordain.   And then the several persons of the said convent, being ques-tioned one by one by the said reverend father, submitted themselves to the said reverend father's ordinance and will as regards the premises in high and low.   And then, after such submissions had been accepted by the said reverend father, the same reverend father willed, ordained and decreed that the said abbot shall have the administration of the temporal goods of the said monastery from henceforth throughout the two years next to come, taking into union with him the said four monks; and, if any one of them be hindered by death, bodily weakness or other lawful cause from being able to attend to these things, another person shall be chosen from the convent by the abbot in the place of the first so hindered, and in the place of the second so hindered another shall be chosen by the convent, and so ever shall others be chosen by the abbot and convent separately in the places of those hindered, and without the accession of the counsel, advice and consent of these four the abbot shall do no great or serious business, nor shall he sell or make presents of copses not meet for cutting or do aught else which may be taken to mean dilapidation; and that during the said space of two years he shall dwell in the cell of Oxney with one monk of repute as his chaplain, two gentlemen, three yeomen and two grooms, honest folk of good report and name, not lewd fellows or of ill report or name, and, as often as may be needful, he shall have recourse to the monastery to survey such the administration and governance of the monastery as regards the observance of the rule and divine worship, without staying there long; and that if, during the said

moraturus; quodque si *nec* sic monasterium ab ere alieno quo iam grauiter deprimitur[1] poterit releuari nec in aliis debite reformari durante dicto biennio, idem abbas in alto et in basso stabit et parebit voluntati et ordinacioni dicti reuerendi patris vt super mora sua, videlicet in quibus partibus, cum quantis personis, sub qua forma et quantis expensis, ad tempus vel tempora per dictum reuerendum patrem in hac parte assignanda *et moderanda*; ad que omnia tam dictus abbas quam singulares persone dicti conuentus expresse consensierunt. Sed quia grauis clamor erat tunc in conuentu de infamia publice volante tam ad intra quam ad extra super criminibus adulterii cum dictis tribus mulieribus et abbate, petitumque erat a dicto reuerendo patre quod ipse mulieres procul a monasterio eliminarentur, ita quod abbas ad eas nec ipse ad abbatem habere possent accessum, nam per eorum communicacionem suspectam continuatam monasterium grauiter apud omnes tam interius quam exterius diffamatur; ideo [fo. 127][2] idem reuerendus pater monuit eundem in virtute obediencie et . . . . [et sub pena priuacionis a statu et] dignitate sui abbacialibus quod in administracione temporalium dicti monasterii . . . . et quod ipsam formam in administracione huiusmodi nullatinus . . . . . . quodque ab omni communicacione, confabulacione et . . . . cum dictis mulieribus penitus et omnino se abstineat; denuncians et denunciauit eidem abbati publice tunc ibidem quod si et quatenus contingat imposterum dictum abbatem super premissorum aliquo canonice conuinci quod contra eum secundum canonicas sancciones et cum rigore procedet. Et hiis sic habitis idem reuerendus pater continuauit visitacionem suam huiusmodi in statu quo tunc erat vsque in proximum diem iuridicum post dominicam qua cantatur officium Misericordia Domini proxime futuram et ad quemlibet diem citra de quo . . . . eos premunierit presentibus abbate et toto conuentu et Johanne Malyns. Subsequenter vero eisdem die ix[o] Februarii et domo capitulari coram dicto reuerendo patre idem abbas genuflectendo iurauit ad Sancta Dei euangelia corporaliter tacta [per eum] quod ipse singulis monachis dicti conuentus salaria siue stipendia sibi per abbatem solui consueta singulis terminis [debitis] secundum consuetudinem monasterii absque dilacione persoluet nisi talis ineuitabilis necessitas ingruerit quod a solucione huiusmodi terminis suis ob maiorem vtilitatem monasterii eciam de consensu maioris partis[3] conuentus pro tempore ipsum [abbatem] abstinere oportebit. In quo casu cicius quo poterit conuentui satisfaciat; presentibus priore Ricardo Harletone . : . . . et pluribus aliis monachis et me Colstone.

[Fo. 96 *sched.*] Memorandum quod tercio die Decembris, anno Domini mcccc[m]o xl sexto in parlora reuerendi patris domini Willelmi, Dei gracia Lincolniensis episcopi, infra manerium suum apud Lidyngtone, sue Lincolniensis diocesis, situata, comparuit coram eodem reuerendo

---

[1] *d* and *nec* cancelled.
[2] The top of this leaf is torn and the writing is much obliterated.
[3] *consens* cancelled.

[1] The words *et abb'* in the original MS. seem to have been written carelessly as an afterthought: this is the only construction that they will bear.
[2] *I.e.* the second Sunday after Easter, which fell on 23 April in 1447.
[3] This schedule refers to a date between the visitation and Alnwick's final visit to the monastery in February, 1446-7.

space of two years, the monastery may neither be relieved of the debts wherewith it is now brought grievously low nor be duly reformed in other matters, the same abbot shall abide by and obey the will and ordinance of the said reverend father in high and in low as touching his abode, to wit in what parts, with how many persons, under what form and at what cost, for a time or times to be appointed and limited in this behalf by the said reverend father; and to all these things the said abbot, as well as the several persons of the said convent, gave their express consent. But because there was then grievous complaint in the convent concerning the ill fame that was publicly current, both within and without [the monastery], touching the crimes of adultery with the said three women and [touching] the abbot,[1] and prayer had been made of the said reverend father that the same women should be removed far from the threshold of the monastery, so that the abbot could have no recourse to them nor they to the abbot, for by the continuance of the suspect intercourse between them the monastery is grievously defamed among all men both within and without; therefore the same reverend father admonished him in virtue of obedience and . . . . [and under penalty of deprivation from his estate and] dignity of abbot, that, in the administration of the temporalities of the said monastery . . . . and that he shall in no wise . . . the same form in such administration . . . . and that he shall utterly and entirely abstain from all communication, conversation and . . . . . with the said women; and, making announcement, he announced to the same abbot that, if and so far as it may happen hereafter that the said abbot is canonically convicted touching any one of the premises, he will proceed against him vigorously according to the sanctions of canon law.   And, after these things had thus taken place, ·the same reverend father adjourned such his visitation in the state wherein it then was until the next law day after Sunday whereon is sung the office *Misericordia Domini* next to come,[2] and to any day on this side thereof, of which he shall . . . . give them notice, there being present the abbot and the whole convent and John Malyns.   And thereafter, on the same ninth day of February and in the same chapter-house before the said reverend father, the same abbot, bending on his knee, sware upon the holy gospels of God, which were touched [by him] bodily, to pay without delay to each monk of the said convent the salary or stipend accustomed to be paid him by the abbot at each term [whereon it is due] according to the custom of the monastery, unless there shall arise such unavoidable necessity that the same [abbot] must needs abstain from such payment at their several terms for the time being, for the sake of the greater advantage of the monastery, and also with the consent of the more part of the convent.   In which case he shall make satisfaction to the convent with what speed he can; there being present the prior, Richard Harletone . . . . and several other monks and I Colstone.

It is to be noted[3] that on the third day of December, in the year of our Lord 1446, in the parlour of the reverend father, the lord William, by the grace of God bishop of Lincoln, which is situate within his manor of Liddington,[4] of his diocese of Lincoln, there appeared in person before

---

[4] Doubtless the chamber at the west end of the hall, described in *Visitations* II, xxiv.

patre personaliter in iudicio Margareta Clerk, vxor Willelmi Clerke de Burgo,[1] *et iurata de veritate dicenda,* obiecto sibi crimine adulterii et incestus cum fratre Ricardo Asshtone, abbate monasterii de Burgo, huiusmodi crimen ab omni tempore constanter negauit. Tandem euocato dicto Willelmo Clerke predicto[2] ad presenciam dicti reuerendi patris, idem reuerendus pater retulit dicto Willelmo Clerke quod dicta Margareta vxor sua articulum predictum sibi obiectum negauit. Propterea[3] idem reuerendus pater, pensato quod dictus abbas fuit et est prelatus egregius ecclesie, vt asseruit, et propterea eius honor debeat in quantum possit illesus obseruari, dixit se velle ipsam Margaretam fauorabilius per-tractare, in *casu* quo ipsi Willelmus et Margareta a loco habitacionis sue, qui locus est contiguus monasterio, et ad scandalum euitandum se amouere vellent seu disponerent cum effectu. Tandem idem reuerendus pater prefixit et assignauit dictis Willelmo et Margarete terminum citra festum Purificacionis proximum ad amouendum se ab illo habitacionis sue loco, et in casu quo huiusmodi decreto domini parere curauerint cum effectu, voluit exhibere eis fauorem; et interim sub bona gestura dixit quod vellet ab vlteriori processu in hac parte supersedere, presentibus Thorpe, Malyns et Bugg.

Alicia, vxor Willelmi Parker, notatur cum eodem abbate dicto tercio die Decembris, etc. Negat articulum, etc. Tandem postea dictus Willelmus obligauit se per suum scriptum obligatorium dicto reuerendo patri in xl li., etc.; cuius condicio est quod in casu quo amoueat vxorem suam[4] ab Ibery citra festum Purificacionis vel interim, nullatinus ibidem permansuram cum familia, tunc pro nulla habeatur: alioquin in suo robore stet et effectu.

LXI.

[Fo. 44].

Visitacio RAMESEY.[5]

Frater Johannes Stowe, abbas, examinatus super contingentibus sui statum monasterii in spiritualibus et temporalibus petit inducias vt deponere valeat [in] scriptis.

---

[1] *et* cancelled.
[2] *Sic.*
[3] Altered from *propteri.*
[4] *cum ad* cancelled.
[5] Ff. 40-43 are lost. They probably contained the opening part of this visitation.

[1] Abbot Assheton continued to rule the monastery for twenty-five years after this date. Apparently great things had been hoped from his rule, and the state of the monastery in 1442 was satisfactory, unless there was collusion to hide faults from the visitor. To assume collusion, however, without positive evidence to that effect, would be prejudiced. It is clear, however, that by 1446 the abbot had dis-appointed expectations. Subsequently there is reason to think that he re-estab-lished his good name. The monastery did not decline under his rule, and after his death in 1471 there were thirty-seven monks in it. It was during the later part of his rule that the Peterborough *Ordinale,* usually referred to as a *Consuetudinarium,* now in the library at Lambeth palace, was compiled.

[2] It is unfortunate that three leaves have disappeared at this point in the MS., as they may have contained a full account of the process, similar to that which prefaces the depositions in the Peterborough visitation of 1437 (No. LVIII).

the same reverend father in judgment Margaret Clerk, the wife of William Clerke of Peterborough, and, being sworn to tell the truth, when the guilt of adultery and incest with brother Richard Asshtone, the abbot of the monastery of Peterborough, had been laid to her charge, she steadfastly denied such guilt at any time.   At length, when William Clerke aforesaid had been summoned to the said reverend father's presence, the same reverend father told the said William Clerke that the said Margaret his wife denied the article aforesaid which was laid to her charge.   Therefore the same reverend father, perpending that the said abbot has been and is a distinguished prelate of the church, as he averred, and therefore his honour should be preserved from hurt, in so far as it may, said that he would deal more favourably with the same Margaret, in the case that the same William and Margaret should be willing or should arrange effectually to remove for the avoidance of scandal from the place of their dwelling, the which place is adjoining to the monastery.   At last the same reverend father appointed beforehand and assigned to the said William and Margaret a term on this side the feast of the Purification next, to remove from that place of their dwelling, and in the case that they take order to obey effectually such my lord's decree, he would show them favour; and meanwhile, on condition of their good behaviour, he said that he would stay further process in this behalf, there being present Thorpe, Malyns and Bugg.

Alice, the wife of William Parker, is defamed with the same abbot on the said third day of December, etc.   She denies the article, etc.   At length thereafter the said William bound himself by his written bond to the said reverend father in forty pounds, etc.; the condition whereof is that, in the case that he shall take his wife away from Eyebury on this side the feast of the Purification or in the meantime, so that she shall in no wise abide there with her household, then it shall be held for naught: otherwise it shall stand in its full strength and effect.[1]

LXI.

The Visitation of Ramsey.[2]

Brother John Stowe, the abbot,[3] examined concerning matters touching the state of his monastery in things spiritual and temporal, prays for delay, so that he may be able to make his deposition [in] writing.

---

[3] Abbot Stowe entered office in 1436, during the voidance of the see of Lincoln after bishop Gray's death.   The *congé d'élire* on the death of abbot John Croweland was granted 24 March, 1435-6; the royal assent was given on 4 April following; and, after the confirmation of Stowe's election by Peter Partrich, official *sede vacante*, the temporalities were restored on 6 April (*Cal. Pat.* 1429-36, pp. 508, 510).   Stowe resigned by 27 Aug. 1468 (*ibid.* 1467-77, p. 107).

Forty-four monks were present at this visitation.   Of thirty-six surnames, twelve are those of places in Huntingdonshire, borne by seventeen monks, viz., Alconbury (2), Bury, Chesterton, Ellington (2), Glatton, Hamerton, Houghton, Ramsey (3), St. Ives, Stow, Stukeley (2), and Yaxley.   From adjoining counties come Cambridge (3), Morden, Whittlesey, and possibly Hinton, Cambs.; Eyworth (2) and Meppershall, Beds.; Berkhampstead and Therfield, Herts; Burgh (Peterborough), Clyffe (Kingscliffe) and Titchmarsh (3), Northants.   Swaffham and Walsoken come from Norfolk; Lavenham from Suffolk; Deeping from Lincolnshire. Seven names are of doubtful origin, viz. Bemwell, Bernere, Burton, Marcheford, Mitford, Papeley (possibly Paveley, *i.e.* Pavilly) and Stokes.

[Frater] Johannes Styuecle, prior, dicit de pluralitate locorum vescendi, per quod religio multum leditur et temporalia dissipantur in victua[lib]us; quod incommodum potest remediari per hoc quod hec pluralitas ad loca pauciora reducatur: quia religio in hiis *locis* non seruatur.

[I]temque[1] dicit quod frater Johannes Lauenham, elemosinarius, tenet frequenter nimis familiam apud Bury in domo officii [sui] ibidem nimium sumptuosam et monasterio dispendiosam; attrahit namque ad se multitudinem populorum[2] inutilium ad locum [ill]um et eciam monachos.

Item dicit quod sacrista nimis frequenter tenet sumptuosam familiam in officio extra tempus necessitatis, attrahens sibi [m]onachos et alios per quos monasterium dampnificatur.

Frater *Ricardus*[3] Elyngtone, degens in cella Sancti Iuonis, dicit omnia bene quo ad scire suum.

Frater Robertus Caumbrig, degens in cella Sancti Iuonis, dicit quod elemosinarius *in officio suo* et in infirmaria[4] locus qui dicitur commune borde.[5]

Item quod frater Robertus Eyworthe et Johannes Burtone *Sancti Iuonis* conducunt crofta et terras a laicis et ea seminant cum wode et aliis seminibus ad commoda [prop]ria et non monasterii aut celle Sancti Iuonis; nam iste Burtone *ad hoc* destruxit crocum crescens[6] apud Sanctum Iuonis[7], et per hec diffamantur in partibus super mercandizacione et proprietate.

Item dicit quod cum pertineat ad officium sacriste Sancti Iuonis reparacio tocius ecclesie celle ibidem, in defectu fratris Johannis Burtone, sacriste ibidem, ecclesia illa maximam patitur ruinam.

Frater Johannes Hamertone dicit quod omnia bene.

+Frater Johannes Alcumbury, prior celle Sancti Iuonis, dicit quod quando fuit tonsuratus non fuerunt nisi tria domicilia in monasterio, videlicet aula vel camera abbatis, refectorium et aula minucionum,[8] et iam sunt perplurima, propter quod religio perit et bona consumuntur. Petit igitur vt huiusmodi abusus ad pristinum vsum reducatur.

+Item dicit quod aliquociens elemosinarius apud Bury, aliquociens apud ly spitelle tenet domicilium siue familiam suam superfluam ad magnum domus scandalum et detrimentum.

+Item monachi stantes cum abbate apud le Byggyng in refeccione meridiana, vbi post illam directe[9] redirent ad monasterium, hoc relicto

---

[1] *Sic.*
[2] *inul* cancelled.
[3] Interlined above *Rogerus* cancelled.
[4] *q* erased.
[5] The sentence is as above, but there is some omission, and it is possible to supply only the general sense.
[6] *in* cancelled.
[7] *Sic*: for *Iuonem.*
[8] Written *mumucionum.*
[9] *accederent ad* cancelled.

[1] Bury in Hurstingstone hundred, Hunts., a mile south of Ramsey.
[2] For St. Ives priory, see *Visitations* I, 155. The relation of St. Ives to Ramsey resembled that of Oxney to Peterborough. At the present time there were six monks there.

[Brother] John Styuecle, the prior, says that they have many places for meals, whereby religious discipline is greatly damaged, and their temporal goods are wasted in victuals; the which disadvantage may be remedied by bringing these many places down to a few: inasmuch as in these places religious discipline is not observed.

Also he says that brother John Lavenham, the almoner, exceedingly often keeps a household at Bury[1] in the house of [his] office there, which is exceedingly costly and expensive to the monastery; for he draws to him at that place a multitude of unprofitable folk, and monks as well.

Also he says that the sacrist too often keeps a costly household in his office at seasons when there is no need, drawing to him monks and other persons by whom the monastery suffers loss.

Brother Richard Elyngtone, dwelling in the cell of St. Ives,[2] says that, so far as he knows, all things are well.

Brother Robert Caumbrig, dwelling in the cell of St. Ives, says that the almoner [keeps open house] in his office, and [that] in the infirmary [there is] a place which is called ' commune borde.'[3]

Also that brother Robert Eyworthe and John Burtone of St. Ives[4] hire crofts and lands from lay-folk and sow them with woad and other seeds to their own profit, and not to that of the monastery or of the cell of St. Ives; for this Burtone did for this purpose destroy the saffron growing at St. Ives, and by reason hereof they are defamed of bargaining and private gain in the neighbourhood.

Also he says that, whereas it appertains to the office of the sacrist of St. Ives to repair the whole church of the cell there, that church, in default of brother John Burtone, the sacrist in that place, suffers very great dilapidation.

Brother John Hamertone says that all things are well.

+Brother John Alcumbury, prior of the cell of St. Ives, says that, when he was tonsured, there were only three household places[5] in the monastery, to wit, the abbot's hall or chamber, the frater, and the seyny hall, and now there are very many, by reason whereof religious discipline comes to naught and their goods are wasted. He prays therefore that for such abuse the former use be restored.

+Also he says that the almoner, sometimes at Bury, sometimes at the Spital,[6] keeps his lodging or household in excess, to the great offence and damage of the monastery.

+Also the monks who are with the abbot at his noonday meal at le Byggyng,[7] whereas they should return to the monastery as soon as

---

[3] This is evidently the sense. The term ' commune borde ' could be applied to the entertainment furnished by the almoner at Bury.

[4] Burtone was also a monk, though here ' brother ' is inadvertently used of Eyworthe alone.

[5] *I.e.* places where a separate table was kept.

[6] The Spital was probably the name given to the almshouse at the gate of the monastery.

[7] This was in the town of Ramsey, and was known in later times as Biggin house. The name survives, and one of the streets in Ramsey is called Biggin lane. Biggin = building: cf. the Biggin in Benefield parish, Northants, near Oundle.

nulla petita licencia vel obtenta, accedant[1] ad Bury et ibi cum elemosinario intendunt potacionibus, comesacionibus et aliis insolenciis vsque medias noctes.

+Item dicit quod monachi dicto completorio non accedunt ad dormitorium, sed intendunt vigiliis et potacionibus vsque x^{am}, aliquociens xj^{am} vel vlteriorem horam de nocte. Petit igitur vt hoc emendetur.

+Item dicit quod sunt quidam monachi dicentes se infirmos et non posse sequi chorum, et tamen sunt bene comedentes et bibentes, et indies visitant omnes quasi officinas monasterii domosque et ortos contra antiquam consuetudinem.

+Item dicit de elemosina distribuenda vt omnino distribuatur ad portas monasterii et nullatinus in infirmaria, sicut iam solito distribuitur, per quod datur occasio secularibus ingrediendi septa claustralia contra bonum religionis. Petit igitur vt hoc omnino remedietur.

+Item petit vt sacrista Sancti Iuonis compellatur ad reparacionem ecclesie ibidem secundum quod congruit officio suo, et quod computet priori ibidem de reparacione annua facta ibidem.

+Item dicit quod mulieres multociens admittuntur ad familiaritatem nimiam infra monasterium, vt ad potaciones et alias insolencias. Petit igitur vt ista cohibeantur.

+Item dicit quod per pueros et alios seculares fiunt conclamaciones et strepitus in infirmaria ad grauem inquietatem monachorum infirmancium.

+Item petit quod in correccionibus grauium defectuum monachorum faciendis aduocet prior abbatem ad sibi succurrendum.

[Fo. 44 *d.*] Frater Robertus Eyworthe dicit omnia bene.

+Frater Johannes Tychemersshe dicit quod aliquociens fiunt potaciones post completorium.

+Frater Rogerus Hoghtone dicit quod in horis canonicis de die perpauci sequuntur chorum, in tantum quod aliquociens non sunt vltra iiij, v vel vj in choro. Hore eciam debite *contemplacionis* non seruantur in claustro. Post completorium eciàm plures exeunt claustrum, omisso dormitorio, intendentes potacionibus et aliis insolenciis.

+Item dicit quod a pluribus annis non fuit compotus redditus in communi secundum exigenciam ordinis et statutorum.

Frater Robertus Alcumbury [deput]atur abbati pro custodia feretri Sancti Iuonis vt pro miraculis ibidem factis publicandis.

+Frater Willelmus Caumbrige dicit quod capella beate Marie ibidem est dotata in temporalibus vt custos illius exhibeat lumen coram ymagine eiusdem in eadem capella continue ardens de die et nocte, et iam extinguitur ad vij horam de nocte et non accenditur ante vij[2] horam in mane, et hoc in defectu custodis.

---

[1] *Sic*: for *accedunt*: *accedent ap* cancelled.
[2] Or *viij*.

[1] Cf. the state of things at Peterborough in 1437 (No. LVIII).
[2] Literally ' is deputed to the abbot,' but ' deputed by the abbot ' must be meant.

it is over, neglect to do this, and, without asking or obtaining leave, go to Bury and do there spend their time with the almoner in drinking, feasting and other irregular doings until midnight.

+Also he says that, when compline has been said, the monks do not go to the dorter, but keep late watches and drinkings until ten, sometimes until eleven o'clock or a later hour of the night. He prays therefore that this be amended.

+Also he says that there are some monks who say that they are ailing and cannot attend quire, and yet they are good eaters and drinkers, and daily visit almost all the offices of the monastery and its outbuildings and orchards, contrary to the ancient custom.

+Also concerning the distribution of alms, he says that it should be distributed altogether at the gatehouse of the monastery, and in no wise in the infirmary, as the customary distribution now is, whereby opportunity is given to secular folk to enter the cloister precincts, contrary to the welfare of religion. He prays therefore that this be altogether remedied.

+Also he prays that the sacrist of St. Ives be compelled to repair the church in that place, as befits his office, and that he render account to the prior there of the yearly repairs done therein.

+Also he says that women are oftentimes admitted to excessive intimacy within the monastery, to wit, to drinkings and other irregularities. He prays therefore that these things be kept in check.

+Also he says that bawling and uproar are made by boys and other secular persons in the infirmary, to the grievous disquiet of the monks that are ailing.

+Also he prays that, in making corrections of the grievous defaults of the monks, the prior may call the abbot to his aid.

Brother Robert Eyworthe says all things are well.

+Brother John Tychemersshe says that sometimes drinkings take place after compline.

+Brother Roger Hoghtone says that at the canonical day-hours very few attend quire regularly, insomuch that sometimes there are in quire not more than four, five or six.[1] The due hours for contemplation also are not kept in cloister. After compline also many go out of cloister, neglecting the dorter, and spend time in drinkings and other irregular doings.

+Also he says that for several years back no account has been rendered in common, as the order and statutes require.

Brother Robert Alcumbury is the abbot's deputy[2] as warden of the shrine of St. Ives, in such matters as the publication of the miracles done there.

+Brother William Caumbrige says that the chapel of St. Mary there[3] is endowed with temporal property, to the end that its warden may provide the light before her image in the same chapel, to burn continually day and night; and it is now put out at seven o'clock at night and is not lighted before seven o'clock in the morning, and this is in the warden's default.

---

[3] *I.e.*, the Lady chapel at Ramsey.

+Item dicit quod pulsaciones ad horas de die non fiunt prolixe secundum antiquam consuetudinem monasterii, sed adeo breui quod post cessacionem seniores non possunt commode accedere ad chorum ante inchoacionem horarum.

Frater Willelmus Clyffe dicit omnia bene.

Frater Ricardus Hyntone dicit omnia bene.

Frater Robertus Mitford dicit omnia bene.

Frater Thomas Ramesey dicit quod omnia bene, preter hoc quod est nimia raritas monachorum in conuentu, vt sibi videtur.

Frater Johannes Glattone dicit quod omnia bene.

Frater Johannes Depyng iuuenis est et dicit quod omnia bene.

Frater Willelmus Wytlesey nouissimus dicit omnia bene.

Frater Johannes Swafham dicit omnia bene.

Frater Willelmus Tychemersshe dicit quod aliquociens non est presidens in refectorio qui presideat religioni diebus illis presertim quibus carnes comeduntur ad extra, et sic obseruancie regulares non ibi obseruantur.

Frater Thomas Eyworthe dicit de pulsacione breui ad horas canonicas de die et ad collaciones vt supra.

Item dicit de miraculis publicandis vt supra.

Item dicit quod elemosinarius, sacrista, camerarius et cellerarius exhiberent equos monachis euntibus et redeuntibus a Ramesey ad Sanctum Iuonem et retro, et hec fuit causa tardi aduentus sui isto die a Sancto Iuone vsque Ramesey, eo quod nullum habuit equum ad hoc destinatum.

[Fo. 45.] +Frater Robertus Moredone, monachus *domus* Sancti Iuonis, dicit quod propter defectum reparacionis ecclesie ibidem pluuia dampnificat ecclesiam.

+Frater Johannes Burtone, monachus domus Sancti Iuonis, dicit quod sacrista, celararius, elemosinarius et camerarius ac magister operum *monasterii de Ramesey*[1] exhiberent equos propter monachos *qui* de Ramesey vsque *domum* Sancti Iuonis ibidem pro tempore moraturi transmittuntur, set sic[2] equos prouidere sepius omittunt, vnde huiusmodi monachi sic transmissi pedestres itinerare coguntur.

Frater Ricardus Walsokene, monachus domus Sancti Iuonis, dicit per totum cum primo examinato.

---

[1] *sunt necglig* cancelled.

[2] *non sepius* cancelled.

[1] For bell-ringing in a monastery see the elaborate directions in *Consuetud. S. Aug. Cantuar.* (Henry Bradshaw Soc.) ii, 291-317. The ordinary method for matins and vespers was to ring three chimes, viz. *primus motus*, one bell, *secundus motus*, two bells, *tertius motus*, the whole peal; but this order varied according to the season, and, of course, in different churches. For the minimum period to be occupied by a chime there seem to be no directions; but see Bradshaw and Wordsworth, *Lincoln Cath. Statutes* i, 366, ii, 102, for ' prolix ' ringing in the secular churches of Lincoln and York.

[2] *I.e.* that the number of monks who were together in the convent at one time was too small. The total number, though probably falling short of the full complement possible, was equal to that found at Peterborough in the previous year, and represents the average in the larger English monasteries at this period. No injunction was made with regard to a general increase in number.

+Also he says that the bells for the day hours are not rung at full length, according to the ancient custom of the monastery,[1] but for so short a time that, after they have stopped, the elder monks cannot get to quire conveniently before the hours begin.

Brother William Clyffe says all things are well.

Brother Richard Hyntone says all things are well.

Brother Robert Mitford says all things are well.

Brother Thomas Ramesey says that all things are well save this, that, as it seems to him, there are too few monks in the convent.[2]

Brother John Glattone says that all things are well.

Brother John Depyng is a young [monk] and says that all things are well.

Brother William Wytlesey, very lately professed,[3] says all things are well.

Brother John Swafham says all things are well.

Brother William Tychemersshe says that sometimes there is no president in frater to preside over religion, especially on those days whereon meat is eaten outside,[4] and so the regular observances are not kept there.

Brother Thomas Eyworthe says as above concerning the shortness of the bell-ringing for the canonical day-hours and collations.[5]

Also he says as above concerning the publication of miracles.

Also he says that the almoner, sacrist, chamberlain and cellarer should provide horses for the monks when they go and return from Ramsey to St. Ives and back again,[6] and this was the reason of his own late arrival to-day at Ramsey from St. Ives, because he had no horse appointed for this purpose.

+Brother Robert Moredone, monk of the house of St. Ives, says that, by reason of default in the repair of the church there, the rain does damage to the church.

+Brother John Burtone, monk of the house of St. Ives, says that the sacrist, cellarer, almoner and chamberlain and the master of the works[7] of the monastery of Ramsey should provide horses for the monks who are sent from Ramsey to the house of St. Ives to stay there for a season; but they very often neglect so to provide horses, whereby such monks, so sent, are compelled to make the journey on foot.

Brother Richard Walsokene, monk of the house of St. Ives, says altogether as does the first examined.[8]

---

[3] This is apparently the meaning of *novissimus*. William Witlesey, B.D., succeeded Stowe as abbot: royal assent 9 Sept., temporalities restored 20 Oct., 1468 (*Cal. Pat.*, 1467-77, pp. 107, 98). He died before 5 Sept., 1473 (*ibid.*, p. 394).

[4] *I.e.*, outside the frater. This seems to imply that at Ramsey, as in Cistercian monasteries (see p. 249, note 4), the frater was reserved for vegetarian diet, and meat was eaten in the misericord or some similar chamber. The ' loft ' at Durham became the habitual dining-room of the monks in the later middle ages (*Rites of Durham* [Surtees Soc.], pp. 86, 87): cf. the *deportum* at Christchurch, Canterbury (Willis, *Monastery of Christchurch*, pp. 59-61.)

[5] See p. 234, note 4.

[6] Cf. with the arrangement at Croyland, *Visitations* II, 55, 56, by which two horses were provided by the almoner, and two by the master of the works, for officers and monks going on journeys: see the memoranda to this effect, *ibid.* 57, 58.

[7] The master of the works is here added to the four other officers.

[8] *I.e.* the previous examinee.

+Frater Thomas Papeley, monachus *senex*, moram continuam trahens in infirmaria, dicit quod non seruitur infirmatis ibidem in cibis subtilibus et sanatiuis, set in grossis tantum, vtpote in bouinis et bacon.

+Item dicit quod magna est carencia vasorum eneorum et aliorum *coquine* ad infirmariam pertinentis in defectu[1] infirmarii et celarar[ii].

Frater Johannes Therfield, senex stagiarius in infirmaria, dicit quod omnia bene sunt et sana.

Frater Thomas Elyngtone dicit omnia bene.

Frater Johannes Jakesley dicit quod sana sunt omnia, etc.

Frater Johannes Mepsale[2] dicit omnia bene, etc.

Frater Johannes Ramesey iunior, capellanus abbatis, dicit omnia sana esse et congrua.

Frater Thomas Chestertone dicit quod sunt omnia bene.

Frater Henricus Berkhamstede dicit omnia bene.

Frater Johannes Lauenham, elemosinarius, dicit omnia bene esse et sana.

Frater Johannes Cambrygge dicit omnia bene esse, etc.

Frater Henricus Tichemersshe dicit omnia bene.

Frater Ricardus Stokes dicit omnia bene et[3]

Frater Willelmus Bemwelle[4] dicit omnia bene.

Frater Johannes Stucley iunior dicit omnia bene et[3]

Frater Willelmus Bury dicit omnia bene esse.

Frater Willelmus Burghe dicit omnia bene esse et sana.

Frater Johannes Marche*ford* dicit omnia bene.

[Fo. 45 *d.*] Frater Johannes Ramesey senior dicit omnia bene, etc.

Frater Johannes Seynt Ives dicit omnia bene.

Frater Johannes Bernere dicit omnia bene.[5]

[Fo. 46.] Quod prior et ceteri ordinis presidentes in monasterio quotidie corrigant defectus quotidianos secundum personarum qualitatem et delicti quantitatem absque omni personarum accepcione.

Quod in maioribus delictis et criminibus ipsi prior et presidentes aduocent abbatem vt eius presidio et assistencia crimina et delicta huiusmodi debite corrigantur secundum regulam.

Quod maior numerus fratrum solito sequatur chorum tempore horarum diurnarum, cum vix sint presentes in huiusmodi horis iiij aut v aut vj monachi in choro.

Quod pulsaciones ad horas diurnas et ad collacionem prolixius solito pulsentur secundum antiquam monasterii consuetudinem, quia

---

[1] *fri* (*fratris*) erased.
[2] *Sic*: probably for *Mepersale*.
[3] *Sic*: sc. *sana.*
[4] Possibly *Beniwelle*.
[5] *Frater Willelmus Wytleshey* cancelled.

[1] See p. 273, note 1. The phrase ' old stager ' is by no means modern.
[2] *I.e.* Meppershall, Beds.
[3] Compared with the carefully drawn up admonitions and the unusually elaborate injunctions, the depositions show a remarkable reticence. We can conclude only that the faults of the house were so patent that Alnwick attached no great importance to the repetition of ' omnia bene ' by nearly two-thirds of the convent. As has been said before (p. 302, note 1) it is wrong to assume that a chorus of such

+Brother Thomas Papeley, an old monk, abiding continually in the infirmary, says that the ailing monks therein are not served with delicate and health-giving food, but with coarse food only, such as beef and bacon.

+Also he says that there is a great lack of brass and other vessels in the kitchen belonging to the infirmary, in the infirmarer's and cellarer's default.

Brother John Therfield, an old man stagiary[1] in the infirmary, says that all things are well and wholesome.

Brother Thomas Elyngtone says all things are well.

Brother John Jakesley says that all things are wholesome, etc.

Brother John Mepsale[2] says all things are well, etc.

Brother John Ramesey the younger, the abbot's chaplain, says all things are wholesome and suitable.

Brother Thomas Chestertone says that all things are well.

Brother Henry Berkhamstede says all things are well.

Brother John Lavenham, the almoner, says that all things are well and sound.

Brother John Cambrygge says that all things are well, etc.

Brother Henry Tichemersshe says all things are well.

Brother Richard Stokes says all things are well and [sound].

Brother William Bemwelle says all things are well.

Brother John Stucley the younger says all things are well and [sound].

Brother William Bury says all things are well.

Brother William Burghe says that all things are well and sound.

Brother John Marcheford says all things are well.

Brother John Ramesey the elder says all things are well, etc.

Brother John Seynt Ives says all things are well.

Brother John Bernere says all things are well.[3]

That the prior and the other presidents of the order in the monastery shall correct daily defaults every day according to the quality of the persons and the degree of their transgression without any acceptation of persons.[4]

That in cases of more serious transgressions and crimes the same prior and presidents shall call in the abbot, that by his aid and assistance such crimes and transgressions may duly be corrected according to the rule.[5]

That a greater number of brethren than usual shall attend quire during the day-hours, since at such hours there are scarcely four or five or six monks present in quire.[6]

That the ringings for the day-hours and for collation shall be continued longer than is usual, according to the ancient custom of the

---

answers necessarily implies collusion to deceive the visitor; but there is certainly reason to suspect it in the present case.

[4] This long series of paragraphs embodies the bishop's admonitions *ad interim* and formed the foundation for the written injunctions which followed. To the first none of the depositions correspond. This and the succeeding paragraph form the subject of the eighteenth injunction.

[5] Founded upon the petition at the end of John Alcumbury's depositions.

[6] Founded upon Hoghtone's first *detectum*: cf. Thomas Ramesey's deposition. See the twelfth injunction.

iam adeo abbreuiantur quod ante earum cessacionem seniores non possunt commode ingredi chorum ante incepcionem horarum.

Quod omni die ad minus tercia pars conuentus commedat in refectorio, et sit ibi presidens vnus qui presit religioni, cum[1] aliquociens *non* sit ibi presidens *qui presit religioni*; et aliquociens si presidens sit ibi non sint fratres . . . . eundo[2] in ecclesia cantando gracias nisi presidens et vnus monachus, nam diebus saltem quibus carnes comeduntur ad extra perpauci vescuntur in refectorio.

Quod monachi singuli saltem potentes sequantur chorum et statim dicto completorio dormitorium petant, non exinde exituri ante vij horam diei sequentis, cum plures fingentes se infirmos, cum sint satis fortes vt comedant et bibant et ad exteriora vagentur, subtrahant se a sequela chori, et plures post completorium exeunt[3] claustrum intendentes potacionibus et aliis insolenciis vsque x horam de nocte, exceptis officiariis qui de nocte absque quesito colore in officiis suis occupantur; quodque decetero nulle fiant potaciones post completorium vt solito.

+Quod hore debite contemplacionis secundum regulam seruentur indies in claustro, cum modernis diebus quasi nulle obseruentur ibidem.

+Quod monachi stantes in refeccione meridiana cum abbate apud Byggyng statim post refeccionem illam directe redeant ad monasterium et nullatinus vsque Bury vt solito, vbi *nulla petita vel obtenta licencia* intendunt potacionibus et aliis insolenciis cum secularibus, eciam mulieribus suspectis pro quibus mittunt, et si mittere non audeant pro eis, accedunt ad eas in cotagiis suis, vbi morantur expectantes ibidem et extra monasterium vsque ad x vel xj horam de nocte.

+Quod in monasterio secundum antiquam laudabilem eius consuetudinem sint dumtaxat tria loca pro refeccione . . . videlicet aula vel camera abbatis, refectorium et aula minucionum, cum iam[4] exerceantur per monachos in refeccionibus suis plura alia et quasi indeterminata loca ad eorum refecciones, vbi[5] religio [non solum] . . . . . natur[6] sed quasi totaliter perit, et fragmenta mensarum suarum non ad elemosinam donantur, sed . . . . . . mode consumuntur.

+Quod monachis de facto infirmis in infirmaria seruiatur de cibariis laucioribus et subtilioribus quibus . . . . refici poterunt ad eorum sanitatem, cum iam solum seruiatur illis de grossis cibariis, videlicet carnibus bouinis [et bac]onis et aliis salsis quibus vesci non possunt *propter*[7] eorum debilitatem.

---

[1] *sit* cancelled.
[2] This passage is nearly illegible.
[3] *Sic*: for *exeant*.
[4] *sint* cancelled.
[5] *rell* cancelled.
[6] This portion of the passage is illegible.
[7] Interlined above *obstantibus* cancelled.

[1] Founded upon William Caumbrige's second, and Thomas Eyworthe's first *detecta*. No injunction was made upon this point.
[2] This is intended to remedy the multiplication of 'households,' mentioned in the first *detecta* of the prior and John Alcumbury. See also William Tychemersshe's deposition. The substance is embodied in the third injunction.
[3] Founded upon John Alcumbury's fourth and fifth, John Tychemersshe's, and Hoghtone's first *detecta*. See the first injunction.
[4] None of the depositions touch definitely on this: it was, however, a legitimate inference, and the fact may have been elicited by further questioning. See the third injunction.

monastery, because now they are made so short that, before they have stopped, the elder monks cannot conveniently enter quire before the hours have begun.[1]

That every day at least the third part of the convent shall eat together in frater, and there shall be one president there to be over religious discipline, since sometimes there is no president there in charge of religion; and sometimes, if the president be there, there are no brethren to go together into church, singing grace, save the president and a single monk, for at any rate on days when meat is eaten outside very few eat in frater.[2]

That each monk, who at any rate is able, shall attend quire and, immediately after compline has been said, shall go to the dorter, nor go out therefrom before seven o'clock on the following day; whereas many, feigning themselves to be sick, though they be strong enough to eat and drink and roam out of doors, withdraw themselves from attendance in quire, and many go out of cloister after compline and spend the time in drinkings and other irregularities until ten o'clock at night, except the officers who without feigned excuse are busied in their offices by night; and that henceforward no drinkings shall be held after compline, as is customary.[3]

+That the due hours for contemplation according to the rule shall be observed daily in cloister, since at the present time hardly any are kept therein.[4]

+That the monks who stay with the abbot at Byggyng at the noonday meal shall immediately after that repast return straight to the monastery, and in no wise go, as is their wont, to Bury, where, without asking or obtaining leave, they spend their time in drinkings and other irregular doings with secular persons, even with suspect women for whom they send; and, if they dare not send for them, they go to them in their cottages, where they stay, tarrying there and outside the monastery until ten or eleven o'clock at night.[5]

+That there shall be in the monastery, according to its ancient and laudable custom, three places for meals . . . . to wit, the abbot's hall or chamber, the frater and the seyny hall, since at their meals several other places which are hardly defined are used by the monks for their meals, wherein religious discipline [not only is damaged] but almost entirely comes to naught, and the fragments from their tables are not given to the alms, but are wasted in [divers] ways.[6]

+That the monks who are actually ailing in the infirmary shall be served with richer and more delicate foods, whereby they may [best] be restored to their health, whereas they are now served with coarse food only, to wit, with beef and bacon and other salt meats which because of their weakness they cannot eat.[7]

---

[5] Founded upon John Alcumbury's third *detectum*. The circumstantial detail added here indicates that further inquiry had been held on this point. See the fourth injunction.

[6] Founded upon the prior's and John Alcumbury's first *detecta*. Cf. the fifth paragraph of this series. See the second injunction.

[7] Founded upon Papeley's first *detectum*. For this and the next paragraph see the tenth injunction.

+Quod in infirmaria *aut cameris monachorum ibidem* non sint tot pueri de nocte aut aliis[1] seculares, cum hiis diebus sint ibidem ad [minus] iiij[or] vel plures pueri *qui* faciunt ibidem strepitus et clamores ad grauem inquietacionem infirmancium [ibidem, et] cum sint in infirmaria vnus barbitonsor et vnus lotor qui seruiant infirmis non sunt necesse tot [pueri].

+Quod de die et nocte sit continue lumen ardens in capella beate Marie secundum eius dotacionem et fundacionem; nam in defectu custodis non ponitur ibi in nocte nisi vna candela vnius pollicis in vij[a] hora de nocte, que cito comburitur et alia non accenditur ante vij horam diei sequentis.

+Quod sacrista celle Sancti Iuonis faciat reparari ecclesiam conuentualem ibidem, que maximos patitur [defectus] minantes ruinam; et quod omni anno reddat compotum de officio suo priori loci illius, nam . . . . sacrista modernus reparaciones et [2] occupans officium illud[3] pro tempore redd . . . . non reddito;[4] et quod distribuat poma monachis singulis sextis feriis vt est consuetum.

+Quod elemosina monasterii integre distribuatur temporibus debitis ad portas monasterii et nullatinus ad infirmariam vel alia loca claustralia vt hiis diebus, ne seculares aut mulieres colorem aut occasionem habeant loca illa ingrediendi.

+Quod mulieres quantumcunque honeste, exceptis hiis de quibus nichil seui[5] criminis iura suspicantur admittantur[6] ad aliquam familiaritatem infra loca claustralia nec ibi pascantur aut conuiuentur, sed in locis publicis et honesta comitiua, sic quod mali suspicio super hoc non oriatur.

[Fo. 46 *d*.] +Quod elemosinarius non aduocet ad se vsque Bury vel ly Spitelle monachos aliquos ad refecciones vel potaciones; nam sic aduocando[7] pro quolibet monacho sic vocato *percipit* vnum iuste[8] ceruisie continens vnam lagenam et vnam quartam, vnum panem monachile[9] et integrum ferculum de coquina, et vbi victualia vnius monachi sufficerent ad refeccionem omnium illorum monachorum tunc presencium, idem elemosinarius applicat[10] in vsus proprios totum residuum, quod tendit in magnum detrimentum refectorii et elemosine, et sic quod per

---

[1] *Sic*: for *alii*.

[2] *quilibet* cancelled.

[3] *dimitten* cancelled.

[4] The edge of the leaf is much faded and torn, and some of this passage is illegible.

[5] *Sic*: possibly the beginning of a word which should have been cancelled.

[6] *Sic*: *non* omitted.

[7] A letter cancelled.

[8] *Sic*: for *iustam*.

[9] *Sic*: for *monachalem*.

[10] *totum residuum* interlined and cancelled.

[1] The partition of the infirmary into separate cells, common in the fifteenth century, is here alluded to. See *Visitations* I, 40, note 1.

[2] Founded upon John Alcumbury's ninth *detectum*, with added detail.

[3] Founded upon William Caumbrige's first *detectum*, with added detail. See the fourteenth injunction.

[4] On fruit at meals see *Consuetud. S. Aug. Cantuar.* I, 178; II, 124. The gardener at Westminster was expected to find apples for monks supping in the misericord during times of indulgence and on Septuagesima Sunday (*ibid.* II, 91).

+That there shall not be in the infirmary or in the chambers of the monks therein[1] so many boys by night or other secular persons, whereas in these days there are at least four or more boys there, who make uproar and outcries therein to the grievous disquiet of them that are ailing there, and, seeing that there are a barber and a washerman in the infirmary to serve the sick, so many boys are not a necessity.[2]

+That there shall be by day and night a light continually burning in the chapel of St. Mary, according to its endowment and foundation, for in the warden's default there is set there at night only a one-inch candle at seven o'clock at night, which is quickly burned up, and another is not lighted before seven o'clock on the day following.[3]

+That the sacrist of the cell of St. Ives shall cause the conventual church there to be repaired, which suffers very serious [defaults] that threaten ruin; and that he shall render every year an account of his office to the prior of that place, for the sacrist that now is [neglects] repairs, and, occupying that office for the time being, [leaves it] without rendering [an account]; and that he shall distribute apples[4] to the monks every Friday, as is accustomed.[5]

+That the alms of the monastery shall be distributed in their entirety at the due seasons at the gatehouse of the monastery, and in no wise, as in these days, at the infirmary or at other places in cloister, so that secular persons or women may have no excuse or opportunity for entering those places.[6]

+That women, how honest soever they be, except such as the laws suspect of no heinous crime, shall [not] be admitted to any familiar conversation within the cloister buildings, nor shall they be fed or regaled there, but in public places and honest company, so that no suspicion of evil may arise touching this.[7]

+That the almoner shall not invite any monks to come to him at Bury or the Spital for repasts or drinkings; for, at such invitations he receives for every monk so invited a pot[8] of ale containing a gallon and a quarter, a monk's loaf[9] and an entire dish from the kitchen, and, whereas a single monk's victuals should be enough for the repast of all those monks then present, the same almoner applies the whole of the remainder to his own uses, which tends to the great damage of the frater and the alms; and thus [it happens] that by such repasts, drinkings or

---

[5] Founded, as regards the first part, on Robert Caumbrig's third, John Alcumbury's seventh, and Moredone's *detecta*. The rest is founded upon additional information. See the sixteenth injunction.

[6] Founded upon John Alcumbury's sixth *detectum*. See the ninth injunction.

[7] Founded upon John Alcumbury's eighth *detectum*. See the seventh injunction.

[8] Literally a 'joust.' *Justa=justa mensura.*

[9] *I.e.* the daily allowance of bread for a monk. The rule of St. Benedict, cap. xxxix, laid down a pound of bread as a sufficient allowance for a day. Among the petitions of the general chapter (early 14th cent.) for the mitigation of the rule (*Consuetud. S. Aug. Cantuar.* I, 396) is one for uniformity in the amount of bread baked, as custom varied in different monasteries. The ordinary *panis monachalis* at St. Augustine's, Canterbury, consisted of a loaf of wastel bread and another of leavened bread, to be shared by two monks (*ibid.* I, 170). The loaf of wastel bread was the loaf usually called ' miche ' (*ibid.* II, 98; see *Visitations* I, 41, note 3). The *panis monachalis* is distinguished from the secondary quality known as *panis militum*: at Peterborough the white loaves used in convent were called ' prikkidbreed,' the brown loaves supplied to servants ' yomannesbreed ' (Reg. Assheton, fo. 64).

tales refecciones, potaciones aut ingurgitaciones meridianas subtrahit monachos a vesperis aliquociens a monasterio vsque x horam de nocte.

+Quod idem elemosinarius non teneat tot domicilia vt solito; nam habet vnum apud Bury et aliud apud le Spitelle, ad que loca dicti monachi vt prefertur habent accessus suos lasciuos: ista nempe domicilia sunt monasterio multum dampnosa, et ipsemet elemosinarius occasione huiusmodi domiciliorum non intendit monasterio sed solum *iconomie*[1] sue superuidendo, cum posset habere vnum iconomum qui ista superuideret, et sic ipse posset in monasterio residere.

+Quod idem elemosinarius distribuat elemosinam monasterii pauperibus magis indigentibus et nullatinus amicis vel seruientibus suis vt solito.

+Quod elemosinarius, cellerarius, sacrista et camerarius, prout eorum officiis incumbit, exhibeant equos competentes monachis euntibus ad Sanctum Iuonem et redeuntibus ad monasterium, nam huiusmodi equos sic exhibere dedicunt; *nam* dicent[2] equos quos habent fore suos proprios, et propter hoc contingit aliquociens priorem Sancti Iuonis esse ibidem solum absque confratre aliquo, exceptis cellerario et sacrista: super isto articulo sepius fuit antea in diuersis visitacionibus querelatum, et tamen nullum secutum est hucusque remedium.

Cum foret obseruatum in monasterio pro statuto vt nullus natus in villa Ramesey tonsoretur ibidem in monachum, quia per tales dissipata erat elemosina monasterii, cum eam largirentur aliis secularibus quam eorum parentibus, iam etenim contrarium huiusmodi statuti obseruatur: prouideatur igitur via aliqua vt elemosina deinceps non sic dissipetur.[3]

Frater Henricus Tichemersshe, hostilarius, tenet in officio *suo* vnum hospicium, videlicet ix monachorum perendinancium apud Sanctum Iuonem vt in eundo et redeundo; et preter illud tenet sepius in mensa sua omni šeptimana pro maiori parte alios fratres quorum fercula, iustes et panes integre percipit, de quibus modicum expendit, sed[4] seruiciam *rema[nentem]* pon[it] in dolea et desicatam ac residuum ferculorum et panum meliori foro vendit et sibi applicat.

Quod sacrista[5] non teneat *superfluum*[6] domicilium in officio suo, nam ibidem plures sumptuose expense extra casum necessitatis fiunt in magnum dispendium monasterii.

---

[1] Interlined above *officio* cancelled.
[2] *Sic*: for *dicunt*.
[3] This clause is cancelled.
[4] *et residuam eciam* cancelled.
[5] *nec* cancelled.
[6] Interlined above *aliquod* cancelled.

[1] Founded upon the prior's second and John Alcumbury's second and third *detecta*, with additional detail. Cf. the eighth paragraph above. See the fifth injunction for this and the next paragraph.

[2] This is founded upon the same evidence as the previous paragraph, with fuller detail.

[3] Founded apparently upon information arising from John Alcumbury's sixth *detectum*. No injunction deals with this.

[4] *I.e.* the cellarer and sacrist of St. Ives, who were bound to stay there for their term of office. It is noteworthy that, whereas at Oxney, the corresponding cell or priory of Peterborough, the only obedientiary in charge was the warden, St. Ives had its prior, cellarer and sacrist.

[5] Founded upon Thomas Eyeworthe's third and Moredone's *detecta*. See the thirteenth injunction.

noontide surfeitings he keeps the monks away from vespers [and] some-times from the monastery until ten o'clock at night.[1]

+That the same almoner shall not keep so many household places as usual; for he has one at Bury and another at the Spital, to which places, as is aforesaid, the said monks have recourse at their wanton will: verily these household places are very damaging to the monastery, and, because of such places, the same almoner takes heed, not to the monas-tery, but only in looking after his stewardship, whereas he could have a steward to watch over these places, and so he himself could dwell in the monastery.[2]

+That the same almoner shall distribute the alms of the monastery to the poor who are most in need, and in no wise, as he is wont, to his friends or serving-folk.[3]

+That the almoner, sacrist, cellarer and chamberlain, as is the duty of their offices, shall furnish suitable horses to the monks when they go to St. Ives and return to the monastery, for they decline so to furnish such horses; for they say that the horses which they have are their own, and by reason hereof it sometimes happens that the prior of St. Ives is there by himself without any of his brethren, save the cellarer and sacrist.[4] Touching this article complaint has very often been made before now at divers visitations, and yet no remedy has followed hitherto.[5]

+Whereas it was observed in the monastery as a statute that no man born in the town of Ramsey should be tonsured as a monk therein, because by such persons the alms of the monastery were wasted, since they bestowed them upon secular folk other than their relations, now, how-ever,[6] the contrary of such statute is observed. Let some way therefore be provided that the alms henceforth may not be thus wasted.[7]

Brother Henry Tichemersshe, the guest-master, keeps in his office an inn, to wit, for the nine monks who stay at St. Ives, on their journeys to and fro;[8] and besides this he very often keeps at his board, every week for the most part, other brethren whose dishes, flagons and loaves he receives in full, distributing but a small quantity of them, but, putting the ale that is left in cask, he sells it when it is stale, with the remainder of the dishes and loaves, at the highest price and applies [the proceeds] to his own use.[9]

That the sacrist shall not keep an unnecessary household place in his office, for therein there is much costly expense when there is no need-ful occasion, to the great waste of the monastery.[10]

---

[6] The force of *etenim* in the original is emphatic: but it is possible that it is a mistake for *tamen*.

[7] None of the depositions bears directly upon this, nor is any injunction founded upon it.

[8] Nine was apparently the maximum number which could be accommodated at St. Ives. It is not very clear whether this lodging or inn was a half-way house belonging to the office or obedience of the guest-master, or whether it was actually in the monastery of Ramsey and was kept for the entertainment of monks who, during their sojourn at St. Ives, paid occasional visits to the parent monastery. The distance from Ramsey to St. Ives is about ten miles: there can have been no lack of opportunity for refreshment on the way, as the almoner's house at Bury also lay on the road.

[9] This is a *compertum* obtained from a source unrecorded in the depositions. For this and the next paragraph see the sixth injunction.

[10] Founded upon the prior's third *detectum*.

Quod monachi non conducant agros vel terras aut eos seminent aliquibus seminibus vt ea occasione habeant libertatem vagandi ad extra.   Nam fratre[1] Johannes Eywort conduxit similia terras et crofta *in Ramesey* et ea fecit seminari [*fatetur et monitus est quod abstineat decetero*], et[2] frater Johannes Burtone destruxit crocum existens in magna copia apud Sanctum Iuonem et ibidem seminauit wode [*fatetur et non permittitur pro hoc anno*]; per ista namque diffamantur in partibus super mercandizacione et proprietate, nam seminantes huiusmodi wodde dicunt se posse perquirere de vna acra xx libras vel x vel v, et tamen indebitantur.

Quod monachi cohibeantur a villa de Rameseye, nam ad illam habent publicum accessum et ibidem intendunt tabernis publicis potacionibus et aliis insolenciis.

Item conuentus exigit certas[3] conuiuaciones per annum a cellerario, subcellerario, infirmario et precentore ad summam vj^{li}. vj^s v[iij^d], propter quod eorum officia multum dampnificantur.   Cohibeantur propterea tales conuiuaciones.

Quod deputetur cuilibet monacho sic delicato quod nesciat se prudenter regere vnus[4] tutor qui stipendia sua recipiat et necessaria sibi ministret, et in fine anni domino abbati de administracione sua computet, nam aliqui sic indiscrete se habent quod multipliciter indebitantur et eorum debita post mortem suam ab abbate exiguntur.

Quod hostilarius non dimittat ad firmam fratribus suis cameras aut gardina colenda; nam per huiusmodi fratres subtrahuntur a religione et seculares inducuntur.

Quod singulis annis reddatur compotus in communi, nam pluribus annis retroactis nullus fuit redditus.

De miraculis factis ad feretrum Sancti Iuonis publicandis.

De numero monachorum augendo.

+De carencia vasorum enneorum et aliorum necessariorum in coquina infirmarie deficiencium.

Iniuncciones Ramesey.

[Fo. 48.]   Willelmus, permissione diuina Lincolniensis episcopus, dilectis filiis abbati et conuentui monasterii de Ramsey, ordinis Sancti Benedicti, nostre diocesis, salutem, graciam et benediccionem.   Sanc-

---

[1] *Sic.* Altered imperfectly from *fratres*.
[2] *dictus* cancelled.
[3] *festa* cancelled.
[4] *coad* cancelled.

[1] Presumably to reside at St. Ives.
[2] Founded upon Robert Caumbrig's second *detectum*.   Inquiry seems to have been made meantime into the economic details of the question.   See the eighth injunction.
[3] Not definitely stated, but easily to be inferred from the depositions.   See the second injunction.
[4] For this and the next two paragraphs there is no evidence in the depositions. See the fifteenth injunction.
[5] See p. 238, note 2.
[6] See the eleventh injunction.
[7] See the eighth injunction.
[8] Founded upon Hoghtone's second *detectum*.   See the seventeenth injunction.

That the monks shall not hire fields or lands or sow them with any seeds, that by reason thereof they may have freedom to roam outside. For brother John Eywort did hire such lands and crofts in Ramsey and caused them to be sown (he confesses it, and was warned to abstain therefrom henceforward), and brother John Burton destroyed the saffron which is in great abundance at St. Ives, and there did he sow woad (he confesses it and is refused permission for this year);[1] whereby they are both defamed in those parts of bargaining and private gain, for they that sow such woad say that from a single acre they can get five, ten or twenty pounds, and yet they are in debt.[2]

That the monks shall be restrained from the town of Ramsey; for they have public recourse thereunto, and there do they pass the time in the taverns, in public drinkings, and other breaches of rule.[3]

Also the convent requires certain banquets a year of the cellarer, subcellarer, infirmarer and precentor, to the sum of £6 6s. [8d.], whereby their offices are greatly endamaged. Let such banquetings therefore be kept in check.[4]

That to every monk who is so given to fine living that he cannot control himself with prudence there shall be appointed a guardian, who shall receive his pay[5] and furnish him with things needful, and at the end of the year shall give an account of his ministry to the lord abbot; for there are some who bear themselves so imprudently that they are on manifold accounts in debt, and after their death their debts are required of the abbot.[6]

That the guest-master shall not let chambers or gardens for cultivation to his brethren to farm; for by such things the brethren are withdrawn from religion and secular folk are brought in.[7]

That an account be rendered in common each year, for none has been rendered for several years gone by.[8]

Concerning the publication of the miracles wrought at the shrine of St. Ives.[9]

Concerning the increase of the number of monks.[10]

Concerning the lack of brass vessels and of other necessaries that are wanting in the infirmary kitchen.[11]

INJUNCTIONS FOR RAMSEY[12]

William, by divine permission bishop of Lincoln, to our beloved sons the abbot and convent of the monastery of Ramsey, of the order of St. Benet, of our diocese, health, grace and blessing. The authority of

[9] See Thomas Eyworthe's second and Alcumbury's *detecta*. No injunction.
[10] See Thomas Ramesey's *detectum* and the note thereon (p. 305, note 2). No injunction.
[11] See Papeley's second *detectum*. See the tenth injunction.
[12] These injunctions, which are written in a hand different from Colstone's and leave much more room for marginal additions and interlineations than he usually employed, are the most elaborate series in this collection. They are of special value for their full rehearsal of the *comperta* which were their occasion. These have already been indicated by the previous series of *ad interim* paragraphs, and are now repeated with careful detail. It should be noted that the *comperta* are stated in their original form of *detecta* or *delata*, i.e. they have been founded on definite evidence, which, as already noted, was clearly supplemented by inquiries of which no report is given. The *sollertia* of the inquiry is mentioned in the preamble.

torum patrum sanxiuit auctoritas vt ecclesiarum prelati ad corrigendum subditorum excessus et reformandos mores eorundem prudenter ac diligenter intendant, ne sanguis eorum de manibus suis requiratur, nec admittitur pastoris excusacio si ipso nesciente oues luporum morsibus dilanientur, cum ab eo tacente et sic consenciente permittatur securitas delinquendi. Horum siquidem ammonicione vt ad vos et vestrum monasterium visitandum descenderemus cura nostra pastoralis necessario nos coegit. Verum quia per inquisicionem diligentem et solertem per nos in huiusmodi visitacione nostra factam comperimus nonnulla puritati religionis inimica et contraria indies committi, *et dictum monasterium per inprouidam*[1] *disposicionem et necligenciam in suis facultatibus et emolumentis irrecuperabile quasi pati dispendium*, infrascripta mandata nostra, iniuncciones ac ordinaciones vobis destinamus sub penis infrascriptis inuiolabiliter obseruanda.

In primis cum iuxta sacros canones ac regularia vestri ordinis instituta in vno dormitorio et sub vno *tecto*[2] simul de nocte quiescere et dormire, simul in vna domo refeccionem sumere silenciumque in ecclesia, dormitorio, refectorio et claustro seruare ac leccioni et contemplacioni debitis horis in claustro intendere teneamini et debeatis; nobisque in huiusmodi visitacione nostra detectum existat pariter et delatum quod nonnulli monachi dicti vestri monasterii, premissa non ponderantes sed ea que carni et non spiritui placeant sectantes, post *prandium et* completorium potacionibus intendunt, claustrum exeunt et circumvagantur, et non in dormitorio sed seorsum in cameris separatis de nocte dormiunt et quiescunt; quodque non in locis debitis secundum regulam sed in plerisque locis priuatis et latebris vescuntur, sicque per huiusmodi refeccionis locorum multitudinem bona monasterii dissipantur, religio perit, elemosina consumitur, sed nec temporibus refeccionis lecciones habentur, neque in claustro hore contemplacionum et leccionum debite obseruantur, silenciumque rumpitur horis et locis quibus[3] iuxta regulam seruari deberet: iniungimus igitur vobis sub penis infrascriptis vt omnes et singuli monachi dicti monasterii, exceptis hiis qui absque ficcione aliqua adeo infirmantur quod eos infirmariam ea racione omnino sequi oportet, et exceptis hiis qui exterioribus officiis deputati adeo occupantur quod hoc facere[4] commode non poterunt, omni die statim dicto completorio dormitorium petant *et adeant ac*[5] ibidem quiescant, non inde exituri nisi ad matutinas dumtaxat vsque septimam horam diei sequentis, sub pena quam cuilibet monacho in hoc delinquenti infligimus, videlicet vt proxima sexta feria ieiunet in pane et aqua pro prima vice, et pro secunda vice quarta et sexta *feria*, et pro tercia vice quarta, sexta feria et Sabbato *similiter ieiunet in pane et aqua et sic quociens*[6] creuerit culpa tociens aggrauetur pena;[7] quodque non liceat alicui monacho claustrum post completorium vllatinus exire nec potaciones sumere nisi ex vrgenti necessitate priori exposita et licencia super hoc ab eo petita et obtenta,

---

[1] *et necgligentem* cancelled.
[2] Interlined above *tego* cancelled.
[3] *quibus* repeated and cancelled.
[4] Part of a word cancelled.
[5] Interlined above *et* cancelled.
[6] Interlined above *pro prima vice et pro secunda* cancelled.
[7] *et pro tercia* cancelled.

the holy fathers has given sanction that the prelates of churches should with prudence and diligence take heed to correct the transgressions of them that are set under them and to reform their manners, that their blood may not be required at their hands; nor is the shepherd's excuse accepted, if, in his ignorance, the sheep be torn in pieces by the bites of wolves, whereas by his silence, and therefore by his consent, liberty to offend is freely allowed. It was, then, by the warning of these [fathers] that our care as a shepherd necessarily constrained us to come down to visit your monastery. Moreover, because by the diligent and dexterous inquiry held by us in such our visitation we have discovered that certain things hostile and contrary to the purity of religion are being committed daily, and that, by imprudent management and negligence the said monastery is suffering almost irrecoverable waste in respect of its resources and profits, we direct to you our commands, injunctions, and ordinances hereunder written, to be observed without breach under the penalties written beneath.

In the first place, whereas, according to the sacred canons and the regular institutes of your order, you are bound and ought to take rest and sleep at night together in one dorter and under one roof, to take your meals together in one house, and to keep silence in the church, dorter, frater and cloister, and to take heed to reading and contemplation at the due hours in cloister; and it is disclosed and likewise reported to us in such our visitation that some monks of your said monastery, not considering the things aforeset, but following after those things that are pleasing to the flesh, and not to the spirit, after breakfast and compline spend their time in drinkings, go out of cloister and roam about, and sleep and take their rest of a night, not in the dorter, but apart in separate chambers; and that they take their food, not in the due places according to the rule, but in many privy places and lurking-holes, and so by reason of the multitude of such places of refreshment the goods of the monastery are squandered, religious discipline comes to naught, the alms are consumed, nor are readings kept at meal-times, nor are the due hours for reading and contemplation observed in cloister, and silence is broken at the hours and in the places when and where it should be kept according to the rule: we therefore enjoin upon you, under the penalties written hereunder, that all and several the monks of the said monastery, except such as without any pretence are so ailing that on that account they must altogether abide in the infirmary, and except such as, being put in charge of external offices, are so busy that they cannot conveniently do this, shall every day, immediately after compline has been said, seek the dorter and go thither and take their rest therein, and go not out therefrom save only to matins until seven o'clock on the following day, under the penalty which we inflict upon every monk who offends herein, to wit, that on the next Friday he shall fast upon bread and water for the first time, and for the second time he shall likewise fast upon bread and water on Wednesday, Friday and Saturday, and so, as often as his fault is repeated, so often shall the penalty be increased; and that it shall be lawful for no monk in any wise to go out of cloister after compline or take drink, unless it be for urgent need set forth to the prior, and with licence asked and had of him touching this, under penalty to every monk

sub pena cuilibet monacho in hiis delinquenti vt abstineat [fo. 48 *d.*] *a carnibus per vnam ebdomodam* pro prima vice, et pro secunda vice per quindenam, et pro tercia vice per tres ebdomadas.

Item iniungimus vobis quod decetero tribus locis ad refecciones sumendas in dicto monasterio, videlicet aula abbatis in eius *presencia*[1] et ad eius vocacionem, refectorio et aula minucionum saltem sani absque pluribus aliis locis contenti nulla alia loca publica vel priuata ad refecciones exerceant vllo modo, nec ad villam de Ramsey aut alias [villas] in circuitu accedant, neque in eis vel apud Bury vel in *le*[2] Spitelle apud Ramsey bibant, comedant aut expectent ibidem, sub pena cuilibet monacho in horum aliquo delinquenti, pro prima vice vt custodiat claustrum et loca claustralia per vnam ebdomadam,[3] pro secunda vice per duas[4] ebdomadas, et pro tercia vice per tres ebdomadas loca illa per tempora huiusmodi nullatinus exiturus.

Item cum similiter nobis sit detectum quod aliquociens adeo pauci monachi sunt in refectorio quod presidens cum vno solo monacho post prandium gracias decantando ad ecclesiam accedat, iniungimus vobis abbati et priori *ac cuilibet alii ordini in dicto monasterio pro tempore presidenti* vt diligenter superintendatis quod, exceptis *vobis* abbate et *capellano vestro*[5] et quos ad mensam *vestram iuxta regulam inuitare decreueritis,*[6] notabiliter eciam infirmis et ad extra[7] necessario occupatis *et in minucionibus pro tempore existentibus,* ad minus tercia pars conuentus in refectorio comedat[8] omni die; et quod tempore refeccionis, eciam extra refectorium, leccio aliqua de sacra scriptura coram discumbentibus ad eorum edificacionem habeatur; quodque omni die hore[9] leccionum et contemplacionum *debite et consuete in claustro* secundum regulam,[10] et eciam[11] quod silencium horis et locis debitis ab omnibus obseruentur[12] . . . . . *priori* . . . . *cuilibet presidenti* . . . . . *necgligenter* . . . . *acione* . . . . *ebdomadam* . . . . *inmediate* . . . . . *in hoc deliquerit vestrum aliquis* . . . . . . *in* . . . .[13]

Item quia in eadem visitacione nostra nobis detectum extitit et delatum quod monachi stantes cum abbate in refeccione meridiana apud ly Byggyng, sumpta refeccione non directe ad monasterium redeunt, sed lasciue vsque Bury diuertunt, ibidem cum te, elemosinarie, potacionibus, commesacionibus et miserarum mulierolarum quas ad se ibidem aduocant, et si sic ad se vocare non audeant, ad earum cotagia et domos accedentes prauis colloquiis, vt de aliis taceamus, intendunt, ex quibus

---

[1] Interlined above *absencia* altered into *presencia* and cancelled.
[2] Interlined above *lez* cancelled.
[3] Several cancelled words. The penalties here and elsewhere in the injunctions have been filled in after the main part of the text had been written.
[4] *se* cancelled (*septimanas*).
[5] Interlined (*vestro* instead of *suo* cancelled) above *capellanis suis* cancelled.
[6] Interlined (*iuxta regulam* further interlined, and *inuitare* altered from *inuitatis*) above *suam vult vocare* cancelled.
[7] *ex* cancelled.
[8] Altered from *comedant.*
[9] *debite et consuete* cancelled.
[10] *in claustro* cancelled.
[11] *quod* cancelled.
[12] Sic: *sub pena cuilibet monacho in horum aliquo delinquenti pro prima vice, pro secunda et pro tercia* cancelled.

who offends herein that for the first time he shall abstain from meat for a week, and for the second time for a fortnight, and for the third time for three weeks.[1]

Also we enjoin upon you that henceforward those of you at any rate who are sound in health shall be content with three places wherein to take your meals in the said monastery, to wit, in the abbot's hall in his presence and at his invitation, in the frater and in the hall for seynies, and with no more, and shall in no wise resort for meals to other places public or private, or go to the town of Ramsey or to other towns in the neighbourhood; nor shall they drink or eat in them, or at Bury or in the spital at Ramsey, or linger there, under pain to every monk offending in any of these matters of confinement to cloister and the cloister buildings, for a week, for his first offence, for two weeks the second time, and for three weeks the third; and during such periods he shall in no wise leave these limits.[2]

Also, since it has been discovered to us in like manner that sometimes there are so few monks in frater that the president goes to church with a single monk only, when they sing grace after breakfast, we enjoin upon you the abbot and prior, and upon every other president of the order in the said monastery for the time being,[3] that you keep diligent watch that at least the third part of the convent shall take its meals in the frater every day, with the exception of you the abbot and your chaplain, and such as you decide to invite to your table according to the rule, and in especial also those that are infirm, and those who have necessary business abroad, and those who are in their seynies for the time being; and that at meal-time, even outside the frater, some lesson from holy scripture shall be read in the presence of them that sit at meat to their edification; and that every day the due and accustomed hours for reading and meditation in cloister shall be observed according to the rule, and that silence be kept by all at the due times and places, [under pain] to the prior and to any [other] president [of the order who shall behave himself] neglectfully [herein, of keeping . . . . for] the week immediately [following the occasion] of an offence by any of you in [such matters].[4]

Also because in our same visitation it was disclosed and reported to us that the monks who stay with the abbot at the noonday meal at the Byggyng, do not go back straight to the monastery after taking their food, but ramble wantonly to Bury [and] there spend their time with you, the almoner, in drinking, eating and vile chattering, to say nothing of aught else, with the wretched queans whom they bid come to them there, going, if they dare not so invite them, to their cottages and houses;

---

[13] This marginal addition is nearly illegible and much torn.

[1] The injunction is expanded from the sixth of the preceding paragraphs. The comprehensive preamble embodies a summary of the chief points which go to the finding of general disorderliness.

[2] See the ninth and twenty-fourth paragraphs.

[3] The holders of the various offices, apart from the prior, almoner, and prior of St. Ives, are not identified in the depositions; but, in a monastery of the size, there were probably a subprior and third and fourth priors or *custodes ordinis*.

[4] See the fifth and seventh paragraphs: the directions for reading in frater and silence in cloister are added as corollaries.

plura feda *que*[1] timemus subsequuntur in ipsius monasterii scandalum[2] et personarum eiusdem perniciosum exemplum: iniungimus propterea vniuersis monachis cum abbate in forma predicta refectis vt statim post refeccionem huiusmodi absque omni mora directe ad monasterium et nullatinus ad alia loca quecunque accedant, hiis que religioni congruunt sedule intendentes, sub pena cuilibet monacho in hiis delinquenti custodie claustralis per vnam ebdomodam pro prima vice [fo. 49], et pro secunda vice per duas ebdomadas et pro tercia per vnum mensem, et sic quociens excreuerit *culpa*,[3] superaddatur et pena.

Item quia in eadem visitacione nostra ex clamore valido et facto patenti reperimus detectum et delatum quod tu, elemosinarie, qui sepius plures monachos vsque Bury vel le Spitelle aduocas et fercula illa siue dietas que vel quas in monasterio pro die illo haberent percipis, videlicet panes iustas et fercula coquine, et vbi modicum huiusmodi victualium sufficeret monachis ipsis, tu totum residuum tibi coaceruas et inter seruientes tuos vel alibi pro voluntate tua expendis; quodque multociens vbi ipsos monachos in mensa in meridie habere non poteris, eos post meridies ad Bury et post completorium vsque ly Spitelle aduocas, vbi similibus potacionibus, comesacionibus, ingurgitacionibus prauisque et vanis colloquiis intendunt, sicque et alias multipliciter ipsos monachos vsque decimam vel xj horam de nocte a monasterio, claustro et dormitorio retrahis, sicque bona et elemosine monasterii in domiciliis et familiis tuis que apud Bury in ly Spitelle in magnum detrimentum monasterii et scandalum foues et tenes per te et tuos indebite et inordinate consumuntur et dissipantur: iniungimus igitur et mandamus tibi et cuilibet tibi in dicto officio substituendo, *teque et quemlibet huiusmodi successorem tuum*[4] *primo, secundo et tercio*[5] *monemus sub [pena excommunicacionis] maioris quam [in personam] tuam et cuiuslibet s[uccessoris] tui in illo officio [substituendo] si monicionibus [nostris huiusmodi non] parueris aut [paruerint secundum] effectum tuis et suis [crimine] dolo et offensa [nostraque trina] monicione premissa [in hac parte] precedentibus et . . . . . . tibus ferimus in [hiis scriptis]*,[6] vt a premissis omnibus que *in* tantum animarum periculum monasterii que dispendium tendunt omnino et decetero penitus abstineas; quodque inantea nullum tale domicilium locis predictis aut eorum aliquo foueas aut teneas.[7] Sustinemus tamen vt si necesse habeas iconomiam et seruientes tuos apud Bury superuidere horis competentibus de licencia abbatis vel prioris ad hoc petita *et*[8] obtenta cum vno monacho socio mature etatis et discrecionis, in religione approbato et Deum timente tibi per abbatem vel priorem ad hoc assignato ad illa visenda et disponenda, et non frequenter nimis accedere valeas, dummodo illo negocio absque mora expedito vsque ad monasterium ad maiores missas ad minus et ad refecciones absque pluri accedas.

---

[1] Interlined above *quod* cancelled.
[2] *monasterii* cancelled.
[3] Interlined above *pena* cancelled.
[4] *monemus* cancelled.
[5] *su* cancelled.
[6] Much torn.
[7] *sub pena pro prima vice pro secunda et pro tercia* cancelled.

wherefrom do follow many foul things whereof we are afraid, to the scandal of the same monastery and the disastrous example of the persons of the same: we enjoin therefore upon all the monks who have taken their meals with the abbot in the form aforesaid that immediately after such meals they go straight to the monastery without any delay, and in no wise to any other places, and take busy heed to such things as are agreeable to religion, under pain to every monk who offends herein of confinement to cloister, for a week for the first time, and for two weeks the second time, and for a month the third; and so, as often as the fault is repeated, shall the penalty be also increased.[1]

Also, because in our same visitation we found it disclosed and reported to us, by loud rumour and as an evident fact, that you, the almoner, who very often invite several monks to Bury or the Spital and receive the dishes or daily allowances which they should have for that day in the monastery, to wit, loaves, flagons and kitchen dishes, and, whereas a small quantity of such victuals should be enough for the same monks, you heap together the whole residue for yourself and expend it among your serving folk or elsewhere at your will; and that many times, whereas you may be unable to have the same monks at your board at noonday, you invite them to Bury after noon and to the Spital after compline, where they spend their time in like drinking, eating, surfeiting, and vile and empty talking, and thus and in other manifold ways you keep the same monks from the monastery, cloister and dorter until ten or eleven o'clock at night, and so the goods and alms of the monastery are unduly and in disorderly wise spent and squandered by you and your folk in your households and retinues which you maintain and keep at Bury [and] in the Spital to the great harm and scandal of the monastery: we therefore enjoin and command you and every one who shall take your place in the said office, and admonish you and every such successor of yours a first, second and third time, under [pain] of the greater [excommunication], which in these writings we lay [upon] your [person] and that of every [successor] of yours [who shall take your place] in that office, if you or [they] obey not [such our] admonitions [according to their] effect, as a consequence of your and their [guilt], craft and transgression, [and of our threefold] admonition aforeset [in this behalf . . . . .], that wholly and utterly henceforward you refrain from all things aforeset which tend to do great peril to souls and expense to the monastery, and that henceforth you shall maintain or keep no such household in the places aforesaid or any one of them. Nevertheless we allow that, if you have necessity to look after your stewardship and serving folk at Bury, you may go to visit and order them at fitting seasons, with leave to this effect asked and had of the abbot or prior, with one monk in your company of ripe age and discretion, approved in religion and God-fearing, appointed to you for this purpose by the abbot or prior, and not too often, provided that, after finishing your business without delay, you go, without longer stay, to the monastery for high mass at least and for meals.[2]

---

[8] Interlined above *vel* cancelled.

[1] Founded on the eighth paragraph with strong emphasis.
[2] See the sixteenth and seventeenth paragraphs.

Similiter quia reperimus nobis detectum quod vos, sacrista et *hostilarius*,[1] similia in officiis vestris tenetis domicilia *monasterio* dispendiosa: iniungimus vobis *et vestrum vtrique* sub *pena*[2] *obseruacionis refectorii per septimanam continuam pro qualibet vice qua in hoc deliqueritis vel deliquerit aliquis vestrum ne*[3] amodo talia domicilia *ullatinus*[4] teneatis in officiis vestris [fo. 49 *d.*] antedictis.

(*Ne mulieres recipiantur.*) Item quia repperimus nobis detectum quod nonnulle mulieres infra septa claustralia quampluries receptantur et conuiuantur, ex quo grauia pericula formidantur euenire scandalaque plurima monasterio hactenus euenerunt: iniungimus vobis vniuersis et singulis presentibus et futuris vosque monemus primo, secundo et tercio, sub pena excommunicacionis maioris quam in singulares personas vestras in hiis delinquentes, suis dolo et culpa nostraque trina monicione premissa in hac parte precedentibus, exnunc prout extunc et extunc prout exnunc ferimus in hiis scriptis, ne aliquas mulieres quantumcunque honestas infra septa claustralia dicti monasterii introducatis nec ab aliis introductas ad familiaritatem aliquam admittatis seu vestrum aliquis admittat, illis personis dumtaxat exceptis de quibus nichil mali iura posse presumi suspicantur, sed et si *alique*[5] tales ad monasterium accesserint, alicubi seorsum a septis claustralibus in comitiua honesta receptentur et conuiuentur.

Cumque, prout eciam detectum nobis existit, plures de monachis dicti monasterii nonnulla agros, gardina, ortos et crofta in villa de Ramesey et aliis vicinis a secularibus, eciam infra septa monasterii a suis confratribus officiariis, conducant eaque colant diuersisque seminibus serant, sicque occasiones se *a* diuinis et chori sequela et aliis regularibus obseruanciis retrahendi sumentes, et ad extra inter seculares, eciam mulieres inhonestas quas ad colendum predicta loca ex affeccione conducunt, vagentur et se huiusmodi secularibus negociis et occupacionibus[6] non absque suspicione mali contra doctrinam apostoli immiscent: vobis firmiter iniungimus et mandamus vt ab omnibus huiusmodi per que cultus religionis impeditur vel quauis[7] vagandi occasio detur inantea penitus abstineatis, nullis talibus vel similibus decetero vllatinus intendendo, sub pena cuilibet delinquenti custodie claustri *in monasterio* per vnum mensem pro prima vice, per duas mensas[8] pro secunda, per tres menses pro tercia vice.

Et quia, prout nobis detegitur, elemosina dicti monasterii, que per tot loca refeccionum clam surripitur pro maiori sui parte et consumitur indebite, ita vt modica pars remaneat distribuenda, et tamen non ad portas monasterii vt solito sed in infirmaria, per quod secularibus loca claustralia ingrediendi contra regulam [fo. 50][9] datur occasio lasciua, hiis diebus distribuitur: iniungimus et mandamus tibi nunc et annis

---

[1] Interlined above *hostiarius* cancelled.
[2] Interlined above *eisdem* cancelled.
[3] Interlined above *penis vt* cancelled.
[4] Altered from *nullatinus.*
[5] Interlined above *que* cancelled.
[6] *contra doctrinam apostoli* cancelled.
[7] *Sic*: for *queuis.*
[8] *Sic*: for *menses.*
[9] Wrongly numbered 49 in original.

[1] See the twenty-first and twenty-second paragraphs.

Likewise, because we found it disclosed to us that you, the sacrist and guestmaster, keep like households in your offices to the wasteful expense of the monastery: we enjoin upon you and either of you, under pain of keeping frater for a week on end, for every time wherein you or any one of you transgress herein, that henceforth you in no wise keep such households in your offices aforesaid.[1]

Also, because we found it discovered to us that certain women are very often received and entertained within the cloister precincts, wherefrom grievous dangers are feared to arise, and very many scandals have hitherto arisen to the monastery: we enjoin upon you all and singular that now are and shall be, and admonish you the first, second and third time, under pain of the greater excommunication, which we lay in these writings, from now as from then and from then as from now, upon the several persons of you who shall offend in such things, as a consequence of their craft and fault and our threefold admonition aforeset in this behalf, that you shall bring in no women, howsoever honest, within the cloister precincts of the said monastery, or admit them, you or any of you, if they be brought in by others, to any familiar converse, saving only those persons of whom the law suspects that no evil may be presumed; but, even if any such come to the monastery, they shall be received and entertained in honest company in some other place apart from the cloister enclosure.[2]

And whereas, as it is also discovered to us, many of the monks of the said monastery hire certain fields, gardens, orchards and crofts in the town of Ramsey and other neighbouring towns from secular folk, and also within the precincts of the monastery from the officers their brethren, and till them and sow them with divers seeds, and so, taking opportunities of withdrawing themselves from divine service and from attendance in quire and from the other regular observances, roam abroad among secular folk, and women of ill fame also whom out of their liking they hire to till the aforesaid places, and, contrary to the doctrine of the apostle,[3] do intermeddle with such worldly businesses and employments, not without suspicion of evil: we firmly enjoin and command you that from henceforth you utterly refrain from all such things whereby the observance of religion is hindered or any opportunity of roaming abroad may be given, in no wise henceforward paying heed to such or the like matters, under pain to every transgressor of confinement to cloister in the monastery, for one month the first time, for two months the second, and for three months the third time.[4]

And because, as it is disclosed to us, the alms of the said monastery, which, by reason that there are so many places for meals, are, for their greater part, privily carried off and unduly consumed, so that a scanty share is left for distribution, and [this] nevertheless is distributed in these days, not at the gates of the monastery, as was customary, but in the infirmary, by reason whereof wanton occasion is given to secular folk to enter the cloister buildings, contrary to the rule: we enjoin and command you who are now the almoner, and him who shall be in years

---

[2] See the fifteenth paragraph.
[3] No special text is quoted; but such texts as Rom. xii, 2, and St. James i, 27, are implied by the allusion.
[4] See the twenty-third and twenty-seventh paragraphs.

futuris elemosinario tuique et eius subelemosinario vt totalem elemosinam dicti monasterii fideliter et integre congreges et congregat[1] ac congregari facias et faciat, congregatamque absque diminucione, pueris tamen elemosinarie qui de dicta elemosina [refici] consueuerunt prius exinde refectis, ad portas monasterii et non alibi temporibus debitis distribuas et distribuat seu distribui facias et faciat, sub pena ieiunandi in pane et aqua *proxima*[2] sexta feria quociens in hoc deliqueris vel aliquis vestrum deliquerit.

Item cum in *in*firmaria monachorumque cellulis ibidem, prout nobis detectum existat,[3] tanti per pueros insolentes qui ibidem aliter quam expediat vel egeat in excessiuo sunt numero strepitus et clamores tumultuosi fiant quod infirmancium et aliorum[4] inibi degencium quies multipliciter turbetur, non obstante quod in eodem officio sunt continue vnus barbitonsor et vnus lotor qui infirmis ad votum deseruiant; quodque infirmantibus huiusmodi non ministratur de talibus[5] cibis quibus ad sanitatem valeant melius refici: vobis vniuersis et singulis firmiter iniungimus et mandamus quatinus solum dictis duobus seruitoribus in infirmaria ad deseruiendum infirmis retentis omnes huiusmodi pueri penitus amoueantur et decetero nullatinus iterato admittantur, sub pena cuilibet in hoc delinquenti tales pueros decetero admittendo seu retinendo sub pena[6] abstinencie ab esu carnium quolibet die quo sic deliquerit aliquis eorundem tales *pueros contra formam huiusmodi nostre iniunccionis*[7] *acceptando.* Vosque, abbas, superintendatis diligenter vt infirmis ipsis vel in minucionibus seu in infirmaria vel refectorio existentibus de cibariis eis iuxta quod[8] melius conualescere poterunt congruentibus, absque tamen aliorum scandalo, congrue faciatis prouideri; quodque in coquina infirmarie prouideatur competenter *infra duos menses proximos post recepcionem presencium* de vasis stanneis et enneis et aliis necessariis pro seruiendo infirmis, que omnino ibi desunt vt informamur; et hec sub pena dicendi vij psalmos penitenciales *quotidie*[9] *quousque de vasis huius-modi* [*prouideri*] *competenter* [*feceritis*].[10]

Cumque, vt accepimus, nonnulli monachi diuersis officiis prefecti ita indiscrete se habent in eisdem, vt in cessione vel dimissione officiorum huiusmodi seu ipsorum monachorum decessu ipsi *monachi reddunt*[11] monasterium in magnis et notabilibus summis indebitatum, *aliique plures*[12] sic se indiscrete habent et delicate viuunt quod ipsum monasterium eciam relinquunt grauiter indebitatum; que omnia post eorum cessionem vel decessum ab abbate et ipso monasterio exiguntur: iniungimus ipsis et mandamus vobis abbati et conuentui predictis vt talibus et aliis se in disposicione peculii sui quod ex permissu abbatis possident sic necgligentibus vnus solidus, maturus et discretus monachus [fo. 50 *d.*] assignetur in tutorem, qui peculia ipsorum monachorum recipiat, eis

---

[1] *Sic*: for *congreget.*
[2] Interlined above a word cancelled.
[3] *Sic*: for *existit.*
[4] *ib* cancelled.
[5] *cibus* cancelled (*cibz*).
[6] *Sic*: repeated.
[7] *attemptando* cancelled.
[8] Altered from *quos.*
[9] *de v* cancelled.
[10] Interlined (nearly illegible) above *quociens in hoc deliqueritis* cancelled.

to come, and your and his sub-almoner, to gather and cause to be gathered together faithfully and entirely the whole alms of the said monastery, and to distribute it when gathered together, or cause it to be distributed at the gates of the monastery and not elsewhere at due seasons without diminishment, but after the boys of the almonry,[1] who were wont to have refreshment out of the said alms, have been first refreshed therefrom, under pain of fasting upon bread and water the next Friday after, as often as you or any one of you transgress herein.[2]

Also, whereas in the infirmary and the cells of the monks therein, as is disclosed to us, such great uproar and outcries are made by the unruly boys who are therein in excessive number, otherwise than is expedient or necessary, that the rest of those that are ailing and of the others that abide therein is broken in manifold ways, notwithstanding that there are continually in the same office a barber and a washerman, to do service to the infirm at their request; and because such infirm persons are not served with such meats as by means of which they may best be restored to health: we strictly enjoin and command you all and singular that, keeping only the said two serving-men in the infirmary to do service to the infirm, all such boys be utterly removed and in no wise be admitted again henceforward, under penalty, to everyone who transgresses herein by admitting or keeping such boys henceforth, of abstinence from eating flesh-meat every day whereon any one of the same shall so transgress by receiving such boys contrary to the form of such our injunction. And you the abbot shall keep diligent watch that you cause fitting provision to be made for the same infirm persons who are either in their seynies or in the infirmary or the frater of food suitable to them, according as they may best be able to recover health, but without cause of offence to others, and that competent provision be made in the kitchen of the infirmary, within the two months next after you receive these presents, of vessels of tin and brass and other things that are needful for the service of the infirm, which, as we are told, are altogether wanting there; and this under pain of saying the seven penitential psalms daily, until [you have caused] sufficient [provision to be made] of such vessels.[3]

And whereas, as we have heard, certain monks who are set over divers offices behave themselves so indiscreetly in the same, that, when they resign or demise such offices, or at the decease of the same monks, the same monks leave the monastery in debt in great and notable sums, and several others behave themselves so indiscreetly and live so delicately that they also leave the same monastery grievously in debt; and all these things, after their resignation or decease, are required of the abbot and of the same monastery: we enjoin upon the same and command you, the abbot and convent aforesaid, that to such persons and others who so neglect their duty in laying out their money which they possess by the abbot's permission, there be appointed as guardian a sound, ripe and discreet monk, who shall receive the money of the same monks, furnish

---

[11] Above *mon' tradunt* cancelled.
[12] Interlined above *aliisque pluribus* cancelled.

[1] See *Visitations* I, 23, note 1, and 232.
[2] See the fourteenth paragraph. There is no allusion to the eighteenth paragraph, which might have been referred to in this injunction.
[3] See the tenth, eleventh and thirty-first paragraphs.

necessaria subministret, eorum debita persoluat et abbati qui tempore fuerit de administracione sua in premissis in fine cuiuslibet anni fidelem reddat racionem, sic quod monasterium talibus insolenciis decetero non grauetur.

Item quia in eadem visitacione nostra nobis extitit detectum quod monachi a sequela chori de die tanto subtrahant quod horis diurnis vix iiij, v vel vj monachi ipsis horis intersint, quod inconsonum est religioni, presertim vbi tct in numero sunt in conuentu: iniungimus idcirco et mandamus vt cuilibet hore diei eciam magne misse omnes monachi dicti monasterii, saltem non legitime impediti vel de licencia abbatis vel prioris absentes, intersint in choro psallentes, preter eos qui altari tempore missarum huiusmodi deseruiunt, sub pena sub pena[1] sequendi chorum continue singulis horis nocturnis et diurnis per vnam ebdomadam pro prima vice, per duas ebdomadas pro secunda et per tres ebdomadas pro tercia vice.

Similiter nobis in eadem visitacione detectum extitit pariter et delatum et quasi ab omnibus generaliter querelatum quod hii qui officiis elemosinarii, cellerarii, sacriste et camerarii in ipso monasterio preficiuntur racione officiorum suorum huiusmodi et ipsorum sumptibus et expensis teneantur et debeant exhibere equos et equitaturas conuenientes et honestas monachis euntibus de monasterio ad cellam Sancti Iuonis et abinde vsque ad monasterium redeuntibus in quolibet huiusmodi eorum egressu[2] et regressu secundum eiusdem monasterii laudabilem consuetudinem approbatam: moderni tamen elemosinarius, cellarius,[3] sacrista et camerarius habentes equos quos dicunt proprios, cum execrandum sit monachum habere proprium, monachis sic euntibus et redeuntibus huiusmodi equos et equitaturas iuxta consuetudinem predictam exhibere non curant, ymo recusant in tantum, quod aliquociens oportebit monachos huiusmodi *solos et absque comite* pedestres ire et redire: vobis igitur abbati sub pena infrascripta firmiter iniungimus et mandamus quatinus nostra auctoritate dictos elemosinarium, cellerarium, sacristam et camerarium *et eorum quemlibet* pro tempore existentem ad exhibicionem equorum et equitaturarum *competencium* dictis monachis euntibus et redeuntibus in quolibet eorum egressu et regressu *compellatis et[4] in hiis ex affectu delinquentes[5]* ab eorum huiusmodi officiis *finaliter amoueatis,*[6] ad quod vobis vices nostras committimus per presentes.

Item cum similiter nobis detectum sit inibi et delatum quod capella beate Marie in possessionibus *et* presertim ad exhibendum quendam cereum in ipsa capella continue die ac [fo. 51] nocte ardentem sit dotata, possessionesque huiusmodi ad hoc et cetera onera eidem capelle incumbencia sufficiant, per negligenciam tamen sacriste pro tempore existentis ipse cereus quampluries extinctus dimittitur: iniungimus igitur sacriste

----

[1] *Sic.*

[2] Altered from *regressu.*

[3] *Sic:* for *cellerarius.*

[4] Originally written *compellatis et quemlibet eorum hoc non facientem: hoc non facientem* was then altered to *in hoc deficientem:* the whole was then struck out and *compellatis* interlined.

[5] Originally *pena amocionis finalis,* for which *alioquin deficientes huiusmodi* was then substituted and struck out.

[6] *et pro qualibet vice qua sic defecerit acriter puniatis* cancelled.

[1] See the twenty-sixth paragraph.

them with necessaries, pay their debts, and at the end of every year render a faithful account to the abbot for the time being of his steward-ship in the premises, so that the monastery be not burdened hence-forward by such breaches of discipline.[1]

Also, inasmuch as in the same our visitation it was disclosed to us that the monks so greatly withdraw [themselves] from attendance in quire by day, that at the day-hours hardly four, five or six monks are present at the same hours, which is out of keeping with religious disci-pline, especially where there are so many in number in the convent: we therefore enjoin and command that all the monks of the said monas-tery, at any rate such as are not lawfully hindered or are [not] absent with leave of the abbot or prior, shall be present and sing in quire at every hour of the day, and also at high mass, except those who are serving the altar at the time of such masses, under pain of continual attendance in quire, at each hour of the night and day, for a week the first time, for two weeks the second, and for three weeks the third time.[2]

In like manner in the same visitation it was discovered and likewise reported, and general complaint was made to us almost by all, that [whereas] they who in the same monastery are set in charge of the offices of almoner, cellarer, sacrist and chamberlain are bound and ought, by reason of such their offices and at the charges and costs of the same, to furnish horses and suitable and decent equipments to the monks when they go from the monastery to the cell of St. Ives and return there-from to the monastery, at every such their setting forth and returning, according to the praiseworthy [and] approved custom of the same monas-tery: nevertheless the almoner, cellarer, sacrist and chamberlain that are now, having horses that they call their own, albeit it is an accursed thing for a monk to have aught of his own, take no order to furnish such horses and equipments, according to the custom aforesaid, to the monks thus going and returning, but refuse to do so, insomuch that such monks have sometimes to go and return on foot by themselves and without company: we therefore strictly enjoin and command you the abbot, under the penalty written below, that by our authority you compel the said almoner, cellarer, sacrist and chamberlain, and every one of them for the time being, to provide horses and sufficient equipments to the said monks when they go and return, at each of their outgoings and return journeys, and that you summarily remove from such their offices those who wilfully transgress herein, for which purpose we commit to you our own part by these presents.[3]

Also, whereas it was likewise disclosed and reported to us in that place that the chapel of blessed Mary is endowed with possessions, and especially in order that a wax taper should be provided to burn con-tinually day and night in the same chapel, and that such possessions are sufficient for this and the other burthens incumbent upon the same chapel, nevertheless by reason of the carelessness of the sacrist for the time being the same taper is very often left extinguished: we therefore

---

[2] See the third paragraph. The principle of attendance in quire by rotation seems to be recognized by the terms of the penalty: the injunction, however, requires the attendance of the whole monastery at the day-hours and high mass, without laying similar stress upon the night office.

[3] See the nineteenth paragraph.

cuilibet dicti monasterii pro tempore existenti quod diligenter super-
intendat vt dictus cereus decetero in forma predicta continue exhibeatur
sub pena ieiunii in pane et aqua proxima sexta feria quociens in hoc
deliquerit.

Et quia detectum simili modo inuenimus et delatum quod conuentus
dicti monasterii nonnullas ab officiis cellerarii, subcellerarii, infirmarii et
precentoris exigunt[1] annuatim graues et magnas expensas *ad* conuiuaciones, cum nec egestas nec honestas requisita in hoc subsistat, sed pocius
ex hiis causantur insolencie, dissoluciones et forte ebrietates et similia,
et ex industria possent huiusmodi impense vtilius in commodum et vsus
monasterii conuerti: iniungimus igitur vobis personis singularibus de
dicto conuentu presentibus et futuris ne dictas decetero exigatis conuiuaciones, sed impense que in talibus conuiuacionibus effunderentur in
vtilitatem dicti[2] monasterii per communem assensum disponantur, eo
presertim quod vobis in cibis ad vestra magna solacia vltra necessariam
sustentacionem habundancius sit prouisum, ne ingluuiei videamini
intendere pocius quam religioni, et hoc sub pena standi in refectorio per
vnam septimanam[3] cibis refectorii *tantummodo* contenti.

Similiter cum in eadem visitacione nostra nobis detectum existat
quod onus reparacionis ecclesie conuentualis Sancti Iuonis ad officium
sacriste loci eiusdem pertineat, quodque sacrista huiusmodi omni sexta
feria confratribus suis monachis ibidem residentibus poma debeat ministrare, quodque eo quod sacriste huiusmodi compotos de officio suo perantea non reddiderunt dictum officium permaximum patitur detrimentum:
iniungimus igitur tibi sacriste dicti loci et cuilibet tibi in eodem officio
substituendo ac volumus, mandamus et ordinamus vt defectus in dicta
ecclesia et alibi ibidem ad tuam curam pertinentes debite et competenter
facias reparari pomaque in forma predicta *si haberi possint* ministrari,
quodque fidelem compotum atque plenum certo cuiuslibet anni termino
per abbatem dicti monasterii ad hoc assignato de omni administracione
tua in huiusmodi officio facta priori dicte celle vel alii ad hoc per abbatem
deputato reddere teneamini et reddatis, sub pena *totalis* amocionis ab
officio huiusmodi et custodie claustralis infra dictum monasterium per
vnum mensem continuum.

Item quia comperimus nobis simili modo detectum quod pluribus
annis iam transactis nullus fuit in communi exhibitus compotus de
administracione spiritualium vel temporalium ad ipsum monasterium
pertinencium sic quod timetur[4] ipsum monasterium est graui onere eris
alieni depressum: iniungimus vobis abbati quod omni anno inter festa
Sancti Michaelis et Omnium Sanctorum exhibeatis plenum compotum
administracionis omnium bonorum spiritualium et temporalium eidem
monasterio seu cuiuis officio in eodem monasterio vel extra illud
qualitercunque spectancium in loco capitulari coram toto conuentu
vel saltem certis discretis et fidedignis personis de conuentu per

---

[1] *Sic*: plural for singular.
[2] *alios vsus* cancelled.
[3] *cib* and *refeccione* cancelled.
[4] *Sic*: but the word appears to be underlined as if to be cancelled.

[1] See the twelfth paragraph.
[2] See the twenty-fifth paragraph.

enjoin upon every sacrist of the said monastery for the time being that he take diligent heed that the said taper be provided continually henceforward in form aforesaid, under pain of fasting upon bread and water the next Friday after, as often as he transgresses herein.[1]

And because we have found it in like manner disclosed and reported that the convent of the said monastery yearly demand of the offices of the cellarer, subcellarer, infirmarer and precentor certain heavy and great expenses for banquetings, whereas in this there is no underlying need or seemly requirement, but rather there are brought about hereby breaches of discipline, dissolute manners, and perchance drunkenness and the like, and such expenses might by diligence be converted more profitably to the advantage and uses of the monastery: we therefore enjoin upon you, the several persons of the said convent that are and shall be, that henceforward you demand not the said banquetings, but that the expenses which might be lavished upon such banquetings be laid out by common assent to the profit of the said monastery, seeing especially that you have very abundant provision of food for your great comfort, over and above your needful means of support; lest you seem to pay heed to surfeiting rather than to religion; and this under pain of staying in frater for a week, during which you shall be content with the food of the frater only.[2]

Likewise, whereas it is disclosed to us in the same our visitation that the burthen of the repair of the conventual church of St. Ives should belong to the office of the sacrist of the same place, and that such sacrist ought to furnish apples every Friday to his brethren the monks there resident, and that, because such sacrists have not rendered accounts of their office aforetime, the said office suffers very great damage: we therefore enjoin upon you, the sacrist of the said place, and everyone who shall take your place in the same office, and we will, command and ordain that you cause the defaults in the said church and elsewhere in that place which appertain to your charge to be duly and sufficiently repaired, and the apples, if they may be had, to be ministered in form aforesaid, and that you shall be bound to render and shall render a faithful and full account, at a certain term in every year appointed for this purpose by the abbot of the said monastery, of all your administration done in such office to the prior of the said cell or another person deputed by the abbot to this end, under pain of entire removal from such office, and of confinement to cloister within the said monastery for a month on end.[3]

Also, because we found it disclosed to us in like manner that for several years now past no account has been furnished in common of the administration of the spiritualities or temporalities appertaining to the same monastery, so that there is fear that the same monastery is bowed down with a heavy weight of debt: we enjoin upon you who are abbot that every year between the feasts of St. Michael and All Saints you present a full account of the administration of all the spiritual and temporal goods which belong in any way whatsoever to the same monastery or to any office in the same monastery or without it, in the place of chapter in presence of the whole convent, or at any rate of certain discreet and trustworthy persons of the convent, to be appointed to this end by the

---

[3] See the thirteenth paragraph.

ipsum conuentum ad hoc assignandis exhibeatis[1] plenarie et reddatis sub pena suspensionis ab omni huiusmodi administracione.

[Fo. 51 *d.*] Et quia frustra foret condere leges nisi contra earum transgressores debitis modis horis[2] exequantur, vobisque abbati et priori ex sanctorum sentencia canonum incumbat vt vos, abbas, quanto frequencius poteritis sitis cum fratribus in conuentu vigilem curam et diligentem solicitudinem de omnibus gerendo, vt de officio vobis commisso dignam Deo possitis reddere racionem, vosque, prior, in quo post abbatem requitur[3] potencia in opere et sermone, vt exemplo vite verboque doctrine fratres vestros et instruere in bono et de malo reuocare possitis, zelo religionis secundum scienciam delinquentes corrigendo et castigando obedientesque fouendo pariter et confortando: vobis igitur in virtute sancte obediencie et sub pena grauis contemptus firmiter iniungimus et mandamus, vosque abbatem monemus primo, secundo et tercio peremptorie sub pena perpetue amocionis et priuacionis vestri ab omni administracione et dignitate vestra abbaciali, vosque priorem eciam monemus sub pena maioris excommunicacionis quam in personam vestram si non feceritis quod mandamus intendimus fulminare quatinus omnia et singula premissa nostra iniuncciones, mandata et ordinaciones, quatenus vos et vestrum vtrumque concernunt, in personis vestris inuiolabiliter obseruetis et per singulos vestros confratres et commonachos presentes et futuros, quatenus eos et eorum quemlibet in genere vel in specie concernunt, faciatis consimiliter obseruari, penasque contemptoribus aut ea non seruantibus superius per nos iniunctis[4] absque omni affeccione, fauore aut amore exequamini realiter cum effectu; vosque, abbas, ad capitulum pro corrigendis maioribus et rebellium criminibus et excessibus quociens per priorem fueritis requisiti accedere nullatinus omittatis, sicuti periculum monicionum nostrarum vobis superius factarum volueritis euitare, super gregem dominicum vestre custodie et cure commissum iuxta formam sacrorum canonum superius descriptam diligentissime intendendo, vt in extremo examine *dicere valeatis* 'quos dedisti michi seruaui.'[5]

Qualiter autem premissa nostra iniuncciones, ordinaciones, *moniciones* et mandata obseruaueritis et feceritis *ab aliis* obseruari, qualiterque *commonachi dicti monasterii obedierint eisdem et ea obseruauerint, et si penas predictas*[6] iuxta formam suprascriptam debite et cum diligencia *fueritis* executi, in fine anni cuiuslibet futuri absque omni *desidia aut* torpore vigilancius inquiremus et faciemus inquiri, et quos in premissis desides, necgligentes *seu*[7] rebelles inuenerimus iuxta delicti quantitatem nulli parcentes seuerius puniemus, vt pena et non impunitas sit posteris in exemplum, quod vobis omnibus harum serie intimamus. Et vt nullus vestrum presencium aut futurorum huiusmodi iniunccionum, monicionum, ordinacionum *aut*[8] mandatorum *nostrorum* ignoranciam

---

[1] *Sic*: repeated.
[2] *Sic*: for *horisque*.
[3] *Sic*: for *requiritur*.
[4] *Sic*: for *iniunctas*.
[5] St. John xvii, 12 (*quos dedisti mihi custodivi*). The final clause of the injunctions is an addition. *Dat'* was written at this point and then cancelled.
[6] *fueritis executi debite* cancelled.
[7] Interlined above *et* cancelled.
[8] *et* cancelled.

same convent, [and] shall present it in full and render it, under pain of suspension from all such administration.[1]

And because it would be vain to make laws, unless they be executed in due manner [and] season against them that transgress them, and whereas, according to the sentence of the holy canons, it is incumbent upon you, the abbot and the prior, that you, the abbot, shall be as much and as often as you can with your brethren in the convent, taking watchful care and diligent anxiety for all things, that you may be able to render a worthy reckoning to God of the office entrusted to you, and you [also], the prior, in whom there is required, next to the abbot, power in deed and speech, that, by the example of your life and by the word of doctrine you may be able both to instruct your brethren in good and to recall them from evil, correcting and chastising offenders with zeal for religion according to knowledge, and cherishing and likewise comforting the obedient: we therefore strictly enjoin and command you in virtue of holy obedience and under pain of grievous contempt, and we admonish you, the abbot, a first, second and third time peremptorily, under pain of your perpetual removal and deprivation from all administration and from your dignity of abbot, and we also admonish you, the prior, under pain of the greater excommunication, which, if you do not that which we command, we intend to fulminate against your person, that you observe without breach all and sundry our aforeset injunctions, commands and ordinances in your own persons, and cause them to be observed likewise by each of your brethren and fellow-monks that are and shall be, so far as they concern them and each one of them in general or in special, and that you execute really and effectually, without any inclination, favour or love, the penalties enjoined above by us upon those who despise them or observe them not; and you, the abbot, shall in no wise omit to go to chapter, to correct the more serious faults, and the crimes and transgressions of the rebellious, as often as you shall be asked by the prior, even as you wish to avoid the peril of our admonitions made to you above, taking most diligent heed over the Lord's flock which is entrusted to your wardship and care, according to the form of the sacred canons above written, so that at the last judgment you may be able to say, 'Those whom Thou hast given me I have kept.'[2]

Now in what wise you shall observe and cause to be observed by the others our aforesaid injunctions, ordinances, admonitions and mandates, and in what wise your fellow-monks of the said monastery shall obey the same and keep them, and whether you have executed duly and with diligence the penalties aforesaid after the form above written, we shall most watchfully, without any sloth or laziness, make inquiry and cause inquiry to be made at the end of every year to come; and those whom we find slothful, careless or rebellious in the premises, we shall punish most severely, sparing no-one, according to the degree of their misdoing, so that their penalty, and not their freedom from punishment, may be for an example to them that come after, of the which we give you notice in the serial order of these letters. And, that no one of you that are now or shall be may be able to pretend ignorance in any manner whatsoever of such our injunctions, admonitions, ordinances or commands,

---

[1] See the twenty-eighth paragraph.
[2] See the first and second paragraphs.

pretendere valeat modo quouis, iniungimus vobis abbati et priori predictis sub penis supradictis vt premissa omnia *quater singulis annis*[1]
in pleno capitulo coram omnibus distincte ac de verbo in verbum eo
sensu quo melius intelligi valeant legi et in aliquo loco *patenti*[2] infra
dormitorium vestrum, vt ad ea intuenda et inspicienda facilior haberi
possit recursus, affigi faciatis. Data sub sigillo nostro in manerio nostro
de Nettelham xiij die mensis Junii anno Domini mccccxxxix⁰, nostrarumque consecracionis anno xiij⁰ et translacionis tercio.

LXII.

[Fo. 38.]

VISITACIO PRIORATUS MONIALIUM DE ROTHEWELLE, ORDINIS SANCTI
AUGUSTINI, LINCOLNIENSIS DIOCESIS, FACTA IN DOMO CAPITULARI
IBIDEM XXIJ⁰ DIE MENSIS JULII, ANNO DOMINI MCCCCXLIJ⁰, PER
REUERENDUM IN CHRISTO PATREM ET DOMINUM, DOMINUM WILLEL-
MUM, DEI GRACIA LINCOLNIENSEM EPISCOPUM, ANNO SUARUM
CONSECRACIONIS XVJ⁰ ET TRANSLACIONIS VJᵗᵒ.

In primis sedente dicto reuerendo patre iudicialiter pro tribunali
in huiusmodi visitacionis sue negocio die et loco et anno predictis, comparuerunt coram eo priorissa et conuentus dicti prioratus, parate vt
apparuit ad subeundum visitacionem huiusmodi; et deinde primo et
ante omnia propositum fuit verbum Dei iuxta actus futuri congruenciam
per venerabilem virum magistrum Thomam Twyere, in artibus magistrum, sequentem hoc thema ' Ne timeas, Maria,' etc.[3] Quo laudabiliter
finito, priorissa loco certificatorii ministrauit nomina monialium, et
deinde iurauit obedienciam. Et interrogata de statu domus dicit quod
domus indebitatur in vj marcis diuersis creditoribus et habent in stauro
c oues, braseum, frumentum et alia minora catalla que omnia prouveniunt
ex rectoria de Desburghe eis appropriata.

Soror Margareta Staple, priorissa, dicit quod ipsamet vtitur vno
velo cerico.

Soror Margareta Claybroke dicit omnia bene.

Soror Johanna Burghe dicit omnia bene.

Soror Agatha Holme dicit omnia bene. Iniunctum est sibi quod
habeat velum ad supercilia.

Soror Margareta Crosse dicit omnia bene. Iniunctum est similiter
de velo.

---

[1] Interlined above *singulis septimanis* cancelled.
[2] *publico* cancelled.
[3] St. Luke I, 30.

[1] The precise date of the visitation has unfortunately been lost. It may have
taken place about the middle of May, when Alnwick was for a short time at Buckden
(*Visitations* II, xxxiii). The series of admonitions and suggestions for injunctions
contains so much that is additional to the actual depositions, that the visitation
may well have been adjourned from an earlier period, to allow of further inquiry.
It is not unlikely that it may have been begun in August, September or October,
1438, a period in which the bishop visited several religious houses which were in
need of reform.

we enjoin upon you, the abbot and prior aforesaid, under the penalties abovesaid, that you cause all the premises to be read four times in each year in full chapter in the presence of all, distinctly and word for word in that sense wherein they may best be understood, and to be fastened up in some open place within your dorter, that the easiest recourse may be had to look upon and view them.   Given under our seal in our manor of Nettleham on the thirteenth day of the month of June in the year of our Lord 1439, and the thirteenth year of our consecration and of our translation the third.[1]

LXII.

THE VISITATION OF THE PRIORY OF THE NUNS OF ROTHWELL, OF THE ORDER OF ST. AUSTIN, OF THE DIOCESE OF LINCOLN, PERFORMED IN THE CHAPTER-HOUSE THEREIN ON THE TWENTY-SECOND DAY OF THE MONTH OF JULY, IN THE YEAR OF OUR LORD 1442, BY THE REVEREND FATHER IN CHRIST AND LORD, THE LORD WILLIAM, BY THE GRACE OF GOD BISHOP OF LINCOLN, IN THE SIXTEENTH YEAR OF HIS CONSECRATION AND THE SIXTH OF HIS TRANSLATION.

In the first place, as the said reverend father was sitting in his capacity of judge as a tribunal in the business of such his visitation on and in the day and place and year aforesaid, there appeared before him the prioress and convent of the said priory, in readiness, as was apparent, to undergo such visitation; and then first and before all else the word of God was set forth as was agreeable with the process about to take place by the worshipful master Thomas Twyere, master in arts, after this text, ' Fear not, Mary,' etc.   And when this was come to a praiseworthy end, the prioress furnished the names of the nuns in lieu of a certificate, and then sware obedience.   And, being interrogated concerning the state of the house, she says that the house is six marks in debt to divers creditors, and they have in stock a hundred sheep, malt, wheat and other petty chattels which all proceed out of the rectory of Desborough, which is appropriated to them.[2]

Sister Margaret Staple, the prioress,[3] says that she herself wears a silken veil.

Sister Margaret Claybroke says all things are well.

Sister Joan Burghe says all things are well.

Sister Agatha Holme says all things are well.   She was enjoined to wear her veil [down] to her eyebrows.

Sister Margaret Crosse says all things are well.   [She] was likewise enjoined touching her veil.

---

[2] Desborough church was appropriated to the priory by bishop Buckingham, 4 Jan., 1387-8, in pursuance of a bull of Urban VI, 21 Nov., 1386.   A vicarage was ordained 9 Jan., 1388-9 (Reg. XII, ff. 348-9).

[3] Her election is not recorded.   See *Visitations* I, 109, note 2.   Three place-names occur among the surnames of the nuns, viz. Claybroke (Claybrooke in Leicestershire, near Lutterworth), Burghe (probably Peterborough) and Holme.

Soror Agnes Mershe dicit omnia bene, in Londoniis nata. Iniunctum est sibi similiter de velo.

Soror Johanna Chace. Iniunctum est sibi similiter de velo.

Quibus examinatis et iterum ad capitulum euocatis, iniunctum est omnibus quod non vtantur velis, etc.

LXIII.

[Fo. 52 (50)].

VISITACIO PRIORATUS DE SANCTO NEOTO, ORDINIS SANCTI BENEDICTI, LINCOLNIENSIS DIOCESIS, FACTA IN DOMO CAPITULARI IBIDEM PER REUERENDUM IN CHRISTO PATREM ET DOMINUM DOMINUM[1] WILLELMUM, DEI GRACIA LINCOLNIENSEM EPISCOPUM, SALTEM INCEPTIUE XXVIIJ⁰ DIE MENSIS SEPTEMBRIS, ANNO DOMINI MCCCCXXXIX⁰, DICTIQUE REUERENDI PATRIS CONSECRACIONIS XIIIJ⁰ ET TRANSLACIONIS QUARTO ANNO.

In primis sedente dicto reuerendo patre iudicialiter in huiusmodi visitacionis sue inchoande negocio, die et loco antedictis, comparuerunt coram eo prior et conuentus dicti loci, visitacionem huiusmodi vt apparuit subituri; et deinde primo et ante omnia propositum fuit verbum Dei per egregium virum magistrum Thomam Duffelde, in sacra theologia bacallarium, sequentem hoc thema, ' Peccator morietur quia non habuit disciplinam,'[2] etc. Quo in lingua latina finito, prior certificatorium mandati domini eidem priori pro visitacione huiusmodi directi dicto reuerendo patri porrexit; quo recepto et perlecto, prior confirmacionem eleccionis sue et installacionem suam auctoritate magistri Petri Partryche, officialis Lincolniensis, sede vacante factam primo, deinde fundacionem domus per Rohesiam vxorem Richardi filii comitis Gisleberti tempore regis Henrici primi, et tercio bullam apostolicam de liberacione ipsius prioratus a potestate et dominio domus de Becco, confirmacionem apostolicam secundum modum antiquum Romane curie factam, et postea statum domus vnum post aliud successiue exhibuit. Quibus visis mandauit dominus priori, vt confirmacionem, installacionem, fundacionem domus et eius status[3] faceret copiari et copias huiusmodi penes registrum dimitteret. Tenor vero talis certificatorii sequitur in hec verba ' Reuerendo in Christo patri,' etc.; quibus exhibitis dominus

---

[1] *Dei* cancelled.
[2] This text appears to come from some other source than the Vulgate.
[3] *Sic*: for *statum*.

[1] *I.e.* the veils should not be worn above their foreheads, as in previous cases. See *Visitations* II, **47**, note **3**.
[2] *I.e.* in the interval between Gray's death in Feb. 1435-6 and Alnwick's translation in the following September. There is no record of the confirmation or installation. Cf. the similar case of the prior of Newnham, p. 231, note 7.
[3] The accepted date was 1113. See *Monasticon* III, 473. This was, however, a refoundation as a cell of Bec of the earlier house mentioned *D.B.* I, fo. 207. For a confirmation and *inspeximus* of charters, 1 July, 1438, see *Cal. Pat.* 1436-41, pp. 173,174. The chartulary (MS. Cotton, Faustina A. iv) is summarised in *Monasticon* III, 465-8.

Sister Agnes Mershe, born in London, says all things are well. She was likewise enjoined touching her veil.

Sister Joan Chace. She was likewise enjoined touching her veil.

Now when these had been examined and had been summoned a second time to the chapter-house, all were enjoined that they should not wear their veils, etc.[1]

LXIII.

THE VISITATION OF THE PRIORY OF ST. NEOT, OF THE ORDER OF ST. BENET, OF THE DIOCESE OF LINCOLN, PERFORMED IN THE CHAPTER-HOUSE THEREIN BY THE REVEREND FATHER IN CHRIST AND LORD, THE LORD WILLIAM, BY THE GRACE OF GOD BISHOP OF LINCOLN, AT ANY RATE IN ITS INITIAL STAGE, ON THE TWENTY-EIGHTH DAY OF THE MONTH OF SEPTEMBER, IN THE YEAR OF OUR LORD 1439, AND THE FOURTEENTH YEAR OF THE CONSECRATION OF THE SAID REVEREND FATHER, AND THE FOURTH OF HIS TRANSLATION.

In the first place, as the said reverend father was sitting in his capacity of judge in the business of such the beginning of his visitation, on and in the day and place aforesaid, there appeared before him the prior and convent of the said place, to undergo, as was apparent, such visitation; and then, first and before all else, the word of God was set forth by the excellent master Thomas Duffelde, bachelor in sacred theology, after this text, ' The sinner shall die, because he hath had no chastisement,' etc. Now, when this was come to an end in the Latin tongue, the prior presented to the said reverend father the certificate of my lord's mandate addressed to the same prior for such visitation; and, when this had been received and read through, the prior exhibited, one after another in succession, first, the confirmation of his election, and his installation, executed by the authority of master Peter Partryche, the official of Lincoln, during the vacancy of the see;[2] then the foundation of the house by Rohese, wife of Richard son of earl Gilbert, in the time of king Henry I,[3] and in the third place the apostolic bull concerning the deliverance of the same priory from the power and lordship of the house of Bec, [with] the apostolic confirmation made according to the ancient manner of the court of Rome,[4] and thereafter the state of the house. And, having seen these, my lord ordered the prior to cause his confirmation, installation, the foundation of the house and its state to be copied, and to leave such copies in the hands of the registrar. Now, the purport of such certificate follows in these words, ' To the reverend father in Christ,' etc.; and, when these things had been exhibited, my lord pro-

---

[4] In 1113 the church and monastery had been granted as a cell to the abbey of Bec-Hellouin (Eure). The house, however, remained conventual and did not become, like most ' alien priories,' a mere temporal dependency of the foreign monastery. Its prior was perpetual, and not merely an obedientiary of the parent house who could be recalled at pleasure. On these grounds it received letters patent of denization, 14 May, 1409, (*Cal. Pat.* 1408-13, p. 76: printed in *Monasticon* III, 479). The bull exempting it from obedience to Bec bears date 22 March, 1411-12, and mentions that, since the death of the last French prior, William of St. Waast, all the foreign monks except two had returned to France (*Cal. Papal Letters*, VI, 250).

processit ad examinacionem prioris et singulorum monachorum, qui examinati dicunt ea que sequuntur.

Frater Robertus Etone, prior, dicit quod quidam de monachis adeo sunt sompnolenti quod male surgunt de nocte ad matutinas.

Item quod monachi non seruant silencium in ecclesia, sed adeo confabulantur ibidem cum secularibus ac si essent in foro.

Et dictus reuerendus pater vidit oculata fide rupturam murorum prioratus, vbi intrinseci exire et extrinseci intrare loca interiora prioratus de facili possunt.

O Item prior dicit quod monachi ex consuetudine frequenti inducunt extraneos, nedum amicos sed eciam inimicos suos in prioratum, quibus faciunt omnimoda cibaria habundanter ministrari, per quod domus grauiter oneratur et opprimitur; et per tales qui non sunt beneuoli domus grauiter diffamatur. Et deinde iurauit idem[1] prior iurauit[2] canonicam obedienciam in forma consueta.

Frater Robertus de Sancto Neoto, supprior, dicit quod domus indebitatur, sed nescit in quanto, quia prior non reddit plenum compotum in communi.

Item dicit quod diuinum seruicium non debito modo decantatur de nocte et die.

Item dicit de ruptura clausure circa prioratum vt dominus vidit.

+ Frater Henricus de Sancto Neoto dicit quod conuentum erat inter priorem nunc et quendam Bulloke de Etone quod idem Bullok laboraret quod idem prior eligeretur in priorem in vltima vacacione et pro laboribus et expensis suis idem prior sibi satisfaceret, et super *hoc* fiunt inter eos certe obligaciones et certe alie euidencie, et idem prior soluit dicto Bullok xliiij marcas vel eo amplius, et[3] per hoc domus multum depauperatur, et timetur de peioi.[4]

Item dicit quod non habetur locus pro refectorio vbi monachi commedentes omnino possent obseruare religionem; nam vbi iam commedunt fuit dudum ordinatum pro refectorio, sed inibi sedent omnes extranei seculares, eciam seruientes domus, temporibus refeccionum monachorum.

Item dicit quod ecclesia, presertim chorus, adeo est ruinosus quod tempore pluuie non possunt habere vnum librum apertum.

Item dicit quod prior de mane egreditur prioratum et tota die occupat se inter seruientes et seculares, vix audiendo missam in die, et nescitur an dicat horas canonicas, sed non celebrat a dominica in dominicam.

Item dicit de clausura siue cinctura circa prioratum non reparata vt supra.

Frater Willelmus Eynesbury dicit quod non seruitur ministris, officiariis et seruientibus domus de salariis suis, et de hoc est magnum murmur in populo.

---

[1] *reuerendus pater* cancelled.
[2] *Sic*: repeated.
[3] *post* cancelled.
[4] *Sic*: for *peiori*.

[1] Of the nine monks, including the apostate Byllyng, four came from St. Neots. Eynesbury bore the name of an adjacent village, and Etone probably came from

ceeded to the examination of the prior and the several monks, who, upon examination, say these things which follow.

Brother Robert Etone,[1] the prior, says that certain of the monks are so sleepy that they are ill risers to matins of a night.

Also that the monks do not keep silence in the church, but so chatter therein with secular folk as though they were at market.

And the said reverend father saw with the testimony of his own eyes the breach in the walls of the priory, where the inmates can go out and folk from outside can easily enter the inner parts of the priory.

O   Also the prior says that the monks of frequent custom bring in strangers, not only their friends, but also their enemies, into the priory, and cause all manner of meats to be served to them in abundance, whereby the house is grievously burthened and harassed; and the house is grievously defamed by such as are not well-wishers.   And then the same prior sware canonical obedience in form accustomed.

Brother Robert of St. Neots, the subprior, says that the house is in debt, but he knows not how far, because the prior does not render a full account in common.

Also he says that divine service is not chanted in due manner by night and day.

Also he says concerning the breach of the enclosure about the priory, as my lord hath seen.

+   Brother Henry of St. Neots says that it was agreed between the present prior and one Bulloke of Eaton,[2] that the same Bullok should do his endeavour for the election of the same prior to be prior at the last voidance, and that for his trouble and expense the same prior should give him satisfaction; and touching this there are certain bonds and certain other deeds made between them; and the same prior paid the said Bullok forty-four marks or more, and hereby the house is much impoverished, and there is fear of worse things.

Also he says that they have no place for frater, where the monks at meals could observe religious discipline at all; for the place where they now eat was aforetime ordained to be their frater, but therein do sit all the secular folk from outside, even the serving-folk of the house, while the monks take their meals.

Also he says that the church, especially the quire, is in such decay that in rainy weather they cannot keep a book open.

Also he says that the prior goes out of the priory early in the morning, and is busy the whole day among the servants and secular folk, scarcely hearing mass during the day; and it is not known whether he says the canonical hours, but he does not celebrate from one Sunday to another.

Also he says as above concerning the enclosure or boundary wall about the priory, that it is not repaired.

Brother William Eynesbury says that the stewards, officers and serving-folk of the house are not supplied with their salaries, and concerning this there is great talk among the people.

Eaton Socon, the adjoining village in Bedfordshire.   Caxton is in Cambridgeshire, about eight miles to the east.   Harwedone (Harrowden in Northants, near Wellingborough) and Witleseye (Whittlesey) came from more distant districts.

[2] *I.e.* Eaton Socon.

Item dicit de pecuniis quas Robertus Bullok habebit de domo vt supra.

Frater Willelmus Harwedone dicit de diuino obsequio et ruina clausurarum et ecclesie ac domorum vt supra et campanilis, et hoc in defectu prioris, qui non curat de hiis que Dei sunt, ecclesie vel religionis, sed que sunt in domo, quibus semper se implicat.

Item dicit quod silencium nullicubi seruatur, nec leccio habetur in mensa nec contemplacio in claustro propter accessum secularium, eciam mulierum.

Item dicit quod adeo in tantis summis creditoribus diuersis indebitatur domus quod non possint exire ad nundinas ad extra propter arestacionem equórum et aliorum bonorum domus; nam creditores semper explorant talia.

Item dicit quod[1] prior non reddidit compotum de anno in annum vt deberet, et dicit de materia inter Bullok et priorem vt supra.

Item prior reputatur multum suspectus cum quadam muliere coniugata de Herdewyk nominata Agnete Actone.

Frater Robertus Byllyng de Sancto Neoto, monachus loci illius, est in apostasia, sed vbi nescitur pro certo: creditur tamen quod est apud Wynchelsye.

[Fo. 52 *d.* (50 *d.*)]. Frater Johannes Caxtone dicit de diuino obsequio vt supra, et hoc in defectu prioris, qui ista non attendit, et eciam propter raritatem monachorum.

Item prior non iacet in dormitorio sed in camera prioris, nec accedit ad matutinas.

Item dicit quod supprior non est totus integer mente sed quodammodo alienatus mente, et tamen passus est stare in officio ne deterius sibi contingat.

Item dicit de tarde venientibus ad matutinas vt supra.

Item dicit de ruina et non reparacione prioratus, etc., vt supra.

Frater Thomas Seyntnedo deponit de hiis que tangunt Bullok prout superius depositum est.

Item de clausuris dicit quod tanto dirupte sunt quod monachi exire et extranei quicunque per eas intrare possunt cum voluerint.

Item dicit de stipendiis seruiencium vt supra.

Item dicit de ruina ecclesie et campanilis vt supra.

Frater Johannes Witleseye dicit de stipendiis seruiencium non solutis vt supra, cuius rei causa clamant vindictam a Deo de priore et eius conuentu.

Quibus examinatis, idem reuerendus pater continuauit visitacionem suam huiusmodi vsque post prandium eiusdem diei in eodem loco, presentibus J. Depyng et Thoma Thorpe. Post nonas vero eiusdem diei xxviij[2] Septembris anno predicto in domo capitulari predicta coram eodem

---

[1] *comp* cancelled.
[2] *die* cancelled.

[1] The priory church was distinct and at some distance from the parish church, the splendid tower of which was built c. 1500. The parish church is mentioned in the *comperta* and articles included in this visitation.
[2] *I.e.*, ' for fear lest the horses, etc., may be arrested.'
[3] Probably Monks Hardwick, a mile east of the priory.

Also he says as above concerning the monies which Robert Bullok shall have of the house.

Brother William Harwedone says as above concerning divine service and the ruinous state of the enclosures and the church and buildings, and also of the bell-tower;[1] and this is in the prior's default, who cares not for those things which are of God, the church, or religion, but for those things which are in the house, wherein he is ever engrossed.

Also he says that silence is kept nowhere, nor have they reading at table or contemplation in cloister, because of the resort of secular folk, even of women.

Also he says that the house is so in debt to divers creditors in such large sums that they cannot go abroad to fairs, because of the arrest of the horses and other goods of the house;[2] for the creditors are always spying out such things.

Also he says that the prior has not rendered an account from year to year as he ought, and he says as above concerning the business between Bullok and the prior.

Also the prior has a very suspect reputation with a married woman of Hardwick,[3] named Agnes Actone.

Brother Robert Byllyng of St. Neots, monk of that place, is in apostasy; but where he is is not known for certain, but it is believed that he is at Winchelsea.[4]

Brother John Caxtone says as above concerning divine service; and this is in the prior's default, who heeds not these things, and it is also because there are so few monks.

Also the prior lies not in the dorter, but in the prior's lodging, and he comes not to matins.

Also he says that the subprior is not entirely sound in mind, but is to some degree out of his wits; and yet he is suffered to stay in office lest a worse thing happen to him.

Also he says as above concerning them that come late to matins.

Also he says as above concerning the ruinous state and lack of repair of the priory, etc.

Brother Thomas Seyntnedo[5] deposes concerning these things which touch Bullok, even as it has been deposed above.

Also concerning the enclosures he says that they are so greatly broken that the monks can go out and any strangers can enter in through them whenever they will.

Also he says as above concerning the stipends of the serving-folk.

Also he says as above concerning the ruinous state of the church and bell-tower.

Brother John Witleseye says as above concerning the non-payment of the stipends of the serving-folk, because whereof they call for vengeance from God upon the prior and his convent.

Now, when these had been examined, the same reverend father adjourned such his visitation until after breakfast of the same day in the same place, there being present J. Depyng and Thomas Thorpe. And after nones of the same twenty-eighth day of September in the year

---

[4] For a similar case of an apostate whose presence in a distant place was known or suspected, see *Visitations* II, 37.

[5] A curious form of St. Neots.

reuerendo patre in visitacionis sue huiusmodi negocio iudicialiter sedente
et ad vlteriora in eodem procedente comparuerunt personaliter dicti
prior et conuentus omnes et singuli; et deinde quia dominus inuenit
dictam domum ere alieno grauiter oneratam nec de facili posse[1] ex huiusmodi onere absque eo quod alie vie reperiantur, per quas sumptus
excessiui inibi[2] per monachos et aliorum indiscretam gubernacionem tam
in spiritualibus et temporalibus[3] solercius releuentur; quodque dictus
prioratus tam in ecclesia et campanili aliisque domibus, edificiis et
clausuris tales et tantos paciuntur[4] defectus et ruinas tam interius quam[5]
exterius quod, nisi cicius remedium apponatur, omnia tendent ad ruinam,
vt de viis et remediis huiusmodi per eiusdem reuerendi patris sani consilii
dictorum prioris et conuentus interim prouideatur;[6] ex hiis et aliis causis
ipsum reuerendum patrem in hac parte mouentibus visitacionem suam
huiusmodi in statu quo tunc erat vsque in diem Lune proximum post
festum Sancti Dionisii proxime futurum continuauit assignans, et
assignauit eisdem priori et conuentui eosdem diem et locum ad procedendum et procedi[7] videndum in huiusmodi visitacionis negocio secundum
inuenta et comperta in eadem ac alias prout de iure [competit] procedendum ac ad cetera facienda et recipienda, etc., presentibus magistro
J. Depyng, T. Thorpe et me Colstone.   Quibus termino et loco ac anno,
dicto reuerendo patre in huiusmodi visitacionis sue negocio iudicialiter
sedente pro tribunali,[8] comparuerunt coram eo dicti prior et conuentus
omnes et singuli iuxta assignacionem supradictam; et deinde idem reuerendus pater publicauit detecta et comperta in huiusmodi visitacione sua,
et obiectis dicto priori omnibus et[9] articulis qui ipsum tangebant[10] et per
eum quodammodo recognitis et confessatis, exceptis articulis adulterii
et simonie, quas omnino negauit, dominus assignauit eidem priori terminum, ad primam videlicet pulsacionem horilogii post nonas eiusdem
diei, xij videlicet mensis Octobris anno Domini supradicto, in eadem
domo capitulari et coram eo ad purgandum se cum tribus confratribus
suis de huiusmodi negatis, *et ad proponendum in forma iuris quare iuxta
confessata sua non debet pronunciare ipsum consumptorem et dilapiditorem*[11]
bonorum dicti prioratus, et ad cetera facienda et recipienda, etc.   Quantum
vero ad recognita et confessata per priorem ipse prior submisit se in
alto et in basso gracie, correccioni et reformacioni domini, spondens se
facturum et subiturum omnia que in ipsis idem dominus decreuerit,
ordinauerit et voluerit ipsum fore facturum.   Et deinde idem reuerendus
pater continuauit eandem visitacionem suam in statu quo tunc erat
vsque post prandium eiusdem diei xij in eadem domo, etc., presentibus
magistro J. Depyng *et* Thoma Thorpe et me Colstone.   In quibus termino
et loco idem reuerendus pater, vt prius dictis priore et monachis omnibus

---

[1] *releuari* is needed to complete the sense.
[2] *facti* interlined and cancelled: *facilius* cancelled.
[3] A letter cancelled.
[4] *Sic*: for *patitur*.
[5] *extere* written before *exterius*, and left uncancelled.
[6] The sentence is written as above, but the construction is senseless.
[7] Altered from *procedend'*
[8] *primo et ante omnia* cancelled.
[9] *Sic*: *singulis* omitted.
[10] *presertim adulterii* cancelled.
[11] *Sic*: for *dilapidatorem*.

aforesaid, there appeared in person in the chapter house aforesaid, before the same reverend father as he sat in his capacity of judge in such the business of his visitation and was proceeding to further business in the same, the said prior and convent, all and singular. And then, because my lord found that the said house was grievously burthened with debt and could not easily [be relieved] of such burthen unless other ways be found whereby the excessive expenses therein, by reason of the monks and of the indiscreet governance of others in matters both spiritual and temporal, may most skilfully be lightened; and because the said priory is suffering such and so great defects and decay, both inside and outside, as regards both the church and the bell-tower and the other houses, buildings and enclosures, that, unless a remedy be applied with all speed, all things will go to ruin, in order that meanwhile provision may be made of such ways and remedies [for the relief] of the said prior and convent with [the help] of the sound advice of the same reverend father—for these and other reasons moving the same reverend father in this behalf, he adjourned such his visitation in the state wherein it then was with assignation until Monday next after the feast of St. Denis next to come,[1] and he assigned the same day and place to the same prior and convent for proceeding and viewing process in the business of such his visitation according to the matters found and discovered in the same, and for proceeding otherwise even as is competent in law, and for doing and receiving all else, etc., there being present master J. Depyng, T. Thorpe and I Colstone. At and in the which term and place and year, as the said reverend father was sitting in his capacity of judge as a tribunal in the business of such his visitation, there appeared before him the said prior and convent, all and singular, according to the assignation above-said; and then the same reverend father made public the matters dis-closed and discovered in such his visitation; and when all and [sundry] the articles which touched him had been put to the said prior and had in some measure been acknowledged and confessed by him, except the articles of adultery and simony, which he altogether denied, my lord assigned a term to the same prior, to wit, at the first stroke of the clock after nones of the same day, the twelfth day, to wit, of the month of October in the year of our Lord abovesaid, to make his purgation in the same chapter-house and before him concerning such matters denied by him with three of his brethren, and to set forth in form of law where-fore [my lord], according to those things which he confessed, should not declare him to be a waster and dilapidator of the goods of the said priory, and to do and receive all else, etc. Now, as far as regards the matters acknowledged and confessed by the prior, the same prior sub-mitted himself in high and low to my lord's grace, correction and reforma-tion, promising that he would do and undergo all things which the same my lord shall decree, ordain and will that he should do as regards the same. And then the same reverend father adjourned the same his visitation in the state wherein it then was until after breakfast of the same twelfth day in the same house, etc., there being present master J. Depyng and Thomas Thorpe and I Colstone. At and in the which term and place the same reverend father, the said prior and monks, all and

---

[1] *I.e.* 12 October.

et singulis,[1] primo et ante omnia[2] peciit a dicto priore an paratus foret ad purgandum se in forma sibi indicta super sibi superius obiectis et per eum negatis.　Qui dixit quod sic, et ad hoc produxit fratres Henricum de Sancto Neoto, Willelmum Eynesbury, Johannem Wytlesey et Thomam de Sancto Neoto; quibus productis idem reuerendus pater iterato obiecit et articulabatur eidem priori articulum simonie huiusmodi vt *in* parte proximi folii proxime[3] sequentis, adiciens eidem articulo in specie quod idem prior promisit cuidam Roberto Bullok certas et magnas pecuniarum summas ad effectum vt ipse mediis et viis suis taliter operaretur et laboraret quod dominus Johannes Turvey, vltimus et inmediatus prior dicti loci cederet, et ipse loco sui per eleccionem posset subrogari, quodque dictus Robertus sic operatus est quod dictus frater Johannes, tunc prior, cessit et ipse ex post electus est et confirmatus, et quod idem nunc prior in parte solucionis dictarum maiorum summarum soluit dicto Roberto Bullok xxj li. vj s. viij d. *simoniam committendo.* Ad istum articulum et ad adiectum eidem dictus prior respondens negat omnem dilapidacionem et in sui super hoc excusacionem et in parte probacionis innocencie sue in hac parte exhibet quendam rotulum continentem debita domus et nomina debencium et eciam creditorum et summas eidem debitas de data vigilie Sancti Michaelis, anno regni regis Henrici sexti xv et anno Domini mccccxxxvj[to], qui rotulus remanet penes registrum: fatetur tamen quod domus isto die oneratur grauiori ere alieno et plus indebitatur quam fuit tempore cessionis dicti fratris Johannis Turvey prioris, non tamen dicit causam.　Fatetur eciam defectus reparacionum et ruinam imminentem in ecclesia, edificiis et clausuris prioratus.　Negat insuper crimen huiusmodi simonie contentum in articulo et eciam adiecto eidem, vnde dominis assignauit et indixit sibi purgacionem super hiis adiectis vt supra; qui tandem dicens et confitens se non posse purgare se super hiis adiectis et sibi articulatis submisit se gracie et correccioni domini. Tandem dominus obiecit eidem priori quod ipse vt prior obligauit se dicto Roberto Bullok in cc li. per duo scripta obligatoria sigillo officii sui sigillata, quod quidem *sic* sibi obiectum idem prior expresse negauit. Obiecit eciam idem reuerendus pater eidem priori quod idem prior per quandam billam manu sua propria scriptam et sigillo officii sui sigillatam fatebatur et recognouit se sic se obligasse dicto Roberto vt obicitur in cc li. per duo scripta obligatoria et debere dicto Roberto huiusmodi cc li. Fatetur et recognoscit idem prior se sic et per talem billam manu sua scriptam obligatum fore recognouisse.　Fatetur eciam idem prior et recognoscit quod scripsit dicto Roberto Bullok, dicens quod si idem exponeret[4] [fo. **53** *d.* (**51** *d.*)] centum li. ad effectum vt posset promoueri ad honores in ipso prioratu in euentu futuro cessionis predicti fratris Johannis Turvey tunc prioris quod[5] habebat amicos qui de tanto et eo

---

[1] *presentibus* omitted.

[2] *ob* erased.

[3] An erasure.

[4] A note is written at foot of fo. 52 *d*. . . . *alia parte* . . . *rep' ad* ⊙ The mark ⊙ is at the head of fo. 53 *d*, the obverse of fo. 53 being filled with the detailed articles founded on the depositions.

[5] *Sic*: repeated.

[1] *I.e.* the fourth and seventeenth of the series of articles embodied in this visitation.

[2] See *Visitations*, I, 111, note 3.

singular, [being present] as before, first and before all else asked of the said prior whether he was ready to make his purgation in the form enjoined upon him touching the charges previously put to him and denied by him.   And he said yes, and to this end brought forward brothers Henry of St. Neots, William Eynesbury, John Wytlesey and Thomas of St. Neots; and, when these had been produced, the same reverend father a second time put to the same prior and charged him in detail with the article of such simony, as [appears] in part of the next leaf next following,[1] adding to the same article in special that the same prior promised to one Robert Bullok certain and great sums of monies, to the effect that he by means and ways of his own should so contrive and endeavour that dan John Turvey, the last immediate prior of the said place,[2] should resign, and he himself might be substituted in his place by election, and that the said Robert so contrived that the said brother John, then the prior, resigned, and he himself was thereafter elected and confirmed, and that the same present prior, in part payment of the said greater sums, paid to the said Robert Bullok £21 6s. 8d., committing simony.   To this article and to the addition thereunto the said prior in answer denies all dilapidation, and for an excuse for himself touching this and in part proof of his innocence in this behalf he exhibits a roll containing the debts of the house and the names of the debtors and also of the creditors and the sums due to the same, bearing date on the eve of St. Michael[3] in the fifteenth year of the reign of king Henry VI and in the year of our Lord 1436, the which roll remains in the hands of the registrar; but he confesses that the house is burthened to-day with heavier debt and is more in debt than it was at the time of the resignation of the said brother John Turvey the prior: he does not, however, say the reason.   He confesses also the defaults of repairs and the imminent ruin in the church, buildings and enclosures of the priory.   He denies moreover the guilt of such simony contained in the article and also in the addition thereunto, wherefore my lord appointed and enjoined that he should make purgation touching these additional charges as above; and he at length, saying and confessing that he could not make his purgation touching these additional charges and the articles put to him, submitted himself to my lord's grace and correction.   At last my lord put it to the said prior, that he as prior bound himself to the said Robert Bullok in two hundrèd pounds by two deeds of obligation sealed with the seal of his office, the which charge so put to him the prior expressly denied. The same reverend father also put it to the same prior that the same prior, by a bill written with his own hand and sealed with the seal of his office confessed and acknowledged that he had so bound himself to the said Robert, as he is charged, in two hundred pounds by two deeds of obligation, and that he owes such two hundred pounds to the said Robert. The same prior confesses and acknowledges that he was so bound and by such bill written with his hand.   The same prior also confesses and acknowledges that he wrote to the said Robert Bullok, saying that if the same Bullok would lay out a hundred pounds to the effect that, in the future event of the resignation of the aforesaid brother John Turvey, then the prior, he could be promoted to honour in the same priory, he

---

[3] 28 September. This roll was drawn up very soon after he had entered upon office.

ampliori satisfacerent. Fatebatur eciam idem nunc prior quod de sciencia sua idem Robertus Bullok effectualiter laborabat ad cessionem dicti fratris Turvey tunc prioris, qui postea cessit et iste nunc prior, tunc gremialis, electus est in priorem et confirmatus. Subsequenter vero obiecto sibi articulo adulterii cum dicta Agnete Actone, negat omne crimen cum ipsa muliere post assumpcionem suam ad officium prioris, et sic purgauit se super eodem crimine a dicto tempore cum confratribus suis predictis per eum superius prius ad hoc productis. Nichilominus tamen abiurauit omnem familiaritatem et omnem communicacionem et omne crimen cum dicta Agnete et ipsam eandem Agnetem decetero et inantea, tactis euangeliis. Postea idem reuerendus pater obiecit dicto fratri Johanni Caxtone crimen adulterii cum Johanna . . . .[1] de Sancto Neoto, coniugata muliere; quod crimen idem frater Johannes negat et super eodem crimine ad assignacionem dicti reuerendi patris cum iiij confratribus suis se purgauit tunc ibidem. Nichilominus tamen abiurauit eandem Johannam ac omnem familiaritatem et communicacionem suspectam et omne crimen cum eadem decetero et in antea, tactis euangeliis. Tandem ex certis notabilibus et magnis causis euidentem *vtilitatem et vrgentem necessitatem* dicti prioratus concernentibus ipsum reuerendum patrem intime mouentibus, idem reuerendus pater negocium sue visitacionis huiusmodi, quin ymmo ipsam visitacionem suam in statu quo tunc erat vsque ad [primum] proximum[2] diem iuridicum post festum Exaltacionis Sancte Crucis proximum et ad omnem diem iuridicum citra continuauit et prorogauit assignans, et assignauit eisdem priori et monachis eundem diem *proximum iuridicum*[3] et quemlibet diem iuridicum citra de quo idem reuerendus pater eos fecerit premuniri in eadem domo capitulari ad procedendum et procedi videndum ad vlteriora in dicte visitacionis negocio iuxta formam retroactorum in eadem habitorum et ad cetera facienda et recipienda que iuris sunt, presentibus magistro Johanne Depyng, Thoma Thorpe et me Thoma Colstone.[4]

Fo. 53 [51]. Prior non reddidit plenum compotum tempore suo in communi: ideo status domus penitus ignoratur.

Ecclesia conuentualis et chorus ac campanile eiusdem multos paciuntur defectus in coopertura et aliis, in tantum quod timetur de eorum ruina nisi cicius reparentur, in tanto quod tempore pluuioso non possunt tenere vnum librum apertum in choro.

Clausura circa prioratum est multum et intanto rupta quod extrinseci ad loca interiora eciam claustralia ingredi et intrinseci exire de facili possunt.

---

[1] The name is illegible: it appears from fo. 53 to have been Coke.
[2] *fest'* cancelled. This part of the visitation is much faded and obscured by mending. The passage possibly should read *vsque ad annum proximum et ad primum*, etc.
[3] Interlined above *crastinum* cancelled.
[4] The rest of fo. 53 *d.* and the obverse of fo. 54 are blank, and were probably left for the rest of the visitation.
[5] *extra* cancelled.

[1] *I.e.* after 14 Sept., 1440.
[2] This formal report is followed by the *comperta* administered on 12 October in the form of articles as above described.

had friends who would give satisfaction for as much and even more. The same present prior also confessed that with his knowledge the same Robert Bullok worked with effect for the resignation of the said brother Turvey, then the prior, who afterwards resigned, and this present prior, at that time a member of the house, was elected and confirmed as prior. Afterwards, when the article of adultery with the said Agnes Actone had been put to him, he denies all guilt with the same woman after his promotion to the office of prior, and so he made his purgation touching the same crime since the said period with his brethren aforesaid, who, as above, had been previously brought forward by him for this purpose. Yet he nevertheless abjured all familiar conversation and all communication and all guilt with the said Agnes, and the same Agnes herself henceforward and for the future, having touched the gospels. Thereafter the same reverend father put to the said brother John Caxtone the crime of adultery with Joan [Coke] of St. Neots, a married woman; the which crime the same brother John denies, and touching the same crime he made his purgation there and then at the appointment of the said reverend father with four of his brethren. Yet he nevertheless abjured the same Joan and all familiar converse and suspect communication and all guilt with her henceforward and for the future, having touched the gospels. At length, because of certain notable and great reasons concerning the evident profit and urgent necessity of the same priory, which deeply moved the same reverend father, the same reverend father adjourned and prorogued the business of such his visitation, nay, rather his same visitation in the state wherein it then was with assignation until the [first] law-day next after the feast of the Exaltation of the Holy Cross next to come,[1] and to any law-day on this side thereof, and he assigned to the same prior and monks the same next law-day and any law-day whatever on this side thereof concerning which the same reverend father shall cause them to be warned beforehand, in the same chapter-house, to proceed and view process to further matters in the business of the same visitation, according to the form of the past acts held in the same, and to do and receive all else that is lawful, there being present master John Depyng, Thomas Thorpe and I Thomas Colstone.[2]

The prior has not rendered a full account in common during his time: therefore the state of the house is altogether unknown.[3]

The conventual church and quire and the bell-tower of the same are suffering many defaults as regards roofing and other matters, to so great a pitch that there is fear that they will come to ruin unless they be repaired with all haste, in so much as in rainy weather they cannot hold a book open in quire.[4]

The enclosure round the priory is greatly and so far broken that persons from outside can enter to the inner buildings, even those of the cloister, and the inmates can go out easily.[5]

---

[3] See the first *detectum* of Robert of St. Neots, and Harwedone's fourth.

[4] See Henry of St. Neots' third, Harwedone's first, and Thomas Seyntnedo's fourth *detecta*.

[5] See the note among the prior's *detecta*, and the *detecta* of Robert of St. Neots and four others.

Prior indebitauit domum per obligaciones cuidam Bullok de Etone, vt in vltima vacacione eligeretur in priorem, ad cc marcas[1] et eo amplius, vt creditur, de qua summa idem prior soluit dicto Bullok xliiij marcas: vide ad tale signum +.[2]

Omnes hospites seculares et seruientes domus comedunt omni die in refectorio tempore refeccionum monachorum, sic quod ibidem nulla obseruatur religio.

Prior ex consuetudine de mane egreditur prioratum et tota die occupatur in secularibus et inter seculares, vix audiendo missam in die, et nescitur an dicat horas canonicas, sed non celebrat a dominica in dominicam.

Prior non soluit ministris et seruientibus domus stipendia et salaria sua, propter quod domus multum diffamatur, et clamant vindictam de priore et conuentu.

Prior non intendit choro in diuinis nec religioni nec hiis que Dei sunt, sed semper implicat se secularibus, omittendo penitus ea ad que ex voto religionis obligatur, nec hore contemplacionis obseruantur in claustro secundum regulam propter frequentem accessum secularium eciam mulierem.[3]

In defectu prioris domus tanto oneratur ere alieno quod carecte nec alia bona sua exire possunt ad nundinas vel alibi nisi arestentur, quia creditores fiunt in hiis exploratores.

Idem prior multum reputatur suspectus super adulterio cum Agnete Actone de Herdewyk, coniugata. Obiecto sibi articulo negat crimen ab omni tempore: habet terminum ad primam pulsacionem post nonas in eadem domo capitulari ad purgandum se de huiusmodi crimine et eciam simonie cum iij de confratribus suis et ad proponendum quare non debet pronunciare ipsum dilapidatorem et pro dilapidatore iuxta confessata sua et ad cetera facienda, etc., que iuris sunt. Ad faciendum purgacionem pro adulterio produxit fratres Henricum [de Sancto] Neoto, Willelmum [Eynes]bury, Johannem [Wytlesey et] Thomam de Sancto [Neoto], cum quibus purgauit [se de crimine] huiusmodi: post ar . . . . cium prioris . . . [abiurauit] dictam mulierem [et omnem fa]miliaritatem [cum ea] suspec[tam].[4]

Item in defectu prioris non intendentis religioni silencium non seruatur vbi seruari deberet iuxta regulam, nam monachi adeo fabulantur cum secularibus in ecclesia, claustro et refectorio ac si essent in foro, nec habetur leccio in mensa.

Item in defectu prioris, qui non attendit diuinum obsequium, non debite decantatur de nocte et die secundum regulam.

Item monachi sunt multum sompnolenti et necgligentes in surgendo de nocte ad matutinas in defectu prioris, qui non iacet in dormitorio sed in camera sua, nec venit ad matutinas.

---

[1] *Sic.*

[2] This refers to the first paragraph of the evidence of Henry of St. Neots: see p. 321.

[3] *Sic*: for *mulierum.*

[4] This passage is much rubbed and torn.

[1] See Henry of St. Neots' first, Eynesbury's second, Harwedone's fourth, and Thomas Seyntnedo's first *detecta.*

[2] See Henry of St. Neots' second *detectum.*

The prior put the house in debt by bonds to one Bullok of Eaton, in order that at the last vacancy he might be elected prior, to the amount of two hundred marks and more, as it is believed; of the which sum the same prior has paid to the said Bullok forty-four marks.[1] See the sign +.

All the secular guests and serving-folk of the house mess every day in the frater during the monks' repasts, so that no religious discipline is observed therein.[2]

The prior of custom goes out of the priory early in the morning, and is busied all day long in secular matters and among secular folk, scarcely hearing mass in a day; and it is not known whether he says the canonical hours, but he does not celebrate from one Sunday to the next.[3]

The prior does not pay the officers and serving-folk of the house their fees and wages, by reason whereof the house is sorely defamed, and they cry vengeance on the prior and convent.[4]

The prior pays no attention to the quire as regards divine service, or to religion or to those things that are of God, but is always meddling with secular matters, leaving utterly undone those things whereunto he is bound by his vow of religion; nor are the times for contemplation observed in cloister according to the rule, by reason of the often coming of secular folk, even women.[5]

In the prior's default the house is so greatly burthened with debt that the carts and its other goods cannot go out to fairs or elsewhere without being arrested, because its creditors become spies upon such things.[6]

The same prior is reputed to be greatly suspect of adultery with Agnes Actone of Hardwick, married woman.[7] The article having been put to him, he denies his guilt at any time: he has his term at the first stroke after nones in the same chapter-house to clear himself of such guilt, and also of simony, with three of his brethren, and to show cause wherefore [my lord] should not declare him a dilapidator and to be such according to his confessions, and to do all else, etc., which are in course of law. To make purgation for adultery he brought forward brothers Henry [of St.] Neots, William [Eynes]bury, John [Wytlesey] and Thomas of St. [Neots], with whom he cleared [himself of] such guilt: after . . . . . of the prior . . . [he abjured] the said woman [and all] suspect intercourse with her.

Also in default of the prior, who heeds not religion, silence is not kept where it should be kept according to the rule, for the monks so prattle with secular folk in church, cloister and frater, as though they were at market, nor do they have reading at table.[8]

Also in the prior's default, who does not attend divine service, it is not sung by night and day according to the rule.[9]

Also the monks are much given to sleep and careless in rising by night to matins, in the prior's default, who does not lie in the dorter, but in his lodging, and comes not to matins.[10]

---

[3] See Henry of St. Neots' fourth *detectum*.

[4] See Eynesbury's first, Thomas Seyntnedo's third, and Witleseye's *detecta*.

[5] See Harwedone's first and second and Caxtone's first *detecta*.

[6] See Harwedone's third *detectum*.

[7] See Harwedone's fifth *detectum*. The notes which follow were added at the inquiry on 12 October and afterwards incorporated in the report.

[8] See the prior's second, Harwedone's second and Caxtone's first *detecta*.

[9] See Robert of St. Neots' second, Harwedone's first and Caxtone's first *detecta*.

[10] See the prior's first, and Caxtone's second and fourth *detecta*.

Frater Robertus de Sancto Neoto, paciens quodammodo mentis alienacionem, deputatur supprior, cum propter huiusmodi defectum sit ineptus huiusmodi officio.

Domus multum oneratur per extraneos, quos monachi inducunt ad refecciones quotidianas, vt in depositis ad hoc signum O[1]

Item *propter*[2] raritatem monachorum religio in nullo obseruatur.

Prior procurauit plures magnates, eciam dominos temporales, mittere litteras suas conuentui in vltima[3] vacacione domus dirigi[4] vt ipsum eligerent in priorem, et vt *sic* scriberent donauit eisdem scribentibus plura magna dona in vltimatam exinanicionem domus et dilapidacionem, sicque per talia media simoniaca electus est et confirmatus. Negat articulum vt pro simonia: negat eciam dilapidacionem. Fatetur onus eris alieni. Fatetur eciam ruinam in domibus.[5] Fatetur eciam quod domus plus indebitatur pronunc quam tempore cessionis vltimi prioris, sed non reddit causam huiusmodi superuenientis oneris alieni. Isti articulo simonie dominus adicit in specie quod cuidam Roberto Bullok dedisset certas et magnas summas vt ipse operaretur ad cessionem vltimi prioris et suiipsius eleccionem secutam. Negat istud adiectum, vnde dominus indixit sibi purgacionem vt supra; qui respondens dixit non potuit[6] purgare se huiusmodi articulo.[7] Iuratus negat se obligasse se in cc li. dicto Roberto. Fatetur se tamen recognosse per [billam suam] et sub sigillo [officii sui] se taliter fec[isse]. Fatetur eciam se s[cripsisse eidem] Bullok quod si [exponeret] c li. ad eff[ectum vt prom]oueretur ad h[onores in] euentum cessionis [prioris] quod[8] habebat amic[os qui] de tanto sat[isfacerent et de pluri] eciam, et fatetur quod de sciencia [sua] laborabat ad cessionem e[iusdem][9]

Item omni die dominico conficiunt aquam benedictam et panem benedictum infra prioratum et eos ministrant parochianos[10] ecclesie parochialis ibidem, subtrahendo eos ab ecclesia sua diebus eisdem.

Item omni die per continuam[11] pulsacionem vnius campane aduocant eosdem parochianos ad diuina inibi audienda, et sic eos subtrahunt ab ecclesia sua parochiali et priuant eam honore et obediencia et vicarium commodo et oblacionibus, etc.

Item frater Johannes Caxtone est multum suspectus super crimine adulterii cum Johanna Coke de Sancto Neoto, coniugata. Comparuit et obiecto sibi articulo negat crimen ab omni tempore; vnde dominus iniunxit sibi vt statim purget se cum iij confratribus suis in eadem instancia, et sic purgauit se et postea abiurauit eam, etc.

---

[1] See the prior's last deposition, p. 321.

[2] Interlined above *de* cancelled.

[3] Part of a word cancelled.

[4] *Sic*: apparently the construction has been forgotten, and *dirigi* written for *directas*.

[5] *non tamen in sui culpa* cancelled.

[6] *Sic*: *quod* omitted before *non*.

[7] *Sic*: *super* omitted before *huiusmodi*.

[8] *Sic*: *quod* repeated.

[9] The edge is torn, and the actual words at the end of the lines can be thoroughly restored only here and there. The passage, however, is simply an abbreviated note of the matter contained in the visitation.

[10] *Sic*: for *parochianis*.

[11] Altered from *continuacionem*.

Brother Robert of St. Neots, who suffers in some degree from wandering of his wits, is appointed subprior, whereas by reason of such defect he is unfit for such office.[1]

The house is much burthened by the strangers, whom the monks bring in to their daily meals, as [is contained] in the depositions at the sign O.[2]

Also because of the fewness of the monks religion is observed in naught.[3]

The prior procured several persons of importance, even temporal lords, to send their letters directed to the convent at the last vacancy of the house, to the effect that they should elect him to be prior, and, that they might so write, he gave the same who wrote many great gifts to the final impoverishment and dilapidation of the house, and so by such simoniacal means was he elected and confirmed.[4] He denies the article on the charge of simony: he also denies dilapidation. He confesses the burthen of debt. He confesses also that there is ruin in the buildings. He confesses also that the house is more in debt at present than at the time of the resignation of the last prior, but gives no reason for such increase of debt. To this article of simony my lord adds in special that he might have given to one Robert Bullok certain large sums, so that the same [Robert] should work for the resignation of the last prior and for his own election which followed. He denies this added charge: wherefore my lord appointed him his purgation, as above; and he in answer said [that] he could not make his purgation [touching] such article. He denies upon oath that he bound himself in two hundred pounds to the said Robert. He confesses, however, that he made recognisance by [his bill] and under the seal [of his office] that he [had done] so. He confesses also that he had [written] to the same Bullok that, if [he would lay out] a hundred pounds to the end that he might be promoted to [honour in] the event of [the prior's] resignation, he had friends [who] would [give him satisfaction] for so much [and more] also; and he confesses that [Bullok] with [his] knowledge made endeavour for the resignation [of the same].

Also every Sunday they make holy water and blessed bread within the priory, and minister them to the parishioners of the parish church in that place, taking them away from their church on the same days.[5]

Also every day, by the continual ringing of a bell, they call the same parishioners to hear divine service in the priory, and so they take them from their parish church and rob it of honour and obedience, and the vicar of his profit and of the offerings, etc.[5]

Also brother John Caxtone is greatly suspect of the guilt of adultery with Joan Coke of St. Neots, married woman.[5] He appeared, and, the article being put to him, denies his guilt at any time; wherefore my lord enjoined him to clear himself immediately with three of his brethren at the same instant, and so he cleared himself and afterwards abjured her, etc.

---

[1] See Caxtone's third *detectum*.
[2] See the prior's last *detectum*.
[3] See Caxtone's first detectum.
[4] An extension of the fourth article above, with the addition of notes made at the inquiry.
[5] Not in the *detecta*.

LXIV.

[Fo. 60 [58]]

Visitacio prioratus de SPALDYNG, ordinis Sancti Benedicti, Lincolniensis diocesis, facta in domo capitulari ibidem saltem inceptiue, xxj die mensis Augusti, anno Domini MCCCCXXXVIIJ⁰, per reuerendum in Christo patrem et dominum dominum Willelmum, Dei gracia Lincolniensem episcopum, anno suarum consecracionis xiij⁰ et translacionis secundo.

[In] primis sedente dicto reuerendo patre dictis die et loco iudicialiter sedente¹ pro tribunali in huiusmodi visitacionis negocio, comparuerunt [cor]am eo prior et conuentus, parati vt apparuit huiusmodi visitacionem subire; et deinde primo et ante omnia propositum fuit [ve]rbum Dei per honestum virum magistrum Thomam Duffelde, in sacra theologia bacallarium, sequentem hoc thema, ' Visita [vi[n]eam istam,'² etc.; quo in lingua latina laudabiliter finito recedentibusque omnibus de capitulo quos res ista [n]on tangebat, prior liberauit domino certificatorium mandati domini sibi pro hac visitacione inibi exercenda³ in hec [v]erba, ' Reuerendo in Christo,' etc.; quo per dominum recepto et michi per ipsum tradito ad legendum, mandauit michi notario subscripto vt ipsum certificatorium et cetera omnia in huiusmodi visitacionis negocio occurrencia fideliter inactitarem; et deinde lecto dicto certificatorio et preconizatis singulis citatis et comparentibus personaliter, prior primo exhibuit veras copias fundacionis monasterii, vt asseruit, ac tituli confirmacionis eleccionis sue. Exhibuit eciam copiam fundacionis vnius cantarie inibi fundate et iniuncciones factas per dominum Willelmum Grey, nuper Lincolniensem⁴ episcopi;⁵ et postea exhibuit confirmacionem eleccionis sue sub sigillis, cuius cum eius copiis dominus mandauit fieri collacionem. Qua facta dominus, amotis omnibus aliis monachis de domo capitulari, ad examinacionem prioris processit et eum super contingentibus examinauit, qui examinatus dicit ea que sequuntur. Testimoniale installacionis prioratus sigillatur cum sigillo officialis archidiaconi Lincolniensis per dominum Ricardum Caudrey, nunc et non tunc archidiaconum Lincolniensem, de nouo fabricato, in quo sculpta

¹ Sic.
² Ps. lxxx, 14.
³ Sic: directi omitted.
⁴ dioc' cancelled.
⁵ Sic: for episcopum.

¹ The visitation of Spalding was carried out with great care, and the minutes, embodying two series of depositions, are of considerable interest. Reference to Alnwick's itinerary at this period (*Visitations* II, xxxiii) shows that he was at Spalding two days after his visit to Markby (No. XLIII). He does not appear to have been holding a general visitation of the district at this time, and the religious houses visited in 1438 appear to have been chosen because they were in need of special and immediate attention.
² For the details of foundation see *Monasticon* III, 215 sqq. A succinct statement of the somewhat complicated origin of this priory is given in *Visitations* I, 156.

LXIV.

THE VISITATION OF THE PRIORY OF SPALDING, OF THE ORDER OF ST. BENET, OF THE DIOCESE OF LINCOLN, PERFORMED IN THE CHAPTER-HOUSE THEREIN, AT ANY RATE IN ITS INITIAL STAGE, ON THE TWENTY-FIRST DAY OF THE MONTH OF AUGUST, IN THE YEAR OF OUR LORD, 1438, BY THE REVEREND FATHER IN CHRIST AND LORD, THE LORD WILLIAM, BY THE GRACE OF GOD BISHOP OF LINCOLN, IN THE THIRTEENTH YEAR OF HIS CONSECRATION AND THE SECOND OF HIS TRANSLATION.

[In] the first place, as the said reverend father was sitting on and in the said day and place in his capacity of judge as a tribunal in the business of such visitation, there appeared before him the prior and convent, in readiness, as was apparent, to undergo such visitation; and then, first and before all else, the word of God was set forth by the honest master Thomas Duffelde, bachelor in sacred theology, after this text, ' Visit this vine,' etc. And when this was come to a praiseworthy end in the Latin tongue, and when all whom this affair did not concern were gone from the chapter-house, the prior delivered to my lord the certificate of my lord's mandate [which had been addressed] to him for the holding of this visitation in that place, in these words, ' To the reverend [father] in Christ,' etc. And when this had been received by my lord and handed to me by him to read, he commanded me, the notary hereunder written, to put faithfully into the form of acts the same certificate and all else that should occur in the business of such visitation;[1] and then, after the said certificate had been read and each of them that were summoned had been called by name and appeared in person, the prior in the first place presented true copies of the foundation of the monastery,[2] as he asserted, and of the title of confirmation of his election.[3] He exhibited also the copy of the foundation of a chantry founded therein,[4] and the injunctions made by the lord William Grey, late bishop of Lincoln;[5] and thereafter he exhibited the confirmation of his election under seals, of which my lord ordered that collation should be made with the copies thereof. The which having been made, my lord, having removed all the other monks from the chapter-house, proceeded to the examination of the prior and examined him touching those things that concerned him; and he, upon examination, says these things which follow. The testimonial of his installation in the priory is sealed with the seal of the official of the archdeacon of Lincoln, newly made by sir Richard Caudrey, who is now, and was not then, archdeacon of

---

[3] Robert Holand succeeded John Multon as prior of Spalding in 1421-2: his election was confirmed on 13 Jan. by abbot Upton of Croyland, acting as Flemyng's commissary (Reg. xvi, fo. 15 d.).

[4] The identity of this chantry is not certain. See below, p. 340, note 2.

[5] These injunctions have been lost. The quire of injunctions in Reg. xvii is incomplete (see *Visitations* I, 54, note 1), and there is no date in the register which enables us to fix the date of Gray's visitation.

est salutacio *beate Marie et sub ea quoddam scutum talis figure,*[1] *et est littera illa de nouo sigillata et de nouo scripta et de data anteriori.*[2]

Frater Robertus Holande, prior, examinatus et in virtute obediencie prestite oneratus, dicit quod aula in elemosinaria non dum reedificatur, vt vltimus episcopus, Gray, mandauit reedificari.

Quo examinato dominus iniunxit sibi vt exhiberet eidem reuerendo patri statum domus quo eam inuenit tempore installacionis sue et in quo nunc est ac nomina creditorum et debitorum domus.

Frater Willelmus Pynchebek, supprior, dicit quod terrarum suarum in Pynchebek et alibi ad firmam dimissarum acra dimittitur pro xij d. vel ij s. ad omne maius.

Item dicit quod diebus carnium vij monachi, et aliis diebus ieiuniorum et quibus pisces commeduntur xij vel xiiij seruant refectorium.

Item dicit quod monachi non exirent monasterium antequam plene reddiderint et satis experti forent in regularibus obseruanciis, quod hiis diebus non seruatur.

Item dicit quod nonnulla bona monachis et monasterio donata multociens alienantur per mortem huiusmodi monachorum et ad manus secularium ponuntur.

Frater Johannes Ramesey dicit quod omnia bene quantum ad noticiam suam.

Frater Johannes Framptone dicit quod duo monachi non assumuntur in receptores secundum exigenciam iniunccionum domini Willelmi, nuper Lincolniensis episcopi, sed ipse prior ponit se vt vnum receptorem et ad eius veniat[3] substancia domus et alius nominabatur secundus receptor qui modicum recepit.

Item dicit quod prior solus habet sigillum domus ad causas in custodia sua. Similiter omnes compotos domus solus sibi seruat in custodia sua.

Item dicit quod nulla vel modica humanitas exhibetur monachis infirmantibus secundum regulam.

---

[1] Here in the MS. is a rough drawing of a shield with the bearings *a fess and three roundels in chief*. The tinctures are not indicated.
[2] Italicised passage added in margin. *Anteriori* interlined above *posteriori* cancelled.
[3] *Sic*: for *ad eius manus venit*. It is possible that *et . . . veniat* was written in mistake for *ut . . . . veniat*.

[1] For Caudrey see *Visitations* I, 176-8. He became archdeacon of Lincoln in October, 1431. At the time of Holand's election, the archdeacon was Henry Welles, who had collation 6 Feb., 1406-7, and again, on the recovery of presentation by the Crown, on 6 Feb. 1407-8 (Reg. xiv, ff. 473, 479 *d*, 480: cf. *Cal. Pat.* 1405-8, p. 244). Caudrey succeeded on his death.
[2] The type of seal described is familiar. Cf. the seal of Richard Elvet, described by Blair, *Durham Seals (Arch. Ael.* ser. 3, xv, 508), and various seals of archdeacons' officials in the same series (*ibid.* 506, 507).
[3] It is obvious that the letters of confirmation, guaranteed by the seal of the officiality, were an authentic testimonial, according to the common form used on such occasions, supplying the place of an original which the prior had lost. They seem, however, to have included no covering statement to explain the discrepancy between the seal and the date.
[4] Twenty-seven monks appeared at this visitation. When it was continued in Oct., 1439, twenty-six of these gave evidence, Alan Kyrketone having in the meantime gone as prior to Bardney. Twenty-two of these bore Lincolnshire surnames.

Lincoln,[1] whereon is graven the salutation of blessed Mary, and there-under a shield of such a form;[2] and the letter is sealed anew and written anew, and is of earlier date.[3]

Brother Robert Holande,[4] the prior, being examined and charged in virtue of his oath of obedience, says that the hall in the almonry is not yet rebuilt, as the last bishop, Gray, ordered that it should be rebuilt.

And, when he had been examined, my lord enjoined him to exhibit to the same reverend father the state of the house in which he found it at the time of his installation, and in which it now is, and the names of the creditors and debtors of the house.

Brother William Pynchbek, the subprior, says that of their lands that are let to farm in Pinchbeck and elsewhere an acre is let for twelve-pence, or for two shillings at the very most.

Also he says that on flesh-days seven monks, and on other days when they fast and when fish is eaten, twelve or thirteen keep frater.[5]

Also he says that the monks should not go out of the monastery before they have fully rendered [their tasks][6] and are well experienced in the regular observances; but in these days this is not observed.

Also he says that certain goods which were given to the monks and the monastery are oftentimes alienated by the death of such monks, and are put into the hands of secular persons.

Brother John Ramesey says that all things are well, so far as he knows.

Brother John Framptone says that two monks are not chosen to be receivers,[7] as is required by the injunctions of the lord William, late bishop of Lincoln; but the prior himself appoints himself as one receiver, and the substance of the house comes to his [hands]; and another was nominated as second receiver, who has received but a little.

Also he says that the prior by himself has the seal of the house *ad causas* in his keeping. Likewise he keeps in his custody all the accounts of the house for himself alone.

Also he says that no kindness, or very little, is shown to the monks who are infirm, as the rule requires.

The prior, the two Bostons, Frampton, Kyrketon (Kirton), Leeke (Leake), the two Pynchebeks (Pinchbeck), Quaplode (Whaplode), the six Spaldyngs, the two Suttons, Sybsey and Weston evidently came from places in the parts of Holland. Byllyng-burghe (Billingborough) and Repynghale (Rippingale) are names from the edge of the fens in Kesteven, while Grantham is not far to the west. There are two names from Huntingdonshire, Glatton and Ramsey. Redeforde is uncertain: it may be from Nottinghamshire (Radford or Retford). Scorby is doubtful: possibly from some place further north in Lincolnshire, the name suggests Scoreby in the East Riding of Yorkshire, while Seyvelle (Savile or Saywell) is a surname intimately connected with the West Riding.

[5] See the injunction to Ramsey, p. 312 above, which lays down the principle, generally recognised at this period, that at least a third part of the convent should use the frater daily. At a time when separate ' households ' were becoming common, and when the relaxed discipline of meals in the misericord was more popular than the regular observance of frater, this provision was a necessary guarantee against total infringement of the rule. Allowing for the frequent absences of the external officers of the house and for other causes such as were given at Peterborough in 1437 (p. 273), it is possible that seven monks, on an average, represented a third of those usually present in the monastery at meal-times; but the number in frater on fast-days was certainly below what it should have been.

[6] *I.e.* until they knew the services by heart. See p. 255, note 4.

[7] See note on Bursarius, *Visitations* I, 221.

Item dicit quod tempore decessus vltimi prioris domus habuit in thesauro et in debitis leuabilibus plusquam septingintas li., et in quali statu domus nunc est ignorat, quia plenus status non ostenditur in communi.

[Fo. 60 *d.* (58 *d.*).]   Frater Johannes Pynchebek dicit quod omnia bene.

Frater Willelmus Suttone dicit quod frater Alanus Kyrketone, dudum scolaris Oxoniensis, habuit de bonis communibus domus non-nullos libros, xij in numero, et[1] diuersas pecias argenti vsque Oxoniam, et iam tres anni sunt ex quo venit ab Oxonia et nondum restituit ista domui, videlicet bibliam, historiam scolasticam, librum sentenciarum, librum decretalium, vj^{tum} librum decretalium cum glosa cardinalis, constituciones Clementinas, librum decretalium, librum decretorum, epistolas Blesensis, librum concordanciarum, sermones Odonis, flores Bernardi.

Item dicit quod domus non est in adeo bono statu modernis diebus sicut fuit in ingressu prioris nunc, et hoc o . . . .[2] sterilitatem diuersorum annorum subsequencium fore in causa.

Frater Johannes Glattone dicit quod omnia sunt bene.

Frater Johannes Bostone senior, sacrista, dicit omnia bene.

Frater Willelmus Bostone, cellerarius, dicit omnia bene.

Frater Thomas Spaldyng senior dicit omnia bene.

Frater Thomas Quaplode dicit omnia bene.

Frater Robertus Sybsey dicit omnia bene.

Frater Thomas Scorby, custos operum ecclesie, dicit quod non prouidetur sufficienter pro[3] nouo opere campanilis.

Frater Alanus Kyrketone, elemosinarius, dicit de receptoribus deputatis contra formam iniunccionum alias factarum vt supra.

Post meridiem dicti diei xxj[4] examinati fuerunt subscripti per Depyng ex commissione domini.

Frater Rogerus Seyvelle dicit omnia bene.

Frater Simon Byllyngburghe petit vt vendicio vini infra situm prioratus, presertim loca claustralia, omnino cohibeatur.

Frater Nicholaus Suttone petit vt in omni mensa extra refectorium legatur aliquid sacre scripture per vnum clericum de elemosinaria ad edificacionem discumbencium.

---

[1] *duas* cancelled.
[2] The margin is torn here.
[3] *nullo* cancelled.
[4] *p* erased.

[1] The list of books borrowed by a student from the convent library is interesting. It includes five volumes which formed a necessary foundation for the study of canon law, viz. the *Decretum* of Gratian (*liber Decretorum*), two copies of the Decretals, a *Liber Sextus*, and the Clementine constitutions. The ' cardinal's gloss ' is the commentary upon the Decretals by Henry of Susa, ' fons et splendor juris,' bishop of Sisteron 1241, archbishop of Embrun 1250-71, and cardinal bishop of Ostia from 1263. *Biblia* is, of course, the Vulgate or part of it. For the *Historia Scholastica* of Petrus Comestor, see Migne, P.L. cxcviii. *Liber sententiarum* is the work of Peter Lombard, the fundamental text-book of the theological student. The epistles of Peter of Blois are printed in Migne, P.L. ccvii: for their author see the valuable essay in Dr. Armitage Robinson's *Somerset Hist. Essays*, 1921, pp. 100-40. The *Concordantiae* is probably the concordance to Holy Scripture begun by Hugh of

Also he says that at the time of the last prior's decease the house had in the treasury and in debts that might be recovered more than seven hundred pounds, and in what sort of state the house now is he knows not, because the full state is not exhibited in common.

Brother John Pynchebek says that all things are well.

Brother William Suttone says that brother Alan Kyrketone, sometime a scholar at Oxford, took to Oxford of the common goods of the house certain books, twelve in number, and divers pieces of silver; and it is now three years since he came from Oxford, and he has not yet restored these things to the house, to wit, a Bible, an *Historia Scolastica*, a book of the Sentences, a book of the Decretals, the sixth book of the Decretals with the cardinal's gloss, the Clementine constitutions, a book of the Decretals, a book of the Decrees, the letters of [Peter] of Blois, a book of Concordances, the sermons of Odo, the Flowers of Bernard.[1]

Also he says that the house is not at the present time in as good a state as it was at the entry of him who is now prior, and [of] this . . . . the barrenness of divers years that followed is the reason.

Brother John Glattone says that all things are well.

Brother John Bostone the elder,[2] the sacrist, says all things are well.

Brother William Bostone, the cellarer, says all things are well.

Brother Thomas Spaldyng the elder says all things are well.

Brother Thomas Quaplode says all things are well.

Brother Robert Sybsey says all things are well.

Brother Thomas Scorby, warden of the church works, says that there is not sufficient provision for the new work of the bell-tower.[3]

Brother Alan Kyrketone, the almoner, says as above concerning the appointment of receivers contrary to the form of the injunctions made at another time.

After noon of the said twenty-first day the persons hereunder written were examined by Depyng, by my lord's commission.[4]

Brother Roger Seyvelle says all things are well.

Brother Simon Byllyngburghe prays that the sale of wine within the precinct of the priory, especially in the cloister buildings, be altogether repressed.

Brother Nicholas Suttone prays that at every table outside the frater there may be read some passage of holy scripture by a clerk of the almonry,[5] for the edification of them that sit at meat.

St. Cher, prior of the Dominican house of St. Jacques at Paris, and known as *Concordantiae S. Jacobi*, which was amplified by John of Darlington, archbishop of Dublin 1279-86, and by other friars of the same order. *Sermones Odonis* are the sermons of Odo, the famous abbot of Cluny (see Migne, P.L. cxxxiii), and *Flores Bernardi* were a selection of passages from St. Bernard of Clairvaux (*ibid.* clxxxiii).

[2] 'The elder' seems to be an error. No other John Bostone is mentioned now or in the following October, but a monk of that name appears to have died during 1438: see p. 344 below. On 12 July, 1441, John Bostone, monk of Spalding, had a dispensation to be elected to dignities and to hold benefices with or without cure wont to be governed by monks of his order (*Cal. Papal Letters* ix, 205).

[3] At Spalding, as at St. Neots (see p. 322, note 1) the steeple of the parish church remains, while the priory church has altogether perished.

[4] Cf. the procedure adopted at Peterborough, pp. 270-1.

[5] *I.e.* one of the youths brought up in the almonry. This ingenious suggestion may probably be construed as a plea for the toleration of separate 'households' and the consequent disuse of frater.

Item dicit quod maneria de Golwell lathe, Halmere quasi totaliter destruuntur per discursus aquarum defluencium ex procinctu Croylandie.

Item dicitur quod nimis leniter et absque causis conceditur licencia exeundi iuuenibus monachis. Petit vt restringatur huiusmodi licencia.

Frater Johannes Spaldyng dicit omnia bene.

Frater Thomas Westone dicit omnia bene.

Frater Adam Redeforde dicit se velle ministrare billam.

Frater Robertus Leeke dicit omnia bene.

Frater Johannes Grantham scolaris.

[Fo. 61 [59]] Frater Laurencius Spaldyng dicit omnia bene.

Frater Thomas Spaldyng iunior dicit omnia bene.

Frater Willelmus Repynghale, nouicius professus, dicit omnia bene.

Frater Robertus Spaldyng, nouicius professus, dicit omnia bene.

Frater Hugo Spaldyng, nouicius professus, dicit omnia bene.

Quibus examinatis, dominus dictis die et loco iudicialiter sedens in negocio eorum, comparentibusque coram eodem priore et conuentu predictis, continuauit visitacionem suam vsque *in* diem tunc crastinum, xxij videlicet diem dicti mensis Augusti, mandans et iniungebat priori vt ipso termino exhibeat sibi nomina creditorum et debitorum, etc., presentibus Depyng, Bug, Thorpe et me Colstone.

[Fo. 61 *d.* (59 *d.*)]. Quod prior occupat officium[1] vnius receptorum, omnia sibi imbursando, contra formam iniunccionum domini Willelmi Gray nuper Lincolniensis episcopi, et non reddidit compotum. Negat imbursacionem.

Domus habuit in thesauro et debitis leuabilibus plus quam dcc. libras in ingressu istius prioris, et nunc nescitur qualiter stat cum domo, quia prior non ostendit plenum statum in communi. Allegat solum fuisse cciiij[xx]x li. et xj s. cum quibus oneratus est, vt asserit, in primo compoto suo.

Prior solus habet sigillum commune domus ad causas in custodia sua, per quod timetur de magno dampno domus, nam dicit quod preter antiquum sigillum ad causas habetur aliud eiusdem fabrice de nouo et per omnia antiquo simile fabricatum. Monitus est prior in virtute obediencie quod sigillum illud reponat custodiendum cum reliquo sigillo communi, nam dicit quod fregit antiquum et fieri fecit nouum alterius structure dissimile ab antiquo.

Prior non exhibet nec exhiberi facit monachis infirmantibus medicinas nec aliquam aliam humanitatem vnde cicius valeant conualescere. Johannes Glattone, infirmarius, monitus est quod de similibus prouideat de medicinis et aliis si vtilioribus, etc.

---

[1] *rec* cancelled.

[1] These appear to have been S.E. of Spalding, in the direction of Cowbit. The names may survive, but are not upon modern maps.

[2] *I.e.* the university.

[3] The articles of the *comperta* follow, as in the case of St. Neots (No. LXIII) mingled as usual with notes of the business arising out of them.

[4] See Framptone's first and Kyrketone's *detecta*.

[5] See Framptone's fourth *detectum*.

[6] See Framptone's second *detectum*.

Also he says that the manors of Golwell lathe [and] Halmere[1] are almost utterly destroyed by the spreading of the waters that flow down from the neighbourhood of Croyland.

Also it is said that leave to go out is granted very easily and without reasons to the young monks. He prays that such leave may be restrained.

Brother John Spaldyng says all things are well.

Brother Thomas Westone says all things are well.

Brother Adam Redeforde says that he wishes to furnish a bill.

Brother Robert Leeke says all things are well.

Brother John Grantham, at the schools.[2]

Brother Lawrence Spaldyng says all things are well.

Brother Thomas Spaldyng the younger says all things are well.

Brother William Repynghale, novice professed, says all things are well.

Brother Robert Spaldyng, novice professed, says all things are well.

Brother Hugh Spaldyng, novice professed, says all things are well.

Now, when these had been examined, my lord, sitting in his capacity of judge on and in the said day and place in their business, and the prior and convent aforesaid appearing before him, adjourned his visitation until the day which was then the morrow, the twenty-second day to wit of the said month of August, and in his command he enjoined the prior to exhibit to him at the same term the names of the creditors and debtors, etc., there being present Depyng, Bug, Thorpe and I Colstone.[3]

That the prior occupies the office of one of the receivers, putting all things in his purse, contrary to the form of the injunctions of the lord William Gray, late bishop of Lincoln, and has not rendered an account.[4] He denies that he has pocketed [the receipts].

The house, at the entry of this prior, had in the treasury and in debts that might be recovered seven hundred pounds; and now it is not known how it stands with the house, because the prior does not show the full state in common.[5] He avers that there were only £290 11s. with which he was charged, as he asserts, in his first account.

The prior by himself has the common seal *ad causas* of the house in his keeping, by reason whereof there is fear of great damage to the house;[6] for he[7] says that, beside the old seal *ad causas*, they have another of the same workmanship, newly wrought and in all things like to the old. The prior was warned in virtue of obedience to put back that seal, to be kept with the remaining common seal; for he says that he broke the old [seal] and caused a new one to be made of another form, unlike the old.

The prior does not furnish or cause medicines or any other human kindness whereby they may the more quickly be able to recover to be furnished to the monks who are infirm.[8] John Glattone, the infirmarer, was admonished to make provision of medicines in like cases, and of other things, if they may be of more advantage, etc.

---

[7] Apparently the prior's first statement on the point, unless *dicit* is for *dicitur*. This statement implies that the old seal *ad causas* was still in existence: the prior, however, admitted on examination that he had destroyed it, and consequently that the new seal, in his keeping, was the only one in use for the purpose.

[8] See Framptone's third *detectum*.

Bona data domui et monachis ad habendum eorum vsum in vita sua post eorum mortem alienantur, vt creditur, per priorem secularibus, vbi perpetuo deberent remanere domui, et si vendantur, seculares preferuntur monachis in empcione.

Prior licenciat iuuenes monachos sepius exire monasterium antequam reddiderint et perfecti sint in religione, vel saltem tolerat scienter eos *sic* exire contra consuetudinem domus: ideo restringantur huiusmodi licencie. Non exeunt nisi quando vadunt ad minuciones, vt dicit prior.

Prior non facit competentem numerum iuxta quantitatem personarum seruare refectorium, nam diebus carnium soli vij^tem et diebus piscium soli xij vel ad omne maius xiiij seruant refectorium. Dicit prior quod tercia pars omni die seruat refectorium.

Prior recognouit se nichil fecisse quo ad reedificacionem aule in elemosinaria iuxta iniuncciones domini Willelmi, nuper Lincolniensis episcopi. Prior dicit quod est in onere elemosinarii edificare et reparare omnia edificia illius officii.

Prior non ministrat nec facit ministrari sufficienter operi ecclesie et campanilis, attenta eius magnitudine et diutina prolongacione eiusdem, nam vetus campanile oportet cicius reparari vel in proximo erit in periculo ruine, eo quod prior non attendit ad illud reparandum, eo presertim quod decime ecclesie de Sybsey in eius appropriacione ad hoc specialiter assignantur. Videat propterea dominus suggestionem appropriacionis. Monitus est Johannes Bostone, sacrista, quod diligenter attendat super custodia plumby campanilis antiqui cum prosternitur vel aliqua parcella plumbi per tempestates euellatur vel cadat.

Prior permittit vina vendi publice infra loca claustralia per sacristam, ad quod seculares tam viri quam mulieres, eciam suspecti, habent communem recursum in magnum scandalum domus, et tamen domus per hoc non melioratur. Fiat iniunccio de contrario.

Prior habet nimis frequentem, dispendiosam et diutinam moram extra monasterium, ex quo timetur *de* pluribus inconuenienciis[1] suspectis. Dicit prior quod non est absens per septimanam.

Prior non superuidet nec facit diligenter superuideri husbandriam siue yconomiam in magnum dampnum domus. Dicit se velle diligencius superuidere.

Prior est multum segnis in defendendo iura, res et bona domus, propter quod domus incurrit indies notabile detrimentum, vt in submersione maneriorum de Golwelle et Halmere per inundaciones aquarum

---

[1] *et infamia* cancelled.

[1] See William Pynchebek's fourth *detectum*.
[2] See William Pynchebek's third and Nicholas Suttone's third *detecta*.
[3] See William Pynchebek's second *detectum*.
[4] See the prior's deposition.
[5] See Thomas Scorby's deposition. This, as well as the need of a new almonry hall, were matters which the bishop could discover *oculata fide*, and the depositions were probably answers to direct questions on the point, *i.e.* confessions rather than *detecta* voluntarily furnished.
[6] The licence for the appropriation of Sibsey church bears date 21 Nov., **1354** (*Cal. Pat.* 1354-8, p. 144). A bull to this effect was issued by Clement VI, 20 June, 1351, the preamble to which mentions the damage caused by floods to the priory. This appropriation was made to the *mensa* of the priory, and neither it nor the

The goods given to the house and the monks, to have the use thereof in their life, are after their death alienated, as it is believed, by the prior to secular persons, whereas they ought to remain to the house for ever ; and, if they be sold, secular persons are preferred before the monks as purchasers.[1]

The prior very often gives the young monks leave to go out of the monastery before they have said their tasks and are fully acquainted with religious observance, or at any rate he wittingly suffers them so to go out, contrary to the custom of the house : therefore let such licences be restrained.[2] They go out only when they go to their seynies, as the prior says.

The prior does not cause a sufficient number, according to the quantity of persons, to keep frater ; for on flesh-days seven only, and on fish-days only twelve or at the very most fourteen keep frater.[3] The prior says that a third part keeps frater every day.

The prior acknowledged that he had done nothing as regards the rebuilding of the hall in the almonry according to the injunctions of the lord William, late bishop of Lincoln.[4] The prior says that it is in the almoner's charge to build and repair all the buildings belonging to that office.

The prior does not furnish or cause sufficiency to be furnished for the fabric of the church and bell-tower, considering its importance and the long continuance of the same ;[5] for the old bell-tower must be repaired with all speed, or it will be very soon in peril of ruin, because the prior takes no heed to repair it, especially in as much as the tithes of the church of Sibsey are particularly assigned to this purpose in the deed of appropriation thereof.[6] Therefore let my lord see the purport of the appropriation. John Bostone, the sacrist, was admonished to take diligent heed to the keeping of the lead of the old bell-tower, when it is taken down or when any particle of lead is torn off by storms or falls.

The prior suffers wine to be sold in public within the cloister buildings by the sacrist ;[7] to which thing secular folk, both men and women, even suspect persons, have common recourse, to the great scandal of the house, and yet the house is not bettered hereby. Let an injunction be made to the contrary.

The prior makes very frequent, costly and long sojourning outside the monastery, because of which there is fear of many things that are unfitting and suspect.[8] The prior says that he is not absent throughout the week.

The prior does not survey or cause diligent survey to be made of the husbandry or stewardship, to the great damage of the house.[9] He says that he is willing to make more diligent survey.

The prior is very lazy in defending the rights, property and goods of the house, by reason whereof the house daily incurs noteworthy injury, as in the drowning of the manors of Golwell and Halmere by the floods

---

ordination of the vicarage by bishop Buckingham make special reference to the fabric (Reg. x, ff. 79-80 d).

[7] See Byllyngburghe's detectum.

[8] There is no detectum to this effect.

[9] See William Pynchebek's first and Framptone's fourth detecta, the second of which, however, embodies an excuse.

defluencium ex procinctu Croylandie in estate et defluencium a tergo in yeme, et in decimis lini de certis terris que sunt in controuersia an sint in parochia de Westone vel Spaldyng.

Prouideat prior de augmentando numerum monachorum iuxta domus possibilitatem, et quod debite satisfiat in temporibus debitis monacho studenti Cantabrigie de pensione sua tam per ipsum priorem quam alios officiarios domus. Habet duos parate ad tonsurandum; prior promisit se prouisurum vt satisfaciat scolari.

Prior habet in custodia sua omnes rotulos compotorum qui remanerent et reponerentur in cista communi cum aliis euidenciis domus. In preficiendo officiarios domus est acceptor personarum, nam sibi placentes licet ineptos preficit aliquando vni, aliquando duobus officiis, omittendo alios magis ingeniosos licet iuniores. Quo ad primam partem dicit quod huiusmodi rotuli sic reponuntur, nisi sit quod extrahuntur pro informacione; quo ad secundam partem negat prout articulatur, dicens se nunquam aliquos ex affeccione deputasse, sed tantum pro commodo officiorum.

[Fo. 62 (60)]. (Supprior.) Frater Willelmus Pynchebek, supprior, non est diligens in[1] reducendo fratres discordantes in concordiam, ymo fouet discordias exortas, nunc vni, nunc alteri secrete fauendo, et sic non habet se equum ad omnes: ideo non est dignus illo officio. Iniunctum est sibi quod sit indifferens ad omnes.

(Pietanciarius.) Pietanciarius solueret certam pietanciam cuilibet monacho in die[2] Sancti Bartholomei annuatim, quod non eque facit; nam omissis iunioribus satisfacit senioribus in ipso festo, iunioribus autem non ante annum et dimidium anni. Petitur igitur vt ab omni huiusmodi particulari solucione abstineatur, quousque omnibus vno et eodem tempore satisfieri poterit. Monitus est pietanciarius quod omni anno satisfaciat omnibus integre citra festum Omnium Sanctorum.

(Glattone.) Frater Johannes Glattone, cum fuerit *vbi sint*[3] mulieres, est multum insolens et dissolutus, intromittens et publice loquens de secretatibus mulierum,[4] propter quod timetur de lapsu, cum verba sua semper sonent in luxum carnis, et est detractor inter fratres et quasi seminator discordiarum inter eos. Quo ad primum, negat: negat eciam secundum, vnde habet terminum ad medietatem hore ad purgandum se cum iij fratribus suis. Produxit Johannem Bostone, Thomam *Quaplode*[5] et Symonem Byllyngburghe.

Idem cum non sit multum expertus in sacra scriptura publice affirmat quasdam opiniones male sonantes in auribus audiencium: ideo cohibeatur

---

[1] *redud* cancelled.
[2] *Sabbati* cancelled.
[3] Interlined above *inter* cancelled.
[4] Altered from *mulieres*.
[5] Interlined above *Scorby* cancelled.

[1] Partially supplied by Nicholas Suttone's second *detectum*. The text, as regards the floods, seems to imply a curious natural phenomenon. What is meant, however, seems to be that the ordinary water-courses, which drained from the west towards the Wash and were lost in the fens by the way, formed meres which, swollen by the winter rains, spread far inland.
[2] There is no *detectum* relative to the small number of monks. The directions for provision for the Cambridge student, John Grantham, was evidently suggested by the result of the inquiry, given below, into the case of Alan Kyrketone.

of the waters that flow down from the neighbourhood of Croyland in summer and that flow from the opposite direction in winter, and in the tithes of flax from certain lands which are in dispute whether they are in the parish of Weston or in Spalding.[1]

Let the prior take order to increase the number of monks according to the ability of the house, and that proper satisfaction be made of his pension at due seasons to the monk who is studying at Cambridge, both by the prior himself and by the other officers of the house.[2] He has two in readiness to be tonsured: the prior promised that he would take order to satisfy the scholar.

The prior has in his keeping all the rolls of accounts which should abide and be laid in the common chest with the other muniments of the house. In preferring the officers of the house he is an accepter of persons, for he prefers those who please him, albeit they are unfit, sometimes to one, sometimes to two offices, setting aside others who, although they are younger, have more wit.[3] As regards the first part he says that such rolls are so laid by, unless it be that they are taken out for the sake of information: as regards the second, he denies the terms of the article, saying that he never appointed any out of liking, but only for the profit of the offices.

(The subprior.) Brother William Pynchebek, the subprior, is not diligent in bringing the brethren back to concord when they are at variance; nay, he encourages quarrels that have arisen, privily favouring, now one side, now the other, and so he behaves himself without treating all alike: therefore he is not worthy of that office. He was enjoined to treat all indifferently.

(The pittancer.) The pittancer should pay a certain pittance to every monk yearly on St. Bartholomew's day,[4] which he does not do with equity; for he leaves out the younger monks and gives satisfaction to the elder on the same feast, but not to the younger before a year and a half have passed. Prayer therefore is made that all such separate payments may be withheld, until satisfaction can be made to all at one and the same time. The pittancer was admonished to make entire satisfaction to all every year before the feast of All Saints.

(Glattone.) Brother John Glattone, when he is where there are women, is very unruly and dissolute, meddling with and speaking publicly of women's private matters, because of which there is fear of his lapse, seeing that his words always harp upon fleshly lust; and he is a backbiter among the brethren and, as it were, a sower of discord among them. As regards the first [article], he denies it: he denies also the second, wherefore he has a term half an hour hence to make his purgation with three of his brethren. He brought forward John Bostone, Thomas Quaplode, and Simon Byllyngburghe.

The same, whereas he is not greatly skilled in holy scripture, affirms in public certain opinions that sound ill in the ears of them that hear

---

[3] This and the paragraphs which follow are *comperta* evidently obtained after fuller and more detailed examination. Here, as in the case of Ramsey (No. LXI), the numerous *omnia bene* answers were contradicted by searching inquiry.

[4] 24 August. This custom may perhaps be explained as a reminiscence of the early connexion between Spalding priory and the monastery of St. Bartholomew and St. Guthlac at Croyland.

a talibus, quia timetur quod in hiis officit et non proficit.   Decretum
est inquirendum specialiter super hoc articulo: iuratus est quod decetero
non attemptabit talia.

(Seyvelle.)   Frater Rogerus Seyvelle, cum fuit[1] in comitiua mulierum,
multum lasciue habet se cum eis in osculando eas et aliter per vbera vel
alia secreta tractando et tangendo in pessimum scandalum ceterorum
et malum exemplum interessencium.   Comparuit et negat, vnde habet
terminum ad medietatem hore ad purgandum se cum iij confratribus.[2]
Producit Willelmum Bostone, Robertum Sybsey, Nicholaum Suttone,
quibus[3] productis fatetur oscula et abiurauit huiusmodi oscula,[4] excepto
casu peregrinacionis, et de residuis purgauit se; et pro confessis habet
in penitenciam quod non bibat in loco vbi mulier est presens citra Pascha,
excepta vxore fratris sui.

(Omnes.)   Inter omnes est pessimum regimen, nam cum aliquis[5] motus
fuerit aduersus aliquem fratrem suum, statim prorumpit in verba derisus,
opprobrii et[6] improperii et aliter multum vilia, ac si essent garciones.
Petitur igitur vt cohibeantur omnes a talibus reprehensibus[7] presumptiuis
sub graui pena.   Fiat iniunccio.

(Lector.)   Petitur eciam vt in omni mensa monachorum extra
refectorium legatur aliquid de sacra scriptura per aliquem clericum de
elemosinaria in edificacionem discumbencium, nam sic resecabuntur
plura friuola et inutilia.   Fiat iniunccio.

Frater Alanus Kyrketone, dudum scolaris Oxoniensis, habuit de
libris communibus domus vsque Oxoniam, videlicet bibliam, historiam
scolasticam, librum sentenciarum, librum decretalium, sextum librum
decretalium cum glosa cardinalis, constituciones Clementinas, alium
librum decretalium, librum decretorum, epistolas Petri Blesensis, librum
concordanciarum, sermones Odonis et flores Bernardi ac duas pecias
argenti; et iam tres anni sunt ex quo venit ab Oxonia et non dum restituit
ista domui: petitur vt compellatur ad restitucionem.   Monitus est sub
pena excommunicacionis et custodie claustralis per vnum annum quod
faciat omnia ista restitui integre citra proximum festum natalis Domini,
nam fatetur se habuisse omnia premissa et ea impignorasse ob defectum
non solucionis pensionis sue, sed dicit quod prior iam prouidit sibi de
pecuniis in supplementum pensionis huiusmodi sue.   Et deinde dominus
continuauit visitacionem suam huiusmodi in statu quo nunc est vsque
in diem Lune proximum post festum Sancti Alphegi martyris proxime
futurum, hoc est crastinum dominice qua cantatur officium Misericordia

---

[1] *Sic*: for *fuerit.*
[2] *W* cancelled.
[3] *fatetur* cancelled.
[4] *nisi* cancelled.
[5] *modis* cancelled.
[6] *impropri* cancelled.
[7] *Sic*: for *reprehensionibus.*

[1] Probably irreverent conjectures which might be suspected of Lollard ten-
dencies.
[2] Kisses given to fellow-pilgrims by way of greeting were *oscula sancta*, and
might be justified by apostolic injunction, *e.g.* Rom. xvi, 16.   See the general note
in Lyndwood (tit. *de Haer.* cap. *Nullus*, ver. *deosculationibus*; ed. 1679, p. 298):
' quae sunt religionis: unde dicitur, *Recepit eum in osculo pacis*,' etc.   See also

him:[1] therefore let him be restrained from such [doings], because it is feared that in these things he gives hindrance and not profit. It was decreed that special inquiry should be made touching this article: he was sworn that from henceforth he will attempt nothing of the kind.

(Seyvelle.) Brother Roger Seyvelle, when he is in the company of women, behaves himself very wantonly with them, kissing them and otherwise handling and touching them lasciviously, to the foul scandal of the rest and to the bad example of those that are present. He appeared and makes denial, wherefore he has a term half an hour hence to make his purgation with three of his brethren. He produces William Bostone, Robert Sybsey, Nicholas Suttone; and, having brought them forward, confesses to kissing, and abjured such kisses, except in case of pilgrimage;[2] and concerning the remainder he made his purgation. And as a penance for his confessions he has that he shall not drink before Easter in a place where a woman is present, except his brother's wife.

(All.) There is very ill rule among all, for, when anyone is moved against any of his brethren, he straightway breaks out into words of derision, reviling and reproach, and very base words of other sorts, as though they were grooms. Prayer therefore is made that all be restrained from such presumptuous upbraidings under grievous penalty. Let an injunction be made.

(Reader.) Prayer is made also that at every table of the monks outside the frater there be read some passage of holy scripture by some clerk of the almonry, for the edification of them that sit at meat, for in this wise shall many trifling and unprofitable things be kept in check.[3] Let an injunction be made.

Brother Alan Kyrketone, sometime at the schools of Oxford, took to Oxford of the common books of the house a Bible to wit, an *Historia Scolastica*, a book of the Sentences, a book of the Decretals, the sixth book of the Decretals with the cardinal's gloss, the Clementine constitutions, another book of Decretals, a book of the Decrees, the letters of Peter of Blois, a book of Concordances, the sermons of Odo and the Flowers of Bernard and two pieces of silver; and it is now three years since he came from Oxford, and he has not yet restored these things to the house: prayer is made that he may be compelled to restore them.[4] He was admonished, under penalty of excommunication and of confinement to cloister for a year, to cause all these things to be entirely restored before the next feast of Christmas, for he confesses that he had all the things aforeset and pawned them, because of default in the non-payment of his pension; but he says that the prior has now provided him with money as a supplement to such his pension.[5] And then my lord adjourned such his visitation in the state wherein it now is with assignation until Monday next after the feast of St. Alphege the martyr next to come, that is, the morrow of Sunday whereon is sung the office *Misericordia*

Aquinas II, 2, quaest, cliv, art. 4: ' possunt enim haec (sc. oscula, etc.) absque libidine fieri, vel propter consuetudinem patriae, vel propter aliquam necessitatem, aut rationabilem causam.'

[3] See the petition at the opening of Nicholas Suttone's deposition.

[4] See William Suttone's first *detectum*.

[5] No formal report was drawn up from these paragraphs; but at this point Colstone, having made very full notes upon the cases which arose, continued them as a report of the inquiry.

Domini proxime future, assignans et assignauit ipsum diem Lune priori dicti loci in domo capitulari ibidem ad plenarie et plane exhibendum sibi statum domus quo fuit tempore installacionis sue et quo *dicto* die Lune fuerit et eciam vera nomina omnium creditorum et debitorum domus et ad cetera facienda, etc., presentibus Depyng, Bug, Thorpe et me Colstone.[1]

Familie in prioratu, videlicet

Aula vel camera prioris.

Refectorium.

Aula infirmarii

Aula minucionum infra prioratum.

Minuciones apud Wykham.

Quo in termino, quia dominus non vacauit intendere vlteriori processui in sua huiusmodi vacacione,[2] continuauit eandem visitacionem suam in statu quo tunc erat vsque in diem Jouis proximum post festum Sancti Michaelis archangeli tunc proxime futurum, prout patet per litteras suas patentes, quarum tenor continetur in libro memorandorum. In quo termino, videlicet primo die mensis Octobris, anno Domini supradicto,[3] in dicta domo capitulari coram magistro Johanne Depyng, legibus[4] licenciato, ecclesie Lincolniensis canonico, dicto reuerendi patris commissario, in huiusmodi negocio visitacionis iudicialiter sedente pro tribunali, comparuerunt dicti prior et singuli monachi dicti loci, excepto fratre Alano Kyrketone, qui fungitur officio prioris apud Bardeney iuxta effectum constitucionis Benedictine, etc.; et deinde idem commissarius fecit commissionem legi in publica audiencia; qua lecta, nichil contradicto contra eam, personam suam aut potestatem, etc., pronunciauit pro iurisdiccione sua, et deinde volens, vt asseruit, informari *si* que emerserint citra[5] inchoacionem visitacionis domini necessario corrigenda, dixit se velle procedere ad singularem examinacionem, et sic de consensu omnium processit, et sic primo examinauit priorem, qui examinatus dicit vt sequitur.

[Fo. 62 *d.* (60 *d.*)]. + Frater Robertus Holande, prior, dicit quod quo ad statum domus quo eam inuenit tempore ingressus sui, prior vltimus habuit in thesauro in pecunia ccc li., de quibus soluit archidiacono Lincolniensi, videlicet in recompensacione debiti quod debebat eidem

---

[1] The text, crowded into the page, continues directly with the words *Quo in termino.* The note which follows was written before the account of the proceedings on 20 April.

[2] *Sic*: for *visitacione.*

[3] *Sic*: The year (1439) has not been mentioned before.

[4] *Sic*: for *in legibus.*

[5] *v* cancelled.

[1] *I.e.* 20 April, 1439. St. Alphege's day (19 April) coincided in that year with the second Sunday after Easter, the introit for which is *Misericordia Domini plena est terra* (Ps. xxxiii, 5).

[2] This note was probably made for the purpose of a detailed preamble to an injunction prescribing the proper use of the frater. The 'hall of seynies' shows that there was a misericord distinct from the infirmary hall. For Wykeham, see the note on archbishop Courtenay's visitation of Spalding in 1389 (*Visitations* I, xxviii). The grange at Wykeham, with its beautiful fourteenth-century chapel, now roofless, is possibly the best example of a 'seyny place' now remaining in England.

Domini next to come,[1] and he assigned the same Monday to the prior of the said place in the chapter-house therein, to exhibit to him fully and clearly the state of the house wherein it was at the time of his installation, and wherein it shall be on the said Monday, and also the true names of the creditors and debtors of the house, and to do all else, etc., there being present Depyng, Bug, Thorpe and I Colstone.

The households in the priory, to wit,

The prior's hall or chamber.

The frater.

The infirmary hall.

The hall of seynies within the priory.

The seynies at Wykeham.[2]

At the which term, because my lord was not at leisure to attend to the further process in such his visitation, he adjourned his same visitation in the state wherein it then was until Thursday next after the feast of St. Michael the archangel then next to come,[3] as appears by his letters patent, the tenor whereof is contained in the book of memoranda.[4] At the which term, to wit on the first day of the month of October in the year of our Lord abovesaid, in the said chapter-house in the presence of master John Depyng, licentiate in laws, canon of the church of Lincoln, commissary of the said reverend father, who was sitting in his capacity of judge as a tribunal in such business of visitation, there appeared the said prior and the several monks of the said place, except brother Alan Kyrketone, who is performing the office of prior at Bardney according to the effect of the Benedictine constitution, etc.;[5] and then the same commissary caused his commission to be read in the public hearing. And when this had been read and nothing was said on the other side against it, his person or power, etc., he made declaration on behalf of his jurisdiction, and then, wishing, as he asserted, to be informed of anything that may have come to light since the beginning of my lord's visitation, as calling for necessary correction, he said that he would proceed to examine them one by one, and so he proceeded with the consent of all.   And so in the first place he examined the prior, who upon examination says as follows.

+ Brother Robert Holande, the prior, says that, as regards the state of the house wherein he found it at the time of his entry, the last prior had in the treasury three hundred pounds in money, whereof he paid to the archdeacon of Lincoln,[6] to wit, in recompense of the debt

---

[3] 1 Oct., 1439.

[4] There is no mandate of this kind addressed to Spalding among the memoranda in Reg. XVIII. It is possible, however, that the reference is to the common form given there (fo. 32 and *d.*), which has been printed in full in *Visitations* II, lxvi, lxvii. This form, as is suggested there, may have been drawn up primarily for the visitation of Peterborough in 1437, and could not be used in the present case without adaptation to a case of adjournment, as well as to the form required by letters patent; but the essential clauses could easily be altered or selected to suit the necessary form.

[5] See *Visitations* II, 25. The constitution referred to is cap. 32 of the constitutions of Benedict XII (see Wilkins, *Concilia* II, 610-11).

[6] Evidently Henry Welles: see p. 329, note 1. The circumstantial account in this and the next paragraph contradicts the assertion made in August, 1438, by Framptone that the house could raise £700 from its treasury and debtors at the period referred to. Framptone, however, adhered to his previous statement.

archidiacono, cclxx li., et sic debebant[1] dicto archidiacono vltra soluta xxx libras. Postea idem tunc prior infirmatus et videns se ex hac infirmitate moriturum et habens tunc in thesauro xl li., soluit dicto archidiacono xxx li. in plenam solucionem dicti debiti sui, et de residuis x li. supprior et conuentus liberarunt tempore vacacionis domus officio cellarii[2] domus c s. et residui c s. exponebantur in eleccione nunc prioris.

+ Item dicit quod remanserunt in manibus certorum debitorum domus tempore mortis vltimi prioris cciiij[xxx]x li. et xj s., quos idem nunc prior leuauit et recepit tempore suo, vt liquet per compotum suum.

+ Frater Willelmus Pynchebek, supprior, adiuratus in periculum anime sue, etc. dicit quod omnia bene.

Frater Johannes Ramesey dicit quod frater Alanus Kyrketone, dudum scolaris, non dum restituit domui libros, pecias argenteas, murras et alia domus vtensilia que habuit secum ad studium, prout monitus erat.

(Bostone +.) Item dicit quod in operibus ecclesie tempore vltimi magistri operum huiusmodi habebantur lathomi in hiisdem operibus, et postquam prior exonerauerat ipsum tunc magistrum et substituerat fratrem Johannem Bostone seniorem in officium illud, idem Johannes sic substitutus ipsos lathomos totaliter repulit, sic quod opus non progreditur in magnum scandalum domus. Dicit quod exposuit in officio lx s. et nichil adhuc recepit, et quo ad lathomos expulsos dicit quod magister lathomus noluit expectare,[3] nisi habuisset vnam perpetuitatem de monasterio ad terminum vite, non obstante quod obtulerunt sibi xij marcas annuatim. Monitus est quod diligenter attendat huic operi vt progrediatur, sic quod videri possit ad oculum, sub pena amocionis ab officio illo.

(Subcellerarius.) Item dicit quod subcellarius[4] occupat duo officia, videlicet subcellerarii et custodis capelle beate Marie, et tanto occupatur circa vnum quod aliud necgligit. Occupat officium sacriste per se aut suos, vt asserit.

Item dicit quod solebat exhiberi in capella beate Marie vnus cereus continue ardens nocte et die, pro quo iam vicissim habetur lampas ibidem, sed pro maiori nec ardet ibidem lampas neque cereus.[5] Prouentus officii non sufficiunt ad huiusmodi onus, tamen concedit exhibere lampadem.

+ Frater Johannes Framptone dicit quod, vt credit, in morte vltimi prioris domus habebat in thesauro et debitis leuabilibus dcc li.,

---

[1] *vltra* cancelled.
[2] *Sic*: for *cellerarii*.
[3] *nichil* (*nl.*) cancelled.
[4] *Sic*: for *subcellerarius*.
[5] *officium* cancelled.

[1] His depositions in August, 1438, were couched in somewhat general terms and were not very serious.
[2] Ramesey had answered *omnia bene* on the previous occasion, and his present *detecta* refer to the interval which had taken place since.
[3] The list of the goods abstracted by Kyrketone is extended to plate.
[4] Thomas Scorby had been master of the fabric in 1438, when Bostone was sacrist.
[5] The incident is interesting, especially on account of the glimpse which it affords of the relations between the master of the fabric or clerk of the works and the master-mason or architect. Upon the organisation of medieval building, see the present editor's paper on *Cathedral Builders of the Middle Ages* in *History* x, 139-50,

which he owed the same archdeacon, £270, and so they owed the said archdeacon thirty pounds beyond what was paid.   Thereafter the same prior who then was, being stricken with infirmity and seeing that he would die of this sickness, and having at that time forty pounds in the treasury, paid the said archdeacon thirty pounds in full payment of his said debt; and of the remaining ten pounds the subprior and convent, àt the time when the house was void, delivered a hundred shillings to the office of the cellarer of the house, and the remaining hundred shillings were laid out at the election of the present prior.

+   Also he says that there remained in the hands of certain debtors of the house at the time of the last prior's death, £290 11s., which the same who is now prior levied and received in his time, as is clear by his account.

+   Brother William Pynchebek, the subprior, sworn in peril of his soul, etc., says that all things are well.[1]

Brother John Ramesey[2] says that brother Alan Kyrketone, some-time at the schools, has not yet restored to the house the books, silver pieces, mazers and other furniture of the house which he had with him at the university,[3] as he was admonished to do.

(Bostone +.)   Also he says that, as regards the church works, in the time of the last master of such works there were stone-masons kept at the same works, and, after the prior had discharged the same who was then master and had substituted brother John Bostone the elder in that office,[4] the same John, so substituted, utterly drove away the same masons, so that the work does not advance, to the great scandal of the house.   He says that he has laid out sixty shillings in the office and has received nothing as yet, and, as regards the masons that were driven away, he says that the master mason would not stay, unless he might have had a perpetual pension from the monastery for the term of his life, notwithstanding that they offered him twelve marks yearly.[5]   He was admonished to take diligent heed to this work, that it may go forward so that it may be apparent to the eye, under penalty of removal from that office.

(The subcellarer.)   Also he says that the subcellarer occupies two offices, to wit, those of subcellarer and warden of the chapel of blessed Mary,[6] and he is so busy with the one that he neglects the other.   He occupies the office of sacrist in person or by his ministers, as he asserts.

Also he says that there was wont to be provided in the chapel of blessed Mary a wax taper continually burning night and day, instead whereof a lamp is now kept there, but for the most part neither the lamp nor the taper is burning there.   The revenues of the office are not enough for such a charge, but he grants that he will provide the lamp.

+   Brother John Framptone says that, as he believes, at the death of the last prior the house had in the treasury and in debts that might be recovered seven hundred pounds, and he says further that, two years

---

where the relative positions of the *magister* or *custos operis* and the *magister caemen-tarius* or *lathomus* are discussed.   See also the very full and valuable paper by Mr. F. B. Andrews on *The Mediaeval Builder and his Methods* (*Trans. Birmingham Archaeol. Soc.* XLVIII, 1-99), which draws upon a very large amount of material.

[6] Presumably the Lady chapel of the priory church.   A similar office has been noted at Ramsey (p. 304).

et dicit vlterius quod[1] biennium postquam prior nunc fuit confirmatus idem prior peciit allocacionem sibi de ccc li. tanquam de parcella dicte maioris summe vt de illeuabilibus.

(+ Prior et cellerarius.) Item dicit quod officium cellararii[2] pendet ex officio receptoris occupato per priorem, et dicit quod nullus redditur compotus de officiis illis, saltem de pluribus annis. Prior fatetur compotos aretro de[3] vno anno tantum, et hoc p. . . . .[4] preterito.

(+ Prior.) Item dicit quod prior in reddendo compotos dicit se soluisse c marcas pro debitis, vbi non *soluit*[5] c denarios. Dicit prior se non dicere solutum quicquam fuisse nisi sit solutum.

(+ Prior.) Item dicit quod prior cum bonis monasterii communibus emit certa tenementa in Spaldyng et commodum illorum sibi inbursat. Negat articulum, asserens tenementa illa fuisse empta cum bonis filii fratris prioris et non cum bonis domus.

(+ Prior.) Item dicit quod nullum cariagium monasterii potest excedere fines suos versus Bostone propter timorem arestacionum per creditores domus. Prior dicit quod domus non debet vltra xj li. : dicit tamen quod fuit quedam controuersia inter domum et exteros, et propterea fuit carecta arestata et non ex alia causa.

(+ Prior.) Item vbi deducitur in debitare[6] quod domus debet Henrico Newman xv li., dicit iste plane quod citra vltimum festum Pasche liberata fuit eidem Henrico vna obligacio c marcarum sub sigillo communi, et dicit quod citra id festum Pasche emanarunt sub sigillo communi quinque obligaciones[7] maiorum summarum diuersis[8] hominibus. Quo ad primam partem dicit[9] talis facta est obligacio pro xv li. ex parte prioris, xxv li. ex parte receptoris et xlviij li. pro braseo empto a dicto Henrico, et dicit quod tres alie obligaciones facte sunt pro pensione domini Roberti Rocheforthe.

(+ Prior.) Item dicit[9] ecclesia conuentualis patitur magnam ruinam in tectura, et quod nisi apponatur cicius remedium cito tendet ad ruinam. Johannes Bostone, sacrista, monitus vt diligenter attendat ad huiusmodi reparacionem.

(+ Prior.) Item dicit quod in appropriacione ecclesie de Sybsey fructus illius assignabantur ad reparacionem fabrice ecclesie, recepcionem hospitum, et tamen prior recipit totum et nichil exponitur ad fabricam ecclesie, quia prius . . . .[10]

[Fo. 63 (61)]. (+ Prior.) Item dicit quod *licet* de diuersis officiis quibus *iste deponens, videlicet Framptone,* diuersis vicibus prefuit debean-

---

[1] *post* cancelled.

[2] *Sic*: for *cellerarii.*

[3] *duobus annis* cancelled.

[4] Word lost by hole in MS., possibly *proximo.*

[5] Interlined above *debebantur* cancelled.

[6] *Sic*: for *debitale.*

[7] *in* cancelled.

[8] *creditori* cancelled.

[9] *quod* omitted.

[10] This deposition is left unfinished.

[1] Frampton's statement means that, in presenting his account in 1424, the prior demanded that an item of £300, arising out of irrecoverable debts for the levying of which he was responsible, should be written off the debit side. This is suspiciously like the £290 11s. which the prior claimed to have recovered, and, as there are no *comperta* or injunctions surviving, the real truth of the case cannot be

after the present prior was confirmed, the same prior asked for himself an allowance of three hundred pounds, as being parcel of the said larger sum arising from irrecoverable debts.[1]

(+   The prior and cellarer.)   Also he says that the office of cellarer depends upon the office of receiver filled by the prior,[2] and he says that there is no account rendered of those offices, at any rate for several years. The prior confesses that his accounts are one year only in arrear, and this [the year last] past.

(+   The prior.)   Also he says that the prior, in rendering accounts, says that he has paid a hundred marks for debts, whereas he has not paid a hundred pence.   The prior says that he does not say that anything has been paid, unless it has been paid.

(+   The prior.)   Also he says that the prior bought certain tenements in Spaiding with the common goods of the monastery, and pockets their profits for himself.   He denies the article, asserting that those tenements were bought with the goods of the prior's brother's son, and not with the goods of the house.

(+   The prior.)   Also he says that no carriage of the monastery can go outside its bounds in the direction of Boston, for fear of arrest by the creditors of the house.   The prior says that the house does not owe more than eleven pounds: he says, however, that there was a quarrel between the house and persons outside, and for that cause and for no other reason a cart was arrested.

(+   The prior.)   Also whereas it is brought into the list of debts that the house owes Henry Newman fifteen pounds, this deponent plainly says that since Easter last a bond for a hundred marks was delivered to the same Henry under the common seal; and he says that since that Easter there have been issued under the common seal five bonds for larger sums to divers men.   As regards the first part, [the prior] says [that] such a bond was made for fifteen pounds on the prior's part, twenty-five pounds on that of the receiver, and forty-eight pounds for malt bought from the said Henry,[3] and he says that three other bonds were made for the pension of sir Robert Rocheforthe.[4]

(+   The prior.)   Also he says [that] the conventual church suffers great ruin as regards the roof, and, unless a remedy be speedily applied, it will quickly come to ruin.   John Bostone, the sacrist, was admonished to take diligent heed to such repair.

(+   The prior.)   Also he says that, in the appropriation of the church of Sibsey, its fruits were assigned to the repair of the fabric of the church [and] the reception of guests, and yet the prior receives the whole and nothing is laid out upon the fabric of the church, because before . . .

(+   The prior.)   Also he says that, albeit certain noteworthy sums are due from the divers offices over which this deponent, to wit Framptone,

---

arrived at.   Depyng had to decide between two opposite stories, each of which, of course, was given *in camera*.

[2] The statement should probably be put in the opposite way, viz. that the cellarer *pro tem.* was *ex officio* receiver.

[3] It thus appears that, in the account submitted on this occasion, the prior entered only the amount of the bond for which he himself, as prior, was personally responsible.

[4] I am unable to trace the history of this pension.   The surname of the pensioner referred to appears in Stoke Rochford, near Grantham; and he was probably a member of that family.

tur[1] certe notabiles *summe* tam *sibi* de peculio suo qu*am*[2] de pecunia de aliis personis mutuata, idemque prior de magna parte summarum huiusmodi satisfecerit, prout hec omnia in quadam billa inde inter eos indentata plenius continetur,[3] idem tamen prior de residuo summarum huiusmodi adhuc debitarum satisfecere[4] non curat. Prior dicit quod monitus fuit iste Framptone per quemlibet priorem loci quod non excederet in expensis in officio cui prefuit, et hoc in virtute obediencie,[5] et ideo excessum huiusmodi habere non debet nisi committat inobedienciam: quam monicionem idem Framptone fatetur, dicit tamen quod nunquam excessit nisi de voluntate prioris. Prior negat scienciam operis in ecclesia Sancte Crucis. *Prior vult de sciencia conuentus contentare istum Framptone de excessu in officio pietanciarii infra viij dies.*[6]

(+ Prior.) Item dicit quod licet quiscumque officiarius domus exoneratus de officio suo indebitetur racione officii sui, prior tamen non vult satisfacere de vno denario debiti huiusmodi, quamquam officiarius ille plenum reddiderit compotum de administracione sua: ideo sit prior informatus de operibus excessuum, ita quod de eius consensu procedant, et tunc prior subeat onus excessuum huiusmodi.

(+[7].) Item dicit quod nullo vnquam tempore redditur plenus plenarius compotus in communi: propter[8] nescitur quod stat de statu domus.

(+[9].) Item dicit quod non ministratur senibus et infirmis de cibis subtilioribus quibus melius refici possent.

(+ Prior.) Frater Johannes Pynchebek petit melioracionem panis et ceruisie pro conuentu. Prior concedit quod in euentu melioris facture emendentur huiusmodi panis et ceruisia.

(+ Prior.) Frater Willelmus Suttone petit vt dominus videat[10] compotum vltimo factum per Johannem Multone in vita sua, et sic procedendo de anno in annum vsque hunc annum, et sic videbit dominus an compoti sint rasi vel cancellati et qualiter domus prosperatur.

Item de statu domus ignoratur, vt deponit Framptone.

Item dicit de libris, ij peciis, ij murris et vj coclearibus argenteis adhuc non restitutis per Alanum Kyrketone.

(+ Prior.) Item dicit quod non est[11] satisfactum seruientibus secularibus de stipendiis suis per vnum, duos, per tres annos. Prior monitus est quod quamcito accomode poterit satisfaciat de huiusmodi stipendiis.

---

[1] *a* interlined above an erasure.
[2] Altered from *quod*.
[3] *Sic*: for *continentur*.
[4] *Sic*: for *satisfacere*.
[5] *quam monicionem il* cancelled.
[6] Italicised passage added in margin.
[7] *Prior* cancelled.
[8] *Sic*: for *propterea*.
[9] *Prior* cancelled.
[10] *vlti* cancelled.
[11] *sas* cancelled.

[1] It is difficult to say to what church this refers, or to explain how it is pertinent to the case. It is possible that the original dedication of the parish church of Spalding was to the Holy Cross, and that Framptone, possibly as master of the works, may at some period have committed himself to repairs there without taking

has been set at divers times, both to himself of his own private money and of money borrowed from other persons, and the same prior has made satisfaction for a great part of such sums, even as all these things are more fully contained in a bill made thereon by indenture between them, nevertheless the same prior takes no heed to give satisfaction for the residue of such sums that are still owing. The prior says that this Framptone was admonished by every prior of the place not to go beyond bounds in expenses in the office over which he was set, and this in virtue of obedience, and therefore he should not have such an excess without committing disobedience. The which admonition the same Framptone confesses, but says that he never passed bounds without the knowledge of the prior. The prior denies knowledge of the work in the church of Holy Cross.[1] The prior is willing, with the knowledge of the convent, to content this Framptone for the excess in the office of pittancer within eight days.

(+ The prior.) Also he says that, albeit every officer of the house, when he is discharged of his office, is in debt by reason of his office, nevertheless the prior will not give satisfaction for a penny of such debt, although such officer may have rendered a full account of his stewardship: therefore let the prior be informed of works involving excess, so that they may go forward with his consent, and then let the prior meet the charge of such excesses.

(+) Also he says that never at any time is a full [and] perfect account rendered in common: therefore it is unknown how it goes with the state of the house.

(+) Also he says that the old and infirm are not provided with more delicate meats, wherewith they might be better refreshed.

(+ The prior.) Brother John Pynchebek prays for the amendment of the bread and beer for the convent. The prior grants that, in the event of a better way of making, such bread and beer shall be improved.

(+ The prior.) Brother William Suttone prays that my lord will see the account last made by John Multone[2] in his life-time, and so [see further], going on from year to year until this year; and so shall my lord see whether the accounts are erased or cancelled,[3] and how the house prospers.

Also nothing is known of the state of the house, as Framptone deposes.

Also he speaks of the books, two pieces, two mazers, and six spoons of silver, which have not yet been restored by Alan Kyrketone.

(+ The prior.) Also he says that satisfaction of their wages has not been made to the secular serving-folk for one, two or three years. The prior was admonished to make satisfaction of such wages as quickly as he conveniently can.

---

counsel with the prior. But there is abundant evidence that the parish church was dedicated to St. Mary: the present double dedication of St. Mary and St. Nicholas seems to have come into use after the suppression of the priory.

[2] The previous prior.

[3] The vitiating effect of an erasure or other alteration in an official document needs no comment. Cf. *Dial. de Scaccario* I, v, where erasure of the Pipe roll is forbidden, and cancellation is permitted only in the modified form ' linea subtili subducta.' Cf. also the familiar attestation of the authenticity of papal letters ' non vitiatae, non cancellatae, nec in aliqua sui parte abolitae, sanae, integrae, omni vitio et sinistra suspicione carentes.'

(Tomsone.) Item dicit quod est ibidem in prioratu[1] eius sumptibus sustentatus quidam capellanus nomine dominus Johannes Tomsone, qui domui non est necessarius nec ad alicuius talis exhibicionem domus tenetur, sed et si *aliquis persona* prioratus paciatur lapsum carnis, iste dominus Johannes est *in causa, quia reputatur* pronuba.

(+ Prior.) Item prior habet in consuetudine quod omni die in nocte amouet a se omnes confratres et generosos et bonos valettos et aduocat sibi duos vel tres garciones de stabulo et cum eis confabulatur edendo et bibendo, ac si essent socii, in magnum scandalum et incontinencie vt timetur fomentum. Prior dicit quod recedentibus monachis et aliis nullus penitus remanet nisi camerarius et garcio camere.

(+ Warnere.) Item dicit quod quidam Robertus Warnere, garcio camere prioris, est multum elatus et monachis quodammodo infestus, nec aliquam inpendit monachis reuerenciam cum eis obuiauerit. Monitus est prior quod attendat quod seruientes sui faciant et exhibeant monachis debitam reuerenciam.

Frater Johannes Glattone dicit omnia bene.

(+ Prior, cellarius.[2]) Frater Johannes *Bostone,*[3] magister operum, dicit quod magnus defectus[4] in prouisione stauri domus, videlicet allecibus, piscibus duris et salsis, vinis et liberaturis, quia omnia capiuntur sub mutuo et cariori precio in magnum domus detrimentum. Fiat iniunccio.

(+ Officiarii.) Item dicit quod *receptor,*[5] cellerarius, subcellarius[6] et elemosinarius non veniunt ad matutinas de nocte nec ad processiones pro statu ecclesie et regni. Fiat iniunccio.

Item dicit quod pertinent officio magistri operis redditus xiij s. iiij d. et x s. de duobus cotagiis, ix s. redditus assise ac decima lane et lini ecclesie de Pynchebek de certo, et non plus nisi de elemosina fidelium.

(+ Gardiani in minucionibus.) Item petit quod gardiani stancium in minucionibus apud Wykham onerentur quod non paciantur confratres ibidem stantes exire gardinum nisi ex causa racionabili et in comitiua[7] honesta. Fiat iniunccio.

(Juuenes.) Item dicit quod iuuenes monachi sunt quodammodo rebelles suis senioribus et ceteris ordinis presidentibus et non preueniunt eos honore.

(De onerosa multitudine seruiencium.) Frater Willelmus Bostone dicit de multitudine seruiencium vt supra, et dicit quod credit priorem velle pocius minuere numerum monachorum quam seruiencium. Et hiis examinatis, continuauit visitacionem huiusmodi in statu quo tunc

---

[1] Altered from *prioratus.*
[2] *Sic:* for *cellerarius.*
[3] Interlined above *Pynchebek* cancelled.
[4] *Sic: est* omitted.
[5] Interlined above *senescallus* cancelled.
[6] *Sic:* for *subcellerarius.*
[7] *rel* cancelled.

[1] If the house was not bound to pay this man, he can have been neither the parish chaplain nor a chantry priest. From a subsequent deposition, his duties appear to have lain in the almonry.
[2] The division of a prelate's or nobleman's immediate dependents into gentlemen, esquires or donzels (*domicelli, armigeri*), yeomen (*valetti*) and grooms (*garciones*), was habitual. See, *e.g. Consuetud. St. Aug. Cantuar,* I, 63. The prior of Spalding

(Tomsone.)   Also he says that there is in that place in the priory, maintained at its cost, a chaplain, by name sir John Tomsone,[1] who is not necessary to the house, nor is the house bound to the payment of any such person; but also, if any person of the priory suffers from fleshly lapse, this sir John is part of the reason, for he is reputed to be a pander.

(+   The prior.)   Also it is the prior's custom that every day at night-time he removes all his brethren and his gentlemen and honest yeomen from him, and summons to him two or three grooms of the stable,[2] and chatters with them, eating and drinking, as though they were his equals, to his great scandal and, as it is feared, to the encouragement of incontinence.   The prior says that, when the monks and the others are gone, no-one at all is left but the chamberlain and the groom of the chamber.

(+   Warnere.)   Also he says that one Robert Warnere, the groom of the prior's chamber, is greatly puffed up and somewhat ill disposed to the monks, nor does he pay the monks any reverence when he meets them.   The prior was admonished to take heed that his serving-men shall do and pay due reverence to the monks.

Brother John Glattone says all things are well.[3]

(+   The prior, the cellarer.)   Brother John Bostone, master of the works,[4] says that [there is] great default in the provision of the store of the house, to wit in herrings, stockfish and salt fish, wines and liveries, because all things are received on credit and at a dearer price, to the great disadvantage of the house.   Let an injunction be made.

(+   The officers.)   Also he says that the receiver, the cellarer, the subcellarer and the almoner do not come to matins by night, or to processions for the state of the church and realm.[5]   Let an injunction be made.

Also he says that there belong to the office of the master of the fabric rents of 13s. 4d. and ten shillings from two cottages, nine shillings of rent of assize, and the tithe of wool and flax of the church of Pinchbeck for certain, and no more, unless [what comes] of the alms of the faithful.

(+   The wardens in seynies.)   Also he prays that the wardens of them that stay in their seynies at Wykeham be charged that they do not suffer their brethren who are staying there to go out of the garden, save for a reasonable cause and in honest company.   Let an injunction be made.

(The young.)   Also he says that the young monks are somewhat rebellious against their elders and the other presidents of the order, and do not prefer them in honour.

(Concerning the burdensome multitude of serving men.)   Brother William Bostone says of the multitude of serving men as above, and says that he believes that the prior would lessen the number of monks rather than that of the servants.   And, when these had been examined, [Depyng] adjourned such visitation in the state wherein it then was until the

---

evidently had his separate lodging and household, with the chamberlain as his chief official, and the groom of the chamber as his personal attendant.

[3] As on the previous occasion.

[4] Previously sacrist.

[5] As ordered by the constitution of Ottobon *Justus et misericors*, and by diocesan bishops on special occasions.

erat vsque in diem tunc crastinum, presentibus Willelmo Bostone, Roberto Sybsey et me Colstone. In quo termino ad vlteriorem inquisicionem processit in hunc modum. Committitur priori et[1] conuentui vt communicato eorum communi consilio inter eos ordinent prout viderint faciendum.

Frater Thomas Quaplode dicit de compotis vt supra et de stipendiis seruiencium non solutis vt supra.

(+ Prior.) Item dicit quod prior est nimis tepidus et remissus in veniendo ad capitulum et corrigendo excessus delinquencium, presertim in hiis quibus aliorum presidencium non sufficit potestas siue auctoritas. Moniti sunt presidentes quod in necessitatibus requirant priorem, nam prior presens est in capitulo omni die dominica ad omne minus, vt dicit.

(+ Prior.) Inquiratur a priore[2] de fundacione cantarie pro anima domini Gilberti Favne, videlicet quid actum est de superplusagio reddituum et prouentuum *eiusdem*[3] cantarie post exhibicionem capellani, nam extendunt se ad x li. huiusmodi prouentus. Dicit quod redditus extendit se solum ad vj li. viij s., modicum plus vel minus, de quibus capellanus percipit viij marcas et residuum exponitur in reparacionibus tenementorum.

(+ Prior.) Item petatur quid factum est de illis x li. quas[4] frater Ricardus Swyneshede de voluntate et consensu prioris disposuit ad vnum calicem faciendum pro summo altari loco alterius calicis surrepti. Dicit quod huiusmodi x libre fuerunt in debitis accommodatis per eundem Ricardum certis[5] debitoribus, de quibus prior recepit solum ij marcas et residuum est illeuabile.

[Fo. 63 *d.* (61 *d.*)]. Frater Thomas Spaldynge senior dicit quod tempore vltimi compoti redditi per fratrem Simonem Holbeche, tunc receptorem, in vita sua redditi[6] in illo officio, quatenus liquere potuit per illum compotum, domus non indebitabatur, qualiter enim nunc stat cum domo nescit.

+ Frater Thomas Scorby, elemosinarius, dicit de compotis non redditis vt supra: ideo non constat de statu domus.

Item dicit quod in compotis reddendis non vocantur monachi secundum formam constitucionis legatine, etc.

(Tomsone.) Item dicit quod dominus Johannes Tomsone, capellanus, manens in prioratu, reputatur pronuba inter priorem et alios monachos, inducendo mulieres in prioratum suspecto modo: nam familiarissimus

---

[1] *communica* cancelled.

[2] Altered from *prioracione* (*sic*).

[3] *eius* was interlined above *eiusdem* cancelled, and afterwards altered into *eiusdem*.

[4] *pr* cancelled.

[5] *v* cancelled.

[6] *Sic*: repeated.

[1] One of those who had previously returned *omnia bene*.

[2] Gilbert Faune was vicar of Spalding at the close of the fourteenth century, and was one of the founders of the gild of the Holy Trinity in 1393 (*Cal. Pat.* 1391-6, p. 310). He also joined with John Thorneton of Spalding in 1395 in alienating lands and rent in Spalding and the neighbourhood to the prior and convent, for the celebration of the obit of bishop Buckingham in St. Mary's, *i.e.* the parish church

day which was then the morrow, there being present William Bostone, Robert Sybsey, and I Colstone. At the which term he proceeded to further inquiry after this wise. Commission is made to the prior and convent that, having taken their common counsel together among them, they shall make ordinances as they shall see fit to do.

Brother Thomas Quaplode[1] says of the accounts as above, and of the non-payment of the serving-men's wages as above.

(+ The prior.) Also he says that the prior is exceedingly lukewarm and slack in coming to chapter and correcting the transgressions of offenders, especially in those things wherein the power or authority of the other presidents is not sufficient. The presidents were admonished to have recourse to the prior in case of necessity, for the prior is present in chapter every Sunday at the very least, as he says.

(+ The prior.) Let an inquiry be made of the prior concerning the foundation of the chantry for the soul of sir Gilbert Faune,[2] to wit, what has been done with the surplus of the rents and revenues of the same chantry after the payment of the chaplain; for such revenues amount to ten pounds. He says that the rent amounts only to £6 8s., rather more or less, of which the chaplain receives eight marks, and the residue is laid out in the repairs of the tenements.

(+ The prior.) Also let it be asked what has been done with those ten pounds which brother Richard Swyneshede, with the prior's will and consent, appointed for the making of a chalice for the high altar, in place of another chalice which had been stolen. He says that such ten pounds consisted of debts from loans furnished by the same Richard to certain debtors, whereof the prior has received two marks only, and the residue cannot be recovered.

Brother Thomas Spaldynge the elder[3] says that, at the time of the last account rendered by brother Simon Holbeche, at that time the receiver, in his life-time as regards that office, so far as might appear by that account, the house was not in debt; for how it now stands with the house he knows not.

+ Brother Thomas Scorby, the almoner,[4] says of the accounts as above that they are not rendered: therefore there is no certainty of the state of the house.

Also he says that at the rendering of accounts the monks are not invited according to the form of the legatine constitution, etc.[5]

(Tomsone.) Also he says that sir John Tomsone, chaplain, abiding in the priory, is reputed to be a pander with the prior and the other monks, bringing women into the priory in manner suspect; for he is

---

(*ibid.* p. 641). This may possibly have been perpetuated as a chantry for Faune's soul: there is no record of another chantry founded by him. No doubt, Faune's chantry is that referred to earlier (p. 328).

[3] *Omnia bene* at the last visitation.

[4] Previously master of the works.

[5] The constitution of Ottobon, *De prelatis*, to which this alludes, has no special reference to the formal invitation of the members of a convent to the audit of accounts, but offers the usual alternatives to the presence of the whole house: ' praesente toto conventu, vel aliquibus de senioribus vel prudentioribus, ad hoc a capitulo deputatis.' Stephen Langton's provincial constitution *Ut rectius* requires only a section to be present: ' coram fratribus a conventu ad hoc deputatis, vel coram superioribus juxta monasterii consuetudinem reddant de receptis et expensis omnibus rationem.'

est cum hiis qui reputantur suspecti super incontinencia; et dicitur quod idem exportat vinum prioris in villam, nam dicitur quod plus vini huiusmodi expenditur *in anno* in villa quam inter monachos.

(Prior.)[1] Item dicit[2] ex consuetudine laudabili monasterii solebant exire de cellaria conuentu[3] ad domum elemosinarie pro reficiendis pauperibus extraneis qui superueniunt indies in multitudine xlvj mortes in anno, et quodlibet mort continet sex panes conuentuales, et sex lagene ceruisie, vt pro animabus fratrum defunctorum: solebat eciam exire de eadem cellaria quolibet die vnus panis ad refeccionem vnius pauperis, et ad vsum elemosinarii ij panes, *et vocantur mandata,* et certa mensura ceruisie: que omnia subtrahuntur de mandato prioris preter ceruisiam datam nomine mandati.

(Tomson.) Frater Robertus Sybsey dicit quod bonum foret pro honestate domus quod dominus Johannes Tomsone non habeat tantam familiaritatem cum priore, sed omnino con*ten*tetur cum officio suo in elemosinaria: alioquin de prioratu totaliter expellatur, nam habet infra prioratum vnam cameram ad quam mulieres habent frequentem accessum.

+ Frater Rogerus Sayvyle dicit quod non constat sibi de aliquo compoto reddito in officio receptoris post mortem fratris Simonis Holbeche.

+ Frater Simon Byllyngburghe dicit quod omni tempore supprior, tercius prior, *cantor*[4] et sacrista sunt gardiani, vnus videlicet post alium, et regimen habent stancium in minucionibus apud Wykham.

+ Item dicit quod non constat sibi de statu domus, cum nunquam interfuerit compotis redditis.

+ Item dicit de domino Johanne Tomsone, videlicet quod est suspectus et mali nominis, etc.

+ Frater Nicholaus Suttone dicit de tarda solucione pietanciarum que solui deberet[5] in festo Bartholomei monachis.

+ Item dicit de libris et aliis iocalibus non restitutis per fratrem Alanum Kyrketone.

(+ Bostone.) Item dicit quod frater Johannes Bostone *nunquam fuit vtilis sed* semper[6] dampnosus[7] officiis quibus[8] *prefuit,*[9] nam supplantauit occupantem sacristiam et illud[10] male rexit, et iam supplantauit occupantem officium magistri operis et nichil agit in eo. Computabit de officio sacristie ad festum Michaelis nunc.

+ Item dicit de iij panibus subtractis ab officio elemosinarie per vnum annum vt supra.

---

[1] This clause is cancelled.
[2] *quod* omitted.
[3] *Sic*: for *conuentus.*
[4] Interlined above *elemosinarius* cancelled.
[5] *Sic*: for *deberent.*
[6] *fuit et est* cancelled.
[7] *in* cancelled.
[8] Altered from *officio quo.*
[9] Interlined above *stetit* cancelled.
[10] *illud=officium sacristie.*

[1] Apparently so called as being alms given for the salvation of the souls of dead benefactors.
[2] *I.e.* doles, so called from the *mandatum novum* contained in St. John XIII, 34.

upon the closest terms with such as have a suspect reputation of incontinence; and it is said that he also takes out the prior's wine into the town, for it is said that more of such wine is spent in the town in a year than among the monks.

(The prior.) Also he says [that] according to the praiseworthy custom of the monastery there used to go out of the convent cellar to the house of the almonry, for the refreshment of the poor folk from outside, who come daily in great numbers, forty-six morts[1] a year, and every mort contains six loaves of convent bread, and six gallons of beer, to wit for the souls of the brethren deceased: there used also to go out of the same cellar every day a loaf for the refreshment of one poor person, and for the almoner's use two loaves, and they are called maundies,[2] and a certain measure of beer; and all these are now withheld by the prior's command except the beer, which is given under the name of maundy.

(Tomson.) Brother Robert Sybsey says that it would be a good thing for the fair fame of the house that sir John Tomsone should not be so friendly with the prior, but should be altogether content with his office in the almonry: otherwise he should be utterly expelled from the priory, for he has a chamber within the priory to which women have often access.

+   Brother Roger Sayvyle says that he has no sure knowledge of any account that has been rendered in the office of the receiver after the death of brother Simon Holbeche.

+   Brother Simon Byllyngburghe says that the subprior, third prior, chanter and sacrist are all the time wardens,[3] one to wit after the other, and have the governance of them that stay in their seynies at Wykeham.

+   Also he says that he is not certain of the state of the house, since he has never been present when accounts are rendered.

+   Also he says of sir John Tomsone, to wit that he is suspect and of ill fame, etc.

+   Brother Nicholas Suttone speaks of the tardy payment of the pittances which ought to be paid to the monks at the feast of St. Bartholomew.[4]

+   Also he speaks of the books and other treasures that have not been restored by brother Alan Kyrketone.

(+   Bostone.) Also he says that brother John Bostone was never profitable, but was always a source of damage to the offices over which he was set, for he supplanted him that held the office of sacrist, and he ruled it ill; and now he has supplanted him that held the office of master of the fabric, and he does nothing therein. He shall render account of his office as sacrist at the present feast of St. Michael.

+   Also he says as above concerning the three loaves that have been withdrawn for a year from the almoner's office.[5]

---

[3] *I.e.* wardens of the ' seny place ' at Wykeham.   Cf. the *gardianus* of Oxney at Peterborough.

[4] See p. 333 above.

[5] See Scorby's fourth *detectum*.

(Prior.) Item dicit quod credit ecclesiam conuentualem, *cum sit parochialis*, non dedicari, cum nullum obseruent festum dedicacionis nec festum reliquiarum, et *tamen*[1] plures sunt ibi reliquie sanctorum, nec remanent aliqua signa dedicacionis. Dicunt omnes quod ecclesia non est finita: attamen habent licenciam apostolicam necessariam. Habent terminum ad exhibendum domino licenciam huiusmodi citra proximum festum Omnium Sanctorum, sinautem extunc interdicitur eis inibi celebracio.

(+ Prior.) Item dicit de defectibus in ecclesia, claustro, refectorio et in infirmaria ob defectum reparacionis in tantum quod volte lapidee in ecclesia ex verisimili funditus destruentur in fine nisi remedium apponatur. Monitus est prior quod diligenter attendat reparacionibus omnium huiusmodi locorum preter ecclesie, que est in onere sacriste.

(+ Nota.) Item dicit quod si vnus delinquat omnes indiscrete[2] puniuntur, videlicet si vnus loquatur cum muliere, omnes propterea includentur. Prior respondet et dicit quod non nouit tale quid attemptatum, sed cum constiterit de vno delinquente ille punitur et non alius pro huiusmodi delicto.

(+ Prior.) Item dicit quod frater Simon Byllyngburghe sepius absque causa licenciatur ad exeundum et aliquando stat extra monasterium per septimanam, cum non habeat iustam causam absencie. Monitus est prior quod non sit facilis in concedendo huiusmodi licencias.

+ Item dicit quod iura monasterii pereunt in defectu prioris, et non est qui prosequitur pro recuperacione.

(Supprior.) Item quod supprior adeo familiaris et insolens *est* in vultu cum monachis quod non curant de eo sed quasi vilipendunt eum, nec eius correccionibus obtemperant propter puerilem eius gesturam.

(Nota.) Item quod contemplacio et studium non obseruantur in claustro temporibus debitis, sed monachi vacant ocio et vanis fabulacionibus. Supprior et tercius prior moniti sunt quod diligenter superintendant vt contemplacio et studium ac silencium horis debitis obseruentur et quod in hiis delinquentes debite puniantur secundum regulam.

+ Item petit quod habeatur leccio tempore refeccionis in aula minucionum.

(+ Nota.) Item dicit quod consuetudo, ymo corruptela in monasterio ex longo vsu habetur quod monachi a festo Omnium Sanctorum

---

[1] Interlined above *cum* erased.
[2] A short word interlined above and cancelled.

[1] The priory church was originally the parish church of Spalding, though it is uncertain how long the parish altar remained within the building, and whether a separate parish church was not built within the precincts of the monastery. At an unspecified date, probably in the later part of the thirteenth century, the prior and convent entered into an agreement with the parishioners to build a new church on the east side of the Welland on the site and within the churchyard of the earlier chapel of St. Thomas the Martyr. This chapel may have been incorporated in the new church, to which the dedication of St. Mary was transferred. It is said that the present parish church on this site was largely built by prior William of Littleport in 1284; but at the time of Alnwick's visitation it was evidently undergoing extensive repair. By the agreement with the parishioners (printed in *Monasticon* III, 228-9) the priory church reserved to some extent its parochial rights, asserting that the parish church was entirely dependent upon it, and requiring the parishioners to-

(The prior.)   Also he says that he believes that the church of the convent, although it is a parish church,[1] is not dedicated, seeing that they observe no feast of the dedication or feast of the relics,[2] and nevertheless there are many relics of the saints therein; nor do any marks of the dedication remain.   They all say that the church is not finished, but they have the papal licence which is necessary.[3]   They have a term to show such licence to my lord before the next feast of All Saints; but, if they do not, they are forbidden to celebrate therein from that date.

(+   The prior.)   Also he says that there are defaults in the church, cloister, frater and infirmary for lack of repair, to so great an extent that the stone vaults in the church will in all likelihood be utterly destroyed in the end, unless a remedy be applied.   The prior was admonished to take diligent heed to the repairs of all such places, save those of the church, which is in the sacrist's charge.

(+   Note.)   Also he says that, if one man sin, all are punished indifferently, to wit, if one man speak with a woman, all shall be included on that account.   The prior answers and says that he knows that nothing of this kind has been attempted, but, whensoever one man is known to have sinned, he and no other is punished for such transgression.

(+   The prior.)   Also he says that brother Simon Byllyngburghe is very often given leave to go out without cause, and sometimes stays outside the monastery for a week, although he has no just reason for absence.   The prior was admonished not to be easy in granting such licences.

+   Also he says that the rights of the monastery are coming to naught in the prior's default, and there is no-one who makes suit for their recovery.

(The subprior.)   Also that the subprior is on such homely terms and bears so unruly a countenance with the monks that they take no heed of him but almost hold him cheap; nor do they obey his corrections because of his childish behaviour.

(Note.)   Also that contemplation and study are not observed in the cloister at the due seasons, but the monks spend their time in idleness and empty chattering.   The subprior and third prior were warned to keep diligent watch that contemplation and study and silence be observed at due times, and that they who sin in these matters be duly punished according to the rule.

+   Also he prays that there may be reading during meals in the seyny hall.[4]

(+   Note.)   Also he says that there exists of long use in the monastery the custom, or rather the corrupt practice that from the feast of

---

make their oblations at the priory on the three principal festivals.   Thus the statement that the conventual church was a parish church, though not exactly true in the full sense of the term, was still partially correct.

[2] The *festum reliquiarum* at Lincoln was observed on Sunday after the Translation of St. Thomas the Martyr (7 July), following the custom of Salisbury as ordained by bishop Mortival in 1319 (Bradshaw and Wordsworth III, 818: cf. Wordsworth and Macleane, *Stat. of Salis. Cath.*, p. 248).

[3] See *Cal. Papal Letters* v, 436-8, for the confirmation by Boniface IX of the rebuilding and transference of the parish church, 14 July, 1401.

[4] A repetition of his previous request at the earlier stage of the visitation. Here he confines his request to a single place outside the frater.

vsque festum¹ Purificacionis cenabunt,² qui in refectorio ante, qui in aula minucionum post completorium, quod est contra regulam et quibusdam ad tedium. Consulatur dominus super isto detecto.

+ Frater Johannes Spaldyng dicit de festo dedicacionis non obseruato vt supra.

[Fo. 64 (62)]. + Frater Thomas Westone dicit de officio camerariatus in non soluendo monachis in festo Bartholomei vt supra.

+ Frater Adam Redeforde dicit de multitudine onerosa seruiencium tam ad infra quam ad extra.

+ Item dicit de fama laborante contra dominum Johannem Tomsone vt supra, et quod vina et victualia monasterii consumuntur per eum in villa.

(+ Sacrista.)³ Frater Robertus Leek dicit quod bonum foret vt scientifici artifices bene et substancialiter videant et examinent interius et exterius antiquum campanile, et si possit commode reparari, reparetur: alioquin superior pars eiusdem, cum sit multum debilis, prosternatur, et conseruetur plumbum ad vtilitatem ecclesie.

+ Item dicit de cereo et lampade in⁴ capella beate Marie vt supra.

(+ Quaplode.) Item dicit quod frater Thomas Quaplode ex lapsu lingue detrahit confratribus suis tam ipsis fratribus quam eciam laicis, et eciam penes⁵ priorem, propter quod creditur quod monachi habentur in minore⁶ reputacione. Negat articulum, tamen monitus est sub pena custodie claustralis per vj dies continuos quod decetero abstineat a similibus.

Frater Johannes⁷ Grantham dicit quod omnia bene.

Frater Thomas Spaldyng junior dicit omnia bona. Capellanus prioris est iste.

(+ Prior.) Frater Willelmus Repynghale dicit quod de consuetudine monasterii est quod quilibet nouicius habeat tutorem vsque promoueatur ad sacerdocium, qui recipiat peculium suum et ministret sibi necessaria, et dicit quod frater Simon Holbeche, qui fuit tutor suus, iam defunctus, debuit sibi de peculio suo in morte ipsius Simonis iiij marcas, et citra mortem ipsius Simonis prior recepit peculium suum, et de toto illo peculio et dictis iiijᵒʳ marcis non recepit iste Willelmus nisi *tantum* xxx solidos in omnibus. Frater *Robertus Sybsey*⁸ deputatus est sibi tutor⁹ per priorem.

(+ Prior.) Item dicit quod vbi bona fratrum decedencium deueniunt ad manus prioris, prout consuetudo est, statim alienantur vel

---

¹ *omnium* cancelled.
² Altered from *cenant*.
³ *Prior* cancelled in right-hand margin: *sacrista* added in left.
⁴ *b* cancelled.
⁵ *reg* cancelled.
⁶ *recommendacione* cancelled.
⁷ *granh* cancelled.
⁸ Interlined above *Willelmus Suttone* cancelled.
⁹ Altered from *subtutor*.

¹ Previously this duty has been referred to the pittancer. It appears from this passage that the dole was charged either upon the prior's *camera* or upon the revenues appropriated to the office of the chamberlain of the monastery. The prior's chamberlain, probably one of his esquires, has been mentioned already; but we hear of no chamberlain *ex parte conventus*.

All Saints to the feast of the Purification, those monks who are in frater shall sup before, and those who are in the seyny hall shall sup after compline, which is contrary to the rule and is an annoyance to certain persons. Let my lord be consulted touching this disclosure.

+ Brother John Spaldyng says as above that the feast of the dedication is not observed.

+ Brother Thomas Westone says of the office of the chamberlain-ship as above,[1] that he does not pay the monks on the feast of St. Bartholomew.

+ Brother Adam Redeforde speaks of the burthensome multitude of serving-folk both within and without [the priory].

+ Also he says as above concerning the report that is current against sir John Tomsone, and that the wine and victuals of the monastery are wasted by him in the town.

(+ The sacrist.) Brother Robert Leek says that it would be a good thing that cunning craftsmen[2] should well and substantially view and examine the old bell-tower within and without, and that it should be repaired, if it may be repaired conveniently: otherwise the upper part of the same, since it is very weak, should be taken down, and the lead preserved for the profit of the church.

+ Also he says as above concerning the taper and lamp in the chapel of blessed Mary.

(+ Quaplode.) Also he says that brother Thomas Quaplode. with his slippery tongue, slanders his brethren both to the brethren themselves and also to lay-folk, and even in presence of the prior, for which reason it is thought that the monks are held in less reputation, He denies the article, but was warned, under pain of confinement to cloister for six days continually, to abstain from the like practices henceforward.

Brother John Grantham[3] says that all things are well.

Brother Thomas Spaldyng the younger says that all things are good. This is the prior's chaplain.

(+ The prior.) Brother William Repynghale says that it is of the custom of the monastery that every novice should have a tutor until he be promoted to the priesthood, who shall receive his private allowance and furnish him with things needful; and he says that brother Simon Holbeche, who was his tutor, now deceased, owed him of his allowance at the death of the same Simon four marks, and since the death of the same Simon the prior has received his allowance,[4] and of all that allowance and the said four marks this William has received nothing but thirty shillings in all. Brother Robert Sybsey was appointed his tutor by the prior.

(+ The prior.) Also he says that, whereas the goods of the brethren when they die come into the prior's hands, as the custom is, they are

---

[2] For the architectural use of the word *artifex* see the sources mentioned above, p. 336, note 5. A conspicuous example occurs in the famous account of the rebuilding of the quire of Canterbury cathedral after the fire of 1174 (Gervase of Cant. [Rolls ser.] I, 3 sqq.) : ' Convocati sunt igitur artifices Franci et Angli : sed et ipsi in dando consilio dissenserunt . . . Advenerat autem inter alios artifices quidam Senonensis, Willelmus nomine, vir admodum strenuus, in ligno et lapide artifex subtilissimus.'

[3] At the university, apparently Cambridge, in August, 1438.

[4] Simon, as noted by Thomas Spaldyng the elder, had been one of the receivers.

inter seculares, sic quod nichil de eis ad commodum *monasterii* prouenit, nec monachi in emendo ea sed seculares preferuntur. Conuertuntur in vtilitatem domus, vt dicit prior.

Frater Laurencius Spaldyng dicit quod omnia bene.

Frater Robertus Spaldyng dicit quod omnia bene.

(+   Scorby et ceteri officiarii.)   Frater Hugo Spaldyng dicit quod seniores monachi et *in officiis constituti, ac* presertim frater Thomas Scorby, intitulati ad onera chori non ea exequuntur per se nec per vicarios suos, quos ad hoc in eorum absencia deputare tenentur, nec idem Scorby surgit ad matutinas. Perfecit[1] hucusque et decetero faciet per se vel alium, etc.

Item dicit de ruina ecclesie et domus capitularis in tectura in tantum quod pluit super voltas.

Item elemosinarius debet percipere de cellaria conuentus quotidie pro tribus mandatis faciendis in ly parlour v lagenas fracte ceruisie et tres panes conuentuales de refectorario et nouem oua de receptore. Subtracta sunt ab vltimo Pascha de consensu omnium.

(+   Prior.)   Item debet percipere de cellaria conuentus per annum xlvj morts, quolibet continente vj lagenas ceruisie fracte et sex panes conuentuales. Subtracta sunt ab vltimo Pascha de consensu omnium. Fiat iniunccio quod ista distribuantur magis indigentibus.

Item debet[2] dari pro quolibet fratre mortuo in primo anno obitus sui quolibet die tres potelle ceruisie de doleo conuentus et vnus panis conuentualis et quinque oua et per xl dies post annum huiusmodi; et ista omnia subtrahunter per priorem sine consensu conuentus. Pro fratribus Johanne Bostone et Simone Holbeche non dabatur huiusmodi elemosina; pro istis duobus subtrahuntur ab vltimo Pascha de consensu tocius conuentus.

Eodem secundo die Octobris, facta inquisicione et congregatis omnibus in capitulo, dominus commissarius publicauit detecta, et deinde expeditis omnibus prout continentur in actis superius, preter ea que tangunt priorem, continuauit visitacionem huiusmodi vsque in diem crastinum, presentibus magistro J. Spenser et me Colstone.

---

[1] *ante* cancelled.
[2] *Sic*: for *debent.*

[1] The custom of attending quire in rotation has been already referred to, p. 273, note 1. This passage shows how slight the difference of custom was at this date between monastic and secular churches.
[2] The *locutorium* or parlour was the room or passage through which the cloister was entered from the outer court, and was usually in the western range of cloister buildings. To this passage lay-folk who came on business were admitted: the author of *Rites of Durham* records that merchants came to the parlour to ' utter their wares ' (p. 52), though he appears to refer to the inner or monks' parlour in the eastern range.

immediately alienated, even among secular folk, so that nothing of them comes to the profit of the monastery, nor is the preference in purchasing them given to monks, but to secular persons. They are converted to the profit of the house, as the prior says.

Brother Lawrence Spaldyng says that all things are well.

Brother Robert Spaldyng says that all things are well.

(+ Scorby and the other officers.) Brother Hugh Spaldyng says that the elder monks and they that are set in the offices, and especially brother Thomas Scorby, when they are on the list for duty in quire,[1] perform such duty neither by themselves nor by their deputies, whom they are bound to appoint for this purpose in their absence; nor does the same Scorby get up for matins. He has performed [his duties] fully hitherto, and will perform them henceforward by himself or another, etc.

Also he says that the church and chapter-house are in a ruinous condition as regards roofing, to such a degree that the rain falls upon the vaults.

Also the almoner ought to receive from the convent cellar daily, for the performance of three maundies in the parlour,[2] five gallons of small ale, and three convent loaves from the fraterer, and nine eggs from the receiver. They have been withdrawn from Easter last with the consent of all.

(+ The prior.) Also he ought to receive from the convent cellar forty-six morts a year, each mort containing six gallons of small ale and six convent loaves. They have been withdrawn from Easter last with the consent of all. Let an injunction be made that these things be distributed to them that are most in need.

Also for every brother that is dead there should be given, in the first year after his decease, three quarts of beer every day from the convent cask, and a convent loaf and five eggs, and for forty days after such year, and all these things are withdrawn by the prior without the consent of the convent. Such alms were not given for brothers John Bostone[3] and Simon Holbeche: for these two they are withdrawn from Easter last with the consent of the whole convent.

On the same second day of October, after the inquiry had been made and when all were gathered together in the chapter-house, my lord the commissary made the disclosures public, and then, after all things had been carried out, even as they are contained in the acts above, except those that concern the prior, he adjourned such visitation until the morrow, there being present master J. Spenser and I Colstone.

---

[3] Possibly John Bostone the younger, whose recent existence is implied by the mention of the monk of the same name, at this time master of the works, as 'the elder.' Both Bostone and Holbeche appear to have died in the course of 1438, and the alms distributed for their souls to have been withdrawn before the anniversary of their deaths.

LXV.

[Fo. 77.]

VISITACIO PRIORATUS DE STAYNFELDE, ORDINIS SANCTI BENEDICTI, LINCOLNIENSIS DIOCESIS, FACTA IN DOMO CAPITULARI IBIDEM XXV DIE MENSIS JULII, ANNO DOMINI MCCCCXL⁰, PER REUERENDUM IN CHRISTO PATREM ET DOMINUM, DOMINUM WILLELMUM, DEI GRACIA LINCOLNIENSEM EPISCOPUM, ANNO XIIIJ⁰ [1] ET TRANSLA-CIONIS IIIJ^{to}.

Sedente dicto reuerendo patre iudicialiter pro tribunali in dicte visitacionis sue negocio die, loco et anno supradictis, comparuerunt coram eo priorissa et conuentus dicti loci. Primo et ante omnia propositum fuit verbum Dei per honorabilem virum magistrum Johannem Beuerley, sacre pagine professorem, sequentem hoc thema, ' Ecce elongaui me fugiens et mansi in solitudine.'[2] Quo laudabiliter finito, priorissa liberauit dicto reuerendo patri certificatorium super mandato domini sibi pro hoc negocio directo, factum in hec verba, ' Reuerendo in Christo patri,' etc. Quo perlecto et preconizatis ac comparentibus singulis, Alicia Benyngtone, que alienata mente tenetur in vinculis, dumtaxat excepta, dicta priorissa iurauit obedienciam et fidelitatem in forma consueta. Postea exhibuit eadem priorissa confirmacionem eleccionis sue et installacionem suam. Deinde exhibuit statum domus. Deinde exhibuit fundacionem domus per Willelmum de Percy, et deinde examinata dicit ea que sequuntur.

Domina Margareta Hulle, priorissa, dicit quod omnia bene.

Domina Elizabetha Topclyffe, suppriorissa, dicit quod omnia bene.

Domina Elizabetha Eueringham dicit quod priorissa habet vnam familiam, celleraria aliam et sorores laice aliam.

Domina Johanna Grymescrofte dicit *quod* seculares iacent in dormitorio, et dicit de familiis vt supra.

Domina Felicia Dowode dicit quod omnia bene.

Domina Johanna Ravenesthorpe dicit quod omnia bene.

Domina Johanna fitz Wyllyam dicit quod omnia bene.

Domina Alicia Kervyle dicit quod omnia bene.

Domina Alicia Seynt Qwyntyne dicit quod omnia bene.

Domina Margareta Grymesby dicit quod omnia bene.

Domina Matilda Seynt Qwyntyn dicit quod omnia bene.

---

[1] *Sic*: sc. *consecracionis.*

[2] Ps. LV, 7.

[1] See *Visitations* II, note .

[2] See *Visitations* I, 115, note 3.

[3] See *Visitations* I, 157. Some documents are printed in *Monasticon* IV, 309-11, in which some doubt arises as to the founder. The present statement appears to settle the difficulty and assign the foundation not to Henry Percy, as Leland stated, but to William Percy, the founder of Sawley abbey in Yorkshire (1146-7).

[4] In *Visitations* I, 115, note 3, the occurrence of well-known Yorkshire names, such as Everingham and St. Quintin, in the priory at this date has been remarked. Topcliffe, from which the subprioress derived her name, was the original seat of the Percys in Yorkshire, while the Everinghams and St. Quintins were well-known

LXV.

THE VISITATION OF THE PRIORY OF STAINFIELD, OF THE ORDER OF
ST. BENET, OF THE DIOCESE OF LINCOLN, PERFORMED IN THE
CHAPTER-HOUSE THEREIN ON THE TWENTY-FIFTH DAY OF THE
MONTH OF JULY, IN THE YEAR OF OUR LORD 1440, BY THE
REVEREND FATHER IN CHRIST AND LORD, THE LORD WILLIAM, BY
THE GRACE OF GOD BISHOP OF LINCOLN, IN THE FOURTEENTH
YEAR [OF HIS CONSECRATION] AND THE FOURTH OF HIS TRANSLATION.

As the said reverend father was sitting in his capacity of judge as
a tribunal in the business of his said visitation on and in the day, place
and year abovesaid, there appeared before him the prioress and convent
of the said place. First and before all else the word of God was set
forth by the honourable master John Beverley, professor of holy writ,[1]
after this text, ' Lo, I have fled afar off and have remained in the wilder-
ness.' And when this was come to a praiseworthy end, the prioress
delivered to the said reverend father the certificate touching my lord's
mandate which had been addressed to her for this business, made after
these words, ' To the reverend father in Christ,' etc. And when this
had been read through and the several [nuns] had been called over and
made their appearance, save only Alice Benyngtone, who, being out of
her mind, is kept in bonds, the said prioress sware obedience and fealty
in the form accustomed. Thereafter the same prioress showed the
certificate of confirmation of her election and that of her installation.[2]
Then she exhibited the state of the house. Then she exhibited the
foundation charter of the house granted by William Percy,[3] and then on
examination she says these things which follow.

Dame Margaret Hulle, the prioress,[4] says that all things are well.

Dame Elizabeth Topclyffe, the sub-prioress, says that all things
are well.

Dame Elizabeth Eueringham says that the prioress has one household, the cellaress another and the lay-sisters another.

Dame Joan Grymescrofte says that secular folk do lie in the dorter,
and she says as above concerning the households.

Dame Felise Dowode says that all things are well.

Dame Joan Ravenesthorpe says that all things are well.

Dame Joan fitz Wyllyam says that all things are well.

Dame Alice Kervyle says that all things are well.

Dame Alice Seynt Qwyntyne says that all things are well.

Dame Margaret Grymesby says that all things are well.

Dame Maud Seynt Qwyntyn says that all things are well.

---

families in the East Riding, where the Percys had a large and important house,
Wressle castle on the Derwent.   The surnames derived from places are Hull,
Topclyffe and Everingham, in Yorkshire.   Ravenesthorpe may be Ravensthorpe
in the West Riding, and Malteby may be Maltby near Rotherham.   It may, however,
be one of the Lincolnshire Maltbys. Grymsby (Grimesby), Gaudeby (Gautby),
Laceby, Keleby (Keelby), and probably Cotes (Great or Little Coates near Grimsby),
are Lincolnshire names.   Henour (Heanor) comes from Derbyshire.   Grymescrofte
and Dowode are doubtful.

Domina Margareta Groos dicit quod omnia bene.

Domina Agnes Towres dicit quod omnia bene.

Domina Margeria Malteby dicit quod omnia bene.

Domina Margareta Henour dicit quod omnia bene:[1] dicit tamen de familiis vt supra.

Domina Margareta Gybone dicit quod omnia bene.

Soror Johanna Gaudeby dicit quod omnia bene.

Soror Agnes Laceby dicit quod omnia bene.

Soror Alicia Gregge dicit quod omnia bene.

Soror Elena Keleby dicit quod omnia bene.

Soror Alicia Cotes dicit quod omnia bene.

LXVI.

[Fo. 82 *d.*]

VISITACIO DOMUS SIUE PRIORATUS SANCTI LEONARDI IUXTA STAMFORDIAM, ORDINIS SANCTI BENEDICTI, LINCOLNIENSIS DIOCESIS, QUE EST CELLA MONASTERII DUNELMENSIS, FACTA IN DOMO CAPITULARI IBIDEM XXJ⁰ DIE MENSIS OCTOBRIS, ANNO DOMINI MCCCCXL, PER REUERENDUM IN CHRISTO PATREM ET DOMINUM, DOMINUM WILLELMUM, DEI GRACIA LINCOLNIENSEM EPISCOPUM, ANNO SUARUM CONSECRACIONIS XV⁰ ET TRANSLACIONIS Vᵗᵒ.

In primis, sedente dicto reuerendo patre iudicialiter pro tribunali in dicte visitacionis sue negocio die, anno et loco antedictis, comparuerunt coram eo frater Ricardus Bartone, prior, et frater Thomas Hexham commonachus suus; et cum non sint plures, idem prior liberauit domino mandatum domini quod alias recepit pro visitacione huiusmodi, asserens quod ipsum executus est: petens ex gracia vt ad aliud certificatorium quam[2] hoc oretenus factum non artetur. Quod dominus graciose concessit; et deinde idem prior exhibuit titulum incumbencie sue, et illo exhibito idem prior iurauit obedienciam et fidelitatem domino in forma solita et consueta; et deinde prior examinatus dicit ea que sequuntur.

Idem prior dicit quod domus grauiter oneratur de vna pensione vij librarum quam abbas[3] Croylandie exigit ab isto loco, vt ex concessione dudum prioris et capituli Dunelmensium in commutacionem ecclesie de Ederham, que dudum erat abbatis Croylandie, et iam vnitur prioratui de Coldyngham, qui est cella Dunelmensis; ad quam solucionem

---

[1] *deci* cancelled.

[2] Altered from *quod.*

[3] *exigit* cancelled.

[1] St. Leonard's at Stamford is a parallel case to that of Breedon priory (No. IX), where the convent was merely part of a larger body whose monastery was at a distance. See *Visitations* II, 40, note 1. Such priories were not strictly conventual, and, in spite of the fact that their priors received institution and might therefore be considered 'perpetual,' their tenure of their benefices actually rested upon the will of the head of the parent house. The important and beautiful remains of St. Leonard's show that it was originally intended to hold a larger number of monks than two or three, and it is noticeable that it had its own chapter-house, a feature which would not be often found in such small establishments.

Dame Margaret Groos says that all things are well.

Dame Agnes Towres says that all things are well.

Dame Margery Malteby says that all things are well.

Dame Margaret Henour says that all things are well: howbeit she says as above concerning the households.

Dame Margaret Gybone says that all things are well.

Sister Joan Gaudeby says that all things are well.

Sister Agnes Laceby says that all things are well.

Sister Alice Gregge says that all things are well.

Sister Ellen Keleby says that all things are well.

Sister Alice Cotes says that all things are well.

LXVI.

The visitation of the house or priory of ST. LEONARD BY STAMFORD, of the order of St. Benet, of the diocese of Lincoln, which is a cell of the monastery of Durham, performed in the chapter-house therein on the twenty-first day of the month of October, in the year of our Lord 1440, by the reverend father in Christ and lord, the lord William, by the grace of God bishop of Lincoln, in the fifteenth year of his consecration and the fifth of his translation.

In the first place, as the said reverend father was sitting in his capacity of judge as a tribunal in the business of his said visitation, on and in the day, year and place aforesaid, there appeared before him brother Richard Bartone, the prior, and brother Thomas Hexham, his fellow monk;[1] and seeing that there are no more, the same prior delivered to my lord my lord's mandate, which he received at another time, for such visitation, asserting that he has performed the same, [and] praying as a favour that he may not be compelled to [furnish] any other certificate than this, made by word of mouth.[2] The which my lord graciously granted; and then the same prior exhibited the title of his incumbency, and, having exhibited it, the same prior sware obedience and fealty to my lord in the wonted and accustomed form; and then the prior, upon examination, says these things which follow.

The same prior says that the house is heavily burthened with a pension of seven pounds which the abbot of Croyland exacts from this place, as of the grant aforetime of the prior and chapter of Durham in exchange for the church of Edrom, which belonged sometime to the abbot of Croyland, and is now united to the priory of Coldingham, which is a cell of Durham;[3] for the payment of which sum, in order that the

---

[2] The insignificance of the convent would make the presentation of the usual certificate an unnecessary formality.

[3] Edrom is in Berwickshire, three miles N.E. of Duns. The vills of Edrom and Nesbit, with the church of Edrom and its chapels, were granted to the monks of Durham by Gospatric of Dunbar in or before 1138 (Lawrie, *Early Scottish Charters*, No. cxvii, p. 90), and the grant was confirmed by King David I at Roxburgh, 16 Aug., 1139 (*ibid.* No. cxxi, p. 93). About 1141 H nry, earl of Northumberland, the son of David, confirmed the grant to the monks of St. Mary and Cuthbert at

faciendam vti dictus prioratus Sancti Leonardi haberet recompensam eiusdem, domus Sancti Leonardi perciperet pensionem v marcarum de ecclesia beate Marie ad pontem et xx s. de ecclesia beate Marie de Bynwerke, xl s. de ecclesia de Kyrkeby super Bayn et xiij s. iiij d. de ecclesia de Normantone in comitatu Notinghamie;[1] et iam dicte ecclesie in Stamfordia ad tantam deuenerunt exilitatem quod pensiones predicte ab eis exigi non possunt, sic quod omni anno deterioratur domus per hoc in iiij li. vj s. viij d.; et hoc est causa quod priores loci huius adeo amouentur nec habent voluntatem inibi permanere.

Frater Thomas Hexham dicit quod non surgunt ad matutinas de nocte propter paucitatem.

Hiis habitis dominus dissoluit visitacionem suam.

LXVII.

[Fo. 83.]

VISITACIO[2] DOMUS MONIALIUM SANCTI MICHAELIS EXTRA STAM-
FORDIAM, ORDINIS SANCTI BENEDICTI, LINCOLNIENSIS DIOCESIS,
FACTA IN DOMO CAPITULARI IBIDEM XXJ DIE MENSIS OCTOBRIS,
ANNO DOMINI MCCCCXL, PER VENERABILEM PATREM, DOMINUM
WILLELMUM, LINCOLNIENSEM EPISCOPUM, ANNO SUARUM CONSE-
CRACIONIS XV ET TRANSLACIONIS QUINTO.

In primis, sedente dicto reuerendo patre iudicialiter in dicte visitacionis sue negocio die et loco ac anno predictis, primo et ante[3] propositum
fuit verbum Dei per egregium virum magistrum Thomam Duffelde, in
sacra theologia bacallarium, sequentem hoc thema, ' Querantur regi
virgines et speciose puelle.'[4] Quo laudabiliter finito, licet tamen priorissa
certificatorium in forma super mandato domini sibi pro hoc negocio
directo non confecerat[5] nec statum domus ostenderat, dicit tamen quod
domus indebitabatur tempore installacionis sue in xx li., et iam in xx
marcis; et sic hiis exhibendis non exhibitis priorissa consenciens in diem
iurauit obedienciam in forma et examinata dicit ea que sequuntur.

Coldingham priory, which was a dependency of Durham (*ibid*, No. cxxxiii, pp.
100, 101). For further confirmations to Coldingham see *ibid*. Nos. clxxviii, clxxxiii,
ccxiii, pp. 139, 147, 174. No charter which granted the church to Croyland at
an earlier date survives, nor are the claims of the abbot of Croyland mentioned in
any of the above charters. Waldef, abbot of Croyland 1124-38, was the brother of
Gospatric (*ibid*. pp. 327, 328). As he did not become a monk till somewhat late in
life, it is probable that he held Edrom, with the advowson of the church, under his
brother, and continued to hold it as abbot. This explains the arrangement made,
as described in the text, between Durham and Croyland. In *Valor Eccl.* (Rec.
Comm. v, 306) the rent payable to Croyland ' de diversis terris in villa de Ederham
in Scocia' is reckoned at £6. There is a letter, dated 5 May, 1451, in *Priory of
Coldingham* (Surtees Soc. p. 173), to the effect that the prior of Stamford was then
unable to pay the pension of £6 due to the abbot and convent of Croyland on account
of the church of Edrom.

[1] *iam* cancelled.
[2] At the head of the leaf is written *Prima* (sc. *visitacio*) and the note *Require
iniuncciones factas tempore istius visitacionis in isto tercio folio precedenti.* [Sc.
fo. 81 *d.*].

said priory of St. Leonard might have recompense therefor, the house of St. Leonard should receive a pension of five marks from the church of St. Mary at the bridge and twenty shillings from the church of St. Mary Bynwerke, forty shillings from the church of Kirkby-upon-Bain, and 13 s. 4 d. from the church of Normanton in the county of Nottingham;[1] and now the said churches in Stamford are come to such slenderness of means that the aforesaid pensions cannot be demanded of them, so that every year the house is hereby £4 6 s. 8 d. to the worse; and this is the reason why the priors of this place are so [often] removed, and have not the will to abide therein.

Brother Thomas Hexham says that they do not get up for matins by night because they are few in number.

After these things had been done, my lord prorogued his visitation.

LXVII.

THE VISITATION OF THE HOUSE OF THE NUNS OF ST. MICHAEL WITH-OUT STAMFORD, OF THE ORDER OF ST. BENET, OF THE DIOCESE OF LINCOLN, PERFORMED IN THE CHAPTER-HOUSE THEREIN ON THE TWENTY-FIRST DAY OF THE MONTH OF OCTOBER, IN THE YEAR OF OUR LORD 1440, BY THE WORSHIPFUL FATHER, THE LORD WILLIAM, BISHOP OF LINCOLN, IN THE FIFTEENTH YEAR OF HIS CONSECRATION AND THE FIFTH OF HIS TRANSLATION.

In the first place, as the said reverend father was sitting in his capacity of judge in the business of his said visitation on and in the day and place and year aforesaid, first and before [all else] the word of God was set forth by the excellent master Thomas Duffelde, bachelor in divinity, after this text, ' Let virgins and fair maids be sought for the king.'   And when this was come to a praiseworthy end, albeit it was that the prioress had not composed a formal certificate touching my lord's mandate which had been addressed to her for this business and had not shown the state of the house, nevertheless she says that at the time of her installation[2] the house was twenty pounds and now is twenty marks in debt; and so the prioress, agreeing to a day for exhibiting these things which she had not exhibited, sware formal obedience, and on examination she says these things which follow.

---

[3] *Sic: omnia* omitted.
[4] Esther II, 2: ' Quaerantur regi puellae virgines ac speciose.'
[5] Altered from *confecerit*.

[1] Normanton-on-Soar, near Loughborough. In *Val. Eccl.* v, 305, the pensions from Kirkby-on-Bain and Normanton churches are noted among the ˌrevenues of St. Leonard's, but that from St. Mary's at the bridge is not entered, although its equivalent is included in the £6 payable to Croyland out of Edrom.   The church of St. Mary Bynwerke was one of those destroyed in 1461, when a Lancastrian army sacked Stamford, and was never rebuilt; and this probably accounts for the reduction of the £7 mentioned in 1440 to £6 in 1535.

[2] The date of her election, etc., does not appear to be recorded. See *Visitations* I, 158.   On her own statement, however, it is clear that she succeeded Agnes Leek in 1429.

Domina Elizabetha Weldone, priorissa, dicit quod viij sunt moniales professe et tres nouicie, quarum due steterunt in nouiciatu per duos annos et tercia per vnum annum, et tamen sunt infra.

Item dicit quod omnes simul commedunt in refectorio diebus quibus vescuntur piscibus, et aliis commedunt diebus in aula communi priorisse, exceptis duabus, videlicet domina Agnete Multone, suppriorissa, et Margeria Croylande et Margeria Morwode nouicia, que tres separatim commedunt in aula[1] suppriorisse.

Item dicit quod stetit priorissa xij annis et quod nunquam tempore suo reddidit compotum in communi; et dicit quod domus potest expendere annuatim xl li., vltra x marcas quas credit officium pietanciarie habet sibi applicatum,[2] et preter commoda iconomie.

Item dicit quod moniales hiis diebus nichil percipiunt pro vestura, nec aliquid aliud percipunt nisi tantum vestimenta.

Item dicit quod arant cum duabus carucis, et habent viij boues, vij equos, vnum balliuum, quatuor seruientes, ad carucas vnum bigarium, et vnum qui est pistor et pandoxatarius, cuius vxor conficit braseum.

Item dicit quod quedam Agnes, monialis loci illius, egressa est in apostasia, adherendo cuidam cithariste; et dicit quod manent simul, vt dicitur, in Nouo castro super Tynam.

Item dicit quod domus oneratur ere alieno in annua pensione lx ş.[2] monasterio beate Marie Eboracensi, et hoc pro decimis non valentibus vltra xl d. annuos; et iam est aretro per xx annos et amplius.

Item petit vt vicarius Sancti Andree Stamfordie deputetur eis confessor.

Domina Agneş Multone, suppriorissa, dicit quod omnes iacent in dormitorio preter priorissam, que iacet in camera sua.

Item dicit quod priorissa nunquam reddidit compotum administracionis sue.

Item dicit quod quelibet monialis percipit de domo annuatim panem et ceruisiam et vnam marcam pro pissibus[4] et carnibus et aliis; et quo ad vestitum nichil percipiunt de domo.

Item dicit de sorore Agnete nominata Butylere alias Pery alias Northamptone iam apostata; et dicit quod alias fuit in apostasiam per vnum diem et vnam noctem ducta per fratrem Johannem Harryes, ordinis Augustinensis; et iam per vnum *annum* et dimidium.

Domina Isabella Seytone, sacrista, dicit quod commoda huius officii consistunt in xvj s. annui redditus et oblacionibus ad imaginem Sancti Michaelis, que valent communibus annis v s. vel circa.

---

[1] *pr* cancelled.
[2] *Sic*: for *applicatas*.
[3] *in* cancelled.
[4] *Sic*: for *piscibus*.

[1] The names of the nuns show their local origin. Weldone (Weldon), ten miles S.W. of Stamford, and Wyteryng (Wittering), four miles S.E., are in Northants., while Thornhaugh, where Margaret Mortymere's father lived, is two miles S.E. of Wittering. Multone (Moulton) and Croyland are in Lincolnshire, at no great distance. Seytone (Seaton), nine to ten miles S.W., and Normanton, six to seven miles W., are in Rutland. Wylugby may be either the Lincolnshire or Nottinghamshire place of that name. Margery Morwode (Marwood), the novice, possibly derived her name from some place in the neighbourhood of the priory.

[2] The point is that, by the legatine and Peckham's constitutions, a novice was bound to make profession after a year's residence. Peckham's constitution *Sancti-*

Dame Elizabeth Weldone,[1] the prioress, says that there are eight nuns professed and three novices, two of whom have continued in the noviciate for two years and the third for one year, and nevertheless they are within [the house][2]

Also she says that they all do eat together in the frater on the days whereon they feed on fish, and on the other days they do eat in the prioress's common hall, except two, to wit dame Agnes Multone, the subprioress, and Margery Croylande and Margery Morwode, a novice, the which three do eat apart in the subprioress's hall.

Also she says that she has continued prioress for twelve years and that never in her time has she rendered an account in common; and she says that the house is able to spend forty pounds a year above ten marks which she believes the office of pittancer holds in appropriation to itself, and besides the perquisites of the stewardship.

Also she says that in these days the nuns receive naught for their raiment nor do they receive aught else but their clothing only.

Also she says that they plough with two teams, and they have eight oxen, seven horses, a bailiff, four serving-folk, a carter for the teams and a man who is their baker and brewer, whose wife makes the malt.

Also she says that one Agnes, a nun of that place, has gone away in apostasy, cleaving to a harp-player; and she says that they dwell together, as it is said, in Newcastle-upon-Tyne.

Also she says that the house is burthened with debt as regards a yearly pension of sixty shillings to the monastery of blessed Mary of York,[3] and this for tithes that are not worth more than forty pence a year; and it is now in arrear for twenty years and upwards.

Also she prays that the vicar of St. Andrew's at Stamford[4] be appointed them as confessor.

Dame Agnes Multone, the subprioress, says that they all do lie in the dorter save the prioress, who lies in her lodging.

Also she says that the prioress has never rendered an account of her administration.

Also she says that each nun receives of the house yearly bread and beer and a mark for fish and flesh and other things; and as to their raiment, they receive naught of the house.

Also she says concerning sister Agnes, named Butylere or Pery or Northamptone, who is now an apostate, and says that she was led into apostasy at another time for a day and a night by brother John Harryes, of the order of St. Austin;[5] and now [she has been] for a year and a half.

Dame Isabel Seytone, the sacrist, says that the perquisites of this office consist in sixteen shillings of yearly rent and in the offerings at the image of St. Michael, which are worth on an average five shillings a year or thereabout.

moniales (Lyndwood, ed. 1679, pp. 202, 203) treated novices who stayed longer than a year as ipso facto professed and bound to remain in their convents.
    [3] This pension came out of tithes in Corby and Swayfield, Lincs. (Val. Eccl. [Rec. Comm.] v, 5).
    [4] The church was appropriated to the prioress and convent. Thomas Curteys or Curtes, inst. to the vicarage 31 Dec., 1425 (Reg. XVI, fo. 28 d.), died before 16 Aug., 1458 (Reg. XX, fo. 130 d.). The church disappeared at the sack of Stamford in 1461.
    [5] Presumably an Austin friar.

Item dicit quod priorissa habet vij vel viij pueros, quosdam masculos, quasdam femellas[1] etatis xij annorum vel inferius ad mensam et ad eos erudiendos.

Item petit arbores crescentes in cimiterio conuerti in vsus et commodum officii sui, eo quod prouentus ad illud pertinentes sunt exiles, attento onere incumbente.

Item dicit quod priorissa non iacet de nocte in dormitorio.

Item dicit de apostata vt supra.

[Fo. 83 *d.*] Domina Margeria Croylande dicit de duabus familiis vt supra: ista est precentrix.

Item dicit quod priorissa non iacet in dormitorio de nocte.

Item petit vt habeant aliquid de domo ad vestitum.

Domina Margareta Mortymere dicit quod vltimo quando ipsamet visitauit patrem suum, stetit cum eo per vnam septimanam de licencia priorisse, et hoc apud Thornhawe.

Item dicit de apostata vt supra.

Domina Alicia Wyteryng dicit quod[2] refectorium non seruatur nisi in Aduentu et in Quadragesima.

Item dicit de compoto non reddito per priorissam tempore suo.

Item dicit quod temporalia non superuidentur nec reguntur[3] vtiliter ad commodum domum.[4]

Domina Elizabetha Wylugby dicit quinque moniales stantes in familia priorisse sedent in eadem mensa cum priorissa sole, nisi superueniant alique graues persone seculares.

Item dicit quod solent commedere in refectorio iiij, vj feriis et sabbato omni septimana, excepto quod iam paucis diebus propter rapturas[5] domus sic non potuerunt.

Domina Alicia Normantone dicit quod nichil percipiunt de domo ad vestitum.

Quibus examinatis, dominus iniunxit priorisse sub pena priuacionis a statu suo vt omni anno reddat plenum compotum administracionis sue coram sororibus suis.

Dominus iniunxit suppriorisse quod dimittat familiam suam et stet decetero in familia priorissa.[6]

Item[7] iniunctum est priorisse quod omnes moniales sedeant in vna mensa, et quod nullus seculares[8] sit inter eas, et quod habeant lecciones temporibus refeccionum meridianarum.

Item iniunxit priorisse quod non licenciet aliquam monialem visitare amicos suos vltra tres dies in sanitate, et quod infra sex dies reducat eas ad domum si infirmentur; et quod non sinat moniales loqui cum secularibus nisi audiente alia moniali, excepto parentibus et aliis de quibus est suspicio.[9]

---

[1] *q* cancelled.
[2] *refectum s* cancelled.
[3] *vlt* cancelled.
[4] *Sic*: for *domus.*
[5] *Sic*: for *rupturas.*
[6] *Sic*: for *priorisse.*
[7] *dicit* cancelled.
[8] *Sic*: for *secularis.*
[9] *Sic*: *nulla* omitted.

Also she says that the prioress has seven or eight children, some male, some female, of twelve years of age and less at her board and for the purpose of teaching them.[1]

Also she prays that the trees which grow in the churchyard be applied to the use and profit of her office, inasmuch as the revenues which belong thereto are small in consideration of the charge incumbent upon it.

Also she says that the prioress does not lie in the dorter of a night.

Also she says as above concerning the apostate.

Dame Margery Croylande says as above concerning the two households: she is precentress.

Also she says that the prioress does not lie in the dorter of a night.

Also she prays that they may have somewhat of the house for their raiment.

Dame Margaret Mortymere says that last time when she herself visited her father, she stayed with him for a week with the prioress's leave, and this at Thornhaugh.[2]

Also she says as above concerning the apostate.

Dame Alice Wyteryng says that frater is kept in Advent and Lent only.

Also she says concerning the account, that one has not been rendered in her time by the prioress.

Also she says that the temporalities are not surveyed or governed profitably to the advantage of the house.

Dame Elizabeth Wylugby says [that] the five nuns who abide in the prioress's household do sit with the prioress at the same board by themselves, unless there also come some secular persons of importance.

Also she says that they are wont to eat in the frater on Wednesday, Friday and Saturday every week, save that for a few days lately they have not been able to do so because of the cracks in the building.

Dame Alice Normantone says that they receive naught of the house for their raiment.

Now when these had been examined, my lord enjoined upon the prioress under pain of deprivation from her estate that every year she shall render a full account of her administration in presence of her sisters.

My lord enjoined upon the subprioress that she shall leave off her household and abide henceforth in the household of the prioress.

Also the prioress was enjoined that all the nuns shall sit at one board, and that there be no secular person among them, and that they shall have readings during their mid-day meals.

Also the prioress was enjoined not to give leave to any nun to visit her friends for more than three days when in sound health, and to bring them back to the house within six days if they be infirm; and not to allow the nuns to speak with secular folk save in the hearing of another nun, except with their parents and others of whom there is [no] suspicion.

---

[1] On the subject of nunnery schools, see Power, *Med. English Nunneries*, pp. 237-84.

[2] Thornhaugh was so near, five miles S.E. of Stamford, that a leave extending over a week was in any case excessive and undesirable.

Item iniunctum est singulis monialibus sub pena excommunicacionis quod alio modo non communicent cum secularibus quam superius est expressum.

Item iniunctum est priorisse quod quo commodius poterit reducat dictam apostatam, que recessit vt prefertur cum citharista nomine Roberto Abbot.

Reseruata potestate faciendi iniuncciones ad detecta, dominus dissoluit visitacionem suam.

[Fo. 81 *d*.] Sancte Michaelis Stamfordie.

Wyllyam, by the suffraunce of God bysshope of Lincolne, to our wele belufed doghters in Criste the prioresse and the couent of the priory of seynt Mighelle wythe owte Stamford, of the ordere of Cistewes, of our diocyse,[1] *helthe, grace and our blessyng.* Late we, as hit longes to *vs*,[2] visityng yowe and your saide pryorye, we fonde by *our* inquisicyone[3] diuerse notable defautes in your saide place, for the reformacion where of we sende yowe certeyn *thes* iniunccyons and commaundements as thai are here benethe writene, chargeyng *you and* yche oon of yowe that ye playnly kepe thaym vndere the peynes here benethe wryten.

In the fyrst we enioyne and charge yowe, prioresse, in vertue of your obedience and vndere peyne of contempte, that nyghtly ye lyg in the dormytorye emong your susters, and that euery principale double fest and festes of xij or ix lessouns ye be at matynes, but if grete sekenes lette yowe; and that often tymes ye be at other howres and messes in the qwere, and also that ye be present in chapitres helpyng the supprioresse in correctyng and punisshyng of defautes done *as welle in* diuine service and regulere obseruaunces discretely, not rygorouse to some ne to some fauoryng.[4]

Also we inioyne yow,[5] supprioresse, and all others of the couent vndere payne of cursyng, that ye lefe your householdes and stande alle holy wythe the prioresse in hire householde.[6]

Also[7] we enioyne yowe, prioresse, vndere peyne of contempte, that in tymes of Aduente and Lentyn and also Wedenesdayes, Fridayes and Seturdayes ye kepe the fraytour and othere dayes kepe your halle, so that [ye] hafe a lessone redde before yowe euery daye in tyme of mete.[8]

Also we enioyne yow, prioresse, vndere [the peynes] here obofe and bynethe writen, that ye gyfe no sustere of yours lefe to byde wythe thaire frendes whan thai [visyte] thaym ouere thre dayes in helthe; and if thai falle seke, that ye do feche thaym home wythe yn sex d[ayes],

---

[1] *salutacion in God wythe our blessyng* cancelled.

[2] Interlined above *hus* cancelled.

[3] *then made* cancelled.

[4] Founded on the subprioress's first, Isabel Seytone's fourth and Margery Croylande's second *detecta*, as regards the first part. No other *detecta* touch the remainder.

[5] *pri* cancelled.

[6] Founded on the prioress's second and Margery Croylande's first *detecta*.

[7] Note in margin: *Scribatur et incipe de obseruacione refectorii.*

[8] Note in margin: *non scribatur de non . . . endo.* Founded on the prioress's second, Alice Wyteryng's first and Elizabeth Wylugby's second *detecta*.

Also the several nuns were enjoined under pain of excommunication to hold converse with secular folk in no other wise then is above declared.

Also the prioress was enjoined to bring back as conveniently as she can the said apostate, who has gone away, as is aforesaid, with a harp-player by name Robert Abbot.

Having reserved the power of making injunctions with respect to the disclosures, my lord dissolved his visitation.

---

ne that ye[1] suffre no sustre of yours to speke wythe no seculere persones save fadere and modere and other that by laghe are not suspecte, but if an other sustere approvede in religyone stande by and here and see thayre gouernaunce; ne that ye suffre none of youre sustres to receyve ne to sende owte nothre gyfte ne lettre but ye see the gyftes and wyte what is conteynede in the lettres.[2]

Also we enioyne yche oon of yow of the couent vndere peyne of cursyng that none of yowe hafe ne holde no communicacyone ne talkyng wythe any seculere persone other wyse or in other forme then hit is a fore writene.[3]

Also we enioyne yow, prioresse, vndere peyne of contempte, that ye suffre no seculere persones, women ne children, lyg in the dormytorye be nyght, ne that ye ne none of your susters take ne holde no maner of suiournauntes yong ne olde wythe yn your place, but if ye have licence ther to of hus or our successours bysshopes of Lincolne.[4]

Also we enioyne yow, prioresse, vndere lyke peynes that wythe alle your diligence and hast possyble ye gare seke your sustere Anneys Buty-lere that is owte in apostasye, and bryng hire home to hire cloystere, and so moderly trete hire aftere your rule that she seke no cause eftis to go in apostasye, ne other take non ensample be hire to trespace in lyke wyse.[5]

Also we enioyne yow, pryoresse, that as ferre as the revenues of your house wylle extende, ye ordeyne that your susters hafe somwhat to[6] thaire habite for eschewyng of more harme; and that ye receyve fro hense forthe no mo nunnes into your house then may be competently susteyned of the reuenues of your house; ne that ye exacte no money ne none other gode for the receyvyng other then thai or thaire frendes of thaire fre wylle wythe owten any couenaunt made wylle gyfe yowe.[7]

Also, for as muche as we conceyve that the profytes of the office of the sekresteyn stande alle onely in xvj s. of rent, we wylle and ordeyne that the sekresteyn that is for the tyme hafe alle the advayle of the

---

[1] *sustre of* cancelled.

[2] Founded on Margaret Mortymere's first *detectum*, but extended to cover cases not in the *detecta*.

[3] Founded on Elizabeth Wylugby's first *detectum*.

[4] Founded on Isabel Seytone's second *detectum*.

[5] Founded on the prioress's sixth, the subprioress's fourth and Isabel Sey-tone's fifth *detecta*. There is a Latin note, nearly illegible, in the margin of this injunction: [*quod reduca*]*t monialem apostatantem . . . diocriter tractent quod non habeat* [*causam*] *ulterius apostatandi.*

[6] *h* cancelled.

[7] Founded on the prioress's fourth, the subprioress's third, Margery Croylande's third and Alice Normantone's *detecta*.

trees that growe in your kyrke yerde, so that *hit* do the kyrke to no harme by tempestes for lak of defense by the trees.[1]

Also we enioyne yow, prioresse, vpo peyne of priuacyone of your state, degree and office of prioresse, that euery yere betwix Mighelmesse and Martyne ye showe to your susters in pleyne chapitree a fulle and playne[2] accompte of alle the reuenues that longe to your place and how thai are dispendede.[3]

LXVIII.

[Fo. 39 *d*.][4]

Visitacio prioratus SANCTI MICHAELIS ARCHANGELI EXTRA STAMFORDIAM, ordinis Cisterciensis,[5] Lincolniensis diocesis, facta in domo capitulari ibidem XIX^{no} die mensis Junii, anno Domini mccccxlij, per reuerendum in Christo patrem et dominum Willelmum, Dei gracia Lincolniensem episcopum, anno consecracionis sue xvj⁰, consecracionis[6] vj^{to}.

In primis sedente dicto reuerendo patre iudicialiter in huiusmodi sue visitacionis negocio die, anno et loco antedictis, comparuerunt coram eo priorissa et singule moniales dicti prioratus, visitacionem suam huiusmodi vt apparuit humiliter subiture; et deinde exposita et declarata per eundem reuerendum patrem dictis priorisse et monialibus causa visitacionis sue huiusmodi, videlicet quod iniuncciones quod[7] alias in prima visitacione sua *alias* ibidem facta non fuerunt inibi debite obseruata,[8] processit ad inquisicionem suam preparatoriam et primo priorissam super tangentibus hanc materiam concernenbus,[9] et deinde alias diligenter examinauit. Que examinate dicunt ea que sequuntur.

Domina Elizabetha, priorissa priorissa,[10] inquisita si obseruauit et ab aliis obseruari fecit iniuncciones domini alias eis factas dicit quod quatenus potuit eas obseruauit et fecit[11] ab aliis obseruari: dicit tamen quod non iacet in dormitorio nec seruat refectorium nec eciam seruat claustrum aut ecclesiam iuxta iniunccionem domini, et hoc propter impotenciam corpoream. Et allegat quod dominus super hiis secum dispensauit, quod omnino dominus dedicit.

Item vt cum ipsamet sit impotens ad regendum temporalia nec habeat[12] industrium virum qui ea superuideat ac prouentus domus ad extra leuet et recipiat, redditus domus remanent in manibus tenencium non soluti. Petit igitur vt deputentur due moniales ad regendum temporalia et ad recipiendum et resoluendum.

---

[1] Founded on Isabel Seytone's first and third *detecta*.
[2] *in* cancelled.
[3] Founded on the prioress's third, the sub-prioress's second and Alice Wyteryng's second *detecta*.
[4] *Prima* is written at the head of the page, as in the case of the previous visitation of St. Michael's. The reason probably is that the present visitation, as appears below, was supplementary to Alnwick's primary visitation of the house in 1440.
[5] *Sic.*
[6] *Sic*: for *translacionis*.
[7] *Sic*: *quod alias* should have been cancelled.
[8] *Sic*: for *observate.*

And also vpon the same peyne, vt in xij^a iniunccione Nuncotone *in isto v folio precedenti*, et post hanc.[1]

More over we monysshe alle and yche oon of yowe vndere peyne of cursyng, etc.

LXVIII.

THE VISITATION OF THE PRIORY OF ST. MICHAEL THE ARCHANGEL WITHOUT STAMFORD, OF THE ORDER OF CÎTEAUX,[2] OF THE DIOCESE OF LINCOLN, PERFORMED IN THE CHAPTER-HOUSE THEREIN ON THE NINETEENTH DAY OF THE MONTH OF JUNE IN THE YEAR OF OUR LORD 1442 BY THE REVEREND FATHER IN CHRIST AND LORD WILLIAM, BY THE GRACE OF GOD BISHOP OF LINCOLN, IN THE SIXTEENTH YEAR OF HIS CONSECRATION, THE SIXTH OF HIS TRANSLATION.[3]

In the first place, as the said reverend father was sitting in his capacity of judge in the business of such his visitation on and in the day, year and place aforesaid, there appeared before him the prioress and the several nuns of the said priory, to undergo with lowliness, as was apparent, such his visitation; and then after the cause of such his visitation had been set forth and explained to the said prioress and nuns by the same reverend father, to wit because his injunctions at his first visitation, which had been performed therein at another time, were not duly kept, he proceeded to his preparatory inquiry, and examined diligently, first the prioress and then the others concerning the particulars touching [and] relating to this matter. And she on examination says these things which follow.

Dame Elizabeth,[4] the prioress, being questioned whether she has observed and caused to be observed by the others my lord's injunctions made to them at another time, says that, so far as she has been able, she has kept them and caused them to be kept by the others: howbeit she says that she does not lie in the dorter or keep frater or even keep cloister or church according to my lord's injunction, and this because of her bodily incapacity. And she avers that my lord granted her a dispensation touching these things, the which my lord utterly disavows.

Also that, since she herself is incapable of governing matters temporal and has not a painstaking man to survey them and collect and receive the external revenues of the house, the rents of the house remain in the tenants' hands unpaid. She prays therefore that two nuns be appointed to govern the temporalities and to make receipts and payments.

---

[9] *Sic*: for *concernentibus*.

[10] *Sic*.

[11] *al* cancelled.

[12] *id* cancelled.

[1] The injunction on fo. 77 *d*. (p. 252 above) refers to the granting of corrodies.

[2] The priory was actually Benedictine.

[3] 'Consecration' in the original.

[4] The eight nuns appear as in 1440. Agnes Multone, however, is now called Maud Multone.

Item dicit quod non habent confessorem, quia alias per dominum ad hoc deputatus iam senio infectus dimisit onus.

Domina Matilda Multone dicit quod Ricardus Gray, nuper cum vxore sua perhendinans in[1] priorissa, procreauit prolem de domina Elizabetha Wylugby moniali ibidem, et sic perhendinauit vsque vltimum Pascha contra iniunccionem domini.

Item dicit quod puelle iuuenes vij vel v annorum iacent in dormitorio contra iniunccionem domini.

Item dicit quod nichil ministratur monialibus pro habitu, et quod priorissa sola recipit et expendit redditus domus conuentu inscio.

Domina Isabella Saytone dicit de Ricardo Gray et Elizabetha Wylugby vt supra.

Domina Margeria Croylande dicit quod non habent receptorem vt supra, et de secularibus iacentibus in dormitorio vt supra.

Item dicit de Gray et Wylugby vt supra, et de impotencia priorisse et de perhendinacione Gray vt supra.

Domina Margareta Mortymere dicit quod moniales, eciam ipsamet, loquuntur cum monialibus[2] indifferenter cum secularibus, nulla moniali audiente alia, sciente priorissa, et de scandalo Gray et Wylugby vt supra.

Domina Alicia Wyteryng dicit quod non habent secularem discretum qui regat temporalia sua.

Domina Elizabetha Wylugby supra. Domina Alicia Normantone vt supra.

Quibus examinatis et post prandium iterato in dicta domo capitulari priorissa et conuentu congregatis, dominus de consensu et peticione omnium deputauit[3] Margaretam Mortymere et Aliciam Wyteryng administratrices omnium bonorum spiritualium et temporalium dicti prioratus et eis huiusmodi administracionem commisit, dicta priorissa ab huiusmodi totali administracione prius[4] suspensa, etc., vt patet vt in commissione eisdem monialibus facta et in libro memorandorum de hoc anno registrata. Et deinde reseruata sibi potestate reformandi et corrigendi premissa detecta, dissoluit visitacionem suam huiusmodi.

Memorandum quod tercio die mensis Julii, anno Domini mccccxlij, in ecclesia parochiali de Wendelyngburghe coram dicto reuerendo patre visitacionem suam ordinariam in clero et populo ibidem exercente comparuit personaliter dictus Ricardus Gray, et obiecto sibi articulo sacrilegii et incestus spiritualis cum dicta domina Elizabetha Wylugby, fatebatur crimen; vnde simpliciter abiurauit tacto libro dictum prioratum, dictam Elizabetham et crimen huiusmodi ac omnem familiaritatem, communicacionem et confabulacionem ac omnia loca suspectum[5] cum eadem Elizabetha extunc et inantea; et pro commissis habet quatuor fustigaciones circa ecclesiam beate Marie ad pontem Stamfordie per quatuor

---

[1] Sic: for cum.
[2] cum monialibus ought to have been cancelled in the original.
[3] dominus cancelled.
[4] commissa cancelled.
[5] Sic: for suspecta.

[1] There is no such commission among the memoranda in Reg. XVIII.

Also she says that they have not a confessor, inasmuch as he who was appointed by my lord at another time to this end, being now overtaken by old age, has given up the task.

Dame Maud Multone says that Richard Gray, who of late was together with his wife a lodger with the prioress, has begotten offspring of dame Elizabeth Wylugby, nun in that place, and did so lodge until Easter last contrary to my lord's injunction.

Also she says that little girls of seven or five years of age do lie in the dorter contrary to my lord's injunction.

Also she says that nothing is furnished to the nuns for their habit, and that the prioress receives and spends the rents of the house by herself without the knowledge of the convent.

Dame Isabel Saytone says as above concerning Richard Gray and Elizabeth Wylugby.

Dame Margery Croylande says as above that they have not a receiver, and as above concerning the secular folk that lie in the dorter.

Also she says as above concerning Gray and Wylugby, and as above concerning the incapacity of the prioress and Gray's abiding as a lodger.

Dame Margaret Mortymere says that the nuns, even she herself, do talk with secular folk without distinction in the hearing of no other nun, whereof the prioress is aware, and as above concerning the scandal of Gray and Wylugby.

Dame Alice Wyteryng says that they have not a wary secular person to govern their temporalities.

Dame Elizabeth Wylugby [as] above. Dame Alice Normantone as above.

Now when these had been examined and the prioress and convent had been gathered together a second time in the said chapter-house, my lord with the consent and at the prayer of all charged Margaret Mortymere and Alice Wyteryng with the administration of all the spiritual and temporal goods of the said priory and committed such administration to them, having first suspended the said prioress from such the entire administration, etc., as appears in the commission made to the same nuns and registered in the book of memoranda[1] for this year. And then, having reserved to himself the power of reforming and correcting the aforeset disclosures, he dissolved such his visitation.

It is to be noted that on the third day of the month of July, in the year of our Lord 1442, in the parish church of Wellingborough before the said reverend father, as he was holding his visitation as ordinary among the clergy and people in the same, there appeared in person the said Richard Gray, and, when the article of sacrilege and spiritual incest with the said dame Elizabeth Wylugby had been laid to his charge, he confessed his guilt; wherefore, having touched the book, he made unqualified abjuration of the said priory, the said Elizabeth and such guilt and all familiar fellowship, communication and conversation and all suspect places with the same Elizabeth thenceforth and for the future; and for what he has committed he has four floggings round the church of blessed Mary at the bridge of Stamford[2] for four Sundays or feast-days,

---

[2] *I.e.* the existing church of St. Mary, appropriated to the prior and convent of Durham (see p. 347, note 1). The church of St. Mary Bynwerke, which no longer exists, was a rectory in the same patronage.

dies dominicos seu festiuos, coram processione eiusdem ecclesie portando in manu sua vnum cereum ponderis vnius libre cere, indutus duploide et vestibus suis lineis tantum, et quod vltimo dictorum quatuor dierum post processionem peractam offerat dictum cereum summo altari dicte ecclesie, et quod per quator[1] sextas ferias similem penitenciam in omnibus et per omnia peragat circa forum Stamfordie, offerendo consimilem cereum summo altari in dicta ecclesia vltimo[2] dictarum iiij[or] feriarum, et quod citra proximum festum Sancti Petri ad vincula eques peregrinetur ad ecclesiam Lincolnie, et cum venerit ad quinque milliaria citra Lincolniam pedibus nudatis eat ad ipsam ecclesiam et offerat[3] summo altari ibidem vnum cereum vnius libre more penitentis; presentibus magistris Johanne Depyng, Johanne Leke et me Colstone. Post nonas vero eiusdem diei iij Julii in dicta ecclesia de Wendelyngburghe coram domino iterato venit dictus Ricardus humiliter ad supplicandum vt penitenciam huiusmodi moderari dignaretur; vnde dominus pietate super eum motus penitenciam sibi circa mercatum iniunctam modificauit sub hac forma, vt videlicet citra proximum festum Sancti Petri ad vincula tribuat monialibus dicti prioratus in vsus suos conuertendos viginti solidos, et quod citra proximum festum Assumpcionis beate Marie offerat fabrice ecclesie Lincolniensis xx s. in vsus fabrice ecclesie illius dumtaxat conuertendos, et quod citra dictum festum Assumpcionis deferat domino litteras testimoniales et autenticas de solucione dictorum xl s. et peracte penitencie apud Lincolniam. Et deinde idem reuerendus pater monuit dictum Ricardum primo, secundo et tercio peremptorie sub pena excommunicacionis maioris, quod dictam penitenciam sic sibi iniunctam et modificatam integraliter perficiat, inchoando penitenciam circa ecclesiam beate Marie Stamfordie dominica proxima post festum Sancte Margarete proxime futurum, et continuando de die dominica in dominicam quousque perfecerit penitenciam, presentibus magistris Johanne Depyng, Johanne Leke et me Colstone vt supra. Post hec dominus commisit vices magistro Johanni Leke ad absoluendum dictum Ricardum a sentencia excomunicacionis maioris contra tales generaliter latam quam occasione premissorum incurrebat. Qui quidem magister Johannes auctoritate huiusmodi sibi commissa fungens[4] prefatum Ricardum a dicta sentencia excommunicacionis dicto die tercio Julii in vestibulo dicte ecclesie absoluit, presente me Colstone. Subsequenter vero dominus per litteras formam et modum penitencie predicte continentes mandauit decano Stamfordie ad vocandum eundem Ricardum ad penitenciam predictam; ipse vero Ricardus licet friuoliter appellauit ad curiam Cantuarie. Vnde obtenta a commissario officialis ibidem licencia quod dominus posset procedere contra ipsum Ricardum quatenus concernit

---

[1] *Sic*: for *quatuor*.
[2] *Sic*: for *vltima*.
[3] *ad* cancelled.
[4] This seems to be the word; but it is written carelessly *fu'igens*.

[1] *I.e.* 1 August.
[2] There were two routes from Stamford to Lincoln in the middle ages, one by Grantham, the other by way of the old road known as Sewstern lane and Newark. In this case, the penitent would go barefoot from a point on the road near Thorpe-on-the-Hill; or, if he went by way of Grantham, from Harmston.
[3] *I.e.* 15 August.

carrying in his hand before the procession of the same church a taper of one pound's weight of wax, being clothed in his doublet and linen garments only, and on the last of the said four days, after the procession is finished, [he has] to offer the said taper to the high altar of the said church, and for four Fridays to perform the like penance in all and through all about the market-place of Stamford, offering a like taper to the high altar in the said church on the last of the said four days, and on this side the next feast of St. Peter's chains[1] to make pilgrimage on horseback to the church of Lincoln, and, when he is come to five miles this side of Lincoln,[2] to go barefoot to the same church and offer to the high altar in the same a taper of one pound [weight] in penitent wise; there being present masters John Depyng, John Leke and I Colstone.   But after nones of the same third day of July in the said church of Wellingborough the said Richard came before my lord a second time to make lowly supplication that he would deign to temper such penance; wherefore my lord, moved with compassion on him, modified the penance which had been enjoined upon him about the market under this form, to wit, that on this side the feast of St. Peter's chains he shall pay twenty shillings to the nuns of the said priory, to be applied to their uses, and that on this side the next feast of the Assumption of blessed Mary[3] he shall offer twenty shillings to the fabric of the church of Lincoln,[4] to be applied only to the uses of the fabric of the said church, and that on this side the said feast of the Assumption he shall bring to my lord authentic letters testimonial concerning the payment of the said forty shillings and the performance of the penance at Lincoln.   And then the same reverend father warned the said Richard a first, a second and a third time peremptorily under pain of the greater excommunication, to perform the said penance so enjoined upon him and modified in its entirety, beginning the penance round the church of blessed Mary of Stamford on Sunday next after the feast of St. Margaret next to come,[5] and going on from Sunday to Sunday till he have accomplished his penance; there being present as above masters John Depyng, John Leke and I Colstone. After these things my lord committed his office to master John Leke to absolve the said Richard from the sentence of excommunication levied in general against such persons, the which he incurred by reason of the premises.   The which master John, in fulfilment of such authority committed to him, absolved the aforesaid Richard from the said sentence of excommunication on the said third day of July in the vestry of the said church,[6] I Colstone being present.   Afterwards, however, my lord commanded the dean of Stamford[7] by letters containing the form and manner of the penance aforesaid to summon the same Richard to the penance aforesaid, but the same Richard, albeit without serious cause, appealed to the court of Canterbury.   Wherefore, having obtained licence from the commissary of the official in that court, that my lord might be able to proceed against the same Richard so far as concerns his soul's

---

[4] The permanent fabric fund or 'works.' See *Visitations* I, 142, note 3.

[5] *I.e.* 22 July, 1442. He was excused his floggings and his visit to Lincoln, but the rest of his penance on Sundays was not remitted.

[6] The medieval vestry still remains on the north side of the chancel of Wellingborough church.

[7] *I.e.* the dean of the Christianity of Stamford.

correccionem anime, inhibicione quacumque non obstante, dominus mandauit ipsum Ricardum citari ad diem et locum infrascriptos ad proponendum, etc., quare non debeat excommunicari et pro excommunicato denunciari, eo quod non paruit monicionibus domini in non peragendo penitenciam, etc. Qui sic citatus comparuit per Willelmum Daund procuratorem suum in ecclesia de Bugdene xv die mensis Nouembris, anno Domini mccccxlij, coram Depyng, et exhibito per ipsum Willelmum procuratorio suo, allegauit pro excusacione absencie et non personalis comparicionis ipsius domini sui, quod ipse dominus suus tantis et tam grauibus infirmitatibus febrium et aliis detinetur, in lecto alternis diebus recubans, quod absque graui corporis detrimento non potest ipso die et loco personaliter comparere. Vnde prestito iuramento corporali per ipsum procuratorem de veritate cause absencie domini sui per eum allegate, Depyng expectauit ipsum Ricardum vsque in diem Martis proximum post festum Sancti Nicholai proxime futurum in ecclesia parochiali beate Marie ville Huntingdonie, iniungens eidem procuratori vt hec domino suo denunciet et ipsum dominum suum coram domino aut ipso seu alio commissario domini sistat die et loco antedictis ad faciendum et recipiendum vt supra; presentibus Bug, Thorpe et me Colstone. Instrumentum procuratorii huiusmodi est inter alia memoranda in fine huius libri.

[Fo. 129 *d.*] In Dei nomine, amen. Cum nos Willelmus, permissione diuina Lincolniensis episcopus, contra te Ricardum Gray de Herdewyke, nostre diocesis, occasione criminis incestus et adulterii cum quadam sorore Elizabetha Wylughby, moniali domus Sancti Michaelis extra Stamfordiam, nostre diocesis, per te commissorum et coram nobis iudicialiter confessatorum, adeo processerimus quod tibi pro huiusmodi demeritis tuis, prestito primitus a te de peragendo per nos tibi iniungenda iuramento corporali, certam legitimam, canonicam et moderatam penitenciam iniunxerimus teque monuerimus primo, secundo et tercio peremptorie sub pena excommunicacionis, quod iuramentum tuum huiusmodi obseruares et iniuncta huiusmodi perficeres, tuque ad huiusmodi iniuncta peragenda legitime euocatus ipsa perficere[1] nec monicionibus nostris huiusmodi parere curasti; ideo te ad hos diem et locum ad proponendum in forma iuris quare te occasione premissorum excommunicare et pro excommunicato publice denunciare minime debeamus fecimus *coram nobis* euocari. Tuque huiusmodi die et loco personaliter coram nobis comparens nullam huiusmodi causam, licet sepius interrogatus, saltem canonicam allegare curasti. Vnde te in non sic proponendo pronunciamus contumacem, et in penam contumacie tue huiusmodi viam vlterius quicquam in hac parte proponendi precludimus per decretum, et te[2] occasione premissorum in non parendo iussionibus nostris predictis pronunciamus manifeste contumacem, et in penam huiusmodi manifeste

---

[1] *non curasti* cancelled.
[2] *exigentibus propter* cancelled.

[1] 11 Dec., 1442.
[2] There is no trace of this proxy remaining; but the document which follows appears, with some memoranda of dates in connexion with the Northamptonshire

correction, any inhibition whatsoever notwithstanding, my lord commanded that the same Richard be summoned for and to the day and place written beneath to show cause, etc., why he ought not to be excommunicated and denounced as excommunicate, in that he has disobeyed my lord's admonitions in not performing penance, etc.   And he, being so summoned, appeared in the person of William Daund his proctor in the church of Buckden on the fifteenth day of the month of November, in the year of our Lord 1442, before Depyng, and, after his proxy had been exhibited by the same William, [William] alleged in excuse of the absence and failure to appear in person of the same his principal, that the same his principal is withheld by so many and so sore infirmities of fevers and other kinds, lying in his bed every other day, that he cannot without grievous bodily harm appear in person on and in the same day and place.   Wherefore, after bodily oath had been proffered by the same proctor concerning the truth of the reason of his principal's absence as alleged by him, Depyng put off the same Richard until Tuesday next after the feast of St. Nicholas next to come[1] in the parish church of blessed Mary of the town of Huntingdon, enjoining upon the same proctor that he declare these things to his principal and set the same his principal before my lord or himself or other my lord's commissary on and in the day and place aforesaid to do and receive as above; there being present Bug, Thorpe and I Colstone.   The instrument of such proxy is among the other memoranda at the end of this book.[2]

In the name of God, amen.   Inasmuch as we, William, by divine permission bishop of Lincoln, have so proceeded against you, Richard Gray of Hardwick,[3] of our diocese, because of the guilt of incest and adultery committed by you with one sister Elizabeth Wylughby, nun of the house of St. Michael without Stamford, of our diocese, and confessed before us in our capacity as judge, that we have enjoined upon you for such your demerits, after bodily oath to perform those things to be enjoined upon you by us had first been proffered by you, a certain lawful, canonical and moderate penance, and have admonished you a first, a second and a third time peremptorily under pain of excommunication, to observe such your oath and perform such injunctions, and you, having been lawfully summoned to fulfil such injunctions, have heeded not to perform them or to obey such our admonitions; therefore we have caused you to be summoned before us for and to this day and place to show cause in form of law why on account of the premises we ought not to excommunicate you and denounce you in public as excommunicate.   And you, appearing in person before us on and in such day and place, have taken no heed, albeit after often inquiry, to allege any such at all events canonical cause.   Wherefore we pronounce you, in that you show no such cause, to be contumacious, and as the penalty of such your contumacy we bar by decree the way to showing any further cause in this behalf, and by reason of the premises do pronounce you manifestly contumacious in not obeying our orders aforesaid, and as

---

visitation of 1442, towards the end of the MS., and carries the business one stage further.

    [3] Hardwick in Northamptonshire, three miles N.W. of Wellingborough.   This is evident from the fact that Gray's first summons was to Wellingborough church, while Alnwick's visitation of Rothwell deanery was in progress.

contumacie tue *et propter ipsam manifestam contumaciam huiusmodi* te excommunicamus in hiis scriptis. Lata fuit ista sentencia in ecclesia parochiali beate Marie Huntingdonie xj die mensis Decembris anno Domini mccccxlij, presentibus Depyng, Bug, Eluedene et me Colstone; et deinde dominus decreuit fieri execucionem, etc.

LXIX.

[Fo. 96].

Visitacio prioratus SANCTI MICHAELIS EXTRA STAMFORDIAM inchoata in domo capitulari ibidem vj die mensis augusti, anno Domini mccccxl quinto, per magistrum Johannem Depyng, canonicum Lincolniensem, in legibus licenciatum, reuerendi in Christo patris et domini, domini Willelmi, Dei gracia Lincolniensis episcopi, commissarium in hac parte deputatum et sub hac forma, 'Willelmus, permissione diuina,' etc.

In primis sedente dicto domino commissario iudicialiter pro tribunali in huiusmodi visitacionis inchoande negocio die et loco antedictis, conuenerunt coram eo priorissa et moniales dicti prioratus; et deinde lecta fuit primo et ante omnia predicta commissio. Et hoc lecto, priorissa ministrauit mandatum domini ipsi commissario loco certificatorii vna cum nominibus citatarum. Idem commissarius processit ad examinacionem singularum personarum in hunc modum.

Domina Elizabetha Weldone, priorissa, dicit quod moniales sunt sibi inobedientes, non curantes sibi accedere cum pro eis miserit.

Item dicit quod Alicia Witeryng habet totalem administracionem bonorum spiritualium et temporalium prioratus ex commissione domini; ipsa tamen ignorat de administracione huiusmodi, et non computat dicta Alicia.

Item dicit quod moniales non conueniunt in choro vnanimiter tempore missarum.

Item dicit quod Alicia Wyteryng sumit sibi Aliciam Wermyngtone in adiutorium *ad extra*, non assignatam per dominum nec per priorissam.

Domina Agnes Multone, suppriorissa, iurata et examinata dicit quod Margareta Mortymere concepit et peperit circa nativitatem Sancti Johannis Baptiste, et quod punita est secundum regulam: nescit tamen de quo concepit nec an peperit marem vel feminam. Absens tamen erat a choro per quindenam. Et deponit quod priorissa est impotens.

Domina Isabella Seytone concordat cum suppriorissa quo ad Margaretam Mortymere, preter hoc quod peperit citra Pascha, et de impotencia priorisse.

---

[1] Of the eight nuns in 1440 and 1442 seven remain, Alice Normantone being the exception, though possibly ' Normantone ' in the earlier visitations is a mistake for ' Wermyngtone.' Of the four juniors, Margery Morwode was one of the superannuated novices in 1440. There are three (or two) additional names. Alice Wermyngtone (Warmington) bears a Northamptonshire name. Haxey is in northwest Lincolnshire, in the Isle of Axholme: this surname was borne by the famous

the penalty of such your manifest contumacy and by reason of such the same manifest contumacy do excommunicate you in these writings. This sentence was passed in the parish church of blessed Mary of Huntingdon on the eleventh day of December, in the year of our Lord 1442, there being present Depyng, Bug, Elvedene and I Colstone; and then my lord decreed that execution should be performed, etc.

LXIX.

THE VISITATION OF THE PRIORY OF ST. MICHAEL WITHOUT STAM-FORD, BEGUN IN THE CHAPTER-HOUSE THEREIN ON THE SIXTH DAY OF THE MONTH OF AUGUST, IN THE YEAR OF OUR LORD 1445, BY MASTER JOHN DEPYNG, CANON OF LINCOLN, LICENTIATE IN LAWS, COMMISSARY DEPUTE IN THIS BEHALF AND UNDER THIS FORM, 'WILLIAM, BY DIVINE PERMISSION,' ETC., OF THE REVEREND FATHER IN CHRIST AND LORD, THE LORD WILLIAM, BY THE GRACE OF GOD BISHOP OF LINCOLN.

In the first place, as the said sir commissary was sitting in his capacity of judge as a tribunal in the business of the beginning of such visitation on and in the day and place aforesaid, there came together before him the prioress and nuns of the said priory; and then first and before all else was read the aforesaid commission. And when this had been read, the prioress furnished the same commissary with my lord's mandate in lieu of a certificate together with the names of [the nuns] who had been summoned. The same commissary proceeded to the examination of the several persons on this wise.

Dame Elizabeth Weldone,[1] the prioress, says that the nuns are disobedient to her, taking no heed to come to her when she sends for them.

Also she says that Alice Wyteryng has the whole administration of the spiritual and temporal goods of the priory by my lord's commission, but she herself knows naught of such administration, and the said Alice renders no accounts.

Also she says that the nuns do not come together with one mind in quire at time of mass.

Also she says that Alice Wyteryng takes Alice Wermyngtone to help her abroad,[2] who has not been appointed by my lord or by the prioress.

Dame Agnes Multone, the subprioress, sworn and examined, says that Margaret Mortymere conceived and brought forth about the nativity of St. John the Baptist, and that she was punished according to the rule, but she knows not of whom she conceived or whether she bare male or female. Howbeit she was absent from quire for a fortnight. And she deposes that the prioress is incapable.

Dame Isabel Seytone agrees with the subprioress as regards Margaret Mortymere, save in this, that she brought forth on this side Easter, and concerning the incapacity of the prioress.

Thomas Haxey, treasurer of York and canon of Lincoln, who died in 1425. Nothing certain can be said of the name Daltone.

[2] *I.e.* when she went on journeys outside the house in her capacity of *administratrix temporalium.*

Item dicit quod iiij sunt claues ostii dormitorii,[1] quas habent priorissa, suppriorissa, Wyteryng et ista Seytone sacrista.

Domina Margeria Croyland iurata, examinata dicit quod tres moniales videlicet ipsamet, Wylugby et Mortymere fuerunt nominate[2] super suspicione, sed Mortymere maxime; et de impotencia priorisse dicit vt supra.

Domina Margareta Mortymere fatetur se fuisse grauidam paulo ante festum Purificacionis vltimo ad annum et non citra, et dicit quod de tempore quo administrauit parata est computare, sed Wyteryng nunquam computauit; et de impotencia priorisse deponit.

Domina Alicia Wyteryng, *iurata et examinata,* dicit quod de administracione sua nichil scribit nec computat.

Domina Elizabetha Wylugby, iurata et examinata, dicit de impotencia priorisse, et dicit quod non constat conuentui de statu domus eo quod nullus redditus est compotus, et si Wyteryng foret mortua que habet administracionem, non constaret de statu in quo est; nam credit quod quasi *ad* vltimatam deducitur inopiam.

Domina Alicia Wermyngtone dicit quod priorissa est sibi nimis rigorosa in correccione, nam pro leuibus punit eam rigorose; et dicit de impotencia priorisse.

Domina Margeria Morwode iurata, examinata dicit omnia bene.

Domina Anna Daltone, iurata et examinata, dicit quod fama fuit quod Mortymere peperit citra Pascha.

Domina Alicia Haxey, iurata et examinata, dicit et concordat cum Daltone.

Quibus examinatis et iterum conuocatis, idem commissarius continuauit visitacionem huiusmodi in statu quo nunc est vsque proximum diem iuridicum post festum Purificacionis beate Marie proxime futurum et ad quemlibet diem citra quo dominus declinare vel mittere ad locum voluerit.

LXX.

[Fo. 76].

VISITACIO PRIORATUS DE STYKESWOLDE, ORDINIS CISTERCIENSIS, LINCOLNIENSIS DIOCESIS, FACTA ET INCHOATA IN DOMO CAPITULARI EIUSDEM XXIII⁰ DIE MENSIS JULII, ANNO DOMINI MCCCCXL⁰, PER VENERABILEM VIRUM MAGISTRUM JOHANNEM DEPYNGE, IN LEGIBUS LICENCIATUM, CANONICUM ECCLESIE LINCOLNIENSIS, REUERENDI IN CHRISTO PATRIS ET DOMINI, DOMINI WILLELMI, GRACIA[3] LINCOLNIENSIS EPISCOPI, COMMISSARIUM IN HAC PARTE SPECIALITER DEPUTATUM, ETC.

Sedente dicto domino commissario iudicialiter pro tribunali in dicte visitacionis negocio inchoando die et loco superius descriptis,[4]

---

[1] *Priorissa habet vnam* cancelled.
[2] *Sic*: one would expect *notate.*
[3] *Sic*: *Dei* omitted.
[4] *est* cancelled.

[1] 2 Feb., 1445-6.

Also she says that there are four keys of the dorter door, which the prioress, the subprioress, Wyteryng and this Seytone, who is sacrist, do keep.

Dame Margery Croyland, sworn, says on examination that three nuns, to wit, herself, Wylugby and Mortymere, have been named on suspicion, but Mortymere chiefly; and concerning the incapacity of the prioress she says as above.

Dame Margaret Mortymere confesses that she was pregnant a little before the feast of the Purification a year back, and not since, and she says that she is prepared to account for the time wherein she had administration, but Wyteryng has never accounted; and she deposes concerning the incapacity of the prioress.

Dame Alice Wyteryng, sworn and examined, says that she writes down nothing nor makes an account of her administration.

Dame Elizabeth Wylugby, sworn and examined, speaks of the incapacity of the prioress, and she says that the convent is not certain of the state of the house because no account is rendered, and if Wyteryng, who has the administration, were dead, there would be no certainty of the state in which it is; for she believes that it is brought almost to the extreme point of poverty.

Dame Alice Wermyngtone says that the prioress is too harsh to her when she corrects her; for she punishes her severely for trifles; and she speaks of the incapacity of the prioress.

Dame Margery Morwode, sworn, says on examination all things are well.

Dame Anne Daltone, sworn and examined, says that rumour was that Mortymere brought forth on this side Easter.

Dame Alice Haxey, sworn and examined, says and agrees with Daltone.

Now when these had been examined and called together again, the same commissary adjourned such visitation in the state wherein it now is until the next law-day after the feast of the Purification of blessed Mary next to come,[1] and to any day on this side thereof whereon it shall be my lord's will to come down or to send to the place.

LXX.

THE VISITATION OF THE PRIORY OF STIXWOULD, OF THE ORDER OF CÎTEAUX, OF THE DIOCESE OF LINCOLN, PERFORMED AND BEGUN IN THE CHAPTER-HOUSE OF THE SAME ON THE TWENTY-THIRD DAY OF THE MONTH OF JULY, IN THE YEAR OF OUR LORD 1440, BY THE WORSHIPFUL MASTER JOHN DEPYNGE, LICENTIATE IN LAWS, CANON OF THE CHURCH OF LINCOLN, COMMISSARY SPECIALLY DEPUTE IN THIS BEHALF, ETC., OF THE REVEREND FATHER IN CHRIST AND LORD, THE LORD WILLIAM, BY THE GRACE [OF GOD] BISHOP OF LINCOLN.

As the said sir commissary was sitting in his capacity of judge as a tribunal in the beginning of the business of the said visitation on and in the day and place above described, there appeared before him

comparuerunt personaliter coram eo priorissa et conuentus dicti loci;
et deinde ante omnia propositum fuit verbum Dei per honestum virum
magistrum Thomam Duffelde, in sacra theologia bacallarium, sequentem
hoc thema, 'Querantur regi virgines et speciose puelle,' etc.[1] Quo
finito in lingua materna, priorissa dicti loci liberauit dicto domino commissario certificatorium mandati sibi a domino in hac parte directi,
confectum in hec verba, 'Reuerendo in Christo patri,' etc. Quo recepto
et publice perlecto, priorissa exhibuit dicto domino commissario confirmacionem eleccionis sue factam per dudum magistrum Robertum
Leeke, tunc canonicum Lincolniensem, vigore commissionis domini
Willelmi, nuper Lincolniensis episcopi, sibi in hac parte facte. Exhibuit
eciam installacionem suam per officialem archidiaconi Lincolniensis
factam. Quibus exhibitis, priorissa[2] iurauit obedienciam et fidelitatem
domino in forma consueta; et deinde exhibuit fundacionem prioratus
factam per Luciam, tunc comitissam Lincolnie, in qua nullus certus
habetur numerus monialium habendarum in ipso prioratu. Exhibicionem
status domus et fundaciones cantariarum dictus dominus commissarius
reseruauit ipsi domino.

Domina Elianora Welby, priorissa, petit vt omnes[3] existentes in
choro temporibus horarum et vesperorum et matutinarum, tam in superioribus quam in inferioribus stallis stantes, possint stare et sedere
vniformiter, non obstante consuetudine contraria, que est vt stantes
in superiori gradu stabunt dum in[4] sedent in inferiori.

Domina Margareta Kele, suppriorissa, dicit quod sunt v diuerse
et distincte familie monialium.

Domina Alicia Thorntone dicit quod iuuenes seculares femine viij
vel x annorum iacent de nocte in dormitorio, in lectis tamen separatis.

Item dicit quod in superiori refectorio vescuntur piscibus et lacticiniis,
et in inferiori carnibus.

Item dicit quod domus indebitatur, vt credit, in octoginta marcis
et amplius: nescit tamen quod domus potest expendere.

Item dicit quod domina Elizabetha Dymmok et domina Margareta
Tylney, vidue, sunt perhendinantes cum priorissa, et eciam earum
seruitrices.

Item quod celleraria habet duas adultas mulieres[5] infra claustralia
loca secum perhendinantes.

Item dicit quod quelibet monialis[6] percipit in anno j porcum, vnam
ouem, j quarterium carnis bouine, ij petras butiri, iij petras casei, qualibet
die in Aduentu et Quadragesima iij alleces, vj pisces salsos et xij fungeas
in anno; et solebant habere ad vesturam vj s. viij d., sed iam pluribus
annis nichil de vestura perceperunt.

---

[1] Esther II, 2, slightly altered. Cf. p. 347 above: Duffelde evidently repeated
his sermon from this ingeniously chosen text at St. Michael's, Stamford, on the
following 21 October.

[2] *exhibuit* cancelled.

[3] *s* cancelled.

[4] *Sic*: this should have been cancelled.

[5] *sibi seruientes in officio suo* cancelled.

[6] Altered from *monialibus*.

[1] Neither the commission nor its return remain in Gray's register. See *Visitations* I, 160. For Robert Leek see *ibid.* I, 212 and II, note 1. He died in 1434-5.

in person the prioress and convent of the said place; and then before all else the word of God was set forth by the honest master Thomas Duffelde, bachelor in divinity, after this text, ' Let virgins and fair maids be sought for the king,' etc.   And when this had been brought to an end in the mother tongue, the prioress of the said place delivered to the said sir commissary the certificate of the mandate addressed to her by my lord in this behalf, composed in these words, ' To the reverend father in Christ,' etc.   The which having been received and read through in public, the prioress exhibited to the said sir commissary the certificate of the confirmation of her election made by the late master Robert Leeke, then canon of Lincoln, by virtue of the commission of the lord William, late bishop of Lincoln, given to him in this behalf.   She exhibited also the certificate of her installation performed by the official of the archdeacon of Lincoln.[1]   And having exhibited these, the prioress sware obedience and fealty to my lord in the form accustomed; and then she exhibited the foundation of the priory made by Lucy, then countess of Lincoln, wherein is contained no fixed number of the nuns to be maintained in the same priory.[2]   The presentation of the state of the house and the foundations of the chantries the said sir commissary reserved for my lord himself.

Dame Eleanor Welby, the prioress,[3] prays that all who are in quire during the hours and vespers and matins, both they that have their places in the upper and in the lower stalls, may be able to stand and sit after one manner, notwithstanding the contrary custom, which is that they that have their places in the upper row shall stand while they in the lower do sit.

Dame Margaret Kele, the subprioress, says that there are five different and separate households of nuns.

Dame Alice Thorntone says that young secular folk female, of eight or ten years old, do lie in the dorter, but in separate beds.

Also she says that they feed on flesh and milk-foods in the upper frater and on flesh in the lower.[4]

Also she says that the house, as she believes, is eighty marks and upward in debt: howbeit she knows not what the house is able to spend.

Also she says that dame Elizabeth Dymmok and dame Margaret Tylney, widows, and also their serving-maids, are lodgers with the prioress.

Also that the cellaress has two grown-up women lodging with her within the cloister precincts.

Also she says that every nun receives in the year one pig, one sheep, a quarter of beef, two stones of butter, three stones of cheese, every day in Advent and Lent three herrings, six salt fish and twelve dough-cakes[5] a year; and they were wont to have 6s. 8d. for their raiment, but for several years back as regards raiment they have received nothing.

---

[2] For documents relating to Stixwould, see *Monasticon* v, 724-7.   For the countess Lucy see *Visitations* I, 160.

[3] The names of the nuns, Welby, Pygot, Paynelle, Dymmoke, Folgeham, are those of gentle families in Lincolnshire or near its borders.   Kele (Keal), Thorntone, Leke (Leake) and Bostone are names derived from Lincolnshire places.   Shirwode (Sherwood) appears to come from Nottinghamshire.   Littelbury, Welhouse and Scupholme are uncertain; but the last two at any rate seem to be of local origin.

[4] See note on the Nuncoton visitation, p. 249, note 4.

[5] For *fungeas*, the word in the original, see Ducange, s.v. Fingia.

Item dicit quod, vt credit, sunt mares et femine perhendinantes cum diuersis monialibus circa xviij in numero, non excedentes in etate xiiij vel xvj annos.

Domina Johanna Pygot dicit quod quasi nichil percipiunt nec a pluribus annis, eciam xx, perceperunt ad vesturam suam; et dicit de infantibus iacentibus in dormitorio vt supra.

Item dicit quod ordinatum et iniunctum est per dominum Ricardum, nuper Lincolniensem episcopum, in visitacione sua quod satisfieret omni anno monialibus de habitu suo, et tamen non est eis in aliquo super hoc satisfactum.

Domina Katerina Leke nichil deponit.

Domina Elizabetha Eylewarde dicit quod omnia bene.

Domina Elizabetha Paynelle, stans in infirmaria, dicit quod omnia bene.

Domina Anna Stynt dicit omnia bene.

Domina Elizabetha Welby dicit omnia bene.

Domina Matildis Bostone dicit omnia bene.

Domina Matilda Shirwode dicit de infantibus iacentibus in dormitorio.

Domina Etheldreda Littelbury dicit omnia bene.

Domina Alicia Welhouse dicit omnia bene.

Domina Alicia Paynelle dicit omnia bene.

Est ibidem quedam suspecta mulier manens infra loca claustralia, nomine Johanna Bartone, ad quam quidam Willelmus Traherne habuit suspectum accessum, trahens eam postea in causa matrimoniali coram iudice ecclesiastico, et est multum infesta monialibus.

[Fo. 76 *d.*] Domina Milicencia Leke dicit omnia bene.

Domina Elizabetha Dymmoke dicit quod omnia bene.

Domina Katerina Leke dicit quod stetit monialis quatuor annis, et nichil recepit hoc tempore ad vesturam.

Domina Anna Bate dicit omnia bene.

Domina E*lizabetha*[1] Scupholme dicit[2] omnia bene.

Domina Alicia Folgeham dicit quod per infirmitates adeo est attenuata quod non potest vllo modo ire neque vix portari; et ideo cum[3] non habeat qui ferant eam ad ecclesiam pro missis audiendis, ideo non audit missis[4] nisi cum communicatur vel raro in principalibus festis.

[INJUNCTIONS.]

[Fo. 75 *d.*] Stykeswolde.

Wyllyam, by the suffraunce of God bysshope of Lincolne, to our wele belufede doghters in Criste the pryoresse and the couent of the priory of Stykeswolde, of the ordere of Cistews, of our diocise, *sendethe helthe, grace and his blessyng.*[5] For as mykelle as in our visitacyon late made in your place we fonde certeyn defautes that nede correccyone, we sende yow as for correccyone of the saide defautes certeyn iniunccyones to be keppede as hit is here benethe *conteynede.*

---

[1] Altered from *Elena.*
[2] *ob* cancelled.
[3] *h* cancelled.
[4] *Sic*: for *missas.*

Also she says that, as she believes, there are males and females, about eighteen in number, who board with divers nuns, not passing fourteen or sixteen years in age.

Dame Joan Pygot says that they receive and for several years, even twenty, they have received almost nothing for their raiment; and she says as above concerning the children that lie in the dorter.

Also she says that it was ordained and enjoined by the lord Richard, late bishop of Lincoln, at his visitation,[1] that every year the nuns should have satisfactory provision for their habit, and yet satisfaction has not been done them in aught touching this.

Dame Katherine Leke deposes nothing.

Dame Elizabeth Eylewarde says that all things are well.

Dame Elizabeth Paynelle, abiding in the infirmary, says that all things are well.

Dame Anne Stynt says all things are well.

Dame Elizabeth Welby says all things are well.

Dame Maud Bostone says all things are well.

Dame Maud Shirwode speaks of the children that lie in the dorter.

Dame Audrey Littelbury says all things are well.

Dame Alice Welhouse says all things are well.

Dame Alice Paynelle says all things are well.

There is in the same place a woman suspect who dwells within the cloister precincts, Joan Bartone by name, to whom one William Traherne has had suspicious access, bringing her thereafter before the ecclesiastical judge in a matrimonial suit, and she is very troublesome to the nuns.

Dame Millicent Leke says all things are well.

Dame Elizabeth Dymmoke says that all things are well.

Dame Katherine Leke says that she has continued a nun for four years and during this time has received naught for her raiment.

Dame Anne Bate says all things are well.

Dame Elizabeth Scupholme says all things are well.

Dame Alice Folgeham says that by reason of her infirmities she is worn so thin that she can in no wise walk and scarcely be carried; and therefore, since she has none to bear her to church to hear mass, she hears mass only when communion is given her or now and then on the chief festivals.

In the fyrst, for as muche as we fynde that euery nunne shulde yerely haue of the commune godes of the house to hire vesture vj s. viij d., the whiche somme was not payed this xx yere, and also our predecessour sir Richard Flemmyng, late bysshope of Lincolne, in his visitacyone ordeynede and enioynede that fro that tyme forthe hit shulde be satisfiede to the nunnes of your house of the saide somme, we, folowyng bothe the laudable custome of your house here yn and also the ordynaúnce of our sayde predecessour,[2] chargees[3] yow, prioresse, in vertue of your

---

[5] Written at top of page: *salutacyon in God wythe our blessyng* cancelled.

[1] This is not recorded in Flemyng's register, nor is there any trace of the date of his visitation.

[2] *we* cancelled.

[3] *Sic.*

obedience and vndere peyne of greuous contempte, that fro hense forthe wythe owtene any excusacyone or delaye ye paye to euery nunne the somme aforesaide in forme aforesaide, so that thai haue no cause to please seculers owtwarde for getyng of *goode*. And that this ordynaunce of our saide predecessour has not bene kepped, we reserue the punysshyng ther of to our selfe.[1]

Also we enioyne and charge yow, prioresse, *sicut in 5 iniunccione Nuncotome*.[2]

Also we enioyne and charge *yow*, pryoresse, vndere peynes obofe and benethe here writene, that fro hense forthe ye suffre no seculere persones, women ne children, lyg by nyght in the dormytorye ne wythe yune the cloystere, but[3] suche as are honeste and necessarye seruaundes and not manye; and in especyalle that in alle haste possyble ye remeve oon Janet Bartone fro wythe ynne the cloystere for diuerse causes that meve hus, the whilk we wylle not declare at this tyme.[4]

Also we charge and enioyne yow, prioresse, in lyke wyse that ye receyve ne holde no suiournauntes, men, women ne childerne, wythe ynne your place, and thoe that nowe are there, ye[5] voyde thaym wythe yn a quartere of a yere after the receyvyng of these our lettres, but if

LXXI.

[Fo. 38 *d*.]

Visitacio prioratus de STONLEE, ordinis Sancti Augustini, Lincolniensis diocesis, facta in domo capitulari ibidem XX⁰ die mensis nouembris, anno domini MCCCCXLIJ⁰, per reuerendum in Christo patrem et dominum, dominum Willelmum, Dei gracia Lincolniensem episcopum, anno suarum consecracionis XVIJ⁰ et translacionis VIJ⁰.

In primis sedente dicto reuerendo patre iudicialiter in dicta domo capitulari die et anno predictis comparuerunt coram eo prior et singuli canonici loci illius; et deinde eos allo[que]batur sub hiis vel similibus verbis: ' Cum sim hic iam presens et intendam nunc vel postea visitare vos, adeo equaliter bene possum hoc iam fa[cere] sicuti aliquo futuro tempore; quodque si sic et non nunc oporteret me pro tunc dirigere vobis priori literas pro visitacione huiusmodi facienda, ideo volo exequi officium meum ac si tempus hoc vobis prius assignandum.' Et deinde amotis omnibus a domo capitulari preter priorem processit ad inquisicionem suam preparatoriam et ipsum priorem super corrigendis inquisiuit, qui inquisitus dicit vt sequitur.

---

[1] Founded on Alice Thorntone's sixth, Joan Pygot's first and second and Katherine Leke's *detecta*.

[2] This injunction concerns the receiving of nuns for money or beyond the resources of the house. The evidence appears to depend upon the *detecta* on which the previous injunction is founded.

[3] *of* cancelled.

[4] Founded on Alice Thornton's first, Joan Pygot's first and Maud Shirwode's *detecta*, and the *compertum* inserted after Alice Paynelle's evidence.

[5] *w* cancelled.

ye here yn hafe specyalle licence of hus or our successours, bysshops of Lincolne, except our wele belufede doghters, dame Elizabethe Dymmok and dame Margarete Tylney, by whose abydyng, as we truste, no greve but rathere avayle is procured to your place.[1]

Also we enioyne yowe, prioresse, vndere the same peynes that euery yere betwix Myghelmesse and Martynmesse ye shewe a fulle and a playne accompte of alle the revenues of your place, and how thai are dispendede to the couent in playn chapitre, or to suche persones as the couent wylle assigne ther to, so that the couent mowe hafe knawlage how hit standes wythe your house.[2]

Also we enioyne, etc., *vt in xij iniunccione Nuncotome*.[3]

Also, for as muche as we conceyve ther is custome in your qwere that nunnes in the ouere *stalles*[4] shalle *stande*[5] the while thoe in the nether[6] stalles sytte, at your peticyone, so that your obseruaunces regulere be not hurte ther by, we wylle and ordeyne that alle vnyformely stande or sytte at ones as wele on that one syde of the qwere as of that othere.[7]

More ouer we monysshe yow and yche oon of yowe ones, twyes and thryes peremptoryly, etc.

LXXI.

THE VISITATION OF THE PRIORY OF STONELY, OF THE ORDER OF ST. AUSTIN, OF THE DIOCESE OF LINCOLN, PERFORMED IN THE CHAPTER-HOUSE THERE ON THE TWENTIETH DAY OF THE MONTH OF NOVEMBER, IN THE YEAR OF OUR LORD 1442, BY THE REVEREND FATHER IN CHRIST AND LORD, THE LORD WILLIAM, BY THE GRACE OF GOD BISHOP OF LINCOLN, IN THE SEVENTEENTH YEAR OF HIS CONSE-CRATION AND THE SEVENTH OF HIS TRANSLATION.

In the first place, as the said reverend father was sitting in his capacity of judge in the said chapter-house, on and in the day and year aforesaid, there appeared before him the prior and the several canons of that place; and he then addressed them in these or in like words: ' Seeing that I am now here present, and intend to visit you now or here-after, I can do this now fully as well as at any future time; and because, if I did so [then] and not now, it would be necessary for me for that occasion to address a letter to you the prior for the holding of such visita-tion, I will therefore perform my office as though this were the time that should be appointed you beforehand.'[8] And then, when all save the prior had been removed from the chapter-house, he proceeded to his preliminary inquiry, and made inquiry of the prior touching matters in need of correction; and he upon inquiry says as follows.

---

[1] See Alice Thorntone's fourth, fifth and seventh *detecta*.

[2] See Alice Thorntone's third *detectum*.

[3] This injunction concerns the grant of corrodies, etc., for which in this case there is no direct evidence.

[4] Interlined above *gree* cancelled.

[5] Interlined above *sytte* cancelled.

[6] *gree stande* cancelled.

[7] See the prioress's petition to this effect.

[8] This visitation, conducted informally, was soon followed by the visitation of the rest of the archdeaconry of Huntingdon (*Visitations* II, xxxviii). Stonely, lying close to Kimbolton, was only five to six miles from Buckden, and the bishop probably took advantage of a spare day to visit it.

Frater Henricus, prior, dicit quod frater Willelmus Higham habet frequentes et suspectos accessus ad villam de Kymbolton, bibendo et commedendo ibidem cum secularibus, nulla licencia exeundi a priore petita vel obtenta. Monitus est et sic omnes moniti sunt quod ab[sti]neant penitus a[1] tali exeundi modo non habita licencia a priore vel eius deputato sub pena excomunicacionis.

Item idem frater Willelmus detinet et detinuit[2] a priore a tempore confirmacionis sue et detinet xij vel xj cocliaria argentea de bo[nis] communibus prioratus. Monitus est sub pena excommunicacionis quod ea liberet priori infra xij dies sub pena excommunicacionis.[3]

Item quod frater Johannes Stonlee nuper prior detinet a priore nunc diuersa cartas euidencias et munimenta concernencia possessiones do[mus]. Monitus est sub pena excommunicaciones quod ea liberet priori infra vnum mensem.

Frater Johannes Stonlee nuper prior dicit omnia bene.

Frater Johannes Stokes dicit quod corrodarii habentes de corrodiis suis esculenta et poculenta ad domos suas nichilominus quasi omni die comedunt cum priore sumptibus domus et in sessione in mensa preferentur[4] canonicis, quod egre gerunt canonici. Monitus est prior quod in mensa sua canonicos secularibus preferat, nisi talis grauis vel honesta superuenit persona que ex necessario erit[5] preferenda, et quod corrodiarii contententur corrodiis suis et non sic decetero onerent domum.

Frater Willelmus Derham dicit quod domus oneratur ere alieno sed nescitur in quanto, quia prior non reddit compotum. Prior monitus est sub pena priuacionis quod infra quemlibet annum confirmacionis sue reddat compotum conuentui vel electis per conuentum.

Frater Willelmus Higham dicit quod non constat conuentui de statu domus, quia prior non computauit de tempore suo, et dicit quod prior omnia facit de consilio secularium spreto aduisamento conuentus. Iniunctum est priori quod nichil arduum faciat nisi de consensu conuentus.

Item dicit quod plures de cognacione prioris sustentantur de communibus bonis domus preter voluntatem conuentus.

Frater Walterus de Sancto Neoto dicit quod prior ignorante conuentu conuenit cum quodam capellano de vno corrodio sibi vendendo, et quod iocalia domus impignorantur de sciencia secularium et non conuentus et an restituantur impignorata nescitur: ideo timetur de alienacione. Iniunctum est priori sub pena amocionis et priuacionis perpetue quod nulla decetero vendat corrodia nisi habita licencia diocesani et de consensu conuentus vel maioris partis. Et hiis ita factis reseruata potestate faciendi iniuncciones dissoluit dominus hanc visitacionem.

---

[1] A word cancelled.
[2] *a tempore* cancelled.
[3] *Sic*: repeated.
[4] *Sic*: for *preferuntur*.
[5] Apparently altered from *esse*.

[1] Neither his surname nor the date of his institution are recorded. Apart from Stonlee (Stonely) and St. Neots, the surnames are uncertain. Higham, however, is probably Higham Ferrers, only a few miles distant, and Derham should be Dereham in Norfolk.
[2] The hamlet of Stonely nearly adjoins Kimbolton on S.E.
[3] This appears to be the meaning of the passage as it stands, but the wording is curious. It is not unlikely that *confirmacionis* in the original is an error, and

Brother Henry the prior[1] says that brother William Higham has often and suspect access to the town of Kimbolton,[2] drinking and eating therein with secular folk, having asked or had no leave to go out from the prior. He was admonished, and so all were admonished, to abstain utterly from such manner of going out without leave had of the prior or his deputy, under pain of excommunication.

Also the same brother William withholds and has withheld from the prior, ever since he was confirmed, and [still] withholds twelve or eleven silver spoons of the common goods of the priory. He was admonished under pain of excommunication to deliver them to the prior within twelve days.

Also that brother John Stonlee, the late prior, withholds from the present prior divers charters, title-deeds and muniments which concern the possessions of the house. He was admonished under pain of excommunication to deliver them to the prior within a month.

Brother John Stonlee, the late prior, says all things are well.

Brother John Stokes says that the corrodiers, who have from their corrodies food and drink at their own houses, do nevertheless mess with the prior almost every day at the costs of the house, and, when they sit at table, are put before the canons, which the canons take ill. The prior was admonished to set the canons above secular persons at his board, unless so important or noble a person comes thereto that precedence must necessarily be given to him; and that the corrodiers shall be content with their corrodies and not burthen the house on this wise henceforward.

Brother William Derham says that the house is burthened with debt, but it is not known to what extent, because the prior does not render an account. The prior was admonished under pain of deprivation to render an account [for the period] within every year since his confirmation[3] to the convent or to persons chosen by the convent.

Brother William Higham says that the convent is not certain of the state of the house, because the prior has not rendered an account in his time; and he says that the prior does all things with the advice of secular folk, setting at naught the counsel of the convent. The prior was enjoined to do no weighty business[4] without the consent of the convent.

Also he says that several of the prior's kindred are maintained out of the common goods of the house, contrary to the will of the convent.

Brother Walter of St. Neots says that the prior, without the knowledge of the convent, made a covenant with a certain chaplain to sell him a corrody, and that the jewels of the house are put in pawn with the knowledge of secular folk and not of the convent, and it is not known whether the things put in pawn are restored: therefore there is fear that they are alienated. The prior was enjoined under pain of removal and perpetual deprivation to sell no corrodies henceforth, without having the licence of the diocesan and without the consent of the convent or the more part thereof. And, when these things had been done thus, my lord, having reserved the power of making injunctions, prorogued this visitation.

---

that *administracionis* is the word intended. If so, the meaning is much improved: 'to render an account of his administration within every year.'

  [4] See note on *arduum negotium, Visitations* I, 220.

LXXII.

VISITACIO PRIORATUS DE STODELEY, ORDINIS SANCTI BENEDICTI, LINCOLNIENSIS DIOCESIS, FACTA IN DOMO CAPITULARI IBIDEM XXVJ DIE MENSIS MAII, ANNO DOMINI MCCCCXLV, PER REUERENDUM IN CHRISTO PATREM ET DOMINUM, DOMINUM WILLELMUM ALNE-WYKE, DEI GRACIA LINCOLNIENSEM EPISCOPUM, SUARUM CONSE-CRACIONIS ANNO XIX ET TRANSLACIONIS NONO.

In primis sedente dicto reuerendo patre iudicialiter in huiusmodi visitacione sua die et loco predictis, comparuerunt coram eo priorissa et moniales dicti prioratus, parate vt apparuit ad subeundum visitacionem huiusmodi; et deinde primo et ante omnia honorabilis vir magister Johannes Beuerley, sacre pagine professor, proposuit verbum Dei in lingua vulgari sequens hoc thema ' Surge, propera, amica mea, et veni,' etc.[1] Quo laudabiliter finito priorissa dicti loci certificatorium mandati domini sibi pro huiusmodi visitacione subeunda directi in forma concep-tum dicto reuerendo patri reuerenter liberauit, cuius tenor talis est, ' Reuerendo in Christo,' etc. Quo in publica audiencia perlecto, eadem priorissa liberauit dicto reuerendo patri confirmacionem eleccionis sue. Installacionem vero non exhibuit, quia missa erat Londonias pro libera-cione temporalium. Ideo dominus assignauit sibi quemlibet diem citra festum Sancti Michaelis proxime futurum vbicunque dominus fuerit infra diocesim ad exhibendum installacionem huiusmodi. Et deinde iurauit eadem priorissa canonicam obedienciam et fidelitatem, etc., vt in forma, etc. ; et deinde examinata dicit ea que sequuntur. Et mandatum est ei quod exhibeat fundacionem et statum domus.

Domina Elianora Cobcote, priorissa, dicit quod moniales licenciate sunt de visitando amicos suos non vltra iij vel iiij dies.

Item dicit quod moniales vtuntur velis et velaminibus sericis.

Et iniunctum est quod faciat sorores suas gerere vela sua vsque supercilia.

Soror Margareta Niernute, suppriorissa. Non habent confessorem assignatum per dominum.

Soror Agnes Devyle, tercia priorissa, dicit quod vltima priorissa que stetit lviij annis nunquam reddidit compotum in toto tempore suo, nec ista priorissa que non stetit per vnum annum : ideo ignorat statum domus, nec sciunt quantum possit domus expendere. Dominus iniunxit priorisse et Thome Halle senescallo quod omni anno exhibeant plenum statum domus in comuni coram conuentu.

---

[1] Cant. II, 10 : ' Surge, propera, amica mea, columba mea, formosa mea, et veni.'

[1] No record of these documents remains. See *Visitations* I, 158. It is obvious that Eleanor Cobcote was elected in 1444 or early in 1445.

[2] This charter and others are printed in *Monasticon* IV, 252-5, from a chartulary then in the possession of Thomas Allen, fellow of Gloucester hall (Worcester college), Oxon.

[3] The names of the nuns derived from places, although not to be identified with certainty, suggest a midland and more or less local origin. The names Niernute or Nernewte and Devyle (Deyvile or Dayvile), which appears in Walton D'Eiville.

LXXII.

THE VISITATION OF THE PRIORY OF STUDLEY, OF THE ORDER OF ST. BENET, OF THE DIOCESE OF LINCOLN, PERFORMED IN THE CHAPTER-HOUSE THEREIN ON THE TWENTY-SIXTH DAY OF THE MONTH OF MAY, IN THE YEAR OF OUR LORD 1445, BY THE REVEREND FATHER IN CHRIST AND LORD, THE LORD WILLIAM ALNEWYKE, BY THE GRACE OF GOD BISHOP OF LINCOLN, IN THE NINETEENTH YEAR OF HIS CONSECRATION AND THE NINTH OF HIS TRANSLATION.

In the first place, as the said reverend father was sitting in his capacity of judge in such his visitation on and in the day and place aforesaid, there appeared before him the prioress and nuns of the said priory, in readiness, as was apparent, to undergo such visitation; and then first and before all else the honourable master John Beverley, professor of holy writ, set forth the word of God in the vulgar tongue after this text, 'Arise, make haste, my love, and come,' etc. And when this was come to a praiseworthy end, the prioress of the said place delivered reverently to the said reverend father the certificate of my lord's mandate which had been addressed to her for the undergoing of such visitation, formally composed, the purport whereof is on such wise, 'To the reverend [father] in Christ,' etc. And when this had been read through in the general hearing, the same prioress delivered to the said reverend father the certificate of the confirmation of her election. But that of her installation she did not exhibit, because it had been sent to London for the delivery of the temporalities.[1] Therefore my lord appointed her any day on this side Michaelmas next to come, wheresoever my lord shall be within the diocese, to exhibit such certificate of installation. And then the same prioress sware canonical obedience and fealty, etc., as in form, etc.; and then on examination she says these things which follow. And she was commanded to exhibit the foundation[2] and the state of the house.

Dame Eleanor Cobcote,[3] the prioress, says that the nuns are given leave to visit their friends for not more than three or four days.

Also she says that the nuns wear silken veils and robes.

And she was enjoined to cause her sisters to wear their veils [down] to their eyebrows.

Sister Margaret Niernute, the subprioress. They have not a confessor appointed them by my lord.

Sister Agnes Devyle, the third prioress, says that the last prioress, who continued for fifty-eight years,[4] never rendered an account in all her time, nor has this prioress, who has not continued for a year: therefore she knows naught of the state of the house, nor do they know how much the house may be able to spend. My lord enjoined upon the prioress and Thomas Halle, the steward, that every year they shall exhibit the full state of the house in common before the convent.

Warwicks., are those of gentle families. The Neyrenutes were a Buckinghamshire family, from the neighbourhood of Aylesbury.

[4] She had actually been prioress for some fifty-five or fifty-six years. Agnes Attehall was elected on the death of Elizabeth Fremantell, and her election was confirmed 11 Dec., 1388 (Reg. xi, ff. 309 d., 310).

Soror Elizabetha Nernewte, precentrix, quo ad statum domus et valorem concordat cum tercia priorissa.

Soror Isabella Bartone.

Dicitur quod est magna confluencia hospitum secularium ad[1] predictam Isabellam et ad eius cameram.

Soror Johanna Berewelle dicit omnia bene.

Soror Alicia Merstone, tacite expressa,[2] dicit quod omnia bene.

Soror Cristina Felde, in religione per biennium et etatis xiij annorum, dicit quod Alicia Godefray, seruiens in prioratu, iniecit manus [viole]ntas Alicie Merstone infra ecclesiam.

Petitur quod vicarius de Burcestria, qui reputatur mature discrecionis et etatis ac competentis sciencie, assignetur conuentui in [con]fessorem et nullatinus scolaris Oxoniensis, cum non sit sanum vt scolares Oxonienses habeant causam accedendi ad prioratum.

. . . . die Maii dominus dictis die et loco capitulari iudicialiter sedens, conuocatis coram eo priorissa et conuentu ac reseruata potestate faciendi iniuncciones, hanc [suam vi]sitacionem dissoluit.

LXXIII.

[Fo. 86 d.]

VISITACIO PRIORATUS DE THORNHOLME, ORDINIS SANCTI AUGUSTINI, LINCOLNIENSIS DIOCESIS, FACTA IN DOMO CAPITULARI IBIDEM XIIJ[o3] DIE MENSIS APRILIS, ANNO DOMINI MCCCCXL, PER REUERENDUM IN CHRISTO PATREM ET DOMINUM, DOMINUM WILLELMUM, DEI GRACIA LINCOLNIENSEM EPISCOPUM, ANNO SUARUM CONSECRACIONIS XIIIJ[o] ET TRANSLACIONIS QUARTO.

In primis sedente dicto reuerendo patre in huiusmodi visitacionis sue negocio iudicialiter pro tribunali die, anno et loco predictis, comparuerunt personaliter coram eo prior et vij canonici, conuentum ibidem vt apparuit facientes, parati eciam vt apparuit visitacionem huiusmodi subituri.[4] Et deinde primo et ante omnia propositum fuit verbum Dei sermone latino secundum auditorium et hoc thema, 'Omnia secundum ordinem in vobis fiant,' etc.[5] Quo finito prior dicti loci liberauit dicto reuerendo patri certificatorium mandati domini sibi pro hac visitacione directi sub hac forma, 'Reuerendo,' etc.; quo perlecto et preconizatis omnibus et comparentibus, vno excepto qui infirmatur et in infirmaria residet, et[6] deinde prior exhibuit quandam cartam cuiusdam Maleherbe, primi donatoris loci in quo situs est prioratus, loco et nomine fundacionis.

---

[1] *fam* cancelled.

[2] *Sic*: *professa* appears to be meant.

[3] Altered from xiij[o].

[4] *Sic*: for *subire*.

[5] 1 Cor. XIV, 40: see p. *219*, note 1. The preacher was probably Duffeld, who had chosen this text at Markby and Ulverscroft in 1438.

[6] *Sic*: *et* is otiose.

[1] *I.e.* a novice who had worn the habit for a whole year. See *Visitations* II, 15, note 2, and see p. 348, note 2.

[2] See *Visitations* II, 35, note 4.

Sister Elizabeth Nernewte, the precentress, agrees with the third prioress as regards the state of the house and its worth.

Sister Isabel Bartone.

It is said that there is great recourse of secular guests to the aforesaid Isabel and to her chamber.

Sister Joan Berewelle says all things are well.

Sister Alice Merstone, tacitly professed,[1] says that all things are well.

Sister Christine Felde, for two years in religion and of the age of thirteen years, says that Alice Godefray, servant in the priory, laid violent hands upon Alice Merstone within the church.

It is prayed that the vicar of Bicester,[2] who is reckoned to be of ripe judgment and age and sufficient knowledge, may be appointed as confessor to the convent, and in no wise an Oxford scholar, since it is not healthy that scholars from Oxford should have a reason for coming to the priory.

On the . . . day of May my lord, sitting in his capacity of judge on and in the said day and chapter-house, having called together before him the prioress and convent and reserved the power of making injunctions, dissolved this [his] visitation.

LXXIII.

THE VISITATION OF THE PRIORY OF THORNHOLM, OF THE ORDER OF ST. AUSTIN, OF THE DIOCESE OF LINCOLN, PERFORMED IN THE CHAPTER-HOUSE THEREIN ON THE TWELFTH DAY OF THE MONTH OF APRIL, IN THE YEAR OF OUR LORD 1440, BY THE REVEREND FATHER IN CHRIST AND LORD, THE LORD WILLIAM, BY THE GRACE OF GOD BISHOP OF LINCOLN, IN THE FOURTEENTH YEAR OF HIS CONSECRATION AND THE FOURTH OF HIS TRANSLATION.

In the first place, as the said reverend father was sitting in his capacity of judge as a tribunal in the business of such his visitation, on and in the day, year and place aforesaid, there appeared in person before him the prior and seven canons, constituting, as it was apparent, the convent in that place, and in readiness also, as was apparent, to undergo such visitation. And then, first and before all else, the word of God was set forth in the Latin speech, as befitted the audience and after this text, ' Let all things be done among you in orderly wise,' etc. Now, when this was finished, the prior of the said place delivered to the said reverend father the certificate of my lord's mandate addressed to him for this visitation under this form, ' To the reverend,' etc.; and, when this had been read through and all had been called by name and made their appearance, save one who is ailing and abides in the infirmary, then the prior exhibited a charter of one Maleherbe, the first giver of the place wherein the priory is situate, in lieu and under the name of the foundation.[3]

---

[3] The foundation charter no longer survives. A jury at Lincoln, temp. John (*Monasticon* VI, 356) returned that the king was patron, and from the same return it appears that William Lungespee, who held the manor of Appleby in chief as of the honour of Peverel, subenfeoffed John Maleherbe temp. Henry II. Whatever truth there may have been in the story of the foundation of Thornholm by king Stephen, the Crown did not exercise patronage in the priory.

Postea exhibuit certificatorium abbatis nuper Thorntone, commissarii ad confirmacionem eleccionis istius nunc prioris per bone memorie dominum Willelmum nuper Lincolniensem episcopum in hac parte specialiter deputati, et nichil aliud nomine tituli exhibuit. Deinde exhibuit statum domus abbreuiatum. Requisitus prior si quid aliud habeat exhibendum pro titulo[1] incumbencie eius, dicit ea que sequuntur.

Frater Robertus Nevyle, prior, exhibitis predictis, in ceteris quo ad conuentum et religionem, dicit quod omnia bene.

Frater Willelmus Asshendone quod refectorium non seruatur quotidie secundum regulam, nec habetur lectura temporibus refeccionum.

Item dicit quod prior non visitat fratres infirmantes nec ministrat eis[2] in cibis subtilioribus quibus melius refici poterunt et recreari.

Item dicit quod silencium non seruatur secundum regulam.

Item dicit quod prior non exhibet annuum compotum nec exhibuit tempore suo nisi vnam nudam[3] visum.

Item dicit quod prior est nuper[4] crudelis in correccionibus et rigorose tractat fratres in capitulo et alibi, eciam cum verbis opprobriosis, dicens quod vix sufficiunt ad officium aquebaiulatus.

Item dicit quod prior omnia eciam ardua facit *non communicato consilio, sed*[5] absque consensu et sciencia conuentus, sed cum fecerit, tunc refert conuentui.

Item dicit quod prior vendidit diuersas grossas arbores per se: videatur igitur si precium earum contineatur in billa ministrata per priorem.

Item dicit quod crimina et defectus correcta per priorem in capitulo deteguntur et reuelantur ad extra: nescitur per quem, presumitur tamen quod per priorem.

Item dicit quod vltimo die sabbato Pasche cuidam canonico infirmato, quia non fuit sibi confessus, indixit penitenciam esus piscium in ipso die, et hoc in aula communi coram omnibus religiosis et secularibus in sui opprobrium, non obstante quod prior dedit eidem canonico generalem licenciam confitendi quando vellet.

Frater Ricardus Ellerkere dicit quod si redditus sufficerent, requireretur maior numerus canonicorum ad officiandum in diuinis.

---

[1] A letter cancelled.
[2] *Sic* cancelled.
[3] *Sic*: for *nudum*.
[4] *Sic*: possibly for *nimis*.
[5] Part of a word cancelled.

[1] There is no record of this. The last election recorded before this date is that of William Ayschendone, canon of St. Frideswide's, Oxford, who was provided, at the petition of the convent, by bishop Repyngdon at Sleaford, 8 Nov., 1413, and installed at Thornholm on the following day by the bishop's commissary (Reg. xiv, f. 136 and *d.*). This prior must have resigned by 1436, as he was still one of the convent at this time. The abbot of Thornton referred to was John Hoton, abbot 1422-39: see *Visitations* I, 122.

[2] The prior, the two Lincolns, Amcotes, Burgh, and probably Bavens, bore surnames for which it is not necessary to seek further than Lincolnshire. Asshendone, who came from St. Frideswide's, Oxford, may have derived his name from Ashendon, Bucks, or Ashdown, Berks. Ellerker and Burstall are names from the East Riding of Yorkshire.

Thereafter he exhibited the certificate of the late abbot of Thornton, the commissary for the confirmation of the election of this present prior, specially deputed in this behalf by the lord William of honest memory, late bishop of Lincoln,[1] and exhibiting nothing else under the name of title. Then he exhibited the state of the house in a shortened form. The prior, being asked if he has aught else to exhibit as the title of his incumbency, says these things which follow.

Brother Robert Nevyle, the prior,[2] having exhibited the things aforesaid, says that in other respects, as regards the convent and religious discipline, all things are well.

Brother William Asshendone [says] that frater is not kept every day according to the rule, nor do they have reading at meal-times.

Also he says that the prior does not visit the brethren who are ailing, nor does he furnish them with more delicate food wherewith they may best be refreshed and restored to health.

Also he says that silence is not observed according to the rule.

Also he says that the prior does not exhibit a yearly account, nor has he exhibited aught in his time save a bare view.[3]

Also he says that the prior is very harsh in his corrections and treats the brethren hardly in chapter and elsewhere, even with reviling words, saying that they are hardly sufficient for the office of parish clerk.[4]

Also he says that the prior does all things, even important matters, without imparting his counsel, but without the consent and knowledge of the convent; and then, after he has done them, he tells the convent.

Also he says that the prior has sold divers great trees on his own account: let it be seen therefore whether their price be contained in the bill furnished by the prior.

Also he says that the crimes and defaults corrected by the prior in chapter are disclosed and made known outside: it is not known by whom, but it is presumed that the prior is responsible.

Also he says that on last Easter Even he bade a canon who was ill do penance by eating fish on that day, because he did not confess to him, and this in the common hall in front of all the religious and secular folk to his disgrace, notwithstanding that the prior gave the same canon a general licence to confess when he would.[5]

Brother Richard Ellerkere says that, if their rents were enough, a greater number of canons would be required to do their office in divine worship.

---

[3] *I.e.* a summary exhibition of the state of the house, probably confined to mere totals of receipts and expenses.

[4] *Aquebaiulus*, the common term for the parish clerk, whose clerical status arose from his duty of carrying holy water for the *asperges* in church. The constitution of archbishop Boniface of Savoy *A nostris* (Lyndwood, ed. 1679, pp. 142, 143) decreed ' quod clericis pauperibus aquae benedictae beneficia conferantur.' The collation of the office was reserved to parochial incumbents, who were required to choose persons ' qui juxta corda eorum sciant et valeant in diuinis officiis sibi congrue deseruire, et suis velint obtemperare mandatis.' On *sciant* Lyndwood remarks that requisite knowledge included ability to read the lessons and epistles, and sing the responsories, graduals, etc.

[5] The prior might very well have argued that, even if the canon had such a licence, unwillingness to confess at Easter was a sign of unreadiness to choose any opportunity for confession.

Item dicit quod prior est quodammodo multum iracundus et de leui mouetur contra fratres.

Item dicit quod certi redditus *in Bostone* deputati ad vesturam canonicorum remanent in manibus tenencium non soluti in defectu prioris non exigentis redditus huiusmodi.

Item dicit quod propter defectum reparacionis intus et extra defectus patent ad oculum intuentis.

Frater Willelmus Lincolne dicit quod defectus ruine non reparantur, vt patet oculum[1]: ideo timetur de maiori ruina.

Item dicit de redditu non leuato vt supra.

Item dicit quod prior vendidit cuidam Edwardo vnum corrodium pro quo recepit xx li., quod stat in vij panibus certi *et melioris* ponderis quam panes et[2] conuentus, et totidem lagenas,[3] et vnam domum pro habitacione sua, certum focale nescit quantum, vnum porcum pro lardaria et vnum modum[4] pro farina.

Item vendidit aliud corrodium Johanni Cutylere ad terminum vite et coniugis sue ipso mortuo ad medietatem pro xx marcis, quod consistit in sua habitacione ad reparacionem prioris, septem similibus panibus et vij lagenis ceruisie.

Et preter ista sunt v alia corrodia antiquitus vendita.

[Fo. 87]. Frater Ricardus Burstalle dicit de[5] reparacione non facta vt supra, et hoc in defectu prioris, quia solus omnia recipit et omnia facit absque communicato consilio conuentus.

Item dicit de compoto non reddito vt supra.

Item dicit quod pecunie recepte pro boscis venditis per priorem extendunt se ad c marcas, et quod edificia propter non reparacionem deteriorantur ad xl li.[6] in defectu prioris; et istud dampnum euenit tempore istius prioris propter ipsius incuriam.

Item dicit quod habent piscatores qui capiunt victualia et stipendia de domo et nichil prosunt, et hoc propter defectum retium et propter non reparacionem ly weres et garthes in aquis.

Item dicit quod vbi iam sunt tres vel quatuor balliui vnus sufficeret ad colleccionem reddituum et emolumentorum.

Item dicit quod Willelmus Wryght, balliuus prioris ad infra, est multum infestus et improperans canonicis, nec magis eos reueretur quam vilissimum garcionem domus.

Item dicit quod prior expensis domus sustentat fratrem suum naturalem et eius filium et sustentauit per biennium, et in nullo prosunt domui.

Item dicit quod in prioratu sunt sex corrodiarii, quorum quilibet valet annuatim ad minus xl s., et duo sunt ad extra.

---

[1] *Sic*: for *oculo.*
[2] *Sic.*
[3] *Sic*: for *lagenis.* The remaining accusatives in the sentence should be ablatives.
[4] *Sic*: probably for *modium.*
[5] *non* cancelled.
[6] *li* written over some other word.

[1] Sc. of beer.
[2] A fish-garth is a dam or weir in connexion with a fishery. Thus the various fisheries in the Witham belonging to Bardney abbey were known as garths.

Also he says that the prior is, so to speak, very wrathful and is easily moved against the brethren.

Also he says that certain rents in Boston, which are applied to the raiment of the canons, remain in the hands of the tenants unpaid, in the prior's default, who does not demand such rents.

Also he says that, because of failure to make repairs, defaults are apparent within and without to the eye of one that looks thereon.

Brother William Lincolne says that defaults in ruinous buildings are not repaired, as is evident to the eye: therefore there is fear of greater dilapidation.

Also he says as above concerning the rent that is not levied.

Also he says that the prior sold to one Edward a corrody for which he received twenty pounds, consisting of seven loaves of a certain and better weight than the loaves of the convent, and as many gallons,[1] and a house for his dwelling, a certain amount of fuel, he knows not how much, a pig for his larder and a measure for meal.

Also he sold another corrody to John Cutylere for the term of his life, and for that of his wife after the same John's death to half the amount, for twenty marks, which consists of his dwelling, which the prior is bound to repair, seven loaves of a like kind and seven gallons of beer.

And besides these there are five other corrodies which were sold of old time.

Brother Richard Burstalle says as above, that repairs are not done, and this in the prior's default, because he receives all things by himself and does all things, without taking common counsel with the convent.

Also he says as above, that no account is rendered.

Also he says that the monies received for the sale of woods by the prior amount to a hundred marks, and that the buildings, because they are not repaired, suffer damage to the extent of forty pounds in the prior's default; and this loss has taken place in the time of this prior by reason of his negligence.

Also he says that they have fishermen who receive victuals and wages from the house, and are of no profit, and this because their nets are faulty and because the weirs and garths[2] in the streams are not repaired.

Also he says that, whereas there are now three or four bailiffs, one would be enough for the collection of their rents and profits.

Also he says that William Wryght, the prior's internal bailiff,[3] is very troublesome and saucy of speech to the canons, and has no more reverence for them than for the lowest groom of the house.

Also he says that the prior maintains his natural brother and his son, and has maintained them for two years, at the costs of the house, and they are of profit to the house in naught.

Also he says that in the priory there are six corrodiers, each one of whom is worth yearly at least forty shillings,[4] and there are two outside.

---

[3] This appears to mean the bailiff who was a member of the prior's household and managed its affairs within the precinct and immediate neighbourhood of the monastery, as distinct from the bailiffs who managed the external manors of the house.

[4] We should say 'costs the house at least forty shillings a year.'

Item dicit quod[1] prior intendit dirimere dormitorium et cameras pro hospitibus, et hoc pro valore quod[2] proueniret ex plumbo, dicens quod vellet ad maius commodum domus facere fieri ly plate rofes.

Item dicit quod granaria pro medietate diripiuntur.

Item dicit quod, quia iste deponens conquerebatur de strictitudine panis, commisit ipsum carceri.

Item dicit quod prior vna vice solus habuit custodiam omnium clauium sub quibus sigillum commune seruatur, et propterea timetur de aliqua iactura siue dampno inferendo domui, vtpote per alienacionem vel alio modo, etc.

Frater Ricardus Burghe dicit de non reparacione vt supra; et de redditu apud Bostone vt supra; et de compoto non reddito.

Frater Willelmus Bavens dicit de non reparacionibus, etc.; et de creditoribus, etc., in defectu prioris.

Item dicit quod canonici non licenciantur ad faciendum gardina ad eorum recreaciones et decorem monasterii.

Item dicit quod prior solus omnia facit, et, si quid canonici iuuenes dixerint pro commodo domus, spernuntur.

Item dicit quod *non* seruitur canonicis competenter quod[3] vestura et cibariis sapidis.

Frater Ricardus Amcotes dicit de non reparacionibus, etc.; de creditoribus, etc.; et de compoto non reddito, etc.; et de redditu in Bostone.

Item dicit[4] redditus in Bostone fuisset recuperandus partim cum pecunia recepta pro vno corrodio vendito, etc., et alia pars solueretur pro decimis regis; et tamen ita non fuit expendita, sed aliunde absque sciencia conuentus.

Frater Simon Lincolne, infirmus, dicit quod prior inhumaniter tractat infirmos, et presertim istum deponentem, vt in cibariis[5] ad eius sanitatem.

Item dicit quod prior minabatur sibi quod, si conquerentur[6] in visitacione, luerent post visitacionem.

Item quod seruitur isti et ceteris de rigido pane et priori de meliori.

Item dicit de fratre prioris et eius filio vt supra.

Item dicit quod prior recipit ad mensam filios generosorum et nichil recipit[7] ab eisdem, non obstante quod prioratus oneratur ere alieno et aliis grauibus.

Item dicit de compoto non reddito et de vendicione nemorum absque *consensu* conuentus, etc., et de eo quod prior solus omnia facit.

---

[1] *diu* cancelled.

[2] *Sic*: for *qui*.

[3] *Sic*: for *quoad*. *Vestimentis videlicet* cancelled: *vestura*, etc., should be in the accusative.

[4] *quod* omitted.

[5] *nichi* cancelled.

[6] *Sic*: for *conquererentur*.

[7] *non* cancelled.

[1] Presumably the buildings in question had retained their old high-pitched roofs until this time. The very general custom of lowering the pitch of roofs in the fifteenth century was due primarily to the decaying of the outer ends of the main timbers, which could be cut off and the timbers relaid at a lower level.

Also he says that the prior intends to dismantle the dorter and the guest chambers, and this for the value which might arise from the lead, saying that he would cause flat roofs to be made for the greater advantage of the house.[1]

Also he says that the granaries, as regards half of them, are stripped.[2]

Also he says that, because this deponent complained of straitness of bread, [the prior] put him into the prison.

Also he says that on one occasion the prior had all the keys under which the common seal is kept in his sole custody, and therefore it is feared that some loss or damage may be caused to the house, to wit, by alienation or in some other way, etc.

Brother Richard Burghe says as above concerning lack of repair, and of the rent at Boston as above, and that no account is rendered.

Brother William Bavens says concerning lack of repairs, etc., and concerning the creditors, etc., in the prior's default.

Also he says that the canons are not given leave to make gardens for their amusement and for the beautifying of the monastery.[3]

Also he says that the prior does all things by himself, and, if the young canons say aught for the profit of the house, they are treated with scorn.

Also he says that the canons are not served sufficiently as regards their raiment and savoury food.

Brother Richard Amcotes says concerning lack of repairs, etc., concerning the creditors, etc., and concerning the account, that it is not rendered, etc., and concerning the rent in Boston.

Also he says [that] the rent in Boston ought to have been recovered, partly with the money received for the sale of a corrody, etc., while the other part might be paid to meet the king's tenths; and yet it has not been spent thus, but in other directions without the knowledge of the convent.

Brother Simon Lincolne, who is infirm, says that the prior treats the infirm, and particularly this deponent, unkindly, to wit, as regards food for his health.

Also he says that the prior threatened him that, if they should make complaints at the visitation, they should pay for it after the visitation

Also that he and the others are served with stale bread, and the prior with a better sort.

Also he says as above, concerning the brother of the prior and his son.

Also he says that the prior receives gentlemen's sons at his board and takes nothing from them, notwithstanding that the priory is laden with debt and other heavy burthens.

Also he says concerning the failure to render account, and concerning the sale of woods without the consent of the convent, etc., and concerning the fact that the prior does all things by himself.

---

[2] The meaning of this is not clear. It may refer to the actual buildings or to their contents: either they were half roofless, or half their stores had been plundered.

[3] Such depositions show the discouragement of manual labour by monks and canons, which was a departure from the original ideals of the monastic system.

[Fo. 87 *d.*] Post prandium vero eiusdem diei xiij Aprilis in domo capitulari dicti prioratus coram prefato reuerendo patre in huiusmodi sue visitacionis negocio iudicialiter sedente, in eodem iuxta inuenta et comperta per inquisicionem per eundem reuerendum patrem factum[1] ad vlteriora procedente, comparuerunt personaliter dicti prior et canonici omnes et singuli, dicto infirmo dumtaxat excepto, et deinde obiectis priori articulis de eo detectis et per eum partim negatis et partim confessatis, et in specie confessato quod mandauit quendam canonicum suum incarcerari, eciam postquam se sibi et ordini submiserat, tandem communicacione habita de meliori regimine prioratus in spiritualibus et temporalibus, cum dominus inuenerat priorem, nedum per compotum suum valide exiliter et obscure conceptum et exhibitum, verum eciam per oculi inspeccionem, indiscrete valde se habuisse in regimine prioratus illius, dominus ex hiis et aliis infrascriptis causis continuauit visitacionem suam huiusmodi vsque ad et in primum diem mensis Junii[2] proxime futuri, assignans et assignauit *eidem*[3] prior[4] eundem diem in ipsa domo capitulari coram ipso aut commissario suo ad plene exhibendum de titulo incumbencie sue, videlicet confirmacionem eleccionis sue et installacionem sua[5] et induccionem, cum de nullo horum antea exhibuerat, et prius quam in hiis plene docuerit, ipsum pro priore declarare et acceptare non intendit idem reuerendus pater; et eciam ad plenius exhibendum de totali statu dicti prioratus et de totali et plena administracione ipsius prioris per ipsum in bonis spiritualibus et temporalibus ipsius prioratus toto tempore suo facta, necnon ipsis priori et conuentui ad exquirendum vias per quas status dicti prioratus vtilius poterit dirigi, et ad vlterius faciendum et recipiendum, etc., que iuris sunt, presentibus magistris Johanne Depyng, Thoma Skayman et me Colstone. Quibus termino et loco, videlicet primo die Junii, anno proxime supradicto in dicta domo capitulari coram dicto reuerendo patre in huiusmodi visitacionis sue negocio iudicialiter sedente et iuxta formam retroactorum procedere intendente et de facto procedente comparuerunt personaliter prior et singuli canonici dicti loci qui alias similiter comparuerunt, fratre Ricardo Ellerkere defuncto dumtaxat excepto; et deinde idem reuerendus[6] peciit a dicto priore si quid aliud habeat exhibendum pro iure et titulo suis in dignitate et officio prioratus quam alias exhibuit. Dicit quod non. Interrogatus si habeat clarum statum domus iuxta assignacionem sibi factam exhibendum, exhibet vt asserit statum in plena forma conceptum de iiij[or] annis et de anno proxime elapso, per quod apparet domum indebitatam in cxix li. et modico vltra, videlicet totidem expendisse vltra omnes prouentus domus. Et deinde quantum ad regimen de consensu omnium dominus ordinauit quod omnia ponantur ad firmam et viuant in communi, et percipiat quilibet xiij d. in septimana et prior

---

[1] *Sic*: for *factam.*
[2] *anno* cancelled.
[3] Interlined above *eisdem* cancelled.
[4] *Sic*: for *priori.*
[5] *Sic*: for *suam.*
[6] *Sic*: *pater* omitted.

[1] From the opening details of the visitation, however, he appears to have exhibited the certificate of his confirmation as prior.
[2] See *Visitations* II, 163, note 4.

Now, after breakfast on the same thirteenth day of April, there appeared in person in the chapter-house of the said priory, before the aforesaid reverend father, as he sat in his capacity of judge in the business of such his visitation, to make further process in the same according to the matters found and discovered by the inquiry made by the same reverend father, the said prior and canons all and singular, save only the said infirm canon; and then, after the prior had been charged with the articles disclosed concerning him, and they had been partly denied and partly confessed by him, and he had confessed in special that he ordered one of his canons to be imprisoned, even after he had made submission to him and the order, at length, when counsel had been taken concerning the better governance of the priory in things spiritual and temporal, whereas my lord had found, not only by his account, which was very scantily and obscurely drawn up and exhibited, but also by ocular examination, that the prior had behaved himself very indiscreetly in the governance of that priory, my lord, for these and the other reasons herein written, adjourned such his visitation with assignation until and to the first day of the month of June next to come, and assigned to the same prior the same day in the same chapter-house, to make full exhibition before him or his commissary of the title of his incumbency, to wit, the confirmation of his election and his installation and induction, seeing that he had made exhibition of none of these beforehand[1]—and, before he has given a full explanation in these respects, the same reverend father does not intend to declare and accept him as prior—and also to make fuller exhibition of the entire state of the said priory and of the entire and full administration of the same prior done by him in his whole time as regards the spiritual and temporal goods of the same priory; and [he assigned the same term] to the same prior and convent, to seek out ways whereby the state of the said priory may be most profitably set straight, and to do and receive further, etc., what the law requires, there being present masters John Depyng, Thomas Skayman[2] and I Colstone. At and in the which term and place, to wit on the first day of June, in the year last abovesaid, there appeared in person in the said chapter-house before the said reverend father, as he sat in his capacity of judge in the business of such his visitation, with the intention of proceeding according to the form of the past acts, and was in fact so proceeding, the prior and the several canons of the said place, who likewise appeared at the other time, save only brother Richard Ellerkere, deceased; and the same reverend father asked of the said prior whether he has aught else to exhibit, on behalf of his right and title in the dignity and office of his priorship, than he exhibited at the other time.   He says no.   Upon interrogation whether he has the clear state of the house for exhibition, according to the appointment made him, he exhibits, as he asserts, the state made up in full form for four years and for the year last past, whereby it appears that the house is £119 and a little more in debt, to wit, that he had spent so much above all the revenues of the house. And then, as regards governance, my lord ordained with the consent of all that all things be put to farm and that they shall live in common, and each one receive thirteen pence, and the prior 2s. 2d. a week,[3] and

---

[3] This represents the cost of their weekly diet, including necessaries, with a double allowance for the prior.   The total cost for a year would be £22 10s. 8d. for

ij s.[1] ij d., et quod habeatur vnus discretus secularis qui collector sit reddituum firmarum et superuisor reparacionum, et alius qui sit cocus cum j garcione, et clericus ecclesie ad seruiendum eis in mensa, et alius qui seruiat priori. Percipiet quilibet canonicus pro vestura xx s., et prior ij marcas. Tamen quia compoti ministrati non sunt clari, ideo dominus assignauit priori diem Jouis proximum post festum translacionis Sancti Benedicti proxime futurum apud Elsham ad exhibendum domino clarum compotum et ad cetera facienda et recipienda que iuris sunt, etc.

THORNHOLME

Willelmus, permissione diuina Lincolniensis episcopus, dilectis in Christo filiis priori et conuentui prioratus de Thorneholme, ordinis Sancti Augustini, nostre diocesis, presentibus et futuris, salutem, graciam et benediccionem. Vt nobis ex officio nostro pastorali incumbit, visitauimus iam dudum iure nostro ordinaiio vos nunc priorem et conuentum et dictum vestrum prioratum tam in capite quam in membris; et quia per inquisicionem nostram preparatoriam quam tunc fecimus, et eciam publice ad oculum patuit, *reperimus euidenter* quod dictus vester prioratus[2] per improuidum regimen presidencium eidem, vendicionem corrodiorum et nemorum ac alias ruinam domorum et edificiorum dicti[3] prioratus tam interius et exterius adeo *extat* ere alieno[4] depressus, quod attentis onere et ruina domus, preter hoc quod nulla[5] religio vel pene religionis effigies inibi obseruatur, de verisimili tenderet ad non esse, et propterea de vestrum omnium expressis consensu et assensu vt dictus vester prioratus in[6] temporalibus sine quibus presens vita duci non potest vberius prosperetur . . . .[7] ordinauimus, statu*imus*[8] et stabiliuimus, *ac per presentes ordinamus, statuimus et stabilimus* quod vos prior et conuentus, vsque dum aliter ordinauerimus, *simul* viuatis in communi, et quod vos prior singulis septimanis ij s. ij d. *pro communis*, et[9] duas marcas in anno ad vesturam, ac quilibet *canonicus* de conuentu eciam singulis septimanis tresdecim denarios[10] pro communis, et xx s. in anno ad vestitum percipiatis et percipiat de communibus *bonis* domus *vestre* antedicte; quodque deputetur vnus secularis idoneus et discretus qui sit collector reddituum, prouentuum et firmarum ad prioratum pertinencium, ac superuisor reparacionum tam interius quam exterius faciendarum; quodque alius solus sit in domo qui *victualium prouisor et* cocus vester existat, habens sub se vnum solum garcionem in officio illo. Sit et alius qui clericus *ecclesie* existat et tam inibi in diuinis quam vobis priori et conuentui in mensa deseruiat; et preter hoc sit vnus alius dumtaxat

---

the prior and seven canons. There is no indication of the total revenues, which, about a century later, as returned in *Valor Ecclesiasticus*, were £157 0s. 6½d. gross, £106 14s. 0½d net.

[1] *v* cancelled.
[2] A word cancelled.
[3] *petr* cancelled.
[4] *fore* cancelled.
[5] *inibi* cancelled.
[6] *p* cancelled.
[7] An illegible clause added in the margin, which is torn at this point.
[8] Altered from *statuerimus*.

that there be had a discreet secular person, to be collector of the rents [and] farms and surveyor of repairs, and another to be cook with one groom, and the clerk of the church[1] to serve them at table, and another to serve the prior. Each canon shall receive for his raiment twenty shillings, and the prior two marks. Nevertheless, because the accounts furnished are not clear,[2] therefore my lord assigned to the prior Thursday next after the feast of the translation of St. Benet next to come, at Elsham,[3] to exhibit a clear account to my lord, and to do and receive all else which the law requires, etc.

THORNHOLM.

William, by divine permission bishop of Lincoln, to our beloved sons in Christ the prior and convent of the priory of Thornholm, of the order of St. Augustine, of our diocese, that are now and shall be, health, grace and blessing. As by virtue of our office of pastor is incumbent upon us, we heretofore visited, by our right as ordinary, you who are now the prior and convent and your said priory both in its head and members; and because by our preliminary inquiry which we then made, and because it was also manifestly open to the eye, we evidently discovered that your said priory, by reason of the uncircumspect governance of them that preside over the same, the sale of corrodies and of woods, and the dilapidation in other ways of the houses and buildings of the said priory, both within and without, is reduced by debt to so low a state that, considering the burthen[4] and ruinous condition of the house, apart from the fact that no religious discipline, or scarcely the outward form of religion, is observed therein, it would in all likelihood come to naught, we therefore, with the express consent and agreement of you all, in order that your said priory may more abundantly prosper in things temporal, without which this present life may not be passed . . . . did ordain, decree and establish, and by these presents do ordain, decree and establish that you, the prior and convent, until we have ordained otherwise, shall live together in common, and that you, prior, shall receive each week 2s. 2d. for your commons, and two marks a year for raiment, and every canon of the convent also shall receive each week thirteen pence for commons, and twenty shillings a year for raiment out of the common goods of your house aforesaid; and that a fit and discreet secular person shall be appointed to be collector of the rents, revenues and farms appertaining to the priory, and surveyor of the repairs to be done both within and without; and that there shall be another [secular person] only in the house to be your purveyor of victuals and cook, having under him in that office one groom only. There shall also be another who shall be clerk of the church, and shall both serve therein at divine service and serve you, the prior and convent, at table; and beside this there shall

---

[9] *quilibet de* cancelled.
[10] *et x* cancelled.

[1] The provision of a secular church-clerk in a house of canons regular was probably customary at this date, to ring the bells and work under the sacrist's direction.
[2] As previously stated, they had been drawn up insufficiently and obscurely.
[3] 14 July, 1440, the date of the visitation of Elsham priory (No. xviii).
[4] *I.e.* the burthen of debt.

qui obsequiis vestri prioris intendat, qui[1] cocus, garcio eius, clericus et
ille[2] alius[3] de bonis communibus domus[4] stipendia annuatim[5] et victus
de remanentibus mensarum vestrarum quotidie percipiant. Collector
vero predictus victum et stipendia de dictis bonis communibus domus
percipiat annuatim, qui eciam vobis priori et conuentui et singularibus
personis pro communis et vestitutu[6] vestris, prout supra ordinauimus,
ac seruitoribus vestris pro suis stipendiis, prout cum eis poterit con-
cordari, de bonis communibus domus satisfaciat et ministret, compotum-
que plenum de omnibus receptis et solucionibus suis ac reparacionibus
per ipsum factis singulis annis inter festa Sancti Michaelis et Sancti
Martini in yeme nobis vel cui mandabimus reddere teneatur.

Item iniungimus vobis priori et cuilibet successori vestro sub penis
infrascriptis quod nichil omnino contra ordinata nostra predicta quo-
modolibet attemptare presumatis, sed quod religioni et obseruanciis
regularibus sedule intendatis; quodque fratres infirmantes sepius visitetis
et eis de cibariis subtilioribus quibus de infirmitatibus suis melius con-
ualescant de communibus bonis domus faciatis ministrari.

Item cum[7] vobis priori de administracione exteriori stante [dicta]
ordinacione *nostra aliquatinus non* incumbet,[8] vobis in virtute obediencie
et sub pena grauis contemptus,[9] ac vobis de *conuentu*[10] sub pena infrascripta
iniungimus vt omni nocte post[11] completorium decantatum, omissis
potacionibus et comesacionibus, dormitorium ad nocturnam quietam
petatis, exinde nullatinus exituri nisi tantum ad matutinas, vsque dum
die sequenti pulsetur ad primam;[12] quodque silencium *locis requisitis*[13]
horasque contemplacionum in claustro temporibus debitis secundum
ordinem obseruetis.

Item iniungimus vobis priori in virtute obediencie et sub pena
excommunicacionis infrascriptis[14] quod capitulis celebrandis omnino
intersitis, defectus fratrum absque omni opprobrio, sed cum paterna
mansuetudine et caritate corrigatis et reformetis.

Item iniungimus vobis priori sub pena perpetue amocionis vestri
a statu et officio prioratus huiusmodi quod decetero non concedatis,
vendatis vel assignetis persone *cuicunque* quantumcunque honeste
pensiones, corrodia siue annuitatates ad[15] certum tempus, imperpetuum
vel ad terminum vite, nec quod nemora prioratui pertinencia succidatis
vel vendatis seu prosternetis[16] nisi tantum ad[17] *necessariam* reparacionem
domus et pertinencium ad eam ex necessario faciendam; quodque non

---

[1] *collector* erased.
[2] *aliis* cancelled.
[3] *de rei* cancelled.
[4] *victam et* cancelled.
[5] *percipiant* cancelled.
[6] Sic: for *vestitu.*
[7] *nichil* cancelled.
[8] *iniungimus* cancelled.
[9] *vt* cancelled.
[10] Interlined above *contemptu* cancelled.
[11] *dictum* cancelled.
[12] *Item iniungi* cancelled.
[13] Interlined above *locis debitis secundum ordinem* cancelled.
[14] Sic: for *infrascripta.*
[15] Sic: for *annuitates.*

be one other only, who shall be occupied in waiting upon you the prior: the which cook, his groom, the clerk and that other shall receive their wages yearly out of the common goods of the house, and victuals daily from the remnants of your tables. Now the collector aforesaid shall receive victuals and wages yearly out of the said common goods of the house, and he also shall make satisfaction and provision to you, the prior and convent, and your several persons as regards your commons and raiment, even as we have ordained above, and to your serving folk, as regards their wages, even as may be agreed with them, out of the common goods of the house, and shall be bound to render a full account of all manner his receipts and payments, and of the repairs done by him, every year between the feasts of St. Michael and St. Martin in the winter, to us or to him to whom we shall give command.[1]

Also we enjoin upon you the prior, and upon every one of your successors, under the penalties herein written, that you presume not in any way whatever to make any attempt counter to our ordinances aforesaid, but that you take anxious heed to religious discipline and the regular observances; and that you visit more often the brethren when they are ailing, and cause them to be furnished out of the common goods of the house with more delicate food, whereby they may the better recover of their infirmities.[2]

Also, seeing that you, the prior, while our said ordinance stands, will have, as it were, no responsibility for external administration, we enjoin upon you in virtue of obedience and under pain of grievous contempt, and upon you of the convent under the penalty herein written, that every night, after compline has been sung, setting drinkings and messes aside, you go to the dorter to rest for the night, and go out therefrom in no wise, save only to matins, until the bell rings for prime on the following day; and that you keep silence in the requisite places and seasons for contemplation in cloister at the due times according to the rule.[3]

Also we enjoin upon you, the prior, in virtue of obedience and under the pain of excommunication herein written, that you be altogether present at the holding of chapters, [and] correct and amend the faults of your brethren without any reviling, but with fatherly kindness and love.[4]

Also we enjoin upon you, the prior, under pain of your perpetual removal from the estate and office of such priorship, that henceforth you grant not, sell or assign to any person whomsoever, how honest soever he be, pensions, corrodies or annuities for a certain time, in perpetuity or for term of life, and that you cut down, sell or fell not, the woods belonging to the priory, save only for the needful repair of the house and of the things appurtenant thereto, when it must necessarily be done;

---

[16] *Sic*: for *prosternatis*.
[17] *racionabilem* cancelled.

[1] All this rehearses at length the arrangements concluded with the prior and convent on 1 June. The direction to farm out the estates of the monastery, and so to obtain a fixed annual income, is omitted.
[2] See Asshendone's second and Simon Lincolne's first *detecta*.
[3] See Asshendone's third *detectum* as regards observance of silence.
[4] Founded upon Asshendone's fifth and Ellerkere's second *detecta*.

sustineatis quoscunque de parentela vestra sumptibus domus absque nostra seu successorum nostrorum, episcoporum Lincolniensium, *licencia* speciali petita et obtenta, et de consensu expresso maioris et sanioris partis conuentus ad hoc accedente.

Item iniungimus vobis priori sub penis supra et infrascriptis vt ad redditus domus[1] in Bostone et alibi per vestram desidiam necglectos cicius recuperandos omnem diligenciam adhibeatis, cum in hoc super dilapidacione redargui possitis.

Item iniungimus vobis vniuersis et singulis sub penis supra et infrascriptis vt refectorium quotidie obseru*etis*[2] saltem in refeccione meridiana, et leccionem de sacra scriptura vel vitis[3] patrum tempore illo habeatis.

Item iniungimus vobis priori sub pena amocionis predicte quod nichil arduum facere presumatis nisi de communicato consilio *et assensu maioris et sanioris partis conuentus.*

Item iniungimus, volumus et ordinamus quod sigillum commune et omnia munimenta domus [fo. 88] in vna cista sub tribus diuersarum formarum clauibus, quarum vnam habeat prior, aliam supprior, et terciam vnus de conuentu ad hoc per conuentum eligendus omnino conseruentur, et quod nichil penitus cum sigillo communi sigilletur nisi in capitulo et de communi consensu maioris et sanioris partis capituli; quodque munimenta domus nullatinus a sua custodia abstrahantur nisi tantum vt in casu necessitatis et pro iure domus conseruando videantur, et illico in sua custodia interim reponantur.

[Omnes.][4] Item iniungimus vobis vniuersis et singulis sub pena excommunicacionis infrascripte vt secreta capitularia decetero nullatinus inter seculares publicentur vel detegantur.

[Prior. 7.] Item iniungimus vobis priori[5] in virtute sancte obediencie et sub pena grauis contemptus ne decetero confratribus vestris pro suis demeritis penitencias publicas in sui *opprobrium* aut religionis scandalum, nisi incorrigibiles apparcant, iniungere presumatis; quodque in correccionibus vestris faciendis modeste et mansuete et nullatinus iracunde vos habeatis, omnem animi iram penitus abiciendo.

[Prior. 8.] Item iniungimus vobis priori sub penis supra et infrascriptis vt diligenter superintendatis vt piscarie domui pertinentes et omnia eis pertinencia omni celeritate accomoda reficiantur et reparentur, cum vt[6] informamur ex hiis plura notabilia commoda domui obuenirent.

Monemus insuper, etc., vt in Humbrestone.

---

[1] *Sic*: for *domorum.*
[2] Altered from *obseruatis.*
[3] Altered from *vita.*
[4] This and the marginal notes before the two next injunctions are not easy to read, but appear to be as extended in the text.
[5] Altered from *priore.*
[6] A letter cancelled.

[1] Founded upon Asshendone's seventh, William Lincolne's third and fourth, Burstalle's third, seventh and eighth, and Simon Lincolne's fourth, fifth and sixth *detecta.*
[2] Founded upon Ellerkere's third, William Lincolne's second, Burghe's, and Amcotes' first and second *detecta.*

and that you maintain no persons whomsoever of your kindred at the costs of the house, without special licence asked and had of us or of our successors, bishops of Lincoln, and without accession hereunto of the express consent of the more and sounder part of the convent.[1]

Also we enjoin upon you, the prior, under the penalties above and herein written, that you apply all diligence to the most speedy recovery of the rents of houses in Boston and elsewhere, which have been neglected by your slothfulness, seeing that you may be reproved for dilapidation in this matter.[2]

Also we enjoin upon you all and several, under the penalties above and herein written, that you keep frater daily, at any rate at the noontide meal, and have a reading at that time from holy scripture or the lives of the fathers.[3]

Also we enjoin upon you, the prior, under pain of removal aforesaid, that you take upon yourself to do no important business without taking counsel and without the assent of the more and sounder part of the convent.[4]

Also we enjoin, will and ordain that the common seal and all the muniments of the house be altogether kept in one chest under three keys of divers shapes, whereof the prior shall have one, the subprior another, and one of the convent, to be chosen for this purpose by the convent, the third, and that nothing at all be sealed with the common seal, unless it be in chapter and with the common consent of the more and sounder part of the convent; and that the muniments of the house be in no wise taken out of their custody, save only that they may be viewed in case of necessity and for the preservation of the right of the house, and then let them be put back again in their custody.[5]

(All.) Also we enjoin upon you all and several under pain of the excommunication hereunder written, that the secrets of chapter be henceforth in no wise made public or disclosed among secular persons.[6]

(The prior. 7.) Also we enjoin upon you, the prior, in virtue of holy obedience and under pain of grievous contempt, that henceforward you take not upon yourself to enjoin public penances upon your brethren for their ill deserts, to their disgrace or the scandal of religion, unless they are apparently incapable of correction; and that in making your corrections you behave yourself with moderation and kindness and in no wise with anger, utterly casting aside all wrath of spirit.[7]

(The prior. 8.) Also we enjoin upon you, the prior, under the penalties above and hereunder written, that you take diligent heed that the fisheries appertaining to the house and all things that appertain to them be remade and put in repair, seeing that, as we are informed, many notable advantages came to the house from them.[8]

We warn you moreover, etc., as in [the injunctions to] Humberstone.[9]

---

[3] Founded upon Asshendone's first *detectum*.

[4] Founded upon Asshendone's sixth, Burstalle's first, Bavens' third, and Simon Lincolne's sixth *detecta*.

[5] Founded upon Burstalle's twelfth *detectum*.

[6] Founded upon Asshendone's eighth *detectum*.

[7] Founded upon Asshendone's fifth and ninth.

[8] Founded upon Burstalle's fourth *detectum*.

[9] See *Visitations* II, 147. The Humberstone injunctions bear date 8 July in this year.

Volumus, etc., vt ibi.

Data sub sigillo nostro in castro nostro de Sleforde quarto die mensis Augusti, anno Domini mccccxl, nostrarumque consecracionis anno xiiij⁰ et translacionis iiij^{to}.

Terciodecimo die mensis Junii, anno Domini mccccxlij, in capella infra manerium de Nettelham coram domino comparuit frater Robertus Nevyle, prior prioratus de Thorneholme supradicto,[1] habens hos diem et locum ex prefixione, vt fatebatur, dicti reuerendi patris sibi facta ad respondendum super non obseruacione iniunccionum et ordinacionum supradictarum et cetera facienda, etc. ; et recitatis sibi articulatim iniunccionibus et ordinacionibus predictis, fatetur se eas in scriptis et sub sigillo domini recepisse, sed[2] iuxta earum formam et effectum non obseruasse nec de presenti obseruare. Vnde dominus, nolens ipsum priorem per responsa sua repentina illaqueare neque precipitanter procedere contra eundem, assignauit et prefixit eidem priori diem Veneris proximam post festum Sancti Jacobi proxime futurum in ecclesia prebendali de Lidyngtone, Lincolniensis diocesis, coram se aut suo commissario a[d] recipiendum articulum super premissis in scriptis et ad cetera facienda et recipienda que sunt iuris, presentibus abbate de Kyrkestede, magistro Johanne Leek, Johanne Wylles et me Colstone. Postea vero, videlicet xviij die mensis Augusti, anno Domini mccccxlij⁰ in aula infra[3] manerium de Nettelham coram dicto reuerendo patre iudicialiter sedente, venit personaliter dictus frater Robertus prior, cui idem reuerendus pater quendam articulum in scriptis conceptum tradidit et liberauit in hec verba, ' In Dei nomine, amen,' etc., assignans et assignauit eidem priori diem Lune proximam post festum Sancti Jacobi apostoli proxime futurum[4] coram ipso domino aut eius commissario suo[5] vbicunque dominus tunc fuerit infra suas ciuitatem et diocesim ad respondendum huiusmodi articulo et ad cetera facienda et recipienda que iuris sunt, presentibus magistro Thoma Skayman, Thoma Marche et me Colstone.

LXXIV.

[Fo. 72 [70] *d.*]

Visitacio monasterii de THORNETONE, ordinis Sancti Augustini, Lincolniensis diocesis, facta in domo capitulari ibidem xj⁰ die mensis julii, anno Domini mccccxl, per venerabilem in Christo patrem et dominum, dominum Willelmum, Dei gracia Lincolniensem episcopum, anno sue consecracionis xiiij⁰ et translacionis iiij^{to}.

Quibus die et loco coram eodem reuerendo patre in huiusmodi sue visitacionis negocio iudicialiter sedente comparuerunt abbas et conuentus

---

[1] *Sic*: for *supradicta.*
[2] *non* cancelled.
[3] *aulam* cancelled.
[4] A letter cancelled.
[5] *Sic.*

[1] *I.e.* each of the orders contained in the injunctions was recited to him with the charge that he had disregarded it.

We will, etc., as in that place.

Given under our seal in our castle of Sleaford, on the fourth day of the month of August, in the year of our Lord 1442, and the fourteenth year of our consecration and the fourth of our translation.

On the thirteenth day of the month of June, in the year of our Lord 1442, there appeared in the chapel within the manor of Nettleham before my lord brother Robert Nevyle, prior of the priory of Thornholm abovesaid, having this day and place by the previous appointment, as he confesses, of the said reverend father made to him, to make answer touching his non-observance of the injunctions and ordinances abovesaid, and to do all else, etc.; and, when the injunctions and ordinances aforesaid had been recited to him in the form of articles,[1] he confesses that he received them in writing and under my lord's seal, but has not observed them, nor does observe them at present, according to their form and effect. Wherefore my lord, being unwilling to ensnare the same prior by his sudden answers, or to proceed against him with undue haste, assigned and pre-appointed to the same prior Friday next after the feast of St. James next to come,[2] in the prebendal church of Liddington, of the diocese of Lincoln, before himself or his commissary, to receive an article in writing concerning the premises, and to do and receive all else that the law requires, there being present the abbot of Kirkstead, master John Leek, John Wylles and I Colstone. And thereafter, to wit on the eighteenth day of the month of August, in the year of our Lord 1442, in the hall within the manor of Nettleham, before the said reverend father sitting in his capacity of judge, there came in person the said brother Robert the prior, to whom the same reverend father handed and delivered an article drawn up in writing, in these words, ' In the name of God, amen,' etc.; and with assignation he assigned to the same prior Monday next after the feast of St. James the apostle next to come,[3] before the same my lord or his commissary, wheresoever my lord may then be within his city and diocese, to make answer to such article and to do and receive all else that the law requires, there being present master Thomas Skayman, Thomas Marche and I Colstone.

LXXIV.

THE VISITATION OF THE MONASTERY OF THORNTON, OF THE ORDER OF ST. AUSTIN, OF THE DIOCESE OF LINCOLN, PERFORMED IN THE CHAPTER-HOUSE THERE ON THE ELEVENTH DAY OF THE MONTH OF JULY, IN THE YEAR OF OUR LORD 1440, BY THE VENERABLE FATHER IN CHRIST AND LORD, THE LORD WILLIAM, BY THE GRACE OF GOD BISHOP OF LINCOLN, IN THE FOURTEENTH YEAR OF HIS CONSECRATION AND THE FOURTH OF HIS TRANSLATION.

On and in the which day and place, there appeared before the same reverend father, as he was sitting in the business of such his visitation,

---

[2] 27 July, 1442. Probably Alnwick was personally present at Liddington on this date (*Visitations* II, xxxviii); but apparently the prior's appearance was adjourned.

[3] 29 July, 1443. The prior was given a year's grace from the date of the previous assignation at Liddington to fulfil the provisions of the article now delivered to him.

dicti monasterii; et deinde primo et ante omnia propositum fuit verbum Dei per honorabilem virum magistrum Thomam Duffelde, in sacra *theologia*[1] bacallarium, sequentem hoc thema, ' Descendi in ortum meum[2] vt viderem poma conuallium,' etc.[3] Quo finito, abbas liberauit prefato reuerendo patri certificatorium confectum super mandato domini eidem abbati pro hoc negocio directo in hec verba, ' Reuerendo,' etc.; quo perlecto, dictus abbas exhibuit eidem reuerendo patri confirmacionem eleccionis sue et installacionem, et deinde iurauit obedienciam idem abbas dicto reuerendo patri in forma consueta. Deinde exhibuit idem abbas fundacionem monasterii et statum domus, et postmodum examinatus dicit ea que sequuntur.

Frater Walterus Multone, abbas.

Frater Johannes Flynton, prior, dicit quod dominicis et festiuis tempore diuinorum canonici, presertim iuniores, absque causa legitima et absque licencia exeunt chorum, perambulantes huc et illuc in ecclesia et alibi confabulando cum secularibus eciam mulieribus. Petit [igitur][4] vt istud reformetur.

Item dicit quod sunt tria loca in quibus vescuntur canonici, videlicet refectorium, domus minucionum et aula abbatis; et dicit quod sumptus excessiui fiunt in cellario per seruientes domus et alios aduentantes, vbi plura consumuntur ad magnum domus detrimentum.

Item dicit quod diebus dominicis et festiuis est magna confluencia populi ad monasterium temporibus diuinorum ad magnus[5] sumptus monasterii, et sunt de parochianis vicinis.

Frater Thomas Gartone, canonicus cellarii, dicit quod solebant esse in elemosinaria aliquando x, aliquando xij vel viij[6] pueri sustentati de elemosina refectorii et abbatis, nam et ipsemet fuit vnus de illis; et iam non sunt nisi duo tantum.

Item dicit quod tunc habebatur in monasterio vnus qui instruebat tam clericos huiusmodi quam iuuenes canonicos in primitiuis scienciis; et iam nullus habetur talis.

---

[1] Interlined above *religione* cancelled.

[2] *Sic*: for *nucum*.

[3] Cant. vi, 10.

[4] Probably *igitur*, but the word is irrecoverable.

[5] *Sic*: for *magnos*.

[6] *Sic*: probably an error for *xiij*.

[1] The dates are not recorded, but the election must have taken place in 1439, the year of abbot Hoton's death: see *Visitations* I, 122, note 1.

[2] No foundation charter survives: a brief account of the foundation is printed in *Monasticon* VI (i), 326. The earliest charter appears to be the charter of confirmation granted by Richard I at Vézelay, 3 July, 1189 (*ibid*. pp. 326, 327).

[3] There are two main groups of surnames. The Lincolnshire group includes Brawby, Haburghe (Habrough), Irby, Keleby (Keelby), Lymberghe (Limber), Salfletby (Saltfleetby), and Thornton, all places near or at no great distance from the abbey; with Multone (Moulton), Spaldyng and Wrangle, from the Holland district. The East Riding group is from Hull and Holderness, viz. Conyngstone (the Cuningeston of the charter in Farrer, *Early Yorks. Charters* III, 42), Flinton, Garton, Hesell (Hessle) and Hulle (two names): Thornton abbey had property at Flinton, and the church of Garton-in-Holderness, with those of Humbleton and

the abbot and convent of the said monastery; and then, first and before all else, the word of God was set forth by the honourable master Thomas Duffelde, bachelor in sacred theology, after this text, ' I went down into my garden to see the apples of the valleys,' etc. And, when this was finished, the abbot delivered to the aforesaid reverend father the certificate drawn up concerning my lord's mandate, which had been addressed to the same abbot for this business in these words, ' To the reverend,' etc.; and, when this had been read through, the said abbot exhibited to the same reverend father the confirmation of his election and his installation,[1] and then the same abbot sware obedience to the said reverend father in the form accustomed. Then the same abbot exhibited the foundation of the monastery[2] and the state of the house, and afterwards upon examination he says these things which follow.

Brother Walter Multone,[3] the abbot.

Brother John Flynton, the prior, says that on Sundays and feast-days during divine service the canons, especially those that are younger, go out of quire without lawful cause and without leave, walking about hither and thither in the church and elsewhere, chattering with secular persons, even women. He prays [therefore] that this matter be reformed.

Also he says that there are three places wherein the canons feed, to wit the frater, the seyny house and the abbot's hall;[4] and he says that extravagant expenses are caused in the cellar by the serving-folk of the house and others that come thither, and that much is wasted there to the great harm of the house.

Also he says that on Sundays and feast-days there is a great flocking together of people to the monastery during divine service, to the great expense of the monastery; and they are of the people of the neighbouring parishes.

Brother Thomas Gartone, the canon of the cellar,[5] says that there were wont to be in the almonry, sometimes ten, sometimes twelve or eight[6] boys, maintained out of the alms of the frater and the abbot, for he himself also was one of them; and now there are but two only.

Also he says that they had then in the monastery one man who instructed such clerks and the young canons alike in the elementary branches of knowledge; and now they have no such person.[7]

North Frodingham in the same neighbourhood were appropriated to it. Hovyng-ham is from the North Riding, near Malton; Forsette is farther away, and seems to be Forsett in Richmondshire; Medeley (Methley) and Wakefelde (Wakefield) are from the West Riding. Apart from Lancastre, the other names, viz. Castelle, Markaunde, Pertre, Scotes and Thorp, have no distinctive character; but St. Quintin is a well-known surname from the East Riding (cf. the visitation of Stainfield, No. LXV).

[4] There was nothing to be said against this, and at Ramsey Alnwick had recognised that these three ' households ' were necessary (p. 312). The prior of Thornton, faced with the question whether excessive expenditure was due to the multiplication of *familiae*, answers that the three ordinary tables are kept, and that the waste is due to other causes.

[5] The nature of his duties is not clear, as there were a cellarer and subcellarer among the canons.

[6] Thirteen is more likely. Cf. the depositions at Leicester abbey (*Visitations* II, 208).

[7] There were, however, a master and teacher of the novices.

[Item dicit] de hospicio construendo apud Skytermylne pro hospitibus ibidem hospitandis in exoneracionem sumptuum domus.[1]

Item quod causa abbas nunc est magne expense in coquine, magni sumptus circa fossata in Holdernesse et iuxta Humbram . . . . . . animalium et defectus annone iam pluribus annis[2] contingens.

Item dicit quod canonici in minucionibus faciunt sumptuosas expensas temporibus minucionum extra monasterium inter laicos et seculares vt in [bonis] asportatis ab Hulle vel Bartone.

Frater Johannes Hulle dicit quod officiarii domus non reddunt compotos de ministracione sua in officiis suis quater in anno vt tenentur, sic quod non constat eis qualiter stat cum domo.

Item dicit quod[3] nunc abbas sit persona multum commendabilis quo ad se, tamen quo ad monasterium et eius commodum, Deus eum sic visitauit quod non est sue memorie compos ad regendum monasterium in temporalibus et spiritualibus.

Item dicit abbates qui antea fuerunt non reddiderunt plenos compotos de administracione bonorum communium monasterii.

Item dicit quod cellerarius dimittit grangias et maneria ad firmam absque communicacione conuentus, et presertim manerium de Barwe nunc dimittitur vni qui nichil habet in bonis nec potest[4] cauere de fideli solucione et fideliter respondendo, et in fine vltime firme dimittebatur peioratum in x libris; et aliquociens dimittuntur firme pauperibus qui nichil habent.

Item dicit quod pessime seruitur canonicis infirmantibus, et hac de[5] causa quia ministri seruitores in infirmaria adeo occupantur circa existentes in minucionibus quod non possunt intendere ad infirmantes.

[Fo. 73 [71].] (Sacrista.) Item quod sacrista accomodat vestamenta[6] meliora monasterii ludentibus ludos noxios in partibus inter laicos, per quod deteriorantur et scandalum generatur monasterio. Petit igitur vt in istis refrenetur accomodacio.

Item dicit quod non est monasterii aliquis elemosinarius; et dicit quod sunt certe parciales elemosine que dudum dabantur talibus qui dudum fuerunt seruientes in monasterio et aliis canonicorum amicis; et iam diebus[7] venduntur, vna pro v marcis, vna pro c solidis, etc.

Item dicit quod dudum erant in elemosinaria xij vel xiiij pauperes clerici aliti ibidem, qui deseruiebant canonicis in celebracione missarum; et iam ob defectum huiusmodi puerorum quamplures misse omittuntur, eciam centum in anno.

Item dicit quod cibaria preparata pro conuentu quedam sunt insulsa, quedam minus salsa, quedam non bene cocta vel non assata, et sic in omni parte insipida.

---

[1] This and portions of the next four paragraphs are nearly illegible.
[2] Altered from *annue*.
[3] *cum* probably omitted.
[4] *ron* cancelled (i.e. *respondere*).
[5] *casu* cancelled.
[6] *Sic*: for *vestimenta*.
[7] *Sic*: *his* omitted.

[1] The Skitter Beck is the stream which, rising above Brocklesby park, watered the sites of Newhouse and Thornton abbeys, and enters the Humber at East Halton Skitter. The mill is referred to in the charter of confirmation printed in *Mon.* VI (1) 326-7, as ' molendinum de Scittra super Humbram.'

[Also he speaks] of the inn that is to be built at Skytermylne[1] to entertain guests there, to the disburthening of the expenses of the house.

Also that the present abbot is the cause of great expense in the kitchen, [and] of great cost spent upon the dykes in Holderness and by the Humber [and that] now for several years there [has] happened [loss] of beasts and failure in the corn supply.

Also he says that the canons in seynies incur heavy expenses during their seynies outside the monastery among lay folk and secular persons, as in the case of [goods] brought from Hull or Barton.[2]

Brother John Hulle says that the officers of the house do not render accounts of their administration in their offices four times in the year, as they are bound, so that they are not certain how it stands with the house.

Also he says that [whereas] the present abbot is a person worthy of much commendation as regards himself, nevertheless, as regards the monastery and its profit, God has so visited him that he is not sufficiently capable in his memory to govern the monastery in things temporal and spiritual.

Also he says [that] the abbots who were before this time did not render full accounts of the administration of the common goods of the monastery.

Also he says that the cellarer lets the granges and manors to farm with taking common counsel with the convent, and in special the manor of Barrow[3] is now let to one who has nothing in goods and cannot give security for faithful payment and for answering faithfully therefor, and, when the last lease came to an end, it was let at a loss of ten pounds; and sometimes farms are let to poor persons who have nothing.

Also he says that the canons when they are ailing are very ill served, and for this reason, because the ministers who do service in the infirmary are so taken up with those who are in their seynies that they cannot attend to those who are ill.

(The sacrist.) Also that the sacrist lends the best vestments of the monastery to persons who play harmful plays[4] abroad among lay folk, whereby they are impaired and scandal is bred to the monastery. He prays therefore that lending, as regards these things, may be restrained.

Also he says that there is no almoner of the monastery, and he says that there are certain partial alms which were sometime given to such as were formerly serving-folk in the monastery and to other friends of the canons; and now [in these] days they are sold, one for five marks, one for a hundred shillings, etc.[5]

Also he says that there were aforetime in the almonry twelve or fourteen poor clerks nurtured therein, who served the canons at the celebration of masses; and now by reason of the lack of such boys very many masses are omitted, even a hundred in the year.

Also he says that some of the food prepared for the convent is unsalted, some is not sufficiently salted, some is ill-cooked or not boiled, and it is thus altogether tasteless.

---

[2] Barton-on-Humber.
[3] Barrow-on-Humber.
[4] Probably secular plays or interludes.
[5] *I.e.* previous donations given in alms had been converted into corrodies.

Item dicit quod prouisione[1] faciende pro monasterio non fiunt tempore congruo nisi quando fuerint carissimi fori.

Item dicit quod magna necgligencia est ad magnum dampnum monasterii, eo quod reparaciones non fiunt in inicio defectuum contingencium, sed omittuntur quousque requirant nimium excessiuas expensas.

Frater Robertus Wakefelde, custos celle de Thwayte, dicit quod officiarii sepe exonerantur et deputantur, et hoc est maxima causa debitorum monasterii in diuersis officiis.

Item dicit de prouisionibus improuide factis vt supra, et de non reparacione vt supra, et de causis[2] debiti vt supra.

Item dicit quod triennio elapso nouit de statu maneriorum et grangiarum, sed iam non nouit; et dicit quod seruientes seculares in maneriis et grangiis non computarunt xvj annis.

Item dicit quod oportunum foret vt fiant noua rentalia, nouus visus maneriorum, grangiarum, terrarum. tenementorum et ecclesiarum appropriatarum.

Item dicit quod non habent[3] studentes in logica et canonibus vt solitum est. Ideo petit quod habeantur duo canonici, vnus ad legendum canones et alium ad informandum iuuenes in logica.

Item dicit de excessiuis expensis factis per canonicos in minucionibus vt supra, et dicit quod faciunt et exercent potaciones serotinas vsque horam nouenam et decimam in[4] noctibus in officio receptoris, aliquando in camera cellerarii, aliquando in camera refectorarii.

Frater Ricardus Hovyngham, hostilarius, dicit quod venientes ad corrodiarios infra monasterium sunt magno oneri monasterio.

Frater Johannes Thorp, custos ordinis, dicit de carencia puerorum in elemosinaria qui assistanciam canonicis [darent][5] vt supra, et dicit quod in elemosinaria dudum fuerunt vnus pedagogus et vnus capellanus sustenti[6] per monasterium, et iam non habentur; et credit quod propterea domus non prosperatur sed retrocedit.

Item dicit de elemosinis venditis vt supra. Addit quod isti viuentes sic de elemosinis huiusmodi viuerent in communi infra[7] officium elemosinarie, et omni nocte dicerent in capella ibidem certas preces pro fundatoribus et conuentu, [qui] iam dispersim manent infra monasterium intendentes surrepcionibus.

Item dicit quod tenementa sua apud Staylyngburghe et alibi in partibus minantur ruinam.

Item de prouisionibus incommodis et temporibus incongruis vt supra.

---

[1] *Sic*: for *prouisiones*.
[2] *cre* cancelled.
[3] Altered from *habentes*.
[4] *p* cancelled.
[5] Or *preberent*: the word has almost disappeared.
[6] Apparently written so: for *sustentati*. Much of this passage is nearly illegible.
[7] *hospicium* cancelled.

[1] This is the 'locus de Lythelthwait' granted to Thornton, according to the charter printed in *Mon.* VI (1), 326-7, by Matthew of Hamby (Hanby). Thwate hall lies between Welton-le-Marsh and Willoughby, south of Alford. 'Locus' implies that there may have been an early monastic foundation there: see p. 243, note 1. This distant dependency was evidently used as the 'seyny place' for Thornton.

Also he says that the purveyances which should be made for the monastery are not made at the fitting season, but only when prices are highest.

Also he says that there is great carelessness, to the sore damage of the monastery, because repairs are not done at the beginning of casual defaults, but are neglected until they demand highly superfluous expenses.

Brother Robert Wakefelde, warden of the cell of Thwaite,[1] says that the officers are often discharged and appointed, and this is the chief reason of the debts of the monastery as regards divers offices.

Also he says as above concerning the improvident making of purveyances, and concerning lack of repair as above, and concerning the causes of debt as above.

Also he says that during three years past, he knew of the state of the manors and granges, but now he knows it not; and he says that the secular serving folk in the manors and granges have not presented accounts for sixteen years.

Also he says that it would be convenient that new rentals should be made, [and] a fresh view of the manors, granges, lands, tenements and appropriated churches.

Also he says that they have no students in logic and canon law, as is accustomed. Therefore he prays that they may have two canons, one to lecture in canon law, and the other to instruct the young in logic.

Also he says as above concerning the superfluous expenses caused by the canons in seynies, and he says that they hold and carry on drinkings in the evenings until nine and ten o'clock at night in the office of the receiver, sometimes in the cellarer's lodging, [and] sometimes in the fraterer's lodging.

Brother Richard Hovyngham, the guestmaster, says that those who come to the corrodiers within the monastery are to the great burthen of the monastery.

Brother John Thorp, keeper of the order,[2] says as above concerning the lack of boys in the almonry who [should give] assistance to the canons; and he says that there were sometime in the monastery a schoolmaster and a chaplain maintained by the monastery, and now they have them not; and he believes that by reason thereof the house prospers not, but goes backward.

Also he says as above concerning the alms that are sold. He adds that these folk who so live of such alms should live in common within the office of the almonry, and should say every night in the chapel therein certain prayers for the founders and the convent; [but they] now dwell in scattered places within the monastery, minding surreptitious business.

Also he says that their tenements in Stallingborough[3] and elsewhere in those parts threaten to fall into decay.

Also concerning the disadvantageous purveyances made at inconvenient seasons, as above.

---

[2] The *custos ordinis* was one of the *presidentes* responsible for discipline : see Pearce, *Monks of Westminster*, p. 24. At Thornton his office corresponded to that of third prior. At Durham, two *decani ordinis* are found in the place of third and fourth priors (Surtees Soc. cxxvii, 224).

[3] Between Thornton and Grimsby.

Item dicit quod commoda proueniencia de officiis monasterii non relinquuntur futuro substituto ad commodum officiorum, sed reseruantur ad communam, propter quod officia ipsa multum depauperantur, et hoc absque communi consensu conuentus.

Item dicit quod officiarii non subueniunt sibi inuicem in officiis suis cum carectis et aliis necessariis, sicut vacat eis.

[Fo. 73 *d.* [71 *d.*].] Frater Johannes Wrangle, custos infirmarie, dicit quod officium suum dotatum est in xlvijs. iiij*d.* in integro.

Item dicit quod in cella de Thwayte est vna mulier seruiens, que est multum brigosa inter seruientes, et iam desponsatur vni seruienti domus et facit plures turbaciones et dissensiones, per quod locus diffamatur, et eo pocius quod multum intromittit se plus quam decet de negociis domus.

Item dicit de elemosina et de pueris qui[1] solent esse in elemosinaria vt supra, et de vestimentis accomodatis vt supra.

Frater Thomas Hesell, supprior, dicit quod monasterium est indebitatum, sed nescit quibus, in quanto et ob quam causam.

Item dicit quod infirmitas abbatis, nisi cicius conuolescat,[2] causabit magnum dampnum monasterio, absque eo quod resignet, quod foret sumptuosum monasterio vt pro nouo eligendo.

Frater Johannes Scotes, precentor, concordat cum proximo quo ad infirmitatem abbatis.

Frater Ricardus Castelle, capellanus abbatis, dicit de vendicione elemosinarum que dantur fratribus et sororibus, et de carencia puerorum in elemosinaria, et de omissione celebracionis missarum, etc., vt supra, et iste elemosine sic vendite vocantur parua corrodia, et quedam occupantur per mulieres manentes infra situm monasterii, ad quas alie mulieres habent frequentem accessum, per quod monasterium aliquociens diffamatur.

Item visum est sibi vt, cum isti parui corrodiarii perceperint equiualenciam soluti, nec habent aliquam securitatem de monasterio vt pro corrodiis soluendis, vt[3] si non *in* toto tamen in aliquantulo minuantur corrodia sua huiusmodi, vt sic releuetur monasterium; et decetero non sic vendantur, sed habeantur pueri in elemosinaria ad effectum supradictum.

Item quod abbas modernus cepit ab vno quatuor marcas pro concessione ly almesdysshe, quod constat in certo pane et certa mensura ceruisi[4] et aliis victualibus percipiendis omni octaua die.

Item dicit quod frater Robertus Wakefelde, dudum cellerarius et camerarius, est aretro de reddendo compotos de huiusmodi officiis de octo vel ix annis, et sepius requisitus de computando non computat; et ideo non constat de veritate debitorum que petuntur de communa monasterii vt pro ipsis officiis.

---

[1] Altered from *qua.*
[2] *Sic*: for *conualescat.*
[3] *Sic*: repeated.
[4] *Sic*: for *ceruisie.*

[1] He means that it would be better if he resigned, but his resignation would be a doubtful blessing from the point of view of the expense which would be caused by the fees for the various formal processes necessary to complete a new election.

Also he says that the profits arising out of the offices of the monastery are not left for the next holder to the advantage of the offices, but are kept back for the common fund, by reason whereof the same offices are much impoverished, and this without the common consent of the convent.

Also he says that the officers do not afford mutual help to one another in their offices, with carts and other necessaries, as they have opportunity.

Brother John Wrangle, warden of the infirmary, says that the entire endowment of his office is 47 s. 4 d.

Also he says that in the cell of Thwaite there is a serving-woman, who is very quarrelsome among the serving-folk, and she is now espoused to a serving-man of the house and makes many disturbances and bickerings, whereby the place is defamed, and the more so because she intermeddles much more than is seemly with the business of the house.

Also he says as above concerning the alms and concerning the boys who are wont to be in the almonry, and concerning the vestments that are lent, as above.

Brother Thomas Hesell, the subprior, says that the monastery is in debt, but he knows not to whom, in what sum, and for what reason.

Also he says that the abbot's ailment, unless he speedily recovers, will cause great damage to the monastery, apart from the chance of his resignation, which would cause expense to the monastery, to wit, as regards the election of a new abbot.[1]

Brother John Scotes, the precentor, agrees with the last with regard to the abbot's infirmity.

Brother Richard Castelle, the abbot's chaplain,[2] says as above concerning the sale of the alms which are given to the brethren and sisters, and concerning the lack of boys in the almonry, and concerning the omission of the celebration of masses, etc.; and these alms that are thus sold are called the little corrodies, and some of them are held by women who dwell within the site of the monastery, to whom other women have often access, whereby the monastery is sometimes defamed.

Also it has seemed to him that, whereas these little corrodiers have received the equivalent of their payment, and whereas they have no guarantee from the monastery as regards the payment of their corrodies, such their corrodies should be diminished, if not altogether, yet in some small measure, so that the monastery may thus be relieved; and that they should not be thus sold henceforward, but that boys should be had in the almonry to the effect abovesaid.

Also that the present abbot took from one man four marks for the grant of the alms-dish, which consists in a certain loaf[3] and a certain measure of ale, and in other victuals to be received every eighth day.

Also he says that brother Robert Wakefelde, sometime cellarer and chamberlain, is eight or nine years in arrear in rendering the accounts of such offices, and, though oftentimes asked to present his account, does not present it; and therefore they are not certain of the truth of the debts which are demanded from the common fund of the monastery in respect of the same offices.

---

[2] Richard Castell, canon of Thornton, had a licence, dated Buckden, 27 Oct., 1439, as a general preacher in the diocese of Lincoln (Reg. xviii, fo. 44).

[3] *I.e.* a certain allowance of bread.

Item dicit quod vltimus abbas leuauit filios plurium nobilium, vtpote comitis Northumbrie et domini de Welles et aliorum, quibus sic leuatis dedit iocalia domus, videlicet[1] pecias argenteas et deauratas de thesauraria domus ad numerum xij^{cim} et dicit quod monasterium indebitatur vt creditur ad cccc libras.

Frater Johannes Brawby, sacrista, dicit de muliere apud Thwayte amouenda, quia nimis familiaris est et non est multum honesta nec discreta.

Item dicit de officiariis domus non computantibus secundum regulam, et presertim de Wakefelde non computante vt supra: petit igitur vt compoti plene exhibeantur, vt sciatur clarus status monasterii.

Frater Willelmus Conyngstone, bursarius, dicit quod maneria de Stayntone et Lymberghe parua paciuntur ruinam, et dicit de debito monasterii vt supra, et hoc propter improuidam gubernacionem officiariorum.

Item de elemosinis venditis[2] vt supra, et dicit quod Oliuerus, dudum episcopus Lincolniensis, iniunxit abbati et conuentui quod nullatinus venderent elemosinas monasterii sub pena anathematis, etc., et super hoc, vt dicit, habentur in monasterio littere ipsius episcopi.

Item dicit *quod* custos de Thwayte omni anno redderet compotum administracionis sue in monasterio, et dicit quod custodes ibidem non computarunt xij annis et amplius, nec eciam Robertus Wakefelde, custos modernus, de tempore suo.

Item dicit quod non habent aliquem canonicum studentem in studio generali secundum exigenciam[3] constitucionum benedictinarum.

Frater Johannes Thornton, custos refectorii, dicit omnia bene, preterquam de elemosinaria, pueris educandis in eadem ac fratribus et sororibus sustentandis in eadem.

Frater Robertus Pertre dicit de pueris habendis in elemosinaria et iam subtractis vt supra, et dicit quod[4] de prouisionibus indiscrete factis.

Frater Willelmus Irby, cellerarius, dicit de incommodis infirmitatis abbatis. Et dicit de compotis Wakefelde non redditis vt supra.

[Fo. 74 [72].] Frater Johannes de Sancto Quintino, subsacrista, dicit de inconuenienciis que possunt contingere de infirmitatibus abbatis, vt habere capud, qui non potest nec scit regere vt capud, non foret sanum.

Item dicit quod necessarium foret pro bono monasterii quod Robertus Wakefelde reuocetur ad monasterium pro bono et sano consilio adhibendo in agendis.

---

[1] *peci* . . . cancelled.
[2] *et res* cancelled.
[3] *regule* cancelled.
[4] *Sic.*

[1] *leuauit=leuauit ad fontem.* See p. 251, note 1.
[2] Henry Percy, second earl, the son of Hotspur. Out of nine sons, all or most of them probably born before abbot Hoton's death in 1439, it would be difficult to select the probable godson.
[3] Lionel, sixth Lord Welles (d. 1461). For lives of him and his son Richard, see *D.N.B.*
[4] Little Limber, now in Brocklesby park. Stainton appears to be Stainton-le-Hole in Walshcroft wapentake.
[5] *I.e.* Sutton's injunctions sent to the monastery after his visitation.

Also he says that the last abbot was godfather[1] to the sons of several noblemen, such as the earl of Northumberland[2] and lord Welles[3] and others, to whom, when he so stood godfather, he gave the jewels of the house, to wit, silver and silver-gilt pieces from the treasury of the house to the number of twelve, and he says that the monastery is in debt, as it is believed, to the amount of four hundred pounds.

Brother John Brawby, the sacrist, says that the woman at Thwaite should be removed, because she is too much one of the household, and she is not very honest or discreet.

Also he says as above concerning the officers of the house, that they do not render accounts according to the rule, and especially concerning Wakefelde, that he does not render accounts: he prays therefore that the accounts be exhibited in full, so that the state of the house may be clearly known.

Brother William Conyngstone, the bursar, says that the manors of Stainton and Little Limber[4] are suffering decay; and he says as above concerning the debt of the monastery, and this [is] because of the improvident rule of the officers.

Also as above concerning the sale of alms; and he says that Oliver, sometime bishop of Lincoln, enjoined upon the abbot and convent that they should in no wise sell the alms of the monastery under pain of anathema, etc., and concerning this, as he says, they have the letters of the same bishop in the monastery.[5]

Also he says that the warden of Thwaite should render the account of his administration in the monastery every year; and he says that the wardens in that place have not presented accounts for twelve years and more, nor also has Robert Wakefelde, who is now warden in his time.

Also he says that they have not any canon studying at the university, according to the requirement of the Benedictine constitutions.[6]

Brother John Thornton, the warden of the frater, says all things are well, except as regards the almonry, the boys who should be educated in the same, and the brethren and sisters who should be maintained in the same.

Brother Robert Pertre says as above concerning the boys whom they should have in the almonry, and who are now withdrawn; and he says that purveyances are made without discretion.

Brother William Irby, the cellarer, speaks of the disadvantages of the abbot's infirmity. And he says as above concerning the accounts not rendered by Wakefelde.

Brother John of St. Quintin, the subsacrist, says concerning the disadvantages which may come to pass from the abbot's infirmities, to the effect that it would not be wholesome to have one as head, who neither can nor knows how to rule as head.

Also he says that it might be necessary for the good of the monastery that Robert Wakefelde should be recalled to the monastery, to apply good and wholesome counsel in what has to be done.[7]

---

[6] See cap. XI of the constitutions of Benedict XII, *De mittendis ad studia*, ap. Salter, *Chapters of Aug. Canons*, pp. 230-232.

[7] It is evident that there were two opinions in the monastery about Wakefelde. The bishop in the end recalled him from Thwaite and appointed him coadjutor to the abbot after taking the vote of the canons. The attitude of the two parties in

Item dicit de elemosina non distributa vt consuetum est ex antiquo.

Frater Robertus Markaunde, succentor, dicit de insufficiencia abbatis propter infirmitates ad regendum, etc., et quod quidam *propter vtilitatem monasterii* suadent, et quidam volentes habere regimen domus[1] dissuadent abbatem cedere ; et dicit quod male et inhumaniter seruitur infirmantibus.[2]

Item dicit de elemosina diminuta vt supra, et dicit quod non constat conuentui de statu monasterii.

Item dicit quod plures canonici multociens bibunt et comedunt in cellario vel camera cellerarii temporibus vesperorum[3] et aliarum horarum, videlicet Castelle, Irby, Brawby, Medeley et eciam Thorntone quasi ingurgitando ex consuetudine.

Item dicit quod sunt tres vel quatuor[4] habent totale regimen monasterii, quibus abbas non audet contradicere.

Item dicit quod citra recepcionem mandati domini fuit quidam tractatus habitus in capitulo inter omnes de defectibus reformandis inter se ante aduentum domini; et cum quidam conquererentur de certis reformandis,[5] statim fuerunt ab aliis tantis terroribus redarguti quod abbas stringendo manus dixit ' Heu me ! quid faciam ? dampnatus sum ' ; et nisi vi impeditus fuisset et retentus, abcessisset a domo capitulari quasi alenatus[6] mente.

Frater Robertus Lancastre dicit de abbate vt supra impotente ad superuidendum que sunt videnda ad vtilitatem monasterii, et de elemosina vendita concordat cum aliis, et de pueris non habitis in elemosinaria concordat cum aliis.

Item dicit quod cibaria sunt aut insulsa aut insipida vt supra, et de infirmantibus non bene dispositis dicit cum aliis.

Item dicit quod male seruitur canonicis de speciebus[7] et aliis minutis necessariis.

Memorandum de auditore prouidendo ad audiendum compotos monasterii.[8]

Frater Ricardus Forsette dicit quod pro maiori parte canonici sunt iuuenes et sunt quasi . . . .[9] Petit igitur vt deputetur instructor qui eos instruat in canonibus, logica et aliis scienciis.

Frater Thomas Keleby, camerarius, dicit quod domus indebitatur, vt credit, in cccxl libris, et hoc propter indiscretam gubernacionem officiariorum abbatum qui antea fuerunt, et concordat cum Markaund in primo deposito suo.

Dormitorium et capella Sancti Thome infra monasterium paciuntur magnam ruinam in tantum quod pluit ad intra, et vbi consueuerunt

---

the house is defined in Markaunde's first deposition which follows. It seems that Wakefelde's party wished the abbot to remain in his office under supervision, while the other party endeavoured to force his resignation from motives which may or may not have been disinterested. If Wakefelde's administration at Thwaite had not been conspicuously useful, and if the bishop was unwilling to recall him *motu proprio*, his appointment as coadjutor was probably the less of two evils.

[1] *dissi* cancelled.
[2] Altered apparently from *infirmitantibus*.
[3] *Sic*: for *vesperarum*.
[4] *Sic*: *qui* omitted.
[5] *statis* cancelled.
[6] *Sic*: for *alienatus*.
[7] Written *spicebz'*

Also he says that alms are not distributed, as was the custom of old.

Brother Robert Markaunde, the subchanter, says that the abbot is incompetent to govern by reason of his infirmities, etc., and that certain persons persuade the abbot to resign for the sake of the profit of the monastery, and certain persons who wish to have the governance of the house dissuade him therefrom; and he says that those who are infirm are served ill and unkindly.

Also he says as above concerning the decrease in alms, and says that the convent is not certain of the state of the monastery.

Also he says that many of the canons oftentimes drink and eat in the cellar or the cellarer's chamber[1] during vespers and the other hours, to wit Castelle, Irby, Brawby, Medeley and also Thorntone, surfeiting almost as a habit.

Also he says that there are three or four [who] have the governance of the monastery, and the abbot dares not gainsay them.

Also he says that, since my lord's mandate was received, a discussion was held in chapter among them all, concerning defaults that should be reformed among them before my lord's coming; and, when some of them joined in complaining of certain things that ought to be reformed, they were immediately met by the others with such terrible retorts that the abbot said, clasping his hands together, ' Woe is me ! what shall I do ? I am undone '; and, had he not been hindered and kept back by force, he would have gone away from the chapter-house almost like a madman.

Brother Robert Lancastre says of the abbot, as above, that he is incapable of surveying such things as should be viewed for the profit of the monastery, and concerning the sale of alms he agrees with the others, and agrees with the others concerning the fact that they have no boys in the almonry.

Also he says as above that their food is either without salt or tasteless, and concerning those that are infirm, that they are ill appointed for, he says as do the others.

Also he says that the canons are ill served with spices[2] and other small things that are needful.

Be it remembered that an auditor should be provided to audit the accounts of the monastery.

Brother Richard Forsette says that for the more part the canons are young and are almost . . . . . . He prays therefore that an instructor be appointed to instruct them in canon law, logic and the other branches of knowledge.

Brother Thomas Keleby, the chamberlain, says that the house, as he believes, is £340 in debt, and this because of the indiscreet rule of the officers of the abbots who were before this time; and he agrees with Markaund as regards his first deposition.

The dorter and the chapel of St. Thomas within the monastery suffer great decay, in so much that the rain falls inside them, and, whereas

---

[8] A hand in the margin against this entry.

[9] This word is illegible. Some word has been written above it, but apparently has been partially erased, and the original word left uncancelled.

[1] The *camera* was the cellarer's private office or checker. An interesting example of such a *camera* remains on the west side of the western range at Fountains.

[2] See *Visitations* I, 249.

haberi tres lampades de nocte ardentes in dormitorio ad prebendum lumen petentibus lectos et surgentibus, iam nullas [habent] ibidem, quod cedit[1] conuentui ad magnum dispendium.

Abbates qui antea fuerunt solebant post visitaciones episcoporum iniungere omnibus de conuentu ieiunium in pane et aqua quousque confessi sint qui quicquam in huiusmodi visitacionibus detexerunt, et cognitis sic detegentibus vilissime eos reprehenderunt. Petitur vt fiat iniunccio sub pena graui ne talia decetero presumantur.

Frater Johannes Sywarde, instructor nouiciorum, dicit de infirmitatibus et impotencia abbatis et sequentibus incommodis, et dicit quod de noticia sua monasterium non prosperabatur xiiij annis, sed retrocessit, et de pueris non habitis in elemosinaria et de omissione missarum vt supra.

Item dicit de vendicione elemosinarum vt supra. Dicit insuper quod, cum omnium petencium vnanimiter dormitorium quidam cito dormiunt, quidam ad statim non possunt dormire, quod[2] ordinetur vnus locus in domo vocata Routynghouse, in qua non cito dormientes possint vacare aut studio aut oracioni, ne in lecto vigilantes immissionibus malorum spirituum agitentur.

Item dicit de reparacionibus defectuum in domibus ad statim non factis quanta mala ex hoc proueniunt.

Frater Walterus Salfletby dicit de scolari non habito in studio generali, nec de instructore canonicorum in logica et canonibus, etc., secundum exigenciam constitucionum Benedictinarum.

Istis examinatis, dominus continuauit visitacionem suam vsque in crastinum ad horam sextam, presentibus Depyng ac abbate et maiori parte conuentus et me Colstone.

[Fo. 74 *d.* [72 *d.*].] Frater Johannes Haburghe, subcellerarius, dicit de ere alieno vt supra, sed causam dicit esse defectum annone.

Frater Willelmus Hulle, magister nouiciorum, dicit quod omnia bene.

Frater Willelmus Medeley, subbursarius, dicit de compotis non redditis per Wakefelde vt de officiis per eum occupatis vt supra.

Frater Thomas Lymberghe dicit de loco parando in ly Routynghouse infra dormitorium pro canonicis qui velint tempore quo alii dormiunt studere vel oracioni vacare vt supra.

Frater Johannes Spaldyng concordat cum proximo.

Quibus termino et loco, xij⁰ die Junii,[3] anno et loco capitulari predictis, coram dicto reuerendo patre in huiusmodi visitacionis sue negocio iudicialiter sedente, comparuerunt personaliter dicti abbas et singulares persone de conuentu; et deinde idem reuerendus pater publicauit comperta et detecta in huiusmodi sua visitacione. Et quia frater Robertus Wakefelde, nunc custos de Thwayte, fatetur se nunquam

---

[1] *contui* cancelled.
[2] *Sic*: repeated.
[3] *Sic* : for *Julii.*

[1] Apparently the 'snoring-house.' This seems to have been an annexe of the dorter.
[2] See p. 375, note 6.
[3] *Rectius* July.

their custom was that three lamps should be kept burning by night in the dorter, to give them light when they go to bed and get up, now they have none there, which results in great loss to the convent.

They who were abbots before this time were wont, after the visitations of bishops, to enjoin fasting on bread and water upon all of the convent, until they confessed which of them made any disclosures at such visitations, and, when they had learned who they were that had thus disclosed matters, they rebuked them very scandalously. Prayer is made that an injunction be given, under a heavy penalty, that no such proceedings be attempted henceforward.

Brother John Sywarde, the instructor of the novices, speaks of the infirmities and incapacity of the abbot and of the disadvantages arising therefrom; and he says that, of his knowledge, the monastery has had no prosperity for fourteen years, but has gone backward; and concerning the fact that they have no boys in the almonry, and concerning the omission of masses, [he says] as above.

Also he says as above concerning the sale of alms. He says moreover that, whereas, when they all go to the dorter with one consent, some of them go to sleep quickly, [but] some cannot sleep at once, a place should be appointed in the house called Routynghouse,[1] wherein they that go not quickly to sleep may be able to spend time either in study or prayer, so that, while lying awake in bed, they may not be disturbed by the suggestions of evil spirits.

Also, concerning the fact that repairs of defaults in the buildings are not done at once, he says what great evils arise from this source.

Brother Walter Saltfletby says that they have no one in the schools at the university, and that they have no instructor of the canons in logic and canon law, etc., according to the requirement of the Benedictine constitutions.[2]

After these had been examined, my lord adjourned his visitation until six o'clock on the morrow, there being present Depyng and the abbot and the more part of the convent, and I Colstone.

Brother John Haburghe, the subcellarer, says as above concerning the debt, but he says that the reason is the failure of the corn supply.

Brother William Hulle, the master of the novices, says that all things are well.

Brother William Medeley, the under-bursar, says as above, that no accounts have been rendered by Wakefelde in respect of the offices held by him.

Brother Thomas Lymberghe says as above, that a place should be prepared in the Routynghouse within the dorter for the canons who may wish to study or give time to prayer at the time when the others are asleep.

Brother John Spaldyng agrees with the last deponent.

At and in the which term and place, on the twelfth day of June,[3] in the year and place of chapter aforesaid, there appeared in person before the said reverend father, as he sat in judgment in the business of such his visitation, the said abbot and the several persons of the convent; and then the same reverend father made public the matters discovered and disclosed in such his visitation. And because brother Robert Wakefelde, who is now warden of Thwaite, confesses that he has

reddidisse compotum de administracione per eum[1] in officiis in dicto monasterio que perantea occupauit nec eciam de administracione sua apud Thwayte, dominus monuit eum primo, secundo et tercio peremptorie sub pena excommunicacionis maioris in eum, si huiusmodi iniunccionibus non paruerit cum effectu, fulminande, quod infra vnum mensem inmediate post proximum festum Sancti Michaelis archangeli sequentem plenum et fidelem compotum de totalibus administracionibus suis reddat coram conuentu dicti monasterii vt est moris. Et quia nedum per inquisita, verum eciam per aspectum ocularem et examinacionem persone abbatis, idem reuerendus pater repperit ipsum abbatem insufficientem ad regendum dictum monasterium in spiritualibus et temporalibus, vt qui in toto a se abstractus et infatuatus ac discrecione alienatus existit, peciit idem reuerendus pater tam ab ipso abbate quam toto conuentu, si quid haberent proponendum quare non deberet assignare eidem abbati vnum coadiutorem, vnum videlicet de fratribus qui, stante insufficiencia ipsius abbatis, haberet regimen persone abbatis et monasterii in spiritualibus et temporalibus. Vnde, nichil proposito per eorum aliquem, amoto ipso abbate dominus inquisiuit vota singulorum de substituendo vno confratre in huiusmodi coadiutorem, et tandem cum essent xxvij in numero preter abbatem, repertum est xvij nominasse fratrem Robertum Wakefelde. Vnde reuocato abbate ad capitulum dominus deputauit dictum Wakefelde dicto abbati in coadiutorem: vnde idem Wakefelde prestitit iuramentum quod honeste tractabit personam abbatis iuxta statum et gradum *suos* et quod fideliter habebit se in regimine dicti monasterii ac administracione spiritualium et temporalium eiusdem, stante insufficiencia ipsius abbatis, et quod fideliter computabit domino vel cui mandauerit de administracione sua; et deinde iurauit obedienciam domino vt coadiutor et fidelitatem monasterio. Monuit eciam idem reuerendus pater singulares personas de conuentu primo, secundo et tercio peremptorie sub pena excommunicacionis maioris[2] in personas singulares huiusmodi iniunccionibus non parentes intendit fulminare, quod dicto Roberto Wakefelde coadiutori, stante ipso coadiutore in omnibus, que Dei honorem, animarum curam et monasterii vtilitatem[3] fideliter pareant, assistant et intendant. Et quia reperit idem reuerendus pater sibi in hac visitacione sua detectum quod occasione detectorum in prioribus visitacionibus fuisse conuentui grauiter improperatum, dominus simili modo monuit abbatem, priorem et singulares personas conuentus sub simili pena excommunicacionis fulminande quod nullus eorum alteri occasione detectorum in hac visitacione improperet, iniuriam, contumeliam, molestiam calumpniam ve faciat, intimans eorum singulis quod, si constare poterit sibi in futurum quemquam eorum alicui huiusmodi monicionum suarum in aliquo

---

[1] *Sic* : *facta* omitted.
[2] *Sic* : *quam* omitted.
[3] *Sic* : *concernunt* omitted.

[1] The minority of ten, to judge by the character of the depositions, consisted certainly of the five canons who gave evidence against Wakefelde, viz. Castelle, Brawby, Conyngstone, Irby and Medeley, and probably of Wrangle, whose evidence reflected upon the governance of Thwaite, Markaunde, whose evidence tended to show that the abbot ought to resign, and Garton, John Hulle, and Sywarde, who clearly thought the same. On the other hand, there was no unity in this party,

never rendered an account of the administration [performed] by him in the offices which before this time he held in the said monastery, or of his administration also at Thwaite, my lord admonished him the first, second and third time peremptorily, under pain of the greater excommunication, to be pronounced against him, if he obey not such injunctions with effect, that within a month after the feast of St. Michael the archangel next following he shall render a full and faithful account of his entire administrations in presence of the convent of the said monastery, as is the custom. And because, not only by his inquiries, but also by what he saw with his eyes and by examination of the abbot's person, the same reverend father found the same abbot incompetent to govern the said monastery in things spiritual and temporal, as he is a man who is altogether outside himself and full of folly and deprived of wit, the same reverend father asked both of the same abbot and the whole convent, whether they had aught to propound wherefore he should not appoint a coadjutor to the same abbot, one of the brethren to wit, who, while the incompetence of the same abbot lasted, should have the governance of the person of the abbot and of the monastery in things spiritual and temporal. Wherefore, when nothing was propounded by any of them, my lord, having sent out the same abbot, asked for the votes of each of them concerning the appointment of one of their brethren to be such coadjutor; and at length, since they were twenty-seven without the abbot it was found that seventeen had nominated brother Robert Wakefelde,· Wherefore, having summoned the abbot back to the chapter house, my lord deputed the said Wakefelde to be coadjutor to the said abbot; wherefore the same Wakefelde proffered his oath that he will treat the abbot's person honestly according to his estate and degree, and that he will behave himself faithfully in the governance of the said monastery and the administration of the spiritual and temporal affairs of the same, while the incompetence of the same abbot lasts, and that he will render a faithful account to my lord, or to whomsoever he will give order, of his administration; and then he sware obedience as coadjutor to my lord, and fealty to the monastery. The same reverend father also admonished the several persons of the convent the first, second and third time peremptorily, under pain of the greater excommunication, [which] he intends to pronounce against the several persons who do not obey such injunctions, to obey faithfully, give help and hearken to the said Robert Wakefelde the coadjutor, while he remains coadjutor, in all things which [concern] the honour of God, the cure of souls, and the profit of the monastery. And because the same reverend father found it disclosed to him in this his visitation that the convent had been grievously upbraided by reason of the matters disclosed in former visitations, my lord in like wise admonished the abbot, the prior, and the several persons of the convent, under the like pain of excommunication to be pronounced, that no one of them shall upbraid another on account of the matters disclosed in this visitation, or do him wrong, contempt, annoyance or calumny, informing each of them that, if in future he can learn certainly that any one of them has gone counter in aught to any one of such his

---

and four of Wakefelde's critics were accused by Markaunde of wasting time in the cellarer's department, viz. Brawby, Castelle, Irby and Medeley.

contrauenerit[1] et eis non obedierit,[2] quod[3] contra ipsos tanquam clauium ecclesie contemptores et aliter secundum ca*n*ones procedet quod metu pene alii a similibus arcebuntur. Et hiis sic habitis idem reuerendus pater, reseruata sibi potestate faciendi et transmittendi eis iniuncciones salutares, etc., huiusmodi visitacionem suam dissoluit, presentibus Depynde,[4] Skayman et me Colstone.   Monuit insuper idem reuerendus pater die, loco et hora predictis prefatum fratrem Wakefelde vt mulierem illam seruientem in cella de Thwayte manentem infra septem dies a tempore quo proximo idem frater Robertus venerit ad dictam cellam abinde prorsus amoueat, illam vel talem aliam nullatinus simili modo decetero admissurus sub pena excommunicacionis quam in ipsum, si hiis monicionibus non paruerit, intendit fulminare; cui quidem monicioni sic facte, vt apparuit, idem frater Robertus tunc assensiit,[5] etc., presentibus Depyng, Skayman predictis et me Colstone.

[Fo. 78.] Willelmus, permissione diuina Lincolniensis episcopus, dilectis in Christo filiis abbati et conuentui monasterii de Thorneton, ordinis Sancti Augustini, nostre diocesis, presentibus et futuris salutem, graciam et benediccionem. Cum plantatam sacram religionem, etc. (vt in Croylande),[6] exercentes, nonnulla reperimus reformacione notabili et necessaria digna, etc., obseruanda.

In primis iniungimus et mandamus vobis vniuersis et singulis sub penis infrascriptis quod omnes saltem sani et potentes et externis non legitime non[7] impediti omni nocte et die ad matutinas, missas maiores, vesperas et alias horas canonicas ad chorum vniformiter conueniant, et inde ante finem missarum et horarum huiusmodi nullatinus egrediantur nisi ex causa legitima per presidentem in choro approbata et licencia ab eo petita et obtenta; et quod sic egressi in ecclesia vel alibi cum secularibus *non* deambulent aut cum ipsis confabulentur; et si quis huius nostre iniunccionis transgressor repertus fuerit, pro prima vice in pane *et* ceruisia *tantum* prima quarta feria, pro secunda vice in prima quarta et sexta feria[8] in pane et aqua, et pro tercia vice in pane et aqua singulis quartis et sextis feriis per vnum mensem proxime sequentem ieiunet, et sic restante culpa augeatur, et pena.

Item cum in elemosinaria solebant esse xiiij vel xvj pueri ex elemosina sic crescentes, canonicis in celebracione missarum assistentes, ac eciam vnus instructor qui iuuenes canonicos et pueros huiusmodi in primitiuis scienciis et grammaticis *informaret*, necnon vnus capellanus pro fundatoribus et benefactoribus monasterii in capella infra elemosinariam continue celebrans, et iam non habentur huiusmodi capellanus neque instructor, sed neque pueri nisi duo dumtaxat, propter quod nonnulle misse omittuntur in anno ob defectum assistencie huiusmodi; iniungimus

---

[1] *Sic*: for *contrauenisse*.
[2] *Sic*: for *obedisse*.
[3] *Sic*: repeated.
[4] *Sic*: for *Depynge*.
[5] *Sic*: for *assensit* or *assentiuit*.
[6] Bracketed words underlined in original.
[7] *Sic*.
[8] *Sic*: for *feriis*.

[1] See *Visitations* ii, 58. Neither set of injunctions is dated, but they were

admonitions, and has not obeyed them, he will proceed against the same as acting in contempt of the keys of the church, and in other respects according to the canons, so that the others shall be prevented from like doings by fear of the penalty. And, when he had thus finished this business, the same reverend father, after reserving to himself the power of making and conveying healthful injunctions to them, etc., dissolved such his visitation, there being present Depynge, Skayman, and I Colstone. The same reverend father moreover, on and in the day, place and hour aforesaid, admonished the aforesaid brother Wakefelde that, within seven days from the next time at which the same brother Robert shall come to the cell of Thwaite, he shall utterly remove therefrom that serving woman who abides in the said cell, and that he shall in no wise from henceforth admit her or any other such woman in like manner, under the pain of excommunication, which he intends to pronounce against him, if he obeys not these warnings; to the which admonition so made, as it was apparent, the same brother Robert did then assent, etc., there being present Depyng [and] Skayman aforesaid, and I Colstone.

William, by divine permission bishop of Lincoln, to our beloved sons in Christ the abbot and convent of the monastery of Thornton, of the order of St. Augustine, of our diocese, that now are and shall be, health, grace and blessing. Inasmuch as where holy religion is planted, etc. (as in [the injunctions to] Croyland[1]), while holding [our visitation], we found certain things worthy of notable and needful reform, etc.

In the first place, we enjoin and command you all and several, under the penalties written herein, that you all, at any rate those who are sound and able and are not lawfully hindered by external business, come together after one manner to quire every night and day, for matins, high masses, vespers and the other canonical hours, and go not out therefrom in any wise before the end of such masses and hours, unless for a lawful reason approved by him who presides in quire, and with licence asked and had of him; and that they who have so gone out walk not about with secular persons in the church or elsewhere, or chatter with them; and, if any one be found to transgress this our injunction, he shall fast for the first time on bread and beer only on the first Wednesday, for the second time on bread and water on the first Wednesday and Friday, and for the third time on bread and water every Wednesday and Friday for one month next following; and so, while the fault remains, let the penalty also be increased.[2]

Also, whereas there were wont to be in the almonry fourteen or sixteen boys, thus growing up on alms [and] assisting the canons at the celebration of masses, and also an instructor to bring up the young canons and such boys in the elementary branches of knowledge and in grammar, and likewise a chaplain, celebrating continually for the founders and benefactors of the monastery in the chapel within the almonry; and now they have not such chaplain or instructor, and not even the boys save two only, by reason whereof some masses are omitted in the year on account of the lack of such assistance; we enjoin upon you the abbot,

---

probably composed about the same time. The visitation of Croyland had taken place on 18 and 19 June previously.

[2] Founded on the prior's first *detectum*.

vobis abbati[1] in virtute obediencie et sub pena grauis contemptus vt quamcicius commode poteritis et ad omne minus infra vnum annum de tantis pueris, dumtamen honesti, habiles et dociles existant, ac instructore et capellano huiusmodi prouidere curetis, *ac* ipsis pueris alimoniam ab elemosinis vestre et conuentus mensarum et aliis que eorum victum et vestitum abolim assignata fuerunt debite ministrari faciatis.

Item cum vt nobis delatum existat[2] tria loca sunt infra monasterium in quibus canonici vescuntur, videlicet refectorium, aula abbatis et domus minucionum, *et* quod[3] in coquina et cellario magni sumptus et expense excessiue ad magnum domus detrimentum *indies fiunt,* quodque canonici tempore minucionum monasterium exeunt et cum secularibus eciam mulieribus se immiscent et grandia solacia eciam in vinis *et aliis pro* eisdem faciunt ad sui ipsorum et monasterii graue scandalum ; iniungimus vobis vniuersis et singulis *sub*[4] supra et infrascriptis penis vt predictis tribus locis pro refeccione vestra contenti ab aliis penitus abstineatis,[5] ab huiusmodi sumptibus magnis et expensis excessiuis in coquina et cellario omnino precauentes ; quodque non liceat canonicis in minucionibus existentibus *monasterium exire nec hiis vel*[6] aliis quibusuis extra *dictum vestrum monasterium*[7] commedere vel bibere, exceptis hiis qui officiis exterioribus preficiuntur et ad extra agunt in itinere constituti.

Item cum in dicto monasterio sint quedam elemosine dicte parua corrodia, que olim consueuerunt dari seruientibus et canonicorum amicis ad senium vel impotenciam collapsis in *officio*[8] elemosinarie continue in communi viuere et omni nocte in capella ibidem certas oraciones et deuociones pro animabus fundatorum et benefactorum dicere debentibus, et iam huiusmodi elemosine et ly almesdysshe vestri abbatis a pluribus annis non absque vicio simonie *et auaricie* diuersis personis eciam mulieribus infra situm monasterii manentibus vendite sint pro certis summis pecuniarum, ad quas mulieres alie suspecte habent frequentem accessum, per quod monasterium in sua fama multum denigratur; iniungimus omnibus vobis et singulis, presentibus et futuris, sub penis supra et infrascriptis, quod decetero huiusmodi elemosine nullatinus vendantur, nec sub tali sed antiquitus consueta forma donentur, vt prefertur, et assignentur, et hii qui eas emerint [fo. 78 *d.*], presertim mulieres,[9] eciam a situ monasterii penitus eiciantur.

(De poculentis et esculentis.) Item iniungimus subcellerario monasterii pro tempore existenti sub pena ieiunii in pane et aqua proxima quarta vel sexta feria sequenti quociens in hoc defecerit, vt bene, fideliter et diligenter superuideat[10] vt cibaria que pro conuentu preparabuntur quolibet die sint salubria et sa*pida ac*[11] bene et salubriter disposita,

---

1 *huiusmodi* cancelled.
2 *Sic* : for *existit.*
3 *que* cancelled.
4 Interlined above *sub* cancelled.
5 *quodque* cancelled.
6 Interlined above *nec* cancelled.
7 Interlined above *loca claustralia* cancelled.
8 Interlined above *domo* cancelled.
9 *percepta quantitate soluti de ipsis* cancelled.
10 *et superuideat* cancelled.
11 Altered from *salubria et.*

in virtue of obedience and under pain of grievous contempt, that, as speedily as you conveniently can, and at the very least within a year, you take order to make provision of so many boys, provided that they be honest, capable and teachable, and of such an instructor and chaplain, and cause means of nourishment to be supplied to the same boys from the alms of your table and that of the convent, and from the other sources which were assigned aforetime for their victuals and raiment.[1]

Also, whereas, as it is reported to us, there are three places in the monastery wherein the canons feed, to wit the frater, the abbot's hall and the seynies house, and [it is reported] that great costs and super-fluous expenses are incurred daily in the kitchen and cellar, to the great harm of the house, and that the canons during their seynies go out of the monastery and keep company with secular persons, even women, and make great cheer for the same in wines and other things, to their own grievous scandal and that of the monastery; we enjoin upon you all and several, under the penalties above and hereunder written, that you be content with the aforesaid three places for your refreshment, and utterly abstain from others, taking all precaution against such great costs and superfluous expenditure; and that the canons who are in their seynies be not allowed to go out of the monastery, or these or any others soever to eat or drink outside your said monastery, except such as are set in charge of the external offices and do business outside, being on a journey.[2]

Also, whereas in the said monastery there are certain alms called the little corrodies, which were formerly wont to be given to serving folk and to friends of the canons who had fallen upon old age or loss of strength, who were bound to live continually in common in the office of the almonry, and to say every night in the chapel in the same certain prayers and devotions for the souls of the founders and benefactors, and now such alms and your abbot's alms-dish have for many years past been sold for certain sums of money, not without the guilt of simony and avarice, to divers persons, even to women dwelling within the site of the monastery, to which women other suspect women have often access, whereby the monastery is greatly tarnished in its report; we enjoin upon you all and several, that now are and shall be, under the penalties above and here-under written, that henceforward such alms be in no wise sold, or given, as is aforesaid, and assigned under such form, but in the form of old accustomed, and that such as buy them, especially women, be also utterly expelled from the site of the monastery.[3]

(Concerning drinkables and eatables.) Also we enjoin upon the subcellarer of the monastery for the time being, under pain of fasting upon bread and water on the next Wednesday and Friday following, so often as he makes default herein, that he keep good, faithful and diligent watch that the food which shall be prepared for the convent every day be wholesome and savoury, and well and healthfully ordered, cooked and

---

[1] Eight canons testified to the lack of boys in the almonry: five to the need of instructors.

[2] Founded upon the prior's second and third, Garton's fifth and Wakefelde's sixth *detecta.*

[3] Seven canons testified to the abuse of corrodies: see also Hovyngham's *detectum.*

decocta et[1] assata, ne *canonici* ex illis minus sapide dispositis[2] *vescentes illa abhorreant et* infirmitates aliquas incurrant.

Item iniungimus vobis abbati in virtute obediencie et sub pena contemptus vt canonicos in infirmaria infirmantes sepius visitetis et eis de cibis[3] *illis congruentibus* quibus cicius conualescere et melius recreari valeant, ac eciam de seruientibus qui ipsis infirmis in infirmitatibus *suis* congrue deseruiant ministrari et prouideri faciatis.

Item iniungimus vobis vniuersis et singulis sub penis supra et infrascriptis quod a potacionibus serotinis, presertim in officiis recepte et in cameris cellerarii et refectorarii seu aliis locis quibusuis, presertim post completorium, omnino et penitus abstineatis, dormitorium petentes, exinde nullatinus exituri nisi ad matutinas quousque in crastino pulsetur ad primam, hoc solum excepto quod liceat canonicis antea celebrare volentibus in ecclesiam et non extra ingredi.

(De compoto.) Item iniungimus vniuersis et singulis domus officiariis presentibus et futuris quod quater in anno secundum monasterii consuetudinem plenum de administracione sua in officiis suis per ipsos facta reddant compotum coram toto conuentu vel personis ad hoc per conuentum assignandis, et quod remanencia super hiis compotis sic redditis eisdem computantibus vel substitutis in eadem officia per indenturam liberentur, et quod crebro nisi ex causis racionabilibus cognitis ex huiusmodi officiis ea occupantes *non* exonerentur, cum per tales crebras et subitas exoneraciones ipsa officia in pluribus perantea dampnificata sunt; et eciam quod singuli officiarii cum eis vacauerit seinuicem iuuent et auxilientur vt in cariagio et aliis similibus.

(De reparacione.) Item volumus, ordinamus et iniungimus sub penis supra et infrascriptis quod cellerarius pro tempore existens[4] ecclesias monasterio appropriatas, maneria, grangias vel alias possessiones notabiles monasterio pertinentes ad firmam nullatinus dimittere presumat, nisi de hiis prius cum abbate et conuentu tractatus in capitulo habeant,[5] et tunc hii qui firmas accipient in capitulo veniant eas sub indenturis recepturi; quodque cum omni acceleracione ecclesie appropriate, maneria, grangie et tenementa pertinencia monasterio cum matura deliberacione superuideantur, et defectus in eis, *presertim in dormitorio et capella Sancti Thome existentes et* reperti cicius in inicio reparentur, *ne postquam excreuerint de facili vel leui non poterint reparari*; et quod noua[6] rentalia de nouo conficiantur, et quod prouisiones fiende pro monasterio tempore congruo et dum venalia sunt in *leui* foro[7] fiant, et comparanda[8] comparentur.

Item iniungimus et mandamus sacriste dicti monasterii pro tempore existenti sub penis supra et infrascriptis, ne vestimenta dicti monasterii

---

[1] *assig* cancelled.
[2] *tan* cancelled.
[3] *subtilioribus* cancelled.
[4] *si* cancelled.
[5] *Sic*: for *habeat* or *habeatur*.
[6] *reta* cancelled.
[7] *modico* cancelled.
[8] *et* cancelled.

[1] Founded upon John Hulle's ninth and Lancastre's second *detecta*.
[2] Founded upon John Hulle's fifth and Lancastre's third *detecta*.
[3] Founded upon Wakefelde's sixth and Markaunde's third *detecta*.

boiled, so that the canons, feeding upon victuals less savourily ordered, may not shrink from them and incur any ailments.[1]

Also we enjoin upon you, the abbot, in virtue of obedience and under pain of contempt, that you visit the canons more often who are ailing in the infirmary, and that you cause them to be furnished and provided with food suitable to them, whereby they may be able to recover health more speedily and be better refreshed, and also with serving folk to do fitting service to the same infirm persons in their ailments.[2]

Also we enjoin upon you all and singular, under the penalties above and hereunder written, that you altogether and utterly abstain from drinkings in the evening, especially in the offices of receipt and in the cellarer's and fraterer's lodgings, or in any other places whatsoever, in particular after compline, but go to the dorter, and in no wise go out therefrom, save to matins, until the bell ring for prime on the morrow, with this only exception, that it shall be lawful for canons who wish to celebrate before that time to go into church, but not outside it.[3]

(Concerning the account.) Also we enjoin upon all and singular the officers of the house that now are and shall be, that four times a year, according to the custom of the monastery, they render a full account of their administration done by them in their offices before the whole convent or persons to be appointed by the convent for this purpose, and that what remains over and above the accounts so rendered be delivered by indenture to the same who make account or to those who have been preferred to the same offices in their place; and that those who hold such offices be not frequently discharged from them, unless for reasonable causes ascertained, seeing that heretofore the same offices have suffered damage in many ways by such frequent and sudden discharges; and also that the several officers, when they have opportunity, give help and aid to one another, to wit, in carriage and other like matters.[4]

(Concerning repair.) Also we will, ordain and enjoin, under the penalties above and hereunder written, that the cellarer for the time being shall in no wise presume to let to farm the churches appropriated to the monastery, the manors, granges, or other notable possessions appertaining to the monastery, without previously holding treaty in chapter with the abbot and convent concerning these things; and then such as will take farms shall come to receive them in chapter under indentures; and that with all speediness the appropriated churches, manors, granges and tenements appertaining to the monastery be surveyed with ripe deliberation, and the defaults which are and are found in them, especially in the dorter and the chapel of St. Thomas, be speedily repaired at the beginning, lest, after they have increased, they may not be easily or lightly repaired; and that new rentals be drawn up afresh, and that the purveyances which should be made for the monastery be made, and its needful purchases be bought at a fitting time, and while goods are for sale in a cheap market.[5]

Also we enjoin and command the sacrist of the said monastery for the time being, under the penalties above and hereunder written, that

---

[4] See John Hulle's first and third, Wakefelde's first and third, and Castelle's sixth *detecta*; also the evidence of the five canons (p. 378, note 1), who brought special charges against Wakefelde.

[5] Founded upon John Hulle's fourth and eleventh, and Wakefelde's second and fourth *detecta*. For specified instances of lack of repair, see Thorp's third, Conyngstone's first, Keleby's second, and Sywarde's third *detecta*.

quecunque ad aliquos ludos[1] in partibus inter populares vel ad alia ludibria vel spectacula quouismodo accomodare presumat, cum per talem accomodacionem multum deteriorata sunt vestimenta huiusmodi, et non liceat[2] *humanis* vsibus prophanari que semel Deo dedicata existunt.

Item inhibemus vobis vniuersis et singulis, presentibus et futuris, ne proles quascunque in baptismo vel confirmacione absque[3] nostra vel successorum nostrorum, episcoporum Lincolniensium, petita et obtenta leuare presumatis sub penis supra et infrascriptis, cum per tales leuaciones intelligamus monasterium in suis iocalibus et thesauro multipliciter dampnificatum.

Item cum nobis delatum sit quod ex consuetudine laudabili monasterii consuerunt haberi in monasterio vnus instructor, qui canonicos in logica et alius in canonibus instrueret, et quod secundum constituciones benedictinas de quolibet numero vicenario vnus canonicus haberetur in studio generali studens, et iam *non* sint inibi huiusmodi instructores nec canonicus studens, iniungimus vobis abbati in virtute obediencie et sub pena contemptus vt sic consuetudo se habeat de talibus instructoribus et secundum dictas constituciones de canonicis studentibus iuxta numerum canonicorum in conuentu omnino prouidere et ordinare curetis;[4] quodque in dormitorio sint ad minus due lampades continue de nocte ardentes que lumen prebeant canonicis ingredientibus et egredientibus.

Item iniungimus vobis vniuersis et singulis sub penis supra et infrascriptis ne quis vestrum alteri occasione detectorum siue delatorum in hac nostra visitacione quouismodo improperare presumat supermittendo alicui quod ipse talia vel talia detulit vel detexit, quod si quis huic nostre iniunccioni aliquis[5] vestrum contrafecerit, ipsum taliter pro presumpcione,[6] Deo duce, puniemus quod ceteri animum non habebunt similia perpetrandi.

Item si qui sint canonici qui postquam dormitorium petierint non cito petant lectos vel dormientibus aliter sint infesti, volumus vt pro talibus in ly Routynghouse ordinetur vt ab aliorum inquietacione abstineant et sibi ipsis pro sua quiete valeant prouidere.[7]

Item volumus et iniungimus et ordinamus quod deputetur vnus secularis auditor in hoc expertus, qui compotos singulorum officiariorum monasterii iuxta forma iniunccionis nostre supradicte vna cum aliis personis de conuentu ad hoc assignatis omni anno audiat et terminet. Monemus.[8]

---

[1] A word cancelled: the word to be substituted was not written, though a caret is left for it.

[2] *humanibus* cancelled.

[3] *licencia* omitted.

[4] There is a caret here, with a sign referring to the margin, where, in the process of revision, the bishop or his chancellor has added a note, which, owing to the torn condition of the paper, is only partially legible : . . *ra trium necesse* . . . . *spicium de* . . . . *seu canonicis* (?) . . . . (*intend* cancelled) . . . *dis alio* . . . . *dium nec* (?) . . . *in ea parte* (interlined) . . . *suplere* . . . . *mus vos.*

[5] *Sic*: repeated from *quis* above.

[6] *taliter* cancelled.

[7] *Monemus in hoc vos omnes et singulos* cancelled. This alteration followed the revision of the injunctions by the bishop or his chancellor, who, among various emendations and additions, wrote in the margin the note *Fiat iniunccio de auditore seculari idoneo et experto.*

[8] The clause is unfinished.

he take upon himself in no wise to lend any vestments whatsoever of the said monastery for any plays among the general folk in the neighbourhood, or for other games or spectacles, seeing that by lending of this kind such vestments are greatly injured, and since it is not lawful that things which have once been dedicated to God should be profaned by the use of man.[1]

Also we inhibit you all and sundry, that now are and shall be, from taking upon yourselves to be sponsors to any children whatsoever in baptism or confirmation, without [licence] asked and had of us or our successors, bishops of Lincoln, under the penalties above and hereunder written, seeing that by such acts of sponsorship we understand that the monastery is in manifold wise damaged in its jewels and treasure.[2]

Also, seeing that it is reported to us that, of the praiseworthy custom of the monastery, there were wont to be had in the monastery one instructor to instruct the canons in logic, and another in canon law, and that, according to the Benedictine constitutions, one canon out of every twenty should be kept at his studies in the university, and now there are not such instructors therein or such canon at his studies, we enjoin upon you, the abbot, in virtue of obedience and under pain of contempt, that the custom concerning such instructors be kept accordingly, and that you altogether take order to make provision and ordination, according to the said constitutions, of student canons in keeping with the number of the canons in the convent; and that there be in the dorter at least two lamps burning continually by night, to give light to the canons as they go in and out.[3]

Also we enjoin upon you all and several, under the penalties above and hereunder written, that no one of you take upon himself in any wise to reproach another on the ground of matters disclosed or reported at this our visitation, charging anyone with reporting or disclosing this or that; for, if any one of you do contrary to this our injunction, we shall punish him for his presumption, under the guidance of God, on such wise that the rest shall not have the courage to commit like offences.[4]

Also, if there be any canons who, after they have gone to the dorter, do not go to bed quickly or are a nuisance in other ways to them that are asleep, we will that order be taken for such persons in the Routynghouse, that they may abstain from disturbing others and look after themselves as regards their rest.[5]

Also we will and enjoin and ordain that a secular auditor be appointed, with experience in this matter, to hear and determine every year the accounts of the several officers of the monastery, according to the form of our injunction abovesaid, together with other persons of the convent appointed for this purpose.[6]

We admonish [etc.]

---

[1] Founded upon John Hulle's sixth and Wrangle's second *detecta*.

[2] Founded upon Castelle's fifth *detectum*.

[3] See Wakefelde's fifth, Conyngstone's fourth, Forsette's and Salfletby's *detecta*.

[4] See Keleby's third *detectum*.

[5] Founded upon Sywarde's second, Lymberghe's and Spaldyng's *detecta*.

[6] This is added in answer to no special petition, but as a measure of general expediency.

LXXV.

[Fo. 21.]

VISITACIO PRIORATUS DE TORKESEY, ORDINIS SANCTI AUGUSTINI, LINCOLNIENSIS DIOCESIS, FACTA IN DOMO CAPITULARI IBIDEM VJ DIE MENSIS APRILIS ANNO DOMINI MCCCCXL, PER REUERENDUM IN CHRISTO PATREM ET DOMINUM DOMINUM WILLELMUM, DEI GRACIA LINCOLNIENSEM EPISCOPUM, ANNO SUARUM CONSECRACIONIS XIIIJ° ET TRANSLACIONIS PRIMO.[1]

In quo quidem visitacionis negocio, dicto reuerendo patre die, loco et anno predictis iudicialiter sedente, comparuerunt coram eo prior et conuentus dicti loci ad subeundum huiusmodi suam visitacionem; et primo prior liberauit dicto reuerendo patri certificatorium citacionis sui et conuentus auctoritate mandati domini sibi in hac parte directi in hec verba, ' Reuerendissimo,' etc. Quibus perlectis, preconizatisque citatis et comparentibus, iurataque canonica obediencia per priorem, etc., idem prior exhibuit confirmacionem eleccionis sue factam per certos commissarios ad hoc deputatis[2] per dominum Philippum nuper Lincolniensem episcopum, qui commisit vices suas confirmandi eleccionem inibi celebrandam, etc. De installacione sua nichil exhibuit cum de hac vt asserit non habeat scripturam: dicit tamen se posse probare installacionem suam per testes; vnde habet terminum, post meridiem eiusdem diei eodem loco et coram domino ad sufficienter probandum installacionem suam. Exhibuit eciam statum domus, similiter et fundacionem domus. Non sunt alique cantarie in ipso prioratu fundate. Prior non dimisit[3] copias confirmacionis.

Postea prior examinatus dicit quod frater Johannes Gowselle, cum sit eruditus in arte cementaria, non vult missus per priorem intendere operibus ecclesie et prioratus sicut et ipse prior in persona sua, et sic inobediens est ad laborem, et[4] prior ipsum pro laboribus vltra alios remunerabit.

---

[1] *Sic*: for *quarto*.
[2] *Sic*: for *deputatos*.
[3] Some mistake has been made in writing this word, which has been imperfectly altered.
[4] *d* cancelled.

[1] *Rectius* fourth.
[2] His name, not given here, was Richard Hellay. See *Visitations* I, 165. The commissaries referred to were John Southam, archdeacon of Oxford, and Richard Hethe, archdeacon of Huntingdon (Reg. xv, fo. 131). In this small priory there was evidently some difficulty in finding suitable priors *de gremio*. William Cotyngham, elected in 1416, was a canon of Wellow, and Hellay, in 1417, was a canon of Haltemprice.
[3] A confirmation of this and other charters is printed in *Monasticon* VI (i), 426.
[4] A definite statement of this kind, as regards a member of a religious house, has a special interest. How far an intelligent acquaintance with the art of building would enable the canon in question to direct practical operations is, of course, doubtful, and, in view of the fact that the duties of the *magister* or *custos operis*

LXXV.

THE VISITATION OF THE PRIORY OF TORKSEY, OF THE ORDER OF ST. AUSTIN, OF THE DIOCESE OF LINCOLN, PERFORMED IN THE CHAPTER-HOUSE THEREIN ON THE SIXTH DAY OF THE MONTH OF APRIL, IN THE YEAR OF OUR LORD 1440, BY THF REVEREND FATHER IN CHRIST AND LORD, THE LORD WILLIAM, BY THE GRACE OF GOD BISHOP OF LINCOLN, IN THE FOURTEENTH YEAR OF HIS CONSECRATION AND THE FIRST[1] OF HIS TRANSLATION.

In the which business of the visitation, as the said reverend father was sitting in his capacity of judge on and in the day, place and year aforesaid, there appeared before him the prior and convent of the said place to undergo such his visitation; and in the first place the prior delivered to the said reverend father the certificate of the summons of himself and the convent, by the authority of my lord's mandate addressed to him in this behalf, in these words, ' To the right reverend,' etc. And, when this had been read through, and they that were summoned had been called by name and made appearance, and after canonical obedience had been sworn by the prior, etc., the same prior exhibited the confirmation of his election, made by certain commissaries deputed for this purpose by the lord Philip, late bishop of Lincoln, who committed his office of confirming the election to be celebrated therein, etc.[2] Concerning his installation he exhibited nothing, seeing that, as he asserts, he has not written evidence of this: he says, however, that he can prove his installation by means of witnesses; wherefore he has a term after noon of the same day, in the same place and before my lord, to make sufficient proof of his installation. He exhibited also the state of the house, likewise also the foundation of the house.[3] There are no chantries founded in the same priory. The prior did not leave copies of his confirmation.

Thereafter the prior, upon examination, says that brother John Gowselle, albeit he is learned in the art of stone-masonry,[4] will not take heed, when sent by the prior, to the works of the church and priory, as does the prior himself also in his own person; and so he is disobedient as regards his task, and the prior will reward him for his labours beyond the others.

---

in a monastery were financial and disciplinary, it would be unsafe to make too much of this casual allusion to architectural skill. At the same time, there can have been no large resources for the fabric of the priory at Torksey, and it is possible that Gowselle was expected to fill the place which was ordinarily occupied by the master-mason. There are occasional examples of monks and canons in the later middle ages who were capable of acting as master-craftsmen: Edward III engaged Edward of St. Andrews, a canon of Newstead, as master carpenter at the palace of Westminster and St. Stephen's chapel in 1355 and 1360 (*Cal. Close* 1354-60, p. 143; *Cal. Pat.* 1358-61, p. 490). The passage reads as though the canons were trying to undertake repairs themselves: the prior himself was something of an amateur, which may account for Gowselle's refractory conduct.

Item frater Johannes celebrauit vnum annale in diocesi Eboracensi ab vltimo festo natalis vsque nunc, sed tamen absque licencia diocesani proprii.

Frater Robertus Ellay dicit quod non surgunt de nocte ad matutinas, nec dicunt horas canonicas nec aliqua diuina officia cum nota, nec omnes simul conueniunt ad chorum ad diuina obsequia. Iniunctum est omnibus quod de nocte surgant ad matutinas secundum regularia instituta.

Item dicit quod prior plura opera inchoat in edificando et nullum perficit, sic quod opera incepta occasione imperfeccionis magna patiuntur detrimenta, et ideo melius foret vt sibi videtur vt non[1] inchoetur vnum opus[2] nisi prius inceptum debite perficiatur. Iniunctum est priori quod decetero nullum inchoet opus nisi communicato consilio cum fratribus suis et donec prius inchoata sint perfecte completa.

Frater Johannes Gowselle dicit quod omnia bene.

Frater Johannes Devyas dicit quod omnia bene preter hoc quod silencium nec alie regulares obseruancie non seruantur in domo secundum regulam. Iniunctum est eis in generali vt quantum est eis possibile obseruent regulares obseruancias, presertim silencium.

Communicet dominus cum magistro Johanne Southam an ille xl[3] quas dominus Thomas Brette dedit prioratui date erant ad vsum certum in prioratu vel generaliter ad commodum domus.

Dominus monuit priorem et[4] singulares conuentus personas sub pena excomunicacionis maioris quod decetero non commedant vel bibant in villa de Torkesey nisi sint illi qui intendunt curis ecclesiarum ibidem, dummodo se ad hoc non ing[erant] sed inuitentur per aliquas honestas personas.

Reseruata potestate corrigendi detecta in hac visitacione et faciendi iniuncciones, dominus dissoluit hanc suam visitacionem.

COMMISSIO AD INTERDICENDUM ADMINISTRACIONEM PRIORI DE TORKESEY PROPTER DILAPIDACIONEM.

(Reg. XVIII, fo. 59 *d*.)

Willelmus, permissione diuina Lincolniensis episcopus, dilecto in Christo filio et confratri nostro magistro Thome Skyman, ecclesie nostre Lincolniensis thesaurario, salutem, graciam et benediccionem. Relatu fidedigno et facti notorietate se manifestante iam recenter accepimus quod frater Ricardus Ellay, pro priore prioratus de Torksey, ordinis Sancti Augustini, nostre diocesis, se gerens, bona mobilia eiusdem adeo

---

[1] *s'* cancelled.
[2] *no* cancelled.
[3] *Sic*: *libre* omitted.
[4] *conu* cancelled.

[1] Lyndwood (tit. *de cele. miss.* cap. *Sacerdotes*; ed. 1679, p. 228) describes *annalia* as masses to be celebrated ' per anni spatium, vel alias temporaliter, sic quod non sint ad officia talia dicenda intitulati, nec perpetui, sed temporales, et elapso tempore remotiui.' Gowselle's engagement was probably in one of the churches in Nottinghamshire, just across the Trent.

[2] Of the four canons, the two Hellays or Ellays probably came from Elveley (Kirk Ella) in the East Riding, near Haltemprice priory. Gowselle is either Goxhill in Lincolnshire or the place of the same name in Holderness. The surname Devyas has no local connotation.

Also brother John has celebrated an annual in the diocese of York[1] from last Christmas until now, nevertheless without leave from his own diocesan.

Brother Robert Ellay[2] says that they do not get up for matins of a night, neither do they say the canonical hours or any of the divine offices with music,[3] nor do they all come together to quire for divine service. They all were enjoined to get up by night for matins according to the regular institutes.

Also he says that the prior begins many works in building and finishes none of them, so that the works which are begun suffer great damages by reason that they are incomplete; and therefore it would be better, as it seems to him, that a work should not be set on foot, unless that which was begun beforehand be duly finished. The prior was enjoined to begin no work henceforward without first taking common counsel with his brethren, and until the works previously begun be brought to a perfect end.

Brother John Gowselle says that all things are well.

Brother John Devyas[4] says that all things are well, were it not for this, that neither silence nor the other regular observances are kept in the house according to the rule. They were enjoined in general to keep the regular observances, especially silence, as far as lies in their power.

Let my lord take counsel with master John Southam[5] whether those forty [pounds] which sir Thomas Brette[6] gave to the priory were given for a certain use in the priory, or for the profit of the house in general.

My lord admonished the prior and the several persons of the convent, under pain of the greater excommunication, that henceforward they eat not or drink in the town of Torksey, unless they be such as look after the cures of the churches therein,[7] provided that [these] do not introduce themselves to this end, but are invited by some honest persons.

Having reserved the power of correcting the matters disclosed in this visitation, and of making injunctions, my lord dissolved this his visitation.

COMMISSION TO INTERDICT THE PRIOR OF TORKSEY FROM ADMINISTRATION
ON ACCOUNT OF DILAPIDATION.

William, by divine permission bishop of Lincoln, to our beloved son in Christ and brother master Thomas Skyman,[8] treasurer of our church of Lincoln, health, grace and blessing. We have now heard of late, by trustworthy information and by clear evidence of the notoriety of the fact, that brother Richard Ellay, who behaves himself as prior of the priory of Torksey, of the order of St. Austin, of our diocese, has so alienated, wasted and dilapidated the movable goods of the same that

---

[3] In view of the erroneous translations by which *cum nota* is occasionally rendered, Lyndwood's definition (tit. *de maio. et obe.* cap. *Presbyteri*, ed. 1679, p. 70) ' cantu, qui fit per notas,' may be remembered.

[4] Prior of Torksey in 1454 (*Assoc. Soc. R. & P.* xxviii, 528).

[5] Archdeacon of Oxford and a canon residentiary of Lincoln: see *Visitations* I, 182, 183. He died within a year of this date.

[6] There seems to be no other record of this bequest.

[7] The churches in Torksey were three, viz. St. Mary's, All Saints, and St. Peter's. The last was appropriated to the prior and convent in 1385 (*Assoc. Soc. R. & P.* u.s. pp. 502, 503).

[8] Or Skayman. See *Visitations* II, 163, note 4.

alienauit, consumpsit et dilapidauit quod de finali desolacione loci illius verisimiliter formidatur, et quod absque habitatore, quod absit, relinquetur quasi desertus. Ne igitur locus ille Deo sacratus tendat ad non esse nostras solicitudines interponere volentes, vobis committimus et mandamus quatinus ad prioratum illum personaliter descendatis et, si ita vt suggeritur fore repereritis, priorem illum pretensum ab omni et omnimoda administracione bonorum spiritualium et temporalium ad dictum prioratum spectancium, proueniencium et prouenire debencium suspendatis et huiusmodi administracionem interdicatis eidem omniaque et singula res et bona eiusdem prioratus iam existencia et futura[1] in huiusmodi subiaceant, in quibuscumque locis nostre diocesis et quorumcumque nostrorum subditorum manibus existencia, eciam singillum[2] commune dicti prioratus, ne per illius improuidam custodiam alienaciones fiant rerum aut bonorum prioratus illius realiter sequestretis et pro sic sequestratis publice denuncietis, et sequestrum nostrum huiusmodi omnibus quorum interest intimetis et notificetis, ac sequestri vestri[3] huiusmodi custodiam bonorumque sic sequestratorum administracionem plenariam personis idoneis committatis, sigillum predictum nobis remittendo, ceteraque exequamini et faciatis in premissis necessaria et oportuna. Ad que omnia et singula vobis committimus vices nostras et plenariam potestatem, mandantes quatinus nos de omni eo quod feceritis in premissis nos pro loco et tempore oportunis distincte et aperte sub sigillo nostro[4] autentico certificetis presencium cum tenore. Data sub sigillo nostro ad causas in manerio nostro de Bugden v die mensis Septembris, anno Domini mccccxliiij[to] nostrarumque consecracionis anno xix et translacionis viij.

LXXVI.

[Fo. 56 [54].]

VISITACIO PRIORATUS DE VLUESCROFT, ORDINIS SANCTI AUGUSTINI, LINCOLNIENSIS DIOCESIS, FACTA ET INCHOATA IN DOMO CAPITULARI IBIDEM XXIX[no] DIE MENSIS JULII, ANNO DOMINI MCCCCXXXVIIJ[o], PER REUERENDUM IN CHRISTO PATREM ET DOMINUM, DOMINUM WILLELMUM, DEI GRACIA LINCOLNIENSEM EPISCOPUM, ANNO SUE CONSECRACIONIS XIIJ[o] [5] ET TRANSLACIONIS SECUNDO.

In primis, sedente dicto reuerendo patre iudicialiter pro tribunali in huiusmodi visitacionis sue negocio, die, anno et loco predictis, comparuerunt personaliter coram se prior et conuentus dicti prioratus,

---

[1] *Que* (relative) appears to be omitted.
[2] I.e. *sigillum*.
[3] Apparently *vestri*; but the possessive pronouns in the MS. are somewhat ambiguous.
[4] *Sic*: for *vestro*.
[5] Written *xiji*[o], as though Colstone had written *xij* first, and added another i. As a matter of fact, the date falls within the twelfth year of Alnwick's consecration.

[1] His title to the priory was good, as he had been duly confirmed and admitted.
[2] *Rectius* your.

there is fear in all likelihood that that place will end in desolation, and will be left almost abandoned, which God forbid, without any dweller therein. We therefore, wishing to apply our anxious efforts, so that that place, consecrated to God, may not come utterly to naught, entrust and command you to go down in person to that priory, and, if you find that things are as it is hinted, to suspend that pretended prior[1] from all and every sort of administration of the spiritual and temporal goods which belong, accrue or should accrue to the said priory, and interdict the same from such administration, and to sequestrate in reality and pronounce in public to be so sequestrated all and sundry the real property and goods of the same priory that now are and shall be, lying subject within such [administration], in whatsoever places of our diocese and in the hands of whomsoever our subjects they be, [and] also the common seal of the said priory, lest by the improvident custody thereof the real property or goods of that priory may be alienated, and to intimate and give notice of such our sequestration to all who are concerned, and to commit the custody of such your sequestration and the plenary administration of the goods so sequestered, sending us the seal aforesaid, and to fulfil and do all else that is necessary and timely in the premises. For which things all and sundry we commit to you our office and plenary power, commanding you to certify us clearly and openly of all that you do in the premises, as place and time are convenient, under our[2] authentic seal, together with the tenor of these presents. Given under our seal *ad causas* in our manor of Bugden, on the fifth day of the month of September, in the year of our Lord 1444, and the nineteenth year of our consecration and of our translation the eighth.[3]

LXXVI.

The visitation of the priory of ULVERSCROFT, of the order of St. Austin, of the diocese of Lincoln, performed and begun in the chapter-house therein, on the twenty-ninth day of the month of July, in the year of our Lord 1438, by the reverend father in Christ and lord, the lord William, by the grace of God bishop of Lincoln, in the thirteenth[4] year of his consecration, and the second of his translation.

In the first place, as the said reverend father was sitting in his capacity of judge as a tribunal in the business of such his visitation, on and in the day, year and place aforesaid, there appeared in person before

---

[3] In 1453 the priory church was in a state of dilapidation, ' manifesta et notorie ruine subiecta,' according to an indulgence of forty days granted on 19 July in that year at Scrooby by William Bothe, archbishop of York. The indulgence was specially conceded to those ' qui beatissimum confessorum (*sic*) Leonardum . . , cuius vna venerabilis et notabilis corporis porcio, pes videlicet, in dicta ecclesia inter ceteras reliquas (*sic*) contineri perhibetur et pie creditur recondita et inclusa in quadam ymagine eiusdem satis decenter ornata deuote visitauerint et adorauerint' (Reg. W. Bothe, fo. 152 *d*.).

[4] *Rectius* twelfth.

parati vt apparuit ad subeundum visitacionem huiusmodi; et deinde ac primo et ante omnia propositum fuit verbum Dei per magistrum Thomam Duffelde, in sacra theologia bacallarium, sequentem hoc thema, ' Omnia secundum ordinem fiant in vobis.'[1] Deinde prior liberauit domino certificatorium[2] mandati domini eidem priori pro huiusmodi visitacione inibi facienda directi in hec verba, ' Reuerendo in Christo,' etc.; quo perlecto, exhibuit prior partem fundacionis loci, sed non totalem nec primeuam fundacionem. Exhibuit eciam confirmacionem eleccionis ipsius prioris; et deinde, iurata obediencia per dictum priorem in forma consueta, dominus processit ad examinacionem singularium personarum, que singillatim examinate dicunt ea que sequuntur.

Frater Johannes Annesley, prior, dicit quod domus potest expendere de claro lxxxx^{ta} marcas.

Item dicit quod domus indebitatur in c s., vt estimat, et quod centum solidi acquietabunt de omni onere eris alieni.

Item dicit quod frater Johannes Tamworth est multum sibi rebellis.

Interrogatus an secundum exigenciam regulie[3] et constitucionum reddat administracionis[4] sue compotum singulis annis, dicit quod istis proxime preteritis tribus annis nullum reddidit; sed dicit quod in proximo festo Michaelis erit paratus ad reddendum.

Item dicit quod canonici exeunt prioratum et euagantur nulla petita licencia, in tantum quod aliquociens prior solus dimittitur in prioratu absque socio.

Item dicit quod Robertus Rodyngtone discurrit in siluis et nemoribus absque licencia, querendo nidos auium siluestrium et capiendo alias bestias siluestres; et credit quod secreta capitularia reuelantur seruientibus secularibus per istum Robertum, et quod illi seculares ea reuelant in partibus ad magnum scandalum domus. Comparuit et negat omnia ista articulata. Oblato libro renuit iurare. Postea fatetur: vnde i[niunctum est] de peragendo penitenciam et de non exerendo[5] similia decetero: penitencia reseruata. Iniunctum est sub pena excommunicacionis singulis quod nullus exeat absque socio et licencia.

Item dicit quod frater Johannes Tamworthe retin*u*it[6] infra prioratum vnam deploidem defensiuam, et absque licencia exiuit domum vsque Berghdone loge[7] cum quodam carpentario, portando secum dictam deploidem, et postea vendidit eandem deploidem ad carpentarium et precium

---

[1] 1 Cor. xiv, 40.
[2] *cit* [? *citacionis*] cancelled.
[3] *Sic*: for *regule*.
[4] Altered from *administraciones*.
[5] *Sic*: for *exercendo*.
[6] Altered from *retinet*.
[7] *porta* cancelled.

[1] No charter of foundation appears to survive.
[2] There is apparently no record of his election. See *Visitations* I, 165.
[3] Of the eight names, Annesley and Rodyngtone (Ruddington) are from Nottinghamshire, and Whitewyke (Whitwick) from the neighbourhood of Ulverscroft. Broghtone is indefinite, though possibly from the vale of Belvoir, and Tamworth is obvious. Ashby-de-la-Zouch is near at hand, and Zouche may have belonged to that district. Flory and Kynde suggest no locality.
[4] The sequestered site of Ulverscroft, in a well-wooded valley in Charnwood forest, is probably the most picturesque site of a monastic house within the

him the prior and convent of the said priory, in readiness, as was apparent, to undergo such visitation; and then, and first and before all else, the word of God was set forth by master Thomas Duffelde, bachelor in sacred theology, after this text, 'Let all things be done in order among you.' Then the prior delivered to my lord the certificate of my lord's mandate addressed to the same prior for holding such visitation in that place, in these words, 'To the reverend [father] in Christ,' etc.; and, when this had been read through, the prior exhibited part of the foundation of the place, but not the entire or the original foundation.[1] He exhibited also the confirmation of the election of the same prior;[2] and then, after obedience had been sworn by the said prior in the accustomed form, my lord proceeded to the examination of the several persons, who, having been examined one by one, say these things which follow.

Brother John Annesley,[3] the prior, says that the house can spend a clear eighty marks.

Also he says that the house is a hundred shillings in debt, as he thinks, and that a hundred shillings will free it from all burthen of debt.

Also he says that brother John Tamworth is very rebellious against him.

Upon interrogation whether he renders the account of his administration every year, as the rule and constitutions require, he says that for these three years last past he has rendered none, but says that he will be ready to render one next Michaelmas.

Also he says that the canons go out of the priory and roam outside, without asking any leave, in so much that the prior is sometimes left alone in the priory without a companion.

Also he says that Robert Rodyngtone rambles about in the woods and copses without leave, looking for the nests of wood-birds and catching other creatures of the wood;[4] and he believes that the secrets of chapter are revealed by this Robert to the secular serving-folk, and that those secular persons reveal them in the neighbourhood, to the great scandal of the house. He appeared, and denies all these articles put to his charge. When the book was offered him, he refused to swear. Thereafter he confesses; wherefore he was enjoined to perform his penance and to hold no like practices hereafter: the penance was reserved. It was enjoined upon each one, under pain of excommunication, that no one go forth without a companion and a licence.

Also he says that brother John Tamworthe kept a doublet of defence[5] within the priory, and went out of the house without leave to Bardon lodge[6] with a carpenter, carrying the said doublet with him; and thereafter he sold the same doublet to the carpenter and kept the price for

---

ancient diocese of Lincoln: the approach through the woods from Newtown Linford is of remarkable beauty. It is possible that, had the name of Ulverscroft suited his verse, Wordsworth, during his residence at Cole Orton, would have celebrated the priory in preference to the 'ivied ruins of forlorn Gracedieu,' which are less secluded and romantic.

[5] See p. 256, note 4, and p. 290, note 3.

[6] Probably a grange of the monastery at Bardon, two to three miles N.W. of the priory. The striking hill of Bardon, on the edge of the forest, is a well-known landmark. The use of 'lodge' for an outlying farm is still common in forest districts, especially in Northamptonshire and the neighbouring counties.

sibi retinuit. Fatetur se habuisse talem deploidem et vendidisse et pecunias in vsus suos conuertisse: vnde prestito iuramento requisito absolutus est a sentencia excommunicacionis, etc.; et iniunctum est sibi vt septem vicibus dicat vij nocturna psalterii, et quod reuelet priori qualiter expendidit pecunias.

Item frater Johannes Broghtone, priore inscio, recipit pecunias et eas mutuat, et super hoc impetitus per priorem dicit quod vult recipere pecunias a matre, sorore et aliis amicis suis, et de eis pro sua voluntate libere disponere, nullius in mundo licencia petita.

Item dicit quod, quando aliqui hospites declinant ad locum, non solum vnus vel duo exhibent eis solacia, sed omnes ad hoc concurrunt; et tunc fiunt ibi strepitus, clamores, vigile,[1] potaciones et comesaciones absque mensura, eciam post completorium, sicque dissipant et consumunt indebite et dissolute bona domus.

Item dicit quod canonici non obseruant silencium in locis debitis secundum regulam: ymo confabulantur indistincte in choro, circa altare, in claustro et vbique.

[2]Frater Thomas Flory, supprior, dicit quod prior est nimis necgligens et tepidus in corrigendo defectus religionis.

Item dicit quod canonici soli absque licencia petita discurrunt et euagantur per vastum, ex quo scandalum domui generatur.

Item dicit quod prior est nimis capitosus in factis suis, nec petit consilium a senioribus confratribus suis ad agenda; nec petita sequitur, sed semper sectatur proprium velle, est ita capitosus.

Item dicit quod domus rectorie ecclesie sue de Boney, et eciam alia tenementa et edificia pertinencia prioratui, sunt adeo ruinosa quod c. marce non sufficerent ad competentem eorum reparacionem; et cum aliquis confrater siue quisquam sibi[3] dixerit de eorum reparacione, proteruo modo respondet dicens, 'Vellem quod omnia prostrata forent ad terram: satis est michi quod durent tempore meo.'

Item dicit quod, petitus a fratribus et iussus per visitatores ordinis, nullum a multis retroactis temporibus reddidit nec reddere vult de administracione sua compotum siue raciocinium, cum omnia solus recipit et ministrat, et teneat[4] omnia officia domus in manu sua; et credit quod domus ad omne minus indebitatur in xx marcis et amplius; et dimittit firmas domus absque sciencia, voluntate vel consensu conuentus.

Item dicit quod libri qui remanere deberent in libraria exportantur et alienantur, sic quod nescitur a conuentu vbi deueniant.

Item dicit quod libri pro choro non reparantur, adeo quod propter defectum reparacionis quasi totaliter destruuntur.

Item idem prior vendidit et prostrauit quingentas vel circiter ingentes quercus absque consensu conuentus et solum pro viij marcis, in magnam dilapidacionem dicti prioratus.

---

[1] *Sic*: for *vigilie*.
[2] These three paragraphs are bracketed in the original.
[3] I.e. *priori*.
[4] *Sic*: for *tenet*.

[1] *I.e.* the forest. The high land round the priory still preserves much of its old character.
[2] Bunny is in Nottinghamshire, 6½ miles S. of Nottingham. Thomas Ferrers, who had acquired the advowson of the church for that purpose, had licence to alienate

himself. He confesses that he had such a doublet and sold it, and applied the money to his own uses: wherefore, having proffered the requisite oath, he was absolved from the sentence of excommunication, etc.; and it was enjoined upon him that he should say seven nocturns of the psalter seven times, and that he should reveal to the prior how he has spent the money.

Also brother John Broghtone receives money and lends it without the prior's knowledge; and, when impeached by the prior touching this, he says that he will receive money from his mother, sister, and his other friends, and dispose thereof freely at his own will, without asking leave of any one in the world.

Also he says that, when any guests come down to the place, not only one or two give them good cheer, but all hasten together for this purpose; and then noise, clamour, wakes, drinkings and messes go on therein without measure, even after compline; and thus do they unduly and with disorder squander and waste the goods of the house.

Also he says that the canons do not keep silence in the due places according to the rule, but chatter together without distinction in quire, at the altar, in cloister and everywhere.

Brother Thomas Flory, the subprior, says that the prior is exceedingly lax and lukewarm in correcting faults of religious discipline.

Also he says that the canons, without asking leave, ramble and roam about by themselves through the waste,[1] wherefrom scandal is bred to the house.

Also he says that the prior is very obstinate in what he does, nor does he ask advice of his elder brethren as regards what has to be done; and, when it is asked, he does not follow it, but ever runs after his own will, so headstrong is he.

Also he says that the rectory house of their church of Bunny,[2] and also the other tenements and buildings appertaining to the priory, are in such decay that a hundred marks would not be enough to repair them sufficiently; and, when any of his brethren or any person speaks to him of their repair [the prior] answers in saucy fashion, saying, 'I would willingly have them all levelled to the ground: it is enough for me that they last for my time.'

Also he says that [the prior], though asked by the brethren and bidden by the visitors of the order, has rendered no account or reckoning of his administration for a long time past, nor will he render one, whereas he receives and supplies all things by himself, and holds all the offices of the house in his hand; and he believes that the house is at the very least twenty marks or more in debt, and [the prior] lets the farms of the house without the knowledge, will or consent of the convent.

Also he says that the books, which ought to remain in the library, are carried off and alienated, so that the convent does not know where they are gone.

Also he says that the books for the quire are not repaired, so that, for lack of repair, they are almost utterly destroyed.

Also the same prior sold and felled five hundred great oaks or thereabout, without the consent of the convent and for eight marks only, to the sore dilapidation of the said priory.

it in mortmain to the prior and convent, 30 May, 1345, in order to found chantries for the soul of Henry Ferrers (*Cal. Pat.* 1343-5, p. 475).

Item dicit quod consueuerunt habere boues, vaccas et oues, ac alia animalia in magno numero, ex quorum exitu pro maiori parte sustentabatur;[1] sed iam, paucis relictis, omnia perierunt, nec prouidetur domui de nouis, sic quod verisimile est quod domus non potest diu subsistere.

Item dicit quod omnia ostia prioratus sunt absque seruris et stant quasi aperta.

[Fo. 56 [54] *d.*] Item dicit quod cista in qua seruantur et reponuntur euidencie et munimenta domus est adeo debilis quod infantulus posset eam absque magna *vi* frangere et munimenta illa tollere; et similiter sunt ciste alie in quibus vestimenta et alia iocalia et bona domus reponuntur.

Item dicit quod prior, incaute conducens seruientes pro domo, conuenit sic cum eis quod, preter stipendia et vesturas ac victualia, inueniat eis lectisternia.

Item dicit quod prior non est circumspectus in regimine yconomie et operum ruralium; et dicit quod fimus de septem annis remanet in diuersis locis prioratus non abductus ad terras compostandas, ad magnum domus detrimentum, quod[2] terre propter hoc sint[3] quasi steriles.

Item habent duos temporales de consilio; et tamen prior non permittit eos tenere curias, et propter hoc tenementa domus ruunt et tenentes non reddunt seruicia.

Item dicit quod domus haberet decimas arbores de Lyefeld[4] iure domus monachorum de Shene; et tamen prior necgligenter propter complacenciam domini de Ferrariis omittit eas petere aut exigere.

Frater Johannes Tammeworthe deponit vt in billa.

Frater Johannes Broghtone, refectorarius, dicit quod domus bouerie sunt multum ruinose ob defectum debite reparacionis, et cum[5] quicquam infra domum vel tenementum edificauerit,[6] cum fraccinis edificat et extraneis absque consensu conuentus ingentes donat quercus, sic quod edificia per ipsum constructa non sunt vtilia; et si super hoc sit impetitus, respondet ' satis est michi quod duret tempore meo.'

Item prior ex magna imprudencia sumit vaccas fetosas ad coquinam[7] et dimittit alios masculini sexus; et dicit quod credit quod prior multum gubernatur per quendam secularem sibi in camera seruientem.

Item dicit quod prior omnia inordinate et incaute facit, propter quod domus totaliter quasi est in decasu.

Frater Johannes Whitewyke, cantor, dicit quod frater Thomas Flory, nunc supprior, erat ad extra per xx annos, an in apostasia nec ne

---

[1] *Sic*: for *sustentabantur.*
[2] *de* cancelled.
[3] *Sic*: for *sunt.*
[4] Note in margin . . . *dominus dictus de Groby.*
[5] *quemquam* cancelled.
[6] I.e. *prior.*
[7] Altered from *coquinas.*

[1] *I.e.* to give counsel and help in external administration.
[2] This appears to be Leighfield forest in Rutland, near Oakham and on the borders of Leicestershire. It seems from this passage that there had been some exchange of property between Ulverscroft and Shene priories, by which Ulverscroft obtained a right to the tithe in question; but it is not clear how Shene obtained the tithe in the first instance. Presumably the tithe was leased to lord Ferrers, who withheld his yearly rent.

Also he says that they were wont to have oxen, cows and sheep, and other beasts in great number, from the issue whereof they had the more part of their sustenance; but now, but for a few that are left, all are come to naught, nor is provision of new stock made for the house, so that it is likely that the house cannot last long.

Also he says that all the doors of the priory are without locks, and stand almost open.

Also he says that the chest in which the title-deeds and muniments of the monastery are kept and laid is so frail that a little child could break it without great force and carry off those muniments; and the other chests, in which the vestments and the other treasures and goods of the house are laid, are in like condition.

Also he says that the prior, hiring serving-folk for the house without caution, so covenants with them that, beside their wages and clothing and victuals, he shall find them their bedding.

Also he says that the prior is not circumspect in the management of their rural estates and business; and he says that dung seven years old remains in divers places of the priory, without being carried to manure their lands, to the great harm of the house, because for this reason their lands are almost barren.

Also they have two temporal persons of their counsel;[1] and yet the prior does not suffer them to hold courts, and by reason hereof the tenements of the house are falling, and the tenants do not render their services.

Also he says that the house should have the tithe of the trees of Leighfield, in right of the house of the monks of Shene;[2] and nevertheless the prior carelessly neglects to demand or exact them, out of complacency to lord Ferrers.

Brother John Tammeworthe makes deposition, as in his bill.

Brother John Broghtone, the fraterer, says that the ox-houses are greatly in ruin for default of due repair; and, whenever [the prior] builds anything within the house or one of its tenements, he builds it of ash and gives the great oaks to strangers without the consent of the convent, so that the buildings constructed by him are of no profit; and, if he be impeached concerning this, he answers, ' It is enough for me that it should last for my time.'[3]

Also the prior, with great lack of foresight, takes milch cows for the kitchen, and leaves other cattle of the male sex; and he says that he believes that the prior is greatly ruled by a secular person who serves him in his lodging.

Also he says that the prior does all things disorderly and without caution, by reason whereof the house is almost utterly in decay.

Brother John Whitewyke, the chanter,[4] says that brother Thomas Flory, now the subprior, was outside the house for twenty years, whether

---

[3] The prior might have pleaded the pious example of Hezekiah: ' sit pax et veritas in diebus meis ' (2 Kings xx, 19). A considerable amount of building was done at Ulverscroft in the fifteenth century, including the fine west tower of the church and the conversion of the south end of the dorter range into the prior's lodging, well preserved in the farmhouse on the site. This, however, was not till somewhat later, probably about 1470-80, after the financial position of the monastery had been improved by its union with the neighbouring priory of Charley in 1465.

[4] Appointed prior of Charley, 20 May, 1444 (Reg. xviii, fo. 158 d.).

ignorat; et conuentu inscio prior iterato admisit eum in domum, regula non seruata et cum sit conuentui odiosus; et prior commisit sibi officium audiendi confessiones. Quidam abhorrent sibi confiteri, sic quod timet plures inconfessos.

Frater Johannes Zouche, camerarius, dicit quod per improuidum regimen prioris domus est redacta quasi ad vltimatum exterminium; et dicit quod non habent gramina neque blada, oues aut boues, vel alia aliqua ad sufficienciam pasturarum; et dicit quod domus in tantum depauperatur quod non habetur ibi vnus competens lectus pro vno honesto valetto; et dicit quod vtensilia in vnoquoque officio existencia sunt vetusta et quasi vsu consumpta.

Item dicit quod, quia vaccarius, qui vtilis est domui, aliquociens, honeste tamen, contradicit priori et hoc pro commodo domus, prior, habens ipsum ideo[1] exosum, intendit ipsum expellere et alium inutilem cum vxore sua non honesta subinducere.

Frater Robertus Rodyngtone, sacrista, dicit quod sigillum commune solum sub duabus seruris,[2] contra iniunccionem officialis sede vacante; et dicit quod prior non ministrat sibi ceram et oleum necessaria officio illi, et cum petierit a priore, patitur repulsam et tandem cum rubore ministrat in ceteris. Refert se ad billam ministratam per Tamworthe.

Item dicit quod prior non ministrat canonicis pecunias pro necessariis consuetis, nec eciam isti expensas quando vltimo profectus fuit ad ordines suscipiendos.

Item dicit quod omnes clausure domus, vt in muris lapideis, sunt ruinose et in decasu.

[Fo. 57 [55].] Frater Thomas Kynde, nouicius, refert se ad billam ministratam per Tamworthe, et dicit quod prior et supprior sunt indiscreti in correccionibus faciendis et penitenciis iniungendis.

Item dicit quod prior est nimis rigorosus in penitenciis iniungendis in foro anime, quandoque pro leui excessiue iniungendo.

Habitis communicacionibus primo cum priore solo, secundo cum conuentu, absente priore, tercio cum omnibus,[3] appunctuatum est per dominum de consensu prioris expresso et voluntate conuentus quod prior habebit regimen prioratus interius et exterius de hinc vsque proximum[4] festum Sancti Michaelis, et ad ipsum festum dominus disponet vtrum prior resignabit an deputabitur sibi coadiutor; et quod idem prior parebit et obediet ordinacioni domini corporale prestitit iuramentum. Et deinde continuauit dominus visitacionem vsque diem lune proximam post dictum festum Sancti Michaelis,[5] etc., presentibus magistro J. Depyng, Thoma Thorpe et me Colstone.

---

[1] Altered from *adeo*.
[2] *Sic: seruatur* omitted.
[3] *conclusu* cancelled.
[4] *post* cancelled.
[5] *I.e.* 6 Oct., 1438.

[1] This indicates that there had been a special visitation of the convent in 1436.
[2] *I.e.* for the lights of the church.
[3] Much of the dyke which enclosed the site is still in excellent preservation. The wall, however, is gone, and there are no remains of the gatehouse.
[4] He resigned a year later, and was succeeded on 14 July, 1439, by John Pollesworth, canon of aund priory (Reg. xviii, fo. 151 *d.*).

in apostasy or no he knows not; and the prior, without the knowledge of the convent, admitted him to the house a second time, not keeping the rule, and albeit he is detestable to the convent; and the prior committed to him the office of hearing confessions. Certain persons shrink from confessing to him, so that he fears that many are unconfessed.

Brother John Zouche, the chamberlain, says that by the imprudent governance of the prior the house is reduced almost to final destruction; and he says that they have not grass or wheat, sheep or oxen, or aught else for which they have sufficient pasture; and he says that the house is brought to so great poverty that they have not a bed therein suitable for a decent yeoman; and he says that the vessels that are for use in each of their offices are old and almost worn out with use.

Also he says that, because the cowherd, who is of profit to the house, sometimes contradicts the prior, albeit honestly, and this for the advantage of the house, the prior, holding him in hatred on this account, is minded to expel him and to bring in another person of no profit in his place, with his wife, who is unhonest.

Brother Robert Rodyngtone, the sacrist, says that the common seal [is kept] under two locks only, contrary to the injunction of the official during the voidance of the see;[1] and he says that the prior does not furnish him with the wax and oil necessary to that office,[2] and, whenever he asks it of the prior, he suffers refusal, and at length does his ministry in all other matters with shame. He refers himself to the bill presented by Tamworthe.

Also he says that the prior does not provide the canons with money for their accustomed necessaries, nor also [did he provide] this deponent with his expenses, when he set out last time to take orders.

Also he says that all the enclosures of the house, in respect of stone walls, are ruinous and in decay.[3]

Brother Thomas Kynde, novice, refers himself to the bill presented by Tamworthe, and says that the prior and subprior are without discretion in making corrections and enjoining penances.

Also he says that the prior is very strict in his injunction of penances in the spiritual tribunal, sometimes enjoining excessive penance for a light matter.

After converse had been held first with the prior alone, secondly with the convent in the prior's absence, thirdly with all, it was appointed by my lord, with the express consent of the prior and the will of the convent, that the prior shall have the internal and external governance of the priory until Michaelmas next; and at the same feast my lord shall take order whether the prior shall resign or a coadjutor be deputed for him; and the same prior proffered his bodily oath that he will obey and hearken to my lord's ordinance,[4] And then my lord adjourned his visitation until Monday next after the said feast of St. Michael, etc., there being present master J. Depyng, Thomas Thorpe, and I Colstone.[5]

---

[5] The document which follows, though not concerned directly with Ulverscroft, bears upon the condition of a small and almost moribund priory in its immediate neighbourhood. The priory of Charley is sometimes confounded with Ulverscroft: see, e.g., Salter, *Chapters of Augustinian Canons*, pp. 102, 269, 271. Mr. Salter (p. 269) remarks that Ulverscroft and Charley ' are merely two names of the same place '; but see *Visitations* i, 163. Charley, in fact, is about two miles from Ulverscroft. Both priories owed their foundation to the twelfth-century earls of Leicester,

COMMISSIO AD INQUIRENDUM DE DEFECTIBUS PRIORATUS DE CHARLEY.
[Reg. XVIII, fo. 53 *d.*]

Willelmus, permissione diuina Lincolniensis episcopus, dilecto in Christo filio magistro Johanni Wardale, nostro in archidiaconatu nostro Leycestrie et partibus de Kesteuen commissario generali, salutem, graciam et benediccionem. Ex plurium fidedignorum relacione factique notorietate ad nostrum deuenit auditum quod quidam frater Johannes Baltone, gerens se quod prior[1] prioratus de Charley, ordinis Sancti Augustini, nostre diocesis, omissis horis canonicis obsequioque diuino nocturno pariter et diurno, obseruanciis regularibus secundum regulam penitus desolutis,[2] ad nichil aliud vacat nisi potacionibus, ingurgitacionibus et publicis tabernis, in aliis aliter viuens quam deceret, ecclesiamque conuentualem dicti prioratus ceteraque edificia, officinas et domos, clausuras, muros et parietes tam ad intra quam ad extra ruine patere suo defectu patet,[3] cum defectus contingentes in eisdem non reparet, nemora grossa et antiqua non cedua succidit, prosternit et alienat, decimas, iura, redditus et reuentus ac emolumenta alia quecunque eiusdem prioratus consumit et dilapidat; sicque prioratus ille cum possessionibus suis, que per fundatores dabantur in suffragium animarum suarum, per malam et improuidam gubernacionem dicti fratris Johannis tendunt ad non esse, et propterea dictorum fundatorum et donatorum anime suis suffragiis inhumaniter defraudantur. Volentes igitur tam super premissis singulis quam statu dicti prioratus plenius informari, vt contra ea remedium quod possimus apponamus, vobis committimus plenius iniungentes quatinus ad loca in quibus res et possessiones huiusmodi consistunt personaliter accedatis et defectus huiusmodi personali visu[4] supponatis, necnon de vita, conuersacione et totali regimine dicti fratris Johannis, ipso ad hec vocato, per illos inter quos conuersatus est coram vobis iuratos plene et fideliter per omnia inquiratis per omnia[5] veritatem, et quod in premissis inuenire poteritis et faceritis[6] impremissis,[7] sequestrato primitus [fo. 54] nostra auctoritate sigillo communi dicti prioratus et sub salua custodia emisso, nos pro loco et tempore congruis et oportunis distincte et aperte certificetis litteris vestris patentibus habentibus hunc tenorem autentice sigillatis. Data sub sigillo nostro ad causas in manerio nostro de Nettelham viij die mensis Marcii, anno Domini mccccmo xliij nostrarumque consecracionis anno xviij et translacionis viijo.

---

but remained distinct until 1465, when Charley was annexed to Ulverscroft (Reg. xx, fo. 80 and *d.*). It is curious, however, that, as one of the lists cited by Mr. Salter appears to have been written at Laund priory as late as 1510, 'Oluecroft' and 'Charleya' appear in it as distinct monasteries. This list, however, includes 'Twate,' which is probably Thwate in Lincolnshire, a small cell of Thornton (see p. 373 above), and not, as Mr. Salter suggests, Mountjoy or Thweyt in dio. Norwich; so that the priory of Charley may have been preserved as a cell or 'seyny place' to Ulverscroft.

    [1] *Sic*: for *pro priore.*
    [2] *Sic*: for *dissolutis.*
    [3] *Sic*: for *patitur.*
    [4] *Sic*: for *visui.*
    [5] *Sic*: repeated.
    [6] *Sic*: for *feceritis.*
    [7] *Sic*: for *in premissis.*

COMMISSION TO INQUIRE CONCERNING THE DEFAULTS OF THE PRIORY OF CHARLEY.

William, by divine permission bishop of Lincoln, to our beloved son in Christ master John Wardale,[1] our commissary general in our archdeaconry of Leicester and in the parts of Kesteven, health, grace and blessing. By the report of many trustworthy persons and by common knowledge of the fact it has reached our hearing that one brother John Baltone,[2] behaving himself as prior of the priory of Charley, of the order of St. Austin, of our diocese, neglecting the canonical hours and divine service by night and day alike, the regular observances according to the rule being utterly abandoned, gives his time to naught else but drinking, surfeiting and the public taverns, living in other respects otherwise than were seemly, and suffers by his default the conventual church of the said priory, and the other buildings, offices and houses, enclosures, walls and party-walls both within and without to be exposed to ruin, seeing that he does not repair the defaults that occur in the same, cuts down, fells and alienates great and ancient copses that are not fit for cutting, wastes and dilapidates the tithes, rights, rents and revenues, and all other emoluments whatsoever of the same priory; and so that priory with its possessions, which were given by the founders for the succour of their souls, by reason of the ill and improvident governance of the said brother John are coming to an end, and because thereof the souls of the founders and givers are unkindly defrauded of their assistance. We therefore, wishing for fuller information touching each of the premises as well as the state of the priory, so that we may apply what remedy we can to meet them, entrust you with the fullest injunctions to go in person to the places in which such real property and possessions consist, and submit such defaults to your personal view, and also make full and faithful inquiry into the truth by all means, on the oath taken before you of those among whom he has had his conversation, and, having first by our authority sequestrated the common seal of the said priory and put it under safe custody, to certify us clearly and openly, as place and time are agreeable and convenient, of what you can find in the premises and shall do in the same, by your letters patent, having this tenor, authentically sealed. Given under our seal *ad causas* in our manor of Nettleham, on the eighth day of the month of March, in the year of our Lord 1443,[3] and in the eighteenth year of our consecration and of our translation the eighth.

---

[1] John Wardall, priest, LL.D., had collation of Leicester St. Margaret preb. in Lincoln, 7 Nov., 1448, (Reg. XVIII, fo. 109: not 1447, as Le Neve II, 169). He held this till his death, which occurred 4 May, 1472: he also at that date held Twyford preb. in St. Paul's (Hennessy, p. 52). He was inst. to the vicarage of Islington, Middlesex, 16 April, 1455 (*ibid.* p. 230), and to the church, which he held simultaneously, of Great Wigborough, Essex, 17 Sept., 1466 (Newcourt II, 663). His will (P.C.C. 6 Wattys), dated 1 May, was proved 26 May, 1472.

[2] *Rectius* Belton. See *Visitations* I, 163. It seems as though there was no other canon in the priory at the time. For some time past priors had been introduced from other houses: Belton's two immediate predecessors had been canons of Burscough and Repton respectively.

[3] 8 March, 1443-4. Belton resigned, and John Whitewyk was admitted on 20 May following: see p. 388, note 4.

LXXVII.

[Fo. 71 [69].]

VISITACIO MONASTERIJ DE WELHOWE IUXTA GRYMESBY, ORDINIS
SANCTI AUGUSTINI, LINCOLNIENSIS DIOCESIS, FACTA IN DOMO
CAPITULARI IBIDEM VIJ DIE MENSIS JULII, ANNO DOMINI MCCCCXL°,
PER REUERENDUM IN CHRISTO PATREM ET DOMINUM, DOMINUM
WILLELMUM, DEI GRACIA LINCOLNIENSEM EPISCOPUM, SUARUM
CONSECRACIONIS ANNO XIIIJ° ET TRANSLACIONIS QUARTO.

In primis, sedente dicto reuerendo patre iudicialiter in dicte visitacionis sue negocio die et loco antedictis, comparuerunt in eodem negocio
abbas et conuentus dicti monasterii; et deinde primo et ante omnia
propositum fuit verbum Dei iuxta actus futuri congruenciam per fratrem
Johannem Alesby, eiusdem monasterii canonicum, sequentem hoc
thema, ' Pax erit vobis,'[1] etc. Quo finito, abbas exhibuit dicto reuerendo
patri certificatorium mandati sibi a domino pro huiusmodi visitacione
inibi exercenda transmissi, sub hac forma, ' Reuerendo,' etc. Quo
perlecto, idem Robertus[2] exhibuit dicto reuerendo patri confirmacionem
eleccionis sue, sed non exhibet installacionem. Postea exhibuit singulas
euidencias loci et aliarum possessionum in quodam registro contentas.
Postea iurauit abbas obedienciam et fidelitatem vt in forma, et deinde
examinatus dicit ea que sequuntur.

Frater Henricus Suttone, abbas, dicit quod frater Willelmus Elkyngton de proficiscendo ad curiam licenciatus iterum rediit et [erat] admissus.
Secundo absque licencia exiens iterum rediens admissus erat; et tercio
apostatando exiens nunquam rediit, sed semper manet adhuc in apostasia.

Item dicit quod non reddit plenum compotum de administracione
sua coram conuentu singulis annis.

Item quod quilibet canonicus percipit in anno ad vesturam xxvj*s.*
viij*d.*

Frater Johannes Bachilere dicit quod habetur vna cantaria apud
Holme cui deseruitur quotidie per duos canonicos ibidem residentes.

Item Robertus Forman, vnus de consilio monasterii, habet feodum
annuum xiij*s.* iiij*d.* et certas terras apud Germethorpe, quas toto tempore
suo et eciam eius pater tempore suo tenuit de monasterio vt in partem
feodi, nullis indenturis super captura terre huiusmodi factis.

Frater Robertus Humfray dicit omnia bene. Dicit tamen quod
abbas iacet in camera, non in dormitorio.

---

[1] Probably Jer. iv, 10.
[2] *Sic*: an inexplicable error for *abbas*.

[1] For full details of the election see *Visitations* I, 124, 125 (No. LI). At the
time of his election in 1421, abbot Sutton was a canon of Fineshade priory.
[2] No register or chartulary survives.
[3] The name of the abbot, who came to Wellow from a Northamptonshire
monastery, may have been derived from one of the Suttons in those parts, possibly
in the valley of the Welland or Nene. Alesby (Aylesby), Myddeby, Northcotes
(*i.e.* North Somercotes), Somercotes and Westby, with the apostate Elkyngton,
bore Lincolnshire surnames. Chesterfelde is from Derbyshire. The remaining
four bore names of other types.

LXXVII.

THE VISITATION OF THE MONASTERY OF WELLOW BY GRIMSBY, OF THE
ORDER OF ST. AUSTIN, OF THE DIOCESE OF LINCOLN, PERFORMED
IN THE CHAPTER-HOUSE THEREIN ON THE SEVENTH DAY OF THE
MONTH OF JULY, IN THE YEAR OF OUR LORD 1440, BY THE REVEREND
FATHER IN CHRIST AND LORD, THE LORD WILLIAM, BY THE GRACE
OF GOD BISHOP OF LINCOLN, IN THE FOURTEENTH YEAR OF HIS
CONSECRATION AND THE FOURTH OF HIS TRANSLATION.

In the first place, as the said reverend father was sitting in his capacity
of judge in the business of his said visitation, on and in the day and place
aforesaid, there appeared in the same business the abbot and convent
of the said monastery; and then, first and before all else, the word of
God was set forth as befitted the act that was about to take place by
brother John Alesby, canon of the same monastery, after this text,
' Peace shall be unto you,' etc.   And, when this was finished, the abbot
exhibited to the said reverend father the certificate of the mandate
conveyed to him from my lord for holding such visitations in that place,
under this form, ' To the reverend,' etc.   And, after this had been read
through, the same [abbot] exhibited to the said reverend father the
confirmation of his election,[1] but does not exhibit his installation.   Thereafter he exhibited the several title-deeds of the place and of its other
possessions, contained in a register.[2] Afterwards the abbot sware
obedience and fealty as in form, and then upon examination he says
these things which follow.

Brother Henry Suttone,[3] the abbot, says that Brother William
Elkyngton, who had leave to journey to the court [of Rome], came back
again and [was] admitted.   Going forth a second time without leave
[and] coming back again, he was admitted; and the third time he went
forth in apostasy and never returned, but still abides continually in
apostasy.

Also he says that he does not render a full account of his administration before the convent every year.

Also that every canon receives 26s. 8d. in the year for raiment.

Brother John Bachilere says that they have a chantry at Holme,
which is served daily by two canons who reside in the same.[4]

Also Robert Forman, one of the counsel of the monastery,[5] has a
yearly fee of 13s. 4d. and certain lands at Grainthorpe,[6] which he has
held all his time, and his father in his time also held of the monastery
as part of his fee, though no indentures were made touching the taking
of seisin of such land.

Brother Robert Humfray says all things are well.   He says, however,
that the abbot lies in his lodging, not in the dorter.

---

[4] Holme was a manor in the neighbourhood of Clee.

[5] Cf. the two temporal persons who were of the counsel of the prior and convent
of Ulverscroft (p. 388 above).

[6] About ten miles S.E. of Grimsby.

Frater Robertus Somercotes senior, dicit quod abbas solum venit ad matutinas in principalibus.

Frater Thomas Chesterfelde dicit omnia bene.

Frater Johannes Goldsmithe dicit omnia bene.

Frater Willelmus Myddeby dicit quod refectorium non obseruatur, saltem ex quo iste venit ad monasterium.

Frater Johannes Westeby dicit omnia bene.

Frater Johannes Alesby dicit quod deseruit ecclesie de Clee in officio capellani parochialis, et desiderat restitui *ad* claustrum; nam omni die venit ad monasterium ad refeccionem, quod laboriosum est, sed ibi pernoctat.

Item dicit quod ignorat an constituciones legatine sui ordinis[1] siue regula legantur in capitulo necne.

Frater Johannes Tolsone dicit quod defectus est in Roberto Forman, senescallo, quod compotus non redditur in communi.

Item dicit quod abbas vendidit vnum corrodium Johanni Mathewe pro l marcis de consensu conuentus, et constat in tanto quantum percipient duo canonici in esculentis et poculentis; et stetit in eo x annis et amplius.

Frater Robertus Northcotes dicit quod dudum fuerunt in monasterio xviij canonici, aliquociens xvj vel xv, et nunc sunt nisi xj in toto.

Quibus examinatis, dominus sedens dictis die et loco in huiusmodi visitacionis sue negocio iudicialiter publicauit detecta, et deinde iniunxit abbati vt singulis annis inter festa Sancti Michaelis et Omnium Sanctorum ostendat plenum statum domus in communi confratribus suis in capitulo vel certis personis ad hoc deputatis per capitulum, et quod frequencius iaceat in dormitorio et veniat ad matutinas et intersit capitulo pro corrigendis excessibus et defectibus in obseruanciis regularibus et diuino obsequio, et quod frequencius celebret et quod habeat capellanum secum vnum de canonicis suis, qui sit testis conuersacionis sue, etc. Et hiis dictis et gestis dissoluit visitacionem suam, presentibus Depyng, Skayman et me Colstone.

WELHOWE.

[Fo. 77 *d.* [75 *d.*].]

Willelmus, permissione diuina Lincolniensis episcopus, dilectis filiis abbati et conuentui monasterii de Welhowe iuxta Grymesby, ordinis Sancti Augustini, nostre diocesis, salutem, graciam et benediccionem. Cum plantatam sanctam, etc., vt in Croyland.

(1.) In primis iniungimus vobis abbati sub pena grauis contemptus, ac dicti monasterii priori et suppriori ceterisque ordini presidentibus *sub penis infrascriptis*, vt quolibet die quo capitulum celebraueritis

---

[1] *sup* cancelled.

[1] As distinguished from Robert Northcotes.

[2] A vicarage was ordained in the church of Clee, which was barely two miles from the monastery. The document printed at the end of this visitation indicates that vicars had not regularly served the cure, and Alesby's description of himself as parish chaplain, a title never given to vicars, but always denoting a *capellanus amotivus*, shows that the convent had by this time adopted the alternative and irregular method of serving the church by a curate chosen from their number. The last institution to the vicarage of Clee before the suppression of the monasteries bears date 5 April, 1403 (Reg. XIII, fo. 154 *d.*). There is not another till 1590.

Brother Robert Somercotes the elder[1] says that the abbot comes to matins only on the principal feasts.

Brother Thomas Chesterfelde says all things are well.

Brother John Goldsmithe says all things are well.

Brother William Myddeby says that frater is not kept, at any rate since this deponent came to the monastery.

Brother John Westeby says all things are well.

Brother John Alesby says that he serves the church of Clee in the office of parish chaplain, and desires to be restored to cloister; for every day he comes to the monastery for his meals, which is toilsome, but he spends the night at Clee.[2]

Also he says that he does not know whether the legatine constitutions of his order[3] or the rule be read in chapter or not.

Brother John Tolsone says that it is the fault of Robert Forman, the steward, that the account is not rendered in common.

Also he says that the abbot sold a corrody to John Mathewe for fifty marks with the consent of the convent, and it consists of as much as two canons shall receive in meat and drink; and he has been in possession of it for ten years and more.

Brother Robert Northcotes says that aforetime there were in the monastery eighteen canons, sometimes sixteen or fifteen; and now there are but eleven in all.

Now, when these had been examined, my lord, sitting in his capacity of judge on and in the said day and place in the business of such his visitation, made public the matters disclosed, and then enjoined upon the abbot that every year, between the feasts of St. Michael and All Saints, he shall show the full state of the house in common to his brethren in chapter, or to certain persons appointed by the chapter for this purpose, and that he shall lie more often in the dorter, and come to matins and be present in chapter to correct transgressions and shortcomings in the regular observances and divine service, and that he shall celebrate more often, and that he shall have as his chaplain with him one of his canons, to be a witness to his conversation, etc. And, when these things had been said and done, he dissolved his visitation, there being present Depyng, Skayman and I Colstone.

WELLOW.

William, by divine permission bishop of Lincoln, to our beloved sons the abbot and convent of the monastery of Wellow by Grimsby of the order of St. Augustine, of our diocese, health, grace and blessing. Inasmuch, where holy [religion] is planted, etc., as in [the injunctions for] Croyland.[4]

(1.) In the first place, we enjoin upon you the abbot, under pain of grievous contempt, and upon the prior and subprior of the said monastery and the other presidents of the order, under the penalties hereunder

---

[3] The reference to those constitutions of Otho and Ottobon which specially concerned religious houses. This deposition appears to arise out of the last. Alesby had confessed to spending the night at Clee alone. This naturally provoked the question whether he was aware that this was contrary to Ottobon's constitution *Monachos*, which forbade monks or canons regular to dwell alone in manors or churches.

[4] See p. 379, note 1.

constituciones vestri ordinis et legatinas *vos ac dictum ordinem vestrum concernentes*, ac eciam regulam vestram, *seu saltem notabilem partem earundem, ita quod singulis septimanis plene perlegantur*, coram toto conuentu lingua illa que melius intelligi potest in pleno capitulo legi faciatis et ab omnibus penitus obseruari, transgressores secundum regulam taliter punientes vt pena et *non* impunitas sit ceteris in exemplum.

(2. Ad interessendum matutinis.) Item iniungimus vobis abbati in virtute obediencie et sub pena grauis contemptus, vt frequencius solito in dormitorio cum confratribus[1] *vestris* de nocte quiescatis, et ad matutinas personaliter accedatis et eis in choro ac capitulis celebrandis presencialiter intersitis, presidentibus ordini in corrigendo[2] excessus et delicta delinquencium in regularibus obseruanciis et diuino seruicio sedule assistendo.

(3. Ad celebrandum et capellanum habendum.) Item iniungimus vobis abbati sub simili pena preter penas infrascriptas et in remissionem peccaminum vestrorum, quod frequenter confiteamini et celebretis, et vtrobique confratrem vnum vobiscum habeatis capellanum, qui testis sit vestre honeste conuersacionis, quem omni anno, in fine videlicet, mutari volumus et alium loco amoti surrogari.

(4. Ad legendum tempore refeccionis.) Item iniungimus vobis abbati et conuentui sub penis supra et infrascriptis, vt temporibus quadragesimalibus et aduentus Domini ac omni quarta et sexta feria extra[3] tempora *illa* refectorium seruetis et vescamini in eodem, leccionemque aliquam de sacra scriptura vel ali*a*[4] que audientes edificet tempore refeccionum huiusmodi inibi habeatis, nisi aliqui honesti hospites vel extranei aduenerint, quorum occasione vos, abba, a refectorio diebus huiusmodi debeatis ex congruo excusari. (5.) Aliis vero temporibus et diebus anni quibus canonici in aula abbatis vel alibi infra monasterium a refectorio comedunt, volumus et iniungimus sub eisdem penis vt canonici ipsi gracias ante et post prandium in refectorio psallant et cum psalmo ' Miserere ' et aliis suffragiis consuetis *post prandium* a refectorio in ecclesiam psallendo ingrediantur.

(6. Ad conficiendum indenturas de terris, etc.) Item iniungimus vobis abbati sub eisdem penis quod absque expresso consensu conuentus nichil arduum faciatis, sed neque firmas nisi sub indenturis dimittatis; quodque super firma terrarum quas Robertus Forman de monasterio tenet ad firmam in Germethorpe infra annum proxime sequentem indenturas competentes fieri faciatis, ne terre ille in obliuionem deducantur sic quod monasterium[5] *exheredetur.*

(7.) Item iniungimus vobis abbati sub eisdem penis, vt confratrem vestrum fratrem Willelmum Elkyngtone, in apostasia agentem, ad claustrum omni cautela queratis et reducatis, ipsum taliter tractando

---

[1] *suis* cancelled.
[2] Altered from *corregendo.*
[3] *illa* cancelled.
[4] Altered from *aliquo.*
[5] *exheredaretur* cancelled.

[1] Founded upon Alesby's second *detectum.*
[2] Founded upon Humfray's and Robert Somercotes' *detecta.*
[3] There is no *detectum* corresponding to this.
[4] See Myddeby's *detectum.*
[5] Founded upon Bachilere's second and Tolsone's second *detecta.*

written, that, every day whereon you hold chapter, you cause the constitutions of your order and the legatine constitutions which concern you and your said order, and also your rule, or at any rate a notable part of the same [constitutions and rule], so that they may be fully read through every week, to be read in full chapter before the whole convent in that tongue which can be best understood, and to be entirely observed by all, punishing the transgressors on such wise, according to the rule, that their penalty, and not their freedom therefrom, may be for an example to the others [1]

(2. To be present at matins.) Also we enjoin upon you the abbot, in virtue of obedience and under pain of grievous contempt, that you go to rest in the dorter with your brethren of a night more often than is your wont, and that you go to matins in person, and with your presence take part in them in quire and in the celebration of chapters, giving diligent aid to the presidents of the order in correcting the transgressions and defaults of offenders as regards the regular observances and divine service. [2]

(3. To celebrate and have a chaplain.) Also we enjoin upon you the abbot, under the like penalty, besides the penalties hereunder written, and for the remission of your sins, that you make your confessions and celebrate frequently, and have with you everywhere one of your brethren as chaplain, to be a witness to your honest conversation; and it is our will that he be changed every year, and another person, when he is removed, put in his place. [3]

(4. For reading during meal-time.) Also we enjoin upon you the abbot and convent, under the penalties above and hereunder written, that, at the seasons of Lent and the Advent of our Lord, and on every Wednesday and Friday out of those seasons, you keep frater and take your food in the same, and have therein some lesson from holy scripture or from some other writing which may edify the hearers during such meals, unless some honest guests or strangers arrive, by reason of whom you, abbot, should be befittingly excused from frater on such days. (5.) But, at the other seasons and days of the year, wherein the canons eat together in the abbot's hall, or elsewhere within the monastery away from frater, we will and enjoin, under the same penalties, that the same canons chant grace in frater before and after breakfast, and after breakfast go chanting into church from frater with the psalm *Miserere* and the other accustomed suffrages. [4]

(6. To make indentures concerning lands, etc.) Also we enjoin upon you the abbot, under the same penalties, that you do no important business without the express consent of the convent, neither that you let farms, unless under indentures; and that you cause sufficient indentures to be made within the year next following concerning the farm of the lands which Robert Forman holds of the monastery at farm in Grainthorpe, lest those lands come to be forgotten so that the monastery shall lose its heritage. [5]

(7.) Also we enjoin upon you the abbot, under the same penalties, that you seek out with all precaution and bring back to cloister your brother, brother William Elkyngtone, who is living in apostasy, treating him in such wise that you may rejoice one with the other, he for his

vt adinuicem gaudeatis, ipse de reditu suo ad caulam dominicam, et vos *de* filio predicto perdito et inuento.

(8. De compoto.[1]) Item iniungimus vobis abbati et cuilibet successori vestro sub pena suspensionis ab administracione vestra, quod omni anno inter festa Sancti Michaelis Archangeli et Omnium Sanctorum in pleno capitulo coram toto conuentu, vel saltem personis per conuentum *ad hoc* assignatis, exhibeatis et ostendatis plenum et fidelem compotum de omnibus et singulis reuentibus[2] monasterii, et de totali administracione vestra in eodem anno preterito per vos facte[3] absque omni colore fucato.

(9. De corrodiis [et] liberatis.) Item iniungimus vobis abbati et cuilibet successori vestro, sub pena perpetue priuacionis et finalis amocionis vestri a dignitate vestra abbaciali, quod corrodia, liberatas, pensiones aut annuetates cuicunque persone quantumcunque honeste ad terminum vite, imperpetuum vel ad certum tempus nullatinus decetero donetis, concedatis, vendatis vel assignetis, nisi de licencia nostri vel successorum nostrorum, episcoporum Lincolniensium, *in hac parte* specialiter petita et obtenta, et eciam de expresso consensu et assensu maioris et sanioris partis conuentus monasterii antedicti.

Volumus eciam et iniungimus sub penis huiusmodi, vt has nostras iniuncciones et mandata quater in anno in pleno capitulo coram toto conuentu illa lingua que melius potest intelligi legi faciatis, et earum veram copiam in aliquo loco patenti infra dormitorium, vt pateant intueri volenti, affigatis.

Monemus insuper vos omnes et singulos primo, secundo, etc.

MANDATUM AD VOCANDUM REGULAREM PERSONAM DESERUIENTEM CURE AD CLAUSTRUM.
(Reg. XVIII, fo. 44 *d.*)

Willelmus, permissione diuina Lincolniensis episcopus, dilecto in Christo filio fratri Henrico Sutton, abbati monasterii de Welhowe iuxta Grymesby, ordinis Sancti Augustini, nostre diocesis, salutem, graciam et benediccionem. Plurium fidedignorum relatu et facti euidencia didicimus quod ecclesie parochiali de Clee, dicte nostre diocesis, vobis in dicto monasterio abolim appropriate, cui dudum per vicarium perpetuum seu alium capellanum secularem amotiuum in animarum cura deseruiri consueuit, hiis diebus per fratrem Johannem Alesby concanonicum et confratrem vestrum et monasterii vestri, quem pocius iuxta professionem suam claustralibus excubiis intendere deceret quam inter seculares conuersari, non absque consciencie scrupulo, vt inuenimus, in officio capellani parochialis et sacramentorum ministracione, que religiosis quasi aliena videntur, facitis deseruiri. Quanta animarum pericula et corporum dispendia ex religiosorum a claustris suis euagacione et eorum inter seculares mutua conuersacione ex vere simili[4] euenire poterunt non ignorat et prudenter qui attendit. Cum igitur non solum ab omni malo, sed secundum apostolum ab omni specie mali sit abstinendum[5], et vt omnis mali occasio tollatur, vobis in virtute obediencie et

---

[1] Written *compoto*.
[2] Sic: for *reuentionibus* or *prouentibus*.
[3] Sic: for *facta*.
[4] Sic: for *verisimili*.
[5] 1 Thess. v, 22. The Vulgate has 'ab omni specie mala.'

return to the Lord's sheepfold, and you for your son aforesaid, who was lost and is found.[1]

(8. Concerning the account.)   Also we enjoin upon you the abbot, and upon every one who shall succeed you, under pain of suspension from your administration, that every year, between the feasts of St. Michael the archangel and All Saints, you present and show in full chapter before the whole convent, or at any rate before the persons appointed to this end by the convent, a full and faithful account of all and sundry the revenues of the monastery, and of your entire administration done by you in the same during the past year, without any pretended colour.[2]

(9. Concerning corrodies [and] liveries.)   Also we enjoin upon you the abbot and upon every one who shall succeed you, under pain of perpetual deprivation and of your final removal from your dignity of abbot, that you in no wise henceforward give, grant, sell or assign corrodies, liveries, pensions or annuities to any person whomsoever, however honest, for term of life, in perpetuity, or for a certain time, unless with the licence of us or our successors, bishops of Lincoln, specially asked and had in this behalf, and also with the express agreement and assent of the more and sounder part of the convent of the monastery aforesaid.[3]

We will also and enjoin, under such penalties, that you cause these our injunctions and commands to be read four times in the year in full chapter before the whole convent in that tongue which can best be understood, and that you fasten up a true copy of them in some open place within the dorter, that they may be clear to him that will look upon them.

We admonish you moreover, all and several, the first, second [and third] time, etc.

MANDATE FOR THE SUMMONS TO CLOISTER OF A REGULAR PERSON SERVING A CURE.

William, by divine permission bishop of Lincoln, to our beloved son in Christ brother Henry Sutton, abbot of the monastery of Wellow by Grimsby, of the order of St. Austin, of our diocese, health, grace and blessing.   By the information of many trustworthy persons and by actual evidence we have learned that in these days you cause the parish church of Clee, of our said diocese, appropriated of old to you in the said monastery, which was sometime wont to be served, as regards the cure of souls, by a perpetual vicar or another removable secular chaplain, to be served, not without scruple of conscience, as we have found, in the office of parish chaplain and in the administration of the sacraments, which things seem to be almost foreign to religious persons, by brother John Alesby, fellow-canon and brother of you and your monastery, whom it would better beseem to be intent upon watchings in cloister than to have his conversation among secular folk.   How great are the perils to souls and the waste of bodily strength that may very likely arise from the straying of religious persons from their cloisters and their mutual conversation with secular persons, is not unknown to him who also takes prudent heed thereto.   Since therefore we must abstain, not only from all evil, but, according to the apostle, from all appearance of evil, and

[1] Founded upon the abbot's first *detectum*.
[2] Founded upon the abbot's second and Tolsone's first *detecta*.
[3] This arises out of the sixth injunction.

sub pena contemptus firmiter iniungimus et mandamus quatinus prefatum fratrem Johannem ad claustrum absque omnis more defugio[1]
reuocetis, et informacionem[2] aliorum canonicorum et confratrum vestrorum iuniorum in gramatica et regularibus obseruanciis, in quibus, vt
accepimus, sufficienter est imbutus, substituatis, dicteque ecclesie parochiali de Clee et cure eiusdem per capellanum idoneum ibidem continue
nocte et die cubantem et leuantem in officio capellani parochialis faciatis
laudabiliter deseruiri. Que eciam facere duxeritis in premissis nos infra
xx dies post recepcionem presencium immediate sequentes distincte et
aperte certificetis autentico sub sigillo,[3] hoc[4] mandatum nobis remittendo.
Data sub sigillo nostro ad causas in castro nostro de Sleaford xxij°
die Maii, anno Domini mccccxliiij[to], nostrarum consecracionis anno
xliij°[5] et translacionis viij°.

LXXVIII.

[Fo. 122 *d.*]

Visitacio prioratus de WROXTONE, ordinis Sancti Augustini,
    Lincolniensis diocesis, facta in domo capitulari ibidem xvj
    die mensis Junii, anno Domini mccccxl quinto, per reueren-
    dum in Christo patrem et dominum, dominum Willelmum
    Alnewyke, Dei gracia Lincolniensem episcopum, suarum
    consecracionis anno xix° et translacionis nono.

In primis, sedente dicto reuerendo patre iudicialiter pro tribunali
in huiusmodi visitacionis sue negocio exercendo die et loco antedictis,
comparuerunt coram eo prior et conuentus loci illius parati ad subeundem,
vt apparuit, huiusmodi visitacionem; et deinde primo et ante omnia
propositum fuit verbum Dei iuxta actus futuri congruenciam per circumspectum virum magistrum Thomam Twyere, in sacra theologia
scolarem, sequentem hoc thema, ' Vocauit seruos suos,' etc. ;[6] quo laudabiliter in sermone latino finito prior exhibuit dicto reuerendo patri
certificatorium mandati domini sibi pro huiusmodi visitacione exercenda
directi factum in hec verba, ' Reuerendo in Christo patri,' etc. Quo
in publica audiencia perlecto dictus prior exhibuit confirmacionem sue
eleccionis et installacionis, et deinde iurauit fidelitatem et obedienciam
domino in forma consueta; et deinde exhibuit fundacionem domus per
Hugonem Belet tunc dominum de Wrokstone. Deinde exhibet statum
domus: postea exhibet fundacionem vnius cantarie de vno capellano qui
iuxta ordinacionem eius celebrabit in altari Sancte Katerine in ecclesia[7]
conuentuali ibidem sub pena iiij *s.* pro vnaquaque cessacione inuencionis

---

[1] *Sic*: for *diffugio*.
[2] *Sic*: *in* omitted before *informacionem*.
[3] *nostro* cancelled.
[4] *monic* written after *hoc* and left uncancelled.
[5] *Sic*: for xviij°.
[6] St. Matth. xxv, 14.
[7] *Sancte* cancelled.

[1] Alesby, it will be seen, in spite of the inconvenience of which he complained
in 1440, continued to serve the cure for nearly four years afterwards. In 1456 he

in order that every occasion of evil may be removed, we firmly enjoin and command you in virtue of obedience and under pain of contempt to recall the aforesaid brother John to cloister without the lapse of any delay, and depute him to the instruction of your other canons and younger brethren in grammar and the regular observances, in which, as we have heard, he is competently trained, and cause the said parish church of Clee and the cure thereof to be laudably served in the office of parish chaplain by a fit chaplain, lying down and rising up by night and day in the same continually. And of what also you think fit to do in the premises you shall certify us distinctly and openly within twenty days immediately following after the receipt of these presents under authentic seal, sending back this mandate to us. Given under our seal *ad causas* in our castle of Sleaford, on the twenty-second day of May, in the year of our Lord 1444, in the [eighteenth] year of our consecration and of our translation the eighth.[1]

LXXVIII.

THE VISITATION OF THE PRIORY OF WROXTON, OF THE ORDER OF ST. AUSTIN, OF THE DIOCESE OF LINCOLN, PERFORMED IN THE CHAPTER-HOUSE THEREIN ON THE SIXTEENTH DAY OF THE MONTH OF JUNE, IN THE YEAR OF OUR LORD 1445, BY THE REVEREND FATHER IN CHRIST AND LORD, THE LORD WILLIAM ALNEWYKE, BY THE GRACE OF GOD BISHOP OF LINCOLN, IN THE NINETEENTH YEAR OF HIS CONSECRATION AND THE NINTH OF HIS TRANSLATION.

In the first place, as the said reverend father was sitting in his capacity of judge as a tribunal, in the exercise of the business of such his visitation, on and in the day and place aforesaid, there appeared before him the prior and convent of that place, in readiness, as was apparent, to undergo such visitation; and then, first and before all else, the word of God was set forth as befitted the act that was about to take place by the distinguished master Thomas Twyere, scholar in sacred theology, after this text, ' He called his servants,' etc.; and, when this had been brought to a praiseworthy end in the Latin speech, the prior exhibited to the said reverend father the certificate of my lord's mandate addressed to him for the holding of such visitation, drawn up in these words, ' To the reverend father in Christ,' etc. Now, when this had been read through in the public hearing, the said prior exhibited the confirmation of his election and installation;[2] and then he sware fealty and obedience to my lord in form accustomed; and then he exhibited the foundation of the house by Hugh Belet, at that time lord of Wroxton.[3] Then he exhibits the state of the house: thereafter he exhibits the foundation of a chantry of one chaplain, who, according to the ordinance thereof, shall celebrate at the altar of St. Katherine in the conventual church in that place under penalty of four shillings for each cessation for fifteen days of the

---

succeeded Sutton as abbot: the royal assent to his election was given on 2 Sept., and the temporalities restored on 2 Oct. (*Cal. Pat.*, 1452-61, pp. 330, 325).

[2] Records of these are wanting.

[3] See *Monasticon* VI, 485.

capellani huiusmodi per xv dies; et deinde processit dominus ad inquisicionem suam hoc modo.

Frater Johannes Abberbury, prior, dicit quod omnia sunt bene disposita.

Frater Johannes Prescote dicit quod omnia bene.

Frater Johannes Bloxham dicit quod omnia bene.

Frater Thomas Littelworthe dicit quod seculares commedunt in refectorio, seorsum tamen *et* procul a canonicis.

Frater Thomas Westone dicit quod omnia bene.

Frater Thomas Balscote, scolaris, dicit omnia bene.

Frater Johannes Euesham dicit omnia bene.

Frater Thomas Wottone dicit omnia bene.

Frater Willelmus Oxonforde dicit quod raro iacet prior in dormitorio.

Frater Thomas Byfelde dicit quod *cum* Wykham, qui cum vxore sua stans[1] ibidem in mensa, sit ibidem presens, ipse et vxor sua cum feminis et seruis habent communem transitum per claustrum.

Frater Willelmus Bradenham dicit omnia bene.

Frater Ricardus Oxonforde dicit omnia bene.

LXXIX.

[Fo. 113 *d.*]

VISITACIO PRIORATUS DE WYLMUNDELEY, ORDINIS SANCTI AUGUSTINI, LINCOLNIENSIS DIOCESIS, FACTA IN DOMO CAPITULARI IBIDEM VLTIMO DIE MENSIS NOUEMBRIS, ANNO DOMINI MCCCCXLIJ⁰, PER REUERENDUM IN CHRISTO PATREM ET DOMINUM, DOMINUM WILLELMUM, DEI GRACIA LINCOLNIENSEM EPISCOPUM, SUARUM CONSECRACIONIS ANNO XVIJ⁰ ET TRANSLACIONIS VIJ⁰.

In primis sedente dicto reuerendo patre iudicialiter in huiusmodi sue visitacionis negocio inchoando et continuando, die, anno et loco predictis, comparuerunt prior et conuentus dicti loci coram eodem, parati vt apparuit ad subeundum visitacionem suam huiusmodi; et deinde primo et ante omnia propositum fuit verbum Dei iuxta facti futuri congruenciam per honorabilem virum magistrum Johannem Beuerley, sacre professorem pagine, sequentem hoc thema, ' Vestra conuersacio est in celis,' etc.[2] Quo latino sermone multum laudabiliter finito idem reuerendus pater ad vlteriora in huiusmodi negocio processit in hunc modum. Primo prior exhibuit pro titulo suo confirmacionem eleccionis sue factam per magistrum Thomam Tyberay, commissarium

---

[1] *Sic*: for *stat*.

[2] Phil. III, 20: ' Nostra autem conversatio in caelis est.'

[1] This chantry may have been founded out of the revenues obtained from the property granted by Roger Goldston and others, for which a licence was issued 1 Sept., 1392 (*Cal. Pat.*, 1391-6, pp. 143-4). The object of this, however, is stated generally as the performance of works of piety.

[2] Seven names come from Oxfordshire, viz. Abberbury (Adderbury), Balscote (Balscott), Bloxham, the two Oxonfordes, Prescote (Prescott), and Wottone (Wootton). Littelworthe and Westone are indefinite, probably from Oxfordshire

finding of such chaplain;[1] and then my lord proceeded to his inquiry in this wise.

Brother John Abberbury,[2] the prior, says that all things are in good order.

Brother John Prescote says that all things are well.

Brother John Bloxham says that all things are well.

Brother Thomas Littelworthe says that secular persons eat together in frater, but by themselves and at a distance from the canons.

Brother Thomas Westone says that all things are well.

Brother Thomas Balscote,[3] in the schools, says all things are well.

Brother John Evesham says all things are well.

Brother Thomas Wottone says all things are well.

Brother William Oxonforde says that the prior rarely lies in the dorter.

Brother Thomas Byfelde says that, when Wykham, who stays with his wife in that place at their board, is present in the same, he and his wife, with women and servants, have common passage through the cloister.

Brother William Bradenham says all things are well.

Brother Richard Oxonforde says all things are well.

LXXIX.

THE VISITATION OF THE PRIORY OF WYMONDLEY, OF THE ORDER OF ST. AUSTIN, OF THE DIOCESE OF LINCOLN, PERFORMED IN THE CHAPTER-HOUSE THEREIN ON THE LAST DAY OF THE MONTH OF NOVEMBER, IN THE YEAR OF OUR LORD 1442, BY THE REVEREND FATHER IN CHRIST AND LORD, THE LORD WILLIAM, BY THE GRACE OF GOD BISHOP OF LINCOLN, IN THE SEVENTEENTH YEAR OF HIS CONSECRATION AND THE SEVENTH OF HIS TRANSLATION.

In the first place, as the said reverend father was sitting in his capacity of judge in the business, to be begun and continued, of such his visitation, on and in the day, year and place aforesaid, there appeared before the same the prior and convent of the said place, in readiness, as was apparent, to undergo such his visitation; and then, first and before all else, the word of God was set forth, as befitted the act that was about to take place, by the honourable master John Beverley, professor of holy writ, after this text, ' Your conversation is in heaven,' etc. And, when this had come to a very praiseworthy end in the Latin speech, the same reverend father proceeded to further matters in such business on this wise. First, the prior exhibited as his title the confirmation of his election made by master Thomas Tyberay, the commissary of [the lord]

---

or Northamptonshire. Byfelde is Byfield, Northants. Bradenham is from Buckinghamshire, and Evesham from Worcestershire.

[3] See p. 262, note 1. Thomas Balnescotte, canon of Wroxton, bachelor of canon law, had a papal dispensation to hold a benefice with cure, 23 Sept., 1441 (*Cal. Papal Letters* IX, 217).

Philippi, et eiusdem auctoritate, de qua in litteris ipsis nulla facta est mencio: similiter installacionem factam per officialem archidiaconi Huntingdonie simili forma cum tenore litterarum commissarii sed non episcopi committentis. Exhibuit eciam pro fundacione loci et appropriacione ecclesie de Wylmundeley parua cartam[1] Hugonis episcopi Lincolniensis ipsius episcopi ac decani et capituli Lincolniensium et Ricardi de Argente[in] fundatoris sigillis pendentibus consignatas, in quibus plane cauetur quod dictus Ricardus donauit eidem episcopo et successoribus suis ac decano et capitulo Lincolniensibus aduocacionem prioratus illius qui in limine fundacionis nominabatur hospitale.   Deinde examinatus dicit ea que sequuntur, iurata primitus obediencia et fidelitate domino in forma consueta.

Frater Ricardus Chapman, prior, dicit quod domus potest expendere vt credit de claro xx li.[2]

Item dicit quod domus indebitatur in ij marcis vltra precium campanarum de nouo emptarum et vltra stipendia famulorum.

Frater Johannes Swyneshede dicit quod omnia bene.

Frater Laurencius Whyte dicit quod omnia bene.

Frater Johannes Litlyngtone dicit quod omnia bene.

Frater Willelmus Waterman dicit omnia bene.

---

[1] *Sic*: for *cartas*.
[2] *et* cancelled.

Philip, and by the authority of the same, concerning which there is no mention made in the same letters:[1] likewise his installation, performed by the official of the archdeacon of Huntingdon in like form, with the tenor of the commissary's letters, but not of those of the bishop giving him commission. He exhibited also, for the foundation of the place and the appropriation of the church of Little Wymondley, the charter[s] of Hugh, bishop of Lincoln, sealed with the pendant seals of the same bishop, and of the dean and chapter of Lincoln, and of Richard de Argente[in] the founder, wherein notice is clearly given that the said Richard gave to the same bishop and his successors, and to the dean and chapter of Lincoln, the advowson of that priory, which at the beginning of the foundation was called a hospital.[2] Then, upon examination, he says these things which follow, having first sworn obedience and fealty to my lord in form accustomed.

Brother Richard Chapman,[3] the prior, says that the house, as he believes, is able to spend twenty pounds clear.

Also he says that the house is two marks in debt, over and above the price of the bells that are newly bought, and over and above the wages of the servants.

Brother John Swyneshede says that all things are well.
Brother Lawrence Whyte says that all things are well.
Brother John Litlyngtone says that all things are well.
Brother William Waterman says all things are well.

---

[1] There is no record of this in Reg. xiv. Of the commissary, little appears to be known. Hennessy, note v, 241, mentions 'Thomas de Tybbay,' instituted rector of St. Matthew's, Friday Street, 9 June, 1399 (*ibid.* p. 435), which he exchanged for Parham, Sussex, in 1401. He was also rector of Calbourne, I.W., and made his will in 1421. This may be the man: he was probably a brother of John Tibbay, archdeacon of Huntingdon, who died in 1414 during Repyngdon's episcopate.

[2] These documents do not appear to survive.

[3] None of the five names belong to places in the immediate neighbourhood. Swyneshede is probably Swineshead, now in Bedfordshire, near Kimbolton, and Litlyngtone is Lidlington, also in Bedfordshire.

APPENDIX I

SUPPLEMENTARY DOCUMENTS

(A)   Among the minutes of visitations contained in this series occur a few memoranda made in the course of visitation, which bear upon points not immediately concerned with monastic life and discipline.

(*a*)   On the dorse of fo. 8 are two memoranda, subsequently cancelled.   This is a narrow leaf, folded over from fo. 2, and, forming part of an imperfectly cut sheet, was used during the visitation of 1438 for miscellaneous notes, but was subsequently employed for the visitation of Irthlingborough in 1442, and was then filled up.

The first of these is a note of a series of mandates dispatched to the rural deans of Holland in the archdeaconry of Lincoln and Weldon in that of Northampton, to summon certain persons to appear before the bishop at Peterborough on Wednesday after Passion Sunday (2 April, 1438), with another summons to an individual priest and notes upon two of the offenders thus summoned.

> Ad diem Mercurii post passionem apud Burgum Sancti Petri.
> Decano Holand ad citandum dominum Robertum Ywardeby et Graciam.
> Decano de Weldone ad citandum Thomam Harry.
> Decano de Weldone ac vicario de Geytyngdone[1] ad citandum Agnetem Nayseby personaliter vel per edictum.
> Vicario de Bergham.[2]
> Ricardus Wag ad purgandum se cum viij personis honestis. Cecilia Colfox.
> Gracia Martyn de Tofte latitat.
> Dominus Robertus Iwardeby, rector ecclesie parochialis de Tofte,[3] citatus.

The second is the sentence of suspension pronounced by the bishop's commissary, John Depyng, upon Robert Iwardeby, rector of Fishtoft, for non-appearance in the parish church of St. John at Peterborough on 2 April, 1438, to answer the charge of incontinency brought against him.   It is stated in the previous note that the woman accused with him, Grace Martyn, was in hiding, so that no summons had been served upon her personally.

> In Dei nomine amen. Nos Johannes Depyng, in legibus licenciatus, reuerendi in Christo patris et domini domini Willelmi, Dei gracia Lincolniensis episcopi, commissarius sufficienter deputatus, dominum Robertum Iwardeby, rectorem ecclesie parochialis de Tofte, Lincolniensis diocesis, ad istos diem et locum super graui crimine incontinencie *et incestus spiritualis* cum quadam Gracia Martyn de eadem, seruiente sua familiari et filia sua spirituali, vt

---

[1] Geddington in the deanery of Weldon.   Agnes Nayseby seems to have been included in the same accusation with Thomas Harry.

[2] Barholm, Lincs.

[3] Fishtoft, Lincs.

dicitur, commissi responsurum, legitime citatum, sepius preconiza-
tum et diucius expectatum et nullo modo comparentem pronunciamus contumacem et in penam contumacie sue huiusmodi
ipsum dominum Robertum ab ingressu ecclesie suspendimus in
hiis scriptis.   Lecta in ecclesia Sancti Johannis de[1] Burgo Sancti
Petri, Lincolniensis diocesis,[2] et per Depyng admissa secundo die
Aprilis anno Domini mccccxxxviij, presentibus magistro Willelmo
Appeltone, socio collegii de Foderynghey,[3] Henrico Wyles, canonico,
et me Colstone.

(b)   On the dorse of fo. 129, the second document on which, arising
out of the visitation of St. Michael's priory at Stamford in 1442, is printed
(p. 354 above), is a memorandum of dates of adjourned visitations of
monasteries, made during the visitation of the archdeaconry of
Northampton in that year.

. . . te[4] anno Domini mccccxlij.

Irtlyngburgh.   Visitacio collegii de Irtlyngburghe vsque in
crastinum Sancti Luce et ad quemlibet diem[5] citra.

Moniales Northamptonie.   Visitacio monialium Northamptonie vsque diem Lune proximum post dictum festum et ad quemlibet diem citra.[6]

Dauentre.   Visitacio prioratus de Dauentre vsque in diem
Lune proximum post festum Sancti Andree et ad quemlibet diem
citra.[7]

Catesby.   Visitacio prioratus de Catesby vsque diem Martis
tunc proxime sequentem et ad quemlibet diem citra.[8]

(B)   The portfolio in which these records of visitations are now kept
also contains a sheet of parchment, folded into three parts, on which is
written the mandate of Robert [Fitzhugh], bishop of London, as dean of
the province of Canterbury, dated at Stepney, 22 October, 1439, summoning Alnwick and, through him, the dean and chapter of Lincoln,
the archdeacons, heads of religious houses and clergy of his diocese to
convocation at St. Paul's on 21 November following, in pursuance of
the mandate of Henry [Chichele], archbishop of Canterbury, dated at
Lambeth, 15 October in the same year, which embodies the king's writ
issued at Kennington on 14 October.   As this is in the usual form, it
need not be printed here.   It bears the endorsement: 'Recepta apud
Bugden xxviij die Octobris anno Domini mccccxxxix.'

The sheet was used subsequently for a number of rough notes of
acts during visitations, and on the dorse appear the following.

---

[1] *P* cancelled.
[2] *secundo* cancelled.
[3] See *Visitations* ii, 98.
[4] Possibly *Dies date.*
[5] *supra* cancelled.   For the date see *Visitations* ii, 164.
[6] No record of this visitation of Delapré abbey remains.
[7] Cf. *Visitations* ii, 64.
[8] Cf. *Visitations* ii, 50.

(*a*) Scrutetur registrum Flemmyng pro litteris ordinum fratris Willelmi Coleworthe, canonici de Assheby canonicorum, circa annum Domini mccccxxiiij.[1]

(*b*)[2] Item rectori de Whytchurch[3] pro littera directa episcopo Herfordensi ad inquirendum de . . . . . suo	j s.
Item de presentacione domino Johanni Cristyane, capellano, cui dominus contulit vicariam de Prestone[4]	xij s.
Item de oratoriis Eustachii Burneby et Thome Boghtone	viij s.
Item pro citacione Turvey	vj d.
Priorissa de Rothewelle pro pensione	vj s. viij d.
Item commissio reconsiliacionis cimiterii ecclesie de Redeburne[5] apud Bulwyk xxiij die Julii xiij s. iiij d. xij d.	
Item presentaciones ecclesie de Croweltone[6] et medietatis de Bechamptone[7] apud Sleford xxviij die Julii	xxiiij s.
Item presentacio ad medietatem ecclesie de Bechamtone alterius eisdem die et loco	xij s.
Item eisdem die et loco de Thoma Smythe de Ormesby pro composicione ad recipiendum eius purgacionem	ix s. xij d.
Item ibidem vltimo die Julii de magistro Roberto Matfene[8]	vj s. vi ij d. xij d.
Item primo die Augusti ibidem de rectore de Dene[9] pro composicione ad recipiendum eius purgacionem	xij s. viij d. xij d.
Item eisdem die et loco de collatar[10] vicario de Mumby	xij s.

                                                          xviij li. xj s. ij d.

---

[1] For William Coleworth (Culworth), formerly prior of Canons Ashby, see *Visitations* I, 34, 35. There is no mention of him in 1442, when he was possibly still in apostasy.

[2] This list of receipts, arising from fines and fees for licences, apparently belongs to the end of the visitation of the archdeaconry of Northampton in 1442. It has been cancelled, and lines have been drawn through some of the entries, so that it is difficult to read, and in places nearly illegible.

[3] Probably Whitchurch in the deanery of Henley, archdeaconry of Oxford.

[4] Preston Deanery, Northants, to which John Crystyan was instituted, 20 July, 1442 (Bridges, *Hist. Northants* I, 380).

[5] Probably Redbourn in Lincolnshire: Redbourne in Hertfordshire was in the jurisdiction of St. Albans.

[6] Croughton in Brackley deanery, Northants. There was an institution on 28 July, 1442 (Bridges, op. cit. I, 160).

[7] Beachampton in the deanery and archdeaconry of Buckingham.

[8] Possibly the canon of the Newarke at Leicester, for whom see *Visitations* II, 190, 191, 194. He was rector of North Luffenham in Rutland deanery, and, although called *dominus* in 1440, was certainly *magister* at his death.

[9] Deene in Weldon deanery, the parish adjoining Bulwick on the S. The rector at this date was William Watkyngs *alias* David (Bridges, op. cit. II, 303).

[10] *Sic: collacione* is apparently meant.

(c) Anno Domini mccccxlij⁰ indiccione quinta, pontificatu domini Eugenii pape quarti anno xij, mensis[1] . . . . de Brackeley in presencia magistrorum Johannis Depyng, canonici Lincolniensis, Thome Mortone, magistri[2] . . . . notarii publici, meique Thome Colstone, clerici Lincolniensis diocesis, auctoritate apostolica notarii publici, personaliter constituit honorabilis vir magister Willelmus Scrope, archidiaconus Stowe in ecclesia Lincolniensi,[3] constituit[4] procuratores suos coniunctim et diuisim magistros Thomam Ryngstede,[5] canonicum residentem, etc., Thomam Ludham[6] et Johannem Walpole,[7] canonicos Lincolnienses non residentes, ita quod non sit, etc., ad comparendum coram reuerendo in Christo patre et domino, domino Willelmo, Dei gracia Lincolniensi episcopo, in conuocacione sua, decani videlicet et canonicorum Lincolniensis ecclesie et alios[8] dignitates, etc., quibuscumque diebus horis et locis per ipsum reuerendum patrem prefixis et assignatis et imposterum prefigendis et statuendis, et cum dicto reuerendo patre ac aliis super per eundem reuerendum patrem adtunc exprimendis et iam expositis tractandum et concludendum et factis et processibus ipsius reuerendi patris iam habitis et eciam habendis consenciendo vel consenciendum, et presertim nouo registro pro regimine dicte ecclesie Lincolniensis et ministrorum eiusdem per dictum reuerendum patrem iam edito, laudumque per eundem reuerendum patrem, compromissarium et aliorum arbitratorem, laudatorem et diffinitorem per decanum et capitulum electum ecclesie Lincolniensis concorditer assumptum super diuersis materiis controuersiarum et dissensionum inter eos exortarum, latum omologandum, iuramentum quodcunque presertim de obseruando dictum laudum in omnibus suis capitulis et non contraueniendo eisdem nec eis contrauenientibus vel ea enervare volentibus vel intentibus[9] consenciendo et[10] generaliter omnia alia, etc., et cum clausulis substituendis et ratihabicionis, etc.

(d) Frater Johannes Forman, canonicus de Croxtone,[11] iuratus coram domino in ecclesia de Cotyngham[12] xxiij die Julii anno Domini mccccxlij, deponit quod ipse idem deponens ac fratres Thomas Chilwelle et Johannes Wertone, eiusdem monasterii canonici confratres sui in

---

[1] The top of the sheet has been torn off at this point. The date is probably 11 July, 1442: see *Visitations* II, xxxviii.

[2] See *Visitations* II, 39.

[3] See *Visitations* I, 185, and an additional note in Surtees Soc. cxxvII, 255.

[4] *Sic*: repeated.

[5] Prebendary of Brampton, 14 Dec., 1440 (Le Neve II, 117), and of Caistor c. 1451-4 (*ibid.* 127). He had been dean of St. Mary in the Fields at Norwich; and in Appendix II will be found the record of a visitation held by him as bishop's commissary, during Alnwick's tenure of the see of Norwich.

[6] Prebendary of North Kelsey 20 July, 1438; of Louth, 1446-54 (Reg. xvIII, ff. 107 *d.*, 110; xx, fo. 205).

[7] Prebendary of Leicester St. Margaret 1441-5 (Le Neve II, 169). See p. note .

[8] *Sic*: for *aliorum*.

[9] *Sic*: for *intendentibus*.

[10] A word cancelled.

[11] The Premonstratensian abbey of Croxton in Leicestershire.

[12] Cottingham in Weldon deanery, archdeaconry of Northampton. An entry in (b) above shows that Alnwick was at Bulwick, a few miles away, on the same day. This adds something to the dates given in *Visitations* II, xxxviii.

ordine diaconatus constituti, ordinati fuerunt in sacerdotes die Sabbati quatuor temporum mensis Septembris anno xv vel xvj iam proxime preterito in ecclesia[1] de Sleforde prebendali per dominum Ancoradensem, suffraganeum domini Ricardi tunc Lincolniensis episcopi.

(*e*) xxiij die mensis Julii, anno Domini mccccxlij, in ecclesia de Cotyngham, dominus monuit primo, secundo, tercio et peremptorie dominum Johannem Clement, rectorem ecclesie parochialis de Market Ouertone[2] coram eo in iudicio personaliter constitutum et in dicta ecclesia sua non residentem, quod infra vnam septimanam proximam post proximum festum Michaelis inmediate sequentem se ad dictam ecclesiam suam transferat et in ea personaliter resideat et curam suam agnoscat et exerceat sub pena priuacionis, etc.; et deinde corporale prestitit iuramentum ad sancta Dei euangelia tacto libro, quod monicioni huiusmodi obediet et iuxta eam in dicta ecclesia sua personaliter residebit; et subsequenter idem reuerendus pater monuit eundem rectoriem[3] sub pena excommunicacionis quod huiusmodi iuramentum suum obseruet, et exinde dominus relaxauit sentenciam suspensionis contra eum latam eo quod non comparuit coram domino in visitacione apud Cotesmore,[4] et iniunxit eidem rectori vt tribus pauperibus parochianis suis magis indigentibus equaliter tribuat xij *d.*, que omnia idem rector promisit se facturum sub penis supradictis, presentibus magistro Johanne Leke, Johanne Beuues, capellano domini, et rectore de Cotyngham et me Colstone.

(*f*) Ad diem Lune proximam post festum Sancti Jacobi apud Sleforde.

Dominus Walterus Luffenham, canonicus de Irtlyngburghe, ad proponendum quare non debeat priuari.[5]

(*g*) xxiij die Julii anno Domini mccccxlij in[6] ecclesia de Cotyngham, reuerendus pater dominus Lincolniensis episcopus quendam dominum Johannem Alueriche, rectorem *medietatis* parochialis ecclesie de Segbroke[7] coram eo personaliter constitutum et se in dicto beneficio a diu non resedisse nec residere publice confitentem, monuit primo, secundo et tercio peremptorie quod infra proxime sequentes sex *septimanas*[8] in dicto beneficio resideat et curam eius secundum ipsius qualitatem exerceat sub pena priuacionis, presentibus Wylles, Bretone et me Colstone. Et assignauit eidem diem Lune proximam post festum Sancti Michaelis proxime futurum in ecclesia de Sleforde ad proponendum quare non

---

[1] *Lincolniensi* cancelled.

[2] In the deanery of Rutland.

[3] *Sic*: for *rectorem*.

[4] Possibly the deanery of Rutland, or part of it, was visited at Cottesmore in June, 1442, probably between the 19th and 22d of the month.

[5] See *Visitations* II, 163.

[6] *capella beate Marie Magdalene in cimiterio* cancelled. Probably Colstone was thinking of the chapel of St. Mary and St. Anne in the churchyard of Bulwick, where he was on the same day. The church of Cottingham is dedicated to St. Mary Magdalene.

[7] Sedgebrook, Lincs.

[8] Interlined above *menses* cancelled.

debeat pronunciari institucionem vt surrepticiose obtentam, eo quod non concordat cum registris, nullam fore et inualidum et sic beneficium fore vacans, et scribere patrono ad presentandum, etc., presentibus vt supra.

(*h*) Ad diem Sabbati post Jacobi apud Sleforde.
Causa matrimonialis de Ernesby, in quo[1] transmittendus est processus commissarii Leycestrie in eodem habitus.

(*i*) Memorandum quod xxiij die Aprilis, anno Domini mccccxliij, indiccione vj, pontificatus domini Eugenii quarti anno xiij°, in aula infra manerium de Netelham, Lincolniensis diocesis, magister Adelardus Welby, canonicus Lincolniensis et prebendarius prebende de Nortone episcopi in eadem[2] constituit procuratores suos magistros Thomam Skayman, thesaurarium, Thomam Ryngsted et Thomam Ludham, canonicos residentes dicte ecclesie Lincolniensis, in forma qua Scrope superius constituit procuratores vt supra, presentibus dominis Johanne Wylles et Johanne Beuues,[3] de Whethamstede et Waldegraue, Lincolniensis diocesis, rectoribus et me Colstone.

(*k*) Scrutetur registrum memorandorum de tempore Philippi pro dispensacione Johannis Stevenes, rectoris ecclesie de Wolde,[4] iuxta constitucionem cum ex eo[5] de anno xvij consecracionis dicti domini Philippi.
apud Rothewelle . . . de
Dominus Walterus Luffenham, canonicus de Irtlyngburghe.
Dominus Willelmus Taylour de Bucketone, capellanus.[6]

APPENDIX II
Records of Alnwick's Episcopate at Norwich

Something has been said, in the introduction to the second volume of this series of visitation records, of Alnwick's administration of the diocese of Norwich. In the summer of 1923 the present writer, by the kindness of his friend, Mr. Leonard G. Bolingbroke, the diocesan registrar, had the opportunity of examining Alnwick's register as bishop of Norwich, which, with the other episcopal registers, is kept in the western triforium gallery of the south transept of the cathedral church. This, like most of its companion volumes, is devoted almost entirely to records of institutions to benefices, which were entered carefully and with great regularity;

---

[1] *Sic*: for *qua*.
[2] *Sic*: *ecclesie* has been omitted after *Lincolniensis*. Adlard Welby had collation of this prebend 2 April, 1438 (Reg. xviii, ff. 107 *d*., 108 *d*.).
[3] Beuues (Bewes) was instituted to Waldegrave, Northants, 17 Dec., 1442 (Bridges, op. cit. ii, 129).
[4] Wold or Old in the deanery of Rothwell. The institution of Stevenes is not recorded (Bridges, op. cit. ii, 132).
[5] The constitution of Boniface viii (Sext. lib. i, c. 34, tit. *de electione*) dispensing a student at a university from proceeding to higher orders for seven years, and from residence on his benefice in the meantime, while receiving its fruits.
[6] See *Visitations* ii, 47, 58, 49.

but at the end of the book are a few supplementary documents. These are mainly concerned with the bishop's attempt to enforce his jurisdiction upon the exempt abbey of Bury St. Edmunds, and, as such, are of a purely formal character. The interesting account of the visitation of the nunnery at Redlingfield, near Eye in Suffolk, is of another type, and is printed here as a valuable supplement to the records preserved at Lincoln. It belongs, however, to the period before Alnwick had come to reside in his diocese; and of his personal visitations of the numerous monasteries of Norfolk and Suffolk neither minutes nor injunctions remain.

The dates in his register provide some idea of his activities. On the day after his consecration, 19 August, 1426, he appointed a vicar-general and a suffragan, to administer a diocese which his public duties prevented him from visiting at present. Of the suffragan, Robert, ' episcopus Gradensis,' nothing appears to be known. He continued to act throughout Alnwick's tenure of the see, holding frequent ordinations at the regular seasons, usually in the chapel of the bishop's palace at Norwich.[1] The vicar-general, William Bernham, had combined the same office with that of official principal or chancellor of the diocese for some years before Alnwick's accession,[2] and continued to exercise them until May, 1434, when master John Saresson or Wygenhale succeeded to his place.[3] It need hardly be said that the duties of the suffragan were confined purely to rites and functions for which the presence of a bishop was indispensable: he held no administrative position, nor had he any status in the cathedral church. In the absence of the bishop of the diocese, his official acts were performed by the vicar-general and by special commissaries.

As Alnwick continued to be keeper of the privy seal for nearly two years after his consecration, he appears to have resided in London during most of that period, with St. James' hospital as his headquarters. He did not appear in his diocese until the Christmas of 1427, when, after holding his first ordination at Thetford on 20 December, he was enthroned at Norwich two days later. He spent Christmas at Norwich, and visited Walsingham and Lynn in January; but he did not begin to reside habitually in his diocese until August, 1428. The itinerary which follows shows that, although his visits to London were fairly frequent after that time, they were not prolonged, and that he showed an attention to the duties of his see which he exhibited even more noticeably after his translation to Lincoln.

The episcopal manor-houses within the diocese were comparatively few in number, and most of Alnwick's time was spent at Thorpe, in the immediate neighbourhood of Norwich, with frequent visits to the palace

---

[1] The suffragan held ordinations as follows: 1426, 21 Sept., 21 Dec.; 1426-7, 15 March; 1427, 5 April, 14 June, 20 Sept.; 1427-8, 28 Feb., 20 March; 1428, 3 April (in ' Sculton ' (? Sculthorpe) church), 29 May; 1428-9, 19 Feb.; 1429, 21 May, 24 Sept., 17 Dec.; 1430, 10 June, 23 Dec.; 1430-1, 24 Feb., 17 March; 1431, 26 May, 22 Sept., 22 Dec.; 1433-4, 20 March (Mountjoy priory); 1434, 22 May; 1435, 16 April, 24 Sept., 17 Dec; 1436, 7 April, 22 Dec. In all, 28 ordinations out of 57 held during Alnwick's episcopate.

[2] Le Neve II, 495.

[3] Reg. Alnwick, fo. 69.

at Norwich, which he used with more freedom than bishops were accustomed to use with regard to their residences in cathedral cities. There are records of three visits to the manor of Thornage in the north of the county, during the Lent seasons of 1430, 1433 and 1435; and he held his September ordination there in the last of these years. From 1429 to 1436 he spent Easter at Norwich, with one exception in 1434, when he was either at Bury St. Edmunds or in London. For the Christmas feast there is less information: he was at Norwich in 1427 and 1432, and probably at Bury St. Edmunds in 1433, at a time when he found occasion to be often there at short intervals. There is evidence for several visits to Hoxne, which was conveniently situated on the borders of Norfolk and Suffolk; and he spent long periods there in the summers of 1432 and 1436. His visits to Lynn, near which, at Gaywood, was a house belonging to the see, were few and short. Outside the diocese, he had a residence at Terling, near Chelmsford, which, as in 1432 and 1433, was a useful halting-place between Hoxne and London. His ordinary route from Norwich to London was the more westerly road by way of Newmarket. He apparently entered his diocese by this route in 1427, deviating from the direct road to hold an ordination at Thetford.[1] In Sept., 1429, he clearly took the straight road by Brandon and Newmarket. In Feb., 1432-3 we find him two days from Norwich at Babraham, S.W. of Newmarket, from which he evidently went to London by Royston and Ware, as he was at Barkway on the following day. He returned by Bury St. Edmunds, and again, towards the end of the year and in 1433-4, Bury is the only landmark on his journeys to and from London. This, however, is easily explained by the fact that Henry VI was at Bury St. Edmunds from Christmas, 1433, until the later part of the following April.[2] During Alnwick's later journeys, he appears to have favoured the eastern route to London, breaking his journey at Hoxne, which lay near the road.

Incidentally, the Norwich register throws some doubt upon a date which comes from another source. The record of the consecration of Marmaduke Lumley as bishop of Carlisle, which took place in St. Thomas' chapel at the East bridge, Canterbury, on 16 April (Easter day), 1430, includes the name of Alnwick among the consecrators.[3] As Alnwick held his Easter ordination in Norwich cathedral on 15 April, his presence at Canterbury on the following day seems highly improbable. It is possible that there is some error in the record, and that 'Willelmus episcopus Norwycensis' was substituted by mistake for some other prelate.[4]

The itinerary provides only a slight amount of information with regard to Alnwick's methods of visitation. The diocese, divided into

---

[1] He may possibly have come to Thetford on 19 Dec. from Terling, where he was on 8 Oct.; but during the interval between these dates it is more likely that he returned to London.

[2] See *Archaeologia* xv, 65-71, and *Monasticon* III, 113, note d., for the account of this visit from abbot Curteys' register. The presence of Alnwick at Cirencester on 5 Nov., 1434, is similarly explained by the king's movements: see *Cal. Pat. Rolls* 1431-6, p. 3.

[3] Stubbs, *Reg. Sac. Angl.*, p. 87.

[4] Two other English bishops bore the name William at this period, viz. Gray of London and Heyworth of Coventry and Lichfield.

four archdeaconries, viz. Norwich, Norfolk, Suffolk and Sudbury, comprised the whole of Norfolk and Suffolk, with a strip of Cambridgeshire which formed a rural deanery in the archdeaconry of Sudbury. The twenty-five rural deaneries in Norfolk were divided among the two archdeaconries in such a way that neither represented a compact geographical area. On the other hand, the nine deaneries of the archdeaconry of Sudbury formed a compact group in west Suffolk, while the archdeaconry of Suffolk, with fourteen deaneries, covered the eastern part of the county. Parishes in East Anglia are small, and churches are thickly set, so that most of the rural deaneries, within areas corresponding, speaking generally, to a single hundred or a group of hundreds, contained a large number of parishes. A curious point, though not without parallel, is that the office of rural dean in Norfolk and Suffolk was a freehold benefice with a small endowment in the gift of the bishop. Institutions to rural deaneries are recorded in great numbers in the registers of the bishops of Norwich, and such benefices were open to the custom of exchange which was so prevalent throughout England in the fourteenth and fifteenth centuries.

Monasteries in Norfolk and Suffolk were extremely numerous, and it is probable that Alnwick visited them with some thoroughness. The dates in the register, however, furnish no very clear view of his system of visitation. A visit to Lavenham on 5 Sept., 1428, may mark the beginning of the visitation of Sudbury archdeaconry. It is noticeable that the bishop returned there for an ordination on 18 December, a few days before which he was staying at Bury St. Edmunds, so that here we may have a clue to the opening of his primary visitation. He may also at this time have made his first attempt to assert his authority over the exempt house at Bury. It was a favourable opportunity, for abbot Excetre was near his end, and died during the following month;[1] but Alnwick's quarrel with the great monastery did not mature till later, when Excetre was succeeded by abbot Curteys, and the archdeacon of Sudbury who acted as his chief assistant in the dispute was not appointed until April, 1429.[2]

After this, there is no immediate indication that the work of visitation was pursued with systematic vigour. Bromhill priory, on 16 Sept., 1429, appears to connote a special visitation in the course of a journey to London; but there is room for a few days here in the deaneries of Cranwich and Fincham, for which the register contains otherwise no evidence. Similarly, on 23 August, 1430, the specific mention of the chapel of St. Edmund at Hoxne points to a beginning in the archdeaconry of Suffolk; but it was not until more than a year later, so far as we can tell, that Alnwick visited any further portion of this section of his diocese. Needham Market, on 4 October, 1431, is an isolated date: the place, however, the large church of which was a chapel subordinate to the parish church of Barking, was a convenient centre for the deanery of Bosmere, and may have been one of several visited during a special tour.

---

[1] The *congé d'élire* following his death was issued on 30 Jan., 1428-9 (*Cal. Pat. Rolls* 1422-9, p. 527).

[2] *Cal. Pat. Rolls* 1422-9, pp. 531, 532.

The record in Amundesham's chronicle of Alnwick's attempt to visit Binham priory, a cell of the exempt abbey of St. Albans, places the incident in the twelfth year of abbot Whethamstede, *i.e.* 1431-2.[1] As it took place on a Saturday, the writer took the opportunity of contrasting it with the pious visit of the Maries to our Lord's sepulchre, and an incautious reader might interpret the passage as referring to the Easter Even of 1432 (19 April). On that date, however, the bishop was holding an ordination at Norwich; and the writer distinctly says that the Saturday in question was the first Saturday of Whethamstede's twelfth year. Whethamstede actually succeeded to the abbacy of St. Albans in Oct., 1420, his temporalities being restored on the 23d of that month,[2] so that Saturday, 26 Oct., 1431, is the latest date which can be assigned to this abortive proceeding. Alnwick must thus have come from Needham Market and its neighbourhood to the north-east part of the diocese during October, and possibly went to Binham from his house at Thornage.

In May, 1432, he was certainly active in the deaneries of Sudbury and Clare: the landmarks are Kersey priory and the colleges of St. Gregory at Sudbury and Stoke-by-Clare. He appears to have returned specially from London in June to hold an ordination at St. Gregory's. On the following 24 July he left Hoxne to visit the archdeaconry of Suffolk. His progress through the deaneries of Wangford (Bungay), Dunwich (Blythburgh), Orford (Snape) and Wilford (Wickham Market) to Holy Trinity priory, Ipswich, is clearly marked: on 18 August he was at Bricett priory in the deanery of Bosmere and back at Hoxne three days later. The intervals between Snape and Wickham Market and Ipswich and Bricett give room for a considerable amount of business in the various deaneries, and this tour probably involved a very thorough visitation of the archdeaconry. A second visit to Holy Trinity or Christchurch priory at Ipswich in October was evidently undertaken specially, probably to conclude adjourned proceedings.

November and December of the same year seem to have been devoted to a similar tour in Norfolk. On three successive days the bishop was at Acle in the deanery of Blofield, Great Yarmouth in that of Flegg, and the important abbey of St. Benet or Hulme in its lonely situation by the windings of the Bure. Here he may have stayed a few days, as it was not till five days later that he was at Ingham in the deanery of Waxham. Two days more brought him to Cawston in the deanery of Ingworth, after which eight days elapse until we find him at Walsingham. From Walsingham he went to Fakenham in Burnham deanery, and probably spent some time subsequently at Gaywood, as he was at Lynn during the first fortnight in December. He returned to Norwich for Christmas, visiting East Dereham on the way. This gives evidence for a careful visitation of the eastern, northern and central parts of Norfolk, with time for inspecting the monasteries of the district. It would be possible to fill in the dates which are wanting with reasonable conjectures. In the following January he completed the districts immediately round Norwich, as he was at Loddon in Brooke deanery on 16 January, and at the priory of Horsham St. Faith's, a few miles north of Norwich, on the

---

[1] See *Visitations* II, xx.
[2] *Cal. Pat.* 1416-22, p. 302.

23d. Reason has already been given for supposing that he had visited the south-western part of the county much earlier, and for the southern portion Hoxne was always a convenient base of operation.

After this, apart from his prolonged visits to Bury St. Edmunds during Henry VI's Christmas visit in 1433-4, Alnwick's movements in his diocese were limited, and the only sign of a visitation is his presence at West Wretham in Rockland deanery in March, 1434-5. It thus seems that his primary visitation was spread over a large part of his episcopate, as at this period was often the case. Although the dates in the register form a mere skeleton, they yet show that he managed to gain personal acquaintance with every part of a large and populous diocese, and that the thoroughness with which in later years he perambulated the wider area of the diocese of Lincoln was a continuation of the conscientious diligence which gives him a remarkable eminence among the prelates of his age.

The detailed itinerary is as follows:—

1426	19 Aug.	Canterbury. Commissions issued to master William Bernham, Dec. bac., vicar-general, and Robert, 'episcopus Gradensis,' suffragan.
	18, 31 Oct.	St. James' hospital, Westminster.[1]
1427	8 Oct.	Terling (Essex).[2]
	20 Dec.	Ordination at the Blackfriars, Thetford.
	22 Dec.	Enthronement at Norwich.
	24 Dec.	Norwich.
1427-8	4 Jan.	Norwich.
	13 Jan.	Little Walsingham.[3]
	18 Jan.	Bishop's Lynn.
	7 Feb.	St. James' hospital.
1428	17 April	Cottenham (Cambs.)
	11 May	St. James' hospital
	16 Aug.	Palace, Norwich.
	5 Sept.	Lavenham church.
	7-28 Sept.	Palace, Norwich. Ordination in the cathedral on 18 Sept.
	11 Oct.	Ipswich.
	29 Oct.-1 Dec.	Norwich.
	14 Dec.	The George, Bury St. Edmunds.
	18 Dec.	Ordination in Lavenham church.
1428-9	18 Feb.	St. James' hospital.
	1-23 March	Thorpe-by-Norwich (Thorp Episcopi.) Ordination in the cathedral on 12 March.
1429	26 March	Ordination in Norwich cathedral.
	28 March	Norwich.
	31 March	Thorpe.
	20 April, 9 May	St. James' hospital.

[1] Otherwise St. James' hospital by Charing Cross. Alnwick was master of this hospital, and it remained his head-quarters in London during his tenure of the see of Norwich.

[2] A manor of the bishops of Norwich, near Chelmsford.

[3] This probably marks a special visit to the famous shrine at Walsingham priory.

1429	27 Aug.–2 Sept.	Thorpe.
	16 Sept.	Bromhill priory.[1]
	19 Sept.	Newmarket.
1429–30	7 Jan.	St. James' hospital.
	1–11 March	Thorpe.
	16 March	Ordination in Norwich cathedral.
	17–22 March	Thornage.[2]
1430	6, 8 April	Thorpe.
	11 April	Norwich.
	12 April[3]	Palace chapel, Norwich.
	15 April	Ordination in Norwich cathedral.
	23 July	St. James' hospital.
	3–17 Aug.	Norwich.
	23 Aug.	Chapel of St. Edmund, Hoxne.[4]
	2 Sept.	St. James' hospital.
	16 Sept.	Norwich.
	23 Sept.	Ordination in palace chapel, Norwich.
	26 Sept.–3 Oct.	Hoxne.
1430–1	22, 27 Jan.	Norwich.
1431	26 March–10 April	Thorpe. Ordination in Norwich cathedral on 31 March.
	24 April	Norwich.
	12 Sept.	Norwich.
	4 Oct.	Needham Market.
1431–2	15–23 March	Thorpe. Ordination in Norwich cathedral on 15 March.
1432	28 March	Thorpe.
	3 April	Hickling priory.[5]
	5 April	Ordination in Norwich cathedral.
	10–29 April	Thorpe. Ordination in Norwich cathedral on 19 April.
	1 May	Kersey priory.[6]
	5 May	St. Gregory's, Sudbury.
	8 May	Stoke-by-Clare.
	18 May–11 June	Charing-by-Westminster.[7]
	13 June	College (St. Gregory's), Sudbury.
	14 June	Ordination at St. Gregory's, Sudbury.
	26 June	Charing.
	22, 24 July	Hoxne.
	24 July	Bungay.
	30 July	Blythburgh priory.[8]

[1] A house of Austin canons in the parish of Weeting, near Brandon.

[2] Between Holt and Melton Constable.   The manor belonged to the bishops of Norwich.

[3] Wednesday in Holy Week.

[4] In Suffolk, near Diss.   The bishops had a manor-house here.   The chapel probably marked the place where the head of St. Edmund was found, after his martyrdom by the Danes in 870.

[5] Austin canons, near Stalham.

[6] Austin canons, near Hadleigh, Suffolk.

[7] I.e. St. James' hospital by Charing cross.

[8] Austin canons, near Southwold : a cell of St. Osyth.

1432	1 Aug.	Snape.[1]
	8 Aug.	Wickham Market.
	11 Aug.	Holy Trinity priory, Ipswich.[2]
	18 Aug.	Bricett priory.[3]
	21 Aug.–5 Sept.	Hoxne.
	11 Sept.	Terling.
	14 Sept.	Herne, dio. London.
	16 Sept.	Charing.
	5–7 Oct.	Norwich.
	7 Oct.	Thorpe.
	8 Oct.	Norwich.
	9 Oct.	Thorpe.
	13, 14 Oct.	Holy Trinity priory, Ipswich.
	17, 18 Oct.	Thorpe.
	20 Oct.	Norwich.
	23, 27 Oct.	Thorpe.
	31 Oct.	Norwich.
	3 Nov.	Acle.[5]
	4 Nov.	Great Yarmouth.
	5 Nov.	St. Benet's abbey.[6]
	10 Nov.	Ingham priory.[7]
	12 Nov.	Cawston.[8]
	20 Nov.	Walsingham priory.[9]
	22, 23 Nov.	Great Fakenham.
	5, 9 Dec.	Bishop's Lynn.
	17 Dec.	East Dereham.
	20, 23 Dec.	Norwich. Ordination in the cathedral on 20 Dec.
1432-3	5 Jan.	Norwich.
	16 Jan.	Loddon.[10]
	21 Jan.	Horsham St. Faith's priory.[11]
	28 Jan.–4 Feb.	Thorpe.
	6 Feb.	Babraham (Cambs.).
	7 Feb.	Bishop's inn at Barkway (Herts.).[12]
	10, 12 Feb.	Charing.
	18 Feb.	Bury St. Edmunds.
	23 Feb.	Thorpe.

[1] South of Saxmundham.

[2] Or Christchurch: Austin canons. There is another date from this priory on 6 Aug., which is probably wrong.

[3] Austin canons, between Needham Market and Bildeston.

[4] Possibly Herue, which may be Harrow, though, if so, a very unusual form. Harrow was far out of the way from Terling to London.

[5] Between Norwich and Yarmouth.

[6] Benedictine: on the Bure, between Wroxham and Yarmouth.

[7] A Trinitarian house, near Stalham.

[8] Between Aylsham and Reepham.

[9] Austin canons.

[10] Between Norwich and Beccles.

[11] Benedictine, formerly alien cell of Conches (Eure): north of Norwich, on the road to Aylsham.

[12] The bishop, at this place, instituted [John], bishop of Annaghdown, to the church of Long Melford (fo. 60).

1432-3	24, 25 Feb.	Norwich.
	28 Feb.–19 March	Thornage. Ordination in Thornage church on 7 March.
1433	28 March	Ordination in Thornage church.
	31 March–4 April	Thornage.
	6 April	Thorpe.
	7, 10 April	Norwich.
	11 April	Ordination in Norwich cathedral.
	12 April	Thorpe.
	17 April.	Norwich.
	21 April	Thorpe.
	28 April	Norwich.
	11 May	Holy Trinity priory, Ipswich.
	12–24 May	Hoxne.
	5–8 June	Norwich. Ordination in the cathedral on 6 June.
	19–29 June	Hoxne.
	3 July	Terling.
	15 July–5 Aug.	Charing.
	14 Aug.	London.
	18 Aug.	Terling.
	3–12 Sept.	Hoxne.
	18–29 Sept.	Norwich. Ordination in the cathedral on 18 Sept.
	3 Oct.	Thorpe.
	6 Oct.	Norwich.
	10, 12 Oct.	Hoxne.
	13 Oct.	Bury St. Edmunds.
	4–23 Nov.	Charing.
	19 Dec.	Ordination at the Greyfriars, Babbewell by Bury St. Edmunds.
	23 Dec.	Bury St. Edmunds.
1433–4	6, 7 Jan.	Bury St. Edmunds.
	12, 24 Jan.	London.
	25 Jan.	Hoxne.
	5–17 Feb.	Bury St. Edmunds.
	18 Feb.	Bungay.
	20 Feb.–11 March	Thorpe. Ordination in Norwich cathedral on 20 Feb.
	13 March.	Ordination in Norwich cathedral.
	22, 24 March	Bury St. Edmunds.
1434	19 April–11 May	Charing.
	4 June	Thorpe.
	15 July	Norwich.
	20 July	Thorpe.
	5 Aug.–1 Oct.	Hoxne. Ordination in Hoxne church on 18 Sept.
	8–20 Oct.	Charing
	30 Oct.	Norwich.
	5 Nov.	Cirencester (Glouces.)

1434–5	25–28 Jan.	Hoxne.
	9, 20 Feb.	Thorpe.
	10 March	West Wretham church.[1]
	12 March	Norwich.
	14 March	Thorpe.
	17 March	Norwich.
1435	25 March	Norwich.
	29 March	Thorpe.
	1 April	Charing.[2]
	2 April	Ordination in Norwich cathedral.
	31 May–15 July	Ordination in the cathedral on 11 June.
	11 Nov.–6 Dec.	Charing.
1435–6	24 Feb.	Ipswich.
	26 Feb.	Hoxne.
	29 Feb., 2 March	Norwich.
	3 March	Ordination in Norwich cathedral.
	8 March	Bishop's Lynn.
	10–24 March	Thornage. Ordination in Thornage church on 24 March.
1436	26 March–4 June	Norwich. Ordination in Norwich cathedral on 2 June.
	22 June–16 Aug.	Hoxne.
	22 Sept.	Ordination in Thornage church
	24 Sept., 1 Oct.	Norwich.
	12 Oct.	Hoxne church.
	27 Nov.	Charing.
	12, 14 Dec.	Hoxne.
1436–7	21 Jan.	Ipswich.
	22 Jan.	Norwich.
	28 Jan.–4 Feb.	Charing.

It has already been mentioned that the following document is the sole account of the visitation of a monastery preserved in Alnwick's Norwich register. The text is founded upon a transcript made for the editor by Mr. E. Daly and revised by the kind offices of Mr. Fred Johnson, honorary secretary of the Norfolk and Norwich Archaeological Society.

Inquisitio capta in ecclesia conventuali Sancte Marie et Sancti Andree de Redelynnfeld, ordinis Sancti Benedicti, Norwicensis diocesis, die Martis proximo post festum nativitatis Sancte Marie, videlicet nono die mensis Septembris, anno Domini m.cccc^mo vicesimo septimo, indictione quinta, pontificatus domini Martini pape quinti anno decimo, per discretum virum magistrum Thomam Ryngstede, in decretis bacallarium, decanum ecclesie collegiate Sancte Marie de Campis in Norwico, commissarium reverendi in Christo patris et domini, domini Willelmi, Dei gratia Norwicensis episcopi, per suas commissionis litteras patentes, quarum tenor inferius describitur, sufficienter deputatum, de et super nonnullis excessibus, defectibus, criminibus, incomodis et dilapidacionis

---

[1] North of Thetford, in Rockland deanery, archdeaconry of Norfolk.
[2] This date is obviously wrong.

gravaminibus, et aliis incontinentie et dissolutionis viciis in prioratu dicte ecclesie multipliciter pululantibus ac indies nequiter continuatis, in tantum quod totius vicinie populus inde obloquitur, et non modicum scandalum generatur. In primis, citatis peremtorie domina Isabella Hermyte, loci ipsius priorissa, et per ipsam priorissam Alicia Lampet subpriorissa, Margeria Bokenham, Alicia Lynstede, Agnete Brakele, Katerina Felsham, Margareta Shuldham, professis, ac Johanna Bobble et Johanna Tates, non professis, dicte ecclesie commonialibus, ad subeundum visitationem dicti patris eisdem die et loco: quibus quidem priorissa. et commonialibus predictis omnibus et singulis dictis die et loco coram prefato commissario et judice in domo capitulari dicte ecclesie personaliter comparentibus, perlecta commissione dicti commissarii primo in latinis, et deinde ad pleniorem ipsarum monialium intellectum ipsa commissione exposita et declarata in vulgari, facta de mandato judicis proclamatione publica ad hostium dicte domus, quod si aliqua persona voluerit aliquid dicere vel proponere contra dictam commissionem quod compareat dictura et depositura pro suo interesse in hac parte prout ei videretur melius expedire: qua proclamatione facta et nullo comparente in hac parte dicturo vel deposituro contra commissionem huiusmodi, judex decrevit pro jurisdictione domini in hac parte ulterius fore procedendum, precludendo prius omnibus et singulis interesse in hac parte se habere pretendentibus viam quicquid contra hujusmodi commissionem dicendi ulterius vel proponendi. Deinde petito certificatorio a priorissa de executione mandati citatorii dicti patris eidem in hac parte directi exequenda, priorissa fatebatur illud fore per eandem personaliter debite executum, et promisit judici de executione ipsius mandati sibi postmodum certificatorium legitimum exhibere. Deinde vero, proposito per dictum judicem verbo Dei, priorissa predicta prestitit dicto domino Willelmo Norwicensi episcopo et suis successoribus eorumque ministris personale tactis sanctis euangeliis canonice obedientie juramentum; et deinde processit ad examinationem dicte priorisse.

Que examinata et interrogata fatebatur quod vicesimo quinto die mensis Januarii, anno Domini m.ccccxv^{to}, coram magistro [W.] Bernham, tunc custode spiritualitatis episcopatus Norwicensis, sede tunc ibidem vacante, ac Ricardo Walsham, monacho ecclesie cathedralis Norwicensis, tunc commissario reverendissimi in Christo patris et domini, domini Henrici, Dei gratia Cantuariensis archiepiscopi, ad visitandum civitatem et diocesim Norwicenses sufficienter deputatis, in ecclesia cathedrali Norwicensi, eadem priorissa personaliter constituta, tactis sacrosanctis Dei euangeliis, juramentum prestitit corporale quod ipsa priorissa omnes et singulas injunxiones personam suam concernentes, quas dicti magistri Willelmus Bernham et Ricardus Walsham ad dictam priorissam et conventum duxerint transmittendas, sub sigillis officiorum eorundem conscriptas, ipsa admitteret et inviolabiliter observaret quantum ad ipsam pertinerent.

Fatetur etiam prefata priorissa examinata et interrogata quod, post premissas injunxiones factas et transmissas eidem et per ipsam admissas ipsa non fuit confessa alicui monacho, nec de cetero vult alicui monacho confiteri; quod est expresse contra tenorem et effectum injunctionum predictarum.

Item eadem expresse fatetur quod, post admissionem injunxionum predictarum, ipsa non interfuit divinis diebus dominicis, festis duplicibus et principalibus, matutinis vel vesperis ut deberet, contra effectum injunxionum predictarum.

Item eadem priorissa examinata fatetur quod ipsamet priorissa et Johanna Tates, monialis non professa, non dormiunt in dormitorio communi cum aliis commonialibus, sed dormiunt in camera privata ipsius priorisse, contra effectum injunxionum hujusmodi.

Item priorissa examinata fatetur quod non observatur debitus numerus monialium nec presbiterorum in dicto prioratu; quia deberent habere xiij moniales, et non habent nisi novem, et haberent tres capellanos, et non habent nisi unum tantum.

Item compertum est per inquisitionem et etiam per confessionem propriam dicte priorisse quod in festo Sancti Laurentii ultimo elapso eadem priorissa injecit manus temere violentas in Agnetem Brackle, commonialem suam professam, incurrendo sententiam excommunicationis; pro quo quidem articulo submisit se eadem priorissa correctioni dicti judicis, et prestitit juramentum de peragendo penitentiam pro commissis in hac parte sibi injungendam, et absoluta est per judicem ante ulteriorem processum.

Item compertum est per inquisitionem quod, post admissionem injunxionum predictarum, prefata priorissa fuit in societate Thome Langlond ballivi sui, solus cum sola in locis suspectis, videlicet in parva aula ejusdem prioratus, ostiis undique firmiter seratis, exclusis quibuscumque et aliis personis. Et etiam compertum est quod ipsa fuit sola cum eodem in aliis locis suspectis extra dictum prioratum, sub heggerowes et sub boscis; et tunc ipsa exivit prioratum cum aliis servientibus et personis, quas eadem priorissa remisit ad diversa loca remota et bene distantia ab eadem ad colligendas herbas diversas pro aquis faciendis, ut asseruit de eisdem.

Item compertum est quod, quando ipsa priorissa et prefatus Thomas fuerunt sepius in una domo cum aliis monialibus et servientibus, priorissa mandavit ipsis monialibus et servientibus quod exirent ad diversa negotia facienda que ipsa assignavit eisdem, contra formam et effectum injunxionum predictarum. Prescriptum articulum prefatus judex objecit dicte priorisse in domo capitulari publice die mensis xj Septembris predicta, hora octava: quem priorissa negavit, unde judex indixit sibi purgationem cum tertia manu de commonialibus suis ibidem hora nona illius diei.

Item compertum est quod priorissa non reddit compotum singulis annis, ut tenetur juxta exigentiam injunxionum predictarum. Istum articulum etiam negat priorissa sibi iudicialiter objectum, unde indicitur sibi purgatio.

Item compertum est quod obitus defunctorum quos observare tenentur non recitantur in capitulo, nec servitium mortuorum ibidem dicitur in choro. Priorissa etiam negat istum articulum sibi objectum, unde indicta est sibi purgatio in hac parte.

Item compertum est quod dicta priorissa alienavit bona dicti prioratus et eadem dilapidavit, videlicet Thomam Langeland, nativum dicti prioratus de sanguine alienando, ac nonnullas grossas arbores et fabricam capelle de Benyngham et etiam cuidam Willelmo Jonyour de Eye sine

scientia vel consensu conventus vendendo; necnon sex quarteria et duos
bussellos brasii ac tria quarteria frumenti et plura vasa pandoxatoris
et viginti libras lane matri sui ad Wodebrigg commoranti sine consensu
conuentus etiam transmittendo. Istum articulum etiam priorissa negat,
unde judex indixit sibi purgationem cum sexta manu.

Item compertum est quod dicta priorissa non est religiosa, nec ejus
conversatio honesta gestu, factis vel verbis, in tantum quod Johanna
Tates, monialis, interrogata quare commisit crimen incontinentie, dicit
quia ad hoc fuit provocata ex malo exemplo priorisse. Priorissa negat
istum articulum, unde indicta fuit sibi purgatio cum tertia manu.

Item compertum est quod priorissa commisit crimen Lollardie,
informando moniales sibi subditas quod minus malum est eisdem vitium
incontinentie committere quam ad sui preceptum ipsam non sequi.
Ac etiam ipsa priorissa dedit licentiam generalem monialibus suis ut
acciperent viros vel maritos, et sic contra ipsam priorissam non amplius
murmurarunt. Istum articulum priorissa fatetur sibi objectum, et
abjuravit crimen Lollardie inantea.

Item dicta priorissa examinata et interrogata ibidem dixit, asseruit
et affirmavit quod Thomas Langland, ballivus suus, cum quo ipsa fuit
de incontinentia scandalizata, fuit et est liber et libere conditionis et de
optimo sanguine illius ville procreatus, sed quod communis opinio totius
vicineti ipsum Thomam habuit et reputauit nativum dicto prioratui
de sanguine.

Scrutatis rotulis curiarum dicti prioratus ibidem in capitulo, compertum fuit evidenter quod omnes rotuli curiarum hujusmodi, quos ipsa
priorissa habuit in custodia sua, videlicet a tempore regis Ricardi secundi,
fuerunt rasi dumtaxat in omnibus locis quibus aliqua mentio facta fuit
de nomine ejusdem Thome, et nomen ejus totaliter abrasum et deletum,
maxime in suspicionem et maximam ipsius prioratus et bonorum ejusdem
dilapidationem. Quo quidem articulo prescripto dicte priorisse ibidem
in capitulo judicialiter objecto, ipsa priorissa asseruit quod nesciebat quis
faciebat rasuras rotulorum hujusmodi: vnde dictus judex indixit sibi
purgationem cum sexta manu in eodem loco hora secunda post meridiem
illius diei. Et quia non potuit se purgare in hac parte, submisit se
correctioni eodem die xj.

Quibus quidem articulis prescriptis omnibus et singulis per prefatum
judicem dictis die et loco, videlicet die xj Septembris anno predicto, in
domo capitulari predicta coram omnibus comonialibus prescriptis, in
presentia Willelmi Hedelham, magistri Hugonis Atton, et Thome Walsham
testium, judicialiter objectis dicte priorisse, et per ipsam ut premittitur
judicialiter confessatis, et quibusdam aliis articulis denegatis ut prefertur,
judex prefixit dicte priorisse horam secundam post nonam illius diei xj
prescripti ad purgandum se cum numero sibi ut premittitur assignato in
domo capitulari predicta. Et quantum ad articulos periurii, dilapida-
tionis et Lollardie ac alios articulos prescriptos per ipsam judicialiter
confessatos, dictus judex assignavit eidem priorisse eandem horam
secundam post nonam illius diei ad allegandum causam si quam pro se
habeat quare, demeritis suis in hac parte id exigentibus, privari non
debeat prioratu predicto et regimine eiusdem.

Qua quidem hora secunda illius diei adveniente, dicta priorissa in presentia dictarum monialium et testium prescriptorum, in domo capitulari

predicta personaliter comparuit: nichil tamen effectuale proposuit seu, ut asseruit, ad proponendum habuit quare privari non debuit. Et ideo pro omnibus suis commissis per ipsam ut prefertur judicialiter confessatis, necnon contra ipsam per capitulares ibidem detectis, eo quod non potuit se purgare de eisdem, submisit se correctioni dicti judicis. Et deinde, quia dicta priorissa considerauit quod dictus judex voluit ipsam prioratu predicto privasse per suam diffinitionem, de consilio amicorum suorum, ad evitandum magnum scandalum in hac parte, dicto prioratui de Rydelyngfeld in suis juribus et pertinentiis universis pure, sponte, simpliciter et absolute resignavit et dimisit in scriptis, tunc ibidem presentibus omnibus monialibus et testibus suprascriptis.

Deinde vero subsequenter prefatus commissarius inquisivit a dictis commonialibus omnibus et singulis singillatim, si fuerit aliqua distinctio patens inter habitum monialium professarum dicte domus et habitum monialium non professarum. Quelibet de monialibus prescriptis dixit et deposuit quod fuit et est distinctio patens inter easdem, eo quod moniales non professe gerunt peplum de mero lino et velum singulare non duplicatum, et non gerunt annulum in digitis: moniales vero professe gerunt peplum de crispo et velum duplicatum super caput et annulum in digitis.

Et quia compertum fuit quod omnes moniales dicte ecclesie fuerunt proprietarie et inobedientes, judex prescriptus injunxit cuilibet earundem pro suis commissis in hac parte penitentiam jejunandi feria sexta proxime futura in pane et ceruisia, et dicendi unam litaniam.

Et quia allegatum fuit per conventum quod frater Ricardus Walsham, monachus, nuper visitator, in visitatione sua ibidem tempore ultime vacationis episcopatus Norwicensis, licentiavit omnes moniales ibidem quod ipsarum quelibet per se posset recipere usque ad summam vel valorem xij denariorum sine licentia priorisse vel consensu, si donetur eisdem: quam quidem licentiam tunc ibidem prefatus judex in capitulo expresse annullavit et revocavit.

Et quia compertum fuit tam per inquisitionem predictam quam per confessionem dicte Johanne Tates quod ipsa commisit crimen incontinentie cum Thoma Baker conjugato ac cum Johanne Mildenhall soluto, eadem Johanna Tates submisit se correctioni dicti judicis; qui iniunxit eidem pro suis commissis in hac parte penitentiam subscriptam, videlicet ad incedendum coram solemni processione dicti conventus die dominica proxime sequenti more penitentis, corpore curtello solomodo induto, capite velo destituto et flameoia alba induto.

APPENDIX III

The Official Staff at Alnwick's Visitations

It is much to be regretted that the records of Alnwick's diocesan administration are not supplemented by documents which would inform us of the constitution of his household and the management of his finances, with the particularity of those *Intrinseca de camera* which add so greatly to the value of some of the archiepiscopal registers at York. We know something, however, of the clerks who accompanied him on his journeys, and the evidence of the visitation documents on this point may be summed up here.

Throughout the greater part of his episcopate he was aided in the work of visitation by the chancellor of his household, John Depyng, canon of Lincoln and prebendary of Buckden, who had taken an active part in diocesan affairs for some fifteen years at least before Alnwick's accession.[1] There are few occasions between 1437 and the visitation of the archdeaconry of Oxford in 1445 on which he was not present at the acts recorded in the visitation MS. After 1445 such records are scanty, and it is possible that he died before the Peterborough visitation of 1446-7, in connexion with which his name does not occur. The bishop frequently appointed him to hear and terminate the cases which came before him. A portion of the work of examining deponents at Peterborough in 1437 and 1442 was committed to him; he terminated the adjourned visitations of Spalding priory in Oct., 1439, and of Ankerwyke priory in 1442; and, during the Lincoln visitation in July, 1440, he took the place of the bishop at the nunneries of Legbourne and Stixwould. There can also be little doubt that his revising hand is to be seen throughout the series of injunctions composed after the visitations.

John Leek or Leke, prebendary of Holy Cross, was a younger man than Depyng, but had acted under bishop Gray as commissary-general in the archdeaconries of Huntingdon and Bedford.[2] He appears but seldom among those present at visitations of religious houses, but he certainly accompanied Alnwick during the Northampton visitation of 1442. At Peterborough in 1437 he shared the work of personal enquiry with Depyng, and was his fellow commissary at Ankerwyke in 1442. A week later, he was with the bishop at Markyate, where there is no mention of Depyng.

Robert Thornton, archdeacon of Bedford,[3] was present at the visitation of Kyme priory in Oct., 1440, from which Depyng was absent, and at Peterborough in 1442 was deputed with Depyng to examine individual deponents. He was similarly deputed at Peterborough in 1446, when his work was shared by John Derby, then prebendary of Bedford major. Derby went upon the Oxford visitation of 1445, and was Alnwick's commissary at Littlemore priory on 1 June.

Thomas Skayman, who became treasurer of Lincoln in 1442,[4] took part in the Lincoln visitation of 1440, appearing at Thornholm, Thornton, Wellow, Nocton park and Kyme. On a later occasion, in 1442, we find him presiding over the consistory court at Sleaford.

In addition to these clerks, who took their share in judicial business, there were the clerks to whom the duty of preaching was committed Neither Depyng nor any other member of the official staff preached: their business was law, not theology. On the other hand, the theologians appeared now and then, though rarely, as present at the acts of visitation: John Beverley was so present at Nuncoton in 1440. In the earlier visitations, from 1437 to 1439 inclusive, the habitual preacher was Thomas Duffeld, B.D. Duffeld preached at least eight sermons during the Lincoln visitation of 1440, but three were delivered by John Beverley, prebendary of

---

[1] See *Visitations* I, 190.
[2] See *Visitations* I, 91, note 5.
[3] See *ibid.* I, 60, note 3.
[4] See *Visitations* II, 163, note 4.

Aylesbury,[1] at Bourne abbey and Nuncoton and Stainfield priories. In the Leicester visitation of 1440-1, Duffeld preached four times, Beverley two.

Duffeld disappears after 1441, and Beverley preached seven sermons during the Northampton visitation of 1442. Thomas Twyer, rector of Glatton and afterwards of Bringhurst,[2] however, preached twice, at Daventry and Rothwell. Beverley preached at the visitation of Wymondley in 1442, but, during the Bedford visitation in 1442-3, his only sermon was at Dunstable, while Twyer preached three times. In the archdeaconry of Oxford in 1445, Beverley preached five times to Twyer's four; but at Peterborough in 1446, Twyer, who was specially connected with the abbey as the rector of one of the best livings in its gift, was the chosen preacher.

Out of sixty sermons recorded, Duffeld preached nineteen, Beverley eighteen, and Twyer ten. Of the rest, four sermons remain anonymous; in six cases, at Croyland, Laund, Leicester, Peterborough (twice), and Wellow, the sermons were deputed to members of the houses visited; at Oxford, two sermons were preached by members of colleges; and a single discourse, at Northill in 1442, was pronounced by John Sperhawke, a secular clerk who apparently had no connexion with the diocese. On the ingenuity shown in the choice of texts nothing need be said here. It may be noticed, however, that the same text, probably followed by the same sermon, was used more than once. For his nineteen sermons Duffeld had fourteen texts, Beverley twelve texts for his eighteen. Twyer, on the other hand, repeated himself only once.

Among the remaining clerks, who acted as notaries or scribes, the chief, of course, was the diocesan registrar, Thomas Colstone, who had been in the service of six successive bishops. The minutes and injunctions, with some few exceptions, are in his well-known hand. The name of Thomas Thorpe appears on nineteen occasions, and that of John Bug or Bugge on fourteen. Both these men may be classed among the notaries, and it seems that they were sometimes called in by Colstone to take his place. Neither of them are to be found in the later visitations; but it should be added that there are few mentions of the *personnel* of Alnwick's staff in the Oxford visitation of 1445. John Spenser, who was at Spalding in 1439, John Malyns, at Peterborough in 1446, Thomas London, at Breedon and Gracedieu in 1440-1, and Roger Jurdone, mentioned among those present at a court held by Depyng in Rothwell church in 1442, are other names. John Wylby or Wylles, rector of Wheathampstead, and John Bewes, rector of Waldegrave, were at the adjourned visitation of Dorchester in June, 1441, and occur in the miscellaneous documents printed in appendix I; but they were more probably assessors than scribes.

Occasionally, to the names of the staff are added those of monks, canons, or secular clerks, present at the close of a day's visitation, to give completeness to the official record. These, however, need not be detailed; and it is always possible to distinguish them from the persons who formed the bishop's personal companions and helpers in his journeys through the large area of which he was the spiritual ruler.

---

[1] See *Visitations* II, 34, note 3.
[2] See *ibid.* II, 60, note 2.

APPENDIX IV

Addenda et Corrigenda[1]

Since the first volume of these *Visitations* was published, the editor has been able to make a thorough examination of the contemporary archiepiscopal registers at York, which have revealed many details which are needed to rectify the biographical notices in the footnotes of the text and in appendix II. Where dates in the York register agree with those given by Le Neve and other printed authorities, no new reference is given; but, where they differ, the MS. reference is added instead of one to the printed sources.

Volume I

Page xvii, line 12. 31 March, 1421. This is the date at which the mandate for Gray's installation to the deanery was issued (York Reg. Bowet I, fo. 72*d*).

line 24. Ulleskelf. Gray was admitted to this prebend on 27 July, 1425 (York Reg. Sed. Vac. fo. 422*d*).

Page xviii, line 35. *After* archdeaconry *add* Master William Alnewyk, priest, LL.D. had collation of Knaresborough prebend in York, 3 May, 1421 (York Reg. Bowet I, fo. 72). [See vol. II, p. xiv, where this is noted].

Page xxii, line 32. *After* value *add* The register of the London Charterhouse, fo. 13, supplies a further date for the summer of 1428 : 'Anno domini m°ccccxxviii° die xviii° mensis Julii reverendus in Christo pater et dominus dominus Ricardus Flemyng episcopus Lincolniensis licencia sibi prius ab episcopo Londoniensi concessa consecravit solempniter cum cantu campanam nostram majorem et antiquiorem in honore et nomine gloriose virginis Marie hujus domus patrone' (Hope, *Hist. of the London Charterhouse*, 1925, p. 51).

Page xxiii, line 29. *For* 1431-2 *read* 1432-3.

Page 4, line 18. *For* decay *read* condition for cutting. [See also page 101, line 14, and vol. II, page 180 (English), note 4].

Page 14 (English), note 2, line 7. 23 Aug., 1423. This is the date of issue of the mandate for installation. The actual exchange was effected by the bishop of Salisbury at Potterne on 6 Aug., by commission from the archbishop of York, bearing date 28 July (York Reg. Bowet I, fo. 79*d*).

Page 56 (English), note 8. Further information about Robert Thwaites is derived from York Reg. Kempe. He resigned the church of Terrington by 15 Dec., 1440, when his successor was instituted (fo. 396*d*). On 22 June, 1451, Master Robert Twates was instituted to the church of Crofton, Yorks., W.R. (fo. 74*d*), in which he evidently succeeded Robert Flemyng (see p. 205). He resigned Crofton by 27 Sept. following (fo. 442*d*).

Page 68 (English), note 2, line 6. *After* precinct *add* in this particular case. The evidence for Lacock, however, as Mr. Brakspear has pointed out to me upon the spot, seems indisputable.

Page 69 (English), note 1, line 30. The date 24 May, 1436, is that given by Le Neve. In York Reg. Kempe, fo. 16, the collation is placed in March (day left blank), 1436-7 : by an error the name is given as master *William* Makworth. He is called John, however, after his death, when Botevant prebend was filled up on 2 Nov., 1451 (*ibid.*, fo. 75).

Page 123 (English), note 2 (English), line 4. *After* Moresby *insert*, clerk, had collation of North Leverton prebend in Southwell, 14 March, 1413-4 (York Reg. Bowet, I, fo. 51*d*). He exchanged this for the church of Dacre, Cumberland, to which he was instituted 28 Jan., 1417-8 (*ibid.* ff. 59*d*, 60). He

line 9. *After* Yorkshire *insert* He was instituted to Holme-on-Spalding-moor, Yorks. E.R., at the presentation of Robert Constable, lord of Flamborough, 8 Nov., 1424 (York Reg. Sed. Vac., fo. 387*d*).

lines 9-11. *For* In 1427 . . . . . both churches *read* In 1427 he had a papal dispensation to hold the churches of Dacre and Holme together.

line 11. *After* May). *insert* He resigned Holme by 28 Feb., 1430-1 (York Reg. Kempe, fo. 355*d*).

line 15. *For* vicarage *read* rectory.

lines 17, 18. *For* until . . . . York *read*, but exchanged the arch-deaconry for the church of Bringhurst, Leices., 15 Feb., 1442-3 (Reg. XVIII, fo. 155 and *d*), which he resigned by 9 Nov. following (*ibid.*, fo. 157).

line 19. *For* 1443 *read* 12 Feb., 1443-4, when he resigned his prebend in York (York Reg. Kempe, fo. 51).

Page 175, lines 19, 20. *For* 1423, when *read* June, 1421 (Reg. D. & C. Lincoln VII, fo. 7). In 1423

Page 177, lines 11, 12. *For* 27 *read* 25 ; *and for* Le Neve, III, 453 *read* York Reg. Sed. Vac., fo. 423.

Page 177, lines 38, 39. *For* He also . . . . but *read* His prebend in Wells was collated to his successor on the same day (*Wells Reg. Stafford* [Som. Rec. Soc.], p. 115), and his York and Southwell prebends were similarly filled on 22 Oct (York Reg. Kempe, fo. 9*d*).

Page 180, line 2. Bekingham. It may be noted that in the original entry (York Reg. Kempe, fo. 15*d*), the name appears correctly as Bekyngton.

Page 182, line 41. 26 July. The date of the mandate for installation is 23 July : the exchange was effected by the bishop of Coventry and Lichfield at Eccleshall on 18 July, by commission dated 4 July (York Reg. Bowet I, ff. 42*d*, 43).

Page 183, line 32. 28 Feb. In York Reg. Kempe, fo. 47, the year is given as 1441, i.e., 1441-2 ; but this seems to be an error for 1440.

Page 184, line 18. *For* Bainton in 1446 (*Test. Ebor.*, ut sup.), *read* Huggate by 8 Nov., 1446 (York Reg. Kempe, fo. 59).

line 19. *For* Nov. of the same year *read* the same month.

Page 184, lines 25-31. As suggested in the text, the date in *Test. Ebor.* is wrong, and should be 1449-50 (York Reg. Kempe, fo. 68).

line 36. 8 Aug. The date is actually 18 Aug. (York Reg. W. Bothe, fo. 31).

line 40. *After* Beverley *add.* His successors in his prebends at York and Beverley received collation on 23 and 26 July, 1457, respectively, in Cleveland archdeaconry on 12 Aug., while his successor at Bainton was inst. on 22 Sept. (York Reg. W. Bothe, ff. 42 and *d*, 111*d*).

Page 185, line 38. 22 June. The date should be 22 July : the bishop of Lincoln's certificate of the exchange bears date 14 July (York Reg. Kempe, fo. 64 and *d*).

line 46. *After* page 277). *insert* He resigned Skipwith prebend by 2 Aug., 1457 (York Reg. W. Bothe, fo. 131 and *d*). [See some additional notes on William Scrope in Surtees Soc., vol. 127, p. 299].

Page 186, lines 40, 41. *For* (Harl. 6969, p. 108) *read* (York. Reg. Bowet I, fo. 48*d* ; but the entry is cancelled, with the note ' Ista collacio non sortibatur (*sic*) effectum').

Page 187, line 50. *For* Pinkey *read* Pinkney.

Page 190, lines 5-7. *Omit* He had coll. . . . . below). [It is evident that John Marshall, canon of Wells, was a different person].

Page 191, line 27. *For* 18 Sept., 1423 *read* 3 Dec., 1424.

line 28. *For* (*Test. Ebor.*, ut sup.) *read* (York Reg. Sed. Vac., fo. 389*d*).

Page 192, line 47. *After* fo. 34) *insert* On 12 June, 1430, he was inst. to Kirkby-in-Ashfield, Notts., which he res. by 16 Feb., 1432-3 (York Reg. Kempe, ff. 350, 11).

Page 193, lines 3, etc. The career of John Carpenter has been worked out with great care by Richards and Shadwell, *Provosts and Fellows of Oriel College*, 1922. See also Pearce, *Hartlebury Castle*, 1926, pp. 65 sqq., especially p. 67, note 1, which suggests that ' some of the earlier appointments recorded' in the present note 'must be assumed to refer to other men of the same name.'

line 18. 8 June, 1426. The mandate of induction to Clifton prebend (in the diocese of York) bears date 23 Sept., 1431 (York Reg. Kempe, fo. 358*d*).

lines 33-5. *For* He certainly . . . . ii, 428) *read* He exchanged Clifton prebend about 1438 with Thomas Riby for a prebend in St Stephen's, Westminster. No date is given in the entry in York Reg. Kempe, fo. 395*d*.

Page 195, lines 27, 28. *For* He vacated . . . . p. 113) *read* He exchanged his York prebend for Barnby prebend in Howden, 7 Aug., 1420 (York Reg. Bowet I, fo. 72).

line 42. 21 July, 1434. This is the date of the mandate for installation to Barnby prebend. The exchange actually took place on 4 July (York Reg. Kempe, fo. 397*d*).

Page 197, lines 31-33. *For* page 271), and . . . . . Kempe, however, *read* page 271). According to Le Neve (II, 150), Busshebury did not die until 1450 ; but he must have quitted this prebend long before, as Robert Flemyng appears to have obtained it in 1428 (see note below on page 205, line 26). It is therefore

probable that Kempe succeeded him upon his translation to Milton ecclesia prebend in 1430, and Kempe certainly.

line 40. 4 April, 1431. The date of collation in Reg. Kempe, fo. 15, is 26 March, 1435.

line 42. 2 July. The date in Reg. Kempe, fo. 15d, is 21 June.

line 45. *For* 1439 *read* 1438.

line 47. *For* 28 March . . . . year *read* 17 May, on which day he also

line 51. 19 Nov. The date in Reg. Kempe, fo. 48d, is 8 Nov.

Page 198, line 7. *After* page 162). *insert* He had collation of St Mary Magdalene hospital, Ripon, on 27 July, 1445 (York Reg. Kempe, fo. 56d).

lines 7, 8. 25 June. The date in Reg. Kempe, fo. 61d, is 15 May.

Page 198, line 23. *After* page 90). *insert* On the same day his successors were admitted to the archdeaconry of Richmond and the church of Bolton Percy (York Reg. Kempe, fo. 68). The sacristship of the chapel of St Mary and the Holy Angels was also filled up at the same time, and, although no cause of voidance is recorded in the register, and there is no record of Kempe's admission to this office, there is good reason for supposing that this vacancy was due to the same cause as the others.

Page 199, line 29. *After* (Le Neve, I, 513) *insert* According to Hennessy (*Nov. Rep.*) London Reg. Gilbert records his exchange of Chiswick prebend, 29 Sept., 1448, for Wisborough prebend in Chichester, which is not recorded elsewhere.

lines 46-48. *Omit* and it is possible . . . . i, 351). Welbourne still held this prebend in June, 1421 (Reg. D. & C. Linc. VII, fo. 7).

Page 200, lines 33, 34. *For* (see Le Neve, iii, 151). *read*, of which he had collation 2 July, 1430 (York Reg. Kempe, fo. 9).

Page 201, line 4. *After* 1419. *insert* In 1426 Ralph Lowthe, rector of Winthorpe, Notts., presumably the same person, had licence to preach the word of God in the diocese of York (York Reg. Kempe, fo. 29 and d).

lines 8-9. *For* he had . . . . p. 297). *read* it was void by 15 Nov., 1449 (York Reg. Kempe, fo. 67d).

Page 203, lines 34-36. Leyot appears to have held the prebend in June, 1421 (Reg. D. & C. Linc. VII, fo. 7).

Page 205, line 10. *After* quitted it for *insert* Workington, Cumberland, to which he was inst. 28 Aug., 1428 (York Reg. Kempe, fo. 213d), and this for

line 14. *Omit* his successor at Wells.

Page 205, line 26. ROBERT FLEMYNG. Several additions may be made to this note. From York Reg. Kempe, fo. 332 and d, we obtain the information that he had a mandate of induction to the prebendal church of Farndon, 2 April, 1428, which supplies a gap in the Lincoln registers. It is clear, therefore, that, in the list of prebendaries of Farndon, his name must occur between those of Lewis Busshebury and Thomas Kempe, and the note on page 197, lines 29-33, must be modified accordingly. It is probable that he became rector of Crofton, Yorks, W.R., a place with which the Flemyng family was intimately connected, early in his career ; but there appears to be no record of his institution. On 16 Jan.,

1442-3, archbishop Kempe appointed a commission to enquire into the vacancy of the church of Methley, Yorks., W.R., to which Flemyng had been presented by the Crown (York Reg. Kempe, fo. 49 and *d*). On 18 Feb., 1443-4, he had licence, as rector of Crofton and Methley, of non-residence for three years (*ibid.*, fo. 87). He resigned both by 22 June, 1451 (*ibid.*, fo. 74). His tenure of the deanery of Lincoln did not prevent him from holding other cures of souls ; for he was instituted to Almondbury, Yorks., W.R., on 12 Nov., 1457, and to Warton, Lancs., on 26 Nov., 1458 (York Reg. W. Bothe, ff. 10, 136). He held Almondbury until his death : his successor was instituted 25 Sept., 1484 (York Reg. Rotherham, I, fo. 117).

Page 206, line 12. *After* fo. 254). *insert* On 23 Dec., 1432, he had collation of a prebend in Southwell, void by the death of John Wawen (York Reg. Kempe, fo. 11).

line 25. *After* Sussex *add* Mr. Herbert Chitty informs me that Petworth was a benefactor of Winchester college, where his obit was kept on 29 October, in conjunction with that of Robert Thurbern, warden of the college.

Page 210, line 28. *After* benefice with *insert* Pytchley and Stoke prebend, 28 Oct., 1423 (*Cal. Papal Letters* VII, 286), and exch.

line 34. *For* 1427 *read* 1457.

Page 211, line 3. *After* fo. 191). *insert* During the voidance of the see of York after the death of archbishop Bowet, he had licence of non-residence as rector of Cottingham (York Reg. Sed. Vac., fo. 437*d*).

Page 213, line 39. 8 March. In the original entry the date of the month is not given, and 8 March is the date of the preceding entry (York Reg. Bowet I, fo. 67).

lines 39, 40. *For* in 1419 . . . . 203). *read* by 4 May, 1419, when he obtained Howden prebend in Howden (York Reg. Bowet, I, fo. 67*d*).

Page 215, line 10. William, *episcopus Dunkaldensis*, exchanged Meppershall, Beds., for Great Hallingbury : the date in Reg. XVIII, fo. 182, is 20 May. On 20 Dec., 1441, William Gunwardby, *episcopus Dunkaldensis*, had collation of Cople vicarage, Beds., which he resigned by 31 Oct., 1443 (*ibid.*, fo. 183 and *d*). See also Stubbs' list of suffragans in *Reg. Sac. Angl.*, and Dowden, *The Bishops of Scotland*, pp. 94-5.

line 24. *After* missing *add* Leget resigned the hospital by 8 June, 1441, when William Berford (possibly the clerk mentioned on p. 205 above) succeeded him (Reg. XVIII, fo. 182*d*).

Page 216, line 27. *After* p. 394). *insert* He was not instituted to Brompton however, until 21 June, 1427, by commission from the archbishop of York bearing date 15 June (York Reg. Kempe, fo. 327 and *d*).

line 42. *After* ut sup.). *add* He seems to have lived for some time after the date of his will, as his prebend in Howden was not filled until 1 Aug., and the church of Settrington not until 20 Aug., 1449 (York Reg. Kempe, fo. 421 and *d*).

Page 248, line 7. Dr. G. R. Owst, *Preaching in Mediaeval England*, p. 166, note 1, remarks rightly that the explanation of *scamnum, scabellum,* as 'simply a stool' is inadequate, and cites English equivalents 'bynk,' 'benche,' etc., which show a wider application to seats, benches, and possibly pews. Cf. the term *banc d'oeuvre* or the pew opposite the pulpit in foreign churches, which might be translated *scamnum fabrice.*

VOLUME II

Page xxiii, note 4, line 2.   *For Reporis read Reports.*

Page xxix, note 4, line 1.   *For* Castor *read* Caistor.

note 5, line 2.   *For* Norwich *read* Norwich.

Page xl, line 13.   *For* Dorchester priory *read* Dorchester abbey.

Page lviii, line 36.   *For* John *read* William.

Page 10 (English), note 2.   The series referred to in the note is printed in vol. 127 of the publications of the Surtees Society, 1916.

Page 20 (English), note 7, line 2.   *For scruientes read seruientes.*

Page 24 (English), note 3, line 5.   *For pavlmentum read pavimentum.*

Page 50 (English), note 2 (Eng.), line 14.   *For* St Osyth's priory *read* St Osyth's abbey.

Pages 54-60 (English), head of page (Eng.)   *For* MONASTERY *read* ABBEY.

Page 61 (English), note 3, line 7.   *For* Premonstratentian *read* Premonstratensian.

Page 84 (English), note 4.   *For* in *read* is.

Page 93 (English), note 5.   Since this note was written, the present editor has produced a full text of these statutes in *Archaeol. Journal,* LXXV, 241-309, with an introduction in which some comment is made upon the extreme inaccuracy of Dr. Cox's abstract.

Page 95 (English), note 5, line 8.   *For* porch *read* vestry.

note 3 (English), line 1.   *For* ontside *read* outside.

Page 121 (English), line 8.   *For* boaders *read* boarders.

Page 125 (English), note 7, line 1.   *For* Jurdane *read* Jurdone.

Page 156 (English), note 4, line 21.   *Omit bracket after* 428.

Page 190 (English), note 5, line 1.   *For* Leiceester *read* Leicester.

Page 191 (English), line 21.   *For* Halwelle *read* Halywelle.

Page 210 (English) note 4, line 6.   *Omit comma after* Thornton.

VOLUME III

Page 247 (English), note 4.   Mr. R. L. Hine has kindly supplied me with the information that John Sperhawke, S.T.B., was instituted to the vicarage of Hitchin on 7 May, 1453 (Reg. xx, fo. 299*d*), and remained vicar until his death in 1474, a date which supports his identity with the canon of Wells. He was not vicar of Hitchin until ten years after this visitation ; but it is probable that he belonged to the neighbourhood, and that this accounts for his presence at Northill on this occasion.

INDEX OF PERSONS & PLACES

A

Aas, John (Oseney), 263.

Abberbury, John, prior of Wroxton, 396.

—— : *see* Adderbury.

Abbot, Robert, 348, 350.

Abendone, John (Eynsham), 91.

—— : *see* Abingdon.

Abingdon, Abendone, Berks., 72, 79, 91.

——, abbey, xix.

Abkettleby, Leices., 179.

' Acherches,' registers at Peterborough, 284.

Acle, Norfolk, 408-11.

Actone, Agnes, 322, 325.

Adam, John : *see* Odam.

Adderbury, Abberbury, Oxon., 263, 396.

——, Richard (Oseney), 263.

Agincourt, Azincourt (Pas-de-Calais), battle of, 61, 97.

Aix-en-Provence (Bouches-du-Rhône), 157.

Akeley, Leices., deanery of, xxxvi, 174.

Alanston : *see* Alençon.

Alanus de Insulis, *Distinctiones* referred to, 255.

Albi (Tarn), xxx, 157.

Alcester, Alcestre, Warwicks., 53.

Alcestre, Robert (Chacombe), 53.

Alcock, John, bishop of Worcester, his register referred to, 269.

Alconbury, Alcumbury, Hunts., 302.

Alcumbury, John (Ramsey), 303, 304, 306-10.

——, Robert (Ramsey), 304.

Alderbourne, Alderburne, Alerburn, Bucks., 3.

Alderlound, 59.

Aldewyncle, William (Peterborough), 284, 290, 294.

—— : *see* Aldwinkle.

Aldington, Kent, 234.

——, rector of : *see* Rounhale.

Aldwinkle, Aldewyncle, Northants., 270.

Alençon (Orne), Alanston, 158.

Alerburn : *see* Alderbourne.

Alesby, John (Wellow), 391-5.

—— : *see* Aylesby.

Alexander, bishop of Lincoln, 113.

Alford, Alforde, Lincs., xxxv, 220, 373.

Alforde, John (Markby), 220-4.

Alkerton, Alryngtone, Oxon, 263.

Allen, Thomas, fellow of Gloucester hall, Oxon, 361.

Allesley, Halesley, Warwicks., 50.

Allesley, Agnes (Catesby), 46, 48, 50-2.

Aln river, xxvii.

Alnwick, Alnewyk, Alnwyk, Northumberland, xiv-xvi, xxiii, xxvi-vii.

——, abbey, xvii, xxvi.

Alnwick, William, rector of Goldsborough, canon of London, archdeacon of Salisbury, bishop of Norwich and Lincoln, xiv-xxx, and *passim.*

——, ——, canon of Alnwick, xvii.

——, ——, prior of Belvoir, xvii.

——, ——, prior of Wymondham, xvi.

——, ——, confessor of nuns of Syon, xvii-viii.

——, ——, recluse at Westminster, xviii.

Alryngtone, John (Oseney), 263.

—— : *see* Alkerton.

Altone, John (Nutley), 254.

Alueriche, John, rector of a mediety of Sedgebrook, 403.

Ambresdone, William (Eynsham), 91.

Ambrosden, Ambresdone, Oxon, 91.

Amcotes, Richard (Thornholm), 365, 369.

Amcotts, Amcotes, Lincs., 363.

Amounderness, Lancs., 196.

Ampthill, Beds., xxxix.

Amundesham, John, his *Chronicon* referred to, xvii-viii, 407.

Amundeville, Beatrice, 86.

——, Elias, 86.

——, Awtvyle, Walter, 86.

——, William, 86.

Amyas, John, prior of Breedon, 126.

——, John, of Thornhill, 126.

——, William, 126.

Anastasius IV, pope, 149.

Ancestor, The, referred to, 61.

Ancoradensis, suffragan bishop, 403.

Anderby, Richard (Bardney), 33.

——, William (Humberstone), 140-2, 145-6.

Andever, Edmund, prior of St Frideswide's, Oxford, 266.

Andrew, Richard, dean of the New college, Leicester, 191.

Andrews, F. B., *Mediaeval Builder and his Methods* referred to, 336.

INDEX OF PERSONS & PLACES 457

North, sir Dudley, 248.
Northamburgt : *see* Northborough.
Northampton, Northamptone, xxxiii, xxxvii, xl, 45, 48, 50, 55, 206, 272, 277, 286.
——, archdeaconry, visitations of, x, xiii, xxxviii, 275, 354, 418.
——, ——, *Architectural Notices of Churches of*, referred to, 156.
——, ——, deaneries : *see* Brackley, Rothwell, Rutland, Weldon.
Northampton, Northamptone, battle of, 151.
——, countess of : *see* Hereford.
——, friars (Augustinian and Dominican) of, 50.
——, nuns of : *see* Delapré.
——, St Andrew's priory, Benedictine chapters at, 55, 286.
——, St James' abbey, 244-6.
——, ——, abbot of : *see* Watforde, Youn.
——, ——, Augustinian chapter at 264.
——, ——, canons of : *see* Botylere, Braundestone, Everdone, Grene, Mounceux, Olyvere, Orlyngbere, Patteshulle, Pety, Symonde (2), Tryg, Youn (2).
——, St John's hospital, visitation of, xi, xxxviii, 247.
Northamptone, Agnes : *see* Butylere.
——, John (Laund), 179-80.
——, William, prior of Laund, 178.
Northamptonshire Families referred to, 158-9.
Northamptonshire Natural History Society, *Transactions* referred to, 50.
Northamptonshire, sheriff of : *see* Wydvile.
Northborough, Northamburgt, Northants., 57.
Northburgh, Roger, bishop of Coventry and Lichfield, 120.
North Collingham, Notts., 297.
Northcotes, Robert (Wellow), 391, 392.
—— : *see* North Somercotes.
North Frodingham, Yorks., E.R., 371.
Northill, Northyevelle, Beds., college of, xii, xxxviii, 247-8, 419.
——, ——, master of : *see* Hethe.
——, ——, fellows of : *see* Chorletone, Parkere, Patone, Tempford.
North Kelsey, Lincs., prebend in Lincoln cathedral, 217, 402.
North Kilworth, Leices., 210.
North Leigh, Oxon, 263.
North Luffenham, Rutland, 190, 401.
——, —— : *see* Matfene.
North Newbald, Yorks., E.R., prebend in York minster, 39.
Northolme, Lincs., chapel of St Thomas at, 169, 173.

North Somercotes, Northcotes, Lincs., 391.
Northumberland, earls of : *see* Percy.
North Wingfield, Winfield, Wynfeld, Derbyshire, xxxii, xxxvii.
Northyevelle : *see* Northill.
Norton-by-Daventry, Northants., 63.
Nortone Episcopi : *see* Bishop's Norton.
Nortone, Thomas (Fotheringhay), 94, 96-7, 100.
Norwich, 55, 231, 256, 405-6, 408-13.
——, archdeaconry of, 407.
——, bishops of : *see* Alnwick, Bateman, Brouns, Lyhart.
——, ——, officials and vicar-generals of : *see* Bernham, Wygenhale.
——, ——, palace of, 409.
——, ——, chapel, 405, 410.
——, ——, ——, gatehouse, xxiii.
——, ——, registers of, 407.
——, cathedral, xxiii, xxvi-vii, 409-14.
——, —— priory, 55.
——, —— ——, monk of : *see* Walsham.
——, collegiate church of St Mary in the fields, dean of : *see* Ryngstede.
——, friaries, xxvi.
Norys, Alice, 188, 191.
——, John, 114.
Nostell, Yorks., W.R., St Oswald's priory, 41, 241.
Notteley : *see* Nutley.
Nottingham, Notyngham, xxxvii, 184, 270.
——, church of St Mary, chantry priests of, 142.
——, earl of : *see* Ferrers.
Notyngham, Robert (Peterborough), 285.
Novus Locus : *see* Newstead.
Nuncoton, Cotham, Lincs., priory, xi, xxxv, 117, 173, 247-52, 351, 357, 359, 418-19.
——, ——, prioress of : *see* Skypwythe.
——, ——, nuns of : *see* Ascyue, Aunselle, Benyngtone, Est, Estone, Frost, Gray, Jaktone, Malet, Saltmershe, Skotte, Terry, Thorpe.
Nunny, Nunne, Alice (Godstow, afterwards abbess), 114-15.
Nutley, Notteley, Bucks., abbey, xiii, xliii, 253-62.
——, ——, abbot of : *see* Redyng.
——, ——, canons of : *see* Altone, Asshendone, Borewelle, Brehulle, Brystowe, Bury, Crendone, Esyngtone, Ewelme, Londone, Medemenham, Merlowe, Thame, Tylehurst, Walyngford.
Nutteman, William (Bourne), 38.

INDEX OF COUNTIES

CUMBERLAND.

Carlisle.

Workington.

DERBYSHIRE.

Ashbourne.
Chesterfield.
Hathersage.
Heanor.
Kniveton.

Long Eaton.
Melbourne.
Norbury.
North Wingfield.
Repton.

Sawley.
Willington.
Youlgreave.

DEVON.

Aveton Giffard.
Branscombe.
Buckland.

Cutton.
Exeter.
Ottery St Mary.

Torre.
Totnes.

DORSET.

Chardstock.

Ford.

Shaftesbury.

DURHAM.

Darlington.
Durham.

Raby.

Sedgefield.

ESSEX.

Bradwell-juxta-Mare.
Chelmsford.
Consumpta per Mare.
Great Chesterford.
Great Wigborough.

Keton.
Lamarsh.
Pleshy.
Saffron Walden.
St Osyth's.

Terling.
Walden.
West Tilbury.

FLINTSHIRE.

St Asaph.

GLAMORGAN.

Beaupré.
Cowbridge.

Ewenny.

Llandaff.

GLOUCESTERSHIRE.

Bibury.
Bisley.
Bristol.
Chipping Campden.
Cirencester.
Fairford.

Goodringhill.
Hayles.
Moreton Valence.
Quenington.
Quinton.
Tetbury.

Tewkesbury.
Tormarton.
Westbury-on-Tryn
Whaddon.
Winchcombe.

HAMPSHIRE.

Beaulieu abbey.
Hook.
Hurstbourne Tarrant.

Mottisfont.
Netley,
South Warnborough.

Southwick.
Winchester.

HEREFORDSHIRE.

Hereford.

Putson.

HERTFORDSHIRE.

Ashwell.
Barkway.
Berkhampstead.
Hitchin.

Redbourne.
Royston.
St Albans.
Therfield.

Ware.
Wheathampstead.
Wymondley.

LINCOLNSHIRE.

Alford.
Amcotts.
Appleby.
Asteby.
Aveland deanery.
Axholme, isle of.
Aylesby.
Bardney.
Barholm.
Barrow-on-Humber.
Barton-on-Humber.
Baumber.
Beckering.
Beltisloe deanery.
Belton-in-Axholme.
Belton-by-Grantham.
Belvoir priory.
Benington.
Benniworth.
Billingborough.
Bishop's Norton.
Bitchfield.
Blankney.
Blyton.
Bolingbroke deanery.
Boothby Graffoe.
Boothby Pagnell.
Boston.
Boultham.
Bourne.
Brawby.
Brigg.
Brocklesby.
Broughton.
Burgh-le-Marsh.
Burton Pedwardine.
Butterwick.
Caistor.
Calcewaith deanery.
Candleshoe deanery.
Castle Bytham.
Claxby.
Clee.
Cleethorpes.
Colsterworth.
Coningsby.
Corby.
Cowbit.
Croyland.
Deeping.
Doddington Pigot.
Dousedalehouse.
Driby.
Dunholme.
Dunston.
East Halton.
Elkington.
Elsham.
Fistoft.
Flixborough.
Fosse.
Frampton.
Frieston.
Friskney.

Gainsborough.
Gartree deanery.
Gate Burton.
Gautby.
Gedney.
Gokewell.
Gosberton.
Goxhill.
Graffoe deanery.
Grainthorpe.
Grantham.
Grantham deanery.
Great Coates.
Great Hale.
Great Ponton.
Greetham.
Grimsby.
Grimsby deanery.
Habrough.
Hamby.
Hannah.
Harmston.
Haxey.
Heynings.
Hill deanery.
Holbeach.
Holland deanery.
Holland fen.
Holme.
Horncastle.
Horsley.
Hough-on-the-Hill.
Humber river.
Humberstone.
Huttoft.
Ingoldsby.
Irby.
Irnham.
Keal.
Keelby.
Kettleby.
Kingerby.
Kirkby.
Kirkby-on-Bain.
Kirkstead.
Kirton-in-Holland.
Kyme.
Laceby.
Lafford deanery.
Langtoft.
Langworth.
Lawres deanery.
Leake.
Leasingham.
Legbourne.
Leverton.
Limber.
Lincoln.
Little Coates.
Little Limber.
Long Bennington.
Longoboby deanery.
Long Sutton.
Longwood.

Louth.
Louth park.
Louthesk and Ludborough
  deanery.
Loveden deanery.
Ludborough.
Mablethorpe.
Maltby.
Mareham.
Markby.
Market Deeping.
Market Rasen.
Metheringham.
Midby.
Morton.
Moulton.
Mumby.
Ness deanery.
Nettleham.
Newhouse.
Newstead-by-Stamford.
Nocton.
Nocton park.
Nomansland Hurn.
Normanby-le-Wold.
North Kelsey.
Northolme.
North Somercotes.
Nuncoton.
Ormesby.
Osgodby.
Partney.
Pinchbeck.
Redbourne.
Rippingale.
Saltfleetby.
Scamblesby.
Sedgebrook.
Sheep eau.
Sibsey,
Skendleby.
Skitter beck.
Sleaford.
Snarford.
Somerby-by-Brigg.
South eau.
South Ferriby.
South Reston.
Southrey.
Southwood.
Spalding.
Spanby.
Spilsby.
Spital-in-the-Street.
Stain.
Stainfield.
Stainton-le-Hole.
Stallingborough,
Stamford.
Stixwould.
Stoke Rochford.
Stow.
Sutterton.
Swayfield.

NORTHAMPTON—contd.

Grafton Regis.
Great Oakley.
Greens Norton.
Hardwick.
Harrowden.
Hellidon.
Helpston.
Higham Ferrers.
Holmby.
Irthlingborough.
Kettering.
Kingscliffe.
King's Sutton.
Kislingbury.
Lilbourne.
Lilford.
Little Billing.
Little Oakley.
Longthorpe.
Lowick.
Marholm.
Maxey.
Nene river.

Northampton.
Northborough.
Norton-by-Daventry.
Old.
Orlingbury.
Oundle.
Oxney.
Pattishall.
Peakirk.
Peterborough.
Pilton.
Pipewell.
Preston Capes.
Preston Deanery.
Pytchley.
Quinton.
Rockingham.
Rothwell.
Rushton.
Southorpe.
Southwick.
Stanion.
Staverton.

Thenford.
Thornhaugh.
Thorpe Mandeville.
Thrapston.
Titchmarsh.
Twywell.
Waldegrave.
Wansford.
Warmington.
Watford.
Weldon.
Weldon deanery.
Wellingborough.
Welton.
West Haddon.
Weston-Favell.
Weston-by-Welland.
Westwood.
Wittering.
Wollaston.
Woodford.
Yelvertoft.

NORTHUMBERLAND.

Aln river.
Alnwick.
Bamburgh.
Berwick-on-Tweed.

Chatton.
Hexham.
Hulne.
Matfen.

Newcastle-upon-Tyne.
Tynemouth.
Warkworth.

NOTTINGHAMSHIRE.

Annesley.
Basford.
Beckingham.
Blyth.
Bonnington.
Bunny.
Colston Bassett.
Cotgrave.
Cotham.
Cottam.
Cropwell Butler.
Hickling.

Hoveringham.
Kelham.
Mansfield.
Markham.
Newark-on-Trent.
Newstead-in-Sherwood.
Normanton-on-Soar.
North Collingham
Nottingham.
Oxton.
Papplewick.
Radford.

Retford.
Ruddington.
Scrooby.
Shelford,
Sherwood.
Soar river.
Southwell.
Sutton Bonnington.
Sutton-on-Soar.
Willoughby-on-the-
    Wolds.
Winthorpe.

OXFORDSHIRE.

Adderbury.
Alkerton.
Ambrosden
Aston.
Aston deanery.
Balscott.
Bampton.
Banbury.
Bensington.
Bicester.
Bicester deanery.
Bletchingdon.
Bloxham.
Bucknell.
Burcott.
Caversham.

Charlton-on-Otmoor.
Cherwell river.
Chesterton.
Chipping Norton deanery.
Chislehampton.
Clifton Hampden.
Cuddesdon deanery.
Deddington deanery.
Dorchester.
Drayton.
Ewelme.
Ewelme hundred.
Eynsham.
Garsington.
Godstow.
Goring.

Handborough.
Haseley.
Henley deanery.
Hooknorton.
Langford.
Launton.
Littlemore.
Lower Heyford.
Nettlebed.
Newton Purcell.
North Leigh.
Oseney.
Oxford.
Piddington.
Pirton.
Pirton hundred.

OXFORDSHIRE.—*contd.*

PEMBROKESHIRE.

RUTLAND.

SHROPSHIRE.

SOMERSET.

STAFFORDSHIRE.

SUFFOLK.

SURREY.

SUSSEX.

INDEX TO SUBJECTS

A.

Abbot : *see* Head of house.

Abusive language, 19-20, 24, 79-80, 86, 94, 96, 98, 105, 120, 140, 143, 157-9, 220, 246, 266, 279, 294-5, 299, 334, 363, 376.

——— ———, injunctions against, 88, 244.

Accounts, acquittance of, to obedientiary, 158.

———, audit of, insufficient attendance at, 209.

———, ———, orders for, 52-3, 214, 233.

———, ———, provision of auditor, 238, 376, 382.

———, ———, refusal to hold, 160.

———, erasures in, 338.

———, presentation of, injunctions for, 9, 125, 131, 134, 146, 179-80, 182, 186-7, 214, 227, 231, 233, 238, 308, 310, 316-8, 349, 351, 359, 368, 378, 381, 392, 394.

———, ———, invitations to, 340.

———, ———, neglected, 3, 47-9, 62, 68-70, 84, 109-12, 120, 122, 130-1,133, 141-2, 144, 159-64, 174, 179, 189, 207, 219, 223, 233, 245, 253-4, 266, 281, 287, 291-3, 295, 304, 310, 317, 321-2, 325, 337-8, 340, 348-9, 355-6, 360-1, 363, 365, 372-5, 377-8, 386-7, 391-2, 415.

———, separate, presented by obedientiaries, 272.

———, suppression of, by obedientiaries, 33.

———; *see also* Status domus.

Administrators, appointment of, 64, 67-8, 70, 72, 77-8, 148, 151, 258-9, 275, 299-300, 352, 355, 366-7.

———, ———, petition for, 255, 278, 282, 351.

———, ———; *see also* Bursars, Head of house, coadjutors to, Receivers.

Admissions to monasteries, 4.

——— ———, injunctions relating to, 9, 125, 134, 177, 186, 350.

——— ———, negligence in, 98-9.

——— ———, payment for, 117, 133, 175-6, 249.

——— ———, ———, injunctions relating to, 9, 134, 177, 186, 252, 350, 359.

Adultery, accusations of, 11, 18, 22-4, 45, 47-50, 64, 69, 71, 73, 94, 107, 109, 150, 152, 155, 160, 164, 188, 222-3, 232, 257, 294-5, 297, 323, 325-7, 352.

———; *see also* Head of house, incontinency, Incest, Incontinency, Women, suspect.

Alchemy, multiplying, accusation of, 208-12.

Alienation of goods, 2, 14, 21-3, 35-6, 41, 44, 47-9, 56, 62, 70-1, 73, 77, 84, 103-5, 129, 141, 146, 150-3, 155, 160-1, 175, 187, 233-4, 250, 257, 266, 280, 287-9, 293, 329, 332, 343, 360, 375, 381, 415-6.

———; *see also* Jewels, Pawned goods.

Allowances in clothing, food, money, etc., 7, 15-16, 35-7, 47, 49, 70, 72, 78, 81, 84-5, 92, 99, 121-2, 140, 169, 184, 207, 212, 223, 227, 230, 235, 250, 287, 348-9, 352, 357-8, 367, 389, 391.

——— ——— ———, injunctions relating to, 35, 125, 230, 252, 315-6, 350, 358-9

———, remitted by religious for common object, 274, 280.

———, revocation of, 417.

——— to young religious, administration of, 77.

———; *see also* Beer, Bread, Head of house, retired, Salaries.

Almoner, lack of, 234, 372.

———, charges against, 303-4, 308-9, 312-3.

Almonry, boys in, clerks of, 208-9, 214, 315, 330, 334, 371-7.

———, ——— ———, injunctions regarding 214, 379-80.

———, ——— ———, payment for admission of, 208.

———, fines paid to, 190, 200.

———, maintenance of infirm in, 55, 192.

———, ———, abuse of, 192-3.

———, ———, ———, injunction against, 202.

———, payment for admission to, 212.

———; *see also* Bede-folk, Buildings.

Alms, alienation, waste, of, 14, 20-1, 39, 179, 223, 234, 249, 255, 309, 311, 313, 372-5.